THIRD EDITION

The Psychology of EXERCISE

INTEGRATING THEORY AND PRACTICE

Curt L. Lox
SOUTHERN ILLINOIS UNIVERSITY EDWARDSVILLE

Kathleen A. Martin Ginis
McMASTER UNIVERSITY

Steven J. Petruzzello
UNIVERSITY OF ILLINOIS AT URBANA-CHAMPAIGN

Holcomb Hathaway, Publishers
Scottsdale, Arizona 85250

Library of Congress Cataloging-in-Publication Data

Lox, Curt.
The psychology of exercise : integrating theory and practice / Curt L. Lox, Kathleen A. Martin Ginis, Steven J. Petruzzello.—3rd ed.
p. cm.
ISBN 978-1-934432-05-1
1. Exercise—Psychological aspects. 2. Physical fitness—Psychological aspects. I. Martin Ginis, Kathleen A. (Kathleen Anne). II. Petruzzello, Steven J. III. Title.
GV481.2.L69 2010
613.7'1019—dc22

2010015709

Please note: The author and publisher have made every effort to provide current website addresses in this book. However, because web addresses change, it is inevitable that some of the URLs listed here will change following publication of this book.

Holcomb Hathaway, Publishers, Inc.
8700 E. Via de Ventura Blvd., Suite 265
Scottsdale, AZ 85258
480-991-7881
www.hh-pub.com

10 9 8 7 6 5 4 3

ISBN 978-1-934432-05-1

PRINTED IN THE UNITED STATES OF AMERICA.

Brief Contents

Contents

Preface

How else could we possibly begin this Preface other than to say *thank you* for the overwhelming support we've received for this textbook? The positive feedback and helpful suggestions provided by colleagues, adopters, and students encouraged us to undertake a third edition.

Our goal for this edition was to continue with the approach that made the first two editions successful, while also expanding the content into areas desired by users of the book. We have added a new chapter that focuses on the emerging area of exercise and cognitive function. In addition, we have added exhibits and standardized questionnaires in an effort to complement the narrative information and further enhance the visual appeal of the book. One aspect of the book that has not changed, however, is the application of evidence- and theory-based information to "real-world" situations likely to be experienced by readers. Your feedback continues to highlight this and the book's "user friendliness" as its primary strengths.

As in previous editions, the book is divided into two main sections. Part I includes six chapters that will help readers to understand and modify exercise behavior (either their own or the behavior of others). The book opens with a general introduction designed to acquaint readers with the field of exercise psychology, followed by a chapter addressing patterns of physical activity participation. The next two chapters discuss the theories of exercise behavior currently accepted and used by exercise psychology scholars and practitioners. Chapter 5 introduces the compelling social influences (e.g., leadership, social support) documented to impact psychological responses and exercise behavior. The final chapter in Part I addresses intervention approaches aimed at modifying exercise behavior.

Part II of the book is devoted to the more commonly promoted and investigated psychosocial influences and consequences of exercise, including the bi-directional relationships between exercise and concepts such as personality and body image. In addition, this section highlights the impact of exercise on various mental health states such as depression, anxiety, stress, emotional well-being, self-concept/self-esteem, cognitive function, and health-related quality of life.

Special Features

- New and updated exhibits
- Marginal key terms and a comprehensive glossary
- End-of-chapter review questions and learning activities
- Focus boxes, with additional learning activities, highlighting research on physical activity and populations with chronic disease and disability
- Standardized questionnaires, including some of the most frequently used measures in exercise psychology research

We are excited about the continued evolution of this textbook. As always, we welcome your comments regarding this edition and your suggestions for future editions. Please contact us in care of our publisher:

Holcomb Hathaway, Publishers
6207 N. Cattletrack Rd., Suite 5
Scottsdale, AZ 85250
feedback@hh-pub.com

Acknowledgments

Any series of acknowledgments must begin with Colette Kelly for making this all possible. Her patience and leadership are critical to the success of this book, and we thank her for riding shotgun with us again. Thanks also to Gay Pauley and the rest of the Holcomb Hathaway staff, and to John and Rhonda Wincek of Aerocraft Charter Art Service, for their efforts. We also extend our gratitude to the following individuals, who devoted considerable time and energy reviewing sections of this book at various stages of development: Kelly Arbour-Nicitopoulos, University of Toronto; Christina Beaudoin, University of Southern Maine; Jody Brylinsky, Western Michigan University; Eduardo Bustamante, University of Illinois at Chicago; Camille Cassidy, University of Texas of the Permian Basin; Nicole Culos-Reed, University of Calgary; Shawn Dolan, California State University–Long Beach; Panteleimon Ekkekakis, Iowa State University; Kristen Fisher, California State University, Chico; Brian Focht, Eastern Carolina University; Kristin Hoffner, Arizona State University; Matthew S. Johnson, Texas Christian University; Marcus Kilpatrick, University of South Florida; Anthony P. Kontos, University of New Orleans; Karla Kubitz, Towson University; Amy Latimer, Queen's University; David Xavier Marquez, University of Illinois at Chicago; Eva V. Monsma, University of South Carolina; Melissa Murray, University of Southern Mississippi; Lindsay Ross-Stewart, Saint Francis University; Todd Ryska, University of Texas–San Antonio; Catherine M. Sabiston, McGill University; Christopher R. Snell, University of the Pacific; George David Swanson, California State University, Chico; Danielle Symons Downs, The Pennsylvania State University; Phillip D. Tomporowski, The University of Georgia; Sara Wilcox, University of South Carolina; and Sam Zizzi, West Virginia University. Their feedback and suggestions are appreciated and are reflected throughout this edition of the book.

C.L., K.M.G., S.P.

I extend my gratitude once again to Kathleen, Steve, and Colette for their optimism and excitement as we embarked on this new edition. It is indeed an honor and pleasure to work with the three of you. To Shea and Kelsey—thank you for the inspiration you both continue to provide me on a daily basis.

C.L.

Thank you, Curt and Steve, for being such wonderfully dedicated, insightful, and supportive collaborators over the past decade. Thank you also to the faculty, staff, students, and community members of the Centre for Health Promotion and Rehabilitation in McMaster University's Department of Kinesiology. Your passion and commitment inspire me every day. And, of course, I extend my love and gratitude to Spero and Athena, who make everything possible.

K.M.G.

As always, I thank Curt and Kathleen for the opportunity to work with them and for the continued collaboration that has been far better than I think any of us imagined. This revision, like its predecessor, was worth it; we were able to add some timely updates and new material to the book. We wrote this book for the students and it is ultimately for them that we continue to provide substantial revisions. My thanks go out to those colleagues who took the time and effort to offer such thorough reviews and thoughtful revision suggestions. All reviewers can rest assured that their many excellent ideas were considered and may be reflected here or in future revisions. Finally, my thanks and gratitude go to my two "families." To my academic family—former students and continuing collaborators Panteleimon "Paddy" Ekkekakis, Eric Hall, and numerous other graduate students: we have indeed made a difference in changing the way (at least some) people in the field are thinking about the psychological effects of exercise. And to my "everything" family—Wendy, Tony, and Alyssa: your support and encouragement have been unwavering. I couldn't do this work without you and your continual inspiration. Thank you very much.

S.P

About the Authors

Curt L. Lox, Ph.D., is a professor and chair of the Department of Kinesiology and Health Education at Southern Illinois University Edwardsville. His research is focused on the psychological impact of exercise for special populations, including the elderly, overweight and obese children and adults, and individuals infected with HIV. His articles have been published in the *Journal of Sport & Exercise Psychology, Medicine and Science in Sports and Exercise, Journal of Cognitive Rehabilitation, International Journal of Behavioral Medicine, Journal of Health Psychology,* and *Rehabilitation Psychology,* among others. He has coached at the youth and high school levels and continues to serve as a sport psychology consultant to players and coaches at the interscholastic, intercollegiate, and professional levels in the greater St. Louis area.

Kathleen A. Martin Ginis, Ph.D., is a professor of Health and Exercise Psychology at McMaster University's Department of Kinesiology. Her research program focuses on psychosocial influences and consequences of physical activity participation. She has a particular interest in physical activity promotion among people living with spinal cord injury. Martin Ginis received her Ph.D. from the University of Waterloo in 1996 and completed postdoctoral training at Wake Forest University. She has been the recipient of several awards, including the Early Distinguished Career Award from the North American Society for the Psychology of Sport and Physical Activity and a New Investigator Award from the Canadian Institutes of Health Research. She has published more than 100 articles in journals such as *Health Psychology, Journal of Sport & Exercise Psychology, Annals of Behavioral Medicine,* and *Rehabilitation Psychology,* and her work has been featured in publications such as *"O" The Oprah Magazine, Men's Health & Fitness,* and *Shape,* among others.

Steven J. Petruzzello, Ph.D., is an associate professor in the Department of Kinesiology and Community Health at the University of Illinois at Urbana-Champaign. He conducts research in the area of exercise psychology, particularly from a psychophysiological perspective. This research involves the examination of the role of exercise, encapsulated along a physical activity continuum ranging from low-to-moderate forms of exercise (e.g., walking, cycling) to vigorous exercise (e.g., competitive swimming, running) and physical activity performed in extreme environments (e.g., firefighting), on a variety of psychological outcomes, including basic affect, fatigue/energy, anxiety, and depression. He is a Fellow of the American College of Sports Medicine, and a member of the Midwest Chapter of the ACSM, the Society for Psychophysiological Research, and the American Psychological Society. His articles have appeared in *Sports Medicine*, the *Journal of Sport and Exercise Psychology, Medicine and Science in Sports and Exercise,* and *Psychophysiology,* among others.

PART I

Understanding and Modifying Exercise Behavior

1

Introduction to Exercise Psychology

KEY TERMS

acute
adherence
adoption
behavioral medicine
biopsychosocial approach
chronic
exercise
exercise psychology
exercise science
health psychology
medical model
noncompliant
physical activity
psychology
rehabilitation psychology

Pretend, for a moment, that you are an exercise/health professional who has been approached by the following three individuals for assistance. After reviewing each scenario, consider what you might do to modify the thoughts, feelings, and behavior of the individuals described. Think of this activity as a proficiency exam to assess how much you already know about the psychology of exercise.

Case A. Individual A is a college student juggling multiple responsibilities (including classes, a part-time job, and social obligations), which serve as barriers to exercise. She also reports high levels of stress and fatigue.

Case B. Individual B is currently undergoing physical rehabilitation following a complete tear of his anterior cruciate ligament. Although he has always been active, he has never had to cope with such a significant injury, long and (occasionally) painful rehabilitation, and fear with regard to his return to action.

Case C. Individual C is overweight and knows she should exercise to lose weight but is very self-conscious about her body. She has resisted beginning an exercise regimen because she feels apprehensive about exercising in a public setting. She also reports low self-esteem and generally has a negative attitude toward exercise.

What Is Exercise Psychology?

As you probably realized while thinking about these cases, you have already come into contact with principles of exercise psychology without identifying them as such. The individuals just described are fairly typical exercise psychology cases that involve such complex psychological constructs as *adherence, self-esteem, self-efficacy, anxiety,* and *body image* (all of which will be discussed later). But what exactly is exercise psychology? In order to answer this question, we first need to define exercise as it relates to physical activity. For the purpose of our discussions throughout this book, **physical activity** will refer to all bodily movements that cause increases in physical exertion beyond that which occurs during normal activities of daily living. **Exercise** is a form of **leisure** physical activity (as opposed to occupational or household physical activity) that is undertaken in order to achieve a particular objective (e.g., improved appearance, improved cardiovascular fitness, reduced stress, fun).

physical activity ■
exercise ■
leisure ■

Also crucial to understanding the field of exercise psychology is knowledge about the broader disciplines from which the field has emerged. For the purpose of our discussion, refer to the model in Exhibit 1.1. At the top are the two parent disciplines from which the field of exercise psychology emerged. The first is **psychology,** which is the field of study concerned with the various mental processes (e.g., perceptions, cognitions, emotions) people experience and use in all aspects of their lives. The second is **exercise science,** which is devoted to the study of all aspects of sport, recreation, exercise/fitness, and rehabilitative behavior.

psychology ■
exercise science ■

Representing the convergence of exercise science and psychology, the field of **exercise psychology** is concerned with (1) the application of psychological principles to the promotion and maintenance of leisure physical activity (exercise), and (2) the psychological and emotional consequences of leisure physical activity. Consider the individuals described at the beginning of the chapter. As alluded to earlier, each case presents a unique challenge to researchers and practitioners associated with the field of exercise psychology. Case A presents a young woman who perceives multiple barriers (i.e., time, fatigue) that prevent her from

exercise pyschology ■

exhibit 1.1 The "family tree" of exercise psychology.

Psychology		Exercise Science
	Exercise/Rehabilitation Psychology	

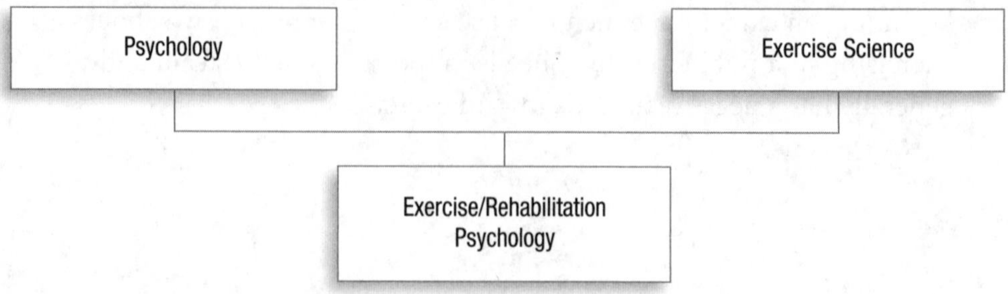

adopting exercise as a regular routine. An individual with knowledge of exercise psychology principles might attempt to find an exercise mode and time that she can work into her busy day and point out that properly prescribed exercise can aid in reducing the stress and fatigue she is experiencing.

In Case B, we find a man beginning the arduous task of physical rehabilitation following a severe injury who is anxious about his return to action and about the entire rehabilitation process. He is also likely struggling with lower than usual confidence in his physical abilities as well as with fear of reinjury. As you will learn in more depth later in this book, the health care practitioner should strive to incorporate exercise psychology concepts into the rehabilitation program. For example, allowing the patient to speak with others who have experienced similar injuries and who have been successfully rehabilitated may help to alleviate anxiety and increase confidence concerning his return to action.

Finally, the woman in Case C is apprehensive about exercise because of a negative body image and concern about others viewing her body in a public exercise setting. Although she needs to become physically active, self-consciousness surrounding her body will likely prevent her from adopting a regimen of exercise. Once again, principles from the field of exercise psychology may help influence the woman's behavior. For instance, we might suggest that she seek out an exercise program geared toward overweight people like herself. This would provide social support and reduce her concern that others (who are not overweight) are viewing her body in a negative fashion.

The reader should note that a "sister" field of exercise psychology is included in Exhibit 1.1. **Rehabilitation psychology** deals with the relationship between psychological factors and the physical rehabilitation process. Thus, this field is concerned with exercise rehabilitation following a disabling event (e.g., injury, heart attack, stroke), as well as the role of physical activity as a complementary strategy for treating disease (e.g., cancer, AIDS, diabetes). In short, the objective is to employ psychological interventions during physical rehabilitation in order to return the individual to a prior, more healthy, physical and/or mental state quickly and effectively, and to maximize residual function and health. Given these goals, researchers and practitioners associated with physical rehabilitation might address the following questions:

■ rehabilitation psychology

1. What psychological issues facilitate or hinder the injury rehabilitation process?
2. What forms and amount of exercise provide psychological benefits for cancer, AIDS, spinal cord injury, or cardiac rehabilitation patients?
3. Can exercise improve quality of life for those individuals dealing with injury, disease, or illness?

Two additional fields tangentially related to exercise psychology are **health psychology** and behavioral medicine. Health psychology is concerned with psychological processes related to health and health care and is therefore not limited to the health behavior of exercise. Nutrition and weight management, smoking cessation, and medication adherence are examples of investigational areas in the

■ health psychology

behavioral medicine ■

field of health psychology. Similarly, **behavioral medicine** focuses on the interrelationships of behavioral, physical, and psychosocial factors in the understanding of healthful living and the treatment of illness, disease, and disability. For example, experts in this field might investigate questions related to the biological and mental factors associated with stress; the immunological, social, and psychological factors associated with AIDS; or the emotional, social, and biological implications of exercise for pregnant women. Readers interested in a somewhat different approach to defining the boundaries of exercise psychology and related fields should consult the seminal article on this topic written by Rejeski and Brawley (1988).

Why Study Exercise Psychology?

adoption ■
adherence ■
noncompliant ■

If it has not yet become obvious, you may be asking yourself why it is necessary or helpful to study the psychology of exercise in the first place. We feel that such an endeavor is relevant for two primary reasons. First, it can help us to understand the psychological antecedents of exercise behavior given that physical activity adoption and adherence rates are so dismal (see Chapter 2). Indeed, researchers have recently suggested that the incidence of regular physical activity participation is considerably lower than we have believed, perhaps less than 5 percent of the adult population (Troiano, Berrigan, Dodd, et al., 2008). **Adoption** refers to the beginning stage of an exercise regimen, while **adherence** refers to maintaining an exercise regimen for a prolonged period of time following the initial adoption phase. Central to adherence is the assumption that the individual voluntarily and independently chooses to engage in the activity. Adherence is generally regarded as a largely psychological issue (see Chapters 3 and 4), and, given the central role of **noncompliant** behavior as it relates to mental and physical health, knowledge of the psychology of exercise becomes paramount in health promotion efforts. The need for this knowledge may be best highlighted by the finding that only one of 13 physical activity and fitness objectives proposed in the federal government's *Healthy People 2000* document was actually met (U.S. Department of Health and Human Services, 2004). These points, as well as information related to the recently updated *Healthy People 2010*, will be further discussed in the next chapter as we review the impact of nonactivity on rates of mortality and morbidity in present-day society.

acute ■
chronic ■

The second primary reason for studying exercise psychology is to understand the psychological consequences of exercise in order to introduce physical activity interventions capable of (1) reducing **acute** (short-term, temporary) and **chronic** (long-term, relatively permanent) negative psychological/emotional states, and (2) promoting acute and chronic positive psychological/emotional states. These goals are especially important in light of the findings described in the U.S. Surgeon General's Report on Mental Health (1999). First, at least one in five people in the United States has a diagnosed mental disorder (approximately 50 million Americans), the majority of whom are not receiving any form of treatment for their illness. Second, the annual combined direct and estimated indirect costs of mental health services in the United States are now more than $150 billion. Clearly, the promotion of physical activity, in conjunction with more traditional mental health interventions (i.e., psychotherapy, pharmacological agents), might enable us to address these staggering statistics. As part of this promotional strategy, prospective exercisers should be made aware of the many benefits of physical activity on physical, psychological, and social well-being. A discussion of these benefits, as well as the barriers to exercise, is presented in the next section.

Changing People's Perceptions About Exercise: Weighing the Pros and Cons

Recognizing and understanding the primary benefits associated with exercise are helpful when attempting to modify exercise behavior (see Chapters 3 and 4 for theories that incorporate both benefits and barriers to exercise behavior). By determining the primary benefits sought out by the client, the exercise leader can tailor the exercise program to meet those outcomes. Additionally, the exercise leader might educate the client about certain benefits of physical activity that the client had not previously considered. The result of this interaction should be enhanced levels of commitment, motivation, and ultimately adherence. In Chapter 2, you will learn about the benefits of physical activity on morbidity and mortality; although these may be the most significant reasons to engage in physical activity, a number of additional benefits exist as well. In general, the list of benefits (see Exhibit 1.2) can be narrowed down to the following four catego-

exhibit 1.2 Common benefits of physical activity.

Common benefits of physical activity.
Lowers morbidity and mortality rates.
Reduces risk of developing diabetes, hypertension, colon cancer, and heart disease.
Helps reduce blood pressure in those with hypertension.
Reduces feelings of depression, anxiety, and general negative mood.
Enhances general positive mood.
Improves body image, self-esteem, and self-concept.
Helps control weight.
Enhances cognitive function.
Helps build and maintain healthy bones, muscles, and joints.
Enhances ability to perform activities of daily living (ADLs).
Provides opportunity to develop social contacts, relationships, and support groups.

ries: improved physiological health/physical fitness; enhanced physical appearance; improved psychological/emotional health; and improved social relations.

Improved Physiological Health/Physical Fitness

As indicated earlier, physical activity provides a number of physiological health benefits including improvements in cardiovascular endurance (fitness), muscle strength/endurance, bone strength, flexibility, lean weight percentage, and resting heart rate. Indeed, participants often choose to engage in exercise for the purposes of preventing or treating poor physical fitness. Relatedly, an increasing number of participants have chosen to embark on an exercise regimen in order to increase sensations of vigor (energy), improve sleep patterns, or reduce levels of pain or fatigue.

Enhanced Physical Appearance

Exercise produces body composition changes considered "desirable" in today's society. For example, long-term engagement in aerobic types of exercise (e.g., walking, running, biking) is associated with body fat reduction. Similarly, long-term resistance training is associated with increased muscle mass. Taken together, reduced body fat and increased lean muscle tissue produce a "toned" body, which is currently portrayed as "ideal" and, more important, attractive for both men and women (see Chapter 9 for a discussion of body image). Enhancing one's physical appearance may also serve to improve elements of psychological health such as self-concept and self-esteem.

Improved Psychological/Emotional Health and Cognitive Function

Improvements in psychological and emotional health are no longer considered secondary benefits of physical activity. Indeed, as discussed throughout the remainder of this book, exercise may play a primary role in reducing negative psychological (e.g., poor body image) and emotional (e.g., depression) states. Exercise can also induce positive psychological (e.g., self-esteem) and emotional (e.g., positive mood) responses. Perhaps most important, the impact of exercise on psychological and emotional health may be both acute and chronic in nature. In other words, while a single bout of exercise may produce immediate temporary benefits, a regular regimen of physical activity may provide enduring benefits. It should also be pointed out that, contrary to popular opinion, many individuals do exercise for reasons of enjoyment.

Finally, as discussed in Chapter 14, physical activity has been shown to exert a positive influence on cognitive function, including reaction time, response accuracy, and ability to process information. A growing body of evidence indicates that moderate exercise can be a useful tool in buffering against and perhaps even preventing the decline in cognitive function and brain deterioration that so often accompanies advancing age.

Improved Social Relations

An often overlooked reason for engaging in physical activity is the social benefits it provides. Exercisers representing all ages and both genders report engaging in physical activity for reasons of social support and camaraderie. For certain segments of society, the social reasons are particularly salient. How often have you seen a group of elderly individuals walking through a mall early in the morning? For pregnant women, group exercise allows them an opportunity to support each other through emotionally and physically challenging times.

As the saying goes, "for every action, there is an equal and opposite reaction." This reality is certainly relevant when it comes to the benefits and barriers of exercise. Thus, while many individuals perceive substantial benefits to adopting a regular exercise regimen, these "pros" are generally balanced (or even overmatched) by the numerous "cons" or barriers to exercise. Simply put, barriers are those elements that prevent an individual from exercising. Barriers may be categorized as either genuine (e.g., inaccessible facilities for persons who use a wheelchair) or perceived (e.g., lack of time). The next section is devoted to some common genuine barriers to physical activity. These include convenience/availability; environmental/ecological factors; and physical limitations.

Convenience/Availability

Inaccessible transportation, lack (or inconvenient location) of facilities, and lack of equipment are just a few of the more popular reasons why people fail to engage in regular physical activity. For example, the elderly are often unable to access transportation, which proves to be an obstacle when attempting to adopt exercise into their lifestyles. Although these factors clearly limit activity mode and, perhaps, the setting in which the activity takes place, a study of Southern California residents indicated that both sedentary and active people have an equivalent number of exercise facilities within a two- to five-kilometer radius of their homes (Sallis, Hovell, Hofstetter, et al., 1990). Interestingly, this same study found that the *perceived* convenience of exercise facilities was completely unrelated to the *actual* proximity of these facilities. Thus, it appears that convenience and availability of facilities are often excuses for failing to be physically active (see review by Brawley, Martin, & Gyurcsik, 1998).

Environmental/Ecological Factors

Aspects of the geographical location, climate, and neighborhood may all serve as genuine barriers to exercise. For example, rain and snowfall, as well as extreme temperatures, may preclude some individuals from engaging in certain outdoor activities. Individuals residing in Colorado might not find exercise enjoyable due to the high altitude and its effect on the respiratory system. Finally, an individual who enjoys running through his neighborhood might not want to do so for safety reasons (e.g., poor lighting, crime).

Physical Limitations

Physical limitations such as injury, disease, and fatigue are real and significant causes of inactivity. Clearly, exercise should be avoided in certain stages/phases of disease or when a body part required for activity is injured. On the other hand, exercise has become a prominent treatment strategy for various diseases (e.g., cancer, AIDS, diabetes, arthritis, obesity) as well as for combating fatigue and pain.

As mentioned earlier, people often fail to exercise due to perceived barriers—things they believe are insurmountable obstacles to exercise. In contrast to many genuine barriers, perceived barriers may be overcome with an effective intervention. Two of the most frequently cited perceived barriers to exercise are lack of time and boredom/lack of enjoyment.

Lack of Time

In most cases, if you ask nonexercisers why they do not engage in physical activity, they will most likely tell you that they do not have time to do so. We can certainly all appreciate such sentiment. A survey of nearly 20,000 Canadians (Shaw, Bonen, & McCabe, 1991), however, found that people who cited "lack of time" as a barrier to physical activity actually performed more hours of activity per week than those who did not consider "lack of time" to be a barrier! This suggests that regular exercisers are employing time-management strategies that nonexercisers are not and, further, that they have made exercise a priority in their lives. Thus, it appears that "lack of time" is merely a convenient excuse for many nonexercisers to not exercise.

Boredom/Lack of Enjoyment

A prominent barrier for many people is the mentality that "physical activity" means running or spinning—highly vigorous activities they find unappealing. This barrier may be best overcome by exposing people to other forms of leisure activity such as dancing, hiking, gardening, or swimming. Additionally, exercising to music or in front of the television may take one's mind off exercising, thereby alleviating boredom. Exercising with others (e.g., family members, coworkers, friends) also tends to make physical activity more enjoyable.

Emergence of Exercise Psychology

Historians have documented widespread physical activity participation as far back as 3,000 years ago when the games of ancient Greece flourished. While sporting events have always been central to society, however, it was not until the Industrial Revolution (late 1700s through the early twentieth century) that the notion of fitness (and its value to the individual and employer) was first recognized. It was this newfound "philosophy of physical fitness," in fact, that paved the way for what came to be known in North America as the "fitness craze" of the 1970s and 1980s. This period was characterized by the emerging popularity of "aerobics," weight training, jogging, and racket sports. In addition, fitness/health clubs and dance studios began popping up in every community, and fashionable exercise attire was introduced. The birth of exercise psychology came on the heels of this fitness frenzy, during the 1980s, as the population was persuaded to alter its collective behavior in order to extend and improve the quality of life. The appearance of exercise psychology, at least in the United States, was also a function of several other societal factors that emerged during the 1960s, '70s, and '80s (Rejeski & Thompson, 1993; Sallis & Owen, 1999). One such factor was the increasing emphasis on the physical appearance of the body. During this time, the image of the full-figured woman was ousted in favor of a new body ideal led by the philosophy that "thin is in." On the male front, simply being "big" was no longer the masculine ideal, unless one's girth was made up of muscle as opposed to fat. The ideal body was thus reconstructed to reflect society's preference for a "lean" and "defined" appearance. Not surprisingly, weight training and aerobics became popular means to achieve the leanness and strength desired by men and women alike.

Heightened levels of stress experienced by members of society during this time may have hastened the emergence of the exercise psychology field. Indeed, with men, women, and children facing more domestic, academic, occupational, and social pressures than ever before, the need to reduce the resulting stress became paramount. Before exercise could be acknowledged as an effective strategy for reducing stress, however, the scientific community first had to embrace the intimate relationship that exists between the mind and body. For example, reducing mental stress also serves to relax the body, and vice versa. Today, this notion has been expanded to include social context and is now referred to as the **biopsychosocial approach** to studying health behaviors (i.e., the belief that the body, mind, and social environment influence one another and, ultimately, behavior).

■ biopsychosocial approach

Finally, during the last few decades we have witnessed a shift in society's perception of who is responsible for maintaining the population's health. Prior to this time, the **medical model**, or the use of traditional forms of medicine (e.g., pharmacology) to improve physical or mental health, dominated health care (and still does, to some extent). In the 1960s, however, people began to recognize that health is largely under the control of the individual and that exercise is one strategy that can be undertaken to address health concerns. Thus, individuals did not have to be passive recipients of treatments or interventions prescribed by health care professionals. Instead, the new philosophy dictated that we could (and should) play an active role in maintaining or improving our health. This change in philosophy corresponded nicely with an increase in the amount of leisure time available to members of society. Specifically, available leisure time hit an all-time high during the 1980s, with people working fewer hours per week than ever before. Unfortunately, this increase in leisure time has not trans-

■ medical model

lated into appreciable increases in physical activity participation. Instead, many individuals in industrialized countries are now working more hours (thereby reducing available leisure time) in less active jobs (thanks to technological advances), and they have seen significant increases in their waistlines and overall sedentary rate.

In summary, physical activity became highly valued by society as a means of relieving stress, improving health, and enhancing physical appearance during the 1960s, '70s, and '80s. As a result, the door was opened for the emergence of a new field of study focused on the psychological antecedents and consequences of leisure physical activity. In recognition of this, 1988 saw the first issues of the *Journal of Sport Psychology,* a scientific publication for sport and exercise psychology researchers, appropriately renamed the *Journal of Sport and Exercise Psychology*. Readers interested in learning more about the roots of exercise psychology may wish to consult a special edition of *The Sport Psychologist* (December 1995, Vol. 9, No. 4), which was devoted specifically to a historical analysis of sport and exercise psychology.

Learning More About Exercise Psychology

We recommend that individuals who wish to obtain information and learn more about exercise psychology contact the prominent professional organizations and review applied and theoretical research articles published in the numerous journals devoted to the field. Because exercise psychology crosses over a variety of disciplines (e.g., psychology, nursing/medicine/health, physical education/kinesiology), however, the task of locating literature related to the field can be challenging. Indeed, it is likely that interested readers will need to look at a number of resources in order to gain a complete understanding. Fortunately, a number of excellent electronic databases (some available via the Internet) exist to help you accomplish this task. Exhibit 1.3 lists some of the most useful databases associated with the field of exercise psychology.

exhibit 1.3 Databases used in exercise psychology research.

- ERIC (Education Resources Information Center) (www.eric.ed.gov)
- MEDLINE (www.ncbi.nlm.nih.gov/pubmed)
- PsycINFO (www.apa.org/pubs/database/psycinfo/index.aspx)
- CINAHL (Cumulative Index to Nursing and Allied Health Literature) (www.ebscohost.com/cinahl)
- SIRC (Sport Information Resource Centre) (www.sirc.ca)
- Physical Education Index (www.csa.com/factsheets/pei-set-c.php)

Professional Organizations Associated with Exercise Psychology

The formation of organizations or associations is central to the progress of any field of study or industry. Such organizations permit individuals with similar interests to come together to share ideas and research related to their particular field. These organizations also serve as important links to the public sector, by publicizing the field and providing information regarding their members to the consumer. Some organizations may be responsible for the development of public policy, guidelines, or standards. A number of organizations currently serve exercise psychology researchers and professionals; the following are the most prominent organizations related to the field.

Association for Applied Sport Psychology (AASP), www.appliedsportpsych.org ■ The purpose of this association, founded in 1986, is to promote the development of psychological theory, research, and intervention strategies in the fields of sport, exercise, and health psychology. The organization consists of three interest areas: intervention/performance enhancement, health and exercise psychology, and social psychology.

American College of Sports Medicine (ACSM), www.acsm.org ■ This multidisciplinary organization, founded in 1954, promotes and integrates scientific research, education, and practical applications of sports medicine and exercise science to maintain and enhance physical performance, fitness, health, and quality of life. ACSM is the largest, most respected sports medicine and exercise science organization in the world.

APA Division 47 (Exercise and Sport Psychology), www.apa47.org ■ Founded in 1986, this division of the American Psychological Association (APA) aims to further the scientific, educational, and clinical foundations of exercise and sport psychology.

APA Division 38 (Health Psychology), www.health-psych.org ■ The mission of this division of the American Psychological Association is to facilitate collaboration among psychologists and other health science and health care professionals interested in the psychological and behavioral aspects of physical and mental health.

Canadian Society for Psychomotor Learning and Sport Psychology (SCAPPS), www.scapps.org ■ Founded in 1977, this society aims to promote the study of motor control, motor learning, motor development, and sport/exercise psychology in Canada and to encourage the exchange of views and scientific information in the fields related to psychomotor learning and sport/exercise psychology.

European Federation of Sport Psychology (FEPSAC), www.fepsac.com ■ This federation is composed of national societies in Europe dealing with sport and exercise psychology, including the German Association of Sport Psychology (ASP) and the British Association of Sport and Exercise Sciences (BASES).

International Society of Sport Psychology (ISSP), www.issponline.org ■ Founded in 1965, this society promotes the study of human behavior of individuals and groups associated with sport and physical activity. The ISSP is the only worldwide organization of scholars explicitly concerned with sport, exercise, and health psychology.

North American Society for the Psychology of Sport and Physical Activity (NASPSPA), www.naspspa.org ■ Founded in 1967, this society aims to develop and advance the scientific study of human behavior in the sport and physical activity arenas. The association is composed of three interest areas: sport and exercise psychology, motor development, and motor learning/control.

Society of Behavioral Medicine (SBM), www.sbm.org ■ The mission of this society, founded in 1978, is to foster the development and application of knowledge concerning the interrelationships of health, illness, and behavior. The goal of this multidisciplinary society is to form an interactive network for education and collaboration on common research and public policy.

Scientific Journals Associated with Exercise Psychology

In addition to organizations, emerging fields of study also require publication outlets for the research they generate. For exercise psychology researchers, a wide spectrum of both applied and theoretical journals is available, with more publications being introduced every year. Theoretical journals are highly technical in nature and are generally written by scientists for fellow scientists in the field. Applied journals, on the other hand, are written for the practitioner (e.g., rehabilitation specialist, exercise leader) and include useful (and less technical) information often based on research. Exhibit 1.4 lists some of the more popular journals associated with the field of exercise psychology.

exhibit 1.4 **Scientific journals containing research from the field of exercise psychology.**

JOURNAL	ASSOCIATION (IF APPLICABLE)
Adapted Physical Activity Quarterly	International Federation of Adapted Physical Activity
Advances in Mind/Body Medicine	
Annals of Behavioral Medicine	Society of Behavioral Medicine
Applied and Preventive Psychology	
Australian Journal of Sports Medicine	Australian Sports Medicine Federation
Basic and Applied Social Psychology	

(continued)

Continued. **exhibit 1.4**

British Journal of Health Psychology	The British Psychological Society
British Journal of Sports Medicine	British Association of Sports and Exercise Medicine
Health Psychology	American Psychological Association, Division 38—Health Psychology
International Journal of Behavioral Medicine	International Society of Behavioral Medicine
International Journal of Sport and Exercise Psychology	The International Society of Sports Psychology
Journal of Aging and Physical Activity	International Coalition for Aging and Physical Activity
Journal of Applied Biobehavioral Research	
Journal of Applied Sport Psychology	Association for Applied Sport Psychology
Journal of Behavioral Medicine	
Journal of Health and Social Behavior	American Sociological Association
Journal of Health Psychology	
Journal of Physical Activity and Health	
Journal of Physical Education, Recreation and Dance	American Alliance for Health, Physical Education, Recreation and Dance
Journal of Psychosocial Oncology	Association of Oncology Social Work
Journal of Psychosomatic Research	The European Association for Consultation Liaison Psychiatry and Psychosomatics and International College of Psychosomatic Medicine
Journal of Sport and Exercise Psychology	North American Society for the Psychology of Sport and Physical Activity
Journal of Sport Behavior	
Journal of Sports Sciences	British Association of Sport and Exercise Sciences
Journal of Teaching in Physical Education	
Measurement in Physical Education and Exercise Science	American Association for Physical Activity and Recreation—Measurement & Evaluation Council
Medicine and Science in Sports and Exercise	American College of Sports Medicine
Perceptual and Motor Skills	
Psychology and Health	European Health Psychology Society
Psychology, Health and Medicine	
Psychology of Sport and Exercise	European Federation of Sport Psychology
Psychosomatic Medicine	The American Psychosomatic Society
Rehabilitation Psychology	American Psychological Association, Division 22—Rehabilitation Psychology
Research Quarterly for Exercise and Sport	American Alliance for Heath, Physical Education, Recreation, and Dance Research Consortium
The Sport Psychologist	

Training Opportunities in Exercise Psychology

Prior to embarking on a career in exercise psychology, an individual must first learn the skills and knowledge of the field at an institution of higher education that offers a program of exercise psychology–related content. Generally, such coursework is *not* found at community/junior college or professional psychology schools. In fact, even some four-year colleges and universities do not offer a stand-alone course in exercise psychology. Nonetheless, those universities that do offer courses or programs that include elements of exercise psychology generally house them in one of these departments.

Kinesiology. This is clearly the most likely department in which to find an exercise psychology course or program. A program would be found only at the graduate level, while courses may be found at both the undergraduate and graduate levels. At the undergraduate level, the fields of sport and exercise psychology may be covered within the same course. Related departments include Physical Education, Movement Studies, Exercise Science, Human Performance, Sport Studies, and many others.

Psychology. Although it is quite rare to find a course focused on exercise psychology in a Psychology department, one is even less likely to find a program of study here. Some Psychology departments offer a health psychology or behavioral medicine program. These multidisciplinary programs focus on the interrelationships among mental, physical, and behavioral factors in health, disease, and disability.

Occupational Opportunities Incorporating Exercise Psychology

Individuals with a background in exercise psychology might be found in positions such as those listed here.

Higher education. This is the primary occupation for individuals trained in the field of exercise psychology. Job responsibilities at the university level generally consist of teaching academic courses and conducting research related to the field of exercise psychology.

Primary/secondary education. Elementary through high school physical education instructors and coaches use principles of behavioral modification and group dynamics for teams and physical education classes. Additionally, knowledge of exercise psychology principles might enable an instructor to increase the self-esteem of a student or provide support for someone experiencing body image concerns.

Fitness and wellness. The fitness and wellness field includes personal trainers as well as directors of corporate fitness and wellness programs. In these positions, the ability to apply motivational techniques and adherence strategies would be particularly valuable.

Rehabilitation. Rehabilitation personnel include athletic trainers, physical therapists, and cardiac rehabilitation staff. The ability to increase confidence and reduce stress in an individual participating in rehabilitation would be extremely useful in this setting. However, it is important that exercise/fitness professionals recognize their limitations when it comes to consultations with clients. While such professionals are often able to deal with "typical" fears (e.g., fear of pain) and low-level anxiety that clients embarking on a rehabilitation regimen may experience, clients with more serious mental and emotional barriers should always be referred to a mental health professional.

Business. Consultants and administrators in the business world may employ principles of exercise psychology related to effective leadership and group dynamics to aid in the functioning of a corporate unit. Knowledge of behavioral modification techniques would be beneficial for anyone leading others.

Conclusion

The field of exercise psychology is inherently interesting and important. It deals with issues to which most of us can relate and is an invaluable resource in our fight to improve public health. Although it maintains strong theoretical roots, the field is extremely practical in that many thoughts, feelings, and behaviors are sensitive to intervention. This practical focus is not surprising given that exercise psychology emerged from two very applied fields, psychology and exercise science. The psychology of exercise focuses on both the psychosocial antecedents and consequences of exercise behavior. Thus, researchers seek to determine (1) the psychosocial factors that can influence exercise behavior, and (2) the psychosocial outcomes of exercise participation. As a "sister" field of exercise psychology, rehabilitation psychology focuses on the relationship between psychological/emotional factors and the physical rehabilitation process.

Given the state of ill health and exceptionally poor rates of physical activity adoption and adherence in our society, exercise psychology is poised to contribute mightily to the war against inactivity. Growing out of the "fitness craze" of the 1970s and '80s, the field has become a mainstay in the exercise science, behavioral medicine, and health psychology literatures. In addition, the number of higher education courses and training programs offered throughout the world has increased tremendously over the past three decades, and many professional organizations and occupations incorporating exercise psychology now exist.

Although we have barely scratched the surface, we hope that you now have a practical idea of where and how exercise psychology fits into our daily lives and the central role that it can play in improving the psychological and physical well-being of our society. As you will learn in the next several chapters, modifying physical activity patterns is no small feat. Based on the contemporary philosophy that the mind and body are inseparable and substantially influence one another, exercise psychology has much to offer fitness professionals, medical personnel, and the mental health profession. We conclude this introduction with the following quotes from a pair of nineteenth-century writers who lived long before the field of exercise psychology was born. Enjoy the journey!

> "Me thinks that the moment my legs begin to move, my thoughts begin to flow."
>
> **HENRY DAVID THOREAU**

> "By too much sitting still the body becomes unhealthy, and soon the mind."
>
> **HENRY WADSWORTH LONGFELLOW**

what do you know?

1. Discuss the parent disciplines from which the field of exercise psychology emerged.
2. Define the fields of exercise psychology and rehabilitation psychology.
3. Why is it important to study the psychology of exercise?
4. Discuss the primary benefits associated with exercise participation.
5. Identify and provide examples of the two categories of exercise-related barriers.
6. What historical and societal factors helped to give rise to the field of exercise psychology?
7. In what university departments are you likely to find courses or programs in exercise psychology?
8. Discuss occupational opportunities incorporating principles of exercise psychology.

learning activities

1. Complete the "proficiency exam" provided at the beginning of the chapter. Save your answers and review them at the end of the course. Would you do anything differently after finishing the course than what you had proposed at the beginning?
2. Learn more about the field of exercise psychology by looking up one of the websites listed in the chapter. Alternatively, conduct a search for new sites.
3. Review articles in one or more of the journals listed in Exhibit 1.4 to gain a feel for the topics and research methodology in the field of exercise psychology.

references

Brawley, L.R., Martin, K.A., & Gyurcsik, N.C. (1998). Problems in assessing perceived barriers to exercise: Confusing obstacles with attributions and excuses. In J.L. Duda (Ed.), *Advances in sport and exercise psychology measurement*. Morgantown, WV: Fitness Information Technology.

Rejeski, W.J., & Brawley, L.R. (1988). Defining the boundaries of sport psychology. The *Sport Psychologist?*, *2,* 231–242.

Rejeski, W.J., & Thompson, A. (1993). Historical and conceptual roots of exercise psychology. In P. Seraganian (Ed.), *Exercise psychology: The influence of physical exercise on psychological processes*. New York: John Wiley & Sons.

Sallis, J.F., Hovell, M.F., Hofstetter, C.R., Elder, J.P., Hackley, M., Caspersen, C.J., & Powell, K.E. (1990). Distance between homes and exercise facilities related to frequency of exercise among San Diego residents. *Public Health Reports,* 2, 179–185.

Sallis, J.F., & Owen, N. (1999). *Physical activity and behavioral medicine*. Thousand Oaks, CA: Sage Publications.

Shaw, S.M., Bonen, A., & McCabe, J.F. (1991). Do more constraints mean less leisure? Examining the relationship between constraints and participation. *Journal of Leisure Research, 23,* 286–300.

Troiano, R.P., Berrigan, D., Dodd, K.W., Mâsse, L.C., Tilert, T., & McDowell, M. (2008). Physical activity in the United States measured by accelerometer. *Medicine & Science in Sports & Exercise, 40,* 181–188.

U.S. Department of Health and Human Services. (2004). *Healthy People 2010*. Washington, DC: U.S. Government Printing Office.

U.S. Public Health Service. (1999). *Mental health: A report of the Surgeon General*. Washington, DC: U.S. Department of Health and Human Services.

2

Physical Activity Epidemiology

KEY TERMS

all-cause mortality rates
epidemiology
longitudinal studies
morbidity
sedentary

Today, the types of physical activity we engage in vary tremendously, from organized sport (e.g., basketball) to playground games (e.g., "tag"), and from fitness activities (e.g., jogging) to outdoor recreation (e.g., rock climbing). People from all walks of life (both sexes, all age groups, most ethnic groups) engage in exercise and other forms of physical activity for a variety of reasons. Through these activities, we rehabilitate, obtain membership status in a socially defined group, improve employee productivity, improve our fitness level, feel better about ourselves, relieve stress, and so forth. Unfortunately, a relatively low percentage of people take advantage of the many benefits of physical activity participation, and the negative consequences of this behavioral choice are becoming painfully clear. The U.S. Centers for Disease Control and Prevention (CDC) have reported that physical inactivity, along with poor diet, is responsible for at least 365,000 "preventable" deaths per year (16 percent of all deaths), a number second only to those deaths caused by smoking (Mokdad, Marks, Stroup, et al., 2005). Furthermore, the World Health Organization (WHO) has identified unhealthy diets and inactivity as two of the leading causes of the major noncommunicable diseases (cardiovascular disease, type 2 diabetes, and certain types of cancer), as well as significant contributors to the global burden of disease, death, and disability.

The epidemic of physical inactivity is not limited to North America—the lack of physical activity is a problem in virtually all industrialized nations (Sallis & Owen, 1999). Indeed, the birth of the Industrial Revolution appears to have coincided with the death of widespread involvement in physical activity. Technology, for example, has provided many time- and effort-saving devices (e.g., refrigerators, microwaves, cars, forklifts) as well as means of entertainment (e.g., televisions, cable/satellite/video game systems, DVD players/recorders, computers, the Internet). One consequence of this, as reported by the CDC, is that the number of trips made by walking or bicycling has declined by more than 40 percent since 1977 (USDHHS, 2004). Making matters worse, today's occupations rely much more on mental as opposed to physical capacity, thus increasing mental stress and reducing occupational physical activity. Concern over the inactivity of society has attracted the attention of government agencies, the World Health Organization, and entities such as the task force for the U.S. Healthy People 2010 initiative (see Exhibit 2.1 for examples of Healthy People 2010 objectives). Fortunately, as detailed in Chapter 6, the field of exercise psychology may play a prominent role in improving the rates of physical activity adoption and adherence. Before we discuss how to use exercise psychology principles to improve adoption and adherence rates, however, it is necessary to review current patterns of physical activity participation.

exhibit 2.1 **Examples of Healthy People 2010 physical activity and fitness objectives.***

- Reduce the proportion of adults who engage in no leisure-time physical activity.
- Increase the proportion of adolescents who engage in moderate physical activity for at least 30 minutes on five or more days per week.
- Increase the proportion of adolescents who engage in vigorous physical activity that promotes the development and maintenance of cardiorespiratory fitness three or more days per week for 20 or more minutes per occasion.
- Increase the proportion of adults who perform physical activities that enhance and maintain muscular strength and endurance.
- Increase the proportion of adults who perform physical activities that enhance and maintain flexibility.
- Increase the proportion of the national public and private schools that require daily physical education for all students.
- Increase the proportion of adolescents who spend at least 50 percent of school physical education class time being physically active.
- Increase the proportion of worksites offering employer-sponsored physical activity and fitness programs.
- Increase the proportion of trips made by walking.
- Increase the proportion of trips made by bicycling.

*The Healthy People 2020 objectives are currently under review, and the final objectives will be released in 2010. See www.healthypeople.gov/HP2020/ for more information.

Source: USDHHS, 2004.

A Primer on Measurement of Physical Activity Behavior

The manner in which researchers measure physical activity varies tremendously. This variation includes not only a consideration of mode (e.g., running, biking, weight training), frequency (e.g., three days per week), intensity (e.g., 60 percent of maximum heart rate), and duration (e.g., 45 minutes per session), but also the ways in which adherence to a physical activity regimen is assessed. Although a comprehensive review of measurement is beyond the scope of this text, the issue merits attention before we begin our discussion of activity patterns.

It has been noted that more than 30 different known measures of physical activity exist in the literature (Kriska & Caspersen, 1997). These measures tend to fall into one of three categories based on the primary means of assessment—namely, (1) subjective/self-report, (2) objective/technological, and (3) observation.

SUBJECTIVE/SELF-REPORT

Self-report measures (e.g., questionnaire, interview) are the most widely used because they provide a great deal of information with relatively little time and financial investment. Indeed, the data presented throughout the remainder of this chapter are based on self-report measures, and sample instruments are provided throughout the book. Among the more popular self-report modalities are daily activity "logs" (activities written in notebooks or recorded in a variety of electronic media) and the use of physical activity recall. The latter may be used for varying periods of time with the caveat that, the longer the time frame, the greater the chance of error due to memory limitations. Recall measures ask the respondent to indicate the mode, frequency, intensity, and duration of the activity(ies) performed for a specified period of time. Measures assessing activities performed during a "typical" week (e.g., Godin Leisure Time Exercise Questionnaire, Godin and Shephard, 1985; see Exhibit 2.2) tend to be less accurate than those using recall of a specific time period. The most popular recall time frame appears to be one week (e.g., Seven Day Physical Activity Recall (PAR), Blair, Haskell, Ho, et al., 1985; see Exhibit 2.3), although a number of three-day, one-month, three-month, six-month, and one-year measures also exist in the literature. Overall, although self-report techniques are subject to both intentional (social desirability bias) and involuntary (poor memory) manipulation, most are cost-effective and easy-to-use assessment tools.

OBJECTIVE/TECHNOLOGICAL

The second category of measurement is composed of the various mechanical and electronic devices used to monitor and record physical activity behavior. A significant benefit of technological devices is that many provide direct measures of intensity and duration (e.g., exercise heart rate, distance walked) as well as indirect estimates of energy expenditure (e.g., calories burned, metabolic units). Although these objective measures are not subject to falsified feedback or memory fade concerns that are characteristic of self-report tools, they are more expensive to purchase and maintain, can be somewhat complex to use, and do not provide information related to all aspects of the activity (mode, frequency). Popular examples include the following:

Heart rate monitor. This instrument uses a transmitter attached to a chest band residing over the heart to emit a signal that is displayed on a special wristwatch. It provides constant pulse readings and, depending on the model, a recording of heart rate at regular intervals, a stopwatch function, and the ability to program a desired intensity range with accompanying auditory feedback.

Pedometer. This small device is typically attached to either the waistband or shoe. It works like the odometer on a car to provide data such as the number of steps taken and distance covered over a period of time. Advanced models can "guesstimate" the number of calories you burn when body weight is entered, but the accuracy of such estimates is notoriously poor due to differences in body physiology and fitness levels. Additionally, because stride length increases as you move faster, the distance reported may be underestimated. Conversely, walking at a slower than normal pace may overestimate distance.

Accelerometer. This small device detects acceleration of a limb (e.g., leg, arm) to provide data related to the amount of activity performed over time. The different types of accelerometers vary considerably not only in price ($100 to several thousand dollars including computer interface and

A Primer on Measurement of Physical Activity Behavior, CONTINUED

software) but also in terms of their sensitivity to movement. As in the case of pedometers, accelerometers may overpredict energy expenditure during walking and underpredict energy expenditure in more intense activities and arm ergometry. Unlike pedometers, however, accelerometers are much less user-friendly.

Global positioning system (GPS) units. Today, GPS technology has become mainstream, showing up in our cars, cellular phones, and increasingly in our workouts, including those involving running, biking, and walking. Continuous microwave signals are transmitted to the earth via satellites and are picked up by a GPS receiver that computes estimated energy expenditure by tracking speed, slope, and duration of physical activity (similar to a heart rate monitor).

In addition to its use in daily exercise activity, one of the more popular leisure activities employing GPS technology is geocaching, which incorporates a GPS unit in an updated form of scavenger hunt. In this activity, the goal is to locate containers (geocaches) that have been hidden outdoors, using a GPS, and then later describe the experience online. Successful discoverers then return the cache to its previous location for the next person to find. At present more than 900,000 geocaches are hidden throughout the world. (See www.geocaching.com for more.)

OBSERVATION

The final category of measurement consists of both direct (viewing exercise behavior "live" or "in-person") and indirect (viewing a recorded behavior) methods of observation. Observation allows for documentation of the specific activities engaged in, eliminates the issue of memory recall and self-report biases, and is more cost effective and less complex to use than electronic devices. An example of a simple observational measure would be a fitness leader's recording of participant attendance. The drawbacks of this technique include time costs as well as the potential for atypical behavior on the part of the exerciser as a function of being observed. Additionally, this procedure often requires other people to make difficult subjective judgments about aspects of the activity, such as intensity level.

exhibit 2.2 Godin leisure time exercise questionnaire.

1. During a typical **7-day period** (a week), how many times on the average do you do the following kinds of exercise for **more than 15 minutes** during your free time (write in each square the appropriate number).

   (a) **Strenuous Exercise (heart beats rapidly)** ☐ Times per week
   (e.g., running, jogging, hockey, football, soccer, squash, basketball, cross country skiing, judo, roller skating, vigorous swimming, vigorous long distance bicycling)

   (b) **Moderate Exercise (not exhausting)** ☐ Times per week
   (e.g., fast walking, baseball, tennis, easy bicycling, volleyball, badminton, easy swimming, alpine skiing, popular and folk dancing)

   (c) **Mild Exercise (minimal effort)** ☐ Times per week
   (e.g., yoga, archery, fishing from river bank, bowling, horseshoes, golf, snow-mobiling, easy walking)

2. During a typical **7-day period** (a week), in your **leisure time,** how often do you engage in any regular activity long enough to **work up a sweat** (heart beats rapidly)?
   ☐ Often
   ☐ Sometimes
   ☐ Never/Rarely

"Godin Leisure-time Exercise Questionnaire," adapted from Godin, G., Jobin, J., Bouillon, J. (1986). Assessment of leisure time exercise behavior by self-report: A concurrent validity study. *Canadian Journal of Public Health, 77,* 359–631. Used with permission.

Seven-Day Physical Activity Recall. exhibit 2.3

PAR# 1 2 3 4 5 6 7

ID# ____________________

Participant ____________________

Interviewer ____________ Today is ____________ Today's Date ____________

1. Were you employed in the last seven days? 0 No (Skip to Q#4) 1 Yes
2. How many days of the last seven did you work? ______ days
3. How many total hours did you work in the last seven days? ______ hours last week
4. What two days do you consider your weekend days? ____________________

(mark days below with a squiggle)

WORKSHEET		DAYS						
	SLEEP	1 ____	2 ____	3 ____	4 ____	5 ____	6 ____	7 ____
MORNING	Moderate							
	Hard							
	Very Hard							
AFTERNOON	Moderate							
	Hard							
	Very Hard							
EVENING	Moderate							
	Hard							
	Very Hard							
Total Min Per Day	Strength:							
	Flexibility:							

4a. Compared to your physical activity over the past 3 months, was last week's physical activity more, less, or about the same? 1 More 2 Less 3 About the same

5. Were there any problems with the PAR interview? 0 No 1 Yes *(If yes, go to the back and explain)*

6. Do you think this was a valid PAR interview? 0 No 1 Yes *(If no, go to the back and explain)*

7. Were there any special circumstances concerning this PAR? 0 No 1 Yes *If yes, what were they? (circle)*

1. Injury all week 2. Illness all week
3. Illness part week 4. Injury part week
5. Pregnancy 6. Other:

(continued)

exhibit 2.3 **Continued.**

ID# ______________________________

Worksheet Key:

An asterisk (*) denotes a work-related activity.
A squiggly line through a column (day) denotes a weekend day.

Rounding:

10–22 min. = .25
23–37 min. = .50
38–52 min. = .75
53–1.07 hr/min. = 1.0
1:08–1:22 hr/min. = 1.25

5. Explain why there were problems with this PAR interview:

____

____

____

____

6. If PAR interview was not valid, why was it not valid?

____

____

____

____

7. Please list below any activities reported by the subject that you do not know how to classify.

____

____

____

____

8. Please provide any other comments you may have.

____

____

____

____

Blair, S.N., Haskell, W.L., Ho, P., Paffenbarger, Jr., R.S., Vranizan, K.M., Farquhar, J.W., & Wood, P.D. (1985). Assessment of habitual physical activity by a seven-day recall in a community survey and controlled experiments. *American Journal of Epidemiology, 122,* 794–804. Used with permission.

Physical Activity Participation Patterns–Sampling Across the Globe

One of our goals in this book is to document current patterns of physical activity behavior in society. Such an agenda falls within the domain of **epidemiology**, which, when applied to physical activity, is a field of study devoted to the five "W's": who exercises; where, when, and why they do so; and what they do. Thus, epidemiology related to physical activity may be defined by questions such as, "To what extent are individuals within a particular society physically active?" and "What physical activities are people most engaged in?" Epidemiology of physical activity might also address variations in physical activity patterns across certain groups of individuals (e.g., based on age, gender, race/ethnicity, income level, education level); why certain individuals are physically active while others are not; and the links among physical activity, morbidity, and mortality. Without epidemiological data, we would not know that the proportion of Brazilians who are inactive during their leisure time is considerably higher than in the United States (Monteiro, Conde, Matsudo, et al., 2003). Or that, every year, physical inactivity is responsible for 600,000 deaths in the European Union (about 6 percent of the total), while overweight and obesity cause more than one million more (Cavill, Kahlmeier, & Racioppi, 2006). We almost certainly would not predict that underweight adults in South Australia spend more time, on average, engaged in sedentary activities than obese adults (Gill, Fullerton, & Taylor, 2007; see Exhibit 2.4). Information such as this is paramount as it allows health care professionals to target specific populations of people for intervention, determine the impact of the intervention, and

■ epidemiology

Daily time spent by South Australian adults in sedentary activities, by BMI category. exhibit 2.4

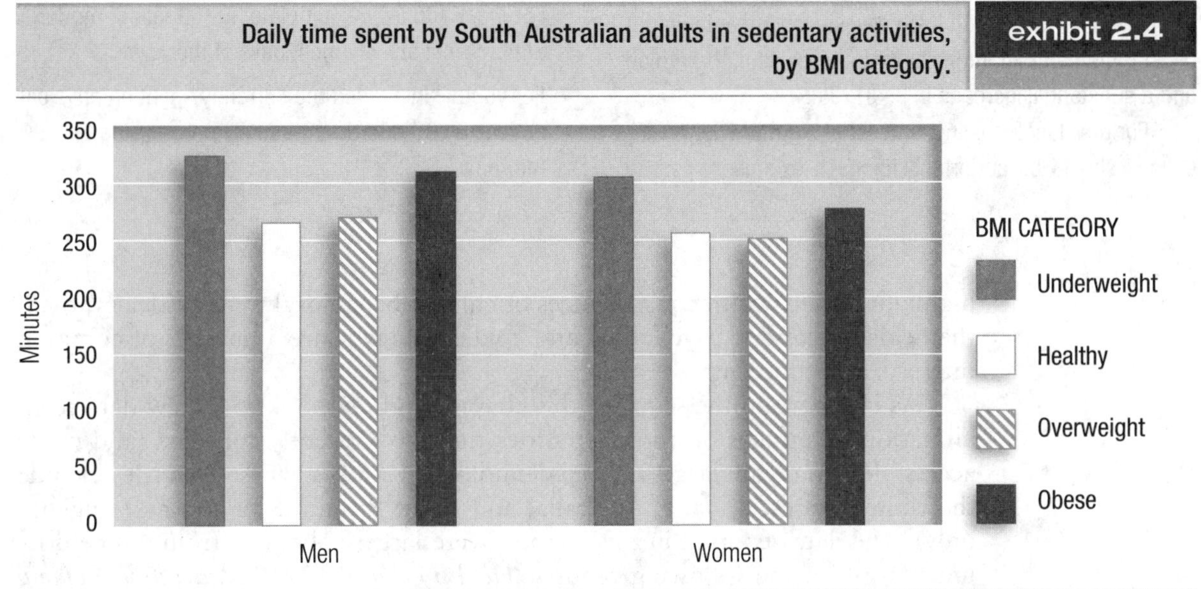

Guidelines for Physical Activity

Most major U.S. organizations (e.g., CDC, National Institute on Aging, U.S. Department of Health and Human Services, American College of Sports Medicine) have guidelines for physical activity for adults, children, and older adults that include recommendations about both aerobic and muscle-strengthening exercises. In addition, exercises to increase/maintain balance and flexibility are often recommended. Because the American College of Sports Medicine (ACSM) is considered the foremost authority on fitness in the United States, we provide the organization's most recently updated recommendations (in partnership with the American Heart Association) for cardiovascular, resistance, and flexibility training suggested for health promotion and disease prevention in adults (Haskell, Lee, Pate, et al., 2007).

For cardiovascular training, individuals should engage in moderately intense activity (e.g., brisk walk) five days per week with each session lasting a minimum of 30 minutes at an intensity that noticeably accelerates the heart rate (see Chapter 6). The time for each session may be reduced to as little as 10 minutes in instances where an individual has chosen to engage in multiple bouts of exercise in a given day. Alternatively, individuals may choose to participate in vigorously intense activity (e.g., jogging) three days per week with each session lasting a minimum of 20 minutes at an intensity that causes rapid breathing and a substantial increase in heart rate.

For resistance training, one set of eight to twelve repetitions should be performed for each exercise. Intensity should be adjusted such that the amount of resistance (e.g., weight) causes the exerciser to experience volitional fatigue upon completing each set. Finally, it is suggested that individuals engage in resistance training twice per week with each session consisting of 8 to 10 different exercises. Because muscle recovery is especially important in resistance training, participants should not train the same muscle groups two or more days in succession.

For flexibility training, three to five sets per stretch should be performed to the point of mild discomfort. Stretches should be held for 10 to 30 seconds, and each major muscle group should be stretched at least three days per week (preferably daily).

Other countries have generated guidelines based on different criteria, such as age. For example, the guidelines developed by the Public Health Agency of Canada (www.phac-aspc.gc.ca/pau-uap/paguide/) are as follows:

- For adults: "Accumulate 60 min of physical activity every day. As you progress to moderate [or vigorous] activity you can decrease the time needed to 30 min, 4 days/week."
- For older adults: "Accumulate 30–60 min of moderate physical activity most days of the week."
- For youth: "Increase time currently spent on physical activity by 30 min/day, gradually progressing to ≥ 90 min/day."

highlight public health consequences of current behavioral trends. Clearly, then, the fields of exercise psychology and epidemiology share a number of common interests and concerns.

As it is beyond the scope of this chapter and textbook to review data from all nations, we focus on those countries that have recently collected (and made accessible) data from large-scale epidemiological studies. These countries include the United States, Canada, Australia, and Great Britain (Scotland and England only). The data reported in this chapter were largely obtained from online documentation of the following reports: *Healthy People 2010 Midcourse Review*

(USDHHS, 2006), the *Health Survey for England 2006* (Craig & Mindell, 2008), the *Scottish Health Survey 2003* (Bromley, Sproston, & Shelton, 2005), the Canadian Fitness and Lifestyle Research Institute's *2007 Physical Activity Monitor,* and *Physical Activity Among South Australian Adults* (Gill, Fullerton, & Taylor, 2007). Where possible, we will also include data from a survey conducted among adults in Brazil (Monteiro, Conde, Matsudo, et al., 2003). We have chosen to focus our review on demographics that are reported fairly consistently across each data set. Therefore, the remainder of this chapter will address the role of physical activity as it relates to age, gender, race/ethnicity, income level, and education level. Before embarking on our discussion, however, we would like to highlight the inherent difficulty in directly comparing the data reported by each of these countries. Specifically, the tremendous variability across nations in definitions of concepts such as "regular activity," "vigorous activity," "minimal activity," "recommended activity," and "sufficient activity" makes comparisons of data between and among countries somewhat impractical. Thus, where disparities in activity rates exist, readers should be cautious about drawing conclusions based solely on country membership.

Adult Patterns of Physical Activity

Not surprisingly, **sedentary** lifestyles (chronic pattern of inactivity) have been consistently identified in four of the five industrialized countries as well as in the newly industrialized country of Brazil. These rates vary tremendously, however, from Australia on the low end (15 percent of adults defined as inactive), the United States representing the middle or average (40 percent), and Brazil on the high end (87 percent). Unfortunately, even when adults do engage in physical activity, they often fail to do so at levels sufficient for health improvements (Exhibit 2.5). Generally speaking, 50 to 70 percent of the industrialized countries' residents do not achieve the recommended amount of regular physical activity, while nearly 97 percent of Brazilian adults fail to perform the minimum recommended amount of physical activity each week. According to a report by the World Health Organization Regional Office for Europe (representing the European Union), two-thirds of the adult population do not reach recommended levels of activity and, more important, the trend is toward less activity, not more (Cavill, Kahlmeier, & Racioppi, 2006).

■ sedentary

Despite these sobering statistics evidence may support a more optimistic view for the future. Indeed, epidemiological data are beginning to emerge that indicate trends toward improvement in physical activity levels in several of these countries. Data from Canada reveal a positive trend in levels of moderate physical activity from 40 percent in 1997 to 49 percent in 2005. In England, only 26 percent of adults in 1997 engaged in activity levels meeting recommendations, compared to 34 percent in 2006. The proportion of Scottish adults engaging in recommended levels of physical activity increased by 3 percent between 1998 and between 2003, while Australia demonstrated a 5-percent increase in sufficient levels of activity between 1998 and 2007. Interestingly, data from the

exhibit 2.5 Percent of population engaging in sufficient levels of physical activity by sex and country.

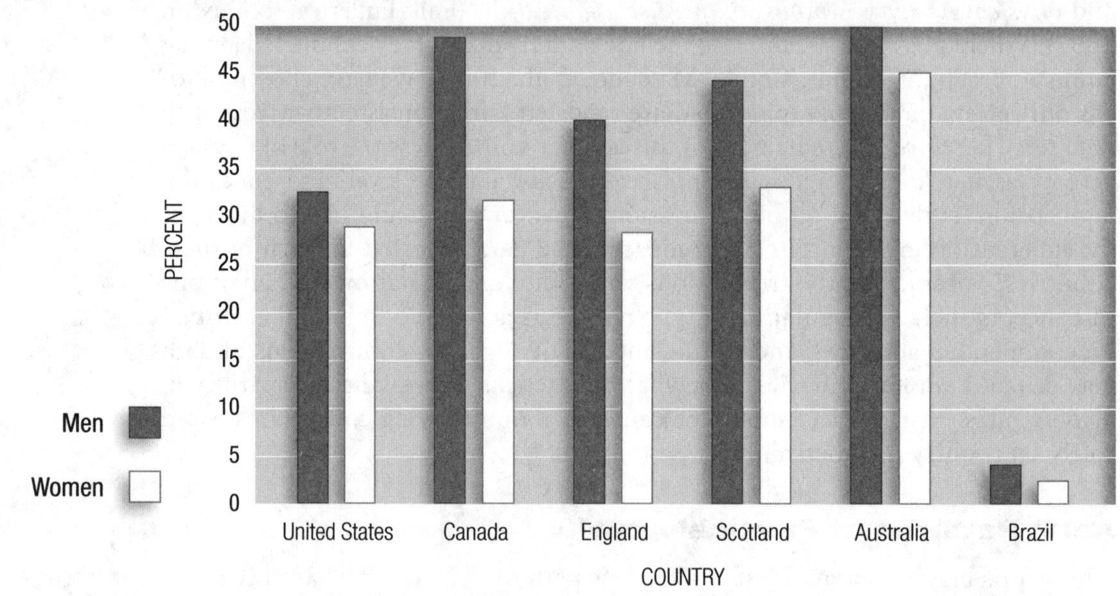

United States have been mixed in recent years and do not reflect the same trends evident in other countries. For example, while sedentary rates in the United States dropped from 40 percent in 1998 to 37 percent in 2003, and rates of moderate to vigorous activity increased from 30 to 33 percent during that time, recent data from 2006 suggest that these rates have regressed back toward the mean (39 percent sedentary, 31 percent engaged in moderate to vigorous activity).

Age and Physical Activity

The trend toward reducing one's level of physical activity as one ages is a widely understood and accepted reality worldwide. What is alarming (and, some would argue, disturbing) are the trends toward increased overweight/obesity and diabetes, increased sedentary behaviors, and reduced physical activity behaviors that plague our youth. Provocative data regarding "sitting" and the physical activity habits of English children revealed that these two behaviors each occupy approximately 10 hours per week in the average life of a three-year-old toddler. By age 15, however, teenagers sit 17 to 18 hours per week and are physically active for only 4 to 8 hours per week.

In Canada, children 1 to 4 years of age spend approximately 28 hours in physically active play each week, while teenagers aged 13 to 17 spend only half that amount of time engaged in physical activity. In fact, more than one-half of Canadian teenagers are sedentary (51 percent sedentary rate for teens 12–14

Daily time spent by Scottish children in sport and exercise activities, by age and sex. **exhibit 2.6**

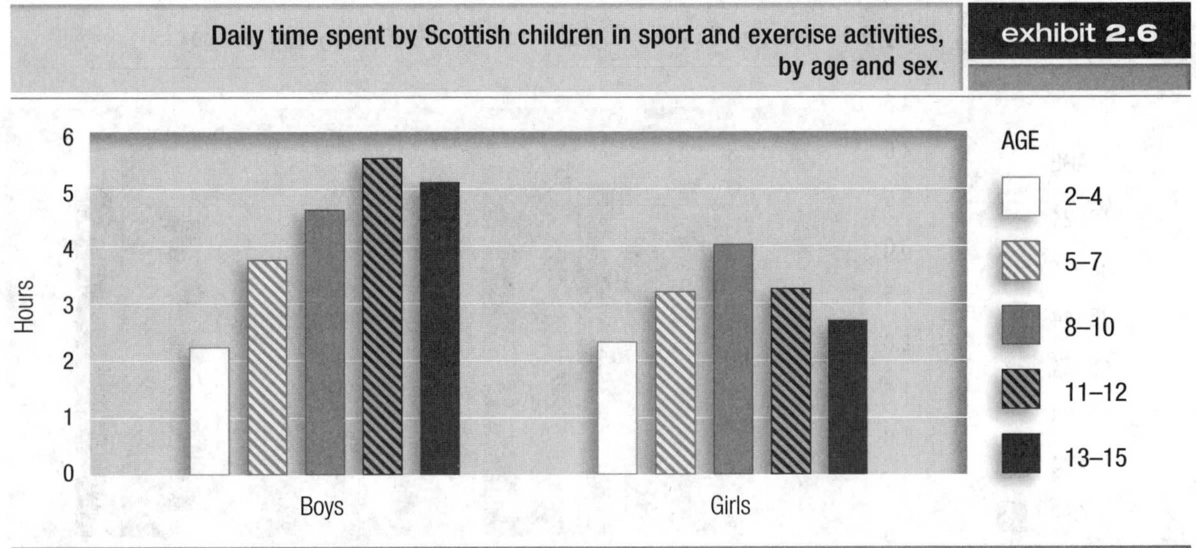

years of age; 59 percent sedentary rate for teens 15–19 years of age). Echoing the results of their adult cohorts, only two-thirds of 11-, 13-, and 15-year-olds in the European Union engage in sufficient physical activity to meet current guidelines and, while boys are more active than girls, physical activity declines with age for both sexes (Cavill et al., 2006).

Recent findings regarding American children are equally disconcerting. For example, while 45 percent of American children view television for more than two hours per school day (and one in four children spend four hours or more each day watching television), only 27 percent of students in grades 9–12 engage in sufficient levels of moderate intensity physical activity. Specific to physical education in schools, only 30 percent of students in grades 9–12 participate in daily physical education.

Finally, data from Scottish children provide insight into the ages at which boys and girls begin to display a drop-off in physical activity (Exhibit 2.6). Specifically, while boys show gradual increases in activity levels through age 12, girls begin to demonstrate reduced levels of physical activity by age 10.

Not surprisingly, the prevalence of physical activity does not improve demonstrably over the life span. For example, data related to Scottish adults sedentary "screen" behaviors (e.g., watching television/videos/DVDs, playing video/computer games, surfing the Internet) indicate that participation in these leisure-time pursuits resembles a J-curve in that activity is greatest in the youngest and oldest age cohorts (Exhibit 2.7). When physical activity is undertaken, clear age trends emerge. For example, data from England indicate a relatively linear decrease in the percentage of adults engaging in high levels of activity, and a relatively linear increase in the percentage of adults engaging in little or no activity, with advancing age (Exhibit 2.8). While similar statistics have been reported by the other industrialized countries, data from Brazil demonstrate a

exhibit 2.7 Daily time spent by Scottish adults in screen activities, by age and sex.

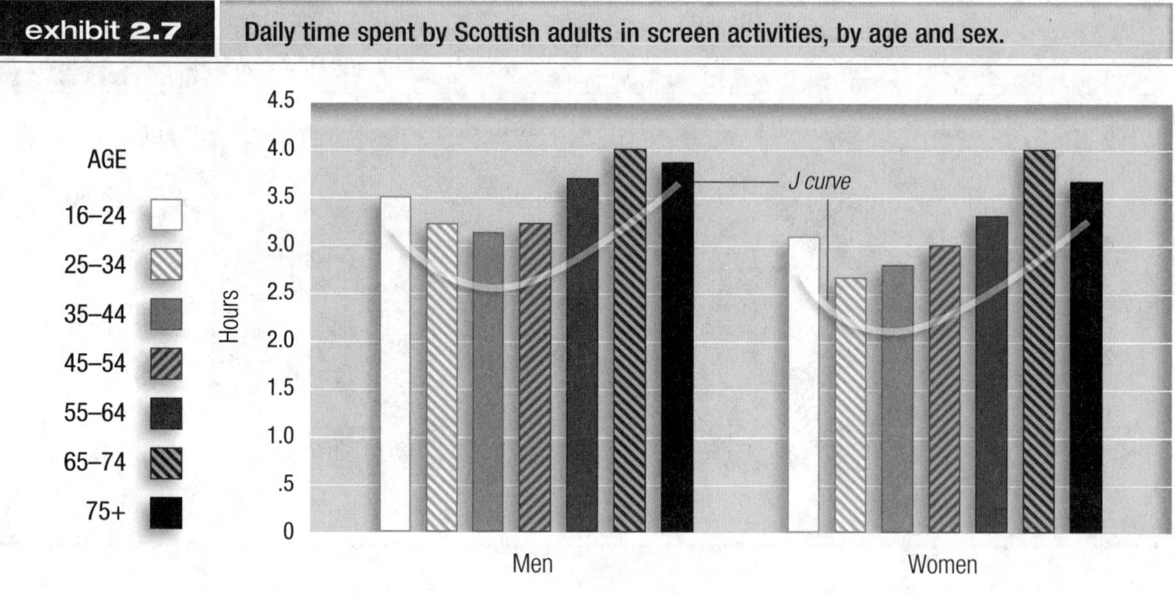

very different physical activity pattern with advanced age (Exhibit 2.9). Specifically, the relationship between age and activity level was direct, indicating that the frequency of physical activity *increases* over the life span.

As a final point regarding age and physical activity, it is interesting to note that physical activity levels present during youth are not related to exercise lev-

exhibit 2.8 Percentage of English population engaged in various levels of physical activity, by age.

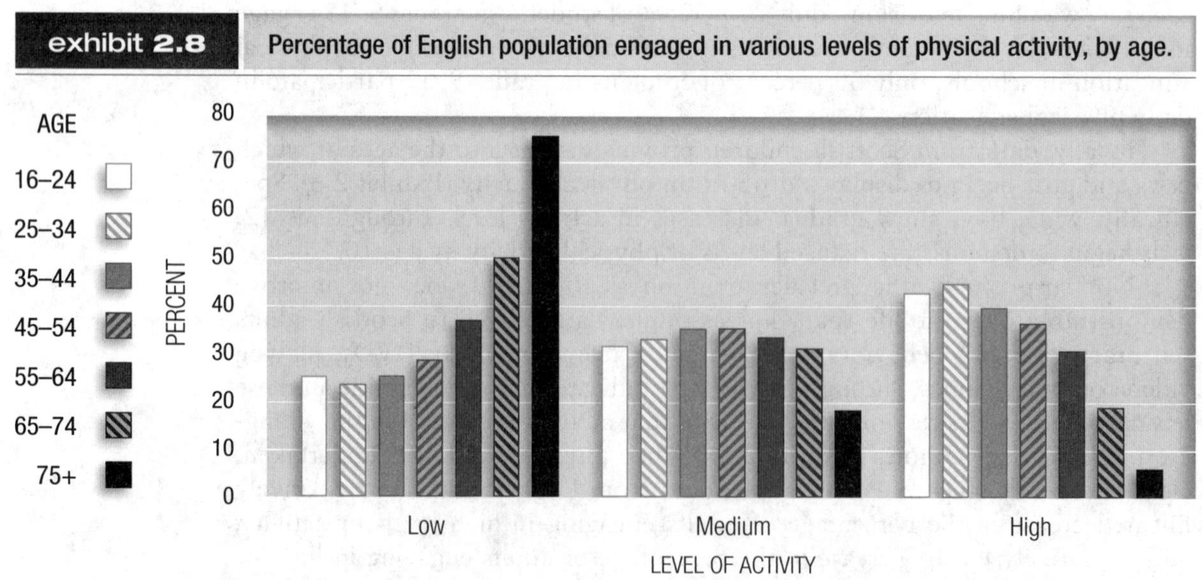

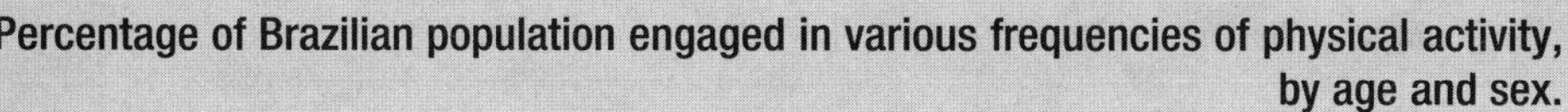
Percentage of Brazilian population engaged in various frequencies of physical activity, by age and sex. exhibit 2.9

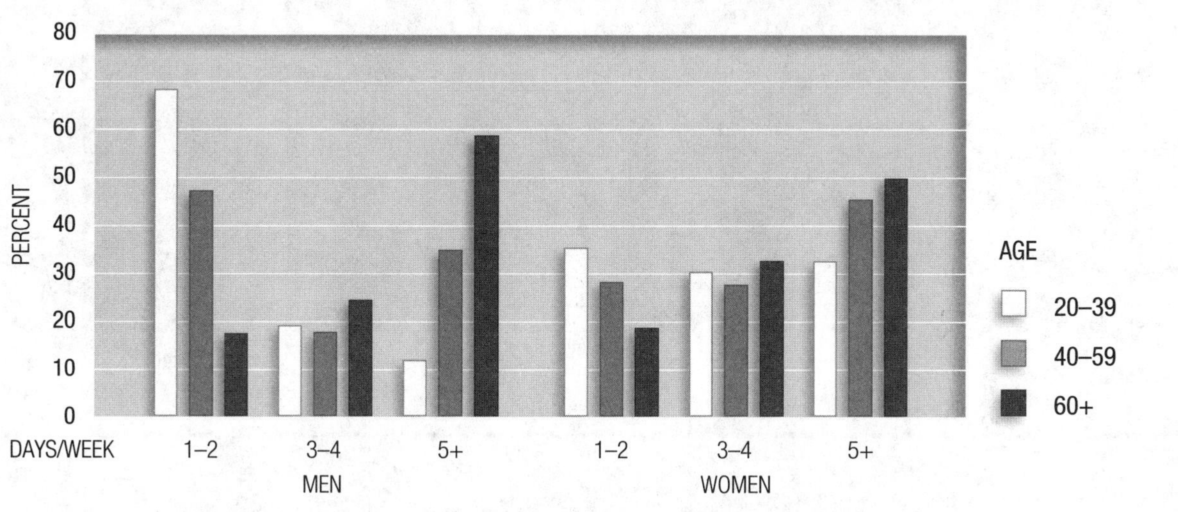

els in adulthood. In other words, highly active youngsters will not necessarily become physically active adults (Trost, Owen, Bauman, Sallis, & Brown, 2002). Clearly, one of the most significant challenges for researchers and practitioners is to determine how to transfer the enjoyment youngsters appear to experience in sport to the "lifetime" physical activities (e.g., tennis, golf, swimming, biking, hiking, dancing) in which active adults typically engage.

Gender and Physical Activity

Although the gap in activity levels has lessened in recent years, males have historically been more physically active than females. For example, while sedentary rates are often relatively similar, American men tend to engage in vigorous intensity activities, as well as muscular strength and endurance activities, to a greater extent than do American women. In England, the proportion of men achieving recommended levels of physical activity exceeds the proportion of women achieving recommended levels by 12 percent (40 percent vs. 28 percent). English males also participate in more hours of physical activity per week (eight) than do their female counterparts (five). When factors such as age or level of activity are considered, however, a somewhat different pattern of results emerges. For example, the proportion of Scottish men engaging in high activity levels decreases markedly with age, while rates for Scottish women remain relatively stable between the ages of 16 and 54. Additionally, males tend to engage in "high levels" of activity to a greater extent than females, while the latter tend to engage in more "low level" and "moderate level" activity (Exhibit 2.10).

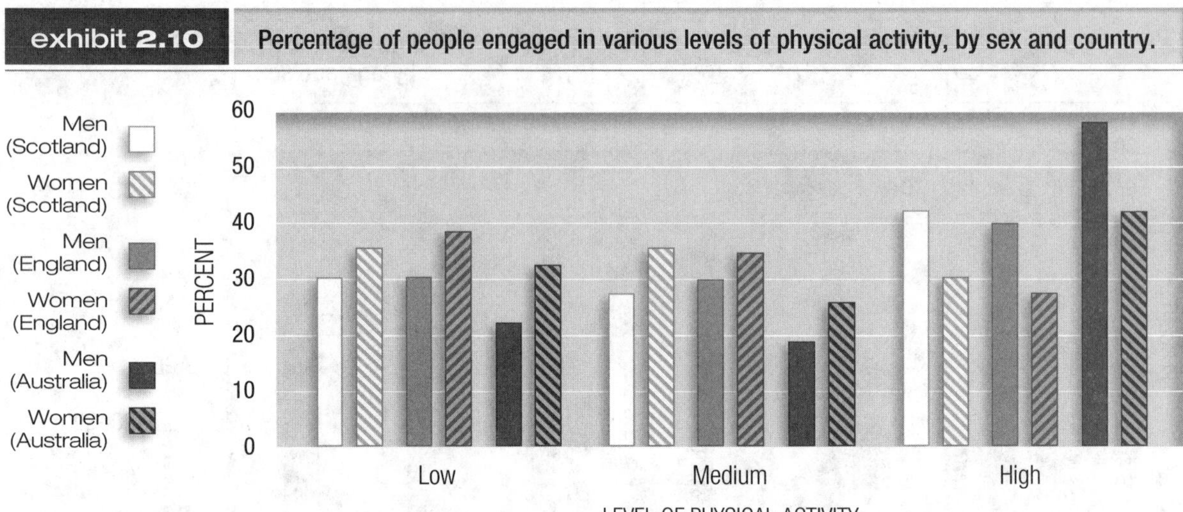

exhibit 2.10 Percentage of people engaged in various levels of physical activity, by sex and country.

Gender differences exist not only in the amount of activity but also in the type of activity performed (Exhibit 2.11). For example, the most common physical activity type for Scottish and English men is sports and exercise, whereas "heavy" housework is the top activity for Scottish and English women. Team sports are the most popular activity for Brazilian men, while walking/jogging is the preferred activity for Brazilian women. On the other hand, the most popular activities for Canadian men and women are the same—namely, walking, followed by gardening/yard work and, finally, "home" exercise.

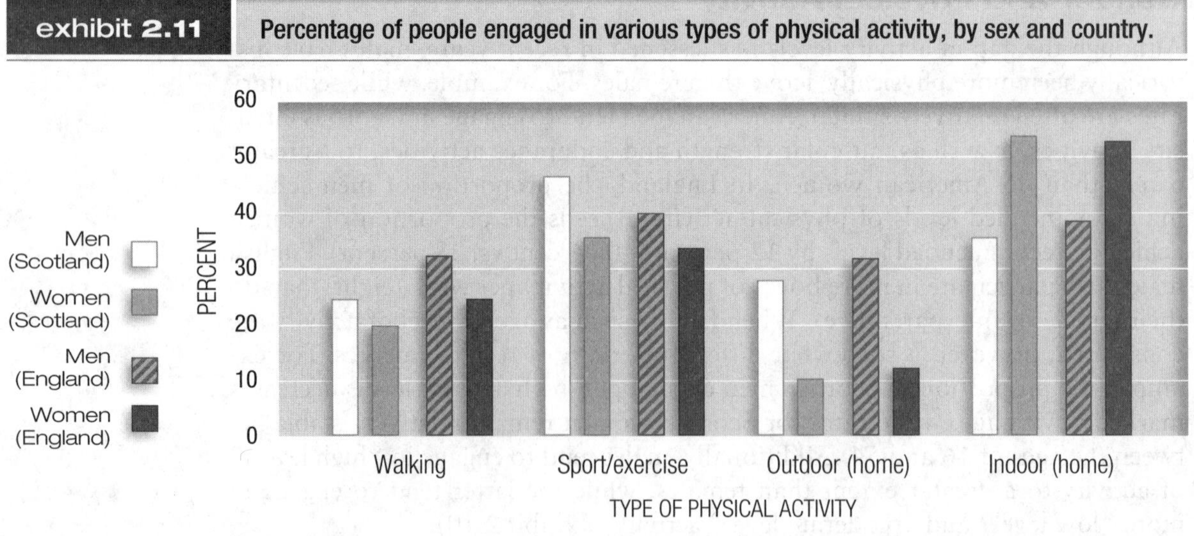

exhibit 2.11 Percentage of people engaged in various types of physical activity, by sex and country.

Sedentary rates in the United States, by race/ethnicity and survey year. **exhibit 2.12**

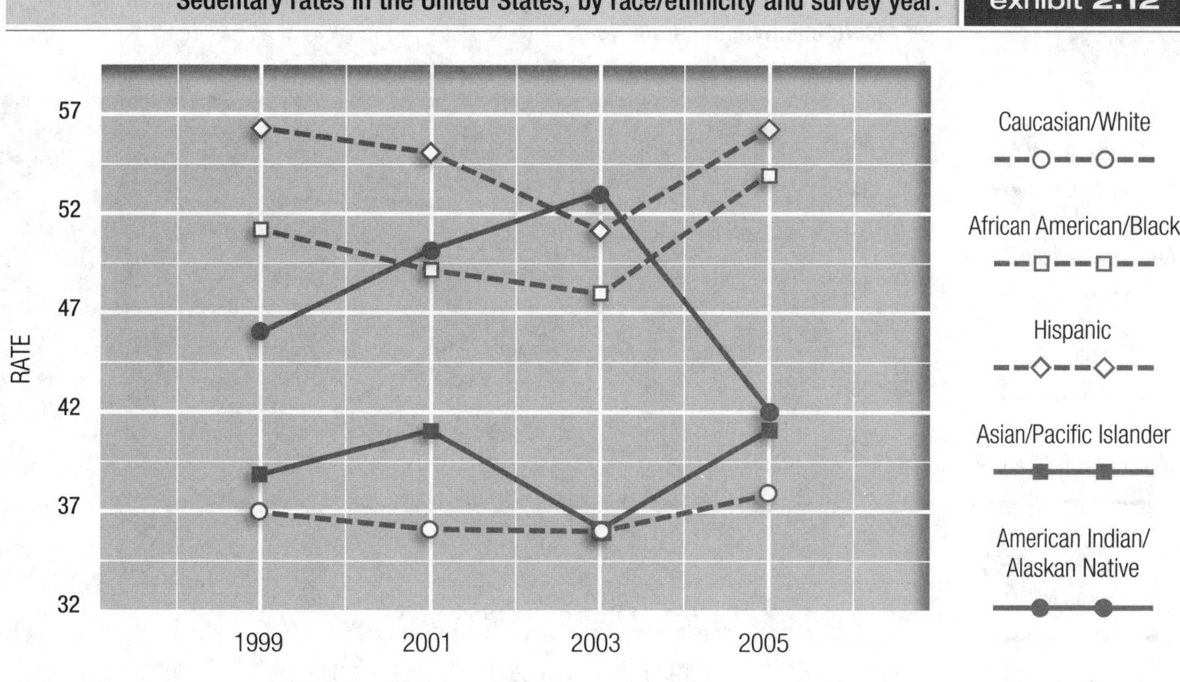

Race/Ethnicity and Physical Activity

With one exception, race/ethnicity is not reported as a demographic factor in the documents of the countries reviewed in this chapter. Thus, the statistics reported in this section are focused solely on data obtained in the United States. In general, these data indicate a trend toward lower physical activity participation in non-Caucasian ethnic groups. For example, the sedentary rate of Caucasian Americans is lower than that of Asian/Pacific Islanders, American Indian/Alaskan Natives, African Americans, and Hispanics (see Exhibit 2.12). Not surprisingly, these trends are reversed when it comes to participation in moderate or vigorous physical activity (Exhibit 2.13).

Similar results have been documented in U.S. adolescents (grades 9–12), although data for American Indian/Alaskan Natives and Asian/Pacific Islanders are not available. Notwithstanding, a larger proportion of Caucasian adolescents (28 percent) engage in moderate physical activity than do Hispanics (25 percent) or African Americans (20 percent). A greater percentage of Caucasians and Hispanics (66 percent each) engage in vigorous physical activity that promotes cardiorespiratory fitness than do African Americans (59 percent). Conversely, a significantly lower proportion (27 percent) of Caucasian high school–aged students report watching television for more than two hours per school day as compared to both Hispanic (43 percent) and African American students (63 percent). Of particular interest is the finding that a greater proportion

exhibit 2.13 Prevalence of regular moderate or vigorous physical activity in the United States, by race/ethnicity and survey year.

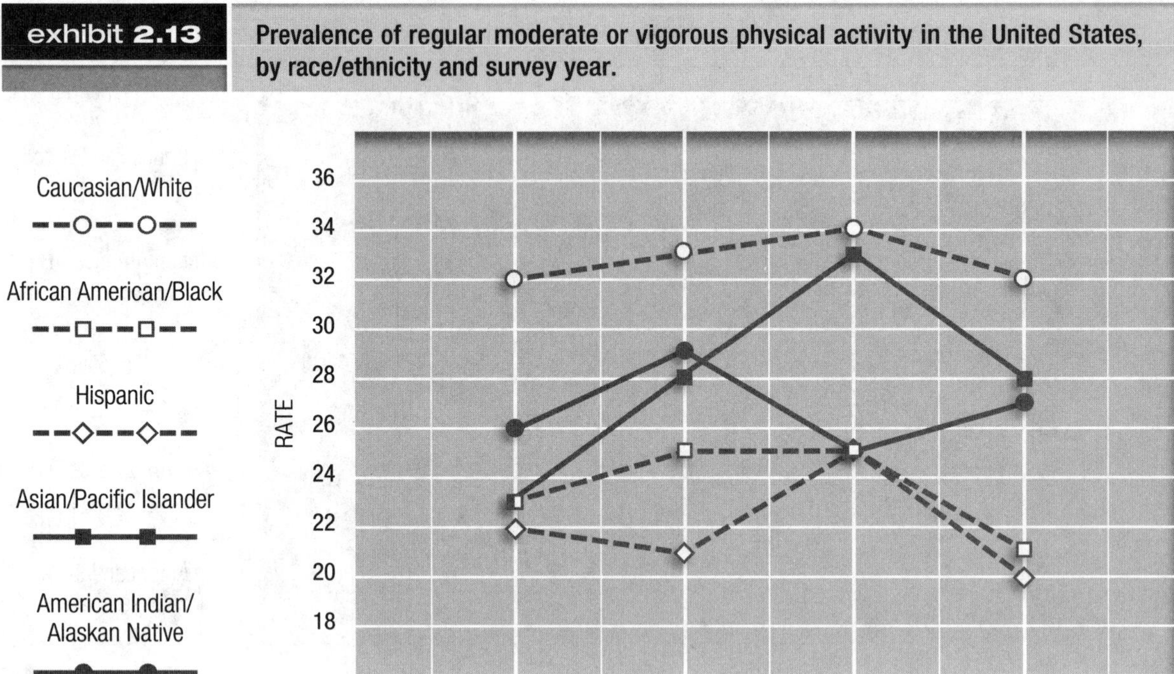

of Hispanics (36 percent) participate in daily physical education in school than do either African Americans (32 percent) or Caucasians (29 percent).

Income Level and Physical Activity

Although the relationship between income level and physical activity participation has typically been viewed as a relatively direct and linear one (e.g., for Canadian and Brazilian adults), such a finding is not consistent across countries and appears to be more complex than originally conceived. For example, sedentary rates, as well as rates of sufficient physical activity participation, in Australian adults support the notion of a direct and linear association (see Exhibit 2.14). When considering those Australian adults who are active at *insufficient* levels, however, no difference is observed in relation to income level.

The prevalence of physical activity based on income is particularly shocking in Brazilian women. Specifically, while 22 percent of women with the highest incomes are sufficiently physically active, only 1 percent of women with the lowest incomes engage in sufficient physical activity. Women in the second (6.5 percent) and third (3.3 percent) quartiles also report exceptionally poor rates of sufficient physical activity.

A somewhat different pattern, however, may be found in Scottish and English adults (see Exhibit 2.15), wherein the highest percentages of the population

Percentage of South Australian population engaging in various levels of physical activity, by income level quartile. exhibit 2.14

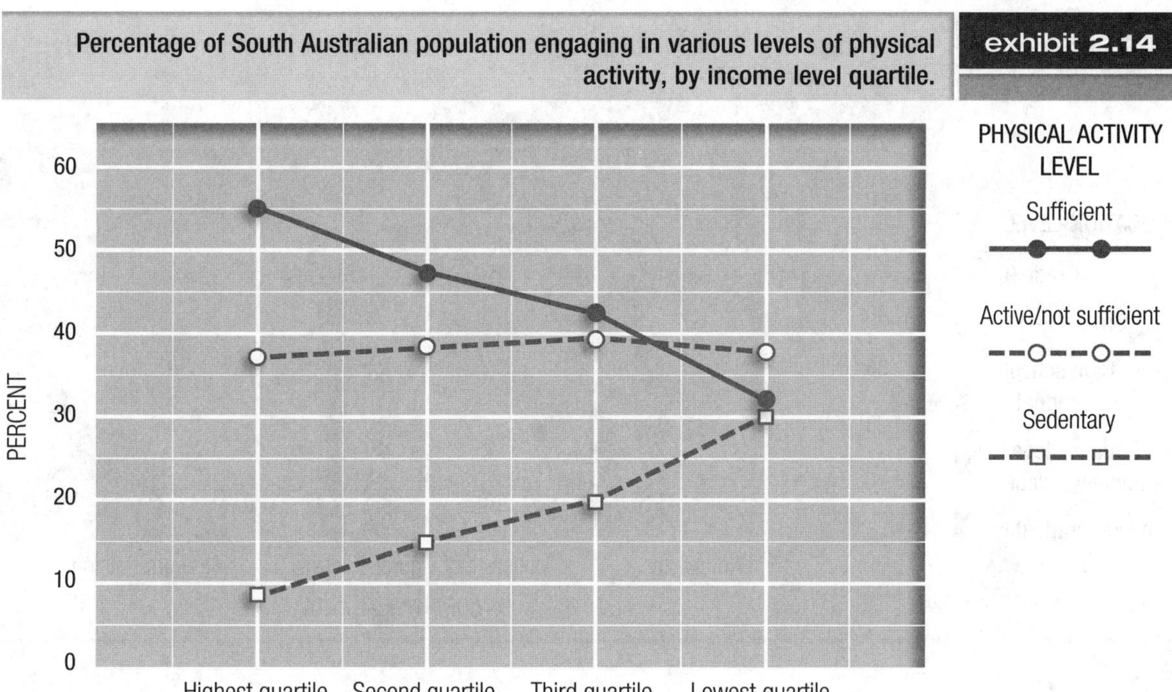

Percentage of population engaged in sufficient physical activity, by income level quintile and country. exhibit 2.15

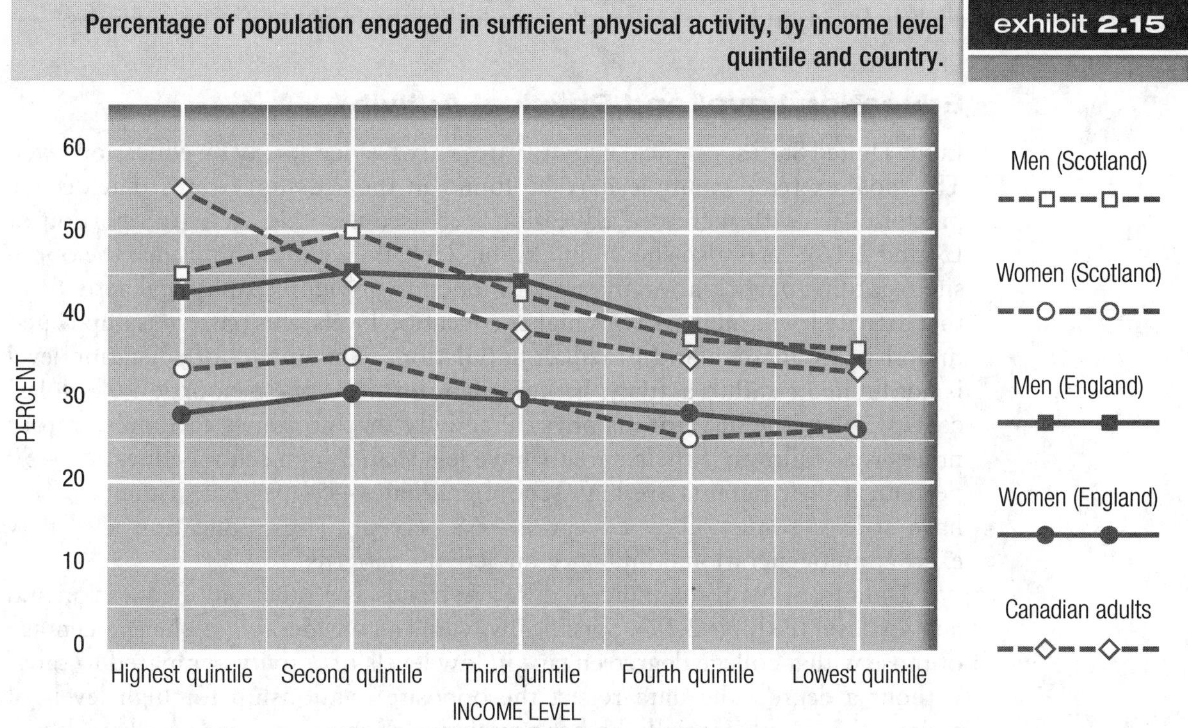

exhibit 2.16 Percentage of U.S. population engaged in various categories of physical activity, by education level.

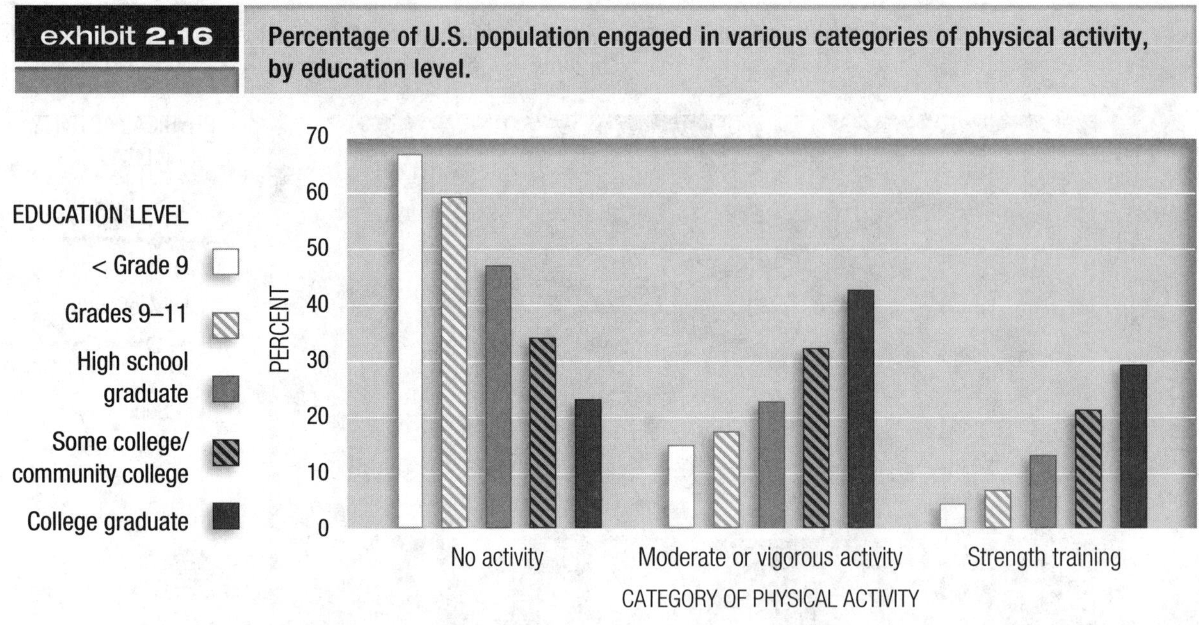

engaging in sufficient physical activity tend to be those in the second quintile (second-highest income level). The first (highest) and third quintiles posted rates slightly lower and were followed, in order, by the fourth and fifth quintiles.

Education Level and Physical Activity

In the United States, physical activity rates vary tremendously by education level. The most extreme example may be found in the sedentary rates that decline precipitously with increased education level (see the "No Activity" portion of Exhibit 2.16). As is also shown in Exhibit 2.16, the relationship is just the opposite regarding participation in regular moderate or vigorous physical activity, in that activity levels increase with higher education levels; this pattern is duplicated in both the Canadian and Brazilian populations. The impact of education level is not limited to adult activity, however. For instance, the proportion of adolescents who engage in vigorous physical activity that promotes cardiorespiratory fitness is as follows: if their parents have less than a high school education—50 percent; if their parents are high school graduates—54 percent; if their parents have at least some college education—68 percent. Thus, education level may exert a multigenerational influence on activity patterns.

Data from Australia indicate different trends as a function of education and activity level (Exhibit 2.17). Specifically, while a considerably higher percentage of those with a college degree engage in low levels of activity compared to those without a degree, the data reflect the opposite relationship for high levels of activity (i.e., a substantially higher percentage of those without a college degree

Percentage of South Australian population engaged in various levels of physical activity, by education level. **exhibit 2.17**

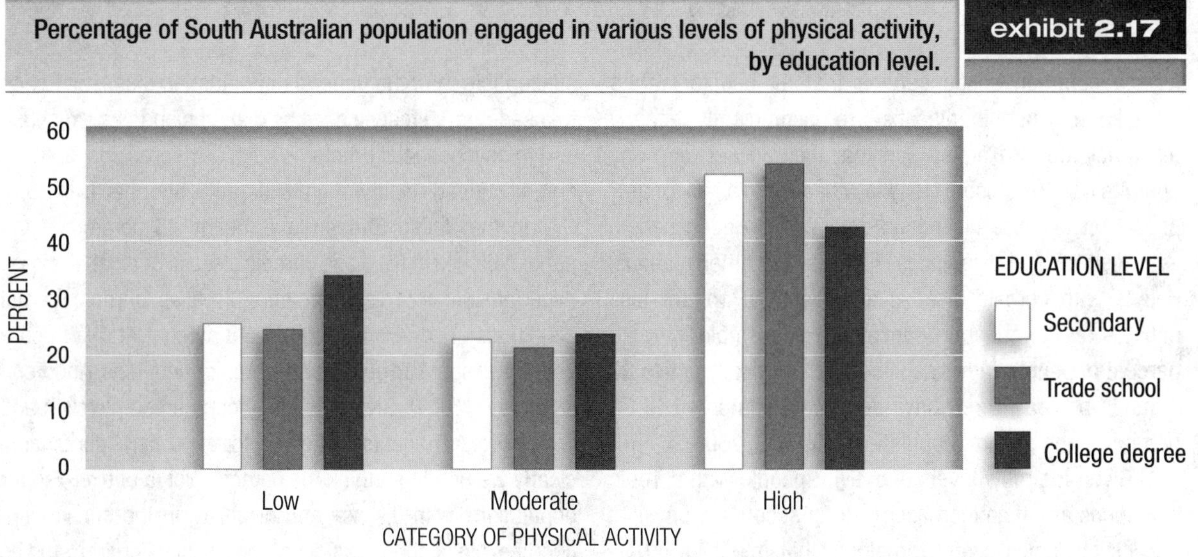

engage in high levels of activity compared to those with a degree). Little to no differences exist in moderate levels of activity based on education level.

Summary of Physical Activity Participation Patterns Across the Globe

Entire university courses are devoted to the study of physical activity epidemiology, and we have barely scratched the surface of the topic in this chapter. The data reviewed here highlight some of the key demographic factors implicated in physical activity behavior patterns across a small sample of industrialized and newly industrialized nations. Taken together, the findings reveal the following trends:

- The number of people worldwide who exercise at the minimal level required to achieve physical benefits is extremely low. A conservative estimate is that at least 50 percent of the population in each of the countries reviewed fail to meet this objective. At least 25 percent do not exercise at all.
- Generally speaking, the amount of time spent engaged in physical activity declines linearly across the life span. Conversely, the amount of time spent in sedentary activities increases linearly across the life span.
- Although males are more likely to participate in vigorous forms of physical activity, women tend to engage in as much, if not more, moderate intensity physical activity.
- Although the differences are relatively small, it appears that low income groups and ethnic minority groups tend to participate in less physical activity than does the overall population. For a discussion of physical activity interventions targeting these groups, the reader is referred to the article by Taylor, Baranowski, and Young (1998).

FOCUS on Special Populations

It is a common misconception that all people with a disability or chronic disease are insufficiently healthy to participate in exercise and that they do not reap any benefits from exercise. This fallacy has led to a lack of emphasis on exercise-promotion activities targeting people with disease and disabilities. For this and other reasons, people with chronic disease and disability are far less active than the general population. For example, only 23 percent of people with disabilities are physically active 20 minutes per day, three days per week, compared to 33 percent of the general population (USDHHS, 2004).

Given their low levels of activity, people with chronic conditions are at an increased risk for secondary physical and psychological health problems that might be otherwise prevented through exercise. For example, people with spinal cord injury (SCI) indicate that physical activity programs are the one service they most desire but are least available to them. With fewer exercise opportunities, it should not be surprising that the SCI population is more susceptible than the general population to diseases linked to a sedentary lifestyle such as diabetes and heart disease and to psychosocial problems such as depression, anxiety, and a reduced quality of life (Noreau & Shephard, 1995).

In the United States alone, nearly 45 percent of the population has at least one chronic disease or disability (e.g., hypertension, arthritis, respiratory diseases, chronic mental conditions). Furthermore, almost 78 percent of health care dollars are spent on people with chronic conditions (Anderson & Horvath, 2004). Given the well-documented physical and psychological benefits of exercise for the general population, clearly we need to rethink the potential value of exercise for populations with disease and disability. In the subsequent chapters, look for the "Focus" boxes highlighting studies that have examined exercise psychology concepts in populations with chronic disease or disability. The boxes will also include a list of related readings and an activity. These materials are designed to get you thinking more about physical activity–related issues in special populations.

- Generally speaking, education level is directly related to physical activity levels (i.e., the more education, the greater the participation in physical activity).

Consequences of Physical Activity and Inactivity

The previous section simply described what certain population segments of the world are doing in regard to engagement in physical activity. More disconcerting than the poor rates of physical activity participation, however, are the eventual consequences of this widespread inactivity. This section highlights the positive health outcomes of physical activity as well as the negative consequences of physical inactivity.

Physical Activity, Morbidity, and Mortality

According to a position paper jointly released by the CDC and the ACSM (Pate, Pratt, Blair, et al., 1995), physically active people outlive their sedentary counterparts, as demonstrated by their lower overall **all-cause mortality rates** (i.e., death by any cause) and by research indicating that a midlife increase in physical activity is associated with a reduced risk of mortality. Indeed, it has been estimated that premature deaths in Canada could be reduced by as much as 20 percent if sedentary and "somewhat active" Canadians became more active.

■ all-cause mortality rates

From a **morbidity** (disease) standpoint, although coronary heart disease (CHD) rates have continued to decline in the United States in recent years, approximately 14 million people still suffer from the disease and more than 1 million experience a heart attack each year. An additional 18 million people have adult-onset diabetes, 50 million people have high blood pressure, and more than 120 million people are overweight (Bassett, Pucher, Buehler, et al., 2008; see Exhibit 2.18). This last statistic is particularly distressing, as the overweight epidemic has found its way into the country's youth as well. Data indicate that approximately 30 percent of children and adolescents (aged 6 through 19) are overweight and 15 percent are obese (National Center for Health Statistics, 2005). Most important, excess weight in childhood and adolescence has been found to predict similar excess weight in adults. Overweight children, aged 10 to 14, with at least one overweight or obese parent, were reported to have a 79 percent likelihood of overweight persisting into adulthood (American Obesity Association, 2005).

■ morbidity

Perhaps the most frustrating aspect of these data is the fact that many of these conditions can be directly and positively impacted by the adoption of a physically active lifestyle. Indeed, several large-scale, descriptive, and longitudinal studies of physical activity level and morbidity/mortality rates support this statement. (**Longitudinal studies** allow researchers to monitor changes in behavior over a relatively long period of time, such as years, in the same group of people.)

■ longitudinal studies

Prevalence of obesity, by sex and country. **exhibit 2.18**

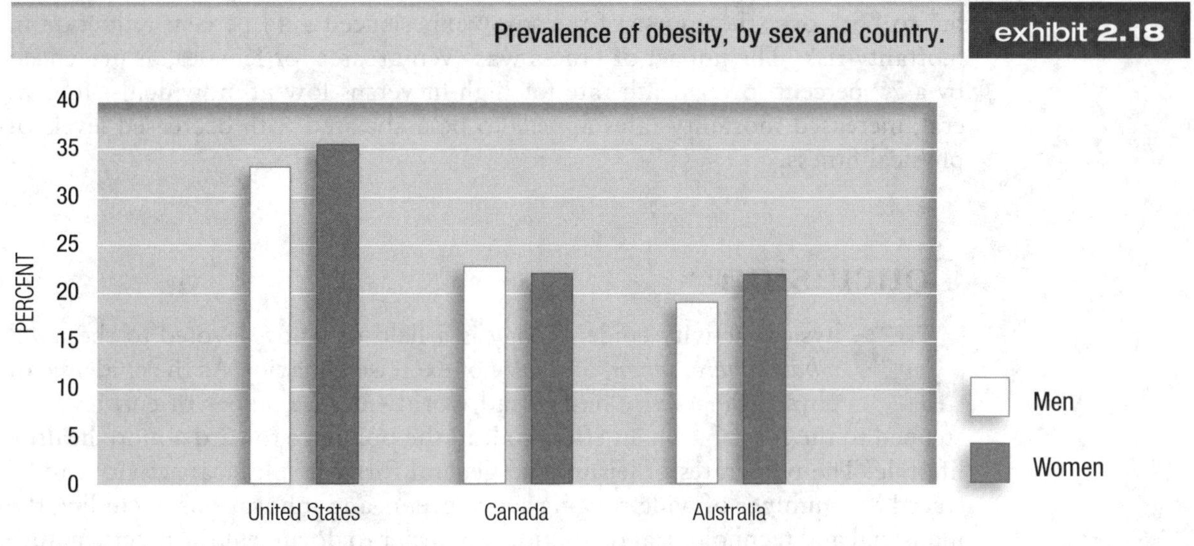

Two of the most recognized studies were conducted with the help of San Francisco longshoremen and Harvard University alumni. The former study (Paffenbarger, Hale, Brand, et al., 1977) involved literally thousands of longshore workers and a 22-year follow-up assessment in which physical work activity (i.e., energy expenditure), coronary heart disease records, and mortality data were obtained. During the 22-year period (1951 to 1972), 11 percent of the longshoremen died of CHD. Men who expended at least 8,500 kilocalories per week on the job, however, were found to possess a significantly lower CHD mortality risk (at any age) than men who were less physically active on the job.

The Harvard study (Paffenbarger, Hyde, Wing, et al., 1986) tracked almost 17,000 alumni from 1962 to 1978. As in the longshoremen study, researchers obtained CHD and mortality data. Unlike the longshoremen study, however, self-reported *leisure-time* physical activity was the focus of the investigation. Results indicated a 53 percent reduction in all-cause mortality among men who participated in at least three hours of sport activity per week as compared with those who engaged in less than one hour of sport activity per week. Additionally, for those engaged in moderate levels of physical activity (at least 10 miles/16 kilometers walked per week), mortality rates were 33 percent lower than among those who walked fewer than three miles/five kilometers per week. Generally speaking, active individuals lived more than two years longer than inactive individuals.

In support of these investigations, a series of studies emanating from the Cooper Institute in the United States (Blair, Haskell, Ho, et al., 1995; Blair, Kohl, Paffenbarger, et al., 1989) has documented the relationship between physical fitness and all-cause mortality among approximately 10,000 men and more than 3,000 women (ages ranging between the 20s and 80s). Baseline and follow-up assessments several years later indicated that males with the highest levels of fitness had a mortality rate 71 percent lower than that of males with the lowest levels of fitness. Those men who improved their physical fitness levels from "unfit" to "fit" over the course of the study experienced a 44 percent reduction in mortality risk. The impact of fitness was even greater for females, as evidenced by a 79 percent lower death rate for high-fit versus low-fit individuals. In general, increased mortality rates appear to be associated with decreased levels of physical fitness.

Conclusion

Physical activity epidemiology is a field of study devoted to the *who, what, where, when,* and *why* of exercise behavior. As the epidemic of physical inactivity has spread worldwide, a number of entities have stepped to the forefront in an effort to lead the populace toward a more healthy lifestyle. The poor rates of leisure and general forms of physical activity can be traced to a number of wide-ranging social events and innovations, including the industrial and technological revolutions. In order to document the precise nature of physical activity patterns, we selectively reviewed physical activity and demographic data from several industrialized countries and one newly industrialized country. We noted that two prominent limitations in much of the epidemiological research concern the definition of physical activity and the variation in physical activity measurement. Physical activity may be assessed through self-report/survey, mechanical/electronic devices, and observation. The pros and cons of each method should be given careful consideration in the design and evaluation of research investigations. Despite these limitations, data indicate that the majority of individuals in our society are either largely or completely inactive. Generally speaking, this inactivity increases with age and varies according to a number of factors, including gender, race/ethnicity, income level, and education level.

Epidemiology is also concerned with consequences of inactivity, such as the rates of morbidity and mortality. In general, an indirect relationship exists between physical activity and morbidity/mortality: those who engage in the greatest amount of activity tend to achieve longer and more healthy lives. Indeed, several large-scale longitudinal research investigations conducted in the United States provide fairly consistent support for this finding.

what do you know?

1. Define the terms *sedentary* and *minimal, recommended,* and *sufficient levels of physical activity.*
2. Why are physical activity participation rates so dismal?
3. What are the five "W's" of physical activity epidemiology?
4. Why is the lack of physical activity participation considered an epidemic?
5. What are the general rates of activity and inactivity across the countries discussed in the chapter?
6. What is the relationship between age and physical activity? Discuss possible explanations for this relationship.
7. What is the relationship between gender and physical activity? Discuss possible explanations for this relationship.
8. What is the relationship between race/ethnicity and physical activity? Discuss possible explanations for this relationship.
9. What is the relationship between income level and physical activity? Discuss possible explanations for this relationship.
10. What is the relationship between education level and physical activity? Discuss possible explanations for this relationship.
11. Does physical activity influence morbidity and mortality? Explain your answer.
12. What did you learn from the San Francisco longshoremen, Harvard University alumni, and Cooper Institute research studies?

learning activities

1. Gather data from each student in the class regarding exercise behavior. (For the purpose of this activity, simply use the number of days per week, on average, each person exercises.) Use variables such as age and gender to create graphical representations of your data.
2. Using the data in the chapter and any additional data you can uncover, draft a "position" paper that discusses physical activity in society and what you believe must be done in order to improve activity levels.
3. As a class, design a longitudinal research study incorporating epidemiological data and at least one psychological measure. In other words, devise an investigation similar to the morbidity/mortality studies, but substitute psychological data for death/disease rates.
4. In 2008, for the first time, the U.S. Department of Health and Human Services came out with guidelines for physical activity. Visit the USDHHS website (www.health.gov/paguidelines/) and note the similarities and differences among the various sets of guidelines discussed in the chapter. If you were to recommend guidelines to a client, which would you choose? Why?
5. Now, choose a country discussed in this chapter. Find the website of governmental organization equivalent to the USDHH for that country and find its guidelines for physical activity. Note the similarities and differences between your chosen country's guidelines and the USDHHS and ACSM guidelines.
6. Visit the geocaching website (www.geocaching.com). Based on the information provided at the site, evaluate whether it would be an effective motivator for physical activity for your peer group.

references

American Obesity Association. (2005). AOA fact sheets. www.obesity.org/subs/fastfacts/aoafactsheets.shtml

Anderson, G., & Horvath, J. (2004). The growing burden of chronic disease in America. *Public Health Reports, 119,* 263–271.

Bassett, Jr., D.R., Pucher, J., Buehler, R., Thompson, D.L., & Crouter, S.E. (2008). Walking, cycling, and obesity rates in Europe, North America, and Australia. *Journal of Physical Activity and Health, 5,* 795–814.

Blair, S.N., Haskell, W.L., Ho, P., Paffenbarger, Jr., R.S., Vranizan, K.M., Farquhar, J.W., & Wood, P.D. (1985). Assessment of habitual physical activity by a seven-day recall in a community survey and controlled experiments. *American Journal of Epidemiology, 122,* 794–804.

Blair, S.N., Kohl, H.W., III, Barlow, C.E., Paffenbarger, R.S., Jr., Gibbons, L.W., & Macera, C.A. (1995). Changes in physical fitness and all-cause mortality. *Journal of the American Medical Association, 273,* 1093–1098.

Blair, S.N., Kohl, H.W., III, Paffenbarger, R.S., Jr., Clark, D.G., Cooper, K.H., & Gibbons, L.W. (1989). Physical fitness and all-cause mortality: A prospective study of healthy men and women. *Journal of the American Medical Association, 262,* 2395–2401.

Bromley, C. Sproston, K., & Shelton, N. (2005). *The Scottish Health Survey 2003.* Edinburgh: Scottish Executive.

Canadian Fitness and Lifestyle Research Institute. (2007). 2007 *Physical Activity Monitor.* Ontario: Health Canada.

Cavill, N., Kahlmeier, S., & Racioppi, F. (2006). *Physical activity and health in Europe: Evidence for action.* Copenhagen: World Health Organization Regional Office for Europe.

Craig, R., & Mindell, J.. (2008). *Health Survey for England 2006.* London: NHS Information Centre.

Gill, T., Fullerton, S., & Taylor, A.W. (2007). *Physical activity among South Australian adults.* Adelaide: SA Health.

Godin, G., & Shephard, R.J. (1985). A simple method to assess exercise behavior in the community. *Canadian Journal of Applied Sport Sciences, 10,* 141–146.

Haskell, W.L., Lee, I., Pate, R.R., Powell, K.E., Blair, S.N., Franklin, B.A., Macera, C.A., Heath, G.W., Thompson, P.D., & Bauman, A. (2007). Physical activity and public health: Updated recommendation for adults from the American College of Sports Medicine and the American Heart Association. *Medicine and Science in Sports and Exercise, 39,* 1423–1434.

Kriska, A.M., & Caspersen, C.J. (1997). A collection of physical activity questionnaires for health-related research. *Medicine and Science in Sports and Exercise, 29,* S43–S45.

Mokdad, A.H., Marks, J.S., Stroup, D.F., & Gerberding, J.L. (2005). Actual causes of death in the United States, 2000. *Journal of the American Medical Association, 293,* 293–294.

Monteiro, C.A., Conde, W.L., Matsudo, S.M., Matsudo, V.R., Bonseñor, I.M., & Lotufo, P.A. (2003). A descriptive epidemiology of leisure-time physical activity in Brazil, 1996-1997. *Pan American Journal of Public Health, 14,* 246–254.

National Center for Health Statistics. (2005). *Health, United States, 2005.* Washington, DC: U.S. Government Printing Office.

Noreau, L., & Shephard, R.J. (1995) Spinal cord injury, exercise and quality of life. *Sports Medicine, 20,* 226–250.

Paffenbarger, R.S., Jr., Hale, W.E., Brand, R.J., & Hyde, R.T. (1977). Work-energy level, personal characteristics, and fatal heart attack: A birth-cohort effect. *American Journal of Epidemiology, 105,* 200–213.

Paffenbarger, R.S., Jr., Hyde, R.T., Wing, A.L., & Hsieh, C. (1986). Physical activity, all-cause mortality, and longevity of college alumni. *New England Journal of Medicine, 314,* 605–613.

Pate, R.R., Pratt, M., Blair, S.N., Haskell, W.L., Macera, C.A., Bouchard, C., Buchner, D., Ettinger, W., Heath, G.W., King, A.C., Kriska, A., Leon, A.S., Marcus, B.H., Morris, J., Paffenbarger, R.S., Jr., Patrick, K., Pollock, M.L., Rippe, J.M., Sallis, J., & Wilmore, J.H. (1995). Physical activity and public health. *Journal of the American Medical Association, 273,* 402–407.

Sallis, J.F., & Owen, N. (1999). *Physical activity and behavioral medicine.* Thousand Oaks, CA: Sage Publications.

Taylor, W.C., Baranowski, T., & Young, D.R. (1998). Physical activity interventions in low-income, ethnic minority, and populations with disability. *American Journal of Preventive Medicine, 15,* 334–343.

Trost, S.G., Owen, N., Bauman, A.E., Sallis, J.F., & Brown, W. (2002). Correlates of adults' participation in physical activity: Review and update. *Medicine and Science in Sports and Exercise, 34,* 1996–2001.

U.S. Department of Health and Human Services. (2004). *Healthy People 2010.* Washington, DC: U.S. Government Printing Office.

U.S. Department of Health and Human Services. (2006). *Healthy People 2010 Midcourse Review.* Washington, DC: U.S. Government Printing Office.

U.S. Department of Health and Human Services. (2008). *Physical Activity Guidelines.* Retrieved February 16, 2010, from www.health.gov/paguidelines/.

3

Theories and Models of Exercise Behavior I

SOCIAL COGNITIVE APPROACHES

Students often become uneasy when their instructors mention theories and models, perhaps because students lack an understanding of how useful models and theories can be. Consider the following case: A woman exercises twice per week, on average, during the course of a calendar year. However, she temporarily reduces (or eliminates completely) her exercise participation for several weeks at a time at various points throughout the year. Following these brief lapses, she always manages to resume her habitual regimen of exercise. A model of this behavioral phenomenon is depicted in Exhibit 3.1. As you can see, a **model** is simply a visual representation of a phenomenon or behavior. Unfortunately, models do not always indicate why the behavior or phenomenon occurs. For example, we might speculate that the woman experiences lapses in her exercise regimen due to seasonal work loads, final exams, or extreme weather patterns. In this way, we are proposing a **theory** to explain why a behavior or phenomenon occurs. Thus, although theories can be graphically represented (modeled) to aid in conceptualization, many models do not include a theoretical explanation.

At this point, you may be wondering why theories are so important (and why we've devoted two full chapters to them). We believe that theories are essential to our discussions of exercise psychology for at least two primary reasons. First, theories allow us to better understand and predict physical activity behavior. Second, theories give us a scientifically validated blueprint from which to formulate effective behavioral interventions. If we are to be successful in our intervention efforts, we must understand the relationships among the many variables believed to influence exercise behavior. As you will see throughout this chapter and the next, theories enable us to organize these variables in a coherent manner.

KEY TERMS

affective state
amotivation
attitude
contextual motivation
coping efficacy
expectancy-value
external regulation
extrinsic
global motivation
identified regulation
imagery
integrated regulation
intrinsic
introjected regulation
mastery
model
motivation
past performance accomplishments
perceived behavioral control (PBC)
physiological state
scheduling efficacy
self-determination
self-efficacy
situational motivation
social cognitive approach
social persuasion
subjective norm
theory
vicarious experiences

- model
- theory

exhibit 3.1 Example of a behavioral model of exercise.

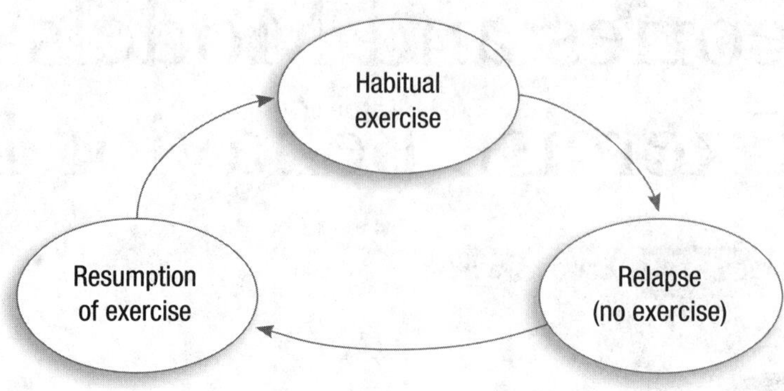

Expectancy-Value Theories: Forerunners to the Social Cognitive Approach

Whether in educational, occupational, sport, health, or exercise environments, theories of behavior have long been rooted in motivation. By **motivation** we mean the degree of determination, drive, or desire with which an individual approaches (or avoids) a behavior. Simply put, it is the direction and intensity of one's effort. Accordingly, motivation is often defined by the behavior itself. For instance, an individual who is highly motivated would be expected to work exceptionally hard at adopting, changing, or accomplishing a behavior. We might also expect a highly motivated individual to persist in her efforts despite repeated failure and minimal improvement. Simply choosing to engage in one activity instead of another implies an element of motivation.

motivation ■

While motivation is often denoted as a singular dimension (ranging from "no motivation" to "high motivation"), researchers and practitioners generally divide motivation into two types based on its origin. Specifically, motivation that emanates from within is termed **intrinsic,** and motivation driven by a force outside the individual is labeled **extrinsic.** Although more will be said about these forms of motivation later in this chapter, examples of each are provided in Exhibit 3.2.

intrinsic ■
extrinsic ■

Early theories of motivation employed what is commonly referred to as an **expectancy-value** approach. Briefly, theorists proposed that motivation (and thus behavior) was predicated on the individual's expected behavioral outcome and on the value (importance) the individual placed on that predicted outcome. For example, a man desires to begin a regimen of exercise but finds that his motivation, although high, is not high enough to entice him to begin the training. From an expectancy-value standpoint, the man's failure to adopt an exercise regimen

expectancy-value ■

Examples of intrinsic and extrinsic motivators for exercise behavior. **exhibit 3.2**

INTRINSIC	EXTRINSIC
Fun	Health (e.g., prevent heart disease)
Sense of challenge	Social recognition/praise
Personal improvement	Tangible reinforcers*

*Include money, certificates, t-shirts, water bottles, etc.

may have three explanations (see Exhibit 3.3). First, although the man may value his prospective exercise habit very highly, he might not believe that he can actually begin and maintain a regular regimen of exercise (expected outcome = inability to maintain exercise) because he failed in a previous attempt (or in multiple attempts). Alternatively, he might feel that he just does not have the discipline to maintain any behavior change for a prolonged period of time. Second, although the man may believe that he can adopt and adhere to his exercise program (expected outcome = ability to maintain exercise), he may decide that he simply does not value (i.e., place enough importance on) physical fitness. Although he likely maintains some degree of value for physical fitness (he would not even consider beginning an exercise regimen if he did not), he probably values an alternative activity (or no activity) to a greater extent. The third explanation is simply a combination of the first two. In other words, the man may not value physical fitness and, furthermore, may not believe that he can successfully maintain a physical activity regimen.

With this discussion as a background, we devote the remainder of this chapter to a review of the more common theories found in the exercise psychology literature that have grown out of the expectancy-value approach. The presentation of each theory consists of the following information:

1. Name of theory, author(s) credited for introducing the theory, and the year the theory was proposed/published
2. Narrative and visual presentation of the theory

Expectancy-value approach applied to exercise behavior. **exhibit 3.3**

		EXPECTED OUTCOME		
		Ability to Maintain Exercise	**Inability to Maintain Exercise**	
VALUE	**Low**	Failure to Adopt Exercise	Failure to Adopt Exercise	**Low**
	High	Successful Adoption	Failure to Adopt Exercise	**High**

3. Example applying the theory
4. A research exemplar
5. Brief discussion of possible intervention techniques
6. Discussion of the usefulness and limitations of the theory
7. Discussion of potential alternative conceptualizations or future avenues of research employing the theory
8. Summary and conclusions

Self-Efficacy Theory

social cognitive approach

One popular category of theories found throughout the exercise psychology literature incorporates a social cognitive philosophy. From a physical activity standpoint, theories based on a **social cognitive approach** view exercise behavior as being influenced by both human cognition (e.g., expectations, intentions, beliefs, attitudes) and external stimuli (e.g., social pressures/experiences). Thus, although someone may intend to be physically active, various external forces, such as family or occupational commitments, might prevent that person from engaging in exercise. Similarly, although social pressures to be physically active exist within our society, some individuals choose to engage in exercise while others do not. These examples support the inclusion of both social and cognitive elements within theories of exercise behavior.

self-efficacy

In 1977, Albert Bandura introduced his self-efficacy theory (SET) in an effort to describe how individuals form perceptions about their ability to engage in a specific behavior. This "perceived capability," known commonly as *self-efficacy*, is a construct that has flourished in the field of exercise psychology. **Self-efficacy** is not concerned with an individual's perception of her abilities; but rather, it focuses on the extent to which the individual feels she will be successful in performing the desired behavior, given the abilities she possesses and the unique situation in which she finds herself. Thus, self-efficacy is generally considered to be a situation-specific form of self-confidence. For example, a woman might, in general, consider herself to be an accomplished runner (high self-confidence for running). If she is used to running on flat courses and must now compete on a hilly course, however, we might find that her self-efficacy for successfully performing on a hilly course is lower than when she competes on a flat course (low self-efficacy for running hills). Similarly, suppose she was scheduled to run on a flat course but had been sick the previous week. Although her overall level of confidence in her running ability likely hasn't subsided, her self-efficacy for this one particular race may be low due to the effects of the illness (e.g., fatigue).

Bandura (1977) postulated four primary sources of self-efficacy: past performance accomplishments, vicarious experiences, social persuasion, and physiological/affective states. These sources are listed in order of their degree of influence in both the following discussion and Exhibit 3.4. Thus, past performances should exert a greater influence on self-efficacy than do vicarious experiences, and so forth.

Diagram of self-efficacy theory. exhibit 3.4

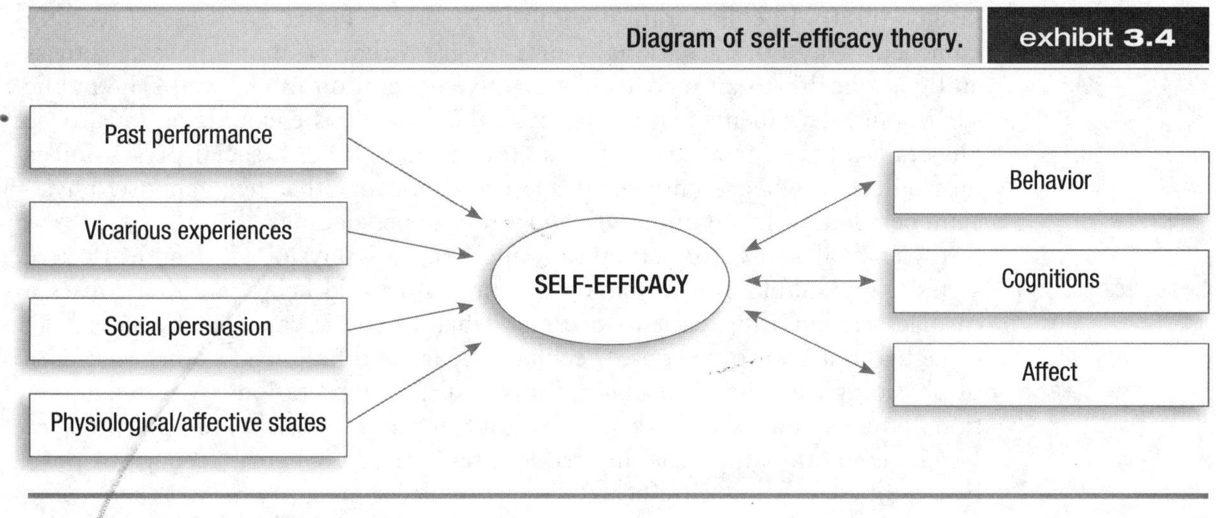

Source: Adapted from Bandura (1986).

Past performance accomplishments refer to the degree of success perceived by an individual who has previously engaged in activities similar to, or the same as, the current behavior. For example, self-efficacy for running may be derived from an individual's previous experiences with jogging, walking, or even biking. Obviously, the degree of similarity between the previously experienced activity and the current activity determines the strength of this source.

■ past performance accomplishments

Vicarious experiences, also known as *modeling,* are those that involve one individual viewing the performance of a behavior by another individual (the model). The greater the perceived similarity between the model and the viewer, the greater the model's influence. Additionally, it should be noted that the model need not be a person known to the viewer, although this is preferable. Instead, the person could be a well-known celebrity of the same age who has initiated an exercise regimen. An unfamiliar person on videotape, if perceived as relatively similar to oneself, might also prove to be an effective model. Recently, researchers have even demonstrated the successful impact of virtual models (e.g., avatars) on exercise behavior (Fox & Bailenson, 2009). Vicarious experience might be employed as an intervention in an instance where a post–myocardial infarction patient is prescribed exercise but is fearful of engaging in strenuous physical activity. Introducing him to an individual who has undergone the same procedure and who has successfully completed cardiac rehabilitation without further incidents might serve to increase self-efficacy. Similarly, the use of **imagery**—a behavior performed in the mind using some or all of the body's senses—would be considered a vicarious source. For example, you might imagine yourself becoming healthier or improving your physical appearance. Alternatively, imagery could be used to mentally rehearse the movements required in an aerobic dance sequence.

■ vicarious experiences

■ imagery

Social persuasion concerns verbal and nonverbal tactics used by others in an attempt to increase a person's self-efficacy. For example, the National Football

■ social persuasion

League (NFL), in collaboration with the American Heart Association, recently launched "Play 60," a national youth program that promotes physical fitness and good health to an increasingly inactive generation of children. The public service announcements feature various NFL superstars encouraging kids to be physically active for at least 60 minutes per day. Indeed, social persuasion is most effective when a knowledgeable or significant other (e.g., spouse, physician, personal trainer, famous athlete) does the persuading.

physiological state ■

affective state ■

The final source of self-efficacy incorporates physiological and affective states. An example of a **physiological state** is a rapid heart rate that causes a cardiac rehabilitation patient to doubt whether she is capable of successfully engaging in a bout of exercise. Feelings of pain and fatigue are other examples of physiological states that might impact efficacy expectations. **Affective** (emotional) **states** can exert both positive and negative influences on self-efficacy. Negative emotionality generally reduces self-efficacy, whereas feelings of positive emotion elevate self-efficacy. For example, a person who is experiencing extremely positive emotions (e.g., happiness, pride) would be expected to view an anticipated exercise bout with higher self-efficacy than would someone experiencing negative emotions (e.g., sadness, disappointment).

Measuring Self-Efficacy

Although a substantial number of self-efficacy "measures" exist in the literature, the traditional and most widely accepted approach to assessing self-efficacy has included measurement of at least two of the three dimensions initially proposed by Bandura (1977): the level and strength of self-efficacy. The *level* of self-efficacy refers to an individual's belief that she can successfully perform various elements of a task (e.g., greater distance, duration, or intensity). The *strength* of self-efficacy indicates the individual's degree of conviction for successfully accomplishing each level of the task. For example, a questionnaire might ask about a person's self-efficacy for jogging incremental distances ranging from one to ten miles. Referring to Exhibit 3.5, a total of 10 levels exist (*a* through *j*), with the strength of each level indicated by the number circled (0% confidence/certainty through 100% confidence/certainty, separated into intervals of 10 percent). In this example, the individual is 100 percent confident/certain that she can jog three miles. As the difficulty of the task (level) increases, the strength of her conviction decreases to the point where she has no confidence at all that she can jog more than six miles. Finally, the generality dimension of self-efficacy concerns the extent to which an individual's efficacy for a specific task carries over to other activities. In our example, self-efficacy for jogging would likely generalize to walking or potentially even biking but might not generalize as well to weight training.

More recently, self-efficacy has been conceptualized as a multidimensional construct (see Rodgers, Hall, Blanchard, et al., 2002, for a detailed discussion). Specifically, researchers have begun to differentiate between traditional notions of self-efficacy for a task (e.g., confidence in one's ability to jog progressively greater distances) and more contemporary (and arguably more cognitively com-

Sample self-efficacy assessment for jogging. **exhibit 3.5**

Using the scale below, circle the number that best represents how confident you are that you can jog each of the following distances during a single session without stopping.

	NO CONFIDENCE AT ALL										EXTREMELY CONFIDENT
a. 1 mile	0	10	20	30	40	50	60	70	80	90	(100)
b. 2 miles	0	10	20	30	40	50	60	70	80	90	(100)
c. 3 miles	0	10	20	30	40	50	60	70	80	90	(100)
d. 4 miles	0	10	20	30	40	50	60	70	(80)	90	100
e. 5 miles	0	10	20	30	40	(50)	60	70	80	90	100
f. 6 miles	0	(10)	20	30	40	50	60	70	80	90	100
g. 7 miles	(0)	10	20	30	40	50	60	70	80	90	100
h. 8 miles	(0)	10	20	30	40	50	60	70	80	90	100
i. 9 miles	(0)	10	20	30	40	50	60	70	80	90	100
j. 10 miles	(0)	10	20	30	40	50	60	70	80	90	100

plex) conceptualizations of efficacy including **coping efficacy** (i.e., self-efficacy for overcoming barriers or challenges to exercise) and **scheduling efficacy** (i.e., confidence in one's abilities to schedule and manage exercise behavior). While measurement of "task efficacy" follows the traditional level and strength approach, measurement of coping and scheduling self-efficacy (often referred to as measures of "self-regulatory efficacy") are somewhat different in that only the strength aspect is relevant. Referring to Exhibit 3.6, note that a level hierarchy does *not* exist as it did in Exhibit 3.5. Thus, each item is independent, and the order of items is irrelevant. The computation of an overall barrier efficacy score, however, is derived in the same manner as discussed earlier.

- coping efficacy
- scheduling efficacy

From Theory to Application

To summarize, Bandura's (1977) theory proposes four primary sources of self-efficacy. These sources may work individually or in conjunction with one another to influence a person's self-efficacy for a specific behavior. Bandura (1986) extended the theory by denoting the primary consequences of self-efficacy (see Exhibit 3.4). In order to explore this theory more fully, let's return to the cardiac rehabilitation example presented earlier. Recall that the man has just recovered from myocardial infarction surgery. He is given an exercise rehabilitation prescription but is afraid to begin any form of strenuous activity for fear that physical activity will produce another heart attack. Both he and his physician

exhibit 3.6 Sample barriers self-efficacy scale.

Using the scale below, circle the number that best represents how confident you are that you can participate in some form of physical activity at least three times per week when:

	NO CONFIDENCE AT ALL										EXTREMELY CONFIDENT
a. You have very little or no time	0	10	20	30	40	50	60	70	80	90	100
b. Your muscles are sore	0	10	20	30	40	50	60	70	80	90	100
c. You have very little or no support from others	0	10	20	30	40	50	60	70	80	90	100
d. You have moved or are on vacation	0	10	20	30	40	50	60	70	80	90	100
e. The weather is bad	0	10	20	30	40	50	60	70	80	90	100
f. You are stressed	0	10	20	30	40	50	60	70	80	90	100
g. Exercise facilities are not convenient	0	10	20	30	40	50	60	70	80	90	100
h. Your work demands and/or travel increase	0	10	20	30	40	50	60	70	80	90	100
i. No child care is available	0	10	20	30	40	50	60	70	80	90	100
j. You are tired	0	10	20	30	40	50	60	70	80	90	100

recognize that his self-efficacy for physical rehabilitation must be increased before he will begin and maintain an exercise regimen. Thus, the physician may attempt one or more of the following interventions:

Past performance accomplishments. Obtain the patient's exercise history in an attempt to increase his sense of mastery based on previous exercise experiences. (**Mastery** refers to the process of accomplishing a goal or the thorough learning and performance of a skill, technique, or behavior.)

mastery ■

Vicarious experience. Show him a video of a former patient who underwent the same surgery and who is now engaging in exercise without incident.

Social persuasion. Strive to be positive and supporting in conversations with the man and enlist the help of his spouse/family in persuading him to begin and maintain the rehabilitation regimen.

Physiological and affective states. Educate the patient in terms of what is a normal physiological response to exercise, so that he does not interpret common exercise symptoms (e.g., heavy breathing, rapid pulse, sweating) as an impending heart attack. This should reduce his anxiety about engaging in physical activity.

As a result of these interventions, we might hypothesize that the man likely maintains a modest level of self-efficacy going into his rehabilitation program.

As he progresses through the rehabilitation (behavior), he begins to realize that he will be capable of doing the things he did before the surgery and experiences increased satisfaction with life (cognitions). Similarly, the man begins to feel a sense of pride (affect) as a result of his behavior. The bi-directional arrows in Exhibit 3.4 reflect the fact that his behavior, feelings of pride, and sense of life satisfaction all serve to elevate his self-efficacy.

The reverse can also occur. For example, a woman with low self-efficacy for maintaining an exercise regimen would not be expected to maintain that regimen. Not only does her self-efficacy affect her behavior, but she also might experience disappointment or shame in herself (affect) and may view herself negatively (as lacking discipline and self-motivation, lazy, etc.). Her unsuccessful behavior, combined with negative affect and cognitions, would further reduce an already low level of self-efficacy.

Research Exemplar

A considerable literature base exists demonstrating the relationship between self-efficacy and a variety of psychological, emotional, and behavioral components of exercise. These relationships are consistent across a wide variety of populations, including African American females with arthritis (Greene, Haldeman, Kaminski, et al., 2006), cardiac rehabilitation patients (Sniehotta, Scholz, & Schwarzer, 2005), German grade-school children (Klein-Hessling, Lohaus, & Ball, 2005), injured athletes undergoing rehabilitation (Milne, Hall, & Forwell, 2005), sedentary obese women in France (Dechamps, Gatta, Bourdel-Marchasson, et al., 2009), adults with intellectual disabilities (Peterson, Lowe, Peterson, et al., 2008), older adults in Italy and the United States (Lucidi, Grano, Barbaranelli, et al., 2006; Umstattd & Hallam, 2007), and undergraduate college students (Hu, Motl, McAuley, et al., 2007).

High school students are yet another population to add to the partial list presented above. In a study aimed at determining whether self-efficacy to overcome exercise barriers was associated with non-school-related moderate and vigorous physical exercise, Winters, Petosa, and Charlton (2003) obtained self-efficacy and typical leisure-time exercise participation information from 248 male and female high school students enrolled in introductory physical education courses in three high schools located within the midwestern United States. Results indicated that self-efficacy to overcome barriers to physical exercise was significantly associated with engagement in moderate and vigorous non-school-related exercise bouts, even after accounting for the influence of gender. Despite this finding, vast differences in the relationship between self-efficacy and exercise behavior did exist between the two levels of intensity and between genders. Specifically, males reported more frequent bouts of vigorous exercise and greater self-efficacy than females. In addition, self-efficacy was more strongly related to vigorous exercise ($r = .34$) than to moderate intensity exercise ($r = .15$). This is, perhaps, not surprising given the proposition underlying self-efficacy theory, which states that self-efficacy is most influential on challenging behaviors. Given our discussions of reduced physical activity participation in schools and with increasing age (see Chapter 2), engaging in vigorous exercise would likely be considered challenging to a large proportion of high school students.

Usefulness, Limitations, and Future Research Avenues of Self-Efficacy Theory

It has been said that few things in life are guaranteed, but the central role of self-efficacy as an antecedent and consequence of exercise behavior may be one of those things. Ample research evidence exists to document the impact of self-efficacy on behavior as well as on various affective/cognitive and physiological training outcomes (McAuley & Blissmer, 2000). Furthermore, self-efficacy has been consistently shown to be a prominent exercise outcome itself. The theory has proven effective in studies employing various forms of physical activity across a wide range of participant samples. It is not without at least one well-acknowledged limitation, however. As mentioned previously, the theory is predictive of behavior only when the behavior is challenging or novel. Indeed, the influence of the efficacy construct is greatly reduced (or eliminated) as exercise behavior becomes well learned and habitual. This might occur, for example, when an individual moves from the adoption to adherence stage.

Notwithstanding this limitation, the outlook for future research employing self-efficacy theory is bright. The substantial literature base might benefit most from investigations that include interventions targeting the key sources of self-efficacy. The results would shed light on the manner in which these sources exert their influence on self-efficacy. Merging self-efficacy theory with other theories composed of similar or shared elements may further enhance the predictive utility of these frameworks (see Lucidi, Grano, Barbaranelli, et al., 2006; Ryan, 2008; Sniehotta, Scholz, & Schwarzer, 2005, for examples). Finally, researchers must revisit the "generality" aspect of self-efficacy proposed by Bandura, because this dimension has largely been ignored in the literature.

Theory of Reasoned Action and Theory of Planned Behavior

Theory of Reasoned Action

Around the same time that Bandura was constructing his self-efficacy theory, Fishbein and Ajzen (1975) were putting the finishing touches on their theory of reasoned action (TRA). Although this theory is also based on the social-cognitive approach, it is markedly different from self-efficacy theory in its predictive intent. While self-efficacy theory is capable of predicting both acute and chronic behavior, the TRA was originally designed to predict voting behavior, which is a single-instance activity. Before applying it to an exercise situation, therefore, we will discuss the theory in relation to its original application, voting.

The behavior of voting, as suggested in Exhibit 3.7, is directly related to a person's *intention* to vote. This intention is determined by two factors—attitude and a sense of subjective norm. **Attitude** simply refers to a person's positive or negative thoughts concerning the performance of the behavior. Two factors serve to influence attitude:

■ attitude

1. An individual's beliefs about the consequences of carrying out a specific action; does the person generally believe that voting is a worthy endeavor?
2. An individual's evaluation (positive or negative) of the consequences; does he feel that his vote is important? Does he care who's running or who wins?

If the answers to these questions are "yes," we can assume that he possesses a favorable attitude toward voting. Thus, attitude has cognitive and affective components.

The second determinant of intention is the person's sense of **subjective norm.** This construct, which focuses on the degree to which a person feels social pressure to perform the behavior, is also predicated on two factors:

■ subjective norm

1. Perceptions about the expectations of significant others; will family, friends, and coworkers be voting?
2. Motivation to comply with the perceived expectations of others; will she be perceived as lazy or uninformed if she does not vote? Does she even care what others think in regard to her voting behavior?

Thus, the more positive the attitude, and the greater the perceived social pressure (subjective norm), the stronger the intention to vote.

Diagram of the theory of reasoned action. **exhibit 3.7**

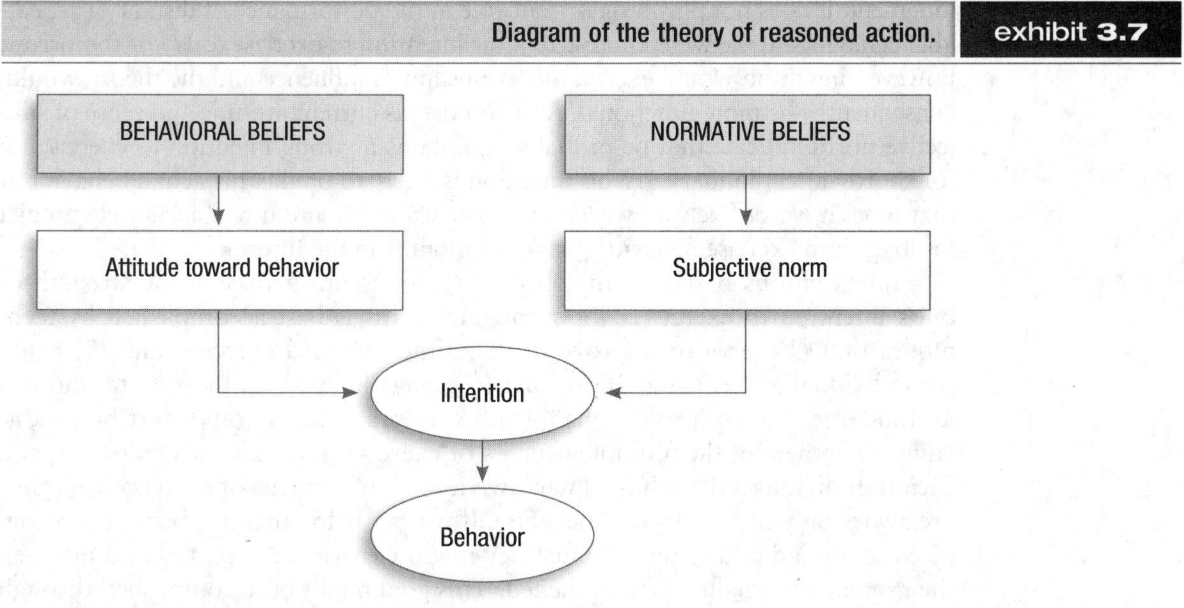

Source: Adapted from Fishbein & Ajzen (1975).

Of course, as the saying goes, "the road to failure is paved with good intentions." In other words, although intention is the single best predictor of behavior within the theory, intentions clearly do not always lead to the intended behavior. This is especially true when we attempt to apply this theory to a repeatable behavior (such as exercise) or to a behavior that is not to be attempted in the immediate future but at some undetermined later time. Thus, intention is the strongest predictor of behavior when that behavior is to be engaged in within a relatively short period of time. As days, weeks, or months pass, however, the strength of the relationship between intention and behavior progressively weakens. In the previous voting example, the intention to vote would likely be a good predictor if the behavior is to be performed the same day as the acknowledged intent. Conversely, intention would likely not be as good a predictor if election day is a number of months away.

From theory to application

Let's summarize this theory with a specific exercise example that most people can probably appreciate. With January 1 rapidly approaching, a man contemplates beginning an exercise regimen as his New Year's resolution. His attitude about exercise is mixed—he knows the benefits and wants to do it but, based on prior experiences, is not sure he will enjoy it. He feels a fairly strong social pressure to exercise because family, friends, coworkers, and even the media are discussing "getting back in shape after the holidays." His intention is to exercise two or three times a week for 30 minutes per session from now until the end of time. Unfortunately, in most cases, this intention is really nothing more than a "hope" of maintaining exercise until the end of time. Once again, because intention is an immediately influencing and fleeting judgment, it does not play a significant role in the performance of distant or repeatable behaviors. If we were interested in his intention to exercise today or tomorrow, however, intention would exert a more substantial influence and the theory would, consequently, be more functional. As it stands, his current attitude and sense of subjective norm indicate that he probably maintains a strong intention to exercise on (or shortly after) January 1. This intention is likely to predict his actual behavior at that time. It is *not* likely, however, that his current intention will accurately predict his long-term exercise behavior (weeks or months in the future).

Interventions based on the TRA must focus on increasing the strength of one's intention to exercise. Not surprisingly, this is best accomplished by techniques that (1) serve to improve one's attitude toward exercise, and (2) cause the individual to feel external pressure to engage in exercise. In order to improve attitude, the exercise professional/health care practitioner could start by heightening awareness of the multiple benefits of exercise (physical, psychological, and social). Individuals often have a narrow view of the benefits of exercise (e.g., they are aware only of the physical benefits). If we can help potential exercisers recognize the myriad additional benefits they might experience (e.g., reduced fatigue), their intentions might be strengthened. This goal might be accomplished through public service announcements, news stories, research, and simply by word of mouth from significant others (particularly those who are physically active).

Modifying one's concept of subjective norm is a somewhat more difficult task. Surrounding oneself with others (i.e., creating a reference group) who are physically active is a good start. Ironically, although we tend to extol the virtue of making our own decisions and resisting peer pressure, this is an instance where "doing what others do" appears to be an acceptable philosophy. It is likely that adherence to exercise, however, will be greater in instances where the individual is physically active for reasons other than those produced by external expectations.

Theory of Planned Behavior

It has been suggested that intention may not be an ideal construct for predicting behaviors that are continuing or repeatable due to the fact that such behaviors pose significant challenges and barriers. To this end, 10 years after the introduction of the TRA, Ajzen (1985) extended the theory by adding the construct of **perceived behavioral control (PBC).** Similar to the self-efficacy construct discussed earlier, PBC refers to the degree of personal control the individual perceives he or she has over the behavior in question. This concept is significant in that it accounts for the many potential barriers to exercise (work, family, weather, facilities, etc.) that people often perceive. Thus, a woman who believes that she has control over (i.e., the ability to overcome) these potential barriers to exercise will be more likely to perform that behavior than if she believes her exercise behavior is influenced by someone or something else. As indicated in the model shown in Exhibit 3.8, attitude, subjective norm, and PBC combine to influence intention. While attitude and subjective norm serve to influence behavior only through their impact on intention, however, PBC is proposed to influence behavior independently (see dashed arrow in Exhibit 3.8) as well as through its effect on intention. Thus, in the theory of planned behavior (TPB), both intention and PBC are hypothesized to be equally influential predictors of behavior.

■ perceived behavioral control (PBC)

Diagram of the theory of planned behavior. **exhibit 3.8**

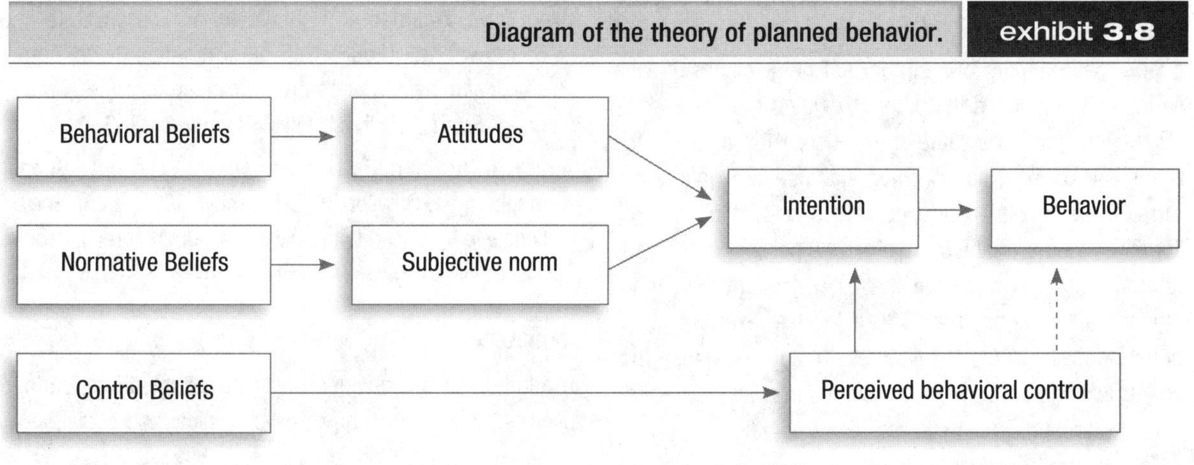

Source: Ajzen (1985).

FOCUS on Cancer

Cancer and its treatments are associated with a wide range of emotional and functional consequences, including depression, anxiety, decreased strength, and fatigue. Accumulating evidence indicates that exercise is an effective strategy for helping to alleviate these problems (Courneya & Friedenreich, 1999). The negative effects of cancer and its treatment can make exercise participation very difficult, however. Indeed, people report significant decreases in their exercise levels even years after their cancer treatment is completed (Courneya & Friedenreich, 1997).

In an attempt to understand factors that might influence exercise behavior after cancer treatment, Courneya and his colleagues conducted a study using the theory of planned behavior (TPB) (Courneya, Friedenreich, Arthur, et al., 1999). They administered measures of the TPB constructs (attitudes, subjective norms, perceived behavioral control, and intention to exercise) to 66 men and women who had undergone surgery for colorectal cancer. For the next four months, the researchers monitored their patients' exercise behavior. The data were then analyzed to determine whether the TPB variables could predict exercise intentions and behavior over the four-month study period.

The results indicated that intention to exercise was determined solely by attitudes toward exercise—neither subjective norms nor perceived behavioral control were influential constructs. These findings suggest that, among cancer patients, the most important determinant of their exercise intentions is the extent to which they hold positive beliefs about the value of exercise. With regard to the prediction of exercise behavior, exercise was jointly determined by intention and perceived behavioral control. Together, these variables explained 30 percent of the variance in exercise, a finding that is consistent with other studies that have used the TPB to explain exercise in the general population. Overall, these results suggest that constructs captured by the TPB can be used to understand exercise among cancer patients.

ADDITIONAL RESOURCES

Courneya, K.S., Friedenreich, C.M., Quinney, H.A., Fields, A.L., Jones, L.W., & Fairey, A.S. (2004). Predictors of adherence and contamination in a randomized trial of exercise in colorectal cancer survivors. *Psycho-Oncology, 13,* 857–866.

Harper, F.W.K., Schmidt, J.E., Beacham, A.O., Salsman, J.M., Averill, A.J., Graves, K.D., & Andrykowski, M.A. (2007). The role of social cognitive processing theory and optimism in positive psychosocial and physical behavior change after cancer diagnosis and treatment. *Psycho-Oncology, 16,* 79–91.

Jones, L.W., Courneya, K.S., Fairey, A.S., & Mackey, J.R. (2005). Does the theory of planned behavior mediate the effects of an oncologist's recommendation to exercise in newly diagnosed breast cancer survivors? Results from a randomized controlled trial. *Health Psychology, 24,* 189–197.

Karvinen, K.H., Courneya, K.S., Campbell, K.L., Pearcey, R.G., Dundas, G., Capstick, V., & Tonkin, K.S. (2007). Correlates of exercise motivation and behavior in a population-based sample of endometrial cancer survivors: An application of the theory of planned behavior. *The International Journal of Behavioral Nutrition and Physical Activity, 4,* 21.

Milne, H.M., Wallman, K.E., Guilfoyle, A., Gordon, S., & Courneya, K.S. (2008). Self-determination theory and physical activity among breast cancer survivors. *Journal of Sport & Exercise Psychology, 30,* 23–38.

Rogers, L.Q., Shah, P., Dunnington, G., Greive, A., Shanmugham, A., Dawson, B., & Courneya, K.S. (2005). Social cognitive theory and physical activity during breast cancer treatment. *Oncology Nursing Forum, 32,* 807–815.

ACTIVITY

In addition to the obvious physical ramifications, cancer involves alterations in one's psychological and social well-being. With this in mind, create a worksheet with the following three columns:

Column 1: Name this column "Variables," and underneath the heading create a list of constructs contained in the theories in this chapter (e.g., self-efficacy, subjective norm, intrinsic motivation). To this list, add other psychological (e.g., mood), social (e.g., isolation), and even physical variables (e.g., fatigue) not discussed in this chapter.

Column 2: Name this column "Cancer," and indicate the predicted impact of the disease on each of the items listed in Column 1.

Column 3: Name this column "Exercise," and indicate the predicted impact of regular physical activity on each of the items listed in Column 1.

When you have completed the worksheet, review your responses. What conclusions can you draw from the results of this activity?

SAMPLE EXCERPT FROM WORKSHEET:

VARIABLES	CANCER	EXERCISE
Fatigue	Increased	Reduced

From theory to application

Let us assume that a woman exhibits a favorable attitude toward exercise and perceives a high degree of social pressure to exercise. According to the TRA, we estimate that her intentions would be relatively strong and, therefore, the likelihood of her engaging in exercise would be relatively high. If she feels she has little control over her exercise behavior (due to a number of potential barriers), however, her behavior will be doubly affected in a negative manner. First, low PBC will weaken her intention to exercise, which in turn will reduce the likelihood that she will engage in exercise. Second, low PBC may present itself, for example, as low confidence (self-efficacy) to overcome barriers, thereby further reducing the likelihood that she will engage in exercise (see self-efficacy theory).

We have already discussed the ways in which we can manipulate attitude and sense of subjective norm in order to modify intention. Our current discussion, therefore, will be limited to intervention techniques aimed at enhancing PBC. Given that PBC affects behavior both directly and indirectly (via intention), it would appear to play a critical role in successful exercise behavior change. Simply put, a strong sense of personal control over one's exercise behavior is essential for adherence. Exercise professionals can promote this sense of control in a number of ways, some of which we identified in our discussion of self-efficacy theory. Allowing exercisers some input when designing their physical activity program should increase feelings of personal control. The way in which we teach prospective exercisers to approach perceived barriers to physical activity is also important (see Chapter 6 for a more detailed discussion). For example, if family or occupational responsibilities prevent a person from engaging in regular exercise, physical activity should be scheduled for those times when one is less busy (e.g., early morning, lunch hour, late evening). Similar allowances might be made for difficulties stemming from weather and facility restrictions. For example, inexpensive and portable resistance bands could be purchased for the home when expensive and inconvenient exercise facilities emerge as limiting factors. Purchasing appropriate clothing to permit exercise in inclement weather or joining a facility with aerobic equipment or an indoor track may also reduce barriers to exercise. Perhaps most notably, setting a regular time in one's schedule for exercise (and physically displaying a reminder with a sticky note or memo in a daily planner) might facilitate activity participation when time is perceived as a significant barrier.

Research exemplar

The theory of reasoned action and the theory of planned behavior have achieved widespread use as theoretical frameworks for explaining exercise behavior. In a study focused specifically on the TPB, Dean, Farrell, Kelley, and colleagues (2006) examined the constructs of the theory to illuminate the factors that influence strength training participation in older adults. Two hundred men and women 55 years of age and older were recruited from community sites frequented by older adults (e.g., churches, bowling leagues, shopping malls) and asked to complete a questionnaire assessing components of the TPB (see sample items in Exhibit 3.9) as well as current physical activity participation. Results indicated that, while attitude, subjective norm, and perceived behavioral control were all significantly related to exercise intention, the latter two variables were most influential. Additionally, intention was the best predictor of strength training participation. Perhaps most noteworthy was the importance of subjective norm over attitude in predicting intention to engage in strength training. This finding runs counter to the majority of the literature, which tends to find little to no impact of subjective norm on intention. As noted by the authors, because older adults often report social motives for exercising, subjective norm may assume a more prominent role in their physical activity cognitions. Taken together, the findings of this investigation suggest that the TPB is a useful framework for understanding exercise intentions and physical activity behavior of older adults.

Usefulness, Limitations, and Future Research Avenues of the TRA and TPB

To summarize the relationships among the various factors incorporated within the TRA and TPB, we turn to several important conclusions of the quantitative literature review conducted by Symons Downs and Hausenblas (2005).

1. The influence of attitude on intention is slightly greater than the influence of perceived behavioral control on intention. The effects of both relationships are large. The influence of subjective norm on intention is considerably less than either attitude or perceived behavioral control.
2. The effect of intention on behavior (large) is greater than the effect of perceived behavioral control on behavior (moderate).
3. Taken together, the results indicate that attitude most strongly influences intention (followed closely by perceived behavioral control), while intention is the strongest determinant of exercise behavior.

Sample measures of theory of planned behavior constructs. **exhibit 3.9**

ATTITUDE

"For me to attend my scheduled exercise classes during my rehabilitation will be . . ."

harmful	1	2	3	4	5	6	7	*beneficial*
useless	1	2	3	4	5	6	7	*useful*
bad	1	2	3	4	5	6	7	*good*
unenjoyable	1	2	3	4	5	6	7	*enjoyable*
unpleasant	1	2	3	4	5	6	7	*pleasant*
boring	1	2	3	4	5	6	7	*fun*

SUBJECTIVE NORM

"Most people who are important to me support me in accumulating 30 minutes of moderate-intensity physical activity at least five days during the next week."

Strongly Disagree	1	2	3	4	5	6	7	*Strongly Agree*

PERCEIVED BEHAVIORAL CONTROL

"During the next week, how much control do you believe you have to accumulate 30 minutes of moderate-intensity physical activity?"

Extreme Lack of Control	1	2	3	4	5	6	7	*Extreme Control*

INTENTION

"During the next week, I intend to accumulate 30 minutes of moderate-intensity physical activity at least five days."

Strongly Disagree	1	2	3	4	5	6	7	*Strongly Agree*

Source: Blanchard et al. (2008).

4. The intention–behavior association was greater in studies that measured intention and behavior within a one-month period compared to studies with a time interval greater than one month. This finding supports the notion that the predictive power of intention decreases as the time between the measurement of intention and behavior increases.

In earlier literature reviews on the topic, Blue (1995) and Godin (1993) proposed that the predictive superiority of the theory of planned behavior (relative to the theory of reasoned action) might be explained by the fact that exercise may not be seen by all participants to be a completely volitional activity. Thus, it may be that the TRA is useful only for predicting behaviors that the individual perceives to be under his or her volitional control. On the other hand, the TPB may offer greater predictive utility given that the individual's perception of control is accounted for in the model by the perceived behavioral control construct. Accordingly, perceived behavioral control may influence behavior by itself (not only via its influence on intention) in situations where the behavior is not perceived to be under the complete control of the individual.

Although the addition of the PBC construct is significant, the TPB still suffers from the same limitations as its predecessor, the TRA. Specifically, the ability of intention to predict behavior is still limited by the elapsed time between the intention and the behavior as well as the repeatability of the behavior. As a result, a relatively distant and/or chronic behavior might be best predicted by the PBC construct. The inclusion of additional variables (e.g., self-efficacy, past behavior) within the model might help to improve the utility of the theory for predicting chronic behaviors such as exercise (Hagger, Chatzisarantis, & Biddle, 2002). Another potential avenue for exploration might involve redefining the subjective norm variable. Just as PBC has been modified to reflect self-efficacy or perceived barriers, it has been suggested that subjective norm might prove more useful if operationalized as perceptions of *social support* for a behavior as opposed to perceived *pressures* to perform a behavior (Rhodes, Jones, & Courneya, 2002). Alternatively, a more sweeping reform of subjective norm has been proposed such that the construct is defined in a multidimensional manner (Jackson, Smith, & Conner, 2003). This would require us to conceptualize subjective norm as a global construct composed of more specific subsets (e.g., descriptive, moral, or personal norms), similar to the self-concept hierarchy described in Chapter 8. Such an approach might allow researchers to identify a specific form or aspect of subjective norm that is meaningfully related to exercise behavior as opposed to a broader, global measure of social pressure.

Future research employing the theory of planned behavior will almost certainly be focused on recent modifications to the attitude construct. Specifically, researchers have begun to separate the affective (e.g., "I enjoy strength training") and instrumental (e.g., "strength training is beneficial to my health") elements of attitude. For example, Blanchard and colleagues (2008) demonstrated that, while both affective and instrumental attitudes were important for predicting physical activity intentions in Caucasian students, only affective attitudes significantly influenced intentions in African American students.

Self-Determination Theory

Much like self-efficacy theory, self-determination theory (SDT; Deci & Ryan, 1985) was designed to better explain affective, cognitive, and behavioral responses within an achievement domain (e.g., academics) and has become popular among exercise psychology researchers. This theory begins with the basic assumption that individuals possess three primary psychosocial needs, namely:

self-determination ■

1. a need for **self-determination** (autonomy, self-dependent behavior)

2. a need to demonstrate competence (experience mastery)
3. a need for relatedness (social interactions)

Thus, individuals seek challenges that serve to satisfy one or more of these needs.

The theory further specifies three forms of motivation capable of driving achievement behaviors. On opposite ends of the continuum (see Exhibit 3.10) are intrinsic motivation and amotivation. As defined earlier, intrinsic motivation refers to the mentality of engaging in a behavior for reasons of inherent pleasure, satisfaction, or personal challenge (e.g., "I exercise because it's fun"). **Amotivation,** on the other hand, is defined as a relative absence of motivation or lack of intention to engage in a behavior. Individuals may be amotivated in regard to exercise for a number of reasons, such as the perception that they lack the ability to adhere to an exercise regimen (e.g., "I'm not disciplined enough to stick with exercise"). They may also believe that exercise is unimportant or unnecessary (e.g., "I'm perfectly healthy and have no need for exercise"), or that exercise will not produce a desired outcome (e.g., reduced body fat).

■ amotivation

Residing between intrinsic motivation and amotivation are four types of extrinsic motivation. The first (and most self-determined) form of extrinsic motivation is **integrated regulation,** which refers to the process of engaging in a behavior in order to confirm one's sense of self (e.g., "I am an exerciser, and

■ integrated regulation

Diagram of self-determination theory, including motives for behavior. **exhibit 3.10**

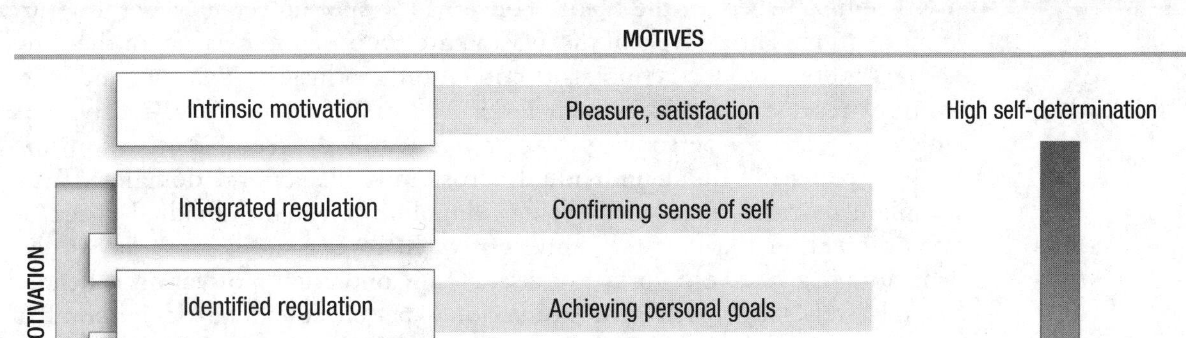

Source: Adapted from Deci & Ryan (1985).

identified regulation ■ introjected regulation ■ external regulation ■

this is what I do"). **Identified regulation** occurs when behavior is motivated by personal goals. Although the behavior is initiated autonomously, identified regulation is considered extrinsic because the decision is guided by an external outcome or product (e.g., improved appearance) as opposed to a feeling of enjoyment or sense of accomplishment. Clearly, this form of extrinsic motivation is one that is commonly employed in the exercise domain. Next on the continuum is **introjected regulation,** which is said to exist when a behavior is dictated by a self-imposed source of pressure (e.g., exercising in order to avoid feelings of guilt). The final (and least self-determining) form of extrinsic motivation is **external regulation,** which refers to the process of engaging in a behavior for the purpose of obtaining an external reward or avoiding an externally applied punishment (e.g., exercising to receive praise from others or because rehabilitation personnel are compelling you to do so).

Self-determination is thought to decrease along the continuum from intrinsic motivation to amotivation. Additionally, the order of the various components is relevant, in that those motivational types closest to one another (e.g., intrinsic motivation and integrated regulation) are hypothesized to be more closely related in terms of their motivational qualities than those more distant from one another (e.g., intrinsic motivation and external regulation). This is important because motivation types that are high in autonomy (self-determination) are thought to be associated with the achievement of a number of positive outcomes, including those related to exercise (see the "Research Exemplar" section later in this section).

global motivation ■ contextual motivation ■ situational motivation ■

The final aspect of the theory concerns the specific versus general nature of motivation. Three levels of motivation are proposed to exist, with the three primary motivation types (intrinsic motivation, extrinsic motivation, and amotivation) represented within each level. The first level is **global motivation,** which, similar to a personality trait, refers to the degree of motivation normally experienced by an individual across most behavioral domains. Thus, we might describe someone as being a highly motivated individual based on our observation that she is highly motivated to engage in most day-to-day behaviors (e.g., school, work, exercise, etc.). **Contextual motivation** is defined as a relatively stable pattern of motivation experienced in a particular context. Here, we might proclaim an individual to be highly motivated to engage in physical activity but poorly motivated to engage in occupational or academic activities. This is important in light of research that suggests that contextual motivation for exercise can significantly influence feeling states experienced following a single bout of activity. For example, self-determined (intrinsic) motivation has been linked with more positive affect following exercise (Lutz, Lochbaum, & Turnbow, 2003). Finally, **situational motivation** refers to motivation experienced in a particular activity at a specific point in time. For example, an individual might be highly motivated to engage in exercise today but poorly motivated tomorrow. Similarly, someone might be highly motivated to run but poorly motivated to lift weights.

From Theory to Application

Based on the predictions of SDT, we can hypothesize that an individual who exercises for reasons reflective of low self-determination (such as the desire to improve appearance) would be less likely to adhere to the regimen than would someone who exercises for the inherent pleasure involved (high self-determination). To this end, we might expect improvements in intrinsic motivation to result from exercise interventions that are aimed at enhancing an individual's sense of competence and autonomy and that are conducted in a positive, mutually supportive environment wherein satisfying social interactions can take place. The latter point would certainly seem to highlight group exercise as a potential strategy for achieving the purpose of relatedness. Promoting a sense of ownership or control over the workout routine should serve to enhance a sense of responsibility and autonomy in regard to exercise behavior. One way to accomplish this would be to allow the exerciser to choose among several activities, all of which are capable of producing the desired result. Additionally, designing a program that leads the individual to feel successful in mastering the activity should help to develop feelings of competence. For example, we might ask novice exercisers to engage in relatively simple, low-intensity, short-duration movements early in the initiation of their exercise program so that they can experience a sense of accomplishment and concomitant feelings of satisfaction and pride.

Research Exemplar

In a study designed to examine the role of self-determined forms of motivation on physical activity behaviors, cognitions, and self-evaluations, Thøgersen-Ntoumani and Ntoumanis (2006) recruited 375 male and female exercisers from 10 fitness clubs and asked them to complete a battery of measures including level of exercise behavior based on a stages of change model (see the discussion of the transtheoretical model in Chapter 4). Briefly, stage models of behavior suggest that individuals pass through a number of sequential steps or "stages" on their way to adopting and maintaining engagement in a particular behavior. These stages range from no consideration of adopting a behavior (the first stage of behavior change) to successful maintenance of the behavior over a period of time (the last stage of behavior change). Self-determination was assessed via the Behavioral Regulation in Exercise Questionnaire, which includes such items as "I take part in exercise because my friends/family/spouse say I should" (external regulation), "I feel guilty when I don't exercise" (introjected regulation), and "I get pleasure and satisfaction from participating in exercise" (intrinsic regulation) (Mullan, Markland, & Ingledew, 1997). The results of the investigation indicated that exercisers reporting higher levels of self-determined motivation (defined as intrinsic motivation and identified regulation) were also more likely to report stronger intentions to exercise, higher self-efficacy to overcome barriers to exercise, greater physical self-worth, and lower social physique anxiety than those reporting lower levels of self-determined motivation (defined as higher scores on external regulation and amotivation). In addition, the authors found that exercisers in the maintenance stage displayed significantly more self-determined motivation to exercise than those in the preparation and action stages of exercise behavior. (Similar results have been reported by Landry and Solmon [2004] in a sample of older, African American females.)

Usefulness, Limitations, and Future Research Avenues of Self-Determination Theory

While self-determination theory is a relative newcomer in the exercise psychology field, an impressive body of literature has begun to emerge focusing on a variety of physical activities and populations (see Hagger & Chatzisarantis, 2008, for a review). This is not surprising given that needs such as competence and autonomy are conceptually similar to constructs such as self-efficacy and perceived behavioral control, which play prominent roles in the more established theories presented in this chapter. As discussed earlier, an understanding of the various types of motivation and where they reside on the self-determination continuum can form a useful foundation for developing physical activity interventions. Practicing exercise professionals could certainly benefit from understanding the various motivational profiles when attempting to modify their clients' exercise behavior. The three primary needs (autonomy, competence, and relatedness) also appear capable of accounting for why some people might enjoy exercise while others avoid it.

With these issues in mind, the future for SDT in the exercise domain appears bright. Clearly, a substantial number of research venues remain to be tested and verified. First, the relationship between self-determination and the experience of interest, enjoyment, and other affective states in the exercise setting warrants additional empirical investigation. Second, we must demonstrate consistent support for the ability of SDT constructs to predict exercise behavior. Specifically, the following questions remain to be answered: Can the various SDT constructs predict exercise participation over an extended period of time (i.e., adherence to an exercise regimen)? How do the levels of SDT constructs vary over time as exercise behavior changes? What interventions are capable of positively or negatively affecting the SDT constructs, and what are the consequences of these interventions to exercise behavior? Not surprisingly, these questions will be best answered as we move beyond cross-sectional designs and toward more longitudinal research methodologies. Finally, future research will also likely build off recent investigations that have successfully combined SDT with concepts contained in other theories (see Chatzisarantis & Hagger, 2009, and Murcia, de San Román, Galindo, et al., 2008, for examples).

Conclusion

The theories and models reviewed in this chapter were designed to help researchers and practitioners better understand and predict physical activity behavior. Theories and models also provide us with a blueprint on which to base interventions. The expectancy-value and social cognitive philosophies are at the core of each theory presented in this chapter. Bandura's (1977, 1986) self-efficacy theory is, arguably, the most popular theory in the exercise psychology literature and offers tremendous opportunity for intervention. The theory of reasoned action and the theory of planned behavior are also sensitive to various intervention strategies and have gained acceptance in the field of exercise psychology for their ability to predict acute physical activity behavior. The relative newcomer on the block, self-determination theory, offers great potential, as it delineates the various forms of motivation that serve to influence achievement behaviors such as exercise.

These theories share a common central construct rooted in self-referent thought—namely, self-efficacy (in SET), perceived behavioral control (in TPB), and the need for autonomy and to demonstrate competence (in SDT). The significance of these self-referencing variables will become clearer when we discuss certain intervention strategies in Chapter 6. As you move through the remainder of this text, try to think in terms of formulating theories in order to gain a more thorough understanding about a particular topic. After all, in the words of noted social psychologist Kurt Lewin, "nothing is so practical as a good theory."

what do you know?

1. What is the difference between a model and a theory?
2. Why is theory important?
3. Describe the social cognitive philosophy of human behavior.
4. What is motivation?
5. What factors determine motivation?
6. Compare and contrast intrinsic and extrinsic forms of motivation.
7. Explain the expectancy-value approach to understanding motivation and behavior.
8. What is self-efficacy? How is it different from self-confidence?
9. Discuss the four sources of self-efficacy.
10. What are the primary consequences of self-efficacy?
11. Describe the two constructs that influence intention in both the TRA and the TPB.
12. What is the relationship between intention and behavior?
13. What construct distinguishes the TRA from the TPB, and why was this construct added?
14. According to SDT, what are our three primary psychosocial needs?
15. Define "self-determined."
16. What are the three primary categories of motivation in SDT?

learning activities

1. Describe a behavior in your life (not related to physical activity) that you feel is a function of both social (learned) experiences and your psychological (cognitive) makeup.
2. Relate a physical activity experience in your life that illustrates one of the theories presented in this chapter.
3. Using the constructs contained in the theories presented in this chapter, construct your own theory or model of exercise psychology/behavior.
4. Complete the sample barriers self-efficacy scale (Exhibit 3.6). Compare your results to those of your classmates. Evaluate the relative strength of your group's self-efficacy to overcome barriers to physical activity.

references

Ajzen, I. (1985). From intention to actions: A theory of planned behavior. In J. Kuhl & J. Beckman (Eds.), *Action control: From cognition to behavior* (pp. 11–39). Heidelberg, Germany: Springer.

Bandura, A. (1977). Self-efficacy: Toward a unifying theory of behavioral change. *Psychological Review, 84,* 191–215.

Bandura, A. (1986). *Social foundations of thought and action.* Englewood Cliffs, NJ: Prentice-Hall.

Blanchard, C., Fisher, J., Sparling, P., Nehl, E., Rhodes, R., Courneya, K., & Baker, F. (2008). Understanding physical activity behavior in African American and Caucasian college students: An application of the Theory of Planned Behavior. *Journal of American College Health, 56,* 341–346.

Blue, C.L. (1995). The predictive capacity of the theory of reasoned action and the theory of planned behavior in exercise research: An integrated literature review. *Research in Nursing and Health, 18,* 105–121.

Chatzisarantis, N.L.D., & Hagger, M.S. (2009). Effects of an intervention based on self-determination theory on self-reported leisure-time physical activity participation. *Psychology and Health, 24,* 29–48.

Courneya, K.S., & Friedenreich, C.M. (1997). Relationship between exercise during treatment and current quality of life among survivors of breast cancer. *Journal of Psychosocial Oncology, 14,* 35–57.

Courneya, K.S., & Friedenreich, C.M. (1999). Physical exercise and quality of life following cancer diagnosis: A literature review. *Annals of Behavioral Medicine, 21,* 171–179.

Courneya, K.S., Friedenreich, C.M., Arthur, K., & Bobick, T.M. (1999). Understanding exercise motivation in colorectal cancer patients: A prospective study using the Theory of Planned behavior. *Rehabilitation Psychology, 44,* 68–84.

Dean, R.N., Farrell, J.M., Kelley, M.L., Taylor, M.J., & Rhodes, R.E. (2006). Testing the efficacy of the theory of planned behavior to explain strength training in older adults. *Journal of Aging and Physical Activity, 15,* 1–12.

Dechamps, A., Gatta, B., Bourdel-Marchasson, I., Tabarin, A., & Roger, P. (2009). Pilot study of a 10-week multidisciplinary tai chi intervention in sedentary obese women. *Clinical Journal of Sport Medicine, 19,* 49–53.

Deci, E.L., & Ryan, R.M. (1985). *Intrinsic motivation and self-determination in human behavior.* New York: Plenum Press.

Fishbein, M., & Ajzen, I. (1975). *Belief, attitude, intention and behavior.* Don Mills, Ontario: Addison Wesley.

Fox, J., & Bailenson, J.N. (2009). Virtual self-modeling: The effects of vicarious reinforcement and identification on exercise behaviors. *Media Psychology, 12,* 1–25.

Godin, G. (1993). The theories of reasoned action and planned behavior: Overview of findings, emerging research problems and usefulness for exercise promotion. *Journal of Applied Sport Psychology, 5,* 141–157.

Greene, B.L., Haldeman, G.F., Kaminski, A., Neal, K., Lim, S.S., & Conn, D.L. (2006). Factors affecting physical activity behavior in urban adults with arthritis who are predominantly African-American and female. *Physical Therapy, 86,* 510–519.

Hagger, M., & Chatzisarantis, N. (2008). Self-Determination Theory and the psychology of exercise. *International Journal of Sport and Exercise Psychology, 1,* 79–103.

Hagger, M.S., Chatzisarantis, N.L.D., & Biddle, S.J.H. (2002). A meta-analytic review of the theories of reasoned action and planned behavior in physical activity: Predictive validity and the contribution of additional variables. *Journal of Sport and Exercise Psychology, 24,* 3–32.

Hu, L., Motl, R.W., McAuley, E., & Konopack, J.F. (2007). Effects of self-efficacy on physical activity enjoyment in college-aged women. *International Journal of Behavioral Medicine, 14,* 92–96.

Jackson, C., Smith, R.A., & Conner, M. (2003). Applying an extended version of the theory of planned behaviour to physical activity. *Journal of Sports Sciences, 21,* 119–133.

Klein-Hessling, J., Lohaus, A., & Ball, J. (2005). Psychological predictors of health-related behaviour in children. *Psychology, Health & Medicine, 10,* 31–43.

Landry, J.B., & Solmon, M.A. (2004). African American women's self-determination across the stages of change for exercise. *Journal of Sport and Exercise Psychology, 26,* 457–469.

Lucidi, F., Grano, C., Barbaranelli, C., & Violani, C. (2006). Social-cognitive determinants of physical activity attendance in older adults. *Journal of Aging and Physical Activity, 14,* 344–359.

Lutz, R., Lochbaum, M., & Turnbow, K. (2003). The role of relative autonomy in post-exercise affect responding. *Journal of Sport Behavior, 26,* 137–154.

McAuley, E., & Blissmer, B. (2000). Self-efficacy determinants and consequences of physical activity. *Exercise and Sport Sciences Reviews, 28,* 85–88.

Milne, M., Hall, C., & Forwell, L. (2005). Self-efficacy, imagery use, and adherence to rehabilitation by injured athletes. *Journal of Sport Rehabilitation, 14,* 150–167.

Mullan, E., Markland, D., & Ingledew, D.K. (1997). Motivation for exercise: Development of a measure of behavioral regulation. *Journal of Sports Sciences, 15,* 98–99.

Murcia, J.A.M., de San Román, M.L., Galindo, C.M., Alonso, N., & González-Cutre, D. (2008). Peers' influence on exercise enjoyment: A self-determination theory approach. *Journal of Sports Science and Medicine, 7,* 23–31.

Peterson, J.J., Lowe, J.B., Peterson, A., Nothwehr, F.K., Janz, K.F., & Lobas, J.G. (2008). Paths to leisure physical activity among adults with intellectual disabilities: Self-efficacy and social support. *American Journal of Health Promotion, 23,* 35–42.

Rhodes, R.E., Jones, L.W., & Courneya, K.S. (2002). Extending the theory of planned behavior in the exercise domain: A comparison of social support and subjective norm. *Research Quarterly for Exercise and Sport, 73,* 193–199.

Rodgers, W.M., Hall, C.R., Blanchard, C.M., McAuley, E., & Munroe, K. (2002). Task and scheduling self-efficacy as predictors of exercise behavior. *Psychology and Health, 17,* 405–416.

Ryan, M.P. (2008). The antidepressant effects of physical activity: Mediating self-esteem and self-efficacy mechanisms. *Psychology and Health, 23,* 279–307.

Sniehotta, F.F., Scholz, U., & Schwarzer, R. (2005). Bridging the intention-behavior gap: Planning, self-efficacy, and action control in the adoption and maintenance of physical exercise. *Psychology and Health, 20,* 143–160.

Symons Downs, D., & Hausenblas, H.A. (2005). The theories of reasoned action and planned behavior applied to exercise: A meta-analytic update. *Journal of Physical Activity and Health, 2,* 76–97.

Thøgersen-Ntoumani, C., & Ntoumanis, N. (2006). The role of self-determined motivation in the understanding of exercise-related behaviours, cognitions and physical self-evaluations. *Journal of Sports Sciences, 24,* 393–404.

Umstattd, M.R., & Hallam, J. (2007). Older adults' exercise behavior: Roles of selected constructs of social-cognitive theory. *Journal of Aging and Physical Activity, 15,* 206–218.

Winters, E.R., Petosa, R.L., & Charlton, T.E. (2003). Using social cognitive theory to explain discretionary, "leisure-time" physical exercise among high school students. *Journal of Adolescent Health, 32,* 436–442.

4

Theories and Models of Exercise Behavior II

STIMULUS–RESPONSE THEORY AND INTEGRATIVE APPROACHES

The previous chapter focused only on theories and models rooted in the social cognitive approach. This chapter continues the discussion of theories and models of exercise behavior by presenting the other frameworks that appear most prominently in the exercise psychology literature.

Social cognitive theories and models assume that people's decisions to exercise are based on a rational decision-making process whereby their thoughts and feelings (e.g., attitudes, self-efficacy beliefs) factor in to their decisions. For instance, the theory of reasoned action holds that people's exercise attitudes and subjective norms influence their decisions or intentions to exercise. Likewise, self-determination theory proposes that the decision to exercise is based on the belief that exercise will satisfy one's psychosocial needs. Other theories, however, do not consider thoughts and feelings about exercise, or even rational decision making, to be necessary determinants of exercise behavior. For example, consider a child who hates to do any type of physical activity but loves to collect stickers. The child's parents influence him to be physically active by providing a packet of stickers for every 30 minutes he spends in active play. Although the child's thoughts and feelings toward exercise may remain negative, his behavior changes. This phenomenon can be explained by the principle of *reinforcement.*

In the first part of this chapter, we look at reinforcement and other principles of stimulus–response theory as an alternative to the social cognitive approach for explaining exercise behavior. In the second part, we examine two models—the transtheoretical model and a preliminary social ecological model of exercise—that have attempted to explain exercise by integrating social cognitive approaches with approaches that look beyond the individual's thoughts, feelings, and decision-making processes.

KEY TERMS

- action stage
- antecedent cue
- behavioral processes
- classical conditioning
- consciousness raising
- consequent reinforcement
- contemplation stage
- decisional balance
- descriptive studies
- ecosystem
- exosystem
- experiential processes
- extinction
- extrinsic reinforcers
- instrumental conditioning
- intervention studies
- intrinsic reinforcers
- macrosystem
- maintenance stage
- mesosystem
- microsystem
- negative reinforcer
- positive reinforcer
- precontemplation stage
- predictive studies
- preparation stage
- punishment
- reinforcement management
- self-liberation
- self-reevaluation
- social ecological models
- stimulus control

Stimulus–Response Theory

B. F. Skinner's (1953) stimulus–response theory (SRT) suggests an explanation for how people learn new behaviors. This theory grew out of the principles of classical conditioning (Pavlov, 1928) and instrumental conditioning (Thorndike, 1898). **Classical conditioning** principles state that a reflexive behavior (e.g., salivating, eye blinking) can be elicited through repeated pairings of the behavior with an **antecedent cue** (i.e., a cue that precedes the behavior). For example, in his famous experiments, Pavlov observed that after repeated pairings of a ringing bell with the delivery of food, dogs would start to salivate whenever the bell rang, even if there was no food present. The dogs salivated because they had learned to associate the ringing bell with the delivery of food (a stimulus that naturally elicits the salivary reflex). **Instrumental conditioning** principles state that a voluntary (i.e., non-reflexive) behavior can be learned by pairing the behavior with **consequent reinforcement** (i.e., a reward that follows the behavior). For example, a dog can learn to sit on command if he is given a cookie every time he responds successfully to the command.

classical conditioning ■

antecedent cue ■

instrumental conditioning ■

consequent reinforcement ■

According to Skinner (1953), although a behavior can be learned through repeated pairings of that behavior with antecedent cues or consequent reinforcers, consequences have a greater impact on behavior than do antecedents. Thus, SRT identifies events that can follow a behavior and the effects these events will have on future behavior. According to SRT, four types of events—positive reinforcement, negative reinforcement, punishment, and extinction—can follow a behavior and will alter the likelihood of that behavior occurring again in the future. (Exhibit 4.1 summarizes information about these events.) Let's look at each of these events within the context of exercise behavior.

Positive Reinforcement

Reinforcement is the key element of stimulus–response theory. A positive reinforcer is an enjoyable or pleasant outcome that makes a person feel good and that strengthens a particular behavior. Within the context of exercise, a **positive rein-**

positive reinforcer ■

exhibit 4.1 Predictions of stimulus–response theory.

EVENTS THAT CAN FOLLOW A BEHAVIOR	DESCRIPTION OF EVENTS	PREDICTED EFFECTS ON FUTURE EXERCISE BEHAVIOR
1. Positive reinforcement	Adding something positive (e.g., money, praise)	Increases exercise
2. Negative reinforcement	Taking away something negative (e.g., pain, depression)	Increases exercise
3. Punishment	Adding something negative (e.g., injury, embarrassment)	Decreases exercise
4. Extinction	Taking away something positive (e.g., opportunities to socialize)	Decreases exercise

forcer is any intrinsic or extrinsic reward that increases the likelihood of a person exercising in the future.

■ intrinsic reinforcers

Intrinsic reinforcers are rewards that come from within the self, such as feeling good about one's body, feeling a sense of accomplishment at the end of a workout, or simply experiencing the physical and emotional sense of well-being that accompanies exercise. **Extrinsic reinforcers** are rewards that come from other people, such as verbal praise from a fitness instructor, t-shirts awarded for perfect attendance at an exercise class, or compliments from friends and family about one's improved physique. According to the principles of SRT, when individuals receive positive reinforcement after exercising, they will be more likely to exercise again in the future.

■ extrinsic reinforcers

Although extrinsic reinforcers have been shown to increase exercise behavior (Noland, 1989), they should be used with caution. For instance, if a parent extrinsically rewards a child every time she is physically active, then she may not choose to be active in situations when the parent is not around to give reinforcement (e.g., when she is playing at a friend's house). In addition, if the child becomes accustomed to receiving some type of reward in return for being active, she may start to think of physical activity as work or a chore—something she does in order to get something that she wants. Another danger with extrinsic rewards is that they can prevent the individual from learning about the intrinsic rewards associated with exercise. The child who is given rewards may be so focused on attaining the extrinsic reinforcement that she never comes to realize the intrinsic rewards associated with being physically active, such as having fun, learning new skills, and making new friends. Finally, people with intrinsic reasons for exercise tend to adhere better over the long term than do those with extrinsic reasons (Ryan, Frederick, Lepes, et al., 1997). It is crucial, therefore, that people of all ages—not just children—realize the intrinsic benefits of physical activity participation.

Negative Reinforcement

■ negative reinforcer

Negative reinforcers are generally unpleasant or aversive stimuli that, when withdrawn after a behavior, will *increase* the frequency of that behavior in the future. (Note that negative reinforcement is not the same as punishment, which is discussed in the next section.) For example, Jacob is a 50-year-old man with arthritis of the knees. He finds that after a long day at work, sitting in front of a computer, his knees ache and become very stiff. At the end of each day, however, Jacob rides his bicycle for half an hour because he finds that this activity significantly reduces his knee discomfort. Thus, for Jacob, a reduction in knee pain serves as a negative reinforcer for exercise. When he exercises, the knee pain is withdrawn, and this increases the likelihood that he will continue to exercise in the future. Of course, Jacob may also derive *positive* reinforcers when he rides his bike, such as experiencing pleasure from being outdoors or receiving praise from his family for being so physically active. The combination of positive and negative reinforcers increases the likelihood that Jacob will continue to ride his bike every day.

Both positive and negative reinforcement will have their greatest effects when people are able to see the relationship between their behavior and the reinforcing outcome. Thus, reinforcement is most effective when it is delivered *frequently* and *immediately* after exercise. This means that outcomes that occur often and soon after an exercise bout (e.g., feelings of satisfaction, changes in pain) will have a bigger effect on future exercise behavior than will outcomes that occur only occasionally or that are accumulated after many exercise sessions (e.g., changes in body composition or cardiovascular fitness). This latter point may explain why so many people who start an exercise program for the purpose of weight loss drop out so quickly. Of course, weight loss does not occur immediately after exercising. Because it may take months for new exercisers to see significant weight loss, weight reduction is a poor reinforcer for exercise. People who exercise only to lose weight often become discouraged and drop out because they fail to derive any immediate reinforcement from their workouts.

Punishment

punishment ■ **Punishment** usually involves presenting an unpleasant or uncomfortable stimulus after a behavior in order to decrease the probability of that behavior happening in the future. If Jacob were to experience even greater pain after cycling, it is unlikely that he would continue to cycle regularly. Under these conditions, pain would be considered a punishment that decreases exercise.

Although pain would likely be considered a punishment by virtually anyone, other exercise consequences that some people consider punishment may be surprising. For example, some women report that they don't want to exercise because they don't like the feeling of being sweaty. For these women, sweat is a punishing stimulus—an uncomfortable consequence of exercise that actually deters them from being physically active. Other consequences—having to go outside with wet hair after a swim or doing additional laundry to clean workout clothing—may not seem particularly unpleasant to many people, but for others they are sufficiently aversive to function as a punishment that deters exercise.

Extinction

extinction ■ **Extinction** involves withholding a positive stimulus after a behavior in order to decrease the likelihood of that behavior happening in the future. According to the principle of extinction, people will decrease their exercise behavior if they stop attaining the positive benefits/reinforcers that they associate with exercise (e.g., losing weight, feeling better physically and psychologically, having an opportunity to socialize). For instance, a woman who starts an exercise program with the sole purpose of losing weight will exercise less or may even quit altogether once she stops losing weight.

From Theory to Application

In real-world exercise settings, trainers, therapists, and others often use the principles of SRT to develop interventions to increase people's exercise behavior.

For instance, gyms and fitness classes frequently offer t-shirts, water bottles, and other rewards as a form of positive reinforcement for adherent exercisers. Likewise, many people motivate themselves to exercise by promising themselves a reward at the end of the exercise session (e.g., a trip to the frozen yogurt shop) or after several months of exercise adherence (e.g., a new outfit). These rewards function as positive reinforcement and are relatively easy to apply as an intervention strategy. Negative reinforcement, however, requires some creativity in its application. One intervention approach is to make exercisers aware of decreases in negative symptoms (e.g., pain) and feelings (e.g., depression) over the course of their exercise program. Like Jacob, people who recognize that exercise causes a decrease in negative sensations may be more likely to continue exercising.

Because punishment is an intervention technique used only to *decrease* behaviors, by definition it cannot be applied to *increase* physical activity. It can, however, be used to decrease sedentary activity, which may, in turn, cause people to increase their physical activity. When people decrease their time spent in sedentary activities, they often fill their spare time with more physically active pursuits (Epstein, Roemmich, Paluch, & Raynor, 2005). Parents who want their children to be more physically active might use punishment to decrease the amount of time the children spend on sedentary activities such as watching television or playing on the computer. For example, parents may assign additional chores (the punishment) to a child who watches too much television. It is important to note that physical activity should *never* be used as a punishment. Children who are given exercise as a punishment may come to see physical activity as something they do only when they misbehave and, thus, as something that is highly aversive. In a similar vein, many adults report that they do not like to exercise because, as children, they had physical education teachers who used running, sit-ups, and other exercise activities as a form of punishment.

Finally, the principle of extinction occurs all too often in fitness settings. When people stop deriving pleasure from exercise, they often quit. For instance, if one's friends leave the exercise group, or a favorite fitness instructor quits, an exerciser may stop exercising if she perceives that she is no longer having fun and deriving the social benefits of exercise that she formerly enjoyed. Fitness professionals can intervene to prevent extinction, however, by helping people to identify what it is that they value and enjoy about exercise, or by pointing out additional benefits that they may not have previously considered. When valued benefits have been identified, the fitness professional can introduce the exerciser to the types of exercise activities and programs that lead to those benefits.

Research Exemplar

In comparison to the social cognitive theories discussed in Chapter 3, relatively little research has applied SRT to the study of exercise behavior. The lack of such research probably reflects exercise psychologists' recognition of the importance of thoughts and feelings in determining exercise behavior. SRT does not take these factors into account, so it tends not to be the theory of choice for many

FOCUS on Overweight Children

The number of overweight children in the United States has tripled since 1980. (Among children, overweight is defined as having a body mass index that is at or above the 95th percentile of BMIs for children of the same sex, age, and height.) Based on data collected from 2003 to 2006, more than 9 million youngsters (16 percent) between the ages of 2 and 19 were classified as overweight (Ogden, Carroll, & Flegal, 2008). Physical activity can play an important role in the treatment of overweight children (Atlantis, Barnes, & Singh, 2006), but it is often difficult to motivate overweight children to become more physically active. In a clever experiment, Epstein, Saelens, Myers, and Vito (1997) applied the principles of stimulus–response theory to the problem of exercise motivation in obese children.

Thirty-four overweight children who were between the ages of 8 and 12 came to a laboratory that contained equipment for four physical activities (a stationary bicycle, a climbing machine, a speed skating slide, and a cross-country skiing machine) and four sedentary activities (a VCR with children's movies, Nintendo video games, books, and coloring materials). On the first day of the experiment, children were given free access to all of the activities for 45 minutes and were then randomized to one of four conditions for the next three days: (1) Children in the *reinforcement condition* were told that they would earn one point for each minute that they did not spend doing their two favorite sedentary activities. (2) Children in the *punishment condition* were instructed that they would lose a point for each minute they spent doing their two favorite sedentary activities. Children in these two conditions could redeem their points for reinforcers such as tickets to a baseball game, passes to the zoo, and video arcade tokens. (3) In the *restriction condition,* the child's two favorite sedentary activities were removed from the lab. (4) In the *control condition,* children were given access to all activities. Children in these latter two conditions were not given any information about gaining or losing points. Each child returned to the lab for three more days. On the fifth day of the experiment, the contingencies (i.e., rewards, punishment, restricted access) were removed, and children were given free access to all eight activities.

When the data were analyzed, it was found that on Days 1 and 5, children in all four conditions engaged in similar amounts of physical activity—on average, only about five or six minutes. On Days 2, 3, and 4 of the experiment (the days on which the contingencies were in effect), children in the reinforcement and punishment conditions were significantly more physically active than children in the control condition. On average, they were active for about 15 minutes. Children in the restricted access condition were only slightly more physically active (about 10 minutes of activity per session) than those in the control condition (about five minutes of activity per session). These results show that in laboratory conditions, the stimulus–response principles of reinforcement and punishment are effective strategies for increasing physical activity in overweight children. Additional research is needed, however, to determine if parents can motivate their children to become more active by using Epstein's laboratory techniques in their homes.

ADDITIONAL RESOURCES

De Bourdeaudhuij, I., Lefevre, J., Deforche, B., Wijndaele, K., Matton, L., & Philippaerts, R. (2005). Physical activity and psychosocial correlates in normal weight and overweight 11 to 19 year olds. *Obesity Research, 13,* 1097–1105.

Marshall, S.J., Biddle, S.J.H., Gorely, T., Cameron, N., & Murdey, I. (2004). Relationships between media use, body fatness and physical activity in children and youth: A meta-analysis. *International Journal of Obesity, 28,* 1238–1246.

Molnar, B.E., Gortmaker, S.L., Bull, F.C., & Buka, S.L. (2004). Unsafe to play? Neighborhood disorder and lack of safety predict reduced physical activity among urban children and adolescents. *American Journal of Health Promotion, 18,* 378–386.

ACTIVITY

Physical activity plays an important role in preventing children from becoming overweight. If researchers can understand the factors that best predict childhood physical activity, then interventions can be developed to modify those factors and to increase physical activity. The articles listed above will give you some ideas about the types of factors that are related (and not related) to physical activity participation among children.

1. Conduct a literature search to identify additional factors that are related to childhood physical activity.
2. Once you have this list of factors, use them to create your own model of physical activity participation among children.
3. Where possible, try to incorporate constructs that are captured in the various theories and models discussed in Chapters 3 and 4 (e.g., "attitudes" from the theory of planned behavior; "environment" from the social ecological models discussed later in this chapter).
4. Based on your model, what types of strategies would be useful for increasing physical activity among children?

researchers. Nonetheless, some studies have demonstrated the utility of SRT principles for altering exercise activity.

For instance, one experiment examined whether reinforcement could increase physical activity among children who watched television and played video games more than 15 hours per week (Roemmich, Gurgol, & Epstein, 2004). Eighteen children between the ages of 8 and 12 were randomly assigned to either a reinforcement or a control condition. For six weeks, the children wore an electronic physical activity monitor to keep track of their daily physical activity levels. At the end of each week, the children and their families met with a member of the research team. For children in the reinforcement condition, the amount of physical activity performed that week was used to determine the amount of time the child would be permitted to watch television during the following week. A child was allowed approximately one minute of television time for each minute spent on moderate or vigorous physical activity. The amount of allowed television time was then programmed into an electronic device placed on every television in the child's home. The child was given a code to activate the device and to turn on the television; when the television allowance ran out, television was not available for the remainder of the week. In the control condition, children were given the goal of engaging in 60 minutes of moderate or vigorous activity per day. They had free access to television regardless of how much activity they performed.

When the data were analyzed, it was found that, over the course of the study, children in the reinforcement condition increased their physical activity by 24 percent and engaged in 32 percent more physical activity and 22 percent less television watching than the control group. Furthermore, the children who had the greatest reductions in television watching also showed reductions in their body mass index (BMI). These results show that, among children, physical activity can be successfully reinforced through access to television.

Another example of SRT is presented in the Focus on Overweight Children box above.

Usefulness, Limitations, and Future Research Avenues of Stimulus–Response Theory

Stimulus–response theory provides a simple and useful framework for understanding the effects of exercise consequences on future exercise behavior. Both reinforcement and punishment have been shown to alter subsequent exercise behavior (Epstein, Paluch, Kilanowski, & Raynor, 2004; Epstein et al., 1997; Noland, 1989). To date, however, no experiments have investigated the effects of negative reinforcement or extinction on exercise behavior. Whether these events can be manipulated to affect exercise behavior remains to be determined in future research.

A major limitation of SRT is that it does not consider the important role of cognition. In SRT, the major role of cognition is to interpret exercise-related outcomes as either positive or negative. Although the theory proposes that these interpretations will determine subsequent exercise behavior (e.g., an outcome interpreted as positive will increase behavior whereas an outcome interpreted as negative will decrease behavior), in reality the relationship between outcomes and exercise behavior is not that simple. If it were, then beginner exercisers would never continue working out beyond the first few painful sessions, and people who felt good after working out would never quit. Of course, many beginners do persist despite the initial discomfort, and many seasoned exercisers quit despite seeing considerable positive outcomes associated with exercise. Clearly, other cognitions pertaining to the outcome—not merely whether it is positive or negative—are involved in determining future exercise behavior. These other cognitions may include *expectations* of deriving a particular outcome again, *perceived control* over attaining that outcome, and the *perceived value* of that outcome (cognitions that were discussed in the previous chapter). Although considerable research has demonstrated the importance of these cognitions in determining exercise behavior, they are not included in the SRT. Consequently, the SRT is limited in its ability to predict and explain exercise behavior.

Another limitation of the SRT in exercise settings is that, although reinforcement has proven to be a useful principle in altering exercise behavior, the other three principles are difficult to manipulate in exercise interventions (e.g., it is difficult and generally unethical to punish people if they miss a workout). The SRT also fails to provide information that can be used to develop interventions to change exercisers' perceptions of a particular outcome as reinforcing or punishing. It has been observed, for example, that some older women can eventually come to see sweating as a reinforcement rather than a punishment. This shift occurs when the women change their beliefs and attitudes toward sweating, yet beliefs and attitudes are cognitions not included in the SRT. In short, the SRT has limited use for predicting future exercise behavior and developing exercise interventions because it ignores the important role of cognition. (For an approach that attempts to integrate SRT with cognition, see the following box.)

Behavioral Economics

AN ALTERNATIVE TO STIMULUS–RESPONSE THEORY

Behavioral economics theory involves the integration of stimulus–response theory with basic research on cognitive psychology and decision making in order to explain how people allocate time and effort to various options. When people are trying to become more physically active, they are often forced to decide whether they will spend their time exercising or performing highly reinforcing, sedentary activities (e.g., watching movies may be reinforced by evoking fun and relaxation). In an exercise context, an understanding of behavioral economics can reveal ways to make highly reinforcing sedentary activities less attractive (Epstein, et al., 2005). Specifically, when the cost of performing sedentary activities increases, people may be less inclined to do them. For example, children may come to see television as less attractive and consequently spend less time watching television if TV access is contingent on the performance of household chores. In contrast, if parents provide noncontingent or "free" access to physical activities, children may see these as less costly and more attractive options than sedentary activities.

Behavioral economics would suggest that information about the reinforcing aspects of *sedentary* activities can be used to identify *physical* activities that may provide the individual with similar reinforcements. For example, consider a group of friends who get together to play board games every Wednesday evening. Upon questioning these individuals, an exercise psychologist discovers that the most reinforcing aspect of their board games is the opportunity to socialize with one another. Recognizing the importance of socializing, the exercise psychologist might suggest that the group go for a walk before starting their game. This extra time together will allow more time to talk with one another and to enjoy one another's company.

Behavioral economics seems to be a promising approach for understanding and promoting physical activity. By understanding factors that alter the reinforcing value of certain activities, exercise psychologists may help people make more healthful choices regarding the ways in which they spend their leisure time.

Integrative Approaches

Integrative approaches pull together concepts from a variety of theories and models in order to explain exercise behavior. They include the transtheoretical model and social ecological models.

Transtheoretical Model

The transtheoretical model (TTM), developed at the University of Rhode Island Cancer Prevention Research Center, was the result of years of studying and observing how people quit smoking (Prochaska & DiClemente, 1983; Prochaska, DiClemente, & Norcross, 1992; Prochaska & Velicer, 1997). The prefix *trans* means "across." The TTM was given its name because it integrates elements from *across* a variety of theories and models of behavior, some of which are social-cognitive in nature and some of which are not.

According to the TTM, behavior change is not a quick process—people do not suddenly decide to quit smoking or to start exercising and then immediately change their behavior. Rather, behavior change is a gradual process whereby the individual progresses through a series of stages. Because the TTM conceptualizes behavior change in this way, it is considered a stage model.

precontemplation stage ■

1. Precontemplation. In the **precontemplation stage,** people have no intention to start exercising in the foreseeable future (the next six months or so). People in this stage consider the cons (disadvantages) of exercising to be greater than the pros (advantages), perhaps because of a lack of information about the health consequences of a sedentary lifestyle or because they have failed at attempts to exercise in the past and have completely given up. Precontemplators are often very defensive when other people try to convince them to change their ways, so it can be difficult to provide them with information regarding the benefits of exercise, or strategies for starting an exercise program. Consequently, the precontemplation stage is very stable, meaning that without intervention, people tend to stay here for long periods of time before moving on to the next stage.

contemplation stage ■

2. Contemplation. People in the **contemplation stage** have intentions to start exercising within the next six months. At this stage, they are aware of the pros of exercising, but they are also equally aware of the cons. These are people who know that exercise is good for them and may feel that they should be exercising, but they are not yet ready to make a commitment to change. People in this stage have ambivalent feelings about exercise, so unless there is some form of intervention, they may remain in this stage for long periods of time.

preparation stage ■

3. Preparation. In the **preparation stage,** people intend to start exercising in the immediate future (i.e., the next month). People in this stage consider the pros of exercising to be greater than the cons. During this stage, people are performing tasks that will prepare them to start an exercise program, such as getting medical clearance to exercise, obtaining information about local exercise facilities and programs, or buying exercise equipment. They may also be making small changes to their current level of physical activity, such as taking the stairs in a building instead of the elevator.

action stage ■

4. Action. In the **action stage,** people are exercising at recommended levels for health and fitness (usually defined as exercise on most days of the week at a moderate intensity for at least 30 minutes duration). Although for people in this stage the pros of exercise outweigh the cons, this is a very unstable stage. In fact, of the five stages, the action stage is the least stable, because people find it so difficult to maintain their new exercise routine. Individuals in the action stage must work hard to avoid falling back into their old sedentary lifestyle.

maintenance stage ■

5. Maintenance. The **maintenance stage** is achieved when people have been exercising at recommended levels for six months. Of course, for maintainers, the pros of exercising continue to outweigh the cons. Maintainers still must work to prevent lapsing into a sedentary lifestyle, but they don't find exercise as difficult to maintain as they did during the action stage. Overall, they are less tempted to relapse and are highly confident that they can continue their exercise program.

How do people move through the stages?

Movement through the stages involves changing:

- how people think about exercise
- how people think about themselves
- aspects of the environment that influence exercise behavior.

According to the TTM, these changes occur through a combination of 10 basic experiential and behavioral processes. These 10 processes are defined in Exhibit 4.2, which also provides examples of interventions that can help people apply each of the processes.

exhibit 4.2 Definitions and examples of interventions associated with each of the processes of change in the transtheoretical model.

PROCESS	DEFINITION	INTERVENTION EXAMPLE
Experiential Processes		
Consciousness raising	Seeking new information and a better understanding of exercise	Read pamphlets, talk to a health care professional about the benefits of exercise
Self-reevaluation	Assessing how one thinks and feels about oneself as an inactive person	Consider whether being inactive is truly in line with one's values
Environmental reevaluation	Considering how inactivity affects the physical and social environment	Find out the costs of inactivity to the health care system
Dramatic relief	Experiencing and expressing feelings about becoming more active or remaining inactive through exercise	Imagine the feelings of regret and loss for not having prevented the loss of health
Social liberation	Increasing awareness of the social and environmental factors that support physical activity	Seek out information about exercise groups and resources in the community, workplace, etc.
Behavioral Processes		
Self-liberation	Engaging in activities that strengthen one's commitment to change and the belief that one can change	Announce one's commitment to exercise to family and friends; stay positive and remind oneself "I can do it!"
Counterconditioning	Substituting physical activities for sedentary activities	Go for a walk after dinner rather than watch television
Stimulus control	Controlling situations and cues that trigger inactivity and skipped workouts	Plan ahead for a busy period at work/school and schedule exercise on a calendar
Reinforcement management	Rewarding oneself for being active	Establish goals and reward oneself for achieving them
Helping relationships	Using support from others during attempts to change	Buddy up with a friend who is also trying to start an exercise regimen

experiential processes ■ self-reevaluation ■ consciousness raising ■

Experiential processes are typically directed toward increasing people's awareness of, and changing their thoughts and feelings about, both themselves and their exercise behavior. For example, the process of **self-reevaluation** involves people carefully considering how they feel about themselves as "couch potatoes" and deciding whether that is an identity they want to maintain. The process of **consciousness raising** involves increasing one's awareness and memory of the benefits of physical activity. Ways to achieve this include providing people with educational literature on physical activity and having them talk with someone who used to be sedentary, but who has since become active and who now recognizes the advantages of exercising.

behavioral processes ■ stimulus control ■ reinforcement management ■

Behavioral processes generally consist of behaviors that a person undertakes in order to change aspects of the environment that may affect exercise participation. For instance, **stimulus control** involves placing cues in the environment that will remind people to be more physically active (e.g., putting your workout clothes by your door) and removing cues that tempt people to be inactive (e.g., taking the batteries out of the television remote control). The process of **reinforcement management** involves developing strategies for rewarding or reinforcing oneself when exercise goals are achieved.

Studies of smoking cessation have shown that people use different types of processes at different stages of change (Prochaska, DiClemente, & Norcross, 1992). Specifically, experiential processes are used more during the earlier stages of smoking cessation, and behavioral processes are used more in the later stages. Yet, for exercise, there does not seem to be a shift across the stages from the use of experiential to behavioral processes (Marshall & Biddle, 2001). Rather, behavioral processes tend to be used just as often as experiential processes across all the stages of physical activity behavior change.

self-liberation ■

For example, the behavioral process of **self-liberation** appears to be particularly important for helping people move through each of the stages (Lowther, Mutrie, & Scott, 2007). Self-liberation involves strategies that strengthen a person's commitment to exercise (e.g., developing a daily exercise plan) and the belief in one's ability to be more physically active (e.g., remembering past successful attempts at becoming more active).

Clearly, behavioral processes are vital to people's progression through the stages. In the next section, we discuss how to determine whether people are indeed progressing.

Indications that people are moving through the stages

According to the TTM, we can determine whether people are moving through the stages by looking for shifts in their decisional balance and an increase in their self-efficacy to overcome the temptation to skip exercise sessions.

decisional balance ■

Shift in decisional balance. The **decisional balance** construct was borrowed from Janis and Mann's (1977) model of decision making. It reflects how people perceive the pros and cons of changing their behavior. We can tell if people are moving through the stages by looking for differences in the number of pros versus cons that they list for exercise. In the precontemplation stage, the cons of exercising will far outweigh the pros. In the contemplation stage, pros and cons will be more equal. In the advanced stages, the pros will outweigh the cons. This relationship is shown in Exhibit 4.3.

Increased self-efficacy to overcome temptations. The self-efficacy construct was borrowed from Bandura's self-efficacy theory (see Chapter 3). In the TTM, self-efficacy represents the situation-specific confidence people have in their ability to deal with high-risk situations that might tempt them to lapse into their old sedentary ways. Situations that might tempt an exerciser to skip a workout include rainy days, a busy work or school schedule, and fatigue. According to the TTM, self-efficacy increases as people move through the five stages. Thus, we can tell whether people are moving through the stages by looking for an increase in their self-efficacy.

Exhibit 4.4 shows levels of self-efficacy that are typically found among people in each of the five stages. In the precontemplation stage, people have virtually no confidence in their ability to successfully handle situations that might tempt them to skip a workout. By the time they reach the action stage and are exercising at recommended levels, their efficacy has increased dramatically. The high level of self-efficacy in the maintenance stage indicates that people are confident that they can resist the temptation to skip a workout in most situations, most of the time.

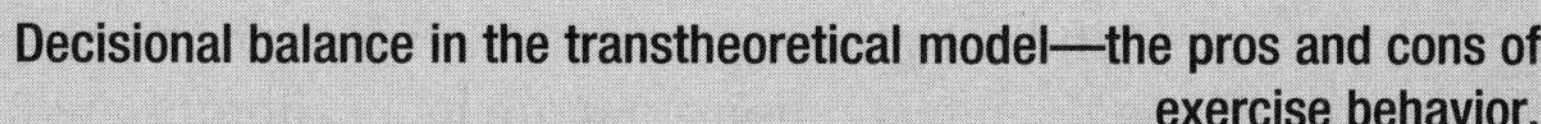

Decisional balance in the transtheoretical model—the pros and cons of exercise behavior.

exhibit 4.3

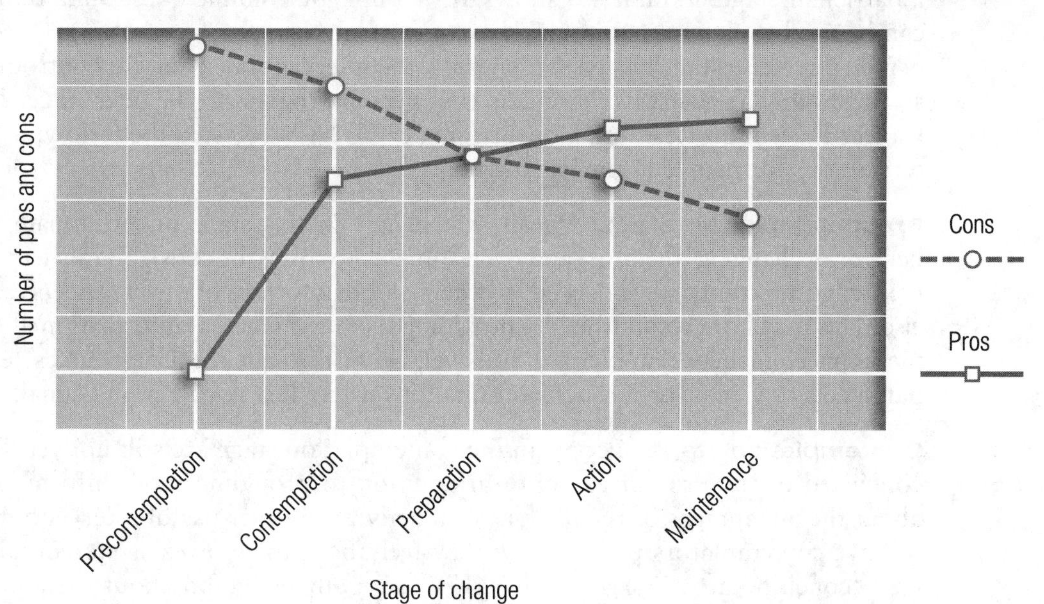

exhibit 4.4 Change in self-efficacy for exercising in high-risk situations across the five stages of the transtheoretical model.

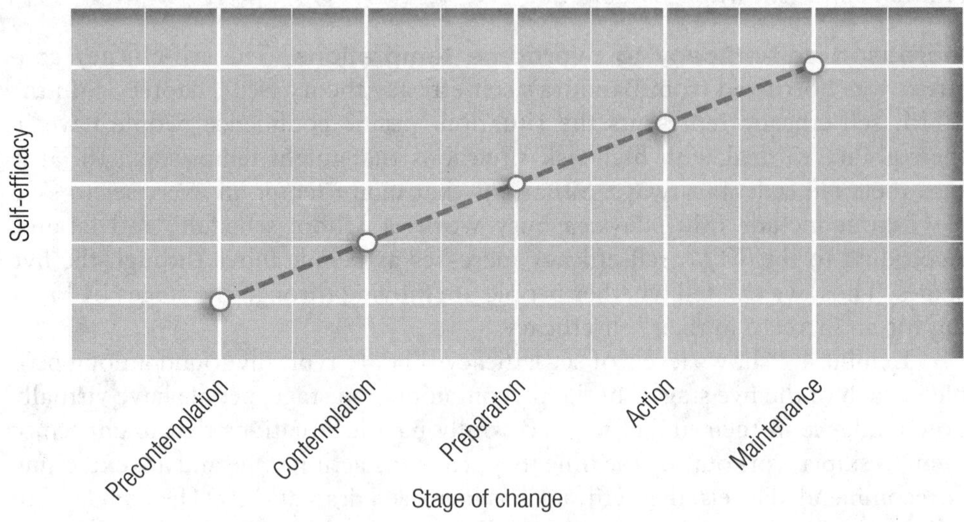

From theory to application

The TTM can be useful for guiding exercise interventions. It provides a framework for identifying the interventions that are most appropriate for a person at a particular stage. Exhibit 4.5 shows an example of a simple questionnaire that can be used to determine in which exercise stage a person currently is. Once a person's exercise stage has been identified, the interventionist can then introduce strategies that are most likely to help that person progress to the next stage. The Cancer Prevention Research Consortium (1995) has suggested the following interventions for people in the various stages of the TTM:

Precontemplation stage. Recall that people in this stage underestimate the benefits of changing (the pros) and overestimate the costs (the cons). To move to the next stage, precontemplators need to become more informed of the benefits of exercise. This may be accomplished by providing them with factual information about the connection between exercise and well-being through media resources (e.g., pamphlets or videos) or through consultations with a health care professional.

Contemplation stage. People in the contemplation stage are still not yet fully convinced of the pros of exercise. In addition to providing more information about the advantages of regular physical activity, another useful intervention is to have contemplators ponder how they feel about themselves as stereotypical lazy "couch potatoes" and whether they can really feel good about themselves if they continue to be sedentary. These questions can spur the contemplator to identify more pros for becoming physically active.

Questionnaire for determining a person's current exercise stage. exhibit 4.5

"Regular exercise" is any planned physical activity (e.g., brisk walking, aerobics, jogging, bicycling, swimming, rowing, etc.) performed to increase physical fitness. Such activity should be performed three to five times per week for 20 to 60 minutes per session.

DO YOU EXERCISE REGULARLY ACCORDING TO THAT DEFINITION?

- ☐ 1. Yes, I have been exercising regularly for MORE than six months.
- ☐ 2. Yes, I have been exercising regularly for LESS than six months.
- ☐ 3. No, but I intend to start exercising regularly in the next 30 days.
- ☐ 4. No, but I intend to start exercising regularly in the next six months.
- ☐ 5. No, and I do NOT intend to start exercising regularly in the next six months.

Results

If you checked the last box, you are in the precontemplation stage.
If you checked the fourth box, you are in the contemplation stage.
If you checked the third box, you are in the preparation stage.
If you checked the second box, you are in the action stage.
If you checked the first box, congratulations! You are in the maintenance stage.

Source: Adapted from the Exercise: Stages of Change–Short Form. Available at www.uri.edu/research/cprc/Measures/Exercise02.htm

Preparation stage. People in the preparation stage are ready to change soon, but they are concerned about failing. Thus, their self-efficacy for exercising is still relatively low. Interventionists can help these people progress through the preparation stage by encouraging them to get organized and start planning for a new physically active lifestyle (e.g., investigate the cost to join a fitness club, decide how exercise will be worked into a busy schedule, identify walking trails) and to seek out support from others (e.g., find an exercise buddy). These strategies provide people with some of the tools and information they will need to change their behavior, which, in turn, can decrease their doubts about their ability to change.

Action stage. People in the action stage are already doing some physical activity, but they can benefit from information that will keep them in the action stage and prevent them from backsliding. Helpful interventions include providing tips on overcoming barriers that might prevent them from adhering, and introducing strategies to help maintain their motivation, such as establishing a contract or setting goals (see Chapter 6 for a discussion of these strategies).

Maintenance stage. People in the maintenance stage have been exercising regularly for at least six months. Interventions that are most useful to maintainers are those that prevent them from slipping back into a sedentary lifestyle. For example, it is particularly valuable for maintainers to plan ahead and to identify situations that might cause them to lapse, such as going on vacation, getting bored with their exercise routine, or being busy at work or school. Strategies can then be developed to deal with these situations, if and when they occur. In Chapter 6, we provide an in-depth description of an intervention to prevent lapses.

It is important to note that these are only a few of the intervention techniques that can be used at each of the TTM stages. Refer also to Exhibit 4.2 and Chapter 6, where we discuss some other interventions that are useful for helping people move through the stages of the TTM.

Research exemplar

Most exercise research involving the TTM can be classified as one of the following:

descriptive studies ■

predictive studies ■

intervention studies ■

1. **Descriptive studies**—studies that *describe* differences between people in the different TTM stages
2. **Predictive studies**—studies that use the TTM constructs to attempt to *predict* future exercise behavior
3. **Intervention studies**—studies that use the TTM to develop exercise *interventions*

Descriptive studies. Considerable research has shown that people in the various stages of the TTM differ in reliable ways in terms of:

- exercise self-efficacy
- attitudes toward exercise
- the use of the processes of change
- exercise behavior.

For example, a study of 819 Canadian high school students found that those who were in the action and maintenance stages of physical activity had greater exercise self-efficacy, perceived more benefits of exercise, and were more likely to use processes of change than were students in any other stage (Nigg & Courneya, 1998). (For a quantitative review of other descriptive studies, see Marshall & Biddle, 2001.)

Predictive studies. Evidence is mixed regarding the TTM's ability to predict exercise stage transition. On the one hand, the TTM does a reasonable job of predicting whether people will progress, regress, or show no movement across the stages. For example, in a study of New Zealand high school students (mean age = 16.4 years), use of the processes of change, self-efficacy, and decision balance was related to whether, in general, students moved forward through the stages, backward, or not at all over a six-month period (Prapavessis, Maddison, & Brading, 2004). On the other hand, the TTM has difficulty predicting which *specific* stage a person will move to. In a study of Canadian high school students (mean age = 14.9 years), Nigg (2001) found that the TTM variables could not predict students' stage of exercise over a three-year period. It seems that the TTM constructs may be more useful for predicting the direction of stage movement than the precise stage that a person will move to.

Intervention studies. Experiments have been conducted to determine the benefits of matching physical activity self-help materials and other motivational materials to a person's stage of change (for reviews, see Adams & White, 2003; van Sluijs, van Poppel, & van Mechelen, 2004). Some studies have found that people who receive materials designed for their particular stage (i.e., stage-matched materials) show greater increases in their activity levels than people who receive standard, generic materials (e.g., Marcus, Bock, Pinto, et al., 1998). Other studies have found no differences in the effectiveness of stage-matched and generic materials for increasing physical activity (e.g., Blissmer & McAuley, 2002). These conflicting findings may reflect between-study differences in the types of people who received the generic materials. Specifically, generic exercise-promotion materials are typically written for people in the preparation, action, and maintenance stages. Generic information could thus be considered "stage-matched" if it is given to people who are in one of these three stages. As a result, in a given study, if most of the participants who receive generic materials are in the preparation, action, or maintenance stages, the generic materials will likely be just as effective as the stage-matched materials. Conversely, if another study is conducted and most of the participants who receive generic materials are precontemplators or contemplators, the generic materials may be less effective than stage-matched materials. Unfortunately, the effectiveness of stage-matched materials has not yet been sufficiently tested to determine the feasibility of this explanation.

Usefulness, limitations, and future research avenues of the transtheoretical model

The TTM has proven to be a useful framework for counselors trying to help people adopt a more physically active lifestyle. In general, people who receive TTM-based physical activity counseling show greater increases in activity than do those who receive no counseling whatsoever (Adams & White, 2003). Many physical activity counselors, including physicians, appreciate the commonsense approach of matching physical activity information to a person's stage of change. The TTM recognizes that when it comes to exercise interventions, one size does not fit all.

The TTM does have a major limitation, however. Measures of the TTM constructs (e.g., processes of change, self-efficacy, decision balance) are very useful for describing differences between people in different stages (Marshall & Biddle, 2001), but the constructs cannot reliably predict which stage a person will move to and when. As a result, the model fails to fully explain the mechanisms by which people change their activity behavior and move across the stages.

Albert Bandura, the father of social cognitive theory, has been particularly critical of the TTM and its limitations. To cite just a few of his many criticisms, Bandura (1997) contends that:

- Deeming a person to be in the maintenance stage after six months of regular exercise is completely arbitrary. There is no justification for choosing six months of exercise as a criterion rather than, say, five months or eight months of regular exercise. Furthermore, the passage of a six-month period, in and of itself, does not cause people to change. Getting people to move from the action stage to the maintenance stage is more complicated than the simple passage of time.

- Most people do not exhibit a stable progression through the stages. Many skip stages or even regress backward through the stages. For example, a person in the contemplation stage could go from being completely sedentary to exercising three times per week. This person would have skipped the preparation stage and gone straight to action. In a similar vein, a beginner exerciser may make it to the preparation stage but decide that he absolutely hates exercising and regress backward to precontemplation. The TTM cannot predict or explain this phenomenon.
- Human functioning is too complex to be categorized into just a few distinct stages.

In an attempt to improve the predictive capabilities of the TTM in exercise settings, future research may identify subgroups of individuals within a particular stage who are most likely to move on to the next stage by the end of an intervention (e.g., Gorely & Bruce, 2000). Presumably, people within a particular stage who have higher self-efficacy, perceive more exercise pros, and are more active at the start of an intervention will be more likely to advance to the next TTM stage than will people who are less efficacious, perceive fewer pros, and are less active. For example, in one study of more than 1,000 adults, some people in the preparation stage were *almost* sufficiently active to be classified as in the action stage, but not quite (Cole, Leonard, Hammond, & Fridinger, 1998). The researchers categorized this subgroup of people in a substage that they labeled "late preparation." After an intervention, people in this group were more likely to move forward to the action stage than were the rest of the people in the preparation stage. Thus, it seems that within the five stages of the TTM, some subgroups of people are more likely to move forward than are others. Further research is needed to determine whether the creation of subcategories or substages improves the predictive power of the TTM.

Social Ecological Models

Stimulus–response theory, the transtheoretical model, and the social cognitive approaches discussed in Chapter 3 emphasize that physical activity participation is largely determined by the *individual*. In other words, how the *individual* thinks and feels about exercise and how the *individual* chooses to respond to exercise consequences (e.g., reinforcement) and antecedents (e.g., cues to action) will have a potent effect on future exercise behavior. In contrast, **social ecological models** take the approach that these individual-level factors are only one of multiple levels of influence on behavior (McLeroy, Bibeau, Steckler, & Glanz, 1988). Social ecological models of health recognize that individuals bear responsibility for engaging in healthful behaviors, but the models also recognize other levels of influence on health behavior, including the physical environment, the community, society, and the government (Green, Richard, & Potvin, 1996; Stokols, 1996).

social ecological models ■

Social ecological models build on the seminal work of Urie Bronfenbrenner (1977, 1989), who developed an ecological theory to explain human development. According to Bronfenbrenner, each person is significantly affected by interactions among a number of overlapping **ecosystems**—systems formed by the interaction of a community of living things with one another and with their physical environment.

■ ecosystems

At the center of Bronfenbrenner's model is the individual, who is surrounded by **microsystems**—the immediate systems in which people interact. Within a physical activity context, we can think of microsystems as environments where people might be physically active or where they might receive support for being physically active, such as physical education classrooms, parks, workplaces, and homes. Interactions between the microsystems take place in the **mesosystem.** An example of a physical activity mesosystem interaction occurs when parents (home microsystem) and physical education teachers (classroom microsystem) coordinate their efforts to increase a child's physical activity levels. Surrounding the microsystems and mesosystem is the **exosystem.** This includes all the external systems that influence the microsystems. For example, school boards could influence what physical activity takes place in the microsystem of a physical education classroom. Health promotion agencies could influence the physical activity that takes place in the microsystem of the home. Finally, the **macrosystem** encompasses all of these other systems. The macrosystem is the larger sociocultural context in which the person resides; it includes cultural values, political philosophies, economic patterns, and social conditions. With reference to physical activity, the macrosystem includes societal values toward physical activity and safe neighborhoods in which one can be physically active (Spence & Lee, 2003).

■ microsystem

■ mesosystem

■ exosystem

■ macrosystem

Social ecological models can be considered an integrative approach because they pull together a variety of models and theories. That is, at each level of influence (e.g., the individual level, the microsystem, the macrosystem), different models and theories may be used to explain physical activity behavior and to bring about change in physical activity. For instance, at the individual level, self-efficacy theory might be used to explain, in part, why so many people have difficulty being physically active. Interventions can then be developed to increase self-efficacy as a means of ultimately increasing physical activity. At higher levels, theories of community organization and government policy may be used to understand some of the barriers people may have to becoming more physically active (e.g., a lack of affordable exercise facilities). These community- and government-level theories can then be applied to bring about environmental and policy changes at the macrosystem level that will help to remove barriers and ultimately increase physical activity.

A social ecological model for physical activity

Exercise participation can be influenced by a wide array of factors that may be beyond the individual's control (e.g., availability of equipment and public facilities). Because social ecological models take these factors into consideration, it makes intuitive sense that a social ecological approach would be useful for understanding and predicting exercise behavior. Unfortunately, such models are not yet well developed, largely because there has been so little research examining the effects of policy and environmental interventions on physical activity. However, a group of Australian and American researchers has created a preliminary social ecological model for physical activity (New South Wales Physical Activity Task Force, 1997; Sallis, Bauman, & Pratt, 1998). Over the past decade and a half, this model has provided the basis for both a growing number of descriptive studies examining the relationship between social ecological factors and physical activity, and a few pilot intervention studies. The model focuses primarily on the exosystem and macrosystem. As illustrated in Exhibit 4.6, the model suggests several ways in which community agencies and groups can influence policies that will provide supportive physical activity environments. According to the social ecological approach, more supportive environments will lead to greater physical activity among community members. To illustrate this chain of events, let's look at two ways in which the model suggests that physical activity can be increased.

1. *Improve availability of and access to facilities and programs.* A social ecological model would predict that if people do not have places where they can be active (e.g., parks, community centers, fitness clubs), then they won't be active. Indeed, the presence of accessible facilities has been shown to correlate positively with physical activity participation. Among both adults (Kruger, Carlson, & Kohl, 2007) and children (Sallis, Nader, Broyles, et al., 1993), those who are more physically active have more facilities for exercise or play near their homes than do those who are less active.
2. *Support active transportation (walking, biking).* Social ecological models highlight the importance of the physical aspects of home, school, and work environments in influencing physically active forms of transportation. For example, because many suburban developments are now built without sidewalks and beyond walking distance of shops, schools, and workplaces, people are often compelled to use sedentary forms of transportation (e.g., buses, automobiles) because it is inconvenient and often unsafe to walk or bike (King, Stokols, Talen, et al., 2002). The social ecological model predicts that physical activity can be increased if agencies develop policies that provide supportive environments for active forms of transportation.

From theory to application

The social ecological model can be applied in numerous ways to develop interventions that enhance availability and access to facilities and programs, and increase active forms of personal transportation.

1. *Improve availability of and access to facilities and programs.* As shown in the model, various agencies can implement policies in the form of organizational statements, rules, or laws that can help to increase facility availability and accessibility. For example, governments could provide funding for more walking and biking trails. Workplaces could subsidize health club memberships for employees. Churches and other houses of worship could make their basements and meeting halls available for community exercise

A preliminary social ecological model of exercise. exhibit 4.6

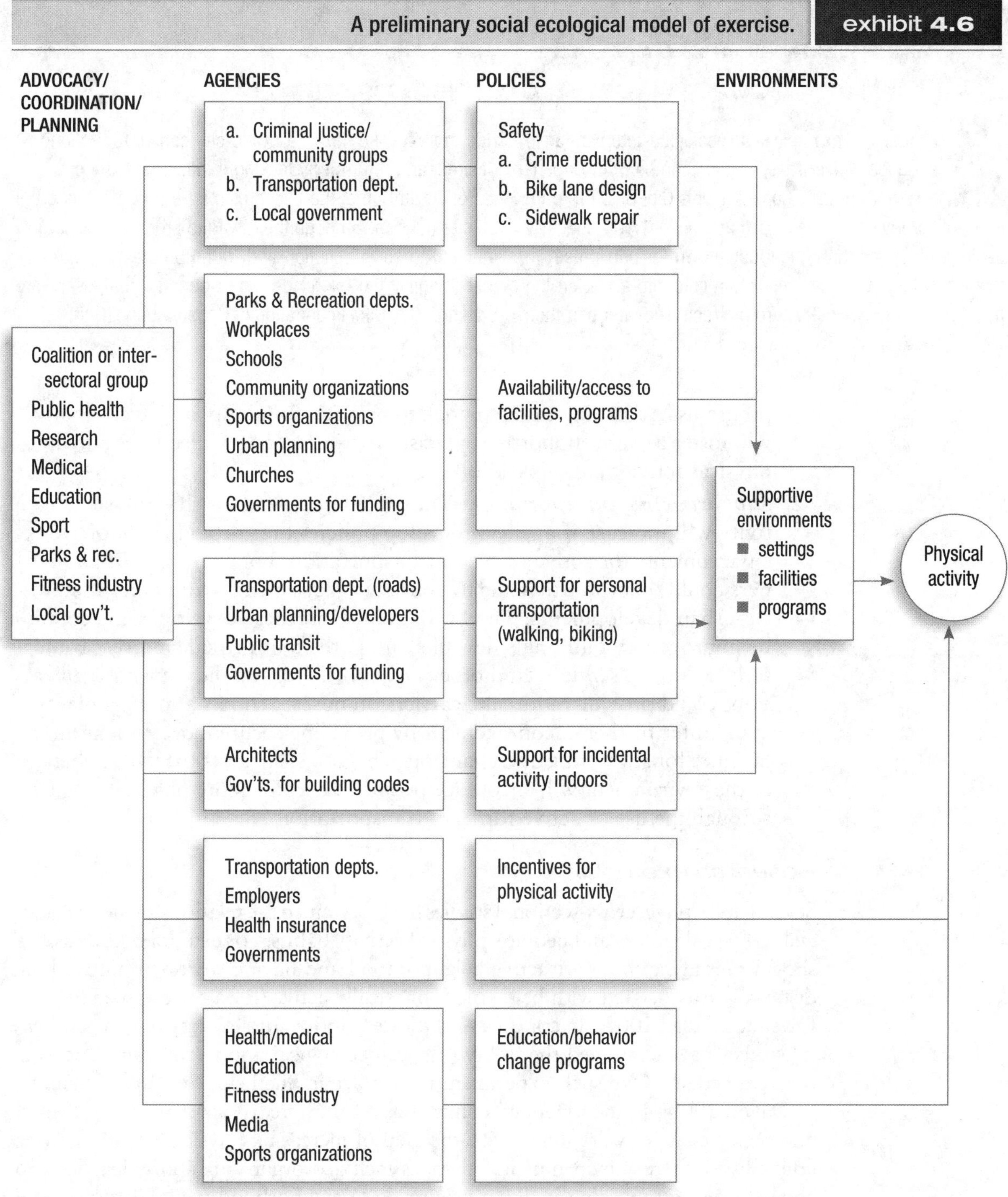

Source: Reprinted with permission from Elsevier Science from *American Journal of Preventive Medicine,* Vol. 15, Sallis, J.F., Bauman, A., and Pratt, M., "Environmental and policy interventions to promote physical activity," page 388. Copyright 1998 by *American Journal of Preventive Medicine.*

The Ecological Model at Work

COPENHAGEN'S CITY BIKE PROGRAM

An ingenious example of an ecological intervention to enhance active transportation comes from Copenhagen, Denmark. Copenhagen's City Bike Program is a public/private partnership that placed 1,100 specially designed bicycles throughout downtown for public use. To use a city bike, the user deposits a coin into a slot on the handlebar, which unlocks it from a rack. The user can then ride the city bike throughout the city center, for as long as desired, and return it by locking it into any of the city bike racks. At that time, the user's coin is returned, making the bike rental free. Although the City Bike program was largely initiated to solve pollution and traffic problems in the city, just imagine the exercise-related benefits that users are gaining! (City Bike Foundation of Copenhagen, 2008)

programs. According to the model, improved availability and accessibility will foster a more supportive exercise environment and, ultimately, greater physical activity participation.

2. *Support active transportation.* The model also predicts that physical activity will increase if agencies develop policies that provide supportive environments for active forms of transportation. For example, urban planners could incorporate plans to construct bicycle paths and lanes in new suburban developments. The "walkability" of these developments could be improved by building sidewalks and paths that provide a direct route to local stores, services, and other neighborhoods. Public transit organizations could provide more bike carriers on buses. Schools and workplaces could offer further encouragement by providing secure bicycle racks and facilities for showering and changing. The model suggests that these changes to the environment will encourage people to become more physically active through the use of active forms of transportation.

Research exemplar

Several descriptive, cross-sectional studies have examined the relationship between social ecological factors and people's physical activity habits. For example, studies have shown that living in an attractive neighborhood and having stores within walking distance are associated with being more physically active (for a review, see Humpel, Owen, & Leslie, 2002). In contrast to these descriptive studies, very few experimental studies have examined the utility of social ecological approaches for increasing physical activity. One such experiment took place in Sheffield, England (Cochrane & Davey, 2008). In the inner-city community of Burngreave, several environmental and policy changes were made with the goal of increasing physical activity among adults living there. Environmental changes included organizing sports leagues and competitions, establishing walking groups and neighborhood walking routes, and increasing access and opportunities to use swimming pools. Policy changes involved encouraging family doctors to refer patients to exercise programs, and arranging for financial support to make some physical activity programs available for free. One year after these changes were implemented, the investigators examined changes in physical activity within a random sample of Burngreave residents. They found that 31 percent of the sample reported an increase in physical activity over the previous year. In contrast, only 14 percent of residents who lived in a control community reported an increase in physical activity over the previous year.

Usefulness, limitations, and future research avenues of social ecological models

The major utility of social ecological models is that they recognize multiple levels of influence on physical activity, and multiple levels of intervention opportunities for increasing physical activity. In other words, an individual's physical activity participation is not solely influenced by that person's thoughts, feelings, and behavior. His or her participation can also be influenced by environmental and policy-related factors beyond the individual's control. As researchers, we can better understand physical activity by understanding the impact of these factors. As interventionists, we can also improve physical activity participation rates by focusing our interventions not just on the individual (e.g., improving attitudes toward exercise or increasing self-efficacy for exercise), but also on the environment (e.g., removing environmental barriers to activity such as unsafe streets) and on public policy (e.g., pressuring city planners to build designated traffic lanes for cyclists). By looking at this "big picture" of variables that can influence physical activity, we increase our ability to understand existing levels of participation and our ability to improve these levels (Stokols, 1996).

Of course, a social ecological approach does have limitations. Environmental and policy changes can take a long time and a lot of money to implement. It is also important to note that social ecological approaches are not intended to be "stand-alone" interventions, with the idea that "if we build it, they will come." Simply building fitness facilities does not mean that people will automatically become more physically active. Rather, social ecological approaches recognize the importance of community-wide educational and incentive programs to motivate individuals to take advantage of activity-promoting environments and policies. These programs themselves can be very expensive and time consuming.

Despite these limitations, social ecological approaches appear to be garnering interest among researchers and interventionists. Given that the Centers for Disease Control and Prevention (2001) have "strongly recommended" environmental and policy approaches to increasing physical activity, a growing number of exercise psychologists are now considering ecological factors in their research. For instance, researchers are now beginning to examine whether the social cognitions that affect physical activity (e.g., self-efficacy, attitudes, and perceived behavioral control) are influenced by aspects of the environment (e.g., the availability of recreation facilities, the quality of sidewalks, and neighborhood safety). So far, the research examining this issue has been primarily descriptive and has produced mixed findings (e.g., Arbour-Nicitopoulos, Martin Ginis, & Wilson, 2010; Cerin, Vandelanotte, Leslie, &

Merom, 2008; de Bruijn, Kremers, Lensvelt-Mulders, et al., 2006). However, future investigators will find it valuable to determine if social ecological interventions that change the environment can in turn change social cognitions and, ultimately, improve physical activity. Researchers might also examine whether changes in public policy—for example, legislation that limits the use of private automobiles along downtown streets—affect attitudes and perceived benefits of physically active commuting.

Conclusion

In this chapter, we have presented stimulus–response theory (SRT), the transtheoretical model (TTM), and a social ecological model of exercise behavior. Unlike the social cognitive approaches discussed in Chapter 3, SRT does not consider the individual's thoughts and feelings to be significant determinants of exercise behavior. Instead, SRT suggests that exercise behavior is contingent on the pairings of exercise with reinforcers and punishers, and suggests also that future exercise behavior depends primarily on whether the exerciser has experienced positive or negative outcomes following previous exercise bouts. Although SRT does have merit, its applicability and explanatory power are reduced by the absence of social cognitions. As demonstrated in Chapter 3, social cognitive variables play a very important role in explaining exercise behavior.

The transtheoretical model represents an attempt to merge some of the best predictors of behavior (e.g., self-efficacy, outcome expectancies) into a single model. Perhaps by integrating theoretical constructs, researchers will be more likely to capture the variety of factors that explain exercise behavior than if they were to rely on any single theory.

Social ecological models go one step further toward integration. The social ecological approach emphasizes the importance of integrating theory, research, and interventions aimed at the individual, with theory, research, and interventions aimed at various other levels of influence including agencies, policies, and the environment.

what do you know?

1. What is the key difference between social cognitive theories and models and SRT?
2. Identify and describe two types of events that can follow a behavior and will increase the likelihood of the behavior occurring again in the future.
3. What is the difference between negative reinforcement and punishment?
4. Describe two limitations of SRT.
5. Describe how people move through the stages of the TTM.
6. What is meant by the term "decisional balance," and how does decisional balance change as one moves through the stages of the TTM?
7. Define and provide examples of experiential processes and behavioral processes.

8. How does self-efficacy change as one moves through the stages of the TTM?
9. Describe two strategies that could help people move through the preparation stage.
10. Describe one benefit and one limitation of the TTM.
11. What sets apart social ecological models from all of the other theories and models discussed in Chapters 3 and 4?
12. Identify two levels of influence in social ecological models and describe how each of these levels can influence physical activity.
13. What types of difficulties might be encountered when using a social ecological approach to change physical activity?

learning activities

1. Visit a fitness center, gym, or exercise rehabilitation facility and identify situations in which reinforcement, punishment, negative reinforcement, and extinction occur.
2. Choose one stage in the transtheoretical model and develop a pamphlet that would provide useful exercise-related information for people currently in that stage.
3. Use the material in Exhibit 4.5 to conduct a survey of students in your class. Ask them to read the definition of "regular exercise" and then indicate which of the five items best describes their exercise patterns. Then complete the following:
   - Graph your results.
   - Write a short paragraph that describes your results.
   - Write a recommendation indicating where exercise-enhancing interventions are most needed (i.e., for people in which stage) and what immediate steps should be taken to help students who are in this stage to move to the next stage.
4. Imagine that you have been hired to increase physical activity within your community. You will be given all the money and resources that you need. Using a social ecological approach, develop a plan for increasing physical activity that will target multiple levels of influence.
5. Make a list of all of the constructs presented in the theories and models discussed in Chapters 3 and 4. Which constructs occur the most often? Which constructs occur the least often? Which constructs would you be most likely to include if you were to develop your own model or theory of exercise behavior, and why?
6. Conduct an Internet search for websites and videos that have been developed to encourage people to become more physically active. Using the list of constructs generated in Learning Activity 5 (above), identify those constructs that are being targeted for change in each website and video. Which constructs are targeted most often? Why do you think these are the most popular theoretical targets for change?

references

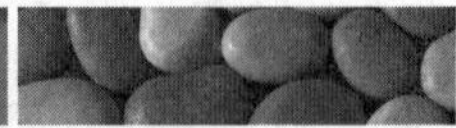

Adams, J., & White, M. (2003). Are activity promotion interventions based on the transtheoretical model effective? A critical review. *British Journal of Sports Medicine, 37,* 106–114.

Arbour-Nicitopoulos, K. P., Martin Ginis, K.A., & Wilson, P. M., (2010). Examining the individual and perceived neighborhood associations of leisure-time physical activity in persons with spinal cord injury. *Annals of Behavioral Medicine, 39*(2), 192–197.

Atlantis, E., Barnes, E.H., & Singh, M.A. (2006). Efficacy of exercise for treating overweight in children and adolescents: A systematic review. *International Journal of Obesity,* 30, 1027–1040.

Bandura, A. (1997). *Self-efficacy: The exercise of control.* New York: WH Freeman.

Blissmer, B., & McAuley, E. (2002). Testing the requirements of stages of physical activity among adults: The comparative effectiveness of stage-matched, mismatched, standard care, and control interventions. *Annals of Behavioral Medicine, 24,* 181–189.

Bronfenbrenner, U. (1977). Toward an experimental ecology of human development. *American Psychologist, 32,* 513–531.

Bronfenbrenner, U. (1989). Ecological systems theory. *Annals of Child Development, 22,* 723–742.

Cancer Prevention Research Consortium. (1995). *Pathways to health.* Kingston, RI: Author.

Centers for Disease Control and Prevention. (2001, October). *Increasing physical activity: A report on recommendations of the task force on community preventive services* (No. RR-18). Atlanta, GA: Author.

Cerin, E., Vandelanotte, C., Leslie, E., & Merom, D. (2008). Recreational facilities and leisure-time physical activity: An analysis of moderators and self-efficacy as a mediator. *Health Psychology,* 27(Suppl. 2), 129–135.

The city bike and Copenhagen. (1988). Retrieved July 21, 2009, from www.bycyclen.dk/englishh/thecitybikeandeopenhagen.aspx

Cochrane, T., & Davey, R.C. (2008). Increasing uptake of physical activity: A social ecological approach. *Journal of the Royal Society for the Promotion of Health, 128,* 31–40.

Cole, G., Leonard, B., Hammond, S., & Fridinger, F. (1998). Using "stages of behavioural change" constructs to measure the short-term effects of a worksite-based intervention to increase moderate physical activity. *Psychological Reports, 82,* 615–618.

de Bruijn, G.-J., Kremers, S.P., Lensvelt-Mulders, G., de Vries, H., van Mechelen, W., & Brug, J. (2006). Modeling individual and physical environmental factors with adolescent physical activity. *American Journal of Preventive Medicine, 30,* 507–512.

Epstein, L.H. (1998). Integrating theoretical approaches to promote physical activity. *American Journal of Preventive Medicine, 15,* 257–265.

Epstein, L.H., Paluch, R.A., Kilanowski, C.K., & Raynor, H.A. (2004). The effect of reinforcement or stimulus control to reduce sedentary behavior in the treatment of pediatric obesity. *Health Psychology,* 23, 371–380.

Epstein, L.H., Raja, S., Gold, S.S., Paluch, R.A., Pak, Y., & Roemmich, J.N. (2006). Reducing sedentary behavior: The relationship between park area and the physical activity of youth. *Psychological Science, 17,* 654–659.

Epstein, L.H., Roemmich, J.N., Paluch, R.A., & Raynor, H.A. (2005). Physical activity as a substitute for sedentary behavior in youth. *Annals of Behavioral Medicine, 29,* 200–209.

Epstein, L.H., Saelens, B.E., Myers, M.D., & Vito, D. (1997). Effects of decreasing sedentary behaviours on activity choice in obese children. *Health Psychology, 16,* 107–113.

Gorely, T., & Bruce, D. (2000). A 6-month investigation of exercise adoption from the contemplation stage of the transtheoretical model. *Psychology of Sport and Exercise, 1,* 89–101.

Greaney, M.L., Riebe, D., Ewing Garber, C., Rossi, J.S., Lees, F.D., Burbank, P.A., Nigg, C.R., Ferrone, C.L., & Clark, P.G. (2008). Long-term effects of a stage-based intervention for changing exercise intentions and behavior in older adults. *The Gerontologist, 48,* 358–367.

Green, L.W., Richard, L., & Potvin, L. (1996). Ecological foundations of health promotion. *American Journal of Health Promotion, 10,* 270–281.

Humpel, N., Owen, N., & Leslie, E. (2002). Environmental factors associated with adults' participation in physical activity. *American Journal of Preventive Medicine, 22,* 188–199.

Janis, I.L., & Mann, L. (1977). *Decision making.* New York: Macmillan.

King, A.C., Stokols, D., Talen, E., Brassington, G.S., & Killingsworth, R. (2002). Theoretical approaches to the promotion of physical activity. Forging a transdisciplinary paradigm. *American Journal of Preventive Medicine, 23,* 15–25.

Kruger, J., Carlson, S.A., & Kohl, H.W. (2007). Fitness facilities for adults: Differences in perceived access and usage. *American Journal of Preventive Medicine, 32,* 500–505.

Lowther, M., Mutrie, N., & Scott, E.M. (2007). Identifying key processes of exercise behaviour change associated with movement through the stages of exercise behaviour change. *Journal of Health Psychology, 12,* 261–272.

Marcus, B.H., Bock, B.C., Pinto, B.M., Forsyth, L.H., Roberts, M.B., & Traficante, R.M. (1998). Efficacy of an individualized, motivationally-tailored physical activity intervention. *Annals of Behavioral Medicine, 20,* 174–180.

Marshall, S.J., & Biddle, J.H. (2001). The transtheoretical model of behavior change: A meta-analysis of applications to physical activity and exercise. *Annals of Behavioral Medicine, 23,* 229–246.

McLeroy, K.R., Bibeau, D., Steckler, A., & Glanz, K. (1988). An ecological perspective on health promotion programs. *Health Education Quarterly, 15,* 351–377.

New South Wales Physical Activity Task Force. (1997). *Simply active every day: A discussion document from the NSW Physical Activity Task Force on proposals to promote physical activity in NSW, 1997–2002.* Summary report. Sydney, Australia: New South Wales Health Department.

Nigg, C.R. (2001). Explaining adolescent exercise behavior change: A longitudinal application of the transtheoretical model. *Annals of Behavioral Medicine, 23,* 11–20.

Nigg, C.R., & Courneya, K.S. (1998). Transtheoretical model: Examining adolescent exercise behaviour. *Journal of Adolescent Health, 22,* 214–224.

Noland, M.P. (1989). The effects of self-monitoring and reinforcement on exercise adherence. *Research Quarterly for Exercise and Sport, 60,* 216–224.

Ogden, C.L., Carroll, M.D., & Flegal, K.M. (2008). High body mass index for age among US children and adolescents, 2003–2006. *Journal of the American Medical Association, 299,* 2401–2405.

Pavlov, I.V. (1928). *Lectures on conditioned reflexes.* (W.H. Gantt, Trans.). New York: International.

Prapavessis, H., Maddison, R., & Brading, F. (2004). Understanding exercise behavior among New Zealand adolescents: A test of the transtheoretical model. *Journal of Adolescent Health, 35,* 346e17–346e27.

Prochaska, J.O., & DiClemente, C.C. (1983). Stages and processes of self-change in smoking: Towards an integrative model of change. *Journal of Consulting and Clinical Psychology, 51,* 390–395.

Prochaska, J.O., DiClemente, C.C., & Norcross, J.C. (1992). In search of how people change: Applications to addictive behaviors. *American Psychologist, 47,* 1102–1114.

Prochaska, J.O., & Velicer, W.F. (1997). The transtheoretical model of behavior change. *American Journal of Health Promotion, 12,* 38–48.

Roemmich, J.N., Gurgol, C.M., & Epstein, L.H. (2004). Open-loop feedback increases physical activity of youth. *Medicine and Science in Sports and Exercise, 36,* 668–673.

Ryan, R.M., Frederick, C.M., Lepes, D., Rubio, N., & Sheldon, K.M. (1997). Intrinsic motivation and exercise adherence. *International Journal of Sport Psychology, 28,* 335–354.

Sallis, J.F., Bauman, A., & Pratt, M. (1998). Environmental and policy interventions to promote physical activity. *American Journal of Preventive Medicine, 15,* 379–397.

Sallis, J.F., Nader, P.R., Broyles, S.L., Berry, C.C., Elder, J.P., McKenzie, T.L., & Nelson, J.A. (1993). Correlates of physical activity at home in Mexican-American and Anglo-American preschool children. *Health Psychology, 12,* 390–398.

Skinner, B.F. (1953). *Science and human behavior.* New York: Macmillan.

Spence, J.C., & Lee, R.E. (2003). Toward a comprehensive model of physical activity. *Psychology of Sport and Exercise, 4,* 7–24.

Stokols, D. (1996). Translating social ecological theory into guidelines for community health promotion. *American Journal of Health Promotion, 10,* 282–298.

Thorndike, E.L. (1898). Some experiments in animal intelligence. *Science, 8,* 818–824.

Van Sluijs, E.M.F., van Poppel, M.N.M., & van Mechelen, W. (2004). Stage-based lifestyle interventions in primary care. Are they effective? *American Journal of Health Promotion, 26,* 330–343.

5

Social Influences on Exercise

KEY TERMS

behavioral reactance
companionship support
effect size
emotional support
group cohesion
informational support
instrumental support
meta-analysis
moderating factors
norm
overprotectiveness
social control
social facilitation
social influence
social support
stereotypes
validation

Social influence refers to real or imagined pressure to change one's behavior, attitudes, or beliefs (Alcock, Carment, & Sadava, 1991). Exercise psychologists are interested in understanding why social influence has an effect on exercise and other forms of physical activity, as well as understanding the conditions under which social influence has its greatest effects. These understandings may lead to the development of interventions that use social influence to increase physical activity participation.

■ social influence

The first part of this chapter focuses on a specific type of social influence—social support. We examine the nature of social support, its measurement, and its relationship with physical activity. The second part of the chapter identifies individuals and groups who provide social support and other forms of social influence in exercise settings (e.g., doctors, fitness leaders, family members). We examine how these people exert social influence and how they impact others' exercise-related thoughts, feelings, and behaviors.

We begin this study of social influences by meeting a woman who is wrestling with changes in behavior and attitudes. In just two months, Lakeisha will be turning 30. To celebrate, Lakeisha and her girlfriends are planning to take a tropical vacation together. This trip, of course, has led to endless talks about bathing suits and how to look good in them. Consequently, at a recent doctor's appointment, Lakeisha asked her family physician to put her on a diet so that she could shed a few pounds. Instead of prescribing a diet, the doctor prescribed an exercise program. Like most people, Lakeisha *knows* that exercise is essential to weight loss—in fact, when she and her friends first started planning their trip, she joined a gym and went to her first aerobics class. Unfortunately, Lakeisha hated the class and vowed never to return. The aerobics instructor seemed to comment on every mistake, which embarrassed Lakeisha and made her feel that everyone was watching her. Working out in the weight training center of the gym was even worse—she felt out of place with so many men in the center, all of whom could lift 10 times the weight she could. Having given up on aerobics and the gym, Lakeisha is feeling the pressure to go on a "quick fix" crash diet. When she mentions this to her doctor, the doctor suggests Lakeisha find a workout partner and that they exercise in a place where Lakeisha is comfortable. Now Lakeisha and her exercise buddy work out five days a week to an exercise video in the privacy of her living room. They depend on each other for motivation and support, and Lakeisha is sticking to their program partly because she doesn't want to let her partner down. Now that she's feeling more confident about her exercise abilities, Lakeisha and her girlfriends have agreed to meet twice a week at the gym to lift weights together. With her best friends by her side, Lakeisha is actually looking forward to going back to the gym!

Social Support

social support ■

Social support is probably the most important type of social influence in exercise and other physical activity settings. In general, the term **social support** refers to the perceived comfort, caring, assistance, and information that a person receives from others. Exercise psychologists are interested in the role that social support plays in influencing exercise behavior. Although one will find many studies of social support in the exercise psychology literature, little agreement exists among researchers as to how social support should be operationally defined.

In general, two types of approaches have been used to operationally define and measure social support among exercisers. The first approach is to measure the size of one's social network, and the second is to measure the amount and type of support that an exerciser receives.

Measuring Social Support: Size of the Social Network

In some exercise studies, social support has been operationally defined as the size of one's social network—that is, the number of social relationships one has. When social support is defined this way, it is typically measured as the number of groups or individuals that an exerciser can turn to for support (e.g., exercise class members, family, friends, doctors, fitness leader, colleagues from work, and so on). This approach, however, does not take into account the quality or type of support provided. Exercisers may have many social contacts, but that does not necessarily mean that they are receiving adequate comfort, caring, assistance, or information from these contacts to help them to exercise.

Measuring Social Support: Amount and Type of Support Provided

Another approach to operationally defining social support is to assess how much of a particular *type* of support is perceived by the exerciser. Five main types of social support exist (Wills & Shinar, 2000), each of which serves a different function. A description of these functions as they apply in exercise settings follows.

- **Instrumental support** involves providing tangible, practical assistance that will help a person achieve exercise goals. Examples of instrumental support include spotting a weightlifter at the gym, driving one's father to his cardiac rehabilitation exercise class, or taking care of a friend's baby while she exercises.

■ instrumental support

- **Emotional support** occurs through the expression of encouragement, caring, empathy, and concern toward a person. Praising an exerciser for her efforts, encouraging her to work harder, and sympathizing with her when she complains about aching muscles are all examples of emotional support. This type of support enhances self-esteem, reduces anxiety, and gives the person a sense of comfort, acceptance, and reassurance of self-worth.

■ emotional support

- **Informational support** includes giving directions, advice, or suggestions about how to exercise and providing feedback regarding the exerciser's progress. Lakeisha received informational support about exercise when she went to see her family physician. Health practitioners and fitness trainers are formal sources of informational support for exercise, but informal sources such as family and friends can also provide informational support by sharing their own exercise experiences and by providing tips for maintaining an active lifestyle.

■ informational support

- **Companionship support** reflects the availability of people with whom one can exercise, such as a friend, family member, or exercise group. Lakeisha received companionship support from her exercise buddy. Companionship support produces positive affect and may distract people from negative exercise-related feelings (e.g., fatigue, pain, boredom) that might interfere with exercise enjoyment and ultimately cause the individual to quit exercising.

■ companionship support

- **Validation** involves comparing oneself with others in order to gauge progress and to confirm (or "validate") that one's thoughts, feelings, problems, and experiences are "normal." For example, many people with chronic health conditions such as heart disease or obesity say that exercising in groups of people similar to themselves gives them the feeling that "if they can do it, so can I," and it provides a sense that they are not alone in their struggle to adhere to the exercise regimen.

■ validation

An example of a scale that has been developed to measure some of these social support functions is presented in Exhibit 5.1. Not only does this scale measure different types of support, it also measures the amount of support received from different sources. As we will see in subsequent sections, researchers are often interested in whether different types of people provide different types of support. Chogahara's (1999) scale (Exhibit 5.1) allows investigators to address this question.

exhibit 5.1 Scale for measuring type and amount of support received.

For each of the following questions, use the scale to describe how often, during the past 12 months, your friends, your family, and health and fitness experts have provided the kind of support described. Place a number from 1 to 4 in each of the corresponding boxes, with 1 being never and 4 being very often.

Scale: 1 *never* 2 3 4 *very often*	Friends	Family	Health and fitness experts
Companionship Support			
Made plans with you for doing a physical activity together?			
Teamed up with you to engage in a physical activity together?			
Promised you that they would participate in a physical activity with you?			
Given you helpful reminders to do a physical activity together with them?			
Changed their schedules so you could do a physical activity together with them?			
Informational Support			
Informed you about the expected positive effects of a physical activity on your health and fitness?			
Explained to you why a physical activity is important to improve your health?			
Clarified for you how you may achieve your health goals through physical activity?			
Suggested a physical activity program or facility that might assist your health?			
Explained to you about the amount or intensity of physical activity necessary for improving your health?			
Emotional Support			
Complimented you on the mastery of a physical activity skill?			
Praised you that your physical activity level is superior to that of other people your age?			
Affirmed that you have done well in your physical activity?			
Shown their respect for your versatility in physical activity?			
Told you that you should be proud of your physical activity skills?			

The scale is scored by calculating the average score for each type of support across each of the three sources (i.e., friends, family, health and fitness experts).

Adapted from Chogahara M. (1999). A multidimensional scale for assessing positive and negative social influences on physical activity in older adults. *The Journal of Gerontology 54B*, 5356–5367.

Research on the Relationship Between Social Support and Physical Activity

Evidence shows that a relationship exists between social support and physical activity, regardless of whether social support is conceptualized and measured in terms of the number of social contacts or the amount and type of support received.

Number of Social Contacts

With regard to the importance of the number of social contacts, a study of more than 2,600 adults demonstrated that those who had more available support sources (e.g., close friends, neighbors, spouse) reported greater levels of physical exertion during leisure-time physical activities than those with fewer support sources (Hibbard, 1988).

Another study of 1,800 Australian adults examined the number of significant others who exercised with each study participant. People who had many significant others to exercise with were more likely to be exercising at recommended levels than people who had few or no significant others with whom to exercise (Giles-Corti & Donovan, 2003).

Amount and Type of Social Support

The importance of receiving adequate amounts of social support for physical activity has also been demonstrated. In a study of nearly 3,000 Australian college students, participants were asked to indicate the amount of exercise support, both companionship and emotional, that they received from family and friends, as well as the amount of physical activity that they had performed in the past two weeks. Among those who were classified as receiving low levels of social support, only 50 percent of the women and 60 percent of the men were sufficiently physically active for good health. In contrast, among those who were classified as receiving high levels of social support, about 65 percent of the women and 80 percent of the men were considered sufficiently active (Leslie, Owen, Salmon, et al., 1999).

Greater amounts of emotional support were also associated with greater levels of physical activity in a study of middle-aged and older women in the United States, even after adjusting for race/ethnicity, marital status, age, income, and education (Eyler, Brownson, Donateller et al., 1999). Specifically, women who reported that their family and friends gave them a great deal of encouragement to exercise (a form of emotional support) were twice as likely to have completed 300 minutes of total weekly activity than women who reported little or no encouragement.

Few studies have looked at multiple types of social support for physical activity and then compared the influence of one type versus another. Thus, little is known about the types of social support that are most related to physical activity participation.

In one study, however, multiple types of perceived social support were measured across an 18-week exercise program for middle-aged and older adults, and then each type was examined in relation to participants' adherence to the program (Duncan, McAuley, Stoolmiller, & Duncan, 1993). The researchers found that as perceptions of emotional support increased (specifically, support that increased feelings of self-esteem and belongingness), so did adherence to the program. In contrast, greater perceptions of instrumental support (specifically, having someone to turn to for exercise information and advice) were not associated with greater adherence to the program. The authors also noted that the relationship between the different types of social support and adherence fluctuated over the course of the study. For example, emotional support was more strongly related to adherence toward the end of the program than at the beginning of the program. These results suggest that as exercisers' needs and coping abilities fluctuate over time, so do their social support requirements.

Another study compared the effects of instrumental and emotional support on exercise performance among patients who reported chronic pain (Patrick & D'Eon, 1996). In this study, spouses were asked to support and motivate their partners (i.e., the patients) while the latter performed an exercise bout on a stationary bicycle. The spouses' behavior was video recorded and subsequently analyzed to determine the amount of *emotional support* (defined as expressions of caring, such as smiling and touching) and *instrumental support* (defined as behaviors designed to facilitate the patient's optimal performance, such as monitoring the duration of the exercise bout) they provided. Analyses revealed that the more emotional support a patient received while exercising, the longer he or she was able to continue cycling. There was no association between the amount of instrumental support received and exercise duration. Moreover, most patients said that they did not consider expressions of instrumental support to be positive, perhaps because they did not like to be reminded of how long they had been exercising. These results suggest that exercisers with chronic pain need emotional support more than they need instrumental support.

Based on the limited research comparing specific types of social support for exercise, it seems that the most effective type of support depends on the exerciser's needs at a given point in time. These needs may vary as a function of changes in the exerciser's thoughts and feelings (e.g., changes in self-efficacy for exercising or changes in mood states) or changes in biophysical factors such as pain and disability. Developmental changes in social support needs may occur, because types of support required by children (e.g., instrumental support in the form of transportation to sports practices) can be very different from the types of support required by adults (e.g., informational support on how to start an exercise program). Some evidence also suggests that sex is related to exercisers' social support needs; emotional support may be more important, and more helpful, to female exercisers than male exercisers (Thrasher, Campbell, & Oates, 2004).

In short, a relationship between social support and physical activity has been demonstrated in a wide variety of populations (e.g., men and women, people of different ages, with varying racial and ethnic backgrounds) and using a wide variety of social support measures (e.g., number of social contacts, amount of encouragement, amount of companionship support). These findings speak to the pervasive relationship between social support and physical activity.

Research on Individual and Group Influences on Exercise

In this section, we examine individuals and groups who provide social support as well as other forms of social influence over exercise. To determine the extent of different individual and group social influences on exercise, Carron, Hausenblas, and Mack (1996) conducted a **meta-analysis** (i.e., a type of quantitative review; see accompanying box) of 87 studies. From these studies, they identified four categories of people who could potentially affect thoughts, feelings, and behaviors relating to exercise. The four categories were: family (e.g., spouse, children), important others (e.g., non–family members such as physicians, friends, work colleagues), fitness instructors or other professionals within the exercise environment, and other exercise participants. The results of the reviewed studies were statistically combined to determine the magnitude of the effect or **effect size,** of social influence on exercise behavior, intentions to exercise, exercise attitudes and satisfaction, and self-efficacy. A summary of some of the results is presented in Exhibit 5.2. Guidelines for interpreting effect sizes are that .20, .50,

■ meta-analysis

■ effect size

■ moderating factors

Defining Meta-Analysis

Meta-analysis is a technique for statistically synthesizing a body of literature. In a meta-analysis, the results of individual studies are statistically combined to produce an estimate of the overall effect across studies. As noted by North, McCullagh, and Tran (1990), meta-analytic methodology has the following primary purposes:

1. Increasing statistical power, or the ability to find differences when they exist: for example, whether levels of depression differ between a group that exercises and a group that doesn't.
2. Resolution of conflicting studies.
3. Better estimates of the magnitude of an effect (referred to as an effect size); for example, how big the difference in depression is between those who exercise and those who don't.
4. Allowing questions to be addressed that may not have been posed in the original studies, because gaps in the knowledge base can now be more readily seen.

One advantage of meta-analysis is that it allows the quantification of the effects of a treatment, exercise in this case, across a variety of moderating factors. **Moderating factors** are variables that could influence or "moderate" treatment effects; for example, variables in exercise research may include mode of exercise, length of the exercise program, exercise intensity, duration, frequency, and so forth. It is worth pointing out that not all exercise scientists are impressed by the advantages offered by meta-analytic techniques (see Morgan, 1994), but the conclusions from the different kinds of reviews (narrative vs. quantitative) seem to converge to the same points regardless.

exhibit 5.2 Selected results from a meta-analysis of the effects of important others, family members, class members, and the exercise class leader on exercise-related behavior, thoughts, and feelings.

VARIABLES	NUMBER OF STUDIES	EFFECT SIZE
The influence of important others on		
Exercise adherence	21	.44
Exercise intentions	6	.44
Exercise attitudes and satisfaction	5	.63
The influence of family members on		
Exercise adherence	53	.36
Exercise intentions	27	.49
Exercise efficacy	3	.40
The influence of class members on		
Exercise adherence	22	.32
The influence of the exercise class leader on		
Exercise adherence	9	.31

Source: Values are based on data presented by Carron et al. (1996).

and .80 represent small, medium, and large effect sizes (Cohen, 1992). As Exhibit 5.2 shows, all of the effect sizes fell in the small to medium range, indicating that family members, important others, exercise class leaders, and class members do exert a modest amount of social influence over various aspects of exercise.

In the remainder of this chapter, we discuss four sources of support and influence (spouses or partners, parents and other family members, physicians, and exercise class leaders), along with the influence of co-exercisers and observers, as well as the broader influence of society.

The Family

Spousal or partner support

Among adults, the positive effects of a supportive spouse or partner on exercise behavior have been consistently demonstrated. For example, healthy married adults who joined a fitness program with their spouse had significantly better attendance and were less likely to drop out of the program than married people who joined without their spouse (Wallace, Raglin, & Jastremski, 1995). Another demonstration of the impact of spousal support comes from a landmark study in which exercise compliance and dropout rates were tracked for participants in a cardiac rehabilitation program (Erling & Oldridge, 1985). As is typical in the exercise compliance literature, approximately 48 percent of patients dropped out within their first six months of joining the program. However, an interesting phenomenon occurred when the exercise program opened its doors to the spouses of the cardiac patients, inviting them to exercise along with their husbands and wives at the rehabilitation center. Six months later, among those patients who were exercising with a spouse, dropout rates had plummeted to 10 percent. Among those patients whose spouse did not exercise with them, the dropout rate was 33 percent. The large difference in dropout rates (10 percent vs. 33 percent) probably reflects the fact that patients who exercised with their spouses had more social support for exercise (emotional support and companionship support) than did those who did not exercise with their spouses.

Spouses and partners who exercise together may also have similar exercise habits. Similarity in exercise habits has been shown to play an important role in couples' perceptions of the support they receive from one another (Hong, Franks, Gonzalez, et al., 2005). Partners who engage in a similar level of exercise are more likely to recognize and appreciate one another's attempts to be supportive than partners with dissimilar exercise habits. Presumably, when both partners are physically active, they have a better understanding of what it takes to adhere to an exercise program, as well as the types of support that an exerciser needs. In contrast, when partners engage in different levels of exercise, their attempts to support one another may not be perceived as helpful. For instance, an inactive partner may not know what types of support the exercising partner needs. Also, when the exercising partner gives reminders and encouragement to be active, the inactive partner might interpret this as nagging.

Partner or spousal support for exercise may be particularly important for mothers with young children, because they often find it difficult to make time for exercise. Although the transition to parenthood can have a negative effect on physical activity among both men and women, new mothers tend to experience a greater decline in activity than new fathers (Bellows-Riecken & Rhodes, 2008). With this issue in mind, Miller, Trost, and Brown (2002) designed an intervention to increase physical activity among mothers of preschool-aged children. One of the intervention components involved encouraging the women to ask their partners for more instrumental support, such as by providing childcare while the mothers exercised. At the end of the eight-week intervention, the women reported significant increases in partner support and physical activity. Furthermore, the women who experienced the greatest improvements in partner support also showed the greatest increases in physical activity. These findings suggest a direct link between partner support and activity levels in mothers of young children.

Parental support

Among children and youth, social support from parents and other family members has been identified as one of the most important determinants of participation in all forms of physical activity, including competitive and recreational sports, structured exercise, and active leisure (USDHHS, 1996). Parental support is important to children's activity levels because parents can provide so many different types of instrumental support (e.g., organizing physical activities, providing transportation and equipment, paying activity fees), emotional support (e.g., encouraging their children), informational support (e.g., giving instruction on how to perform a new physical activity), and companionship support (e.g., playing with their children). Physically active parents may even provide validation support and influence activity patterns by serving as role models for their children, thus establishing norms for a physically active lifestyle (Gustafson & Rhodes, 2006).

Interestingly, mothers and fathers may provide different types of support. Exhibit 5.3 shows a questionnaire developed by Davison, Cutting, and Birch (2003) to measure the amount of instrumental and validation support given by mothers and fathers to their daughters. The first three questionnaire items assess instrumental support, and the final four items assess validation support. In a study of 180 9-year-old girls and their parents, Davison and colleagues

exhibit 5.3 **Activity-related parenting practices scale.**

1. How *active* are you in enrolling your daughter in sports?
   1. I *rarely* enroll my daughter in sports.
   2. I enroll my daughter *once in a while.*
   3. I *frequently* enroll my daughter in sports.
   4. I *go out of my way* to enroll my daughter in sports.
2. How often do you go to your daughter's sporting events with her (e.g., watch your daughter perform in a dance recital or at swim meets)?
   1. Rarely
   2. Sometimes
   3. Usually
   4. Almost always
3. How important is it to *you* to be *actively involved* in your daughter's sporting events?
   1. It is *not particularly* important to me to be involved.
   2. It is *sort of* important to me to be involved.
   3. It is *important* to me to be involved.
   4. It is *extremely* important to me to be involved.
4. How much do you enjoy sport/physical activity?
   1. Don't enjoy
   2. Sort of enjoy
   3. Really enjoy
   4. Thoroughly enjoy
5. How frequently (on average) do you participate in sport/physical activity each week?

   _________ times per week
6. How often does your family use sport/physical activity as a form of family recreation (e.g., going on bike rides together, hiking, ice skating)?
   1. Rarely
   2. Once in a while
   3. Relatively often
   4. Frequently
7. How much do you use *your own behavior* to encourage your daughter to be physically active?
   1. I *don't* use my own behavior to encourage my daughter to be active.
   2. I *rarely* use my own behavior to encourage my daughter to be active.
   3. I *often* use my own behavior to encourage my daughter to be active.
   4. I *constantly* use my own behavior to encourage my daughter to be active.

From Davison, K. K., Cutting, T. M., & Birch, L. L. (2003). "Parents' activity-related parenting practices predict girls' physical activity." *Medicine & Science in Sports & Science 35,* 1589–1595. Reproduced by permission of Lippincott Williams & Wilkins.

THE BUCKETS © United Feature Syndicate, Inc. Reprinted by permission.

found that mothers reported giving significantly more instrumental support than fathers, but fathers reported giving significantly more validation support than mothers. Higher levels of both types of parental support were associated with higher physical activity levels among the daughters.

The most common and most important types of family and parental support probably differ depending on the child's sex and age. However, it is clear that support from one's family is crucial to physical activity participation among boys and girls of all ages. Sallis and colleagues (1999) surveyed a national sample of 1,500 parents and children in Grades 4 through 12. In this cross-sectional study, they found that family support for physical activity was one of the strongest predictors of both boys' and girls' levels of physical activity at all grade levels.

Thus far, we have talked about the effects of parental support on children's participation in various types of *physical activity,* rather than the effects of parental support on children's participation in *structured exercise.* Our discussion of physical activity (as opposed to exercise) reflects the fact that children tend to engage in physical activity through involvement in sports or active games (e.g., tag, skipping) rather than through structured exercise bouts. Some children, however, are prescribed exercise for the treatment or management of a medical condition. For these children, parental involvement and support can play a very important role in compliance with the prescription. For instance, a series of experiments examined the long-term effects of different diet and exercise interventions on childhood obesity (Epstein, Paluch, Roemmich, & Beecher, 2007). After 10 years, children who were part of a treatment that targeted their parents' eating and exercise behaviors as well as their own lost more weight than did children whose treatment targeted only their own behaviors. Presumably, children's compliance was best when their parents took part in the intervention with them because these children perceived the greatest amount of social support.

The downside of family support

behavioral reactance

Sometimes, family support can deter physical activity. When family members pressure or pester their loved one to exercise, or make him or her feel guilty for not exercising, the person may actually respond in the opposite direction and exercise less (Lewis & Rook, 1999). The phenomenon whereby people respond in a direction opposite to the direction being advocated is known as **behavioral reactance.** Behavioral reactance may occur when individuals perceive significant others to be exerting social control, rather than providing social support. Because people generally do not like to be controlled by others (but they do like to be supported), they may try to reestablish a sense of control by doing the opposite of what is being asked of them. For example, a woman who likes to jog short distances for exercise might feel pressured by her husband to run faster and longer. If she perceives this pressure negatively—she feels that her husband is trying to control and change her exercise regimen—she may react by doing the opposite of her husband's request and give up jogging altogether. This would be an example of behavioral reactance. Of course, she could also perceive this pressure positively—if she senses that her husband is providing her with emotional support (encouragement) to work harder—and increase the intensity and duration of her workouts. Whether the woman considers the pressure to be **social control** or social support hinges on how she interprets and perceives the situation.

social control

overprotectiveness

Overprotectiveness is another example of the potential negative effects of social support on physical activity. We say that a person is being "overprotective" when he goes overboard in trying to protect another person from harm. Often, the overprotective person is perceived as being intrusive and controlling. For example, a woman with a chronic disease or disability may have overprotective family members who insist on doing activities that she can and should do for herself (e.g., walking to the store, doing light housework). By refusing to let the patient do these activities, family members undermine her self-efficacy to be active in future situations (Berkhuysen, Nieuwland, Buunk, et al., 1999), thus leading to a vicious cycle of inactivity and further physical decline.

Likewise, overprotective parents may limit their children's participation in physical activities that are perceived to have a high risk of injury due to physical contact (e.g., hockey, football), falls (e.g., inline skating, snowboarding), and other potential hazards (e.g., cycling amid other vehicles). Some parents may be concerned about their child's well-being and discourage participation in these types of activities. A few parents may be so overprotective that they prevent their children from engaging in everyday physical activities such as jumping rope or climbing monkey bars, because they consider the potential for injury to be too great.

On the other hand, we have all heard of parents who are *overly* encouraging and supportive of their children's sport and physical activity participation—signing them up for countless classes and lessons, and yelling and screaming from the sidelines. Unfortunately, children often perceive such strong encouragement as parental pressure. A dislike of pressure has been cited as a reason for children dropping out of physical activity programs (Gould, Feltz, Horn, & Weiss, 1982).

In addition, children who perceive that their parents are too involved in their activities report greater stress and less enjoyment in sport than children who feel that their parents' level of involvement is "just right" (Stein & Raedeke, 1999).

The Physician

Physicians and other health professionals have been identified as important sources of information support for people wishing to become more physically active. For example, in a survey of 2,300 Australians, those who were inactive were asked to choose their preferred source of advice on how to become more physically active. Advice from a doctor or health professional was preferred over all other listed sources, which included books, videotapes, and exercise groups (Booth, Bauman, Owen, & Gore, 1997). Similarly, in a population study of Canadians, nearly a quarter of those surveyed indicated that they looked to health professionals for advice on how to become physically active (Canadian Fitness, 2007). In the United States, likewise, a survey found that nearly two-thirds of patients (65 percent) would be more interested in exercising to stay healthy if advised by their doctor to do so and if given additional resources to help them become more active (ACSM, 2007).

An increasing number of physicians are discussing the benefits of physical activity with their patients. In addition, organizations such as the American College of Sports Medicine have created resources (e.g., information flyers, exercise prescription and referral forms, websites) to make it easier for physicians to counsel their patients to become more physically active (ACSM, 2007). However, activity counseling still occurs during less than half of all patient visits (Heaton & Frede, 2003), and physical activity prescriptions and exercise program referrals are issued by only a small minority of primary care physicians (Leijon, Bendtsen, Nilsen, et al., 2008; Petrella, Lattanzio, & Overend, 2007). Given the importance of regular exercise to health and well-being, why aren't more physicians helping their patients to become physically active? Many still do not view exercise as a critical discussion topic—probably because exercise is not perceived as a treatment that has immediate effects on illness. Other physicians may recognize the importance of exercise, but they don't discuss it with their patients because they feel unqualified to perform exercise counseling and prescription (Pinto, Goldstein, DePue, & Milan, 1998). Even among physicians who do prescribe exercise, few spend more than five minutes on physical activity counseling (Rogers, Bailey, Gutin, et al., 2002). Given the complexity of prescribing exercise and the many questions that patients may have regarding the prescription, five minutes is certainly not enough time to provide adequate information.

To circumvent these barriers to exercise prescription, some physicians have been known to form partnerships with local health clubs so that they can prescribe exercise to their patients and then refer those patients to a fitness consultant at the health club for further exercise information. Another strategy is to place kinesiologists or other certified fitness consultants in physicians' offices so that patients who receive an exercise prescription can go to an on-site expert for further information on how to follow that prescription. Given that these experts have specialized training and dedicated time to talk with patients about exercise,

Dogs as a Social Influence?

Several studies have examined the relationship between dog ownership and physical activity. Although the vast majority of dog owners do not engage in sufficient activity to promote optimal health (Bauman, Russell, Furber, & Dobson, 2001), people who own dogs are more likely to meet recommended activity levels than those who do not (Giles-Corti & Donovan, 2003). How can dogs influence physical activity? Many dog owners report feeling guilty if they do not walk their dog and, as a result, guilt avoidance becomes a powerful incentive for taking daily walks. In addition, dog owners benefit from the companionship support provided by a four-legged exercise partner who never complains that it is too hot, too cold, or too rainy to go for a walk.

they can probably provide more intensive and effective physical activity counseling than physicians (Tulloch, Fortier, & Hogg, 2006).

It is unfortunate that not all physicians prescribe exercise to their patients. Just as Lakeisha took her physician's advice to exercise, many patients are willing to try exercising when it is recommended to them by a health care professional. The impact of physician recommendations to exercise was examined in Project PACE (Patient-Centered Assessment and Counseling for Exercise). This study looked at the effects of brief physical activity counseling delivered to sedentary adults by physicians during a scheduled office visit (Calfas, Long, Sallis, et al., 1996). Self-reported physical activity was measured before the office visit and then four to six weeks later. At follow-up, patients who received PACE counseling increased their minutes of weekly walking by 38.1 compared with 7.5 among the control group. Additionally, 52 percent of the patients who received PACE counseling adopted "some" physical activity compared with just 12 percent of the control group.

Project PACE looked at the short-term effects of physician-based activity counseling. Subsequent studies have demonstrated that exercise advice from a physician can also have longer-term effects on activity participation. For example, adults who received very brief physical activity counseling from a physician reported significant increases in physical activity both 6 and 12 months later (Katz, Shuval, Comerford, et al., 2008). A control group saw no changes in activity levels. In addition, physicians who are regular exercisers themselves have a stronger influence on their patients' exercise behavior than do physicians who are inactive (Harsha, Saywell, Thygerson, & Panozzo, 1996). This observation speaks to the physician's important status as an exercise role model.

The Exercise Class Leader

Exercise class leaders and other fitness professionals (e.g., personal trainers, fitness consultants) can have a powerful social influence on participants. Indeed, fitness leaders are often cited as the single most important determinant of an exerciser's continued participation in an exercise program (Franklin, 1988). The potent influence of fitness leaders is largely due to their ability to provide multiple types of social support. Fitness leaders are in a position to provide informational support regarding what exercises to do and how to do them, as well as emotional support (e.g., providing encouragement and praise), instrumental support (e.g., organizing fitness classes), and companionship support (e.g., providing distractions from feelings of pain, fatigue, and boredom).

The social influence of personal trainers was demonstrated in a study of obese men and women (Jeffery, Wing, Thorson, & Burton, 1998). Participants in one group were each assigned a personal exercise trainer who scheduled exercise sessions, made reminder phone calls to the participant before each session, and attended each session, working out alongside the participant. Another group of study participants was given the same exercise prescription, but not a personal trainer. At the end of the 18-month study, participants who had been assigned a personal exercise trainer attended more than twice as many exercise sessions as those who did not have a personal trainer.

The importance of leadership style

A good exercise leader can have a positive social influence on exercisers and can contribute to increases in their self-efficacy, enjoyment, and motivation to exercise. Conversely, as Lakeisha found out at the beginning of this chapter, a bad leader can have a negative social influence on exercisers and may ultimately cause them to drop out of a fitness program. Given the potential effects of fitness professionals on exercise behavior, it is important to identify the characteristics that make a good exercise leader. To this end, exercise psychologists have conducted a series of experiments comparing the effects of two different exercise leadership styles (Bray, Gyurcsik, Culos-Reed, et al., 2001; Bray, Millen, Eidsness, & Leuzinger, 2005; Fox, Rejeski, & Gauvin, 2000; Martin & Fox, 2001; Turner, Rejeski, & Brawley, 1997).

In these experiments, a single exercise instructor was trained to conduct one exercise class using a socially supportive leadership style, and to conduct another class using a socially bland leadership style. When using a supportive leadership style, the instructor provided exercisers with lots of social support in the form of encouragement, verbal reinforcement, and praise, and showed interest in the participants by addressing them by name and engaging them in casual conversation before and after the exercise session. In contrast, the bland leadership style was characterized by an absence of social support. In this condition, the leader verbally criticized exercisers who made mistakes, did not provide encouragement or praise, failed to address participants by name, and did not interact with them before or after the class.

These experiments showed that, when compared with participants who experienced the bland leadership style, participants who experienced the socially supportive leadership style reported the following:

- Greater exercise self-efficacy
- More energy and enthusiasm
- Less post-exercise fatigue
- Less concern about embarrassing themselves and trying new things during the exercise class
- More enjoyment of the exercise class
- Greater confidence in the instructor's capabilities
- Stronger intentions to join an exercise class in the future

These results indicate that a socially supportive instructor can have positive effects on participants' psychological responses to a *single* exercise class. Presumably, a socially supportive instructor would have similar positive effects on participants' long-term responses to exercise training *programs* and should promote better adherence to exercise than would an unsupportive instructor.

Edmund and colleagues supported this hypothesis in a study involving two aerobics exercise classes at a university fitness center (Edmunds, Ntoumanis, & Duda, 2008). The same female fitness instructor led both classes. In one class (the experimental condition), she employed a leadership style that focused on promoting feelings of autonomy—for example, by providing class members with the opportunity to choose exercises—and displaying interest in the class members. In the other class (the control condition), she employed a leadership style that is typical of most exercise classes. She was also careful to avoid promoting autonomy and showed only minimal interest in her class members. Over the course of the 10-week exercise program, exercisers in the experimental condition attended significantly more classes than those in the control condition. These findings attest to the powerful impact of leadership style on exercise adherence.

The fitness instructor as role model

Many people consider fitness professionals to be reliable sources of health and fitness information. Moreover, many exercisers, particularly those who are just starting an exercise program, look to fitness professionals as role models for their own health and fitness behaviors. Given their potential social influence, fitness instructors must be aware of how their actions can affect other people. For example, instructors who exercise even when they are ill, or who spend exorbitant amounts of time at the gym, are sending a message to class members that it is okay to exercise excessively (see Chapter 13 for a discussion of exercise dependence). This certainly is not the message that fitness professionals should be conveying. Rather, they should use their influence to promote healthy attitudes toward exercise.

To promote healthy exercise attitudes, a fitness instructor can do the following:

- Emphasize the importance of getting adequate rest between workouts and taking the time to recuperate fully when sick or injured

- Emphasize fitness and fun during exercise classes as opposed to fat and calorie burning
- Encourage participants to set realistic fitness and weight loss goals

In addition, instructors need to know that for some exercisers, a few words of praise can be a powerful reinforcement that determines whether that person adheres to or drops out of an exercise program. Instructors should therefore take the time to commend participants for improved exercise ability (e.g., increased intensity and duration) and regular program attendance (Martin & Hausenblas, 1998). Likewise, a few words of advice about future goals from a fitness professional can have potent psychological effects. Elston and Martin Ginis (2004) found significant increases in exercisers' self-efficacy for improving their grip strength after a fitness professional gave them a goal of increasing their grip strength by three pounds. These findings suggest that when a fitness expert conveys goals to an exerciser, it can inspire confidence in the latter by creating the belief that "if an expert thinks I can do it, then I must be able to do it."

The Exercise Group

A growing body of literature indicates that various aspects of exercise groups can serve to promote or to undermine exercise-related thoughts, feelings, and behavior. In this section we look at three aspects of the exercise group and their effects on exercise. These three aspects are group cohesion, group size, and group composition.

Group cohesion

Group cohesion is defined as "a dynamic process reflected in the tendency of a group to stick together and remain united in the pursuit of its instrumental objectives and/or for the satisfaction of member affective needs" (Carron, Brawley, & Widmeyer, 1998, p. 213). The Group Environment Questionnaire (GEQ; Carron et al., 1998) and the Physical Activity Group Environment Questionnaire (PAGEQ, see Exhibit 5.4; Estabrooks & Carron, 2000b) are the most frequently used measures of group cohesion in exercise and physical activity settings. These questionnaires measure how group members feel about social aspects of the group (e.g., their liking of group members, the extent to which they interact with members outside of the exercise setting) as well as task-related aspects of the group (e.g., their liking of group goals and activities). The GEQ and PAGEQ assess group members' level of attraction to the social and task-related aspects of the group and group members' perceptions regarding how integrated they think the group is in terms of its social and task-related activities (see Exhibit 5.5 for a model of cohesion). From this standpoint, a cohesive exercise group would be one in which members are drawn to a common goal and are integrated around the pursuit of that goal and satisfying social interactions and communication.

- group cohesion

exhibit 5.4 The Physical Activity Group Environment Questionnaire.

PART A

The following questions are designed to assess your feelings about *your personal involvement* with your physical activity group. Using the following scale, please fill in a number from 1 to 9 to indicate your level of agreement with each of the statements. If you neither agree nor disagree, respond by using the number 5.

1	2	3	4	5	6	7	8	9
Very strongly disagree	*Strongly disagree*	*Disagree*		*Neither agree nor disagree*		*Agree*	*Strongly agree*	*Very strongly agree*

1. I like the amount of physical activity I get in this program.	①	②	③	④	⑤	⑥	⑦	⑧	⑨
2. This physical activity group is an important social unit for me.	①	②	③	④	⑤	⑥	⑦	⑧	⑨
3. I enjoy my social interactions within this physical activity group.	①	②	③	④	⑤	⑥	⑦	⑧	⑨
4. This physical activity group provides me with a good opportunity to improve in areas of fitness I consider important.	①	②	③	④	⑤	⑥	⑦	⑧	⑨
5. I like meeting the people who come to this physical activity group.	①	②	③	④	⑤	⑥	⑦	⑧	⑨
6. I am happy with the intensity of the physical activity in this program.	①	②	③	④	⑤	⑥	⑦	⑧	⑨
7. I like the program of physical activities done in this group.	①	②	③	④	⑤	⑥	⑦	⑧	⑨
8. If this program were to end, I would miss my contact with the other participants.	①	②	③	④	⑤	⑥	⑦	⑧	⑨
9. I enjoy new exercises done in this physical activity group.	①	②	③	④	⑤	⑥	⑦	⑧	⑨
10. In terms of the social experiences in my life, this physical activity group is very important.	①	②	③	④	⑤	⑥	⑦	⑧	⑨
11. This physical activity group provides me with good opportunities to improve my personal fitness.	①	②	③	④	⑤	⑥	⑦	⑧	⑨
12. The social interactions I have in this physical activity group are important to me.	①	②	③	④	⑤	⑥	⑦	⑧	⑨

Items 1, 4, 6, 7, 9, and 11 measure Attractions to Group–Task (ATG–T). Items 2, 3, 5, 8, 10, and 12 measure Attractions to Group–Social (ATG–S).

The Physical Activity Group Environment Questionnaire is scored by calculating the average rating given for each of the subscales (i.e., for ATG–T, ATG–S, GI–T, and GI–S).

(continued)

The Physical Activity Group Environment Questionnaire, continued. **exhibit 5.4**

PART B

The following questions are designed to assess your feelings about *your physical activity group as a whole.* Using the following scale, indicate your level of agreement with each of the statements. If you neither agree nor disagree, respond by using the number 5.

1	2	3	4	5	6	7	8	9
Very strongly disagree	*Strongly disagree*	*Disagree*		*Neither agree nor disagree*		*Agree*	*Strongly agree*	*Very strongly agree*

1. Members of our physical activity group often socialize during exercise time.	①	②	③	④	⑤	⑥	⑦	⑧	⑨
2. Our group is united in its beliefs about the benefits of the physical activities offered in this program.	①	②	③	④	⑤	⑥	⑦	⑧	⑨
3. Members of our physical activity group would likely spend time together if the program were to end.	①	②	③	④	⑤	⑥	⑦	⑧	⑨
4. Our group is in agreement about the program of physical activities that should be offered.	①	②	③	④	⑤	⑥	⑦	⑧	⑨
5. Members of our group are satisfied with the intensity of physical activity in this program.	①	②	③	④	⑤	⑥	⑦	⑧	⑨
6. Members of our group sometimes socialize together outside of activity time.	①	②	③	④	⑤	⑥	⑦	⑧	⑨
7. We spend time socializing with each other before or after our activity sessions.	①	②	③	④	⑤	⑥	⑦	⑧	⑨
8. Members of our group enjoy helping if work needs to be done to prepare for the activity sessions.	①	②	③	④	⑤	⑥	⑦	⑧	⑨
9. We encourage each other in order to get the most out of the program.	①	②	③	④	⑤	⑥	⑦	⑧	⑨

Items 2, 4, 5, 8, and 9 measure Group Integration–Task (GI–T). Items 1, 3, 6, and 7 measure Group Integration–Social (GI–S). The Physical Activity Group Environment Questionnaire is scored by calculating the average rating given for each of the four subscales (i.e., for ATG–T, ATG–S, GI–T, and GI–S).

exhibit 5.5 Conceptual model of group cohesion as measured by the GEQ and PAGEQ.

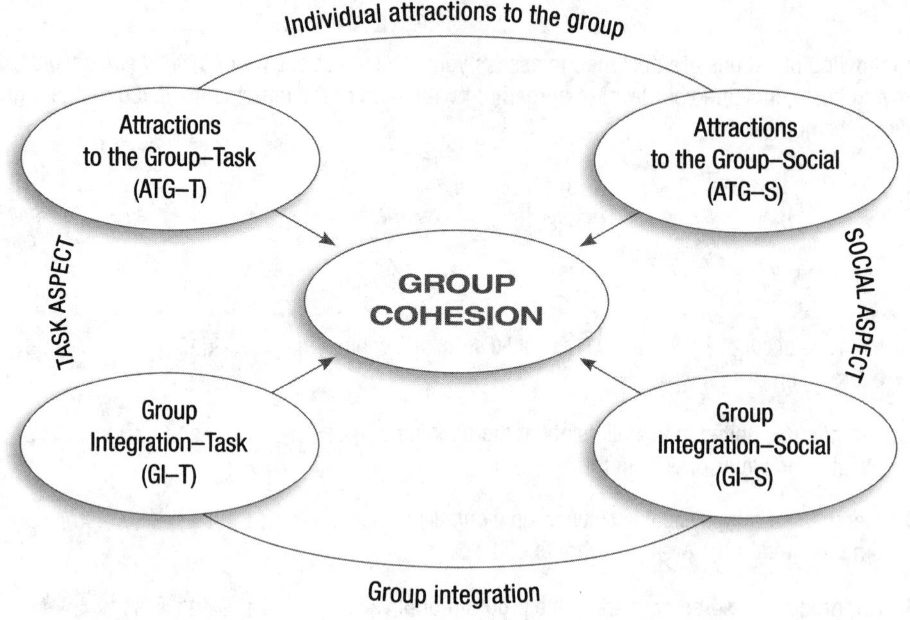

Not surprisingly, more cohesive exercise groups foster greater exercise adherence than do less cohesive exercise groups (Burke, Carron, & Shapcott, 2008). For example, in university-based exercise classes, members who score high on the GEQ measure of attractions to group–task (ATG–T) have been shown to attend more exercise classes and to be less likely to drop out of the program than members who score low on ATG–T (Spink & Carron, 1992, 1993, 1994). Furthermore, most of these university-based studies have found that ATG–T is the only GEQ dimension to distinguish between those who adhere and those who drop out. University-based studies have typically found no difference between adherers and dropouts on the other three dimensions of the GEQ: attractions to group–social (ATG–S), group integration–social (GI–S), and group integration–task (GI–T). In contrast, in a study conducted at a private health club, the two social dimensions (ATG–S and GI–S) were the only dimensions to distinguish adherers from dropouts (Spink & Carron, 1994). No differences existed between these two groups on the task-related dimensions (ATG–T, GI–T). Thus, whereas task cohesion plays a more important role than social cohesion in adherence to university-based exercise programs, the opposite may be true in private fitness clubs. These differences might reflect different motives for joining university versus private fitness centers. People who join private fitness clubs might be more motivated to exercise by the opportunity to meet new people and to socialize with others than are university-based exercisers.

Different types of cohesion (i.e., task vs. social) may be more or less important in different exercise settings (e.g., a university setting vs. a private health club). In any case, it is clear that a sense of cohesion is related to whether an individual adheres to an exercise program. Interestingly, Carron, Hausenblas, and Mack (1996) have noted that task cohesion may be a more important influence on exercise adherence than all of the variables listed in Exhibit 5.2. Carron and colleagues (1996) calculated the overall effects of task cohesion on exercise adherence across six different studies and obtained an effect size of .62. This effect size is larger than any of the effect sizes shown in Exhibit 5.2. When they calculated the effect of social cohesion across four different studies, the effect size was much smaller—only .25. These results suggest that given the potent effects that cohesion—particularly task cohesion—has on adherence, interventions that increase a sense of group cohesion among exercisers could go a long way in improving exercise adherence. In the discussion that follows, we present what studies have shown regarding three important questions concerning group cohesion.

1. How can feelings of cohesion be increased in exercise classes? Carron and Spink (1993) developed a team-building intervention to improve cohesion among exercise class participants. The intervention used five group dynamics principles that have been shown to increase group cohesiveness:

a. *Develop feelings of distinctiveness among group members.* Creating a group name or group uniform can help to create a sense of group identity and a sense of "we" among group members that makes them feel distinct from non–group members.

b. *Assign group roles and/or positions.* Giving group members responsibilities for particular tasks (e.g., distributing equipment) fosters greater interdependence among group members. Also, having members choose their own spot in which to stand during the class, or using specific places in the class for low-, medium-, and high-impact exercisers, contributes to the development of a more stable group structure.

c. *Establish group norms.* The establishment of group norms includes adopting a common goal (e.g., completing 20 minutes of continuous aerobic activity) and a common work ethic among group members (such as, "We keep our feet moving even if we are too tired to keep up with the exercise"). Essentially, the group develops a common set of behavioral expectations for group members. The establishment of group norms, combined with a stable group structure, contributes to a stronger sense of "we," greater conformity, and ultimately greater cohesiveness.

d. *Provide opportunities to make sacrifices for the group.* When individuals make sacrifices to the group, such as agreeing to shorten the aerobic workout time on some days so that the group may have a longer abdominal workout, their commitment to the group increases and their cohesiveness is enhanced.

FOCUS on Cardiovascular Disease

Cardiovascular disease (CVD) is the leading cause of death in the United States, Canada, and the European Union and contributes to nearly one-third of all deaths worldwide (American Heart Association, 2004). Regular physical activity is a cornerstone of programs aimed at reducing risk factors for CVD and for rehabilitating people who have experienced a cardiac event such as a heart attack, but adherence rates for these programs are very low. Recognizing this problem, Rejeski and colleagues (2003) examined whether exercise adherence rates could be improved by providing opportunities for exercise group members to influence one another.

Study participants were 147 sedentary men and women between the ages of 50 and 80 who had either experienced a cardiac event within the past six months or who had two or more major risk factors for CVD. They were randomly assigned to either a standard care or a group-mediated cognitive behavioral change (GMCB) condition. For the first three months of the study, the participants in the standard care condition attended three group exercise sessions per week at the study center, and they received lectures on topics related to CVD. In contrast, the GMCB condition divided their three weekly exercise sessions between group-based exercise at the center and individual exercise at home. Group-based exercise sessions were followed by group discussions, support, goal setting, and problem solving with regard to maintaining an active lifestyle. This aspect of the experiment was designed to maximize group influence on participants' exercise-related thoughts and behaviors. Then, for the next nine months, participants in both conditions were required to do all of their exercise at home. Their exercise adherence was monitored.

Analysis of the exercise adherence data revealed that during the first three months of the study, the participants in the group-mediated condition completed 91 percent of their prescribed exercise sessions, whereas those in the standard care condition completed only 78 percent of their prescribed sessions. During the last nine months of the trial, the GMCB condition reported doing nearly 4.5 hours per week of physical activity, while the standard care group performed only 3.25 hours of activity per week. At the end of the study period, those in the GMCB condition showed greater improvements in cardiovascular fitness than the standard care condition.

These results speak to the important influence of groups for teaching and motivating people with CVD—or those who are at risk for CVD—to initiate and maintain an activity regimen. A group-mediated intervention seems to be far more effective than the standard approach of providing patients with exercise information and then expecting them to use this knowledge successfully without having the support of other people undergoing the same treatment.

ADDITIONAL RESOURCES

Berkhuysen, M.A., Nieuwland, W., Buunk, B.P., Sanderman, R., & Rispens, P. (1999). Change in self-efficacy during cardiac rehabilitation and the role of perceived overprotectiveness. *Patient Education and Counseling, 38,* 21–32.

Carlson, J.J., Norman, G.J., Feltz, D.L., Franklin, B.A., Johnson, J.A., & Locke, S.K. (2001). Self-efficacy, psychosocial factors, and exercise behavior in traditional versus modified cardiac rehabilitation. *Journal of Cardiopulmonary Rehabilitation, 21,* 363–373.

Taylor, C.B., Bandura, A., Ewart, C.K., Miller, N.H., & DeBusk, R.F. (1985). Exercise testing to enhance wives' confidence in their husbands' capability soon after clinically uncomplicated myocardial infarction. *American Journal of Cardiology, 55,* 635–638.

ACTIVITY

Exercise is a primary component of rehabilitation programs for people who have experienced a cardiac event, such as a heart attack, but cardiac patients are often afraid to exercise because they fear that physical activity will bring on another heart attack. These fears are often reinforced by family members who discourage the patient from exercising because they have doubts about the patient's physical capabilities.

Imagine that you are an exercise programmer at a cardiac rehabilitation center. Using information garnered from the articles listed above and the section on self-efficacy theory in Chapter 3, develop a comprehensive intervention for increasing exercise self-efficacy in cardiac patients. The intervention should have the following components:

1. Strategies to increase the patient's self-efficacy for walking on a treadmill and for lifting weights. These strategies should target all four sources of self-efficacy (past performance accomplishments, vicarious experiences, social persuasion, and physiological arousal).
2. Strategies to increase family members' confidence that the patient can exercise safely.
3. Tips for exercise class leaders, physicians, and other sources of social influence, regarding what they can say and do to increase a cardiac patient's exercise self-efficacy.

e. *Provide opportunities for interaction.* Increasing task and social interactions during the class leads to increased perceptions of cohesion. Task interactions can consist of exercises that require participants to "buddy up" with a partner. Examples of social interactions include introducing class members to one another or asking participants to "high-five" the person next to them at the end of the class.

2. What are the benefits of the team-building intervention? The preceding intervention was developed in collaboration with a group of university program fitness instructors who then applied the strategies in their exercise classes (Carron & Spink, 1993). Eight weeks later, the GEQ was administered to exercisers in these classes (experimental condition), as well as to exercisers whose instructors did not apply the intervention (control condition). Exercisers who were part of the experimental condition had significantly greater ATG–T scores than did exercisers who were part of the control group. There were no significant differences on any of the other GEQ subscale scores. When Spink and Carron (1993) implemented their team-building intervention in another university fitness setting, fewer exercisers dropped out of the experimental group (20 percent) than dropped out of the control group (33 percent). Carron and Spink's team-building intervention has also been used with exercise classes for older adults (Brawley, Rejeski, & Fox, 2000; Watson, Martin Ginis, & Spink, 2004) and with a community-based exercise initiative in which adults formed walking groups with their families and friends (Estabrooks, Bradshaw, Dzewaltowski, & Smith-Ray, 2008). All of these studies reported positive effects on exercise participation.

Taken together, these results indicate that a team-building intervention implemented by the class instructor provides an easy and effective way to improve exercise adherence among people of all ages.

3. How does cohesion foster adherence? The exact mechanisms by which cohesion enhances adherence are not known; however, some possible mechanisms have been suggested. One possibility is that more cohesive groups foster more positive attitudes toward class attendance (Courneya & McAuley, 1995);

people may simply feel more positively about exercising in cohesive groups because these groups provide greater social support and interaction than do less cohesive groups. According to the theory of planned behavior (see Chapter 3), more positive attitudes should spur stronger exercise intentions and ultimately greater exercise participation.

A second possibility is that more cohesive groups generate greater self-efficacy in their group members than do less cohesive groups (Estabrooks & Carron, 2000a). For example, highly cohesive exercise groups may provide their members with more efficacy-enhancing verbal persuasion (such as encouraging comments like "You can do it!"). As discussed in Chapter 3, verbal persuasion is a source of self-efficacy. People who have greater exercise self-efficacy adhere better to exercise programs than do those who have low exercise self-efficacy.

Group size

As the number of people in an exercise class increases, perceptions of group cohesion decrease (Carron & Spink, 1995), as does satisfaction with the exercise experience (Carron, Brawley, & Widmeyer, 1990). Presumably, bigger exercise groups result in more crowding and fewer opportunities for participants to interact with one another. Hence, enjoyment and cohesion are diminished.

Group size can also affect perceptions of the instructor. The same aerobics instructor taught a large class (150 to 200 participants), a medium-sized class (50 to 80), and a small class (20 to 30) using the exact same routine, music, instructions, and level of enthusiasm (Prossin & Carron, 1989). At the end of each class, participants rated the instructor on several dimensions, including her effectiveness as a role model, her personableness, her use of feedback, and her general teaching style. Although a panel of fitness instructors observed and confirmed that the aerobic instructor's behavior was exactly the same across all three classes, participants in the medium-sized class rated the instructor less favorably than did participants in the other two classes.

To explain this curvilinear relationship between class size and instructor evaluation, Carron (1990) suggested that the instructor's role is clearest—for both the instructor and the participant—in the largest and the smallest classes. In large classes, participants expect the leader to use a group-oriented approach (i.e., instructors address and reinforce the group as a whole, rather than individual members), and this is the approach that most instructors do indeed use with large classes. In small classes, participants expect, and usually receive, a more individual-oriented approach (i.e., addressing and reinforcing individual members within the group rather than the group as a whole). In medium-sized classes, however, it may be unclear whether a group- or individual-oriented approach is best. Thus, there may be discrepancies between the approach expected by participants and the approach used by the instructor. Perception of these discrepancies could manifest as dissatisfaction with the instructor. In addition, because instructors may be unsure about how to approach a medium-sized class, they may use both styles inconsistently. Such inconsistency in leadership style could also contribute to dissatisfaction with the instructor.

Group composition

The effects of group composition on exercise-related thoughts, feelings, and behaviors are not as well studied as other aspects of the exercise group, such as size and cohesion. Nonetheless, there is some evidence to suggest that characteristics of the people who make up the exercise group can affect responses to the exercise experience.

Sex. The sex of co-exercisers is one group composition factor that can affect an exerciser's comfort level. Like Lakeisha, women often report that they feel uncomfortable in exercise centers where male exercisers are in the majority. Women in cardiac rehabilitation programs, for example, have reported that they feel out of place and a "curiosity" in exercise programs that are dominated by men (Benson, Arthur, & Rideout, 1997). In response to these feelings, some hospitals have established separate programs for female cardiac patients. Similarly, many private health clubs offer fitness classes for women only. We are unaware of any studies that have examined men's level of comfort in exercise classes that are dominated by women (e.g., aerobic dance classes). However, we wonder if there are men who would *like* to participate in aerobic dance and other predominantly female exercise classes, but who avoid them because they don't want to be seen as an "oddity."

Similarity of oneself to other group members. Whether one feels similar to other group members can affect comfort level and motivation. Obese people, for example, indicate that they prefer to exercise in groups of other obese people (Bain, Wilson, & Chaikind, 1989), and their adherence may be compromised if they are required to exercise with nonobese individuals (Treasure, Lox, & Lawton, 1998). Likewise, people generally want to exercise with others of similar fitness levels. Feeling markedly less fit than other group members can deplete an exerciser's self-confidence and motivation (Wasilenko, Kulik & Wanic, 2007).

The age of fellow exercisers is also important. Beauchamp and colleagues surveyed nearly 1,000 people regarding their preferences for exercising in groups composed of younger, middle-aged, and older adults (Beauchamp, Carron, McCutcheon, & Harper, 2007). They found that older and younger adults had a clear preference for exercising in classes composed of similarly aged individuals. For them, exercise settings with considerably younger or older exercisers were not appealing.

Group member enthusiasm. The enthusiasm of group members can affect responses to the exercise experience. Fox, Rejeski, and Gauvin (2000) randomly assigned people who had never done step aerobics to exercise in a class composed of participants who were either enthusiastic, encouraging of one another, and socially interactive (enriched condition), or unenthused, not encouraging of one another, and not socially interactive (bland condition). Not surprisingly, after the exercise class, participants in the enriched condition reported greater enjoyment of the exercise bout and stronger future intentions to join an exercise group than those in the bland condition.

Participants in the enriched condition, however, also reported greater worries about embarrassing themselves and being evaluated by members of the exercise group (Martin & Fox, 2001). Among these first-time exercisers, it seems that encouragement and attention from other group members elicited feelings of self-consciousness and anxiety. These findings suggest that exercise beginners may be more comfortable when the presence of other exercisers is downplayed. Thus, in the early stages of an exercise program for novices, it may be beneficial to focus on helping the exerciser to master exercise skills before introducing any type of team-building intervention that would draw attention to individual participants, such as having exercisers "buddy up" and work out together. As exercisers become more confident in their physical abilities, worries about social evaluation and attention probably dissipate, and an interactive, supportive exercise environment becomes an appealing and welcome feature.

Co-Exercisers and Observers

Even when people are not part of an actual exercise group or class, other individuals in their exercise environment (e.g., the person riding a stationary bike next to them at the gym, the people they pass while jogging through a park) can influence exercise behavior. In this section, we look at the influence of co-exercisers (i.e., people we exercise with) and observers on exercise effort and exertion.

Actual effort

In a clever study, Worringham and Messick (1983) secretly timed solitary joggers as they ran alone along a path. Unknown to the joggers, the researchers had asked a young woman to stand alongside the jogging path. In one condition, the young woman was instructed to watch as the jogger ran by. In the other condition, she was instructed to turn her back when the jogger came by. It was found that both male and female joggers increased their speed when the woman was watching them, but they did not increase their speed when the woman had her back turned to them.

social facilitation ■

The phenomenon in which people increase their effort and performance when others are watching them is known as **social facilitation.** In another study, social facilitation effects were observed in the gym. Researchers compared the maximum amount of weight that participants could bench press both with and without an audience present (Rhea, Landers, Alvar, & Arent, 2003). On average, participants lifted 12 kilograms more when in the presence of an observing audience. Numerous explanations have been put forth to explain social facilitation. In the jogging and weightlifting examples, it's possible that the joggers picked up their pace and the weightlifters tried to lift more weight because they wanted to make a good impression on observers.

Self-reported effort

The presence of others and the desire to make a good impression can influence an exerciser's self-reported effort. For instance, people report lower ratings of perceived exertion (RPE) when they exercise next to a person who is giving the impression that the exercise is very easy than when they exercise alone (Hardy, Hall, & Prestholdt, 1986). Presumably, people want to create the impression that they are just as fit as the people exercising around them. Hence, they may be reluctant to admit that they find a workout to be more strenuous than does the person next to them. Similarly, in exercise-testing situations involving heavy workloads, men have been shown to report lower RPEs when a woman conducts the test than when a man conducts the test (Boutcher, Fleischer-Curtian, & Gines, 1988). The desire to impress the other sex is probably what prompts these men to claim that an objectively hard workout does not actually *feel* all that difficult.

Of course there are dangers associated with trying to create a good impression in exercise settings, whether through putting forth extra effort or claiming that a workout isn't very strenuous when it really is. Some people may exert themselves too strenuously when others are watching, resulting in exhaustion, muscle strain, heat stroke, or even death. People have injured themselves by lifting too much weight at the gym, and in one study these injured parties subsequently indicated that they overlifted because they were concerned that others would perceive them as weak if they reduced the amount of weight already set on a machine or bench (Martin & Leary, 2001). Similarly, in his paper on impression management in sport and exercise, Leary (1992) tells of an acquaintance who died of heat-related complications during a 10K race. The runner refused to quit, arguing that he had boasted to his friends and coworkers of running in the race and he could not face them if he didn't finish. In this case, his concerns about making a good impression literally killed him.

Society

Broadly conceived, the term "society" refers to a group of people who form a single community on the basis of sharing some common characteristic, such as living in the same geographical region (e.g., "western society"), having the same occupation (e.g., "The Law Society of Upper Canada"), or sharing the same leisure interests (e.g., "The Dead Poets Society"). The term "culture" refers to the values, customs, norms, rules, and beliefs that are held by members of a particular society. With regard to physical activity, two aspects of culture that represent social influences on physical activity are *norms* and *stereotyped beliefs*.

Norms for physical activity

A **norm** is a pattern of behaviors or beliefs generally held by members of a particular group (or "society"). Within a given society, norms for physical activity can be reflected by a variety of factors, such as the media's portrayal of physical

■ norm

activity (e.g., do newspapers and magazines frequently feature articles about the benefits of physical activity?), the number of resources dedicated to helping people be physically active (e.g., are public exercise facilities available?), and the visibility of physically active individuals (e.g., is it typical or "normal" to see people outside exercising?). According to the theory of planned behavior (see Chapter 3), norms have an impact on exercise behavior through their effect on behavioral intentions. That is, people will have greater intentions to be physically active if they perceive societal or cultural expectations and encouragement to be active, than if they do not.

One potentially powerful vehicle for conveying social norms for physical activity is the mass media. When popular characters in films and television, and people interviewed in popular magazines, are portrayed as having a physically active lifestyle, they convey the message that exercise is a typical and *normal* thing to do. This message can shape audiences' perceptions of physical activity and perhaps even their behavior. Young audiences may be particularly susceptible to the influences of media-based normative information. Youngsters often identify with, and are influenced by, media figures who engage in such harmful behaviors as smoking cigarettes or losing an extreme amount of weight (Brown & Cantor, 2000).

Although very little data exists regarding media influences on healthful behaviors, one study suggests that media figures can have a positive effect on children and adolescents' physical activity habits. Taveras, Rifas-Shiman, Field, and colleagues (2004) surveyed almost 12,000 American boys and girls who were between the ages of 9 and 16. These study participants provided detailed information on the physical activities they performed over the past year, as well as the extent to which they were trying to look like people they saw on television, in movies, and in magazines. Forty-six percent of the girls and 27 percent of the boys reported making at least some effort to look like figures in the media. Furthermore, as adolescents' desire to look like media figures increased, so did their levels of physical activity. The difference in physical activity between those who did not want to look like people in the media and those who "totally" wanted to look like people in the media was approximately 4 hours of activity per week for girls and 5 hours of activity per week for boys.

Another example of the impact of cultural norms on physical activity can be seen by comparing physical activity rates of older adults living in North America with those of older adults living in China. In Canada and the United States, cultural norms for physical activity among the elderly are not particularly positive. Physical activity among older adults is often considered inappropriate, without benefit, or even dangerous (O'Brien Cousins, 2000). Although efforts have been made in recent years to change these normative beliefs, American and Canadian surveys still indicate that most men and women over the age of 65 are insufficiently active to derive health benefits (Canadian Fitness and Lifestyle Research Institute, 2007; Centers for Disease Control and Prevention, 2007). In China, however, nearly 40 percent of men and women aged 66 to 75 are considered physically active (China National Sports Council, 1997). This difference in participation rates between North American and Chinese elderly may reflect differences in norms for physical activity among the aged. Unlike North Americans, the Chinese have a long tradition of exercise and physical activity among older adults. Every morning, in cities and towns across China, large groups of older adults can be seen performing tai chi quan (a traditional form of Chinese exercise) and other exercises in public parks and squares, on streets and sidewalks—virtually anywhere that provides sufficient space (see Exhibit 5.6). In addition, more than 200,000 physical activity associations throughout China provide physical activity opportunities, including swimming, dancing, and tai chi quan, for older people (Hong & Lu, 1999). Clearly, the Chinese have more positive normative beliefs about the appropriateness of exercise for the elderly than do North Americans. These differences are reflected in the higher physical activity participation rates seen in Chinese society.

In China, cultural norms for older exercisers are very positive.

exhibit 5.6

Stereotyped beliefs

Stereotypes are beliefs—true or false—about the characteristics of people who belong to a particular group. They represent our general expectations or preconceptions for people in that group and are generalized to almost all of the group's members. With regard to physical activity and exercise, stereotypes about the type of people who engage in certain activities can shape our attitudes and our intentions regarding participation in those activities. For example, the stereotyped belief that weight training is a "man's activity" has been cited as a deterrent to women's participation in strength training (Ebben & Jensen, 1998). This is unfortunate because strength training has been identified as an important strategy for reducing the risk of fractures associated with osteoporosis (Kohrt, Bloomfield, Little, et al., 2004)—a disease that afflicts one in three women over the age of 50 and is characterized by low bone mass and deterioration of bone tissue (National Osteoporosis Society, 2000). Some exercise programmers have noted that they must first change women's stereotyped beliefs about strength training before they can convince these women to adopt a strength-training regimen. Such changes have been accomplished through strategies that involve

■ stereotypes

challenging inaccurate beliefs about strength training (such as, "weight training will masculinize my body," "weight training is done by sweaty men in sweaty gyms"), and by "feminizing" the exercise training environment (e.g., by decorating the fitness center in soft colors and using pastel-colored weights; Khoury-Murphy & Murphy, 1992).

In addition to having stereotyped beliefs about the people who engage in specific activities, members of different societal groups may have stereotypes about exercisers and nonexercisers in general. Indeed, studies have shown that North American and Scandinavian university students hold negative stereotypes for nonexercisers and consider them to be lazy and sloppy, with poor self-control (Lindwall & Martin Ginis, 2006; Martin, Sinden, & Fleming, 2000). In contrast, these university students hold highly positive stereotypes for exercisers and consider them to be attractive people who are also intelligent, highly sociable, and hard working. We should note that these stereotypes may be unique to predominantly Caucasian, middle-class university students. People who belong to other segments of society (e.g., older adults, those with less education, or who are less affluent) may not hold the same stereotypes for exercisers and nonexercisers. Nonetheless, it has been suggested that for those people who do hold these stereotypes, some of them may be motivated to exercise simply to avoid the negative stereotypes associated with being a "couch potato."

Practical Recommendations

This chapter has provided information regarding how people can influence one another's physical activity behavior. This information can be applied to promote both the initiation and long-term maintenance of a physical activity program in a number of ways.

First, exercisers should be encouraged to consider their social support needs and preferences. Not all exercisers prefer to work out with other people, so it is important that individuals consider whether they require support in actual exercise settings (e.g., companionship support) or if they need other types of support in order to facilitate their exercise regimen (e.g., instrumental support). Once support needs have been identified, exercisers should then identify people in their lives who can provide these types of support. It is important to note that some people find it difficult to ask others for help, either because they are afraid the other person will say no, or because they do not want to burden the other person. In such cases, these people could be encouraged to find a buddy who also wants help in changing a health habit (e.g., exercising, quitting smoking). Knowing that they are *giving* support to someone may make these people more comfortable about *seeking* support from that person.

Second, people who are in a position of social influence should take every opportunity to encourage and promote physical activity, as their words and actions can have a potent effect on others' activity behavior. For instance, ideally all family physicians (as well as chiropractors, osteopaths, physical therapists, and so on) should discuss and prescribe physical activity with each and every patient. Likewise, parents should act as positive role models and be physically active with their children on a regular basis. There is, of course, a fine balance between encouraging and pressuring a person to become physically active. When exerting social influence, it is important not to belittle people or make them feel guilty for not exercising. These actions could result in individuals giving up exercise altogether.

Third, interventionists can apply several strategies to improve the social aspects of the exercise environment. For instance, the fitness leader can work to develop a positive, socially supportive leadership style. Attending leadership seminars, seeking out feedback from class participants and other fitness leaders, or videotaping and reviewing oneself teaching an exercise class can help in this effort. The social environment can also be improved through the team-building techniques discussed in this chapter to build a more cohesive group. The use of these strategies can help to create a more comfortable group exercise environment that may prevent exercisers like Lakeisha from quitting group exercise programs.

Finally, if physical activity is to become commonplace among all members of society, then there is a need to change some of the cultural norms and stereotypes associated with it. For example, there needs to be a shift from viewing exercise programs for seniors as "unusual," as this normative belief creates the impression that exercise is not a normal part of an older person's lifestyle. If every community had a seniors' fitness program in place (like the Chinese model), physical activity among seniors would be seen as the norm, and more older people would likely be physically active.

Conclusion

Researchers have identified several sources of social support and other types of social influence on physical activity. These sources include the family, the physician and other health care professionals, the exercise class leader, the exercise group, co-exercisers and observers, and society. For better or for worse, these groups and individuals can have a potent impact on our own exercise behavior.

On the positive side, people such as family members and health care professionals may provide social support. This support can take many forms, including instrumental support, emotional support, informational support, companionship support, and validation. Other people within the exercise context, such as the fitness leader and other exercisers, can also exert a positive social influence by building a supportive, cohesive exercise environment. All of these constructive behaviors can lead to more positive exercise-related thoughts, feelings, and behaviors.

On the negative side, people who are trying to be socially supportive may actually come across as controlling, overprotective, or exerting excessive pressure. When supportive behavior is perceived in this negative light, the recipient of the behavior may react by decreasing his or her level of physical activity or quitting an activity program altogether. Likewise, aspects of the fitness leader's behavior—such as being overly critical—and characteristics of the exercise group—such as having poor cohesion—may result in more negative thoughts and feelings toward exercise participation, and ultimately poorer adherence.

what do you know?

1. Briefly describe two ways in which social support can be operationalized.
2. Identify and describe the five main types of social support.
3. Describe two factors that may influence the type of social support an exerciser needs.
4. What is "behavioral reactance"?
5. Why might physician-based activity counseling be a particularly effective way of promoting physical activity among adults?
6. What are some of the challenges that deter physicians from talking to their patients about physical activity?
7. Describe the characteristics of a socially supportive leadership style and three benefits that exercisers experience from being exposed to this style.
8. Define group cohesion.
9. Describe three strategies that can be used to increase perceptions of group cohesion in an exercise class.
10. What is the relationship between group size and group cohesion?
11. Describe two aspects of group composition that can affect exercise-related thoughts, feelings, and behaviors.
12. Provide an example of the social facilitation phenomenon in group exercise settings.
13. How might cultural norms affect physical activity behavior?

learning activities

1. Make three copies of the social support scale shown in Exhibit 5.1. Complete the first copy of the scale by following the instructions printed at the top of the exhibit. Next, reflect on your own childhood and complete the second copy of the social support scale as if you were a 10–12 year old. Finally, think about an elderly friend or relative and complete the third

copy of the scale as you think an older adult might. For each copy of the questionnaire, tally the average score for each type of support across the three sources. Do you see any differences in the types of support that are given to people of different ages? Do these differences reflect changes in our needs for certain types of support over time? Are some sources more likely to give support to a younger than to an older person? What might account for changes in the amount of support we get from different sources over time?

2. Imagine that you are in charge of 50 students living in a college residence. You have been asked to develop a "Get Fit, Stay Active" program for these students. Given what you now know about social influences and physical activity, devise a plan to use social influence to get your students physically active.
3. Test the social influence effects of co-exercisers. In a quiet part of a gym, ask 10 classmates to perform as many sit-ups as they can in a 60-second period. Be sure that each person performs the task without anyone else observing. After all 10 people have completed the task, calculate the average number of sit-ups performed, but do not tell this number to your classmates. Now, ask 10 additional classmates to do the 60-second sit-up task all together, in a group. Calculate the average number of sit-ups that members of this group performed. Is there a difference in the two results?
4. Develop a plan to help physicians become more frequent promoters of physical activity. Check out the Exercise Is Medicine program, managed by the American College of Sports Medicine, at www.exerciseismedicine.org for some ideas and examples of resources that could be used to facilitate physical activity counseling.

references

Alcock, J.E., Carment, D.W., & Sadava, S.W. (1991). *A textbook of social psychology* (2nd ed.). Scarborough, ON: Prentice Hall.

American College of Sports Medicine (2007, November). *ACSM and AMA launch "Exercise Is Medicine" program.* Accessed from www.acsm.org/AM/Template.cfm?Section=Home_Page&TEMPLATE=/CM/ContentDisplay.cfm&CONTENTID=8596

American Heart Association (2004). International cardiovascular disease statistics. Accessed from www.americanheart.org/presenter.jhtml?identifier=3001008

Bain, L.L., Wilson, T., & Chaikind, E. (1989). Participant perceptions of exercise programs for overweight women. *Research Quarterly for Exercise and Sport, 60,* 134–143.

Bauman, A.E., Russell, S.J., Furber, S.E., & Dobson, A.J. (2001). The epidemiology of dog walking: An unmet need for human and canine health. *Medical Journal of Australia, 175,* 632–634.

Beauchamp, M.R., Carron, A.V., McCutcheon, S., & Harper, O. (2007). Older adults' preferences for exercising alone versus in groups: Considering contextual congruence. *Annals of Behavioral Medicine, 33,* 200–206.

Bellows-Riecken, K.H., & Rhodes, R.E. (2008). A birth of inactivity? A review of physical activity and parenthood. *Preventive Medicine, 46,* 99–110.

Benson, G., Arthur, H., & Rideout, E. (1997). Women and heart attack: A study of women's experiences. *Canadian Journal of Cardiovascular Nursing, 8,* 16–23.

Berkhuysen, M.A., Nieuwland, W., Buunk, B.P., Sanderman, R., & Rispens, P. (1999). Change in self-efficacy during cardiac rehabilitation and the role of perceived overprotectiveness. *Patient Education and Counseling, 38,* 21–32.

Booth, M.L., Bauman, A., Owen, N., & Gore, C.J. (1997). Physical activity preferences, preferred sources of assistance, and perceived barriers to increased activity among physically inactive Australians. *Preventive Medicine, 26,* 131–137.

Boutcher, S.H., Fleischer-Curtian, L.A., & Gines, S.D. (1988). The effects of self-presentation on perceived exertion. *Journal of Sport and Exercise Psychology, 10,* 270–280.

Brawley, L.R., Rejeski, W.J., & Fox, L.D. (2000). A group mediated cognitive-behavioural intervention for increasing adherence to physical activity in older adults. *Journal of Applied Biobehavioural Research, 5,* 47–65.

Bray, S.R., Gyurcsik, N.C., Culos-Reed, S.N., Dawson, K.A., & Martin, K.A. (2001). An exploratory investigation of the relationship between proxy efficacy, self-efficacy and exercise attendance. *Journal of Health Psychology, 6,* 425–434.

Bray, S.R., Millen, J.A., Eidsness, J., & Leuzinger, C. (2005). The effects of leadership style and exercise program choreography on enjoyment and intentions to exercise. *Psychology of Sport and Exercise, 6,* 415–425.

Brown, J.D., & Cantor, J. (2000). An agenda for research on youth and the media. *Journal of Adolescent Health, 27 (Suppl),* 2–7.

Burke, S.M., Carron, A.V., & Shapcott, K.M. (2008). Cohesion in exercise groups: An overview. *International Review of Sport and Exercise Psychology, 1,* 107–123.

Calfas, K.J., Long, B.J., Sallis, J.F., Oldenburg, B., & French, M. (1996). Mediators of change in physical activity following an intervention in primary care: PACE. *Preventive Medicine, 26,* 73–81.

Canadian Fitness and Lifestyle Research Institute. (2007). *Physical Activity Monitor.* Accessed May 3, 2010, from www.cflri.ca/eng/statistics/surveys/pam2007.php.

Carron, A.V. (1990). Group size in sport and physical activity: Social psychological and performance consequences. *International Journal of Sport Psychology, 21,* 286–304.

Carron, A.V., Brawley, L.R., & Widmeyer, W.N. (1990). The impact of group size in an exercise setting. *Journal of Sport and Exercise Psychology, 12,* 376–387.

Carron, A.V., Brawley, L.R., & Widmeyer, W.N. (1998). The measurement of cohesiveness in sports groups. In J.L. Duda (Ed.), *Advances in sport and exercise psychology measurement* (pp. 213–226). Morgantown, WV: Fitness Information Technology.

Carron, A.V., Hausenblas, H.A., & Mack, D. (1996). Social influence and exercise: A meta-analysis. *Journal of Sport and Exercise Psychology, 18,* 1–16.

Carron, A.V., & Spink, K.S. (1993). Team building in an exercise setting. *The Sport Psychologist, 7,* 8–18.

Carron, A.V., & Spink, K.S. (1995). The group size–cohesion relationship in minimal groups. *Small Group Research, 26,* 86–105.

Centers for Disease Control and Prevention. (2007). Prevalence of regular physical activity among adults—United States, 2001 and 2005. *Morbidity and Mortality Weekly Report, 56,* 1209–1212.

China National Sports Council. (1997). *Report on China mass sports survey.* Beijing: Author.

Chogaharan, M. (1999). A multidimensional scale for assessing positive and negative social influences on physical activity in older adults. *Journal of Gerontological Social Science, 54B,* 5356–5367.

Cohen, J. (1992). A power primer. *Psychological Bulletin, 112,* 155–159.

Courneya, K.S., & McAuley, E. (1995). Cognitive mediators of the social influence–exercise adherence relationship: A test of the theory of planned behaviour. *Journal of Behavioural Medicine, 18,* 499–515.

Davison, K.K., Cutting, T.M., & Birch, L.L. (2003). Parents' activity-related parenting practices predict girls' physical activity. *Medicine and Science in Sports and Exercise, 35,* 1589–1595.

Duncan, T.E., McAuley, E., Stoolmiller, M., & Duncan, S.C. (1993). Serial fluctuations in exercise behaviour as a function of social support and efficacy cognitions. *Journal of Applied Social Psychology, 23,* 1498–1522.

Ebben, W.P., & Jensen, R.L. (1998). Strength training for women: Debunking myths that block opportunity. *The Physician and Sportsmedicine, 26,* 86–97.

Edmunds, J., Ntoumanis, N., & Duda, J. L. (2008). Testing a self-determination theory-based teaching style intervention in the exercise domain. *European Journal of Social Psychology, 38,* 375–388.

Elston, T., & Martin Ginis, K.A. (2004). The effects of self-set versus assigned goals on exercisers' self-efficacy for an unfamiliar task. *Journal of Sport and Exercise Psychology, 26,* 500–504.

Epstein, L.H., Paluch, R.A., Roemmich, J.N., & Beecher, M.D. (2007). Family-based obesity treatment, then and now: Twenty-five years of pediatric obesity treatment. *Health Psychology, 26,* 381–391.

Erling, J., & Oldridge, N.B. (1985). Effect of a spousal-support program on compliance with cardiac rehabilitation. *Medicine and Science in Sports and Exercise, 17,* 284.

Estabrooks, P.A., Bradshaw, M., Dzewaltowski, D.A., & Smith-Ray, R.L. (2008). Determining the impact of Walk Kansas: Applying a team-building approach to community physical activity promotion. *Annals of Behavioral Medicine, 36,* 1–12.

Estabrooks, P.A., & Carron, A.V. (2000a). Predicting self-efficacy in elderly exercisers: The role of task cohesion. *Journal of Aging and Physical Activity, 8,* 41–50.

Estabrooks, P.A., & Carron, A.V. (2000b). The physical activity group environment questionnaire: An instrument for the assessment of cohesion in exercise classes. *Group Dynamics, 4,* 230–243.

Eyler, A.A., Brownson, R.C., Donateller, R.J., King, A.C., Brown, D., & Sallis, J.F. (1999). Physical activity social support and middle- and older-aged minority women: Results from a U.S. survey. *Social Science and Medicine, 49,* 781–789.

Fox, L.D., Rejeski, W.J., & Gauvin, L. (2000). Effects of leadership style and group dynamics on enjoyment of physical activity. *American Journal of Health Promotion, 14,* 277–283.

Franklin, B.A. (1988). Program factors that influence exercise adherence: Practical adherence skills for the clinical staff. In R.K. Dishman (Ed.), *Exercise adherence: Its impact on public health* (pp. 237–258). Champaign, IL: Human Kinetics.

Gould, D., Feltz, D., Horn, T., & Weiss, M. (1982). Reasons for attrition in competitive youth swimming. *Journal of Sport Behaviour, 5,* 155–165.

Giles-Corti, B., & Donovan, R.J. (2003). Relative influences of individual, social environmental, and physical environmental correlates of walking. *American Journal of Public Health, 93,* 1583–1589.

Gustafson, S.L., & Rhodes, R.E. (2006). Parental correlates of physical activity in children and early adolescents. *Sports Medicine, 36,* 79–97.

Hardy, C.J., Hall, E.G., & Prestholdt, P.H. (1986). The mediational role of social influence in the perception of exertion. *Journal of Sport Psychology, 8,* 88–104.

Harsha, D.M., Saywell, R.M., Thygerson, S., & Panozzo, J. (1996). Physician factors affecting patient willingness to comply with exercise recommendations. *Clinical Journal of Sports Medicine, 6,* 112–118.

Heaton, P.C., & Frede, S.M. (2003). Patients' need for more counseling on diet, exercise, and smoking cessation: Results from the National Ambulatory Medical Care Survey. *Journal of the American Pharmacists Association, 46,* 364–369.

Hibbard, J.H. (1988). Age, social ties and health behaviors: An exploratory study. *Health Education Research, 3,* 131–139.

Hong, T.B., Franks, M.M., Gonzalez, R., Keteyian, S.J., Franklin, B.A., & Artinian, N.T. (2005). A dyadic investigation of exercise support between cardiac patients and their spouses. *Health Psychology, 24,* 430–434.

Hong, Y., & Lu, Y. (1999). Physical activity and health among older adults in China. *Journal of Aging and Physical Activity, 7,* 247–250.

Jeffery, R.W., Wing, R.R., Thorson, C., & Burton, L.R. (1998). Use of personal trainers and financial incentives to increase exercise in a behavioural weight-loss program. *Journal of Consulting and Clinical Psychology, 66,* 777–783.

Katz, D.L., Shuval, K., Comerford, B.P., Faridi, Z., & Njike, V.Y. (2008). Impact of an educational intervention on internal medicine residents' physical activity counseling: The pressure system model. *Journal of Evaluation in Clinical Practice, 14,* 294–299.

Khoury-Murphy, M., & Murphy, M.D. (1992). The cultural problematic of implementing a weight training program among older Southern women. *Play and Culture, 5,* 409–419.

Kohrt, W.M., Bloomfield, S.A., Little, K.D., Nelson, M.E., & Yingling, V.R. (2004). American College of Sports Medicine position stand: Physical activity and bone health. *Medicine and Science in Sports and Exercise, 36,* 1985–1996.

Leary, M.R. (1992). Self-presentational processes in exercise and sport. *Journal of Sport and Exercise Psychology, 14,* 339–351.

Leijon, M.E., Bendtsen, P., Nilsen, P., Ekberg, K., & Stahle, A. (2008). Physical activity referrals in Swedish primary health care—prescriber and patient characteristics, reasons for prescriptions, and prescribed activities. *BMC Health Services Research, 8,* 201–209.

Leslie, E., Owen, N., Salmon, J., Bauman, A., Sallis, J.F., & Lo, S.K. (1999). Insufficiently active Australian college students: Perceived personal, social, and environmental influences. *Preventive Medicine, 28,* 20–27.

Lewis, M.A., & Rook, K.S. (1999). Social control in personal relationships: Impact on health behaviours and psychological distress. *Health Psychology, 18,* 63–71.

Lindwall, M., & Martin Ginis, K. A. (2006). Moving towards a favorable image: The self-presentational benefits of exercise and physical activity. *Scandinavian Journal of Psychology, 47,* 209–217.

Martin, K.A., & Fox, L.D. (2001). Group and leadership effects on social anxiety experienced during an exercise class. *Journal of Applied Social Psychology, 31,* 1000–1016.

Martin, K.A., & Hausenblas, H.A. (1998). Psychological commitment to exercise and eating disorder symptomatology among female aerobic instructors. *The Sport Psychologist, 12,* 180–190.

Martin, K.A., & Leary, M.R. (2001). Self-presentational determinants of health risk behaviour among college freshmen. *Psychology and Health, 16,* 17–27.

Martin, K.A., Sinden, A.R., & Fleming, J.C. (2000). Inactivity may be hazardous to your image: The effects of exercise participation on impression formation. *Journal of Sport and Exercise Psychology, 22,* 283–291.

Miller, Y.D., Trost, S.G., & Brown, W.J. (2002). Mediators of physical activity behavior change among women with young children. *American Journal of Preventive Medicine, 23 (2 Suppl),* 98–103.

Morgan, W.P. (1994). Physical activity, fitness, and depression. In C. Bouchard, R. J. Shephard, & T. Stephens (Eds.), *Physical activity, fitness, and health: International proceedings and consensus statement* (pp. 851–867). Champaign, IL: Human Kinetics.

National Osteoporosis Society. (2000). Osteoporosis [On-line]. Available: www.nos.org.uk.

North, T.C., McCullagh, P., & Tran, Z. V. (1990). Effect of exercise on depression. *Exercise & Sport Sciences Reviews, 18,* 379–415.

O'Brien Cousins, S. (2000). My heart couldn't take it: Older women's beliefs about exercise benefits and risks. *Journals of Gerontology, 55B,* 283–294.

Patrick, L., & D'Eon, J. (1996). Social support and functional status in chronic pain patients. *Canadian Journal of Rehabilitation, 9,* 195–201.

Petrella, R.J., Lattanzio, C.N., & Overend, T.J. (2007). Physical activity counseling and prescription among Canadian primary care physicians. *Archives of Internal Medicine, 167,* 1774–1781.

Pinto, B.M., Goldstein, M.G., DePue, J.D., & Milan, F.B. (1998). Acceptability and feasibility of physician-based activity counseling: The PAL project. *American Journal of Preventive Medicine, 15,* 95–102.

Prossin, A.J., & Carron, A.V. (1989). *The effects of fitness class size on the participants' perception of the leader.* Unpublished manuscript, University of Western Ontario.

Rejeski, W.J., Brawley, L.R., Ambrosius, W.T., Brubaker, P.H., Focht, B.C., Foy, C.G., & Fox, L.D. (2003). Older adults with chronic disease: Benefits of group-mediated counseling in the promotion of physically active lifestyles. *Health Psychology, 4,* 414–423.

Rhea, M.R., Landers, D.M., Alvar, B.A., & Arent, S.M. (2003). The effects of competition and the presence of an audience on weight lifting performance. *Journal of Strength and Conditioning Research, 17,* 303–306.

Rogers, L.Q., Bailey, J.E., Gutin, B., Johnson, K.C., Levine, M.A., Milan, F., Seelig, C.B., & Sherman, S.E. (2002). Teaching resident physicians to provide exercise counseling: A needs assessment. *Academic Medicine, 77,* 841–844.

Sallis, J.M., Prochaska, J.J., Taylor, W.C., Hill, J.O., & Geraci, J.C. (1999). Correlates of physical activity in a national sample of girls and boys in grades 4 through 12. *Health Psychology, 18,* 410–415.

Spink, K.S., & Carron, A.V. (1992). Group cohesion and adherence in exercise classes. *Journal of Sport and Exercise Psychology, 14,* 78–86.

Spink, K.S., & Carron, A.V. (1993). The effects of team building on the adherence patterns of female exercise participants. *Journal of Sport and Exercise Psychology, 15,* 39–49.

Spink, K.S., & Carron, A.V. (1994). Group cohesion effects in exercise classes. *Small Group Research, 25,* 26–42.

Stein, G. L., & Raedeke, T.D. (1999). Children's perceptions of parent sport involvement: It's not how much, but to what degree that's important. *Journal of Sport Behavior, 22,* 591–602.

Taveras, E.M., Rifas-Shiman, S.L., Field, A.E., Frazier, A.L., Colditz, G.A., & Gillman, M.W. (2004). The influence of wanting to look like media figures on adolescent physical activity. *Journal of Adolescent Health, 35,* 41–50.

Thrasher, J.F., Campbell, M.K., & Oates, V. (2004). Behavior-specific social support for healthy behaviors among African American church members: Applying optimal matching theory. *Health Education & Behavior, 31,* 193–205.

Treasure, D.C., Lox, C.L., & Lawton, B.R. (1998). Determinants of physical activity in a sedentary, obese female population. *Journal of Sport and Exercise Psychology, 20,* 218–224.

Tulloch, H., Fortier, M., & Hogg, W. (2006). Physical activity counseling in primary care: Who has and who should be counseling. *Patient Education and Counseling, 64,* 6–20.

Turner, E.E., Rejeski, W.J., & Brawley, L.R. (1997). Psychological benefits of activity are influenced by the social environment. *Journal of Sport and Exercise Psychology, 19,* 119–130.

U.S. Department of Health and Human Services. (1996). *Physical activity and health: A report of the Surgeon General.* McLean, VA: International Medical Publishing.

Wallace, J.P., Raglin, J.S., & Jastremski, C.A. (1995). Twelve month adherence of adults who joined a fitness program with a spouse vs. without a spouse. *Journal of Sports Medicine and Physical Fitness, 35,* 206–213.

Wasilenko, K.A., Kulik, J.A., & Wanic, R.A. (2007). Effects of social comparisons with peers on women's body satisfaction and exercise behavior. *International Journal of Eating Disorders, 40,* 740–745.

Watson, J., Martin Ginis, K.A., & Spink, K.S. (2004). Team building in an exercise class for the elderly. *Activities Adaptation and Aging, 28,* 35–47.

Wills, T.A., & Shinar, O. (2000). Measuring perceived and received social support. In S. Cohen, L.G. Underwood, & B.H. Gottlieb (Eds.), *Social support measurement and intervention* (pp. 86–135). New York: Oxford University Press.

Worringham, C.J., & Messick, D.M. (1983). Social facilitation of running: An unobtrusive study. *Journal of Social Psychology, 121,* 23–29.

6

Physical Activity Interventions

KEY TERMS

abstinence violation effect
action planning
activity log
behavioral approaches
behavioral coping strategies
change talk
cognitive coping strategies
cognitive restructuring
community-wide campaigns
cultural tailoring
empathy
environmental and policy approaches
exercise buddies
exercise contract
fitness appraisals
goal-setting
goal-setting worksheet
health risk appraisals
implementation intentions
informational approaches
lapse
mass media campaigns
motivational interviewing
point-of-decision prompts
rating of perceived exertion (RPE) scale
RE-AIM
self-monitoring
self-talk
social approaches
visualization

In Chapter 2, we reported that physical inactivity has become an epidemic within industrialized nations. Indeed, the vast majority of people living in countries such as the United States, the United Kingdom, Canada, and Australia are insufficiently active. This is a very serious public health issue; inactivity has been cited as a leading cause of noncommunicable disease, disability, and hundreds of thousands of preventable deaths worldwide each year. Given the staggering impact of inactivity on health and well-being, health care costs, workforce productivity, and so on, it is understandable that an ever-increasing number of approaches are being used to try to increase physical activity levels of the populations of these various nations.

You have probably been exposed to many of these approaches. For example, you may have seen billboards or television advertisements telling you about the benefits of being physically active. Pamphlets and brochures may have been distributed on your campus with information about how to become more physically active. Your doctor may even have told you to start an exercise program. But do these strategies work? In this chapter, we describe and evaluate the effectiveness of different approaches that have been used to try to increase people's physical activity levels.

Physical Activity Interventions—An Overview

Effective interventions are developed by making use of theory- and research-based knowledge about the determinants of physical activity. Interventions do not *directly* change behavior, but they modify one or more physical activity determinants, which in turn can increase physical activity. For example, given that several theories conceptualize perceived benefits and barriers to be important determinants of exercise (e.g., theory of planned behavior, transtheoretical model), one intervention strategy might be to teach people to recognize more benefits of exercise and fewer barriers. A change in perceived benefits and barriers would be expected to have a subsequent effect on exercise. It should be noted that interventions that change theory- and research-based determinants of activity might not always be as effective as desired, but they should be more effective than approaches that attempt to alter factors that have not been shown to influence physical activity (Sallis & Owen, 1998).

Because so many different types of physical activity interventions exist, it is helpful to have a strategy to organize and classify them. In 2002, a team of experts conducted a comprehensive review of all studies of physical activity interventions that had been published to that point (Kahn, Ramsey, Brownson, et al., 2002). For each study, they identified the determinants of physical activity purportedly influenced by the intervention. This information was used to classify the interventions as using one of the following four approaches:

informational approaches ■
behavioral approaches ■
social approaches ■
environmental and policy approaches ■

1. **Informational approaches** to change knowledge and attitudes about the benefits of and opportunities for physical activity
2. **Behavioral approaches** to teach people the behavioral management skills necessary for both successful adoption and maintenance of behavior change
3. **Social approaches** to create social environments that facilitate and enhance behavior change
4. **Environmental and policy approaches** to change the structure of physical and organizational environments to provide safe, attractive, and convenient places for physical activity

Exhibit 6.1 shows the four intervention approaches and the determinants of physical activity that they are hypothesized to influence. In subsequent sections, we describe the approaches in further detail and provide examples of activity interventions that use each one.

However, before interventions can take place, the potential recipients should be open to the idea of becoming more physically active. If individuals are not even ready to *think* about changing, then it is unlikely that an intervention will affect their behavior. Motivational interviewing is one technique that can be used to help people become more receptive to physical activity interventions.

Motivational Interviewing

Often, people who don't exercise have mixed feelings about becoming more active. On the one hand, they may know that exercise is good for them and has many positive physical and psychological benefits. On the other hand, however, they may see the benefits of not exercising (e.g., more time to take care of household tasks or watch TV) and may worry about the

Four intervention approaches and the determinants of physical activity they influence. **exhibit 6.1**

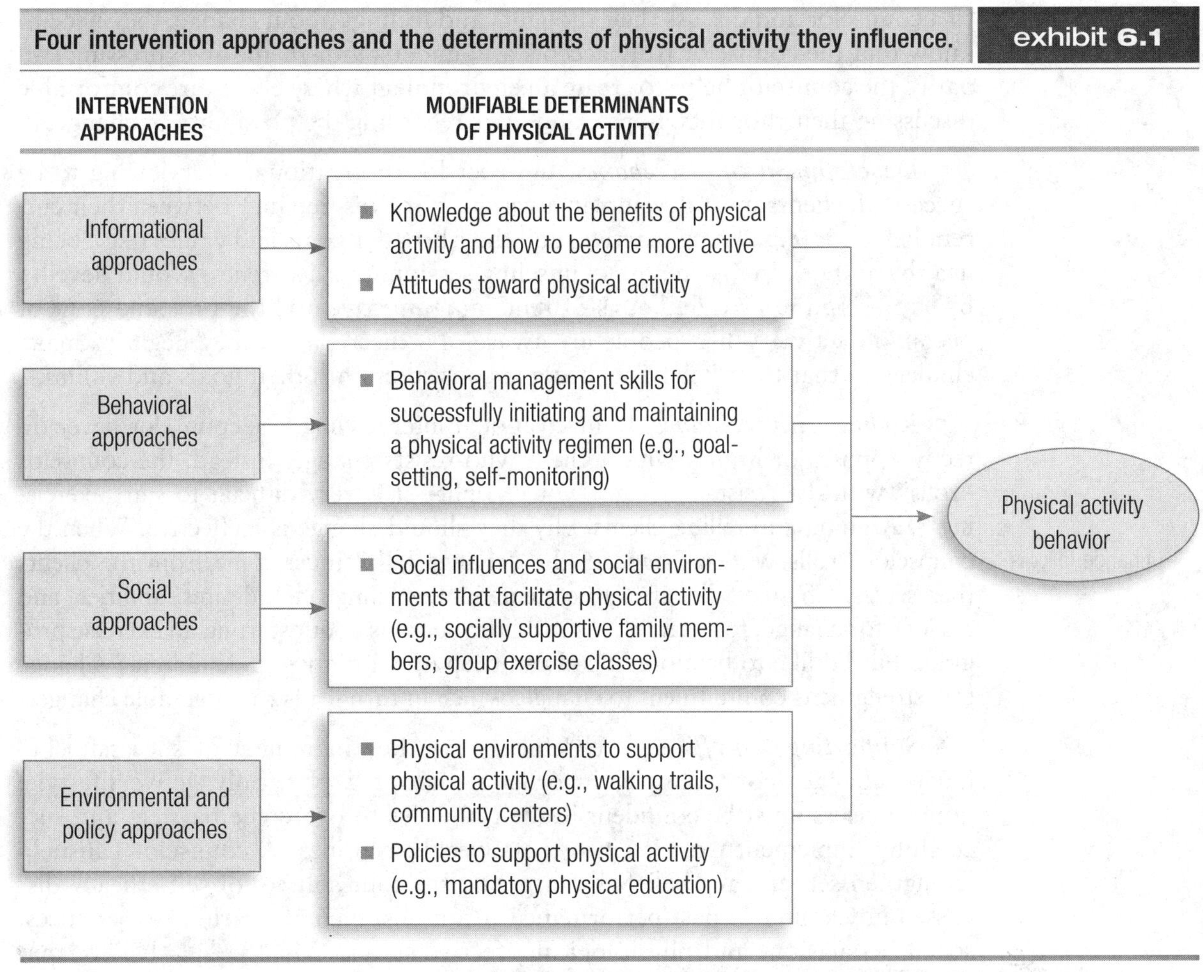

downsides of exercise (e.g., feelings of pain and discomfort). Unfortunately, when attempts are made to persuade ambivalent nonexercisers about the benefits of exercise, they can become even more committed to their arguments against exercise and more resistant to change. **Motivational interviewing** is a counseling technique that provides people with the opportunity to talk about and resolve their mixed feelings so that they can move forward with change (Miller & Rollnick, 2002; Rollnick, Miller, & Butler, 2008). The technique was originally developed as a method to decrease alcohol and drug abuse, but it has since been shown effective for increasing physical activity (Martins & McNeil, 2009).

■ motivational interviewing

In motivational interviewing, the counselor's role is to help the client strengthen his or her intrinsic motivation for change and to provide information on how to change (Miller, 1983). Four basic principles are used to strengthen intrinsic motivation:

■ empathy

■ *Expressions of empathy.* **Empathy** refers to the ability to identify with another person and understand his or her feelings. In order for clients to open up fully to a counselor and discuss their thoughts and feelings about change, they need to know that the counselor truly accepts and understands them. By expressing empathy, the counselor helps to create an environment where clients are comfortable discussing their thoughts, hopes, and fears regarding the possibility of change.

■ *Development of discrepancy.* In order for motivational interviewing to be successful, clients must develop an awareness of a discrepancy between their current behavior (e.g., being inactive) and their broader goals and values (e.g., being healthy and fit). In an exercise counseling session, this awareness would develop by exploring the pros and cons of remaining inactive and the pros and cons of becoming active. When people are aware of a discrepancy, they begin to make changes so that their behaviors become consistent with their goals and values.

■ *Rolling with resistance.* In motivational interviewing, the counselor never directly opposes or argues with a client who resists change. Instead, the counselor "rolls" with the resistance (e.g., "you're right—it is very difficult to start exercising"). Arguing and telling clients why they should change is ineffective. When the counselor "rolls with resistance," the "**change talk**" must come from the clients themselves. Change talk refers to statements regarding one's desires, abilities, and reasons for change; for example, "I'm a little nervous about starting an exercise program, but I'd like to be more fit so I can keep up with my grandchildren." Change talk strengthens commitment to change, which in turn leads to observable change.

change talk ■

■ *Supporting self-efficacy.* Self-efficacy is a key ingredient of successful behavior change. For example, in order to adopt a physically active lifestyle, nonexercisers must be confident in their abilities to overcome barriers and successfully implement exercise into their weekly routines. A counselor can help strengthen self-efficacy beliefs by targeting the four sources of self-efficacy discussed in Chapter 3: past performance accomplishments, vicarious experiences, social persuasion, and physiological/affective states. When people believe that they can change, they are more motivated to change.

Once the client is ready to initiate change, the counselor's next step is to provide information on how to change. However, a defining characteristic of motivational interviewing is the presumption that clients know what is best for themselves. The counselor can provide a menu of intervention approaches (e.g., informational, behavioral), but it is up to the client to decide what will work best.

Now, let's take a closer look at the four types of intervention approaches.

Informational Approaches to Increasing Physical Activity

Despite the best efforts of science, government, educational institutions, and the media, many people still are not aware of the benefits of exercise, why they should value physical activity, or how to start an activity program. Informational approaches are designed to increase physical activity by providing people with the information they need to motivate themselves to exercise and to change their behavior over the short and long term. Generally, informational approaches aim to achieve at least one of the following goals:

- provide information about the benefits of physical activity
- arouse fear or concern about the risks of inactivity
- increase awareness of opportunities for physical activity
- explain techniques to overcome barriers to activity
- provide strategies to overcome negative attitudes toward activity

Provision of this information is expected to influence cognitive determinants of physical activity—such as self-efficacy, attitudes, and perceived behavioral control. In turn, changes in these cognitions are expected to lead to changes in actual physical activity behavior (see Chapters 3 and 4). Three specific types of interventions that use an informational approach are (1) mass media campaigns, (2) community-wide campaigns, and (3) point of decision prompts.

Mass Media Campaigns

Mass media campaigns are interventions that reach people using some medium other than personal contact with a health professional or provider. They offer a means for reaching large numbers of people that is less expensive than face-to-face services (Marcus, Owen, Forsyth, et al., 1998). Physical activity campaigns have been delivered through virtually every type of medium, including broadcast media (television and radio), print-based materials (e.g., pamphlets and posters), audiovisual materials (e.g., PowerPoint presentations, DVD and videotaped information programs), and, of course, the Internet. Some media campaigns have used very simple messages to motivate people, such as Nike's classic "Just Do It!" slogan. Other campaigns have disseminated more extensive information about exercise benefits, opportunities, and activities, such as Health Canada's "Get Active Your Way Every Day—For Life" campaign (www.phac-aspc.gc.ca/hp=ps/hl=msv/pag=gap/start-commence-eng.php), which aims to educate individuals on the appropriate types and amounts of exercise for people of different ages and to provide information on how beginners can start a physical activity program.

■ mass media campaigns

Effectiveness

Mass media campaigns are generally well remembered by the people who see them. A review of mass media interventions (Marcus et al., 1998) found that, on average, 70 percent of people surveyed were able to recall media messages promoting physical activity such as "Exercise: make it part of your day" (Booth, Bauman, Oldenburg, et al., 1992) and "Exercise: take another step" (Owen, Bauman, Booth, et al., 1995). When it comes to increasing physical activity behavior, however, mass media campaigns fall short. In three separate comprehensive reviews of mass media interventions conducted to date, experts have concluded that mass media interventions alone are not effective for increasing physical activity or improving fitness; this is because, in part, they do not provide adequate or sufficient information to help inactive people start an exercise program (Brawley, 1993; Kahn, Ramsey, Brownson, et al., 2002; Marcus et al., 1998).

Drawbacks

Mass media interventions can be considerably expensive, given the costs associated with producing and disseminating newspaper, television, and radio advertisements, and with delivering mailed information to large segments of the population. Furthermore, many intervention materials do not even reach their target audience. For example, people often change the channel during television commercials, health information that arrives in the mail is often thrown out with the other "junk mail" before it is read, and it can be difficult to find credible, usable physical activity advice on the Internet. Nevertheless, as we will see next, mass media interventions might be effective when they are combined with other types of informational interventions to create community-wide campaigns.

Community-Wide Campaigns

community-wide campaigns ■

Community-wide campaigns are interventions that engage different community members and organizations in the development and delivery of information aimed at increasing physical activity. In addition to conveying information through mass-media channels, community-wide campaigns employ a variety of interventions to deliver physical activity information. Examples of these intervention activities include the following:

health risk appraisals ■

■ *Conducting health risk appraisals.* **Health risk appraisals** provide opportunities within the community for people to be screened, without cost, for diseases such as diabetes or cardiovascular disease (CVD). For example, many drugstores have a device that measures people's blood pressure and provides them with immediate feedback about their level of CVD risk. Many workplaces routinely hold "screening days" when employees can have their health risk appraised by a nurse. It is hypothesized that if people are told that they are at increased risk for a particular disease, this information will motivate them to change their health habits, such as increase their level of exercise.

fitness appraisals ■

■ *Conducting fitness appraisals.* Fitness clubs often use informational interventions to motivate people to buy a gym membership. Similar to health risk appraisals, **fitness appraisals** are designed to provide people with personalized information about their level of fitness. The rationale behind this intervention is that people will be motivated to exercise when they learn how unfit they are.

■ *Physician counseling.* Physicians within a community can be trained to provide patients with exercise prescriptions, individually tailored physical activity interventions, and information on local fitness programs. Because physicians are credible, key sources of health information, they can be particularly persuasive in encouraging people to be active.

- *Community health and wellness fairs.* Health and wellness fairs provide a relaxed, informal environment for people to obtain physical activity information. Fairs can be staged virtually anywhere, including worksites, shopping centers, universities, and local sporting events. Information can be disseminated through a variety of mediums including pamphlets, DVDs, PowerPoint presentations, and face-to-face counseling.

Effectiveness

Kahn and her colleagues' (2002) systematic review of published studies of community-wide informational interventions concluded that these interventions are an effective means for increasing

- the percentage of people in a community who are active
- energy expenditure
- the amount of time people spend being physically active

Specifically, looking at the median level of change across all of the reviewed community intervention studies, it was found that community-wide campaigns resulted in a 5 percent increase in the proportion of people who were physically active and a 16 percent increase in energy expenditure. Admittedly, this degree of change is not huge, but it is a trend in the right direction. Given that a 10 percent reduction in physical inactivity in a population can translate into a significant reduction in population disease burden and health care costs (Katzmarzyk, Gledhill, & Shephard, 2000), even relatively small improvements in community-wide activity levels can be of considerable significance.

Drawbacks

Despite the potential effectiveness of community-wide information interventions, they do have some drawbacks. Community-wide interventions require careful planning and coordination, well-trained staff, and sufficient resources to carry out the campaign as planned. Without sufficient resources, the interventions may not reach enough people in the community and the information may not be delivered in sufficient "doses" to change people's knowledge, attitudes, or behavior (Kahn et al., 2002). Furthermore, the success of community interventions is often heavily dependent on the extent to which influential members of the community "buy into" the intervention and provide support for it. For example, some community physical activity interventionists have reported difficulty obtaining the participation of doctors, teachers, and other important community members who can play an influential role in conveying physical activity information to large segments of the community (Estabrooks, Bradshaw, Fox, et al., 2004; Pate, Saunders, Ward, et al., 2003).

FOCUS on Type 2 Diabetes

In 2009, the World Health Organization estimated that, worldwide, more than 220 million people have diabetes. By 2030, this figure is expected to double. Of those with diabetes, approximately 10 percent have type 1 diabetes and the remainder have type 2. With type 1 diabetes, the body makes too little or no insulin. With type 2 diabetes, the body cannot use the insulin that it makes. As a result, glucose builds up in the blood; over time, this can lead to a variety of secondary health problems including blindness, heart disease, and kidney problems (Canadian Diabetes Association, 2004). Type 2 diabetes used to be thought of as an adult concern, but, due to obesity, poor nutrition, and physical inactivity, children as young as eight years are now being diagnosed with type 2 diabetes.

In order to prevent the onset of diabetes-related complications, people with type 2 diabetes need to live a healthy lifestyle that includes following a balanced diet, maintaining a healthy body weight, and engaging in regular physical activity. Unfortunately, because of other competing health care priorities, people with diabetes seldom receive physical activity counseling from their physician or diabetes education programs (McKay, King, Eakin, et al., 2001). Recognizing this shortcoming in diabetes care, Kirk and her colleagues (Kirk, Mutrie, MacIntyre, & Fisher, 2003) examined the effectiveness of an exercise counseling intervention to increase physical activity among sedentary people with type 2 diabetes. Measures of physical activity, glycemic control, and cardiovascular disease risk were assessed in a sample of 70 people who were then randomly assigned to an experimental or control condition. Participants in both conditions received a pamphlet that provided basic information on exercise and its benefits for people with diabetes. Only those participants in the experimental condition received exercise counseling, which consisted of a single 30-minute, one-on-one session with a member of the research team. During the consultation, each participant's stage of change was identified, and stage-matched strategies and techniques were provided to help each person accumulate 30 minutes of moderate physical activity on most days of the week. Six months later, study participants were reassessed.

The investigators found that the group who received the exercise consultation reported significant increases in moderate and total activity per week. Specifically, they reported a median increase of 128 minutes of moderate activity and 153 minutes of total activity per week. The control group reported no significant changes in activity. The experimental group also experienced significant improvements in glycemic control and cardiovascular disease risk factors, whereas the control group showed no change on these dimensions.

These results are very encouraging. They show that a fairly simple, inexpensive intervention can increase physical activity and produce important health benefits among people with type 2 diabetes. The study authors emphasize that, with training, this simple intervention could be conducted by any member of a diabetes care team; they suggest that exercise consultation become a standard component of diabetes care.

ADDITIONAL RESOURCES

Levesque, L., Guilbault, G., Delormier, T., & Potvin, L. (2005). Unpacking the black box: A deconstruction of the programming approach and physical activity interventions implemented in the Kahnawake Schools Diabetes Prevention Project. *Health Promotion and Practice, 6,* 64–71.

Toobert, D.J., Strycker, L.A., Glasgow, R.E., Barrera, M., & Bagdade, J.D. (2004). Enhancing support for health behavior change among women at risk for heart disease: The Mediterranean Lifestyle Trial. *Health Education Research, 17,* 574–585.

Tudor-Locke, C., Bell, R.C., Myers, A.M., Harris, S.B., Ecclestone, N.A., Lauzon, N., & Rodger, N.W. (2004). Controlled outcome evaluation of the First Step Program: A daily physical activity intervention for individuals with type II diabetes. *International Journal of Obesity and Related Metabolic Disorders, 28,* 113–119.

World Health Organization (2009, Nov.). Fact Sheet No. 312, Diabetes. Accessed from www.who.int/mediacentre/factsheets/fs312/en.

ACTIVITY

The studies highlighted here describe a variety of intervention approaches that have been used to try to increase physical activity in people who have or are at risk for type 2 diabetes.

1. Make a list of all of the intervention techniques described in the studies. Then, for each technique, indicate the physical activity determinant being targeted.
2. Make a list of all of the theories and models that were used in the studies. Then, drawing from all of the studies, provide examples of intervention techniques that use the principles of these theories and models.
3. Read the article by Levesque and colleagues (2005), cited in the Additional Resources section, and identify the strategies they used to culturally tailor (see pp. 148–149) their interventions. Choose another cultural group and indicate how you would apply these strategies to make the intervention culturally appropriate for that target group.

Point-of-Decision Prompts

■ point-of-decision prompts

Point-of-decision prompts involve placing a sign at points where people must choose between taking the elevator or escalator versus walking up the stairs, such as in shopping malls, parking garages, train stations, libraries, and other public buildings. The signs typically convey messages about the benefits of stair climbing for health or weight loss, such as "Do your heart a favor, take the stairs" or "Improve your waistline, take the stairs." These messages are believed to be effective either because they inform people about the health benefits of taking the stairs or because they remind people who already want to be more active that they are about to have an opportunity to engage in physical activity (Kahn et al., 2002).

In the seminal study of point-of-decision prompts (Brownell, Stunkard, & Albaum, 1980), researchers placed a prompt at the bottom of an escalator next to a flight of stairs. The prompt consisted of a poster that showed a cartoon healthy heart running up the stairs and an unhealthy heart riding an escalator, with the statement "Your heart needs exercise, here's your chance." The poster was displayed for 15 days. During this period, the proportion of people who took the stairs (instead of the escalator) increased from 11.6 percent to 18.3 percent. One month after the poster was removed, 15.6 percent of people were still taking the stairs; three months after the poster was removed, however, stair use had returned to baseline levels (11.9 percent).

Effectiveness

Researchers have consistently found that more people use the stairs when point-of-decision messages are posted than when such messages are not posted. These messages can increase stair use by about 54 percent in both men and women (Kahn et al., 2002). This is an impressive effect, especially considering how little time, effort, and money it takes to implement a point-of-decision intervention.

Point-of-decision prompts have also been shown to be more effective when their messages are targeted to specific groups of people. For example, one study found that when a sign was posted that linked stair climbing to the potential for weight loss ("Improve your waistline, use the stairs"), obese people were more likely to use the stairs than when a sign was posted that promoted the benefits of stair climbing to heart health ("Your heart needs exercise, use the stairs"; Andersen, Franckowiak, Snyder, et al., 1998). These findings highlight the importance of knowing what benefits of stair use are most valued by particular segments of the population, and then including these benefits in point-of-decision messages.

Interestingly, that same study by Andersen and colleagues showed that the sign was effective for increasing stair use among Caucasians but not African Americans. In a follow-up study, the investigators asked African American men and women to help them design a sign that would promote stair use among African American commuters. Together, they created a sign with the slogan "No time for exercise? Try the stairs!" and a picture of a fit African American woman climbing the stairs. When posted at a subway station, this new sign led to significant increases in stair use among overweight and non-overweight African American men and women (Andersen, Franckowiak, Zuzak, et al., 2006). The results of this study demonstrate that it may also be important to create culturally tailored point-of-decision messages (i.e., messages that take specific cultural characteristics into account) to promote physical activity in minority groups.

Drawbacks

Although point-of-decision prompts are effective, they have several drawbacks. Perhaps their biggest shortcoming is that they are effective only as long as the signs remain posted. Within a couple of weeks after signs are removed, stair use returns to baseline levels (e.g., Brownell et al., 1980). A second drawback is that the effectiveness of the interventions depends on people being able to use the stairways safely. In many buildings, stairways are often difficult to find, poorly lit, or potentially unsafe. And finally, it is not known if people who are prompted to use the stairs subsequently go on to take other opportunities to be physically active in their daily routines. If not, then point-of-decision prompts have limited utility for increasing activity to health-promoting levels.

Developing More Effective Informational Interventions

Adapting or targeting physical activity information to specific populations is an important first step toward making informational interventions more effective. For example, Exhibit 6.2 provides strategies to help target informational interventions to specific cultural groups (i.e., **cultural tailoring**). When people identify with, or relate to, the messages being presented, they are more likely to spend time processing the information; this in turn increases the likelihood that they will remember and act on the information (Cacioppo & Petty, 1984). Once a specific target population has been selected to receive the informational intervention (e.g., minority cultural groups, people at risk for heart disease, older adults, mothers with young children), interventionists can create more effective informational campaigns by adhering to the following guidelines, as outlined by Brawley (1993) and Olson and Zanna (1987):

cultural tailoring ■

1. *Messages should emphasize* specific, *positive consequences of exercise (rather than general consequences) that are personally meaningful to members of the target population.* For example, informational interventions targeting new mothers would likely be more effective if they emphasized the weight loss, stress-reduction, and social benefits of exercise than if they simply referred to the generic benefits of exercise such as a decreased risk of cardiovascular disease and improvements in physical fitness. Chapter 1 discusses a number of more commonly acknowledged benefits of physical activity (see Exhibit 1.2) that would

exhibit 6.2

Strategies to use cultural tailoring with various physical activity informational interventions.

STRATEGIES	DESCRIPTION	EXAMPLES
Design strategies	Materials are presented in ways that convey their relevance to the target group and make them more appealing to that group. This could involve using certain colors, symbols, titles, images, or photos that express the social and cultural world of the target audience.	A brochure targeting Aboriginal people in Canada might be titled "Physical Activity Tips for Aboriginal Canadians" and feature photos of Aboriginals participating in traditional sports and games.
Evidential strategies	Information is presented to enhance the perceived relevance of physical activity, or inactivity, for a particular group. Data are presented showing the impact of physical activity/inactivity on people within that group in order to raise awareness, concern, and perceived vulnerability.	Campaigns to increase physical activity among African Americans could include statements like "In the United States, obesity, hypertension, and diabetes are more common among Blacks than among Whites and other groups. Physical inactivity is a risk factor for each of these conditions, but it can be modified."
Linguistic strategies	Information is presented in the dominant or native language of the target group.	Mandarin- and Cantonese-language billboards could be raised in the predominantly Chinese neighborhoods located in several English-speaking cities (e.g., San Francisco, Toronto, London). These billboards would emphasize the benefits of physical activity.
Constituent-involving strategies	Information is delivered by members of the target group.	Community-wide campaigns to increase physical activity among Hispanic men and women could employ Hispanic nurses, educators, and public health officials to conduct risk factor screening sessions and wellness fairs.
Sociocultural strategies	Information is presented in the context of broader social and/or cultural values and characteristics of the target group. Using this approach, the group's cultural values, beliefs, and behaviors provide context and meaning to information that is given about physical activity and its benefits.	For a group that places a high value on religion, information about the importance of physical activity can be presented within the context of scriptures, or other sacred writings, that emphasize the importance of taking care of one's body.

Source: Adapted from Kreuter, Lukwago, Bucholtz, et al. (2003).

be meaningful for various populations. Information about these benefits can modify attitudes (theory of planned behavior, theory of reasoned action) and intrinsic motives for exercise (self-determination theory), and can increase the number of perceived benefits or "pros" of exercise (transtheoretical model).

2. *Messages should describe* how *to minimize the negative personal consequences of exercise.* For example, new mothers might be concerned that exercise will be too time consuming and will require them to spend lots of time away from their babies. Informational materials could explain that physical activity can be done with their children (e.g., going for a brisk walk while pushing a stroller) or that just 20 minutes of exercise, by themselves, can be a valuable "time-out" that leaves them feeling refreshed, rejuvenated, and re-energized to take care of an infant. This type of information is geared toward changing perceived barriers to exercise, which in turn can influence theoretical determinants of exercise including attitudes and the number of perceived "cons" of exercising.

3. *Messages should create social pressure to exercise.* They should indicate that family members, doctors, community groups, employers, and others encourage exercise. For some people, this information could have an impact on exercise behavior through its influence on subjective norms (theory of planned behavior, theory of reasoned action) and extrinsic forms of motivation (self-determination theory).

4. *Messages should enhance people's beliefs that they have control over their physical activity behavior.* This might be accomplished by explaining how activity can fit into various lifestyles, describing different types of activity, and teaching people how to make sure that they do not work too intensely for their current fitness level. Many people think that the only way to become more physically active is to take up high-intensity activities such as jogging or aerobics—activities for which they lack self-efficacy and that they might find aversive. When people are given information about moderate activities they can do for health benefits, such as walking, dancing, or playing with their children, and when they are taught how to monitor the intensity of these activities by checking their pulse or breathing rates, this information could alter two important determinants of exercise—self-efficacy and perceived behavioral control.

5. *Messages should provide simple but detailed information about how to start an activity program.* This information might consist of maps showing local trails along with tips for starting a walking program, or a schedule of activities at local community centers. Providing "how to" information ensures that once people are motivated to become more active, they have the knowledge to carry through with their good intentions.

These are all important steps toward creating informational interventions that maximize people's awareness of the value of physical activity and their knowledge of how to become more physically active. Yet while awareness and knowledge are important, people often need more than just information in order to make meaningful changes to their behavior (Conn, Hafdahl, Brown, & Brown, 2008). As such, behavioral interventions are a crucial adjunct to informational interventions.

Behavioral Approaches to Increasing Physical Activity

ehavioral interventions aim to increase physical activity by teaching people behavioral skills that will help them initiate and maintain an activity program. In general, these skills involve:

- recognizing cues and opportunities for physical activity
- developing strategies to maintain activity levels
- learning to recognize and manage situations that can sabotage activity plans
- developing strategies to prevent relapse to a sedentary lifestyle

Typically, these skills are taught through some form of counseling intervention—either one-on-one counseling with an exercise or other health expert, or counseling in small groups. The intervention is tailored to specific characteristics of the clients, such as their physical activity preferences, physical limitations, or readiness for change. During the intervention, clients are taught a variety of behavioral techniques to help them begin and maintain an activity regimen. In addition to modifying clients' behavior, these techniques can also influence theoretical determinants of exercise such as perceived barriers, self-efficacy, and exercise motives. Exercise contracts, goal setting, developing action plans and implementation intentions, self-monitoring, and relapse prevention are some examples of commonly used behavioral techniques.

Establishing an Exercise Contract

■ exercise contract

An **exercise contract** specifically describes the amount of exercise to which a person will commit and may also include the promise of a positive reinforcer for fulfilling the contract. As mentioned in Chapter 4, providing reinforcers following successful behavior (contingent rewards) increases the likelihood that the behavior will be repeated in the future. Exhibit 6.3 shows a sample exercise contract. A contract imparts a sense of commitment to exercise and, further, serves as a reminder and an extrinsic motivator to exercise. For example, in a study of patients in a cardiac rehabilitation exercise program (Oldridge & Jones, 1983), those who were asked and who agreed to sign an exercise contract attended more exercise sessions over a 6-month period than those who were not asked to sign a contract or those who were asked to sign a contract but refused to do so.

Goal-Setting

■ goal-setting

Goal-setting is a process that involves assessing one's current level of fitness or performance; creating a specific, measurable, realistic, and challenging goal for one's future level of fitness or performance; and detailing the actions to be taken

exhibit 6.3 Sample exercise contract.

Contract start date: 1/3/11 Award date: 6/1/11

In order to obtain my goal of improving my cardiovascular endurance (increase $\dot{V}O_2$max by 10%) and lose weight (10 pounds), I will

(a) walk one mile through my neighborhood daily after dinner and

(b) ride the stationary bike three times per week (30 mins, 70% of maximum heart rate).

As a reward for accomplishing this goal by the award date shown above, I will be entitled to a shopping spree to purchase all-new exercise attire and equipment (e.g., winter outdoor exercise wear, electronic pedometer, stationary bicycle for home).

Signed Kevin Kelly Date 1/2/11

in order to achieve that goal. Locke and Latham's goal-setting theory (2002) specifies several key ingredients of effective goal-setting:

1. *Goals should be challenging yet realistic.* Goals that are too easy to attain offer minimal reward; goals that are too difficult (or worse, unrealistic) often lead to feelings of failure and, ultimately, poor exercise adherence rates.
2. *Goals should be very specific.* Goals that specify a particular behavioral target (e.g., "my goal is to exercise three times per week for the next six months") are always better than more general goals (e.g., "my goal is to stick to an exercise program for as long as possible") because they provide a defined objective that is more easily quantified and evaluated.
3. *Exercisers should receive feedback regarding progress toward the goal.* The **goal-setting worksheet** in Exhibit 6.4 provides a place for exercisers to record daily progress notes. These notes provide feedback that can be used to indicate whether exercisers are getting closer to their goals or if they need to increase effort in order to reach the goal. Feedback is also crucial to determining when goals have been achieved and when it is time to set new goals.

goal-setting worksheet ■

Although a helpful strategy for even the most advanced exerciser, goal-setting is particularly important during the early adoption stage of exercise. This is because, while the "costs" associated with exercise are often experienced immediately or soon after beginning a physical activity regimen (e.g., soreness, fatigue), many of the desired benefits (e.g., enhanced fitness and appearance) typically are not realized until weeks or even months later. Therefore, it is suggested that exercisers also divide their long-term goals into short-term and intermediate goals that can be met along the way to attaining their ultimate objectives. This will maintain or increase commitment and motivation until the final goal is met. For example, one of the goals in Exhibit 6.4 is a loss of 10 pounds in five months. A short-term goal might be to lose one pound after two weeks and an intermediate goal might be to lose five pounds in two months.

Developing Action Plans and Implementation Intentions

Although many people have good intentions to exercise, they often fail to develop a plan of action to help them follow through with their intentions and achieve their exercise goals. For example, people often make New Year's resolutions to exercise more often, but they rarely devise specific plans for doing so. **Action planning** entails forming concrete plans that specify when, where, and how a person will translate exercise intentions into action. For instance, a college student might develop the action plan of exercising Mondays, Wednesdays, and Fridays at noon, at the campus gym, by running on a treadmill for 30 minutes at 70 percent of his maximum heart rate. In a similar vein, **implementation intentions** involve developing a strong mental association between a situational cue and a specific behavior (Gollwitzer, 1999). The exerciser identifies a particular cue and specifies what will occur when that cue is encountered. For example, that same college student might program his mobile phone to play the *Rocky* theme on Mondays, Wednesdays, and Fridays at noon. His implementation intention would be "when I hear the Rocky theme, then I will go to the gym."

- action planning
- implementation intentions

Sample goal-setting worksheet. **exhibit 6.4**

Contract start date: 1/2/11 Award date: 6/1/11

Goal defined: To improve my cardiovascular endurance ($\dot{V}O_2$max) by 10% and lose weight (10 pounds)

Strategies to achieve goals: (a) walk neighborhood daily after dinner (1 mi) (b) ride stationary bike three times per week (30 min, 70% max heart rate)

Daily progress notes: 1/4/11 – walked after dinner; no bike today; weighed myself at 7:00 a.m. – no change from 2 days ago
1/6/11 – walked after dinner yesterday and today; biked during lunch hour but only made it 20 mins, heart rate around 80% max; lost a pound since 1/4

Self-Monitoring

self-monitoring ■ **Self-monitoring** simply refers to paying attention to one's own thoughts, feelings, and behaviors, and gauging these against a standard. There are at least two aspects of exercise behavior that people should be taught to self-monitor. The first is their level of exercise intensity. One way in which people can monitor their intensity level is to use the **rating of perceived exertion (RPE) scale.** Developed by Gunnar Borg, the rating of perceived exertion scale is a subjective measure of exercise intensity (Borg, 1998). This scale (see Exhibit 6.5) ranges from 6 to 20; each value multiplied

rating of perceived exertion (RPE) scale ■

exhibit 6.5 The Borg–RPE Scale.®

THE SCALE

6	No exertion at all
7	
	Extremely light
8	
9	Very light
10	
11	Light
12	
13	Somewhat hard
14	
15	Hard (heavy)
16	
17	Very hard
18	
19	Extremely hard
20	Maximal exertion

Instructions to the Borg-RPE Scale®

During the work we want you to rate your perception of exertion, i.e., how heavy and strenuous the exercise feels to you and how tired you are. The perception of exertion is mainly felt as strain and fatigue in your muscles and as breathlessness, or aches in the chest. All work requires some effort, even if this is only minimal. This is true also if you only move a little, e.g., walking slowly.

Use this scale from 6 to 20, with 6 meaning "No exertion at all" and 20 meaning "maximal exertion."

6 "No exertion at all" means that you don't feel any exertion whatsoever, e.g., no muscle fatigue, no breathlessness or difficulties breathing.

9 "Very light" exertion, as taking a shorter walk at your own pace.

13 A "somewhat hard" work, but it still feels OK to continue.

15 It is "hard" and tiring, but continuing isn't terribly difficult.

17 "Very hard." This is very strenuous work. You can still go on, but you really have to push yourself and you are very tired.

19 An "extremely" strenuous level. For most people this is the most strenuous work they have ever experienced.

Try to appraise your feeling of exertion and fatigue as spontaneously and as honestly as possible, without thinking about what the actual physical load is. Try not to underestimate and not to overestimate your exertion. It's your own feeling of effort and exertion that is important, not how this compares with other people's. Look at the scale and the expressions and then give a number. Use any number you like on the scale, not just one of those with an explanation behind it.

Any questions?

Note: For correct usage of the scale, the exact design and instructions given in Borg's folders must be followed.

Author's note: The Borg-RPE scale and instructions are reprinted exactly from copyrighted material, with permission.

by 10 would approximate one's heart rate at that particular point in time during or immediately following the exercise bout. For example, if we ask an individual to indicate the value according to the RPE scale that she feels best describes her current exercise exertion level (i.e., how hard she feels she is working), and she reports it to be 14, we would expect that she is exercising at approximately 140 heart beats per minute (14 x 10 = 140). Although the ability of the RPE scale to accurately reflect heart rate in this manner has been questioned, the scale is, nonetheless, a valid and reliable means of determining a person's subjective rating of exertion level. Furthermore, after training individuals on the proper use of the scale, we can use an RPE value or range of values to designate the intensity at which a client or group of clients should be active. (For more information, go to www.borgproducts.com.)

In general, most people who are just starting an exercise program should avoid high-intensity physical activity. If nothing ensures continued behavior like success, then nothing ensures exercise drop-out like the immediate experiences of muscle soreness, fatigue, and injury, all of which serve to decrease self-efficacy and to heighten the perceived cons of exercise. To avoid these negative experiences, novice exercisers should start out at a relatively low intensity and be taught how to self-monitor and measure their heart and respiration rates (e.g., by taking their pulse, checking whether they can maintain a conversation while exercising). This promotes perceived control over their exercise behavior and may help to prevent overexertion and injury.

The second aspect of exercise that people should monitor is their daily physical activity behavior. Exhibit 6.6 provides an example of an **activity log**

■ activity log

Sample seven-day activity log. **exhibit 6.6**

DATE	MODE	DISTANCE	TIME	MY HEART RATE
7/19	Jog	2.0 mi.	16:20	156
7/20	Jog	2.0 mi.	15:47	154
	Swim	15 lengths	7:19	161
7/21	Rest			
7/22	Jog	2.5 mi.	21:08	152
7/23	Jog	2.0 mi.	16:53	159
	Swim	20 lengths	10:22	164
7/24	Rest			
7/25	Jog	3.0 mi.	26:59	150

that exercisers might use for that purpose. A typical activity log might contain information about each exercise session, such as the amount of time spent on a particular activity (e.g., strength training, jogging, walking), one's level of performance on that activity (e.g., amount of weight lifted, distance ran, steps walked), and ratings of affect or perceived exertion following the workout. When completed regularly, these logs become invaluable sources of self-efficacy; the exerciser can refer to the log to determine the amount of progress achieved, thus gaining information about mastery experiences.

Relapse Prevention

lapse ■

abstinence violation effect ■

Relapse is the term used when an individual fails to resume regular exercise following a **lapse** in activity. Although the periodical lapse in an exercise regimen is almost inevitable, lapses can become a cause of concern when they lead to relapse back to a sedentary lifestyle. The relapse prevention model (see Exhibit 6.7) specifies that relapse is triggered by high-risk situations—those instances that challenge an individual's ability to maintain his or her behavioral regimen (Marlatt & Gordon, 1985). As shown in the diagram of the model, the individual's coping response to a high-risk situation (i.e., how he or she psychologically/emotionally responds to the situation) dictates the flow of the model. Specifically, as shown on the right side of the diagram, a negative coping response would lead to (1) decreases in exercise self-efficacy, (2) the anticipation of positive consequences of skipping an exercise session such as having more time to finish a project, and (3) an initial exercise lapse. When an initial lapse causes the exerciser to believe that all future hope of behavior change is lost and that the entire exercise regimen may as well be abandoned (the "all or nothing" approach to exercise), this is known as the **abstinence violation effect.** The effect is typically accompanied by a negative emotional response, such as feelings of guilt or shame, and self-attributions for failure (i.e., self-blame). The combination of these, in turn, leads to an increased probability of relapse. In contrast, as shown on the left-hand side of the diagram, when an exerciser demonstrates a positive coping response, exercise self-efficacy is increased and the probability of relapse is reduced.

The following are some strategies that can be taught as part of an intervention to prevent relapse among exercisers (Knapp, 1988; Marlatt & Gordon, 1985).

Identify high-risk thoughts, feelings, and situations that might prompt a lapse

Novice exercisers should keep a diary of the thoughts, feelings, and situations that tempt them to skip a workout or that actually prevent them from working out. High-risk thoughts might include worries about not having enough time to exercise or thoughts about substituting alternative, sedentary activities that are viewed as more appealing than exercise (e.g., going to a movie with friends). High-risk feelings include the sense that one is too tired to exercise

The relapse prevention model in the exercise domain. exhibit 6.7

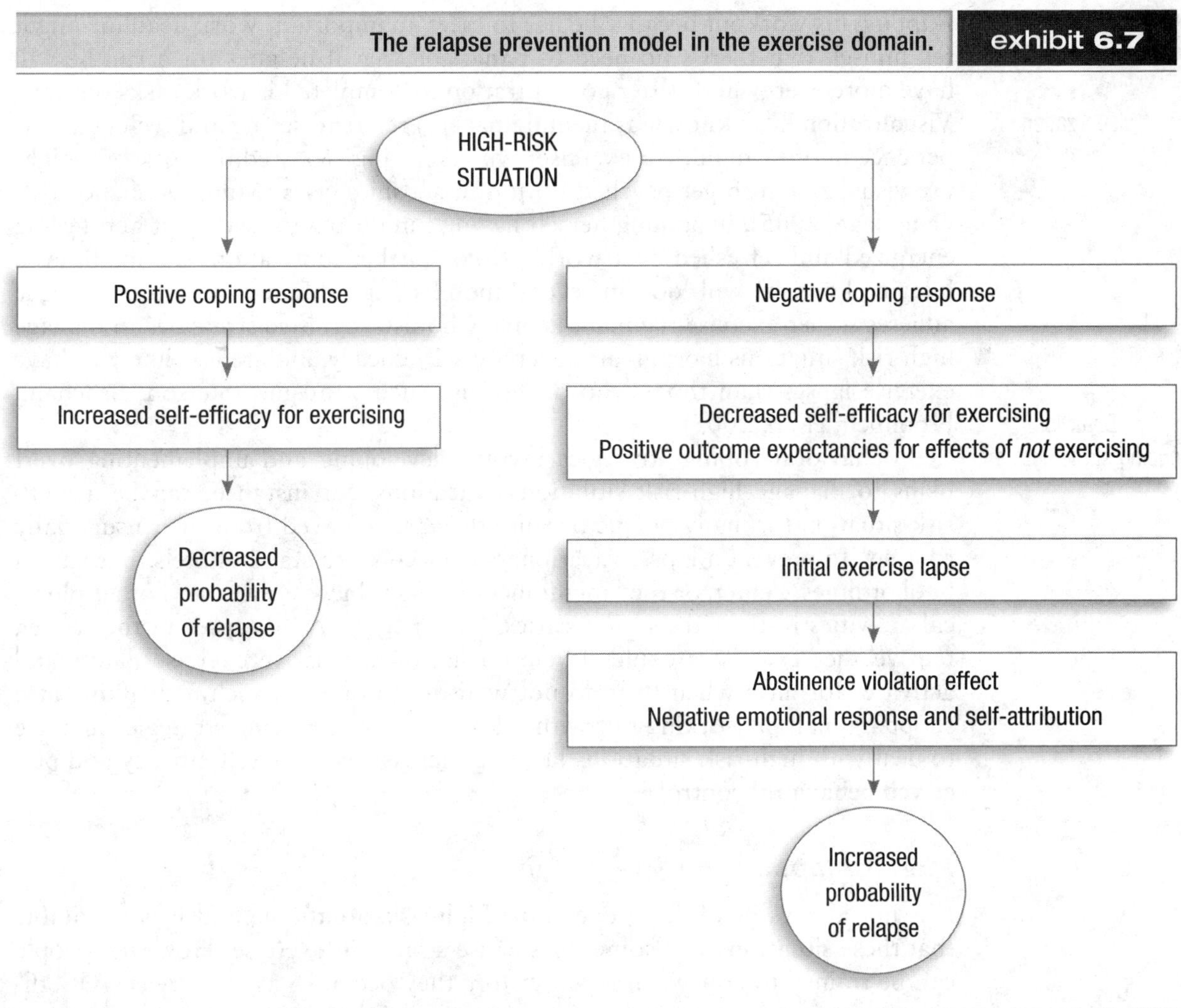

Source: Adapted from Marlatt & George (1984).

or the experience of boredom with one's exercise routine. High-risk situations might include being on vacation and away from one's normal exercise location or experiencing bad weather. By identifying high-risk situations, the exerciser can then focus on trying to avoid those situations and/or developing cognitive and behavioral coping strategies to deal with them as they arise, so they do not prevent exercise in the future.

Cognitive coping strategies involve the use of non–observable thought processes—such as self-talk and visualization—to overcome disruptive thoughts and feelings. **Self-talk** refers to the statements that we make to ourselves and can be used to increase confidence, regulate arousal, and focus effort in order to overcome high-risk situations. For example, an exerciser who is considering

- cognitive coping strategies
- self-talk

skipping his workout because he has to meet an important work deadline might tell himself that there's no need to panic and that if he goes for a run he will have more energy and better concentration to complete his work tasks on time.

visualization ■ **Visualization** (also known as mental imagery) refers to seeing and feeling an experience in one's mind. An exerciser who is feeling too tired to work out might use visualization to get psyched up for an aerobics class (Munroe-Chandler & Gammage, 2005), imagining herself having fun during the workout and feeling energized and refreshed post-workout. For further motivation, she might even imagine how she will look in several months (e.g., thinner, more toned) if she adheres to her exercise regimen. People who use cognitive strategies to manage high-risk situations have greater exercise self-efficacy and are less likely to have exercise lapses than those who do not use such strategies (Stetson, Beacham, Frommelt, et al., 2005).

Behavioral coping strategies ■ **Behavioral coping strategies** involve developing and implementing overt plans to manage high-risk situations. Vacations, for instance, can be a high-risk situation for many people because they are removed from their usual daily routine. To prevent a lapse, vacationers could plan to stay in hotels that have a pool or fitness center, or they might include hikes, bicycle rides, and other physical activities in their travel itineraries. Similarly, to avoid lapses in the winter, fair-weather exercisers could develop a list of alternative exercise places and activities for days when they do not want to go outside, such as walking at a shopping mall or working out with a DVD at home. Having strategies in place to deal with high-risk situations helps to increase exercise self-efficacy and perceived behavioral control.

Plan for lapses

It is not always possible to overcome high-risk situations, and it is inevitable that these situations will sometimes cause a lapse in exercise. However, people can be trained to cope with lapses *before* they occur, so as to increase self-efficacy for returning to exercise after the lapse and thereby preventing a complete relapse. For instance, a novice exerciser might plan ahead for a lapse by identifying an exercise buddy who can be called on after a lapse and who will help the exerciser "get back on the right track" by taking him or her for a walk, bike ride, and so on.

Minimize the abstinence violation effect

cognitive restructuring ■ Exercisers can be taught strategies that will help them cope with the despair they experience when they violate their intention to exercise regularly. One strategy is **cognitive restructuring,** which involves changing how one thinks about a lapse. For example, rather than considering a lapse to be a catastrophe, exercisers should be taught to think of lapses as a normal and inevitable part of the exercise process—something that they can learn from and plan to deal with in the future. Likewise, "all or nothing" thinkers might be encouraged to be more flexible with their exercise goals. For instance, if an exercise session is skipped, the individual could allow himself to "make up" the missed session by adding an exercise session the following week or by adding more time to the next session. Planning ahead for exercise lapses helps to increase exercisers' self-efficacy for dealing with and overcoming these inevitable occurrences.

Effectiveness

Behavioral interventions are probably the most effective way to increase physical activity. In a meta-analytic review of different types of exercise interventions, behavioral approaches were shown to be nearly five times more effective than any other intervention type (Dishman & Buckworth, 1996). Furthermore, in a review of 18 behavior change programs (Kahn et al., 2002), it was shown that behavioral interventions produced a 35 percent increase in the amount of time people spent being physically active. The people in these programs experienced, on average, a nearly 65 percent increase in their energy expenditure. It is encouraging to note that behavioral interventions have been shown to be effective among both men and women and when conducted in a variety of settings, including schools and worksites. Thus, based on this evidence, behavioral approaches represent a highly effective intervention strategy for increasing people's activity levels.

Drawbacks

A couple of drawbacks to behavioral interventions do exist. One drawback is that well-trained counselors are needed to teach people the various behavioral techniques such as self-monitoring and goal-setting. Thus, the success of a behavioral intervention often hinges on having talented, competent staff to carry it out as planned. Another drawback is that the number of activity counselors is limited compared to the huge numbers of inactive people. One-on-one counseling, and even group counseling, are not particularly expeditious approaches for increasing physical activity levels in vast segments of the population.

Social Approaches to Increasing Physical Activity

Social approaches focus on structuring people's social environments to help support their physical activity endeavors. In Chapter 5, we presented a wide array of individuals and groups that can exert social influence on a person's exercise habits, such as friends, family members, coworkers, and members of fitness clubs and programs. Chapter 5 also described the various types of social support that exercisers use. Social interventions recognize the importance of social influence on people's exercise habits, and they are designed to create new social networks and to strengthen existing networks to ensure that people have the necessary support for maintaining an active lifestyle.

A variety of interventions can be used to improve social environments for exercise. Some interventions are quite simple and can be easily implemented by the exercisers themselves, without cost or any special training or assistance from an outside party such as an exercise instructor or counselor. Other interventions are more complicated and might require financial resources, special facilities, or the assistance of an expert. Some examples of social interventions include establishing exercise groups and buddy systems, teaching people to ask for support, developing telephone support systems, and using group support systems.

Establishing Exercise Groups and Buddy Systems

Perhaps the most basic social intervention is simply to bring together people who want to exercise. As discussed in Chapter 5, people are often more motivated by exercising with other people than by exercising alone. Many people prefer to exercise with a group because they like the social support and structure that an exercise group provides. Exercise groups have been established in countless locations such as worksites, shopping malls, after-school clubs, community centers, hospitals, and churches and other houses of worship. Walking, aerobics, strength-training, jogging, and cycling are just a few of the many activities that have been facilitated by the creation of exercise groups.

exercise buddies ■

As an alternative to joining an exercise group, some people prefer to find one or two exercise buddies. **Exercise buddies** provide one another with multiple types of social support—not just during their workouts when they can motivate and distract one another, but also in-between workouts when exercisers might need help overcoming slips in motivation or self-confidence. A good exercise buddy will listen, empathize, and encourage. People with exercise buddies often report that they are less likely to skip a workout because they know that their buddy is depending on them. They do not want to let their buddy down.

Teaching People to Ask for Support

Many people are uncomfortable asking others for support, either because they fear rejection or because they see the need for help as a sign of personal weakness. Yet everyone needs help from time to time, and most people feel good when they are given the opportunity to assist someone else. Interventionists should encourage exercisers to ask others to support them—such as friends, family members, spouses—and interventionists should provide exercisers with a strategy for requesting support. When asking for support, exercisers should be open and candid, explaining why they are trying to become more active and why it is important for them to have the support of others. Most important, exercisers should be very specific about the type of help they need, such as babysitting for half an hour while they exercise or encouragement to reach their exercise goals (Blair, Dunn, Marcus, et al., 2001).

Developing Telephone Support Systems

Several interventions have included regular telephone calls from an exercise counselor or interventionist as a strategy for increasing and maintaining physical activity levels (Eakin, Lawler, Vandelanotte, & Owen, 2007). Phone calls provide the exerciser with a source of emotional and informational support. Interestingly, the content of the phone calls does not seem to be as important as the frequency of the calls. One study showed that people who received weekly phone calls were far more likely to walk regularly than people who received a call every three weeks, even if the purpose of the call was simply to "touch base" and did not provide any exercise information or tips (Lombard, Lombard, & Winnett, 1995). These findings suggest that the social support provided by a weekly telephone call can be an effective intervention for increasing physical activity.

Using Group Support Systems

Interventions can strengthen social networks and enhance social support among groups of exercisers. For example, meetings can be planned for exercisers to get together and discuss common exercise barriers. Group members can share stories of their failures and triumphs in overcoming barriers. These meetings provide participants with the sense that they are not alone with their exercise struggles, and they give exercisers an opportunity to problem solve with their peers in order to bolster self-efficacy and perceived control. Additionally, exercisers might be encouraged to establish a telephone support network, as noted above, in which group members take turns calling one another to check on their exercise progress. Active outings also provide an opportunity for exercisers to commiserate while being active and perhaps to experience a new type of physical activity. For example, group members might organize a hike or bike ride on an unfamiliar trail, or they might arrange to go rock climbing or snowshoeing. These novel experiences can improve attitudes toward different types of activities, enhance motivation, and strengthen self-efficacy beliefs for performing different activities.

Effectiveness

Most tests of the effectiveness of social approaches to increasing physical activity have consisted of examining the effects of simultaneously delivered, multiple social support interventions, or social support interventions that are delivered along with other behavioral or informational interventions. For example, the study highlighted in Chapter 5, in the Focus on Cardiovascular Disease box, combined several social support interventions—including the establishment of an exercise group, buddy systems, group discussions to provide social support, and group problem solving—with behavioral interventions such as goal-setting and self-monitoring (Rejeski, Brawley, Ambrosius, et al., 2003). People who received this combination of interventions were more physically active and had greater improvements in physical fitness than people who did not receive the intervention. However, it is impossible to know which of the interventions had the biggest impact on people's exercise behavior. This interpretational quandary is typical of studies that have used social support interventions to increase physical activity. Because the social interventions are delivered as part of a package of multiple interventions, conclusions cannot be made about the effectiveness of the individual intervention strategies.

Some data suggest, however, that intervention packages that include social support strategies may be more effective in some situations than others. For example, when social support strategies have been applied to community groups—such as members of a church or people who have joined a community exercise program—and worksites, the results have generally been quite favorable. These interventions have been shown to produce, on average, a 44 percent increase in time spent being physically active and a 20 percent increase in the frequency of physical activity. In contrast, interventions aimed at increasing support for physical activity within families have not consistently led to increases in physical activity behavior (Kahn et al., 2002).

Drawbacks

The primary drawback of social approaches is that their success is contingent on the cooperation of group members. If group members hold grudges against one another, or if they are unwilling to work together, social support interventions are doomed to fail. A primary example of this problem comes from the Active Winners program (Pate et al., 2003), a community-based intervention designed to promote physical activity in fifth-grade students. This well-designed program had multiple informational, behavioral, and social interventions, but it failed to increase activity levels. The researchers attributed the program's failure, in part, to long-standing rivalries among children who came from different geographic areas of the participating community. Fights and other disruptions seriously impeded the delivery of the intervention and deterred many children from participating. Clearly, social interventions cannot be implemented if participants are unable to tolerate one another.

Environmental and Policy Approaches to Increasing Physical Activity

Thus far, we have discussed interventions that focus on changing people's thoughts, feelings, and behaviors in order to increase their physical activity levels. The success of these interventions depends on people participating in the interventions—such as reading intervention materials or signing up for exercise counseling—and then successfully applying the intervention's information, skills, and techniques to their daily lives. Although many of these intervention techniques have proven effective, they are limited in their reach because the interventions can work on only those people who receive and use them. Furthermore, the interventions are predicated on the assumption that with enough motivation and knowledge, everybody can be physically active. Yet unfortunately, this is not the case. Some factors beyond the individual's control—such as a lack of equipment or facilities and unsafe neighborhoods and parks—will deter physical activity regardless of motivation or knowledge.

Given these limitations, one needs to look beyond interventions that aim to change the knowledge, behavioral skills, and social networks of every individual exerciser. An alternative approach is to direct interventions toward changing the physical and organizational structures that facilitate or impede activity among an entire population. Accordingly, in this section we examine environmental and policy approaches to increasing physical activity.

Environmental and policy approaches are designed to provide environmental opportunities, support, and cues to help people become more physically active. Interventions are not directed toward individuals but rather to the physical and organizational structures that are represented in the social ecological determinants model of physical activity presented in Chapter 4. The interventions can involve many different sectors (e.g., policy makers, workplaces, local transportation committees, community organizations) that have the common goal of increasing physical activity. Examples of these interventions include:

- Creating transportation policies and changing infrastructure to promote active transport (e.g., walking and bicycling instead of riding cars and buses)
- Using urban planning approaches to ensure that new neighborhoods are built with characteristics that promote physical activity
- Modifying policies and curricula for school-based physical education classes
- Increasing access to places and facilities where people can be physically active

The implementation and evaluation of the first two types of approaches can be a long and difficult process. For example, it can take years for a city council to agree on which streets should become bicycle routes and to then convert existing traffic lanes to bike lanes. Likewise, the design and construction of new neighborhoods may take years or even decades. Because of the novelty of these types of physical activity interventions, coupled with the lengthy durations required for their implementation and evaluation, very few studies have been conducted to examine the effectiveness of active transport and urban planning interventions.

An example of one such study consisted of an evaluation of California's Safe Routes to School (SR2S) program (Boarnet, Anderson, Day, et al., 2005). The SR2S program, intended to make active transit safer and more convenient, was implemented after the California state legislature provided funds for construction projects designed to increase the number of children who walk or bicycle to school. Examples of construction projects included fixing sidewalks, building walking and bike paths, adding crosswalks, and installing traffic signals. Boarnet and colleagues collected data from more than 1,200 parents who had a third-, fourth-, or fifth-grade child living in the vicinity of a recently completed SR2S construction project. Parents were asked whether their child passed the SR2S project on the way to school and if their child had changed his or her biking/walking travel to school since the completion of the project. Fifteen percent of children who passed a completed SR2S project on the way to school increased their walking or biking travel. In comparison, only 4 percent of children who did not pass a completed SR2S project increased their walking and biking travel over the same period.

The results of the study by Boarnet and colleagues are encouraging, insofar as they suggest that policies leading to urban environmental changes (e.g., improvements to sidewalks and pedestrian crossings) can subsequently increase active transportation. However, additional studies on these types of interventions are needed. Currently, insufficient literature is available on which to engage an evidence-based discussion of the implementation and effectiveness of active transport and urban planning interventions. Thus, we focus on two environmental and policy approaches for which adequate evidence exists—modifying policy and curriculum for school-based physical education and creating or enhancing access to physical activity facilities.

Modifying Policy and Curriculum for School-Based Physical Education

Most children in western nations attend school. Thus, physical education (PE) classes represent a tremendous opportunity to increase activity levels in younger segments of the population. Unfortunately, however, the number of students attending daily PE classes has declined significantly over the past decade and a half (Centers for Disease Control and Prevention, 2004). Furthermore, studies suggest that even when children do attend PE classes, they are sedentary for the majority of time spent in the class. For example, one study of PE classes found that children performed vigorous physical activity for only about three minutes out of every 30-minute class (Simons-Morton, Taylor, Snider, et al., 1994). Another study found that children spent only about 30 minutes per week doing *any* type of physical activity during PE classes (McKenzie et al., 1996). Apparently, much of PE class time is spent receiving instruction, waiting to take turns on an apparatus (e.g., gymnastics equipment), or playing sports and games where only one or two players are active at any given time (e.g., baseball). Clearly there is a need for interventions to improve PE programs (Sallis & Owen, 1998).

Interventions that focus on PE classes aim to modify curriculum and policies to increase the amount of time students spend in moderate or vigorous activity (Kahn et al., 2002). This can be done by:

- Increasing the weekly number of PE classes that are offered as part of the PE curriculum and lengthening the duration of existing classes.
- Starting new PE classes that appeal to students who are currently opting not to take PE. For example, students who are uncomfortable playing competitive sports in traditional gym classes may prefer to take a course that focuses on noncompetitive fitness-enhancing activities such as walking, strength-training, cycling, or aerobics.

- Changing the activities performed during PE classes to increase the amount of time spent performing moderate or vigorous activity. For example, rather than playing a single soccer game with the class divided into two teams, multiple soccer games can be played simultaneously, with students divided into multiple three-person teams. Having fewer players on a team requires all players to be continuously active as they work to cover the field. As another example, some PE teachers have begun incorporating active video games, such as Dance Dance Revolution (www.DDRGame.com), into their classes, as a strategy to increase moderate and vigorous activity.
- Educating PE teachers on how to design classes that decrease instruction time and student "standing around" time.

Effectiveness

In a review of studies of interventions aimed at modifying PE curriculum and policies, all of the studies reported significant improvements in students' physical fitness levels (Kahn et al., 2002). On average, the interventions produced an 8 percent increase in aerobic fitness among school-aged children. Increases were also seen in the number of minutes spent in moderate or vigorous physical activity, the percentage of PE class time spent performing moderate or vigorous physical activity, and the overall intensity level of physical activity performed during PE class. The interventions were effective among both boys and girls and in elementary as well as high-school students. It should be noted that many of the PE interventions were implemented along with a package of informational, social, and behavioral skill interventions that were delivered to students during their PE classes. Thus, some of the observed effects may have been partly due to these other types of interventions. Nevertheless, these results indicate that changes to the PE curriculum can increase physical activity in young people. It remains to be determined whether participation in regular physical education throughout childhood and adolescence helps to establish life-long patterns of active living.

Drawbacks

It can be difficult to convince school systems of the importance of devoting time and resources to enhancing PE programs. Schools are often under pressure to eliminate PE to make more time available for academic subjects, and PE teachers themselves often complain that other faculty members do not see its value. There may also be a perception among teachers and parents that by increasing the amount of time devoted to PE, students' academic performance will suffer. However, no evidence exists to support this claim (Kahn et al., 2002).

Creating or Enhancing Access to Facilities for Physical Activity

These interventions focus on providing access to facilities where people can be physically active. Implementation of these interventions often relies on the cooperation of such diverse entities as policy makers, school boards, worksites, local clubs and agencies, neighborhood groups, and municipalities. These entities can work together to change local environments and to create opportunities for physical activity (Kahn et al., 2002). Such efforts might include developing new opportunities to be active, such as building new community or workplace fitness facilities, walking trails, pools, and gymnasiums. Effort may also be directed toward enhancing access to existing physical activity facilities. For example, local clubs and school boards might work together to provide community access to school gymnasiums and pools on weekends and evenings. Policy makers, neighborhood groups and municipalities might work together to make local parks and playgrounds safer, and to eliminate financial barriers (e.g., fees to use pools and recreation centers) and physical obstructions (e.g., the lack of wheelchair-accessible facilities) that can prevent people from using existing fitness facilities. Workplaces might agree to give employees an extra 15 minutes during their lunch breaks in order to give them time to shower and change after a workout.

Effectiveness

To date, most studies of interventions to create or improve access to physical activity facilities have been conducted in workplaces; only a few have been conducted in neighborhood communities. These studies have shown that such interventions can result in a 25 percent increase in the proportion of people who exercise at least three times per week. Most of the studies have also found that the interventions produce weight loss and decreases in body fat among program participants (Kahn et al., 2002). Yet, as with the physical education interventions, most of these studies have also included a variety of informational, behavioral skills, and social interventions, so the relative impact of enhanced access on activity is unclear. Nevertheless, this intervention approach does seem to be effective for enhancing overall activity levels in large population segments.

Drawbacks

The primary drawback to interventions aimed at developing and enhancing physical activity environments is that they are time and resource consuming. Obviously, the construction and staffing of new recreation facilities can be expensive. It is difficult to convince key stakeholders—such as worksite owners and taxpayers—to spend money to develop fitness environments in the face of other financial priorities and obligations.

Another drawback is that simply providing people with opportunities to be physically active is not enough to guarantee that they will actually become more physically active. In other words, we cannot assume that "if we build it, they will come." Ultimately, the success of interventions aimed at enhancing physical activity opportunities will depend on whether people have the information, behavioral skills, and social support networks to take advantage of these opportunities. Thus, environmental and policy approaches have a natural fit with informational, behavioral skill, and social support interventions.

What's Happening in your Gym Environment?

Temperature: Few people would enthusiastically choose to exercise in extreme heat. Studies of swimmers have shown that as the temperature of the pool increases, ratings of enjoyment decrease (Berger & Owen, 1992). Similarly, warmer room temperatures have been associated with reports of greater tension, fatigue, and negative mood during exercise (Hansen, Stevens, & Coast, 2001).

Music: Many people say that they enjoy exercising to music. No wonder—research suggests that music can enhance positive feelings derived from the physical activity experience and can help people to exercise longer before they get tired (Brownley, McMurray, & Hackney, 1995; De Bourdeaudhuiji, Crombez, Deforche, et al., 2002).

Mirrors: Mirror, mirror, on the wall, who's the fittest of them all? Gym mirrors can help people to perfect their technique when lifting weights or trying new aerobics moves. Highly active women report greater feelings of exercise self-efficacy after exercising in front of a mirror than after exercising without a mirror (Katula & McAuley, 2001). However, for inexperienced exercisers, exercising in front of a mirror may lead to an increase in negative mood (Martin Ginis, Jung, & Gauvin, 2003), particularly in group exercise situations (Martin Ginis, Burke, & Gauvin, 2007).

Odors: Some smells in the gym may actually improve your performance. The application of peppermint odor in an exercise environment has been shown to reduce exercisers' perceptions of effort and frustration (Raudenbush, Meyer, & Eppich, 2002). Inhaling peppermint may also improve performance on tasks requiring strength, such as push-ups and sprinting (Raudenbush, Corley, & Eppich, 2001).

Evaluating Physical Activity Interventions in the "Real World"

In this chapter, we have presented descriptions of an array of physical activity interventions and information regarding their effectiveness. For the most part, effectiveness is gauged by the extent to which an intervention increases physical activity when it is administered as part of a research project. However, an intervention that works with a relatively small number of participants in a research setting will not necessarily be successful at increasing activity levels among large segments of the general population in the "real world." This can happen for several reasons.

1. Research study participants may be quite different from the general population along dimensions that could influence the effectiveness of interventions. For example, people who *volunteer* to be in experiments may have greater motivation to exercise than people in the general population. Consequently, exercise interventions could be more effective in experimental than real-world settings.
2. The research staff who deliver an intervention in a research project may have more time, expertise, and motivation to deliver the intervention components than people who are responsible for delivering an intervention in the real world. As a result, an intervention may not be as thoroughly

delivered in the real world as in the research setting. Busy interventionists may even omit key components of an intervention (e.g., risk factor testing, counseling) that are perceived as overly time consuming. Omission of key components could compromise the intervention's effectiveness.

3. Some successful research interventions may not be feasible in the real world. For instance, paying people to exercise could be a potent intervention to increase exercise in a research setting, but it would be virtually impossible to implement this intervention in a community setting.

Given these differences, it cannot be assumed that an intervention that is effective in a research setting will be useful for increasing physical activity in the general population. Before we can decide on the effectiveness of an intervention, we need to evaluate it in realistic settings.

Glasgow and his colleagues (Glasgow, Vogt, & Boles, 1999) created the RE-AIM ■ **RE-AIM** (Reach, Efficacy, Adoption, Implementation, Maintenance) framework to guide the evaluation of physical activity and other health interventions in real-world settings. According to this framework, we should evaluate interventions along five dimensions:

R 1. *Reach* refers to the percentage of people from a given population (e.g., fourth-grade schoolchildren, women with arthritis, factory workers) who participate in the intervention and the characteristics of these people. Ideally, a physical activity intervention should reach as many people as possible, particularly those who are in greatest need of the intervention (i.e., inactive people). Sometimes, the people most likely to participate in a physical activity intervention—people who are already active, for example—are those who need it least.

E 2. *Efficacy* refers to the positive and negative consequences that people experience when they receive all components of an intervention that has been delivered properly. Of course, the positive outcomes should far outweigh the negative ones. Some positive consequences that might result from an exercise intervention are increased physical activity and weight loss; some potential negative consequences are exercise-related injuries, and a decrease in time available for household tasks. When examining the efficacy of a physical activity intervention, it is important to examine quality of life, participant satisfaction, and physiological outcomes, not just changes in physical activity behavior.

A 3. *Adoption* refers to the proportion and representativeness of settings (such as high schools, workplaces, and communities) that adopt a particular intervention. For example, consider an intervention developed for Canadian high school students. Ideally, a large proportion of high schools nationwide would adopt the intervention. Representativeness provides an indication of whether the intervention can be delivered to broad segments of the population or only in settings that have certain characteristics. For instance, if adoption rates were similar among schools in higher- and lower-income neighborhoods, this would suggest that the intervention can be adopted by schools representing a range of socioeconomic strata—not just those in high (or low) income neighborhoods.

I 4. *Implementation* refers to how well the intervention is delivered in the real world. Typically, when physical activity interventions are designed they have a set of instructions that describe how the various intervention activities should be delivered. Implementation is assessed by determining the extent to which the people who deliver the intervention have followed these instructions. The assessment reveals whether it is practical and possible to deliver an intervention properly in real-world settings.

M 5. *Maintenance* refers to the extent to which the intervention is sustained over time. At the individual level, it is necessary to determine how long people continue to participate in the intervention. At an organizational level, it is important to determine if an organization, community, or workplace continues to implement the intervention over the long term. An intervention will have little benefit if individuals and organizations cannot maintain their commitment to it.

To date, very few physical activity interventions have been evaluated with the RE-AIM framework. However, Bopp and her colleagues (Bopp, Wilcox, Laken, et al., 2007) used RE-AIM to evaluate their "Health-e-AME" intervention, a three-year intervention designed to promote physical activity at African Methodist Episcopal (AME) churches across the state of South Carolina. The intervention was culturally tailored for church members, with all intervention activities and messages containing spiritual or religious components. For example, praise aerobics classes (aerobics set to gospel music) were established, and information about the importance of physical activity was posted within the church. Health-e-AME project staff trained church staff on how to organize and deliver the intervention activities. Three years into the project, interviews were conducted with church staff in order to assess reach, adoption, implementation, and maintenance. Data were collected from a random sample of individual church members to assess efficacy.

The results of the RE-AIM analysis of Health-e-AME were as follows:

1. *Reach*. Fifty percent of AME churches in South Carolina were trained in the intervention activities. The majority of intervention participants were women over the age of 40.
2. *Efficacy*. The intervention did not increase the overall number of AME church members who were physically active. However, people who had heard about the intervention were more likely to have increased their activity levels than those who had not heard about it.
3. *Adoption*. About two-thirds of trained churches adopted the intervention. Large churches were more likely to adopt the intervention than small or medium-sized churches. No differences existed in adoption rates based on whether the church was in an urban or rural location, the congregants' ethnicity or race, or the socioeconomic status of the church neighborhood.

4. *Implementation*. Church staff adherence to the intervention delivery principles ranged from 50 to 100 percent.
5. *Maintenance*. Individuals continued their participation in Health-e-AME for as long as their church offered the intervention. However, nearly half of the churches had stopped running the intervention by the second year of the project.

This example illustrates how the RE-AIM framework can be used to identify the strengths and weaknesses of an intervention delivered in a real-world setting. Based on these findings, Health-e-AME was reasonably successful in terms of its reach and adoption. Some churches implemented the intervention better than others, however, and it was difficult for the churches to maintain the program. A RE-AIM analysis can also provide information to explain why the intervention did not successfully increase physical activity participation rates. In the case of Health-e-AME, the efficacy of the intervention was likely compromised by inconsistent implementation and maintenance. Finally, information gleaned from a RE-AIM analysis can be used to choose an appropriate intervention for a particular setting. For instance, based on the above analysis, the Health-e-AME approach might be the intervention of choice for large churches with predominately older, female congregations, and with staff who are committed to implementing the intervention with 100 percent accuracy. In contrast, it might not be a good choice for a small church with a young congregation of both men and women and little staff support for intervention implementation.

Conclusion

In this chapter, we examined various techniques for increasing physical activity. In doing so, we have tried to emphasize the links between specific intervention strategies (e.g., goal-setting, creation of buddy systems) and specific determinants of physical activity (e.g., self-efficacy, social support). The importance of these links cannot be overstated. Intervention techniques based on a sound theoretical and empirical framework offer the greatest potential for altering physical activity behavior.

Four categories of intervention approaches were presented and evaluated—informational, behavioral, social, and policy/environmental. These are summarized in Exhibit 6.8 along with examples of intervention techniques that correspond with each approach. Overall, informational approaches have proven less effective than behavioral, social, and environmental and policy interventions for increasing physical activity. While the latter three have been shown to increase physical activity, little is known about their long-term effects. For example, it is not known how long the effects of self-monitoring or group support systems last, or if people continue exercising after telephone support systems and behavioral contracts end. Further research is needed to determine the long-term effectiveness of these types of interventions and their utility in real-world settings.

Intervention types with examples. **exhibit 6.8**

EXAMPLES OF INTERVENTIONS	EXAMPLES OF SPECIFIC TECHNIQUES
INFORMATIONAL APPROACHES	
Health education classes to change knowledge and attitudes about benefits of exercise, ways to increase exercise	■ School-based knowledge-oriented curriculum ■ Adult health education classes offered by health maintenance organizations
Provider training to change knowledge, attitudes, beliefs, and behavior about physical activity screening and promotion among clinical health care providers	■ Exercise prescription training seminars for health care providers ■ Development of computer-assisted exercise counseling packages for use by physicians
Public information and social marketing campaigns to change knowledge, attitudes, and beliefs about benefits, opportunities for exercise; change social norms about desirability or need for exercise; or create demand for increased opportunities for exercise	■ Mass media campaigns ■ National health initiatives ■ Community-wide campaigns
BEHAVIORAL APPROACHES	
Behavioral skills–oriented health or fitness classes to identify high-risk situations and exercise barriers, develop physical activity and exercise skills, self-management and monitoring skills, and relapse prevention skills	■ Worksite-based physical activity courses ■ Health care–site health promotion classes
Use of **behavioral reinforcers**	■ Use of contingencies, incentives to change exercise and physical activity behavior ■ Exercise contracts
SOCIAL APPROACHES	
Support mechanisms to facilitate and maintain behavior change	■ Telephone support, counseling ■ Physical activity and exercise clubs (e.g., walking, biking clubs) ■ Designation of walking partners ■ Family-based programs ■ School-based social support ■ Faith-based social support
Structured/supervised exercise programs	■ Hospital and cardiac rehabilitation programs ■ Seniors' exercise programs

(continued)

exhibit 6.8 Intervention types with examples, continued.

EXAMPLES OF INTERVENTIONS	EXAMPLES OF SPECIFIC TECHNIQUES
POLICY/ENVIRONMENTAL APPROACHES	
Interventions aimed at changing the **physical environment** to increase exercise opportunities	■ Creation of safe, lighted walking paths ■ Creation of worksite and school fitness facilities ■ Creation of safer pedestrian environments
Organization-based policy interventions to increase exercise opportunities	■ School-based skills-oriented interventions ■ Classroom curricula ■ Physical education curricula
Community-wide policy interventions to increase exercise opportunities	■ Policies or legislation establishing financial incentives for organizations and communities to provide access to exercise opportunities

Reprinted from *American Journal of Preventive Medicine,* Vol. 22 (supplement), Kahn, E. B., Ramsey, L. T., Brownson, R. C., Heath, G. W., Howze, E. H., Powell, K. E., Stone, E. J., Rajab, M. W., Corso, P., & The Task Force on Community Preventive Services, "The Effectiveness of Interventions to Increase Physical Activity. A Systematic Review," pages 73–107, copyright © 2002, with permission from Elsevier.

what do you know?

1. Identify the four general types of intervention approaches and the determinants of physical activity targeted by each.
2. Describe two types of informational approaches and discuss their effectiveness and limitations.
3. Identify and describe five principles for developing effective messages for increasing physical activity.
4. In general, what are people taught to do when they participate in behavioral interventions? Identify and explain three specific techniques that people might be taught during behavioral interventions.
5. Describe three key principles of effective goal-setting.
6. Describe five strategies that can be used to culturally tailor physical activity information.
7. What is the abstinence violation effect?
8. Describe three strategies to reduce the risk of a lapse in activity, as specified by the relapse prevention model.
9. Describe three types of social support interventions. Discuss the overall effectiveness and limitations of social support interventions.

10. What is the primary difference between environmental and policy approaches to increasing physical activity and the three other approaches discussed in this chapter?
11. Describe four strategies that could be used to increase schoolbased physical activity.
12. How effective are environmental and policy interventions? What are their drawbacks?
13. Describe the RE-AIM framework.

learning activities

1. Bowmore & Wembley International is a (fictitious) company that sells dog food over the Internet. Its sales office has 50 employees who spend long days sitting in front of computer terminals, taking orders, and answering customers' questions. Because of their sedentary jobs, many employees have started to gain weight and are now concerned about their increasing risk for diseases associated with a sedentary lifestyle. The company has hired you to help their employees become more active. Using what you have learned about behavioral and social approaches for increasing physical activity, design an intervention program to help the employees increase their activity levels. Your program should include at least three specific behavioral intervention techniques and three specific social intervention techniques.
2. Diabesityville is a rural community with a population of 10,000 people. The town's mayor is concerned about the rising rates of obesity and diabetes among her constituents. She knows that the vast majority of the town's residents are sedentary. The mayor has given you an unlimited budget and the task of getting every man, woman, and child in Diabesityville to become more physically active. Develop an intervention program to increase physical activity in Diabesityville; it should include a community-wide campaign, environmental and social policy approaches, and one other approach of your choosing. Be sure to describe the specific intervention techniques that will be included in your program.
3. Conduct a survey of health and fitness magazines and websites to create a list of tips and techniques that are commonly given to help people become more physically active. Given what you now know about the importance of linking intervention techniques with theory and research-based determinants of physical activity, identify the tips that you think might be most effective and those that will be least effective. Explain the rationale behind your choices.
4. Develop a physical activity information brochure for a particular segment of the population (e.g., a cultural or ethnic group, older adults, people with a health condition). Use the information presented in Exhibit 6.2 to tailor the brochure to the characteristics and needs of this group.

5. Conduct a literature search to identify a study in which a physical activity intervention has been tested in an experimental setting. Using the RE-AIM framework, develop a case for determining whether this intervention will be effective in the real world.

references

Andersen, R.E., Franckowiak, S.C., Snyder, J., Bartlett, S.J., & Fontaine, K.R. (1998). Can inexpensive signs encourage the use of stairs? Results from a community intervention. *Annals of Internal Medicine, 129,* 363–369.

Andersen, R.E., Franckowiak, S.C., Zuzak, K.B., Cummings, E.S., Bartlett, S., & Crespo, C.J. (2006). Effects of a culturally sensitive sign on the use of stairs in African American commuters. *Soz Praventiv Med, 51,* 373–380.

Berger, B.G., & Owen, D.R. (1992). Preliminary analysis of a causal relationship between swimming and stress reduction: Intense exercise may negate the effects. *International Journal of Sport Psychology, 23,* 70–85.

Blair, S.N., Dunn, A.L., Marcus, B.H., Carpenter, R.A., & Jaret, P.E. (2001). *Active living every day.* Champaign, IL: Human Kinetics.

Boarnet, M.G., Anderson, C.L., Day, K., McMillan, T., & Alfonzo, M. (2005). Evaluation of the California Safe Routes to School Legislation: Urban form changes and children's active transportation to school. *American Journal of Preventive Medicine, 28,* 134–140.

Booth, M., Bauman, A., Oldenburg, B., Owen, N., & Magnus, P. (1992). Effects of a national mass-media campaign on physical activity participation. *Health Promotion International, 7,* 241–247.

Bopp, M., Wilcox, S., Laken, M., Hooker, S.P., Saunders, R., Parra-Medina, D., Butler, K., & McClorin, L. (2007). Using the RE-AIM framework to evaluate a physical activity intervention in churches. *Preventing Chronic Disease, 4,* www.cdc.gov/pcd/issues/2007/oct/06_0155.htm.

Borg, G. (1998). *Borg's perceived exertion and pain scales.* Champaign, IL: Human Kinetics.

Brawley, L.R. (1993). Social-psychological aspects of fitness promotion. In P. Seraganian (Ed.), *Exercise psychology: The influence of physical exercise on psychological processes* (pp. 254–298). New York: John Wiley & Sons.

Brownell, K.D., Stunkard, A.J., & Albaum, J.M. (1980). Evaluation and modification of exercise patterns in the natural environment. *American Journal of Psychiatry, 137,* 1540–1545.

Brownley, K.A., McMurray, R.G., & Hackney, A.C. (1995). Effects of music on physiological and affective responses to graded treadmill exercise in trained and untrained runners. *International Journal of Psychophysiology, 19,* 193–201.

Cacioppo, J.T., & Petty, R.E. (1984). The Elaboration Likelihood Model of persuasion. *Advances in Consumer Research, 11,* 673–675.

Canadian Diabetes Association (2004). About diabetes. www.diabetes.ca/Section_About/FactsIndes.asp

Centers for Disease Control and Prevention (2004). Participation in high school physical education—United States, 1991–2003. *Morbidity and Mortality Weekly Report, 53,* 844–847.

Conn, V.S., Hafdahl, A.R., Brown, S.A., & Brown, L.M. (2008). Meta-analysis of patient education interventions to increase physical activity among chronically ill adults. *Patient Education and Counseling,* 70, 157–172.

De Bourdeaudhuiji, I., Crombez, G., Deforche, B., Vinaimont, F., Debode, P., & Bouckaert, J. (2002). Effect of distraction on treadmill running time in severely obese children and adolescents. *International Journal of Obesity and Related Metabolic Disorders, 26,* 1023–1029.

Dishman, R.K., & Buckworth, J. (1996). Increasing physical activity: A quantitative synthesis. *Medicine & Science in Sports & Exercise, 28,* 706–719.

Eakin, E. G., Lawler, S. P., Vandelanotte, C., & Owen, N. (2007). Telephone interventions for physical activity and dietary behavior change: A systematic review. *American Journal of Preventive Medicine, 32,* 419–434.

Estabrooks, P., Bradshaw, M., Fox, E., Berg, J., & Dzewaltowski, D.A. (2004). The relationships between delivery agents' physical activity level and the likelihood of implementing a physical activity program. *American Journal of Health Promotion, 18,* 350–353.

Glasgow, R.E., Vogt, T.M., & Boles, S.M. (1999). Evaluating the public health impact of health promotion interventions: The RE-AIM framework. *American Journal of Public Health, 89,* 1322–1327.

Gollwitzer, P.M. (1999). Implementation intentions: Strong effects of simple plans. *American Psychologist, 54,* 493–503.

Hansen, C.J., Stevens, L.C., & Coast, J.R. (2001). Exercise duration and mood state: How much is enough to feel better? *Health Psychology, 20,* 267–275.

Kahn, E.B., Ramsey, L.T., Brownson, R.C., Heath, G.W., Howze, E.H., Powell, K.E., Stone, E.J., Rajab, M.W., Corso, P., & The Task Force on Community Preventive Services. (2002). The effectiveness of interventions to increase physical activity. A systematic review. *American Journal of Preventive Medicine, 22 (Suppl),* 73–107.

Katula, J.A., & McAuley, E. (2001). The mirror does not lie: Acute exercise and self-efficacy. *Journal of Behavioral Medicine, 8,* 319–326.

Katzmarzyk, P.T., Gledhill, N., & Shephard, R.J. (2000). The economic burden of physical inactivity in Canada. *Canadian Medical Association Journal, 163,* 1435–1440.

Kirk, A., Mutrie, N., MacIntyre, P., & Fisher, M. (2003). Increasing physical activity in people with type 2 diabetes. *Diabetes Care, 26,* 1186–1192.

Knapp, D.N. (1988). Behavioral management techniques and exercise promotion. In R.K. Dishman (Ed.), *Exercise adherence: Its impact on public health* (pp. 203–235). Champaign, IL: Human Kinetics.

Kreuter, M.W., Lukwago, S.N., Bucholtz, D.C., Clark, E.M., & Sanders-Thompson, V. (2003). Achieving cultural appropriateness in health promotion programs: Targeted and tailored approaches. *Health Education & Behavior, 30,* 133–146.

Locke, E. A., & Latham, G.P. (2002). Building a practically useful theory of goal setting and task motivation. *Amerian Psychologist, 57,* 705–717.

Lombard, D.N., Lombard, T.N., & Winnett, R.A. (1995). Walking to meet health guidelines: The effect of prompting frequency and prompt structure. *Health Psychology, 14,* 164–170.

Marcus, B.H., Owen, N., Forsyth, L.H., Cavill, N.A., & Fridlinger, F. (1998). Physical activity interventions using mass media, print media, and information technology. *American Journal of Preventive Medicine, 15,* 362–368.

Marlatt, G.A., & George, W.H. (1984). Relapse prevention: Introduction and overview of the model. *British Journal of Addiction, 79,* 261–273.

Marlatt, G.A., & Gordon, J.R. (1985). *Relapse prevention: Maintenance strategies in the treatment of addictive behaviors.* New York: Guilford Press.

Martin Ginis, K.A., Burke, S.M., & Gauvin, L. (2007). Exercising with others exacerbates the negative effects of mirrored environments on sedentary women's feeling states. *Psychology and Health, 22,* 945–962.

Martin Ginis, K.A., Jung, M.E., & Gauvin, L. (2003). To see or not to see: The effects of exercising in mirrored and unmirrored environments on women's mood states. *Health Psychology, 22,* 354–361.

Martins, R.K., & McNeil, D.W. (2009). Review of motivational interviewing in promoting health behaviors. *Clinical Psychology Review, 29,* 283–293.

McKay, H.G., King, D., Eakin, E.G., Seeley, J.R., & Glasgow, R.E. (2001). The diabetes network internet-based physical activity intervention: A randomized pilot study. *Diabetes Care, 24,* 1328–1334.

McKenzie, T.L., Nader, P.R., Strikmiller, P.K., Yang, M., Stone, E.J., Perry, C.L., Taylor, W.C., Epping, J.N., Feldman, H.A., Luepken, R.V., & Kelden, S.H. (1996). School physical education: Effect of the Child and Adolescent Trial for Cardiovascular Health. *Preventive Medicine, 25,* 423–431.

Miller, W.R. (1983). Motivational interviewing with problem drinkers. *Behavioral Psychotherapy, 11,* 147–172.

Miller, W.R., & Rollnick, S. (2002). *Motivational interviewing: Preparing people for change* (2nd ed.). New York: Guilford.

Munroe-Chandler, K.J., & Gammage, K.L. (2005). Now see this: A new vision of exercise imagery. *Exercise and Sport Sciences Reviews, 33,* 201–205.

Oldridge, N.B., & Jones, N.L. (1983). Improving patient compliance in cardiac exercise rehabilitation: Effects of written agreement and self-monitoring. *Journal of Cardiac Rehabilitation, 3,* 257–262.

Olson, J.M., & Zanna, M.P. (1987). Understanding and promoting exercise: A social psychological perspective. *Canadian Journal of Public Health, 78,* S1–S7.

Owen, N., Bauman, A., Booth, M., Oldenburg, B., & Magnus, P. (1995). Serial mass-media campaigns to promote physical activity: Reinforcing or redundant? *American Journal of Public Health, 85,* 244–248.

Pate, R.R., Saunders, R.P., Ward, D.S., Felton, G., Trost, S.G., & Dowda, M. (2003). Evaluation of a community-based intervention to promote physical activity in youth: Lessons from active winners. *American Journal of Health Promotion, 17,* 171–182.

Raudenbush, B., Corley, N., & Eppich, W. (2001). Enhancing athletic performance through the administration of peppermint odor. *Journal of Sport and Exercise Psychology, 23,* 156–160.

Raudenbush, B., Meyer, B., & Eppich, W. (2002). The effects of odors on objective and subjective measures of athletic performance. *International Sports Journal, 6*, 14–27.

Rejeski, W.J., Brawley, L.R., Ambrosius, W.T., Brubaker, P.H., Focht, B.C., Foy, C.G., & Fox, L.D. (2003). Older adults with chronic disease: Benefits of group-mediated counseling in the promotion of physically active lifestyles. *Health Psychology, 22*, 414–423.

Rollnick, S., Miller, W.R., & Butler, C.C. (2008). *Motivational interviewing in health care: Helping patients change behavior.* New York: Guilford.

Sallis, J.F., & Owen, N. (1998). *Physical activity and behavioral medicine.* Thousand Oaks, CA: Sage.

Simons-Morton, B.G., Taylor, W.C., Snider, S.A., Huang, I.W., & Fulton, J.E. (1994). Observed levels of elementary and middle school children's physical activity during physical education classes. *Preventive Medicine, 23*, 437–441.

Stetson, B.A., Beacham, A.O., Frommelt, S.J., Boutelle, K.N., Cole, J.D., Ziegler, C.H., & Looney, S.W. (2005). Exercise slips in high-risk situations and activity patterns in long-term exercisers: An application of the Relapse Prevention Model. *Annals of Behavioral Medicine, 30*, 25–35.

PART

II

Psychosocial Influences and Consequences of Exercise

7

Personality and Exercise

KEY TERMS

activity trait
androgynous
autonomic nervous system
cerebrotonia
dispositional/trait
ectomorph
endomorph
expressive personality
extraversion–introversion
hardiness
instrumental personality
intensity preference
intensity tolerance
interactionist perspective
learning/situational
limbic system
mesomorph
neuroticism–stability
personality
personality core
psychobiological model
psychoticism–superego
role-related behaviors
somatotonia
type A behavior pattern
typical responses
visceratonia

Jenny is a rather tense person. She always seems to be worrying about something and becomes upset fairly easily. She has a tendency to be suspicious of things and is also timid and apprehensive. Her friend Sarah, who has taken some courses in exercise psychology, suggests that Jenny might try beginning a regular exercise program. Sarah has learned that even something as relatively simple as going for a walk can increase energy and, more important for Jenny, reduce feelings of tension and promote relaxation. Sarah is also smart enough to realize that because of Jenny's timid approach to things, it will be worthwhile for her to have a supervised exercise routine, at least until she becomes comfortable with the process. Sarah notices that, after about six weeks of exercising three to four days per week, Jenny seems to be more relaxed and doesn't get as agitated over the "little things" as she did before she began her exercise program.

As discussed in Chapter 1, exercise psychology has enjoyed a tremendous surge of interest since the 1980s, although the importance of the relationship between bodily movement and the mind has been known for centuries. The ancient Greeks espoused exercise as an important component of both physical and mental health. This philosophy carried over into the sixteenth century, when Christobal Mendez wrote the *Book of Bodily Exercise,* which discussed the effects of exercise on the mind (Mendez, 1553/1960). Noted psychologist and philosopher William James (1899) spoke of the importance of physical activity when he addressed the American Association for the Advancement of Physical Education, saying,

> Everyone knows the effect of physical exercise on the mood: how much more cheerful and courageous one feels when the body has been toned up, than when it is 'run down.' . . .Those feelings are sometimes of worry, breathlessness, anxiety, tension; sometimes of peace and repose. It is certain that physical exercise will tend to train the body toward the latter feelings. The latter feelings are certainly an essential ingredient in all perfect human character.

Although our ancestors recognized the intimate link between body and mind, it wasn't until the late 1960s to early 1970s that any systematic investigation of issues relevant to the psychology of exercise began to emerge. Since its "revival" at that time, exercise psychology has had two primary research objectives that relate to exercise and personality:

1. Determination of the psychological *antecedents* of participation in physical activity
2. Determination of the psychological *consequences* of participation in physical activity.

Examples of the first objective would include research that attempts to determine what personality (or individual difference) factors might lead someone to participate in physical activity. The second objective would be represented by research that examines how an exercise-training program might influence individual difference factors—for example, whether regular exercise might lead one to become less emotional or more emotionally stable.

Defining Personality

Historically, the study of personality has been one of the most popular topics in exercise psychology. In keeping with the aforementioned primary research objectives, scientific inquiries have most often involved attempts at determining whether certain personality attributes are important *antecedents* to physical activity/exercise participation and whether certain personality attributes are developed as the *consequence* of such participation.

personality ■

Personality can be defined as the underlying, relatively stable psychological structures and processes that organize human experience and shape a person's actions and reactions to the environment. More simply, personality is the individual's unique, but consistent, psychological makeup. Personality is consistent in that it is relatively stable over time and across situations. Hollander (1967) described the structure of personality as being composed of the following:

personality core ■

1. The **personality core,** which is developed from early environmental interactions and includes such things as our perceptions of the external world, perceptions of self, basic attitudes, values, interests, motives, and our self-concept; the core is a reflection of who we are. The core is least amenable to change and is relatively unaffected by the context in which a person may be.

typical responses ■

2. **Typical responses,** which characterize our fairly predictable behaviors and ways of reacting to our environment. For example, an outgoing person might be very engaging, introducing herself to people when sitting in a classroom prior to the beginning of a class.

role-related behaviors ■

3. **Role-related behaviors,** which are more variable, daily behaviors influenced by the particular context in which we find ourselves. For example, the same outgoing, engaging person may be quiet and attentive during the class,

likely becoming involved in class discussions or giving input when it is asked for by the instructor, but otherwise fulfilling the role of the "typical" student. Role-related behaviors are most easily changed and most influenced by the environment.

Approaches to the Study of Personality

Personality has been studied from a variety of perspectives. The two most prominent approaches have been the **learning/situational** and **dispositional/trait** approaches, with the emphasis of the latter being on the person while the emphasis of the former has been on the environment. Both approaches endorse what has been termed an **interactionist perspective** to studying personality (see the box below). Such a perspective essentially views both the individual and the situation in which he or she finds himself or herself (i.e., the *interaction* of the person with the environment) as important in determining behavior. Learning approaches include conditioning or behaviorist theories and social learning theories (see Chapters 3 and 4). Dispositional approaches include biological theories and the trait theories; these will be discussed next.

- learning/situational
- dispositional/trait
- interactionist perspective

Biological Theories

Early biological theories of personality related personality to various biological processes. The ancient Greeks focused on body "humors" or fluids. They posited that a preponderance of one of the four basic body fluids (humors) was manifested in discernible personalities. A preponderance of blood predisposed one to be "sanguine" or cheerful and optimistic; yellow bile was related to a "choleric" or irritable disposition; black bile predisposed one to be "melancholic" or sad and depressed; and phlegm was thought to make one "phlegmatic" or apathetic and indifferent. This approach clearly reflects contemporary thinking that mind and body were closely related to one another.

The Person–Situation Debate

The interactionist perspective arose from the debate in the study of personality about whether it was most effective to place the primary focus on the person or on the environment. This was termed the *person–situation debate* and dates to the late 1960s. The person perspective, usually referred to as the *trait approach*, places primary emphasis on the notion that personality is derived from stable, enduring attributes of the individual that lead to consistent responses over time and across situations. The *situation approach*, on the other hand, emphasizes that behavior is best explained by examining the environment and the individual's reaction to that environment. Extreme adherents of either approach basically give no credence to the other position. Over time, a more moderate position—one that considers both the person and the situation and, more important, the interaction between them—has been shown to offer the most utility for understanding the influence of personality on behavior.

ectomorph ■ cerebrotonia ■ endomorph ■ visceratonia ■ mesomorph ■ somatotonic ■

A more recent biological theory of personality, developed by Sheldon (1942), is referred to as *constitutional theory.* According to Sheldon, individuals possess certain body types, or somatotypes. These somatotypes are largely genetically determined, and they predispose the individual toward behavioral consistency. Sheldon's formulation defines three major somatotypes (see Exhibit 7.1). The **ectomorph** has a body type that is characterized by linearity, tallness, and leanness. Sheldon proposed that such a body type was associated with what he referred to as **cerebrotonia.** Individuals possessing such a body type were characterized, Sheldon suggested, by tense, introverted, socially restrained, inhibited personalities. The **endomorph** body type is characterized by plumpness, fatness, and roundness and was purported to be linked with the **visceratonia** personality. This type of individual was characterized by affection, sociability, relaxation, and joviality. Finally, the **mesomorph** is characterized by the classic inverted triangle—wide muscular shoulders and narrower hips. Sheldon referred to this as the classic athletic body type. These individuals have **somatotonic** personalities that

exhibit 7.1 Sheldon's three major somatotypes.

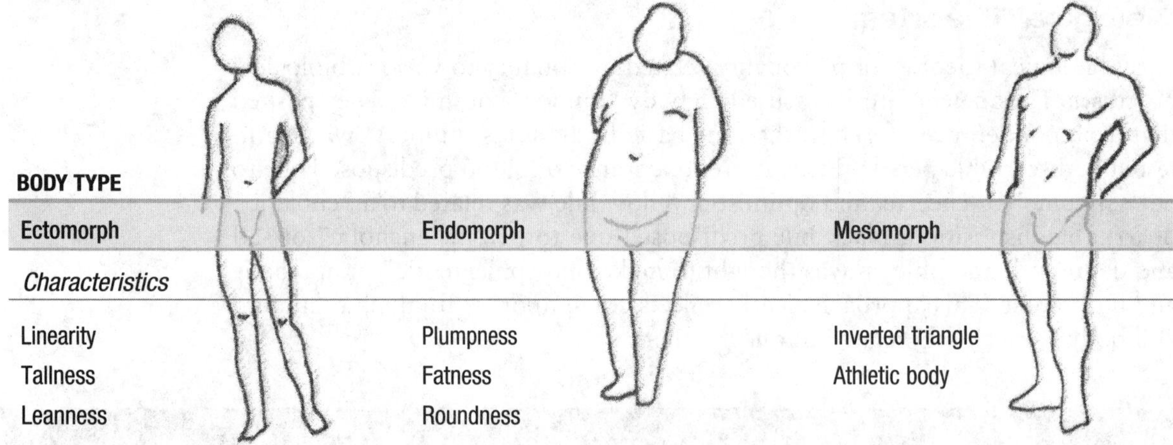

BODY TYPE

Ectomorph	Endomorph	Mesomorph
Characteristics		
Linearity	Plumpness	Inverted triangle
Tallness	Fatness	Athletic body
Leanness	Roundness	

PERSONALITY TYPE

Cerebrotonia	Visceratonia	Somatotonia
Characteristics		
Tense	Affectionate	Adventurous
Introverted	Sociable	Risk-taking
Socially restrained	Relaxed	Dominant
Inhibited	Jovial	Aggressive
		Commanding

predispose them to be adventurous, risk-taking, dominant, and aggressive, and to take charge (i.e., be leaders). Sheldon's initial work with this framework resulted in correlations on the order of .7 or better between the body types and associated personality characteristics. (A *correlation* reflects the degree to which two different things vary with one another. Such values can range from –1.0 to +1.0, the former reflecting a perfect negative correlation and the latter reflecting a perfect positive correlation. In Sheldon's work, for example, as scores on mesomorphy increased so too did scores on traits reflective of somatotonia. A correlation simply means that two factors have a relationship with each other, *not* that a change in one causes the other to change. As the correlation coefficient approaches unity [–1.0, +1.0] the relationship between the two variables becomes stronger.) Such strong relationships have not held up in subsequent work (Eysenck, Nias, & Cox, 1982). It is worth noting, however, that relationships between body types and personality have been shown to be small to moderate in nature, on the order of approximately .3 to .4 (Eysenck et al., 1982). This suggests that there might be a meaningful association between body type and personality.

Trait Theories

Perhaps the most predominant theoretical approach of the "modern" era has involved the examination of *traits,* defined as relatively enduring, highly consistent internal attributes or behavioral dispositions reflective of underlying biopsychological constructs (Rhodes, 2006). Traits are thought to reflect motivational systems that increase adaptation to positive or negative stimuli. Approaches centered on the examination of traits have been referred to as *trait theories.* The emphasis in such theories is placed on the person as opposed to the situation or the environment (see the box on page 185). Trait theories assume personality to consist of more specific facet traits (e.g., moody, anxious, restless, rigid), which are subsumed within more general traits (e.g., neuroticism). Trait theories have emerged that vary with respect to the number of more general traits they propose, ranging from as few as two to as many as seven (Rhodes, 2006). The more prominent and relevant theories for physical activity are presented in the following sections.

Eysenck's Personality Theory

Trait theories have dominated recent work in the area of personality, and the individual perhaps most responsible for their prominence has been Hans Eysenck (see Eysenck et al., 1982). Eysenck proposed that the relationships between traits generated second-order, or what he referred to as *superordinate,* trait dimensions. Within his framework were three superordinate dimensions: Extraversion–Introversion (*E*), Neuroticism (Emotionality)–Stability (*N*), and Psychoticism–Superego (*P*). It is important here to point out that, when dealing with dimensions like those posed in Eysenck's theory (and others to be discussed later), a given individual is not necessarily one or the other—extraverted or introverted, for example. Rather, the endpoints of a given dimension reflect the extremes of that dimension; most people fall somewhere between the extremes, and relatively few people possess the traits that reflect the ends of the dimension. One of the unique aspects of Eysenck's personality framework is that he proposed a biological basis for each of the three dimensions.

Extraversion-introversion. This major dimension of personality is proposed as ranging from Extraversion on one end (a tendency to be outgoing, sociable, impulsive, optimistic, and active) to Introversion on the other (a tendency to be reserved, unsociable, quiet, passive, and careful). An individual can be classified as being somewhere along the continuum between extraversion and introversion. Eysenck proposed that **extraversion–introversion** was driven by level of arousal in the cortex of the brain and is expected to have an influential relationship on pain threshold, pain sensitivity, and/or pain tolerance, essentially reflecting arousability and sensory modulation. From neurophysiological evidence, Eysenck proposed that extraversion–introversion was mediated by the *reticular formation,* a band of neural tissue located primarily in the core of the brainstem that receives input from a variety of locations and is involved in several functions (Bear, Connors, & Paradiso, 2001). (See Exhibit 7.2 for a diagram showing the brain.) With its extensive projections to the cortex, one of the functions of the reticular formation is the mediation of cortical arousal. Eysenck proposed that if the reticular formation is functioning at a high level, the individual feels alert; if it is functioning at a low level, the individual feels drowsy. According to the the-

extraversion–introversion

exhibit 7.2 Diagram showing the location of the reticular formation in the brain.

Note the projections to the cortical regions of the brain, highlighting the interconnectedness of the reticular formation to the rest of the brain.

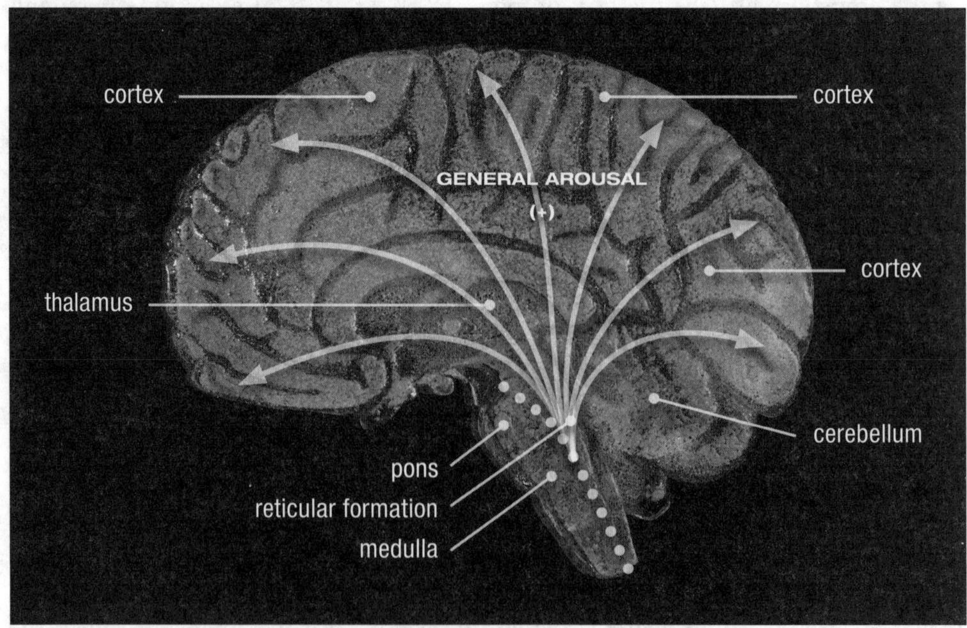

Traits vs. States

The distinction between *traits* and *states* is an important issue in personality research. As noted previously, traits are seen as relatively enduring dispositions that exert a consistent influence on behavior in a variety of situations. States, on the other hand, are viewed as the psychological reaction to the situation in which the individual finds herself, consistent with the individual's traits.

For example, a highly trait-anxious person would tend to be a worrisome, nervous individual regardless of the situation in which she finds herself. When placed in a stressful situation such as standing before an audience to give a speech, this individual would be expected to respond with a high amount of state anxiety. This typically manifests itself cognitively as extreme nervousness or tension and somatically with sweaty palms, tense muscles, and an unsettled stomach.

Carron, in 1980, noted that skeptics had called for abandoning the trait approach altogether because of its failure to account for physical activity behavior. This prompted some scientists to argue that instead of abandoning the trait approach, the approach should be more adequately used. Theorists like Eysenck and Cattell wouldn't necessarily expect broad personality characteristics (i.e., traits) to accurately predict an individual's behavior in physical activity. Coupling such traits with situational factors like psychological states would more accurately predict behavior.

ory, introverts have *higher* base levels of activation, that is, their cortical arousal tends to be higher than the "normal" individual. Because of the relationship between *E* and sensory modulation, the greater arousal at rest that introverts experience results in an augmentation of incoming stimulation. This makes them feel uncomfortable, and thus they *avoid* further stimulation that might increase arousal. Extraverts, on the other hand, have *lower* base levels of activation, that is, lower cortical arousal. This lower arousal results in a reduction of incoming stimulation. This lack of stimulation also makes them uncomfortable; thus extraverts tend to *seek* opportunities and situations that might provide additional stimulation. Additionally, because of this augmentation or reduction of incoming stimulation, introverts tend to have lower pain tolerance whereas extraverts have greater tolerance for painful stimuli.

Neuroticism–stability. This second major dimension of personality is proposed as ranging from Neuroticism (emotional) on one end (a tendency to be tense, anxious, moody, excitable, worried, and indecisive) to Stable on the other (a tendency to be calm, even-tempered, easy-going, and controlled). An individual can be classified as being somewhere along the continuum between neuroticism and stability. It is worth noting that neuroticism (*N*) is related to many forms of negative mental health, including anxiety, depression, hostility, impulsiveness, self-consciousness, and vulnerability. Eysenck proposed that the **neuroticism–stability** dimension was associated with activity of the **limbic system,** sometimes referred to as the emotional brain, and the **autonomic nervous system** (ANS). The ANS is often cited as driving the fight-or-flight response seen when a stressful stimulus is encountered. High *N* individuals tend to have more labile (i.e., readily changeable) and longer-

- neuroticism–stability
- limbic system
- autonomic nervous system

lasting autonomic reactions than do low *N* (i.e., emotionally stable) individuals. For example, if asked to give a short speech (i.e., a stressor) in front of a large group, the high *N* person might respond with a large increase in heart rate and blood pressure, which would remain elevated during and following the speech. Even when the stressor was over, it would take longer for the high *N* person to return to the prestressor resting heart rate and blood pressure. In essence, he continues to process the stressor even when it is no longer present.

psychoticism–superego ■

Psychoticism-superego. The final personality dimension proposed by Eysenck's theory ranges from Psychoticism at one end (a tendency to be impulsive, aggressive, hostile, egocentric, impersonal, and tough-minded) to Superego (a tendency to be empathetic, cooperative, altruistic, and conforming). The biological basis for the **psychoticism–superego** dimension is hypothesized to be driven by hormonal function or, more specifically, by elevated androgen levels (testosterone) and the relative absence of serotonin (neurotransmitter) metabolites; this is reflective of poor neurotransmitter functioning, which has important implications for mental health. Such hormonal function is thought to lead to more aggressiveness, impersonal attitudes, and antisocial behavior. Such traits may be advantageous in certain sporting situations, but it should be pointed out that this last dimension has received relatively little attention in the exercise domain. It is somewhat difficult to imagine situations where an impersonal attitude would be advantageous in the exercise context, but some aspects of psychoticism (e.g., lack of self-discipline, somewhat disordered) may work to inhibit the kind of behaviors that facilitate physical activity.

Eysenck's framework and exercise. With this theoretical basis, specific predictions for physical activity/exercise can be made regarding extraversion–introversion and neuroticism–stability. As mentioned previously, low arousal leads the extravert to seek sensory stimulation through physical activity. Eysenck hypothesized that physical activity/exercise might be one such avenue for increased stimulation. As a result, extraverts would be more likely to adopt and adhere to a physical activity/exercise regimen than would introverts, particularly when the exercise program has variety and excitement. This could be manifested in terms of greater-intensity activity and activity for longer durations. Additionally, the extraverts' higher tolerance of pain is advantageous in such activities.

Although Eysenck does not make specific predictions regarding the Neuroticism dimension, because of its basis in the autonomic nervous system one could surmise that activities that modify ANS function might also affect this personality dimension. Given that exercise training typically results in reductions in heart rate, blood pressure, and numerous other factors, it would seem reasonable to propose that exercise training could also result in a change toward a more stable/less neurotic personality.

In spite of its theoretical foundation, Eysenck's theory has received precious little examination in the exercise domain. (More recent formulations, most notably the five-factor model [see the discussion later in this chapter], have added other dimensions to personality, yet the most prominent theories all contain extraversion–introversion and neuroticism–stability.) In general, individuals involved in physical activity tend to be more extraverted than nonparticipants and also to be more likely to adhere to exercise programs (Courneya & Hellsten, 1998). Again consistent with the theoretical predictions, Shiomi (1980) found that extraverts have greater persistence while exercising. More recently, a review of 36 studies (Rhodes & Smith, 2006) concluded that N was inversely associated with physical activity, albeit with a small effect, whereas E was positively associated with physical activity.

Schnurr, Vaillant, and Vaillant (1990), in a prospective study, found that those individuals possessing vital, well-adjusted personalities as young adults were more likely to engage in frequent exercise 40 years later. Conversely, those with more sensitive, anxious (high *N*) personalities as young adults were likely to exercise less frequently 40 years later. It has also been consistently demonstrated that extraversion is associated with involvement in physical activity (Eysenck et al., 1982; Furnham, 1981; Kirkcaldy & Furnham, 1991). For example, Arai and Hisamichi (1998) noted in a study of more than 22,000 40- to 64-year-old Japanese residents that extraversion was positively related, whereas neuroticism was inversely related, to exercise frequency. Another population-based study of more than 19,000 adolescent and adult twins and their families (De Moor, Beem, Stubbe, et al., 2006) found that exercisers (defined as exercising as least 60 min per week) scored significantly higher on extraversion and lower on neuroticism than those who didn't exercise. Exceptions have been noted in the literature, however. For example, Yeung and Helmsley (1997) found that extraversion was actually inversely related to attendance in an eight-week exercise program.

Extraversion and neuroticism can also influence the behaviors people might engage in to regulate mood. Thayer, Newman, and McClain (1994), in a study examining behaviors that would increase energy and decrease tension, found that extraverts were more likely to exercise to improve energy. Hsiao and Thayer (1998), in a similar study, found that those scoring high on neuroticism reported valuing exercise for its ability to improve mood. Consistent with Eysenck's theoretical tenets, Hsiao and Thayer recommended the following as a way to increase exercise behavior and adherence in those who score high on neuroticism:

> First, the energizing and tension-releasing effects of exercise should be emphasized because these effects are likely to be extremely reinforcing and appealing to the target population. Secondly, exercise regimens should be structured so as to result in minimum physical discomfort. Painful bodily sensation (e.g., soreness of muscle, shortness of breath) could be easily magnified and interpreted as disease symptoms by individuals high on Neuroticism, who then could cease from physical activity altogether. Obviously, the general population can also benefit from following these guidelines. (p. 835)

A fairly substantial body of work has also shown that long-term exercise programs often result in reductions in trait anxiety or neuroticism (see Landers & Petruzzello, 1994). For example, Petruzzello and colleagues (1991), in an extensive review of the literature examining the effects of exercise training programs on trait-anxiety reduction, showed that exercise programs lasting at least 10 weeks resulted in sizable reductions in trait anxiety. Exercise programs lasting longer than 15 weeks resulted in even greater reductions in anxiety. It is worth noting that in their review, Petruzzello and colleagues found significant reductions in trait anxiety occurring only in aerobic exercise programs; such positive effects were generally not seen in nonaerobic (e.g., weight training) programs. As an example of this kind of work, DiLorenzo et al. (1999) conducted a 12-week aerobic fitness training program with a community sample of 82 men and women ages 18 to 39; they compared a variety of psychological outcomes, including trait anxiety, to a waiting-list control group of 29 men and women. In addition to effecting an improvement in fitness, the exercise group also had a significant reduction in trait anxiety, a change not seen in the control group. This work clearly demonstrates the fact that personality can change; that is, it is possible, over a period of weeks, months, or years, for personality to change as a result of regular physical activity. This change is usually in the direction of reduced negative factors (neuroticism) and enhanced positive factors (extraversion), changes that are quite consistent with certain theoretical formulations (e.g., those formulated by Eysenck).

Cattell's Personality Theory

Cattell, a contemporary of Eysenck, likewise proposed a theory of personality based on traits. Personality in this conceptualization was composed of 16 factors, derived through a statistical technique referred to as *factor analysis*. From the many available personality traits, Cattell isolated 16 factors that he felt described the essence of personality (see Exhibit 7.3 for a list of the factors). From this conceptualization, Cattell developed what he called the 16 Personality Factor questionnaire (16PF) to assess these factors. The 16PF has enjoyed widespread use in sport personality studies and has been used to some extent in exercise studies as well. The following are a few sample questions from the 16PF.

- I consider myself a very sociable, outgoing person.

  a. yes b. in between c. no

- People say I'm impatient.

  a. true b. uncertain c. false

- I prefer friends who are:

  a. quiet b. in between c. lively

- When I get upset, I try hard to hide my feelings from others.

  a. true b. in between c. false

Cattell's model and exercise. As with Eysenck's model, Cattell's model has not received much attention in the exercise domain. This is particularly curious given the fact that Cattell, in collaboration with exercise physiologist T.K. Cureton, specifically discussed a possible relationship between fitness and personality.

Cattell's 16 primary personality factors. **exhibit 7.3**

A	Warm, sociable	vs.	Aloof, stiff
B	Intelligent, bright	vs.	Unintelligent, dull
C	Emotionally stable, mature	vs.	Emotional, immature
E	Dominant, ascendant	vs.	Submissive, mild
F	Happy-go-lucky, enthusiastic	vs.	Sober, glum
G	Conscientious, persistent	vs.	Casual, undependable
H	Adventurous, outgoing	vs.	Shy, timid
I	Tender-minded, sensitive	vs.	Tough, realistic
L	Trusting, accepting	vs.	Suspicious, jealous
M	Imaginative, unconventional	vs.	Practical, conventional
N	Naïve, unpretentious	vs.	Shrewd, sophisticated
O	Confident, self-secure	vs.	Timid, apprehensive
Q_1	Radical, experimenting	vs.	Conservative, moralizing
Q_2	Self-sufficient, resourceful	vs.	Group-dependent, conventional
Q_3	Controlled, disciplined	vs.	Uncontrolled, undisciplined
Q_4	Relaxed, composed	vs.	Tense, excitable

Sources: Cattell (1960); Eysenck et al. (1982).

Cattell (1960) suggested that fitness would be related to personality in that individuals with high levels of fitness would be likely to have lower anxiety and neuroticism. Furthermore, he hypothesized that individuals with lower levels of anxiety and neuroticism (i.e., those with greater emotional stability) would respond favorably to intense physical training.

Dienstbier (1984) summarized the results of a number of studies from the mid-1970s to early 1980s that examined the relationship between exercise and personality change using the 16PF. Upon examination of the dimensions thought to be associated with emotionality (conceptually analogous to neuroticism), Dienstbier found support for a link between fitness and emotional stability; that is, higher levels of fitness were associated with greater emotional stability, placidity (or less apprehension), and relaxation (or less tension). He also noted that exercise programs resulting in changes in fitness also tended to result in increases in placidity or relaxation. He speculated that the increased physiological capacity that accompanies physical training might be the reason for the reduced emotionality (i.e., neuroticism).

One of the major conceptual problems with research using the 16PF has been the difficulty of interpreting the complicated findings. Cattell has also described second-order factors, derived through the combination of various primary factors. See Exhibit 7.4 for examples of secondary-order factors and the primary factors from which they are derived. It is interesting that Eysenck has also asserted (as well as demonstrated empirically) that the 16 factors can often be simplified into the two major dimensions of his model (extraversion–introversion, neuroticism–stability) and thus explain the data more parsimoniously. Morgan (1980), perhaps echoing the sentiments of Eysenck, noted that more sophisticated analysis of data using the 16PF might clarify relationships between exercise and personality. In particular, Morgan suggested a greater emphasis on the second-order factors, that is, the relationships among the primary factors, rather than focusing on the primary factors themselves.

The five-factor model (FFM)

The five-factor model (FFM) (Costa & McCrae, 1992; McCrae & John, 1992) has developed relatively recently into the dominant framework for the study of personality. This is also a trait theory that proposes personality to be composed of five dimensions: neuroticism (N), extraversion (E), openness to experience/

exhibit 7.4 Example of secondary-order factors and the primary factors from which they are derived.

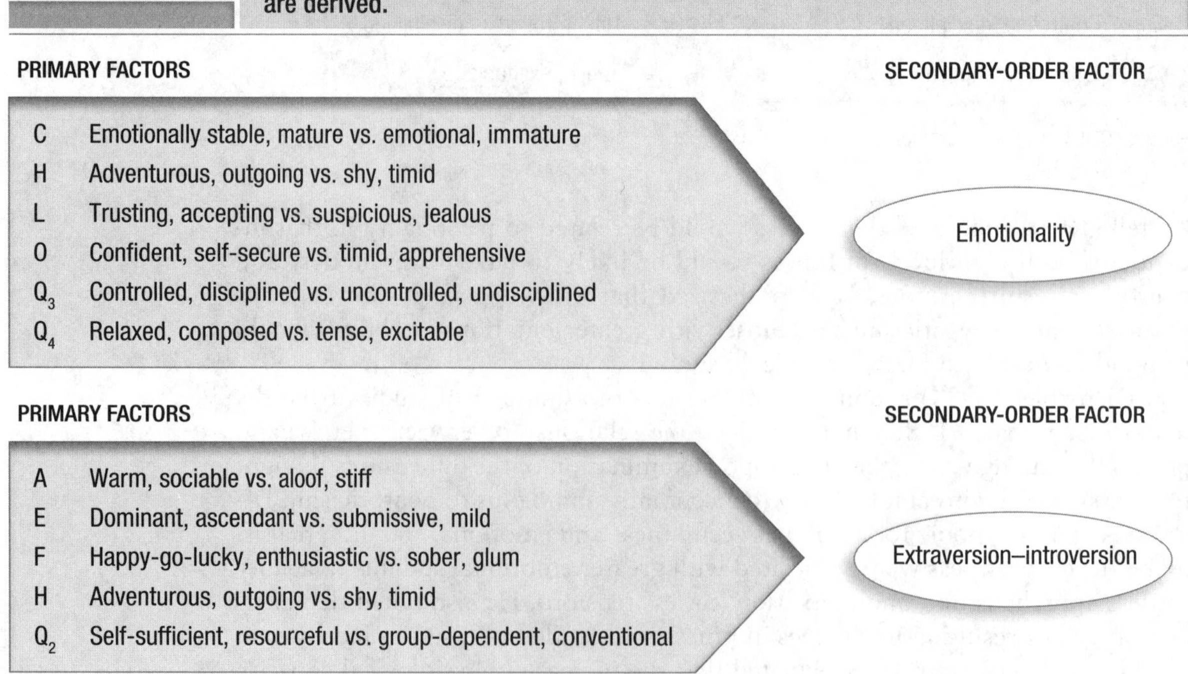

Source: Adapted from Cattall (1960).

intellect (O), agreeableness (A), and conscientiousness (C). Neuroticism and extraversion are similar to the same constructs presented in the earlier models (see Eysenck, Cattell). Openness to experience/intellect refers to a willingness to adjust ideas and activities when presented with new ideas or situations and a tendency to be perceptive, creative, and reflective. Agreeableness refers to compatibility with others (e.g., a tendency to be kind, cooperative, generous), and conscientiousness refers to a tendency to be achievement-oriented, goal-oriented, and self-disciplined. Conscientiousness has been further defined as being determined, strong-willed, and systematic in conducting designated jobs.

The five-factor model and exercise. Because of its relatively recent development, the FFM has not received a great deal of research attention in the exercise domain, with some notable exceptions. Courneya and Hellsten (1998) found E, N, and C to be significantly related to exercise behavior and adherence. Specifically, E and C were positively related to both moderate (e.g., fast walking) and strenuous (e.g., jogging) exercise behavior, and N was a significant predictor of exercise adherence, with greater levels of N predicting lower levels of adherence. Courneya, Bobick, and Schinke (1999) reported that E, N, and C were again all related to exercise behavior in two samples of female undergraduates. E and C were positively related to self-reported exercise (in the first sample of female undergraduates, this was based on both intensity and duration of activity in a "typical" week; in the second sample, this was based on attendance in aerobic classes over an 11-week span), while N was negatively related. Later, Rhodes, Courneya, and Bobick (2001) showed again that E, N, and C were important personality dimensions in examining exercise participation in female breast cancer survivors. Again, E and C were associated with adaptive exercise patterns and more advanced exercise stages, whereas N was associated with maladaptive exercise patterns and less advanced exercise stages (see Exhibit 7.5).

Subsequent to these studies, Courneya and colleagues have continued to examine the role of personality factors in explaining exercise behavior. In addition to the work just cited, they have proposed that the key personality factor may be a sub-trait of extraversion referred to as the **activity trait.** This sub-trait is thought to reflect a tendency to be busy and energetic, and to have a preference for fast-paced living (Rhodes, Courneya, & Jones, 2004). This particular sub-trait of extraversion has been shown to be significantly related to exercise behavior in a number of recent studies (Rhodes & Courneya, 2003; Rhodes et al., 2004).

■ activity trait

Extraversion has also been shown to be related to a preference for a higher level of exercise intensity (Morgan, 1973). Unfortunately, traits related to arousability and sensory modulation (e.g., activity trait) have not been shown to account (reliably) for variability in exercise behavior (e.g., selection of exercise intensity) and responses (e.g., affective responses to varying levels of exercise intensity). The modest relationships between physical activity and extraversion could possibly be due to the fact that

exhibit 7.5 The five-factor model and exercise behavior.

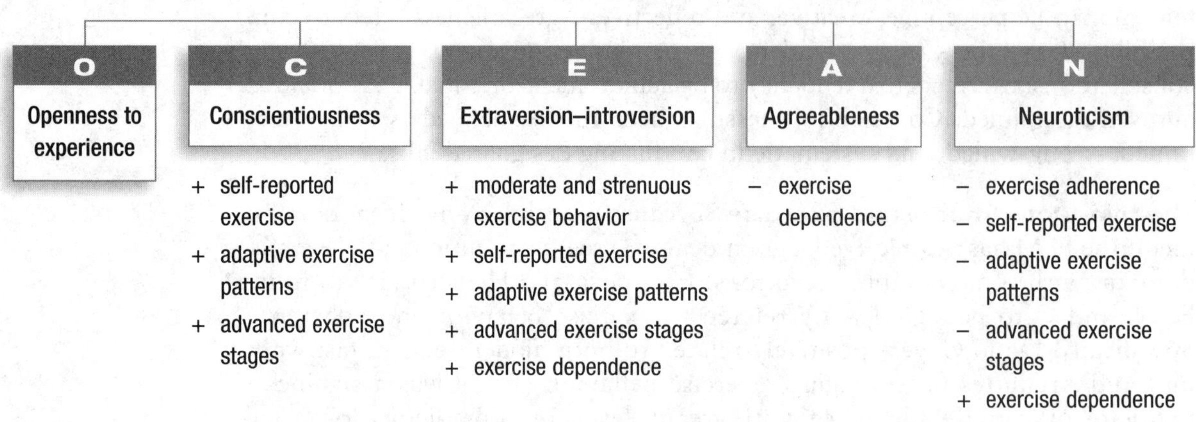

The five factors can be ordered to "spell" the word "ocean" as a mnemonic to remember them.

1. awareness of interoceptive (i.e., internal, physiological) cues relies on different mechanisms than exteroceptive (i.e., environmental, mainly social) cues, and/or
2. most of the available self-report measures of E assess exteroceptive stimuli rather than interoceptive stimuli.

In an attempt to overcome this potential limitation, Ekkekakis, Hall, and Petruzzello (2005) presented the constructs of intensity-preference and intensity-tolerance as genetically determined traits that could help in understanding the exercise intensity–exercise adherence relationship. **Intensity-preference** is defined as "a predisposition to select a particular exercise intensity when given the opportunity (e.g., when engaging in self-selected or unsupervised exercise) (Ekkekakis et al., 2005, p. 354), while **intensity-tolerance** is defined as "a trait that influences one's ability to continue exercising at an imposed level of intensity even when the activity becomes uncomfortable or unpleasant" (p. 354).

intensity-preference ■

intensity-tolerance ■

Evidence supporting the constructs has begun to accumulate. For example, Ekkekakis, Lind, and Jones-Matre (2006) examined whether intensity-preference could predict self-selected exercise intensity in a sample of relatively sedentary middle-aged women. It was shown that intensity-preference did predict self-selected exercise intensity (i.e., those with a preference for greater exercise intensity chose to exercise at greater intensities). Ekkekakis, Lind, Hall, and Petruzzello (2007) sought to examine whether intensity-tolerance would predict time spent exercising after the exercise intensity exceeded the ventilatory threshold, a point at which exercise has been shown to become progressively more unpleasant (see discussion in Chapter 13). This work, consisting of two separate studies, showed that self-reported intensity-tolerance was related to (1) the length of time a sample of young males and females continued to exercise beyond the ventilatory threshold, even after accounting for factors like age, body mass index, exercise frequency, and habitual exercise duration; and (2) the length of time a sample of middle-aged, sedentary women continued to exercise beyond the ventilatory threshold, even after accounting for factors like age, body mass index, and maximal aerobic capacity. Schneider and Graham (2009) have also shown that intensity-preference and intensity-tolerance were positively related to $\dot{V}O_2$peak (peak rate of oxygen consumption) and exercise enjoyment in a sample of healthy adolescents.

Ultimately, the objective of developing such individual difference constructs is to better understand the physical activity adherence/dropout phenomenon and to develop ways to reduce dropout and/or increase adherence. For example, the American College of Sports Medicine (2000) has stated that "individual preferences for exercise must be considered to improve the likelihood that the individual will adhere to the exercise program" (p. 145). Clearly this is an area of research that could be crucial to improving adherence.

Other Personality Factors Examined in Exercise Research

Gender-role orientation

Although the body of literature on gender-role orientations and their role in the exercise domain is not large, the dimensions of masculinity (M) and femininity (F) (Bem, 1974; Spence & Helmreich, 1978) as personality constructs may have important implications for exercise behavior and exercise prescription. Both M and F are conceived of as positive, desirable traits that are possessed by both males and females. It is somewhat unfortunate that these constructs were given the labels they were, because the tendency is to relate them directly to biological sex, when in fact they are not sex-linked. In fact, some formulations have taken to referring to M as "instrumental" and F as "expressive" as a way of avoiding the confusion with biological sex. In essence, the **instrumental personality** is characterized by traits like risk-taking, independence, aggressiveness, and competitiveness. The **expressive personality** is characterized by traits like understanding, sympathy, affection, and compassion. Because the two dimensions are viewed as independent of one another, an individual can possess each to varying degrees. Individuals who score high on the instrumental dimension and low on the expressive dimension are classified as masculine/instrumental; those who score high on the expressive and low on the instrumental dimension are classified as feminine/expressive. Individuals who score high on both dimensions are classified as **androgynous.** (Individuals who score low on both dimensions are classified as *undifferentiated.* Because so few people fall into this category, not much research has been done with this group.)

■ instrumental personality
■ expressive personality
■ androgynous

Gender roles and exercise. Such gender-role personality characteristics have implications for exercise behavior. Cross-gender activities are generally avoided

FOCUS on Anorexia Nervosa

Anorexia nervosa is a psychiatric disorder characterized by the refusal to maintain a minimally normal weight (i.e., at least 85 percent of one's expected weight for age and height), an intense fear of gaining weight even though underweight, body image disturbance, and, in women, the absence of at least three consecutive menstrual cycles (American Psychiatric Association, 1994). It is estimated that, each year, anorexia occurs in 19 out of every 100,000 females and in 2 out of every 100,000 males (Pawluck & Gorey, 1998).

One of the most paradoxical features of anorexia nervosa is that, despite periods of starvation or near-starvation, many anorexics continue to engage in abnormally high levels of physical activity. Dr. Caroline Davis has examined why some patients with anorexia become excessive exercisers and others do not. Part of her research program focuses on the role of the personality traits of addictiveness and obsessive-compulsiveness. The addictive personality type is associated with a tendency toward anxious and depressed mood states, poor impulse control, and the need for intense stimulation. The obsessive-compulsive personality type is associated with being very perseverant, rigid, self-controlled, and in need of orderliness. Adult anorexic patients who exercise excessively score higher on measures of both the addictive personality and the obsessive-compulsive personality than anorexic patients who do not exercise (Davis & Claridge, 1998).

Davis, Katzman, and Kirsh (1999) have also examined why these personality traits might influence anorexic patients' exercise behavior. Using questionnaires, the researchers measured personality, thoughts, and feelings toward exercise, as well as exercise behavior in a sample of 84 female adolescents who had been diagnosed with anorexia. They found that women who scored higher on the addictive and obsessive-compulsive personality measures had more unhealthy thoughts and feelings toward exercise than those who scored lower on these measures. (For example, they were more likely to feel guilty about missing an exercise session or believe that they must exercise even if they were sick or injured.) In turn, patients with more unhealthy exercise thoughts and feelings were more likely to be excessive exercisers. Based on these findings, it seems that the addictive and obsessive-compulsive personality types predispose individuals with anorexia to have unhealthy cognitions regarding exercise. These cognitions become a primary driving force that motivates the anorexic individual to engage in excessive levels of activity.

ADDITIONAL RESOURCES

Adkins, E.C., & Keel, P.K. (2005). Does "excessive" or "compulsive" best describe exercise as a symptom of bulimia nervosa? *International Journal of Eating Disorders, 38,* 24–29.

Bratland-Sanda, S., Sundgot-Borgen J., Rø, Ø., Rosenvinge, J.H., Hoffart, A., & Martinsen, E.W. (2010). Physical activity and exercise dependence during inpatient treatment of longstanding eating disorders: An exploratory study of excessive and non-excessive exercisers, *International Journal of Eating Disorders, 43(3),* 266–273.

Davis, C., Blackmore, E., Katzman, D.K., & Fox, J. (2005). Female adolescents with anorexia nervosa and their parents: A case-control study of exercise attitudes and behaviours. *Psychological Medicine, 35,* 377–386.

Sundgot-Borgen, J., Rosenvinge, J.H., Bahr, R., & Schneider, L.S. (2002). The effect of exercise, cognitive therapy, and nutritional counseling in treating bulimia nervosa. *Medicine and Science in Sports and Exercise, 34,* 190–195.

ACTIVITY

A number of different personality characteristics are described in this chapter. Given the description of the obsessive-compulsive personality type, what other kinds of personality characteristics might be similar? How might the exercise itself (e.g., frequency, intensity, duration, type) or the exercise environment be modified as a way to potentially aid the obsessive-compulsive individual, ideally preventing the unhealthy thoughts and feelings toward exercise (e.g., feelings of guilt when an exercise session is missed and the feeling that general well-being is dependent on not missing an exercise session; the need to continue to exercise in the face of illness or injury)? Describe the changes that you propose and why these would make a difference to the anorexic individual.

by gender-typed individuals. When cross-gender activities are performed, greater psychological discomfort is often reported. For example, feminine (expressive)–typed individuals avoid masculine (instrumental) activities when given a choice. If forced to engage in such an activity, they often have more negative feelings and debilitating perceptions while involved in the activity.

To examine whether gender roles do in fact mediate the perception of strenuous exercise, Rejeski, Best, Griffith, and Kenney (1987) conducted a study with 42 college-aged males. Noting that exercise is typically stereotyped as a masculine task, Rejeski and colleagues hypothesized that feminine-typed males would respond with greater distress to strenuous exercise than would either androgynous or masculine-typed males. Ratings of perceived exertion (RPE) and affective responses were examined using a six-minute exercise bout on a cycle ergometer at an intensity equivalent to 85 percent of each individual's estimated aerobic capacity. The results revealed the following: Feminine-typed males had significantly higher ratings of perceived exertion than either masculine-typed or androgynous males, even though the work load was physiologically equivalent for each group. Feminine-typed males also had significantly greater negative affect compared with the androgynous males, and the trend was in the right direction for the masculine-typed males. Furthermore, immediately following completion of the six-minute exercise bout, subjects were asked to continue exercising at a supramaximal intensity (approximately 110 percent of estimated aerobic capacity) for as long as they could. This behavioral measure indicated that the feminine-typed males, now having the opportunity to withdraw from a potentially uncomfortable activity, exercised for half as long (about 20 seconds) as the masculine-typed males (about 46 seconds) and only about 30 percent as long as the androgynous males (about 67 seconds). Essentially identical findings were shown in an earlier study (Hochstetler, Rejeski, & Best, 1985) with women. Here, feminine-typed females reported less optimism toward a 30-minute exercise bout and reported higher ratings of perceived exertion throughout the run (especially during the last 15 minutes).

Clearly, such personality traits and the psychological discomfort that accompanies the performance of cross-typed activities might predispose one either to avoid exercise altogether or to have negative experiences during the activity. Such findings certainly require further study. It is possible that, if this pattern of findings is reliable, exercise professionals could intervene to help, particularly with feminine-typed individuals. This could involve structuring exercise protocols that would not create such negative psychological effects (e.g., lower intensities).

Type A behavior pattern

"The type A behavior pattern is an action–emotion complex that can be observed in any person who is *aggressively* involved in a *chronic, incessant* struggle to achieve more and more in less and less time, and is required to do so, against the opposing efforts of other things or persons" (Friedman & Rosenman, 1974, p. 67; emphasis in original). The **type A behavior pattern** (TABP) has been thought of as having several characteristic components (Price, 1982), including:

type A behavior pattern ■

- achievement striving
- competitiveness
- sense of time urgency
- aggressiveness
- preoccupation with deadlines
- impatience
- hostility
- hard-driving
- hyperalertness

The TABP has been shown to (1) place one at greater risk for developing cardiovascular disease and (2) be prevalent in those already with heart disease. Not surprisingly, the majority of research examining the TABP has focused primarily on its role in cardiovascular disease and, indeed, it has sometimes been referred to as the *coronary-prone personality.* Friedman and Rosenman (1974) initially posited that it was the sense of time urgency that distinguished the TABP, but more recent investigations have implicated the anger or hostility components of the TABP as the most important features for increased risk of cardiovascular disease. Some researchers have even speculated that it is not just cardiovascular disease but disease in general for which the TABP places one at greater risk (Friedman & Booth-Kewley, 1987). Because of the beneficial effects of exercise programs for those suffering from cardiovascular disease, it has been suspected that exercise could also be beneficial for the type A individual.

TABP and exercise. Exercise has been shown to be effective in reducing the TABP (e.g., Blumenthal, Williams, Williams, & Wallace, 1980), but studies have not produced uniform results. For example, Roskies, Seraganian, Oseasohn, et al. (1986) showed exercise to be less effective than a cognitive–behavioral treatment in reducing heart rate and blood pressure reactivity to stress-inducing laboratory tasks. In contrast, Blumenthal, Emery, Walsh, and colleagues (1988) showed that a 12-week aerobic exercise program did successfully reduce cardiovascular reactivity to psychosocial stressors compared to a strength and flexibility intervention.

There is, however, reason to believe that the TABP might have important implications for individual differences regarding exercise in social contexts. It has been noted that type A individuals tend to have lower adherence rates to exercise programs than do type B individuals (e.g., Oldridge, 1982) and that type As also have higher rates of exercise-related injuries (Fields, Delaney, & Hinkle, 1990). One aspect of the TABP that might explain such findings is the tendency toward involvement in more intense and competitive exercise for type As (e.g., Hinkle, Lyons, & Burke, 1989). Type As have also been shown to exert greater effort, causing greater levels of physiological activation during exercise. They also tend to estimate their perceived exertion and discomfort at lower levels during low to moderate levels of exercise intensity, however (Hassmen, Stahl, & Borg, 1993). Finally, compared to type Bs, type A individuals have greater stress responses at higher exercise intensities (McMurray, Hardy, Roberts, et al., 1989) and more negative affective responses (Hardy, McMurray, & Roberts, 1989) (see Exhibit 7.6).

Hardiness

Whereas the TABP is thought to place one at greater risk for disease, the personality construct of *hardiness* is proposed to be stress buffering. Originally delineated by Kobasa (1979), **hardiness** is theorized to comprise:

■ hardiness

1. a sense of control over events
2. commitment, dedication, or involvement in everyday life
3. a tendency to perceive life events as challenges and opportunities rather than as stressors

Type A and B behavior patterns and exercise. **exhibit 7.6**

TYPE A	TYPE B
↑ Risk of cardiovascular disease	↓ Risk of cardiovascular disease
↓ Adherence rates	↑ Adherence rates
↑ Effort	↓ Effort
↑ Intensity	↓ Intensity
↑ Physiological activation	↓ Physiological activation
↓ Ratings of perceived exertion (RPE)	↑ RPE
↑ Stress responses	↓ Stress responses
↑ Negative affective responses	↓ Negative affective responses

This particular constellation of characteristics is thought to protect against the deleterious effects of stress and to serve as a buffer against illness. Initial studies by Kobasa, Maddi, and Puccetti (1982) and by Kobasa, Maddi, Puccetti, and Zola (1985) were supportive of this notion, largely because of the additive effects of the hardiness personality coupled with exercise behavior. In other words, those higher in hardiness are able to transform stressful events to decrease their stress (e.g., obtaining information, taking action, learning from experience), and exercise serves to buffer against the strain of stressful events.

Hardiness and exercise. Other research examining the link between hardiness and exercise in the stress–illness relationship has been somewhat mixed. Roth, Wiebe, Fillingim, and Shay (1989) found that although fitness and hardiness were negatively related to illness, neither fitness nor hardiness moderated the stress effect. They suggested that, consistent with Kobasa's formulation, hardiness might indirectly affect either the occurrence or interpretation of stressful events. Furthermore, exercise serves to increase fitness, which is indirectly associated with reduced illness. Carson (1993) demonstrated that in long-term AIDS survivors, hardiness was positively associated with, among other things, exercise participation.

At present it appears that hardiness is related to a tendency to engage in more healthful behaviors. Exercise can certainly be included among such behaviors. It should be noted, however, that the majority of research in this area has been correlational in nature. It is not clear whether a hardy personality leads one to engage in exercise or whether exercise participation leads to a hardy personality. This certainly has implications for the impact that exercise might have on reactivity to stress and illness.

Self-motivation

psychobiological model ■

Dishman undertook one attempt at the development of an exercise-specific theory that incorporated personality. He proposed a **psychobiological model** as an attempt to explain exercise adherence (Dishman, 1981). The model specifically advocates consideration of both biological factors (i.e., body composition, body mass) and a psychological factor. The specific psychological factor that Dishman espoused was the construct of *self-motivation* (which is conceptually analogous to the conscientiousness factor from the FFM), defined as a generalized, nonspecific tendency to persist in the absence of extrinsic reinforcement. The Self-Motivation Inventory (Dishman & Ickes, 1981), a questionnaire developed to assess self-motivation, includes statements that reflect the following:

1. low self-motivation (e.g., I'm not very good at committing myself to do things; I never force myself to do things I don't feel like doing) and
2. high self-motivation (e.g., I'm really concerned about developing and maintaining self-discipline; I like to set my goals and work toward them).

Initial work with this model predicted that percentage of body fat and body mass would be negatively related to adherence whereas self-motivation would be positively related to adherence (it is interesting to note that Courneya et al.'s [1999] work with the FFM has also shown conscientiousness to be related to adherence). As with so many other attempts, the initial work was fairly positive, but subsequent research has not supported the model nearly as well (e.g., Gale, Eckhoff, Mogel, & Rodnick, 1984; McAuley & Jacobson, 1991). Thus, while the psychobiological model holds appeal, much more work is needed in this area.

Practical Recommendations

In general, because we currently have such a vague understanding of which personality factors are important for exercise behavior, it is difficult to make straightforward practical recommendations. Given what research has shown, however, it seems reasonable to propose at least a few suggestions. First, individuals who seem to be more emotional (i.e., neurotic) might be encouraged to begin a regular exercise program. The beautiful thing about such a suggestion is that it does not have to be made for the psychological benefits. The current state of fitness for most individuals would allow such a suggestion to be made for the physical benefits, but it seems apparent that the psychological benefits (reduced emotionality in this case) would occur as well. Essentially, the recommended "exercise dose" could be the same as what would be given for improving fitness or encouraging weight loss in terms of frequency, duration, and intensity. The key would appear to be to start slowly, with the realization that improvements will take some time. And second, it also seems reasonable to propose that any exercise program have some type of aerobic activity as a primary component. Although time may well show that resistance activities also influence personality factors, such effects have already been shown for aerobic activities.

Conclusion

It is worth pointing out that the study of personality or individual differences is important for exercise psychology. While regular exercise can clearly be important in both the prevention of chronic diseases and the treatment of such diseases, one of the most vexing problems for the field continues to be an inability to predict accurately those who will adhere to exercise programs and those who will drop out. Certainly, knowledge of factors such as an individual's level of extraversion or neuroticism, or whether the person is more instrumental or expressive, can be helpful in prescribing exercise programs. It also seems fairly apparent that an individual's participation in a regular program of exercise can be important in the development of a more emotionally stable, extraverted personality.

what do you know?

1. What are the three main aspects of an individual's personality?
2. What main feature of Sheldon's constitutional theory is thought to determine personality?
3. What are the three major dimensions of Eysenck's theory?
4. What predictions can be made about Eysenck's personality dimensions with respect to exercise/physical activity?
5. Describe the relationship between fitness and emotionality.
6. What kind of psychological reactions might a feminine-typed individual have to a strenuous bout of exercise?
7. What are the three factors that seem to make up the hardiness personality constellation?
8. What is self-motivation, and is it important in understanding exercise behavior?

learning activities

1. A personal trainer needs to design exercise programs for many different kinds of clients. Based on what you have learned from this chapter, describe a program for an individual who is not particularly self-motivated and who is also overweight. What if the client is feminine-typed? What if the client displays a number of type A behaviors?
2. Return to the opening scenario of this chapter. If you were Sarah, what kind of exercise program would you design for Jenny? Be more specific than the scenario indicated (i.e., more specific than exercising three days per week). What activity or activities would you recommend? How often, how hard, and for how long would you have Jenny do them?
3. Assuming that Sheldon's constitutional theory of personality can be put into practice, what kinds of exercise might be most useful for the ectomorph? Endomorph? Mesomorph?

references

American College of Sports Medicine (2000). *ACSM's guidelines for exercise testing and prescription* (6th ed.). Philadelphia: Lippincott Williams & Wilkins.

American Psychiatric Association (1994). *Diagnostic and statistical manual of mental disorders* (4th ed.). Washington, DC: Author.

Arai, Y., & Hisamichi, S. (1998). Self-reported exercise frequency and personality: A population-based study in Japan. *Perceptual and Motor Skills, 87,* 1371–1375.

Bear, M.F., Connors, B.W., & Paradiso, M.A. (2001). *Neuroscience: Exploring the brain* (2nd ed.). Baltimore: Lippincott Williams & Wilkins.

Bem, S.L. (1974). The measurement of psychological androgyny. *Journal of Consulting and Clinical Psychology, 42,* 155–162.

Blumenthal, J.A., Emery, C.F., Walsh, M.A., Cox, D.K., Kuhn, C.M., Williams, R.B., & Williams, R.S. (1988). Exercise training in healthy type A middle aged men: Effects on behavioral and cardiovascular responses. *Psychosomatic Medicine, 50,* 418–433.

Blumenthal, J.A., Williams, R.S., Williams, R.B., & Wallace, A.G. (1980). Effects of exercise on the type A (coronary prone) behavior pattern. *Psychosomatic Medicine, 42,* 289–296.

Carron, A.V. (1980). *Social psychology of sport.* Ithaca, NY: Mouvement Publications.

Carson, V.B. (1993). Prayer, meditation, exercise, and special diets: Behaviors of the hardy person with HIV/AIDS. *Journal of Associated Nurses AIDS Care, 4*(3), 18–28.

Cattell, R.B. (1960). Some psychological correlates of physical fitness and physique. In S.C. Staley (Ed.), *Exercise and fitness* (pp. 138–151). Chicago: Athletic Institute.

Costa, P.T., & McCrae, R.R. (1992). *The NEO Personality Inventory R: Professional Manual.* Odessa, FL: Psychological Assessment Resources.

Courneya, K.S., Bobick, T.M., & Schinke, R.J. (1999). Does the theory of planned behavior mediate the relation between personality and exercise behavior? *Basic and Applied Social Psychology, 21,* 317–324.

Courneya, K.S., & Hellsten, L.M. (1998). Personality correlates of exercise behavior, motives, barriers and preferences: An application of the five-factor model. *Personality and Individual Differences, 24,* 625–633.

Davis, C., & Claridge, G. (1998). The eating disorders as addiction: A psychobiological perspective. *Addictive Behaviors, 23,* 463–475.

Davis, C., Katzman, D.K., & Kirsh, C. (1999). Compulsive physical activity in adolescents with anorexia nervosa: A psychobiological spiral of pathology. *Journal of Nervous and Mental Disease, 187,* 336–342.

De Moor, M.H., Beem, A.L., Stubbe, J.H., Boomsma, D.I., & De Geus E.J. (2006). Regular exercise, anxiety, depression and personality: a population-based study. *Preventive Medicine, 42*(4), 273–279.

Dienstbier, R.A. (1984). The effect of exercise on personality. In M.L. Sachs & G.W. Buffone (Eds.), *Running as therapy* (pp. 253–272). Lincoln: University of Nebraska Press.

DiLorenzo, T.M., Bargman, E.P., Stucky-Ropp, R., Brassington, G.S., Frensch, P.A., & LaFontaine, T. (1999). Long-term effects of aerobic exercise on psychological outcomes. *Preventive Medicine, 28,* 75–85.

Dishman, R.K. (1981). Biologic influences on exercise adherence. *Research Quarterly for Exercise and Sport, 52,* 143–189.

Dishman, R.K., & Ickes, W. (1981). Self-motivation and adherence to therapeutic exercise. *Journal of Behavioral Medicine, 4,* 421–438.

Ekkekakis, P., Hall, E.E., & Petruzzello, S.J. (2005). Some like it vigorous: Measuring individual differences in the preference for and tolerance of exercise intensity. *Journal of Sport & Exercise Psychology, 27,* 350–374.

Ekkekakis, P., Lind, E., Hall, E.E., & Petruzzello, S.J. (2007). Can self-reported tolerance of exercise intensity play a role in exercise testing? *Medicine & Science in Sports & Exercise, 39,* 1193–1199

Ekkekakis, P., Lind, E., & Jones-Matre, R.R. (2006). Can self-reported preference for exercise intensity predict physiologically defined self-selected exercise intensity? *Research Quarterly for Exercise & Sport, 77,* 81–90.

Eysenck, H.J., Nias, D.K., & Cox, D.N. (1982). Sport and personality. *Advances in Behaviour Research and Therapy, 4,* 1–56.

Fields, K.B., Delaney, M., & Hinkle, J.S. (1990). A prospective study of type A behavior and running injuries. *Journal of Family Practice, 30,* 425–429.

Friedman, H.S., & Booth-Kewley, S. (1987). Personality, type A behavior, and coronary heart disease: The role of emotional expression. *Journal of Personality and Social Psychology, 53,* 783–792.

Friedman, M., & Rosenman, R.H. (1974). *Type A behavior and your heart.* New York: Knopf.

Furnham, A. (1981). Personality and activity preference. *British Journal of Social Psychology, 20,* 57–68.

Gale, J.B., Eckhoff, W.T., Mogel, S.F., & Rodnick, J.E. (1984). Factors related to adherence to an exercise program for healthy adults. *Medicine & Science in Sports & Exercise, 16,* 544–549.

Hardy, C.J., McMurray, R.G., & Roberts, S. (1989). A/B types and psychophysiological responses to exercise stress. *Journal of Sport and Exercise Psychology, 11,* 141–151.

Hassmen, P., Stahl, R., & Borg, G. (1993). Psychophysiological responses to exercise in type A/B men. *Psychosomatic Medicine, 55,* 178–184.

Hinkle, J.S., Lyons, B., & Burke, K.L. (1989). Manifestation of type A behavior pattern among aerobic runners. *Journal of Sport Behavior, 12,* 131–138.

Hochstetler, S.A., Rejeski, W.J., & Best, D.L. (1985). The influence of sex-role orientation on ratings of perceived exertion. *Sex Roles, 12,* 825–835.

Hollander, E.P. (1967). *Principles and methods of social psychology.* New York: Holt.

Hsiao, E.T., & Thayer, R.E. (1998). Exercising for mood regulation: The importance of experience. *Personality and Individual Differences, 24,* 829–836.

James, W. (1899). Physical training in the educational curriculum. *American Physical Education Review, 4,* 220–221.

Kirkcaldy, B., & Furnham, A. (1991). Extraversion, neuroticism, psychoticism and recreational choice. *Personality and Individual Differences, 12,* 737–745.

Kobasa, S.C. (1979). Stressful life events, personality and health: An inquiry into hardiness. *Journal of Personality and Social Psychology, 37,* 1–11.

Kobasa, S.C., Maddi, S.R., & Puccetti, M.C. (1982). Personality and exercise as buffers in the stress-illness relationship. *Journal of Behavioral Medicine, 5,* 391–404.

Kobasa, S.C., Maddi, S.R., Puccetti, M.C., & Zola, M.A. (1985). Effectiveness of hardiness, exercise and social support as resources against illness. *Journal of Psychosomatic Research, 29,* 525–533.

Landers, D.M., & Petruzzello, S.J. (1994). Physical activity, fitness, and anxiety. In C. Bouchard, R.J. Shephard, & T. Stephens (Eds.), *Physical activity, fitness, and health: International proceedings and consensus statement* (pp. 868–882). Champaign, IL: Human Kinetics.

McAuley, E., & Jacobson, L. (1991). Self-efficacy and exercise participation in sedentary adult females. *American Journal of Health Promotion, 5,* 185–207.

McCrae, R.R., & John, O.P. (1992). An introduction to the five-factor model and its applications. *Journal of Personality, 60,* 175–215.

McMurray, R.G., Hardy, C.J., Roberts, S., Forsythe, W.A., & Mar, M.H. (1989). Neuroendocrine responses of type A individuals to exercise. *Behavioral Medicine, 15,* 84–92.

Mendez, C. (1553/1960). *Book of bodily exercise.* Translated by F. Guerra. New Haven, CT: Elizabeth Licht.

Morgan, W.P. (1973). Psychological factors influencing perceived exertion. *Medicine and Science in Sports, 5,* 97–103.

Morgan, W.P. (1980). The trait psychology controversy. *Research Quarterly for Exercise and Sport, 51,* 50–76.

Oldridge, N.B. (1982). Compliance and exercise in primary and secondary prevention of coronary heart disease: A review. *Preventive Medicine, 11,* 56–70.

Pawluck, D.E., & Gorey, K.M. (1998). Secular trends in the incidence of anorexia nervosa: Integrative review of population-based studies. *International Journal of Eating Disorders, 23,* 347–352.

Petruzzello, S.J., Landers, D.M., Hatfield, B.D., Kubitz, K.A., & Salazar, W. (1991). A meta-analysis on the anxiety reducing effects of acute and chronic exercise: Outcomes and mechanisms. *Sports Medicine, 11,* 143–182.

Price, V.A. (1982). The Type A risk factor: Conceptual problems and progress. In V.A. Price, *Type A behavior pattern* (pp. 3–21). New York: Academic Press.

Rejeski, W.J., Best, D.L., Griffith, P., & Kenney, E. (1987). Sex-role orientation and the responses of men to exercise stress. *Research Quarterly for Exercise and Sport, 58,* 260–264.

Rhodes, R.E. (2006). The built-in environment: The role of personality and physical activity. *Exercise & Sports Science Reviews, 34,* 83–88.

Rhodes, R.E., & Courneya, K.S. (2003). Relationships between personality, an extended theory of planned behaviour model and exercise behaviour. *British Journal of Health Psychology, 8,* 19–36.

Rhodes, R.E., Courneya, K.S., & Bobick, T.M. (2001). Personality and exercise participation across the breast cancer experience. *Psycho-Oncology, 10,* 380–388.

Rhodes, R.E., Courneya, K.S., & Jones, L.W. (2004). Personality and social cognitive influences on exercise behavior: Adding the activity trait to the theory of planned behavior. *Psychology of Sport & Exercise, 5,* 243–254.

Rhodes, R.E., & Smith, N.E.I. (2006). Personality correlates of physical activity: A review and meta-analysis. *British Journal of Sports Medicine, 40,* 958–965.

Roskies, E., Seraganian, P., Oseasohn, R., Hanley, J.A., Collu, R., Martin, N., & Smilga, C. (1986). The Montreal Type A intervention project: Major findings. *Health Psychology, 5,* 45–69.

Roth, D.L., Wiebe, D.J., Fillingim, R.B., & Shay, K.A. (1989). Life events, fitness, hardiness, and health: A simultaneous analysis of proposed stress-resistance effects. *Journal of Personality and Social Psychology, 57,* 136–142.

Schneider, M.L., & Graham D.J. (2009). Personality, physical fitness, and affective response to exercise among adolescents. *Medicine & Science in Sports & Exercise, 41,* 947–955.

Schnurr, P.P., Vaillant, C.O., & Vaillant, G.E. (1990). Predicting exercise in late midlife from young adult personality characteristics. *International Journal of Aging and Human Development, 30,* 153–160.

Sheldon, W.H. (1942). *The varieties of temperament: A psychology of constitutional differences.* New York: Harper.

Shiomi, K. (1980). Performance differences between extraverts and introverts on exercise using an ergometer. *Perceptual and Motor Skills, 50,* 356–358.

Spence, J.T., & Helmreich, R.L. (1978). *Masculinity and femininity: Their psychological dimensions, correlates, and antecedents.* Austin: University of Texas Press.

Thayer, R.E., Newman, R., & McClain, T.M. (1994). Self-regulation of mood: Strategies for changing a bad mood, raising energy, and reducing tension. *Journal of Personality and Social Psychology, 67,* 910–925.

Yeung, R.R., & Helmsley, D.R. (1997). Exercise behaviour in an aerobics class: The impact of personality traits and efficacy cognitions. *Personality and Individual Differences, 23,* 425–431.

8

Self-Concept, Self-Esteem, and Exercise

KEY TERMS

academic self-concept
global self-esteem
nonacademic self-concept
perceived competence
physical self-concept
self-concept
self-confidence
self-efficacy
self-esteem
self-schemata
social self-concept

Chris is a high school student who is self-conscious about his body—he feels he is too skinny and lacks muscle definition. Because appearing fit and attractive to others is important to him, his self-esteem is not as strong as he would like it to be. In conversation with his friend Deron, Chris learns that Deron regularly works out at the local fitness club in town. Chris views his friend as fit and recognizes that Deron's self-esteem is very positive. Chris decides to obtain a trial membership at the club and asks Deron to help him get started on a weight-training regimen. Chris develops the habit of working out at the club three times per week with Deron, and he extends his membership to a full year. The physical results of his efforts begin to show, as evidenced by increased muscle size, muscle definition, and weight gain. Perhaps most important, Chris develops a strong sense of pride in his physical fitness and appearance, and his self-esteem improves dramatically.

The Significance of Self-Esteem

In recent years, researchers have confirmed a notion that many in the field of psychology have long understood—that individuals who are popular, rich, and powerful are not necessarily happy. Indeed, Sheldon, Elliot, Kim, and Kasser (2001) found that these components ranked toward the bottom of psychological needs, while self-esteem topped the list of needs that bring happiness to people. This is certainly good news for those of us in the field of exercise psychology, as researchers have repeatedly stated that the greatest potential impact of physical activity may be seen in the participant's self-esteem (Folkins & Sime, 1981; Hughes, 1984; McAuley, 1994). Consider the plight of Chris in the scenario at the beginning of the chapter. The image he maintains of himself as a person is, to some extent, dictated by the specific image he holds of himself as an exerciser. Consequently, we would expect a positive change in both his physical and overall self-concept following successful adoption and maintenance of a physical activity regimen. The findings of Sheldon and colleagues (2001) and other researchers in the field of exercise psychology suggest that promoting the self-esteem–enhancing properties of physical activity might be a viable strategy for improving activity levels in those individuals who view self-esteem as a primary psychological need.

Self-Concept, Self-Esteem, and Related Definitions

self concept ■

self-esteem ■

perceived competence ■

self-confidence ■

self-efficacy ■

Although the constructs of self-concept and self-esteem are closely related and are often used interchangeably, they are not the same. For the purposes of this discussion, we will consider **self-concept** simply to be the way in which we see or define ourselves ("who I am"). You may describe yourself as a son or daughter, student, or salesperson; more specifically, you might consider yourself to be a mature and hard-working student, a loyal spouse, a fitness fanatic, an extravert (outgoing, life-of-the-party type), and so on. **Self-esteem** (synonymous with self-worth) constitutes the evaluative or affective consequence of one's self-concept ("how I feel about who I am"). In other words, self-esteem is the extent to which you feel positively or negatively about your self-concept. Generally, self-concept and self-esteem are considered to be global in nature. That is, one's self-concept and self-esteem influence, and are influenced by, all aspects of an individual's life. Although certain domains of one's life are likely to be particularly influential on self-concept and self-esteem, all domains combine to form an overall sense of each construct. In our earlier example, because Chris values physical activity, his positive physical self-concept is reflected in a relatively high self-esteem.

Self-concept and self-esteem are distinct from other forms of self-referent thought such as perceived competence, self-confidence, and self-efficacy, in that the latter group of constructs is focused primarily on judgments of ability and potential success in specific situations, activities, skills, or domains. For example, we might be interested in assessing an individual's level of **perceived competence** in the physical activity domain. In order to determine this, the individual would have to ask himself questions such as "Do I consider myself to be an 'athletic' individual?" or "Can I perform most physical skills, movements, or activities capably?" **Self-confidence** in the physical activity setting is somewhat more specific in that the individual might perceive herself as capable in activities of daily living (encompassing activities such as walking up and down stairs, and carrying groceries) but not so capable when it comes to engaging in more complex movements (e.g., hiking, dancing, weight training). Finally, as mentioned in Chapter 3, **self-efficacy** is a situation-specific form of self-confidence. In the physical activity domain, this construct generally takes the form of judgments related to a particular skill/ability in a particular situation. For instance, someone might be highly self-efficacious when performing upper-body weight training but not as efficacious when performing lower-body weight training. Similarly, someone might have high self-efficacy for adhering to an exercise regimen in the fall and spring months but might have considerably lower efficacy for adhering in the summer and winter months. In short, these related constructs are more variable than self-concept/self-esteem, but they do contribute meaningfully to an individual's self-concept and self-esteem.

Theoretical Foundations Employed in the Physical Activity Literature

Not surprisingly, initial research investigations concerning exercise and self-concept/self-esteem were generated primarily from theories and models employed in the parent discipline of psychology (social-cognitive psychology, to be exact). This was certainly the case with the self-concept model proposed by Shavelson, Hubner, and Stanton (1976). Later, Sonstroem and Morgan (1989) tailored the model for the exercise setting. These models are the topics of the following sections.

Shavelson, Hubner, and Stanton Model

In 1976, Shavelson and colleagues introduced a multifaceted model of self-concept that asserted that one's general (overall) self-concept was an aggregate construct determined by judgments of self-concept in a number of domains. The model is hierarchically organized so that more situation-specific and unstable evaluations are evident at the lower levels, while more global and stable evaluations are contained within the upper levels (see Exhibit 8.1).

Residing at the top of the model, general self-concept consists of two primary categories—namely, academic and nonacademic self-concept. One's **academic self-concept** encompasses the primary learning domains of English, math, history, and science. **Nonacademic self-concept** is divided into social, emotional, and physical self-concepts. Thus, four domains of self-concept are said to exist. With the exception of emotional self-concept, each domain is influenced by multiple subareas. For example, **physical self-concept** is formulated by the individual's judgments of both general physical abilities and physical appearance. According to the model, individuals with elevated perceptions of their physical abilities and positive feelings regarding their physical appearance would be expected to report a strong, positive physical self-concept. (See Chapter 9 for more detailed discussions of body image and its impact on self-esteem and exercise behavior.) Similarly, **social self-concept** would be enhanced by positive interactions with peers and significant others.

- academic self-concept
- nonacademic self-concept
- physical self-concept
- social self-concept

The base level of the hierarchy is defined by the evaluation of behavior in specific situations. Judgments of physical ability, then, are based on our perceptions

exhibit 8.1 Diagram of the self-concept model.

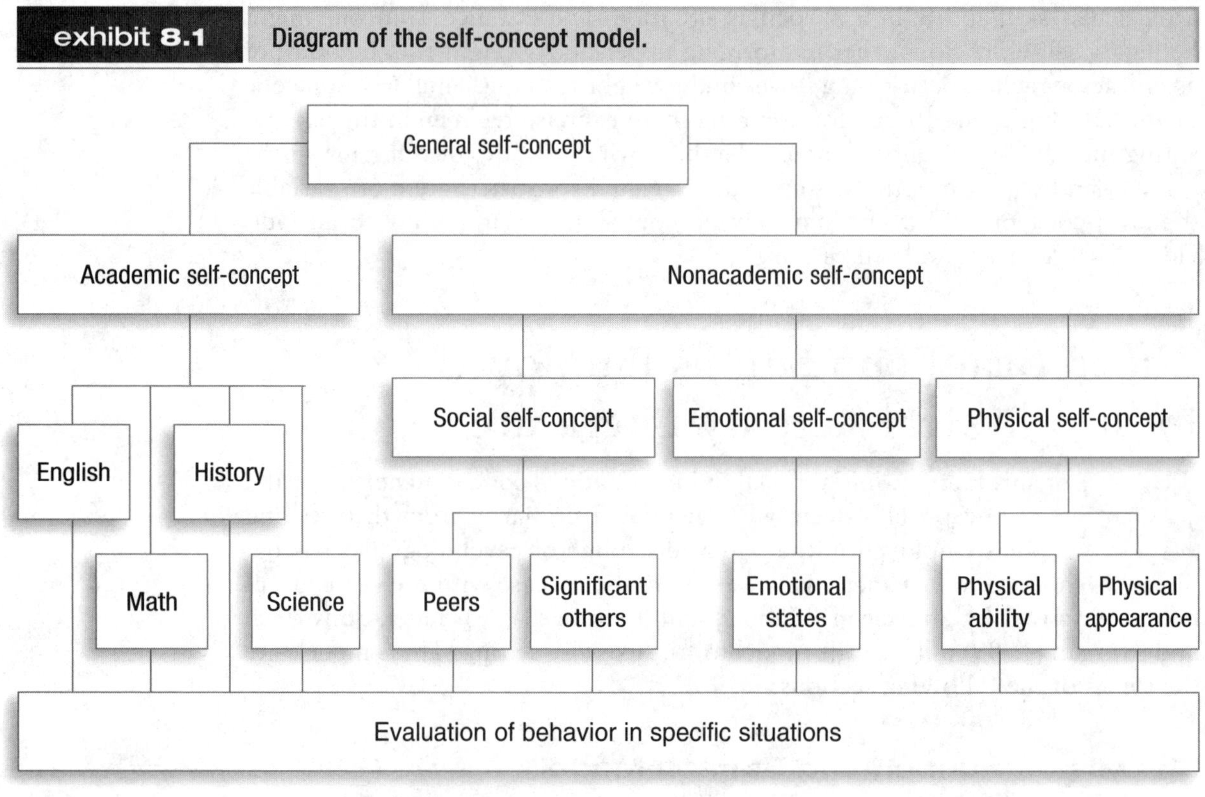

Source: Adapted from Shavelson, Hubner, & Stanton (1976).

of successful and unsuccessful performances in a number of activities engaged in over a prolonged period of time. To use a mathematical analogy, each individually evaluated behavior is assigned a positive (successful) or negative (unsuccessful) number. The sum total of these evaluations indicates whether the perception of physical ability is high or low. Thus, an individual who experiences repeated success in a number of different activities would be expected to maintain a positive physical self-concept.

Unfortunately, this formula is a bit simplistic. Because we value the activities we engage in to varying degrees, the formula must include "weights" for each activity. In other words, a person who places high value on physical ability related to lifetime physical activities (walking, running, strength training, etc.), but little value on physical ability related to sports (tennis, golf, softball, basketball, etc.), will maintain a physical self-concept most consistent with outcomes emanating from lifetime activities. For such a person, a disappointing series of strength-training sessions will have a much greater influence on physical self-concept than will multiple negative performances in golf.

The process is the same for physical appearance. For instance, an individual's perception of her physical appearance might be based predominantly on her body fat content. The fact that she also possesses considerable lean muscle tissue may be of limited consequence in her judgment. Not surprisingly, the result would be a poor evaluation of physical appearance.

Sonstroem and Morgan Model

Building on the model from Shavelson and colleagues, Sonstroem and Morgan (1989) proposed a model of exercise and self-esteem that also featured hierarchically organized constructs leading to predictions of **global** (overall) **self-esteem** (see Exhibit 8.2). The horizontal axis lists the various assessments (two or more) that would be conducted when an intervention is presented. For example, if we were interested in the effect of a 12-month exercise program (intervention) on self-esteem, we would need to obtain a baseline (pre-program) assessment (Test 1) and at least one more assessment (Test 2) following completion of the program. Note that the model specifies an unlimited number of potential assessments beyond the second test (. . . nth test) for research designs incorporating multiple assessments over time. Thus, in the hypothetical 12-month study just

■ global self-esteem

Diagram of the exercise and self-esteem model. **exhibit 8.2**

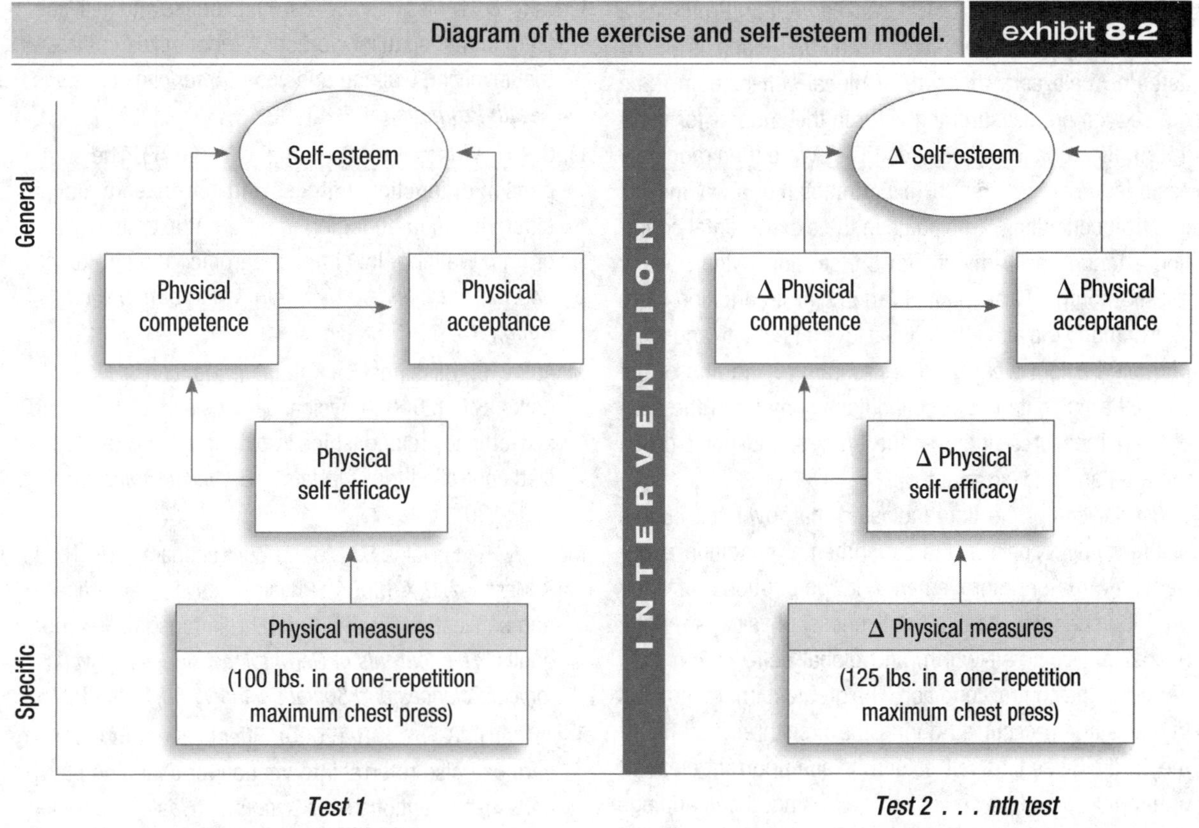

Source: Sonstroem & Morgan (1989).

FOCUS on Aging

Tai Chi, a form of exercise that originates from Chinese culture, is performed as a series of fluid movements that incorporate elements of balance, postural alignment, and concentration. Accumulating data suggest that among older adults, Tai Chi may contribute to a host of physical health benefits—including improvements in balance and strength, cardiovascular and respiratory function, immune system functioning, and flexibility—and psychological benefits such as increased positive affect and decreased negative affect, depression, and psychological distress (Wang, Collet, & Lau, 2004).

Enhanced self-esteem may be another benefit of Tai Chi. This possibility was examined in a randomized controlled trial of 98 older adults with an average age of 73 years (Li, Harmer, Chaumeton, et al., 2002). Study participants completed the Physical Self-Perception Profile as a measure of physical self-esteem, and the Rosenberg Self-Esteem Scale as a measure of global self-esteem. (See the section on measurement later in the chapter for more information on these measures.) They were then randomly assigned to either a Tai Chi (experimental) or a waiting-list (control) condition. Participants in the experimental condition attended a 60-minute Tai Chi session twice a week for six months. Participants in the control condition were instructed to maintain their usual level of activity and were promised a four-week Tai Chi program at the end of the study. Participants in both conditions completed the self-esteem measures again at the study's mid-point (three months) and end (six months).

Analyses of the data indicated that, over the course of the study, people in the experimental condition experienced greater improvements in perceptions of their physical condition, body attractiveness, physical strength, overall physical self-worth, and global self-esteem than people in the control condition. The greatest improvements in self-esteem occurred during the first three months of the study. Given that self-esteem is an important element of happiness and psychological well-being, these findings suggest that Tai Chi may be an important intervention to improve well-being among aging adults who have experienced negative life changes and transitions that may threaten their self-esteem (Li et al., 2002). As Tai Chi offers distinct advantages over other forms of physical activity—it can be performed at any time or place, does not require special equipment, and is less likely to lead to injury or to a chronic condition—it may be an ideal activity for elderly individuals who are constrained by transportation, finances, and other barriers to exercise.

ADDITIONAL RESOURCES

Dioniggi, R.A., & Cannon J. (2009). Older adults' perceived changes in physical self-worth associated with resistance training. *Research Quarterly for Exercise and Sport, 80,* 269–280.

Elavsky, S., & McAuley, E. (2007). Exercise and self-esteem in menopausal women: A randomized controlled trial involving walking and yoga. *American Journal of Health Promotion, 22,* 83–92.

Li, G.S.F., Wang, H.H., & Huang, C.Y. (2007). The comparison of functional fitness and self-esteem among elderly women engaging in different exercise programs: Walking, low impact aerobic, and chi-kung. *Journal of Physical Education & Recreation (Hong Kong), 13,* 49–55.

McAuley, E., Blissmer, B., Katula, J., Duncan, T.E., & Mihalko, S.L. (2000). Physical activity, self-esteem, and self-efficacy relationships in older adults: A randomized controlled trial. *Annals of Behavioral Medicine, 22,* 131–139.

McAuley, E., Elavsky, S., Motl, R.W., Konopack, J.F., Hu, L., & Marquez, D.X. (2005). Physical activity, self-efficacy, and self-esteem: Longitudinal relationships in older adults. *The Journals of Gerontology, Series B Psychological Sciences and Social Sciences, 60,* P268–P275.

Taylor, A.H., & Fox, K.R. (2005). Effectiveness of a primary care exercise referral intervention for changing physical self-perceptions over 9 months. *Health Psychology, 24,* 11–21.

U.S. Department of Health and Human Services. (2008). "Key guidelines for older adults." *Physical Activity Guidelines.* www.health.gov/paguidelines/.

ACTIVITY

Imagine that you are asked to serve on a team that has been given the assignment of designing an exercise gerontology program for the local senior center. Your responsibility on the team is to accomplish the following:

1. Highlight the positive psychological and social benefits of exercise that will be particularly appealing for this population. Develop a list of bullet points that reflect the benefits you will promote in advertisements and in speeches.
2. Using the knowledge you gain from this chapter, discuss the unique features of your program to ensure that the participants will experience enhanced self-concept and/or self-esteem.

mentioned, it may be of interest to assess self-esteem more frequently than simply before and after the program. If this were the case, the model would expand to the right continuously until all the tests were completed, with the intervention maintained between assessments.

The vertical axis has much the same role as in the self-concept model developed by Shavelson and colleagues. The axis is anchored by specific self-perceptions at the base and general self-perception at the top. The process of altering self-esteem is initiated with physical measures located at the base of the model. Physical measures can vary tremendously, ranging from a single measure of a single variable to multiple assessments of a variety of different measures. As indicated on the vertical axis, these measures are highly specific and objective (e.g., number of pounds in a one-repetition maximum chest press). The measures are important only to the extent that they serve as a source of self-efficacy information. A composite physical self-efficacy is formed from the myriad task-specific self-efficacies that the individual maintains. One's physical self-efficacy then informs more generalized judgments of physical competence. For example, an older man who begins a cardiovascular and resistance-training exercise regimen might report substantial improvements in efficacy for these activities. Thus, his physical self-efficacy would likely be enhanced. This improved self-efficacy might also carry over and affect efficacy expectations for other daily physical activities such as carrying heavy bags of groceries or performing yard work. The consequence is that the man now feels relatively competent at performing most physical tasks required or experienced in his life.

As indicated in Exhibit 8.2, physical competence influences self-esteem both independently and through physical acceptance. *Physical acceptance* refers to the extent to which the individual accepts his or her level of physical competence. Thus, global self-esteem is partially driven by the extent to which the person is accepting of who she is physically. A high degree of acceptance enhances global self-esteem. If the individual is not accepting of her physical competence, or has a low degree of physical acceptance, global self-esteem is reduced. For example, one individual might run a 5K race at an eight-minute mile pace and be very satisfied with that level of fitness. Another individual, however, might not view an eight-minute mile as an acceptable display of physical competence. Obviously, the two individuals' global self-esteem will be affected differently.

At this point in our discussion, it is necessary to introduce a critical issue related to self-esteem in general and to Sonstroem and Morgan's model in particular. This issue concerns the relative contributions of objective and subjective interpretations of success to self-esteem. As alluded to in the previous example, different people can have different perceptions of the same performance. It is important to recognize that only the *subjective perception* of success is relevant to one's self-concept/self-esteem. Thus, a personal trainer can tell you a hundred times that you are improving, but if you don't feel that you are making improvements your self-concept/self-esteem will not improve. Conversely, a personal trainer might be concerned about the fact that you have not shown much improvement in your muscular strength. However, you may feel that the training has been a success because you have more energy and are able to perform occupational duties requiring muscular strength more easily than before you began the exercise regimen. Thus, although the objective physiological indicators of improved fitness might not be present, self-concept/self-esteem might improve because your subjective judgment of physical competence has improved.

Measurement

Self-concept and self-esteem have traditionally been defined as unidimensional (global) constructs, and early measures designed to assess these constructs reflected this approach (e.g., self-esteem was represented by a single score indicating a general or overall sense of esteem). Indeed, the most common self-concept/self-esteem tools initially used in the exercise psychology literature (e.g., Coopersmith Self-Esteem Inventory, Piers-Harris Children's Self-Concept Scale, Rosenberg Self-Esteem Scale) employed a single, global dimension of self-concept or self-esteem and usually failed to address elements of physical self-concept (the Tennessee Self-Concept Scale is one exception). Fortunately, these limitations were remedied by the introduction of two physical self-concept/self-esteem inventories in the late 1980s and early 1990s.

The Physical Self-Perception Profile (PSPP; Fox & Corbin, 1989) was based largely on the notions of self-concept proposed by Shavelson and colleagues (1976). The 30-item battery follows a response pattern similar to that successfully employed by Harter (1985), in that two contrasting statements are presented. Respondents are asked to read each pair of statements, decide which of the two statements is most characteristic of themselves, and check a box denoting the extent to which the statement is characteristic of themselves (i.e., "sort of true for me" or "really true for me"). The instrument is divided into five subscales related to beliefs on sports competence, physical conditioning, body appearance/attractiveness, physical/muscular strength, and global physical self-worth. An example of each subscale can be found in Exhibit 8.3. The PSPP has

Sample items from the Physical Self-Perception Profile (PSPP). **exhibit 8.3**

Sports Competence	"Some people feel that they are not very good when it comes to playing sports BUT others feel that they are really good at just about every sport."
Physical Conditioning	"Some people do not usually have a high level of stamina and fitness BUT others always maintain a high level of stamina and fitness."
Body Attractiveness	"Some people are extremely confident about the appearance of their bodies BUT others are a little self-conscious about the appearance of their bodies."
Physical Strength	"Some people feel that they are physically stronger than most people of their sex BUT others feel that they lack physical strength compared to most others of their sex."
Physical Self-Worth	"Some people feel extremely satisfied with the kind of persons they are physically BUT others sometimes feel a little dissatisfied with their physical selves."

Source: Fox & Corbin (1989).

been shown to be a valid and reliable measure across a variety of populations, including middle-aged adults, American and British college students, and overweight adults (Fox & Corbin, 1989; Fox & Dirkin, 1992; Page, Ashford, Fox, & Biddle, 1993; Sonstroem, Speliotis, & Fava, 1992).

Also based on the approach by Shavelson and colleagues (1976) (and sharing certain subscale similarities with the PSPP), the Physical Self-Description Questionnaire (PSDQ; Marsh, Richards, Johnson, et al., 1994) is a 70-item instrument divided into nine components of physical self-concept (general health, coordination, physical activity participation, body fat, sports competence, appearance/attractiveness, muscular strength, flexibility, and cardiovascular endurance) plus two subscales assessing global physical self-concept and global self-esteem. The PSDQ consists of single-statement items and a six-point Likert scale response format ranging from 1 ("false") to 6 ("true"). An example of each subscale can be found in Exhibit 8.4. Marsh and his colleagues have documented considerable support for the validity of the instrument in Australian adolescents (Marsh, 1996, 1997; Marsh & Redmayne, 1994), and the PSDQ appears to provide a comprehensive assessment of physical self-concept with the added feature of global measures of both physical self-concept and self-esteem. Although this breadth in content would appear to favor the PSDQ over the PSPP, researchers should also consider the significant difference in number of questionnaire items as well as the contrasting response formats when making assessment decisions. Because it requires a substantial amount of reading and possesses a more complex response format, certain populations (e.g., children, the elderly) may find the PSPP to be less "user-friendly" than the PSDQ, despite the fact that is it notably shorter. (For a more thorough review concerning various indices of validity with respect to the two scales, see Marsh, Asçi, & Tomás, 2002.)

exhibit 8.4 Sample items from the Physical Self-Description Questionnaire.

Health	"I hardly ever get sick or ill."
Coordination	"I can perform movements smoothly in most physical activities."
Physical Activity	"I often do exercise or activities that make me breathe hard."
Body Fat	"I have too much fat on my body."
Sports Competence	"Most sports are easy for me."
Global Physical	"I feel good about who I am physically."
Appearance	"I am good looking."
Strength	"I am good at lifting heavy objects."
Flexibility	"I think I would perform well on a test measuring flexibility."
Endurance	"I can be physically active for a long period of time without getting tired."
Global Esteem	"Overall, most things I do turn out well."

Source: Marsh et al. (1994).

Selective Research

A number of outstanding reviews of the self-concept/self-esteem literature have been written, and the reader is referred to these publications for extensive discussions of research findings related to these constructs (see Doan & Scherman, 1987; Fox, 2000; Gruber, 1986; McAuley, 1994; Sonstroem, 1984, 1997; Spence, McGannon, & Poon, 2005). Of interest is the increasing number of studies that have been conducted with special populations, including older adults with and without mental retardation (Dungan, Brown, & Ramsey, 1996; Mactavish & Searle, 1992; McAuley, Mihalko, & Bane, 1997), mentally and physically healthy youth and adolescents (see Calfas & Taylor, 1994, for a review), children with learning disabilities or emotional "disturbances" (MacMahon & Gross, 1987; Politino & Smith, 1989), children with spina bifida (Andrade, Kramer, Garber, & Longmuir, 1991), obese children (Gately, Cooke, Butterly, et al., 2000), adults with chronic obstructive pulmonary disease (Weaver, Richmond, & Narsavage, 1997), adults with cancer (Baldwin & Courneya, 1997), injured athletes (see Smith, 1996, for a review), clinically depressed adults (Ossip-Klein, Doyne, Bowman, et al., 1989), adults with brain injury (Driver, 2008; Driver, Rees, O'Connor, & Lox, 2006), and alcoholics (see Donaghy & Mutrie, 1999, for a review). In one of the earliest studies of self-concept and exercise, Collingwood and Willett (1971) enrolled five obese male teenagers in a three-week physical activity program in which participants engaged in daily aquatic and gymnastic activities for one hour. The results indicated significant improvements in body weight, cardiovascular fitness, attitude toward the body and self, and self-acceptance. More recently, Lemmon, Ludwig, Howe, and colleagues (2007) found that African American girls (8–12 years of age) with high levels of self-esteem attended significantly more physical activity sessions per week (3.5 versus 2) than those with low self-esteem.

Employing a more theory-based study rationale, Lau, Cheung, and Ransdell (2008) recruited 320 Chinese children (7–12 years of age) and assessed their self-perceptions of body fat, appearance, strength, global physical self-concept, and global self-concept. The authors tested the proposition that perceptions about body fat, appearance, and strength would impact the children's physical self-concept which would, in turn, influence their overall self-concept. While the relationship held for body fat, appearance, and strength, each had a twofold effect. First, each exerted a significant influence on physical self-concept, as expected. However, perceptions of one's appearance and strength also directly impacted overall self-concept. Put another way, an individual's evaluations of her appearance and strength are sufficient to alter her *overall* self-concept, independent of changes in her *physical* self-concept. A somewhat similar approach to theory-testing was reported by Ryan (2008), who found that perceptions of strength, flexibility, and endurance were associated with enhanced physical self-esteem in male and female college students.

Finally, Driver and colleagues (2006) randomly assigned 18 adults with brain injuries to either an experimental or control group condition and then assessed multiple measures of physical self-concept and global self-esteem pre-and post-intervention. The experimental group participated in exercise sessions consisting of both aerobic and resistance-training activities, each lasting 60 minutes, three times per week for eight weeks. The control group participated in an eight-week vocational rehabilitation program that focused on improving both reading and writing skills. Results revealed significant improvements in perceptions of coordination, body fat, strength, flexibility, endurance, and overall self-esteem from pre- to post-intervention for those participants in the exercise program only.

Although as much as 78 percent of research studies support a positive association between exercise and self-esteem (Fox, 2000), we would be remiss if we did not acknowledge the fact that a number of investigations have failed to provide evidence of an exercise–self-esteem relationship. Indeed, published investigations from various parts of the world in the past decade have demonstrated that Canadian children (Tremblay, Inman, & Willms, 2000), Turkish university students (Asçi, 2003), Finnish older adults (Lampinen & Heikkinen, 2002), Caucasian and African American college-aged men (Russell, 2002), and German middle-aged adults (Alfermann & Stoll, 2000) all failed to report either a significant effect of physical activity participation on self-esteem or a difference in self-esteem between exercise and control conditions. The equivocal nature of the literature is not surprising given that global measures of self-esteem are theoretically difficult to change, while measures of self-concept tend to be more specific to the domain in question. Thus, while self-esteem has historically been included in a substantially greater number of research investigations, self-concept has proven to be a more consistent correlate of physical activity and might, therefore, become the more popular choice for exercise psychology researchers (see Fox, 2000, for a more detailed discussion of this issue).

In addition to the general versus specific nature of self-concept/self-esteem, complications in interpreting the literature have also arisen from the extensive variation in both measurement and research design methodology (i.e., variations in physical activity mode, frequency, intensity, duration, and length of intervention). Regarding this latter point, we currently know very little about the dose–response relationship between exercise and self-concept/self-esteem. Several reviews (Fox, 2000; Spence, et al., 2005) have attempted to shed some light on the dose–response relationship but have yielded little in the way of conclusive evidence. Taken together, these reviews indicate the following:

1. Exercise frequency, intensity, and duration have not proven to be significant influences on global self-esteem, although a nonsignificant trend was reported by Spence and colleagues for frequency (i.e., the more frequent the participation, the larger the increase in global self-esteem).
2. The "jury is out" regarding the influence of program length on self-esteem. Spence and colleagues found no significant effect of program length, while Fox found a trend toward greater changes in global self-esteem as the length of the program increased. As a starting point, Fox suggested that programs should last for at least 12 weeks, with some form of contact continuing for six months or more.
3. Findings are also mixed with respect to the influence of activity mode. Although Spence and colleagues did not find a significant influence of mode on self-esteem, Fox concluded that the research evidence most supported the effectiveness of aerobic exercise and weight training for improving self-perceptions.

Given these research and literature review findings, what definitive conclusions can we make regarding the relationship between exercise and self-concept/self-esteem? First, exercise generally exerts a positive influence on self-concept/self-esteem for all populations. Although we can confidently make such a statement, the reader is reminded that no intervention is 100 percent effective for every individual in every situation. Indeed, as discussed earlier, a number of research studies have failed to demonstrate a significant change in self-concept/self-esteem following a physical activity intervention. It should also be noted, however, that researchers have yet to document a *negative* effect of exercise on self-concept/self-esteem.

Second, the greatest improvements in self-concept/self-esteem are likely to occur in those populations that have the most to gain (physically and psychologically) from exercise participation. Included among these groups are middle-aged and elderly adults; those who are overweight/obese; those suffering from disability/disease; those with low levels of self-confidence, self-concept, or self-esteem; and those who maintain a negative body image.

Third, the influence of exercise on self-concept/self-esteem might not be as strong as has been reported historically. In their quantitative summary of the exercise–self-esteem literature, Spence and colleagues (2005) concluded that the influence of exercise on global self-esteem was, in fact, relatively small.

Mechanisms of Change

Whereas a number of topics throughout this book have benefited from research that has attempted to explain the process by which exercise leads to psychological change, this is not the case for self-concept/self-esteem. In fact, other than the mastery (self-efficacy) hypothesis, no mechanism has been discussed at length in the self-concept/self-esteem literature. Nonetheless, additional explanations do exist, and these are the subject of this section.

Mastery/Self-Efficacy

Although self-efficacy theory is discussed in depth in Chapter 3, we revisit aspects of the theory here in order to demonstrate the impact of behavioral mastery on self-concept/self-esteem. Clearly, such a hypothesis is tenable given the prominent role played by self-efficacy in Sonstroem and Morgan's (1989) model of exercise and self-esteem. Recall that physical measures occupy the base of the model and directly feed physical self-efficacy. The next level of the model's hierarchy shows physical self-efficacy exerting an influence on physical self-concept. Finally, physical self-concept influences global self-esteem both independently and through physical acceptance. Returning to the example provided earlier in the chapter, let's assume that our elderly exerciser has completed a 16-week cardiovascular and resistance-training exercise program. Based on the degree to which he feels he has mastered the skills required to perform the activities successfully, our participant is likely to report improvements in physical self-efficacy. This sense of accomplishment may prove to be so rewarding that it ultimately affects global self-esteem in the manner proposed by the model. Readers interested in the self-efficacy–self-esteem relationship are referred to a study by Ryan (2008) in which he proposed a further modification of Sonstroem, Harlow, and Josephs' (1994) expanded version of the original Sonstroem and Morgan (1989) model.

Body Image/Body Esteem

As detailed in Chapter 9, body image refers to the mental picture we form of our bodies ("what I look like"). Body esteem, then, is the emotional consequence of body image ("how I feel about what I look like"). Thus, perception of one's body (image) elicits either pleasing/satisfying or displeasing/dissatisfying feelings (esteem). The attentive reader will note that these constructs are essentially self-concept and self-esteem applied to the body. It is not surprising, therefore, that body image/esteem would be implicated as a mechanism for improving overall self-concept/self-esteem.

exhibit 8.5 Diagram of possible linkage between body image and self-esteem following chronic exercise.

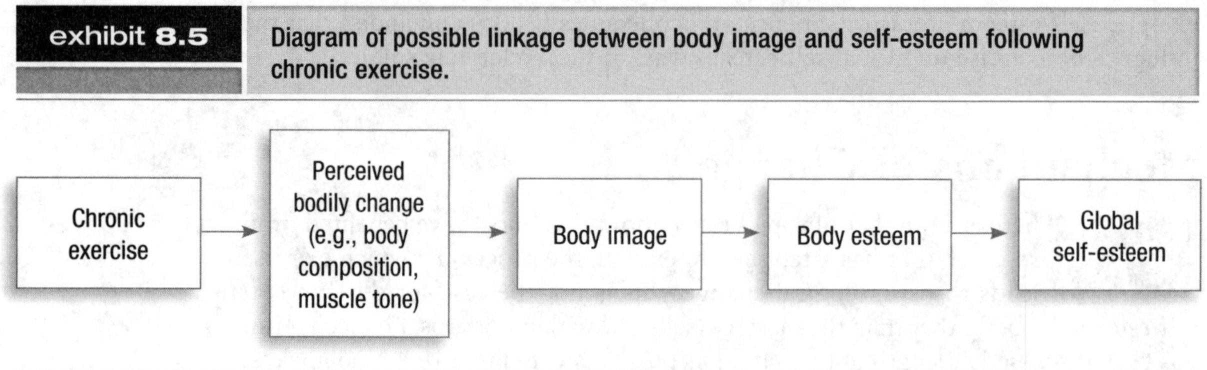

How might this process take place? One relatively simple explanation is diagrammed in Exhibit 8.5. According to the model, prolonged participation in an exercise regimen leads to perceived improvements in body composition, muscule tone, and so forth, independent of whether or not objective change has taken place. Positive perceptions of bodily change, in turn, serve to enhance one's body image. Finally, this improvement in body image would be expected to enhance body esteem, which, if deemed important by the individual, influences global self-esteem. The proposed framework is essentially a duplicate of both the Shavelson et al. (1976) and Sonstroem and Morgan (1989) models. In the model from Shavelson and colleagues, the physical appearance sublevel of self-concept could be readily defined as body-image/esteem. Similarly, the physical acceptance component of Sonstroem and Morgan's model could also be defined as body image/esteem. In all cases, the individual must consider body image/esteem important in order for it to play an influential role in global self-esteem change. In an investigation of the body image–self-esteem relationship, MacKinnon and colleagues (2003) recruited a large sample of male high school football players and found that lower body fat (objectively measured) was associated with higher perceived athletic competence and more positive body image; these, in turn, were associated with higher global self-esteem.

Self-Determination

Although the concept of self-determination has been a mainstay in the contemporary cognitive motivation literature, its relation to self-concept and self-esteem has not been clearly delineated. As discussed in Chapter 3, self-determination refers to an individual's drive to autonomously and successfully perform behaviors important to him or her. With this in mind, self-determination has vast potential to influence self-esteem due to the fact that perceptions of personal control have long been postulated to be associated with positive self-perception, while perceived lack of personal control has been hypothesized to be associated with negative self-perception (DeCharms, 1968). In an achievement setting such as exercise, the realization of achieving a goal such as completing a marathon would likely lead to enhanced judgments of self-determination, because such an accomplishment requires considerable internal capabilities including self-motivation, discipline, and effort. The consequence of assuming responsibility for this successful behavior should be enhanced perceptions of one's physical self. Once again, if the outcome is deemed to be salient to the individual, physical self-concept should positively impact global self-esteem. Exhibit 8.6 details the possible linkage between self-determination and self-concept/self-esteem in the exercise domain. A study of adult exercisers in Great Britain supports such a concept in that self-determined motivation for exercise was significantly and positively associated with physical self-worth (Thøgersen-Ntoumani & Ntoumanis, 2006).

Self-Schemata

A relatively novel explanation of the exercise and self-concept/self-esteem relationship involves the development of domain-specific (e.g., exercise) identities known as **self-schemata.** Although other schemas exist (such as those focused on a particular religious sect or a defined role within a family, occupation, company, team, or school), Kendzierski (1994) has embedded this concept within the domain of exercise and has determined that individuals fall into one of three categories. The first is *exerciser schematics* who describe themselves as exercisers and who rate this self-identification as being critical to their self-image. The second category consists of *nonexerciser schematics* who describe themselves as nonexercisers and who also consider the (deficient) exercise descriptor to be a significant influence on their self-image. Finally, *aschematics* describe themselves as nonexercisers but do not consider this perception to be important to their self-image.

■ self-schemata

Exhibit 8.7 suggests how exercise might impact self-concept/self-esteem through changes in exercise schema. As in the previous discussion of body image/esteem, the process is initiated by a regimen of chronic exercise. In this theory, however, we are not concerned with the potential subjective and objective changes that may occur. Instead, the important element here is that the individual merely begins to identify herself as an exerciser. Assuming that the characteristics of an exerciser are salient to the individual, the self-description will serve to enhance physical self-concept, which in turn will affect global self-esteem. The danger, of course, is that an individual might assign considerable importance to being an exerciser but continue to be unsuccessful in maintaining an exercise regimen. In

Diagram of possible linkage between self-determination and self-concept/self-esteem following an exercise outcome. **exhibit 8.6**

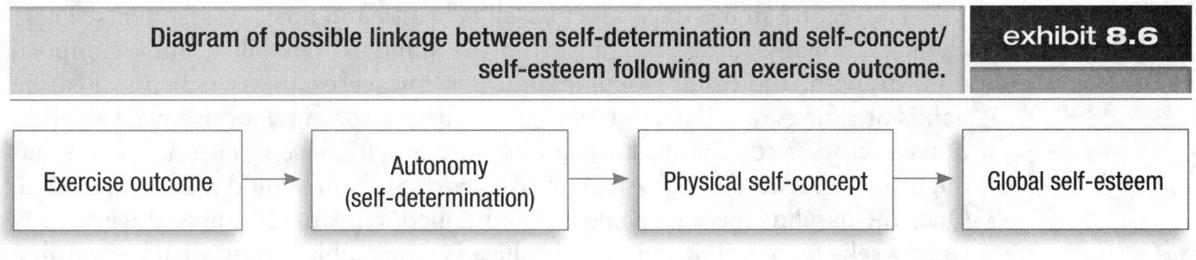

exhibit 8.7 Diagram of possible linkage between exercise schema and self-concept/self-esteem following chronic exercise.

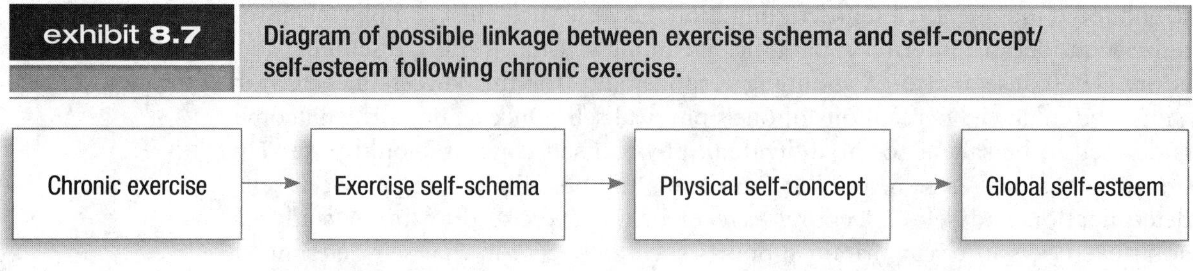

this case, the impact on physical self-concept and global self-esteem would likely be negative.

To date, research regarding self-schemata and self-esteem in the exercise setting has been virtually nonexistent. Nonetheless, support for such a relationship may be established. For example, Yin and Boyd (2000) have demonstrated a relationship between exercise self-schemata and exercise self-efficacy, the latter having been described earlier as being closely related with self-esteem. Additionally, researchers in the general psychology field have documented an association between self-schemata and perceptions of self-worth and self-esteem (Kuiper & McHale, 2009).

Practical Recommendations

Although we still have much to learn about the optimal mode, frequency, intensity, and duration of activity required to yield enhanced self-concept/self-esteem, certain steps can be taken to ensure that the activity engaged in will lead to improvements in these constructs. The first step is to determine *why* the individual is currently interested in an exercise regimen. Generally, one's goals and objectives will provide valuable insight into the factors that are most likely to affect self-concept/self-esteem. For example, if you encounter a man who would like to improve his appearance by "getting bigger," you might prescribe a resistance-training regimen targeting increased muscular hypertrophy. Alternatively, a woman who desires to enhance her social life while becoming physically active should be encouraged to exercise with a buddy or small group, or to join a fitness class.

The second step is to conduct baseline health and fitness assessments. These could take many forms, ranging from the standard flexibility, body composition, strength, and cardiovascular endurance measures, to assessments of eating habits or ratings of satisfaction with one's current social relationships. Any additional factors that might be known to influence self-concept/self-esteem and that might be influenced by physical activity participation should also be included. Once the baseline measures have been obtained, repeating the assessments every eight weeks or so will provide both objective and subjective feedback regarding the progress being made in the exercise program. The exerciser can then use this information to modify self-concept/self-esteem judgments.

The third step is to ensure that exercisers feel a sense of accomplishment and personal control in their exercise routines. Allowing the client some input into decisions regarding the program, and arranging the activities in such a way as to ensure completion and a sense of success, should prove helpful. Highlighting the role of personal control and accomplishment through positive verbal feedback to the client (and avoiding negative verbal feedback) is essential. At the same time, the exercise leader should strive to reward positive self-statements and extinguish negative self-statements made by the exerciser. A good strategy would be to focus on effort and personal improvement while de-emphasizing comparisons with others.

Conclusion

For many of us, the image that we form of ourselves overall (self-concept) is influenced to a large degree by the image that we form of our physical self. This physical self-concept is composed of not only our physical appearance but also the perception of our physical abilities (e.g., to exercise, play sport, or perform house or yard work). Self-esteem, synonymous with self-worth, indicates how one feels about one's self-concept. These distinctions are highlighted in the seminal model of self-concept proposed by Shavelson and colleagues (1976) and in the context-specific model of exercise and self-esteem developed by Sonstroem and Morgan (1989). Both models are constructed in a hierarchical fashion, in which the more situation-specific and unstable evaluations (e.g., running performance) form the foundation upon which the pinnacle—a global, relatively stable judgment of self-concept or self-esteem—is built.

Recently, researchers have sought to complement the unidimensional (global) approach to measurement by positing a multidimensional philosophy whereby the myriad domain-specific self-concepts (i.e., academic, social, emotional, physical) can be assessed individually. This chapter reviewed two measures (PSPP and PSDQ) that show promise for assessing multiple aspects of the physical self. The utility of these measures cannot be overstated, given that these subjective judgments, as opposed to objective measurements of fitness, are primarily responsible for feelings of self-esteem.

At this point, it appears that we cannot make any definitive statements regarding dose–response relationships between exercise and self-concept/self-esteem. Indeed, little systematic research exists concerning the impact of mode, frequency, intensity, or duration on self-concept/self-esteem, and the scant literature addressing these variables has yielded inconclusive results. Clearly, exercise psychology researchers must address dose–response issues in future investigations and, furthermore, must continue to explore potential mechanisms of exercise-induced changes in self-concept/self-esteem.

what do you know?

1. What is the difference between self-concept and self-esteem?
2. What two factors determine physical self-concept in the model from Shavelson and colleagues?
3. Give examples of physical measures in the Sonstroem and Morgan model.
4. What two factors primarily influence global self-esteem in the Sonstroem and Morgan model?
5. Which is most relevant to self-esteem, objective or subjective changes in fitness?
6. Why have more recent self-concept/self-esteem measures (e.g., PSPP, PSDQ) adopted a multidimensional approach rather than the traditional unidimensional approach?
7. How are the PSPP and PSDQ different? In what ways are they the same?
8. Describe the process by which mastery (self-efficacy) may influence self-concept/self-esteem in the exercise setting.
9. Describe the process by which body image/body esteem may influence self-concept/self-esteem in the exercise setting.
10. Describe the process by which self-determination may influence self-concept/self-esteem in the exercise setting.
11. Describe the process by which self-schemata may influence self-concept/self-esteem in the exercise setting.
12. Explain why beginning an exercise program may have little to no effect on global self-esteem/self-worth.

learning activities

1. Obtain a copy of either the PSPP or the PSDQ (either from the appropriate reference in this chapter or from your instructor) and ask each member of the class to complete it. After properly scoring the questionnaire, ask your instructor to correlate each student's questionnaire score and activity score (from Learning Activity 1 in Chapter 2). Discuss the results.
2. Combine the constructs from one or more of the models proposed in Exhibits 8.5, 8.6, or 8.7 with those included in the Sonstroem and Morgan (1989) model, to create your own model. Feel free to be creative and to add, delete, or modify constructs according to your own theory.
3. Review the scenario featuring Chris at the beginning of the chapter. Suppose that he has asked you to design an exercise program for him. Based on the information in this chapter and in Chapter 6, what steps should you take in designing the program? Explain the rationale for your program (i.e., how will it positively affect Chris's self-concept/self-esteem?).

references

Alfermann, D., & Stoll, O. (2000). Effects of physical exercise on self-concept and well-being. *International Journal of Sport Psychology, 30,* 47–65.

Andrade, C.K., Kramer, J., Garber, M., & Longmuir, P. (1991). Changes in self-concept, cardiovascular endurance and muscular strength of children with spina bifida aged 8 to 13 years in response to a 10-week physical-activity programme: A pilot study. *Child: Care, Health and Development, 17,* 183–196.

Asçi, F.H. (2003). The effects of physical fitness training on trait anxiety and physical self-concept of female university students. *Psychology of Sport and Exercise, 4,* 255–264.

Baldwin, M.K., & Courneya, K.S. (1997). Exercise and self-esteem in breast cancer survivors: An application of the exercise and self-esteem model. *Journal of Sport & Exercise Psychology, 19,* 347–358.

Calfas, K.J., & Taylor, W.C. (1994). Effects of physical activity on psychological variables in adolescents. *Pediatric Exercise Science, 6,* 406–423.

Collingwood, T.R., & Willett, L. (1971). The effects of physical training upon self-concept and body attitude. *Journal of Clinical Psychology, 27,* 411–412.

DeCharms, R. (1968). *Personal causation.* New York: Academic Press.

Doan, R.E., & Scherman, A. (1987). The therapeutic effect of physical fitness on measures of personality: A literature review. *Journal of Counseling and Development, 66,* 28–36.

Donaghy, M.E., & Mutrie, N. (1999). Is exercise beneficial in the treatment and rehabilitation of the problem drinker? A critical review. *Physical Therapy Reviews, 4,* 153–166.

Driver, S. (2008). Development of a conceptual model to predict physical activity participation in adults with brain injuries. *Adapted Physical Activity Quarterly, 25,* 289–307.

Driver, S., Rees, K., O'Connor, J., & Lox, C. (2006). Aquatics, health-promoting self-care behaviours and adults with brain injuries. *Brain Injury, 20,* 133–141.

Dungan, J.M., Brown, A.V., & Ramsey, M.A. (1996). Health maintenance for the independent frail older adult: Can it improve physical and mental well-being? *Journal of Advanced Nursing, 23,* 1185–1193.

Folkins, C.H., & Sime, W.E. (1981). Physical fitness training and mental health. *American Psychologist, 36,* 373–389.

Fox, K.R. (2000). Self-esteem, self-perceptions, and exercise. *International Journal of Sport Psychology, 31,* 228–240.

Fox, K.R., & Corbin, C.B. (1989). The Physical Self-Percption Profile: Development and preliminary validation. *Journal of Sport & Exercise Psychology, 11,* 408–430.

Fox, K.R., & Dirkin, G.R. (1992). Psychosocial predictors and outcomes of exercise in patients attending multidisciplinary obesity treatment. *International Journal of Obesity, 16,* 84.

Gately, P.J., Cooke, C.B., Butterly, R.J., Knight, C., & Carroll, S. (2000). The acute effects of an 8-week diet, exercise, and educational camp program on obese children. *Pediatric Exercise Science, 12,* 413–423.

Gruber, J.J. (1986). Physical activity and self-esteem development in children: A meta-analysis. *American Academy of Physical Education Papers, 19,* 30–48.

Harter, S. (1985). *Manual for the self-perception profile for children.* Denver: University of Denver, Colorado.

Hughes, J.R. (1984). Psychological effects of habitual aerobic exercise: A critical review. *Preventive Medicine,* 13, 66–78.

Kendzierski, D. (1994). Schema theory: An information processing focus. In R.K. Dishman (Ed.), *Advances in exercise adherence* (pp. 137–159). Champaign, IL: Human Kinetics.

Kuiper, N.A., & McHale, N. (2009). Humor styles as mediators between self-evaluative standards and psychological well-being. *The Journal of Psychology, 143,* 359–376.

Lampinen, P., & Heikkinen, R. (2002). Gender differences in depressive symptoms and self-esteem in different physical activity categories among older adults. *Women in Sport and Physical Activity Journal, 2,* 171–197.

Lau, P.W.C., Cheung, M.W.L., & Ransdell, L.B. (2008). A structural equation model of the relationship between body perception and self-esteem: Global physical self-concept as the mediator. *Psychology of Sport and Exercise, 9,* 493–509.

Lemmon, C.R., Ludwig, D.A., Howe, C.A., Ferguson-Smith, A., & Barbeau, P. (2007). Correlates of adherence to a physical activity program in young African-American girls. *Obesity, 15,* 695–703.

Li, F., Harmer, P., Chaumeton, N.R., Duncan, T.E., & Duncan, S.C. (2002). Tai Chi as a means to enhance self-esteem: A randomized controlled trial. *The Journal of Applied Gerontology, 21,* 70–89.

MacKinnon, D.P., Goldberg, L., Cheong, J., Elliot, D., Clarke, G., & Moe, E. (2003). Male body esteem and physical measurements: Do leaner, or stronger, high school football players have a more positive body image? *Journal of Sport & Exercise Psychology, 25,* 307–322.

MacMahon, J.R., & Gross, R.T. (1987). Physical and psychological effects of aerobic exercise in boys with learning disabilities. *Developmental and Behavioral Pediatrics, 8,* 274–277.

Mactavish, J.B., & Searle, M.S. (1992). Older individuals with mental retardation and the effect of a physical activity intervention on selected social psychological variables. *Therapeutic Recreation Journal, 1,* 38–47.

Marsh, H.W. (1996). Physical Self-Description Questionnaire: Stability and discriminant validity. *Research Quarterly for Exercise and Sport, 67,* 249–264.

Marsh, H.W. (1997). The measurement of physical self-concept: A construct validation approach. In K.R. Fox (Ed.), *The physical self: From motivation to well-being* (pp. 27–58). Champaign, IL: Human Kinetics.

Marsh, H.W., Asçi, F.H., & Tomás, I.M. (2002). Multitrait-multimethod analyses of two physical self-concept instruments: A cross-cultural perspective. *Journal of Sport & Exercise Psychology, 24,* 99–119.

Marsh, H.W., & Redmayne, R.S. (1994). A multidimensional physical self-concept and its relations to multiple components of physical fitness. *Journal of Sport & Exercise Psychology, 16,* 43–55.

Marsh, H.W., Richards, G.E., Johnson, S., Roche, L., & Tremayne, P. (1994). Physical Self-Description Questionnaire: Psychometric properties and a multitrait-multimethod analysis of relations to existing instruments. *Journal of Sport & Exercise Psychology, 16,* 270–305.

McAuley, E. (1994). Physical activity and psychosocial outcomes. In C. Bouchard, R.J. Shephard, & T. Stephens (Eds.), *Physical activity, fitness, and health* (pp. 551–568). Champaign, IL: Human Kinetics.

McAuley, E., Mihalko, S.L., & Bane, S.M. (1997). Exercise and self-esteem in middle-aged adults: Multidimensional relationships and physical fitness and self-efficacy influences. *Journal of Behavioral Medicine, 20,* 67–83.

Ossip-Klein, D.J., Doyne, E.J., Bowman, E.D., Osborn, K.M., McDougall-Wilson, I.B., & Neimeyer, R.A. (1989). Effects of running or weight lifting on self-concept in clinically depressed women. *Journal of Consulting and Clinical Psychology, 57,* 158–161.

Page, A., Ashford, B., Fox, K.R., & Biddle, S.J.H. (1993). Evidence of cross-cultural validity of the Physical Self-Perception Profile. *Personality and Individual Differences, 14,* 585, 590.

Politino, V., & Smith, S.L. (1989). Attitude toward physical activity and self-concept of emotionally disturbed and normal children. *Adapted Physical Activity Quarterly, 6,* 371–378.

Russell, W.D. (2002). Comparison of self-esteem, body satisfaction, and social physique anxiety across males of different exercise frequency and racial background. *Journal of Sport Behavior, 25,* 74–90.

Ryan, M.P. (2008). The antidepressant effects of physical activity: Mediating self-esteem and self-efficacy mechanisms. *Psychology and Health, 23,* 279–307.

Shavelson, R.J., Hubner, J.J., & Stanton, G.C. (1976). Validation of construct interpretations. *Review of Educational Research, 46,* 407–441.

Sheldon, K.M., Elliot, A.J., Kim, Y., & Kasser, T. (2001). What's satisfying about satisfying events? Comparing ten candidate psychological needs. *Journal of Personality and Social Psychology, 80,* 325–339.

Smith, A. (1996). Psychological impact of injuries in athletes. *Sports Medicine, 22,* 391–405.

Sonstroem, R.J. (1984). Exercise and esteem. *Exercise and Sport Science Reviews, 12,* 123–153.

Sonstroem, R.J. (1997). Physical activity and self-esteem. In W.P. Morgan (Ed.), *Physical activity and mental health* (pp. 128–143). Washington, DC: Taylor & Francis.

Sonstroem, R.J., Harlow, L.L., & Josephs, L. (1994). Exercise and self-esteem: Validity of model expansion and exercise associations. *Journal of Sport & Exercise Psychology, 16,* 29–42.

Sonstroem, R.J., & Morgan, W.P. (1989). Exercise and esteem: Rationale and model. *Medicine and Science in Sports and Exercise, 21,* 329–337.

Sonstroem, R.J., Speliotis, E.D., & Fava, J.L. (1992). Perceived physical competence in adults: An examination of the Physical Self-Perception Profile. *Journal of Sport & Exercise Psychology, 14,* 207–221.

Spence, J.C., McGannon, K.R., & Poon P. (2005). The effect of exercise on global self-esteem: A quantitative review. *Journal of Sport & Exercise Psychology, 27,* 311–334.

Thøgersen-Ntoumani, C. & Ntoumanis, N. (2006). The role of self-determined motivation in the understanding of exercise-related behaviours, cognitions and physical self-evaluations. *Journal of Sports Sciences, 24,* 393–404.

Tremblay, M.S., Inman, J.W., & Willms, J.D. (2000). The relationship between physical activity, self-esteem, and academic achievement in 12-year-old children. *Pediatric Exercise Science, 12,* 312–323.

Wang, C., Collet, J.P., & Lau, J. (2004). The effect of Tai Chi on health outcomes in patients with chronic conditions: A systematic review. *Archives of Internal Medicine, 164,* 493–501.

Weaver, T.E., Richmond, T.S., & Narsavage, G.L. (1997). An explanatory model of functional status in chronic obstructive pulmonary disease. *Nursing Research, 46,* 26–31.

Yin, Z., & Boyd, M.P. (2000). Behavioral and cognitive correlates of exercise self-schemata. *The Journal of Psychology, 134,* 269–282.

9

Body Image and Exercise

June is 19 years old and a college sophomore. Until she went away to college, June trained and competed in dance and gymnastics. An attractive girl, June was often told that much of her success in these activities was due to the appeal of her "all-American good looks." Since retiring from competition two years ago, June has gained 10 pounds, but she is still of average weight for her 5-foot, 2-inch frame. Nonetheless, whenever she looks in the mirror, June sees herself as overweight. She is constantly saying things to herself like "I hate my body," "My hips are too fat," and "What good are you anyway?" Some days, she feels so bad about herself that it takes all of her effort just to get out of bed. Although June's favorite outfits used to consist of fitted jeans and t-shirts, lately she prefers to wear baggy sweat suits that hide the shape of her body. One of June's friends suggests that she might feel better if she exercised more regularly. However, June feels too embarrassed about her body to put on shorts and a t-shirt and attend an exercise class.

June's story is typical of a woman with a poor or disturbed body image. Historically, body image and body image disturbance have been considered issues that affect only young women. Yet today, body image disturbance is common among both men and women of all ages. This is a significant health concern, because body image disturbance may be associated with poorer psychological well-being (e.g., increased risk for depression and eating disorders) and a greater likelihood of engaging in behaviors that put one's physical health at risk (e.g., smoking, over-exercising, or not exercising at all). Given these health concerns, exercise psychologists are interested in understanding how exercise interventions help to improve body image, and how body image can affect physical activity participation.

KEY TERMS

- affective/emotional dimension
- anorexia nervosa
  - binge-eating/purging type
  - restricting type
- avoidance behaviors
- behavioral dimension
- body checking behaviors
- body composition
- body dysmorphic disorder
- body ideal
- body image
- body image disturbance
- body reality
- bulimia nervosa
  - nonpurging type
  - purging type
- cognitive dimension
- healthy body image
- lifestyle behaviors
- muscle dysmorphia
- perceptual dimension
- social physique anxiety

Body Image Defined

body image ■

Body image is a multidimensional construct that reflects how we see our own body, and how we think, feel, and act toward it. Thus, body image is generally defined in terms of four dimensions—perceptual, cognitive, affective, and behavioral.

perceptual dimension ■

The **perceptual dimension** reflects the picture of our own body that we form in our mind. It is how we see our bodies when we look in a mirror and how we imagine ourselves to look—thin or fat, short or tall, muscular or lean, and so on. How we perceive or think that we look is not necessarily the same as how we actually look. As June's story demonstrates, some people may perceive themselves as overweight when they look in a mirror even though they are actually of average weight or even underweight.

cognitive dimension ■

The **cognitive dimension** of body image reflects how we think about and evaluate our body in terms of both its appearance and function. This includes beliefs regarding the attractiveness, strength, and fitness of the body and its various parts, the extent to which we value attractiveness and function, and the things we say to ourselves about our bodies.

affective/emotional dimension ■

The **affective** or **emotional dimension** of body image reflects feelings experienced in relation to the body's appearance and function. People may experience positive feelings about their bodies such as comfort and pride, or negative feelings such as anxiety, shame, and disgust.

behavioral dimension ■

Finally, the **behavioral dimension** represents things we do that reflect our positive or negative perceptions, thoughts, and feelings about our bodies, such as the types of clothing we wear and the activities we choose to engage in.

Healthy Body Image Versus Body Image Disturbance

healthy body image ■

body image disturbance ■

A **healthy body image** is reflected in positive self-evaluations along the four body image dimensions mentioned above. Individuals with a healthy body image have accurate perceptions about their body shape and size, have thoughts and feelings about their body that are predominately positive, and behave in ways that reflect these positive evaluations. In contrast, **body image disturbance** can be seen when the individual has negative self-evaluations along any or all of the body image dimensions. Along the perceptual dimension, body image disturbance is indicated when perceptions of one's body shape and size differ from one's actual shape and size. Along the cognitive and affective dimensions, negative thoughts and feelings about one's body are indicative of disturbance. And along the behavioral dimension, actions performed to hide or change the body's appearance without regard for health implications would be evidence of body image disturbance.

Traditionally, body image disturbance has been seen as a "women's issue." Times are changing, however. In 1973, *Psychology Today* magazine reported that 15 percent of men and 25 percent of women were dissatisfied with their appearance. In 1986, the magazine reported that 34 percent of men and 38 percent of women were dissatisfied with their appearance. In 1997, the dissatisfaction rate was up to 43 percent of men and 56 percent of women. Over the past decade, however, there have been some indications that the prevalence of body image dissatisfaction has declined among women and remained stable among men (Cash, Morrow, Hrabosky, & Perry, 2004). As a result, body image disturbance may now be just as common among men as it is among women.

Factors in Body Image Formation and Disturbance

Body image reflects an interplay between our body reality and our body ideal. **Body reality** refers to our actual physical characteristics—height, weight, body fat, lean body mass, bone structure, fitness, strength, disease, and so on. **Body ideal** refers to how we think our body should look and function. When people's body reality and body ideal are the same or very similar, they usually have a positive, healthy body image. But when people perceive their body reality to be worse than their body ideal—for example, when they judge their bodies to be fatter than they think they should be—this judgment often results in negative thoughts, feelings, perceptions, and behaviors that are indicative of body image disturbance.

- body reality
- body ideal

Where do body ideals come from? A healthy body ideal is derived from a recognition that human bodies naturally come in a wide range of shapes and sizes and that genetic factors are instrumental in determining one's weight and shape. Because genetics limit how much one can reshape the body through diet and exercise (Bouchard, 2008), it would be absurd for everyone to have the same body ideal. Rather, each individual's body ideal should reflect a realistic level of health and fitness for one's own unique and personal body shape.

Media influence

Unfortunately, in our society personal body ideals tend to be displaced by media-driven body ideals. Instead of celebrating a range of body ideals, the media promotes a very strict and narrowly defined image of the ideal body, particularly for women and increasingly so for men. Many people fail to realize that these ideals are unrealistic and unattainable for the vast majority of the population. The predominance of "perfect" bodies in television, magazines, movies, and music videos perpetuates the misconception that the bodies of fashion models and movie stars are the norm.

Cultural influences

Cultural body ideals generally reflect those glamorized in the media. However, people who are part of ethnic groups that reject the media ideal have healthier body images than do those who belong to groups that endorse the media ideal.

For example, although Black women are, on average, heavier than White women, Black women are significantly more satisfied with their bodies than White women (Roberts, Cash, Feingold, & Johnson, 2006). These differences are probably the result of differences in culture-bound values regarding the relative importance of thinness and the acceptance of heavier, more rounded body shapes. Such positive values result in a healthier and more realistic body ideal and, ultimately, better body image (Celio, Zabinski, & Wilfley, 2002).

Interestingly, over the past 10 to 15 years, the difference in body dissatisfaction between White and Black women has narrowed (Roberts et al., 2006). On the one hand, these changes may reflect Black women becoming more dissatisfied with their bodies as they adopt and internalize "White" standards of beauty. On the other hand, diminishing ethnic differences may be due to an increase in body satisfaction among White women (Cash et al., 2004). As Black women and women from other ethnic minorities gain greater prominence in the media, the presence of ethnically diverse body shapes and sizes may help to reshape "White" conceptions of beauty and the cultural body ideal. Thus, White women may come to see a greater range of bodies (including their own) as "ideal."

Activity participation

The activities in which we choose to participate can influence body image by altering perceptions of the body ideal. For example, women who participate in bodybuilding have a greater acceptance of bulkier, more muscular female body shapes, despite the divergence of these shapes from cultural body ideals (Furnham, Titman, & Sleeman, 1994). Likewise, men who participate in bodybuilding have a body ideal that is considerably more hypertrophic (i.e., has greater muscle mass) than the ideal of men who participate in other sports (Blouin & Goldfield, 1995). Whether these ideals are a cause or an effect of participating in bodybuilding is unclear. Nonetheless, continued participation in activities that endorse a particular body ideal can lead the participant to adopt the ideal for that activity and to reject the media or cultural ideal. If the participant is able to achieve a body shape that approximates the new ideal, then body image may improve. However, if the participant is unable to achieve the new ideal, then body image disturbance may become worse. Some researchers have found that bodybuilders have a worse body image than men who play others sports (Blouin & Goldfield, 1995), while others have found that bodybuilders have a better body image than men involved in other physical activities (Pickett, Lewis, & Cash, 2005). These conflicting findings may reflect differences in the bodybuilders' perceptions of success in achieving their ideal body. Men in the first study (Blouin & Goldfield) may have been highly dissatisfied because they perceived that they had not achieved their (potentially extreme and unrealistic) body image ideals. The men in the second study (Pickett et al.) may have felt good about their bodies because they felt that they had achieved their ideal.

Changes to body reality

Body image dissatisfaction has been shown to emerge in children as young as 6 or 7 years old (Ricciardelli & McCabe, 2001) and to get worse at puberty and the transition to adolescence (Eisenberg, Neumark-Sztainer, & Paxton, 2006). As we age, the body grows and alters in size, shape, proportion, and function. These changes can have a profound effect on feelings about oneself and one's body. For example, the growth of facial hair may be a source of pride for a pubescent boy who is eager to take on the appearance of a man. In contrast, a 12-year-old girl may be devastated by the increase in body weight that accompanies puberty. Indeed, normal developmental weight gain during puberty is associated with declines in body satisfaction (Eisenberg et al., 2006). Among older adults, age-related changes in body reality—such as the graying of hair and the wrinkling of skin—can also affect body image (Martin, Leary, & Rejeski, 2000). Thus, not surprisingly, body image dissatisfaction is prevalent among people of all ages—not just young adults. However, the importance that people place on physical appearance does tend to decrease in older adulthood (Tiggemann, 2004).

Sex Differences in Body Image Dissatisfaction

Until recently, it was believed that in general, women have greater body dissatisfaction than men (Feingold & Mazzella, 1998). This belief was based largely on the results of studies that measured body dissatisfaction in terms of people's desire to lose weight. (Participants who wanted to lose more weight were considered to have greater body dissatisfaction.) Overall, these studies showed that regardless of their age, a majority of women—but not men—wanted to lose weight. On the basis of these data, researchers concluded that women were more dissatisfied with their bodies than men. However, this conclusion is now being questioned.

Certainly, for most women, body dissatisfaction stems from a desire to be thinner. Countless studies have shown that among women, body image is positively correlated with body mass index (BMI), such that the smallest women have the lowest levels of body dissatisfaction and the largest women have the greatest body dissatisfaction. Yet, for men, the root of body dissatisfaction is not as straightforward. Among men, the relationship between body image and BMI is curvilinear, such that the largest *and* the smallest men have the greatest body dissatisfaction (Muth & Cash, 1997). This relationship is reflected in studies showing that more than one-third of men want to lose weight, while a similar proportion want to gain weight (McCabe & Ricciardelli, 2004). Of those who want to gain weight, some want to increase their muscle mass, some want to increase their body fat, and some want to increase both muscle and fat mass. Thus, whereas female body dissatisfaction typically stems from concerns about being too fat, male body dissatisfaction can stem from concerns about being too fat, too thin, too scrawny, or a combination of these concerns. If researchers do not measure all of the different ways that men may be dissatisfied with their bodies, the prevalence of male body dissatisfaction may be underestimated. Indeed, when the range of potential male body image concerns is taken into consideration, body image dissatisfaction is probably just as common among men as among women (McCabe & Ricciardelli, 2004).

Differences in the types of body image concerns felt by men and women reflect differences between the male and female body image ideals that are glamorized by the media and endorsed by Westernized culture. These ideals set the standard of female bodily attractiveness as ultra-thin, shapely, and toned. Thus, women who are dissatisfied with their bodies typically want to lose weight so that they can achieve this ideal. The male standard is considered the V-shaped physique: broad, muscular shoulders, toned "six-pack" abdominal muscles, a narrow waist, and muscular legs. As such, men often want to increase their muscle mass and reduce their body fat in order to achieve this ideal.

However, differences in gender-role orientation can influence the extent to which men endorse and pursue the male cultural body ideal (McCabe & Ricciardelli, 2004). Gender-role orientation refers to the extent to which people identify with stereotypically masculine (e.g., strength, assertiveness) versus feminine (e.g., gentleness, affection) traits. Because the male sociocultural body ideal is associated with the possession of typically masculine traits, men who score high on measures of masculinity may be more concerned with obtaining this physique than men who score high on measures of femininity. In contrast, because a smaller, thinner male body is associated with more typically feminine traits, feminine men may be primarily concerned with weight loss and attaining a thinner ideal. Likewise, women with high scores on measures of masculinity may be less concerned with weight loss and thinness than women who score high on measures of femininity. These tendencies suggest that body image comparisons based on biological sex (i.e., whether one is male or female) are overly simplistic. To fully understand differences in body image between men and women, gender-role orientation must also be considered. Comparisons between masculine- and feminine-oriented individuals may be more meaningful than comparisons between male and female individuals.

Why Is Body Image Important?

Relationship to Psychological Well-Being

A healthy body image is related to better psychological well-being in at least two ways: better self-esteem and lowered risk for depression and anxiety. Extreme body dissatisfaction can sometimes be indicative of severe psychological disturbances such as body dysmorphic disorder (see p. 234).

Self-esteem

A positive correlation exists between body image satisfaction and self-esteem (Miller & Downey, 1999), which indicates that people who feel better about their bodies tend to feel better about themselves overall. The positive relationship between body image and self-esteem has been demonstrated in studies of both male and female adolescents (Davison & McCabe, 2006) and adults (Davison & McCabe, 2005). However, the strength of the relationship seems to depend on the extent to which people value their physical appearance. For people who place a good deal of value on their physical appearance, their feelings of self-worth appear to be more influenced by their body image than for people who put less value on their appearance.

"Before you try on any bathing suit, you're required to sign this waiver releasing us from liability should you incur permanent damage to your self-esteem."

CLOSE TO HOME © 1996 John McPherson. Reprinted with permission of Universal Uclick.

Depression and anxiety

A poor body image has been associated with greater anxiety and depressive symptomatology (Cohen & Esther, 1993; Kirkcaldy, Eysenck,

Furnham, & Siefen, 1998). Specifically, depressed and anxious individuals view their appearance more negatively than do nondepressed and nonanxious individuals, despite the fact that there are no differences between these groups' actual body shape or size. Preliminary data suggest that body image disturbance is an antecedent, rather than a consequence, of increased depression (Paxton, Neumark-Sztainer, Hannan, & Eisenberg, 2006) and anxiety (Stice & Whitenton, 2002). In other words, having a poor body image may cause other psychological disturbances.

Body dysmorphic disorder

body dysmorphic disorder ■

In some extreme cases, body dissatisfaction may be indicative of a serious, underlying psychiatric condition known as **body dysmorphic disorder** (BDD). People diagnosed with BDD are excessively preoccupied with an imagined defect in their physical appearance (e.g., breast size, body weight, facial features). Although they may have a minor physical abnormality, people with BDD have grossly excessive anxiety and concern over this aspect of their appearance. They engage in obsessive-compulsive activities such as constantly checking their appearance in a mirror or weighing themselves, and they avoid social situations because they do not want others to see them (Veale, 2009). Given these behaviors, BDD can severely interfere with one's ability to go to school or to work, to have relationships, and, ultimately, to enjoy life.

muscle dysmorphia ■

Muscle dysmorphia (MD) is a particular type of BDD that is characterized by a preoccupation with muscularity (Phillips, O'Sullivan, & Pope, 1997). People with muscle dysmorphia have inaccurate beliefs about their muscularity, believing that they are far less muscular than they actually are. They might use steroids and work out compulsively, yet they remain deeply anxious and dissatisfied with their degree of muscular development.

Currently, the prevalence of BDD and MD in the general population is unknown. It has been estimated, however, that between 0.7 and 2.3 percent of the general population have BDD (Phillips & Dufresne, 2000) and, among those who are diagnosed with BDD, approximately 9 percent are men with MD (Olivardia, 2001).

Relationship to Physical Well-Being

Body image is also related to physical well-being, insofar as it can affect one's tendency to engage in health-damaging and health-promoting behaviors.

Health-damaging behaviors

Eating disorders and unhealthy weight control strategies. Body image disturbance has been identified as a risk factor for the development of eating disorders and is a key feature of eating disorder symptomatology (Polivy & Herman, 2002). A review of more than 60 studies found that women diagnosed with eating disorders reported greater body image dissatisfaction and more distorted body image perceptions than the general population (Cash & Deagle, 1997).

Body image disturbance is also a risk factor for relapse after successful eating disorder treatment. In one study, predictors of relapse were examined among women who had been successfully treated for **bulimia nervosa** or **anorexia nervosa** (Keet et al., 2005). Bulimia nervosa is an eating disorder characterized by binge eating, excessive compensatory behaviors to prevent weight gain, and a self-evaluation that is highly influenced by body shape and weight. Bulimia is further classified as the **purging type** (e.g., regular episodes of self-induced vomiting or the misuse of laxatives or diuretics) or **nonpurging type** (regular use of other compensatory behaviors such as fasting or excessive exercise, but no purging episodes). Anorexia nervosa is an eating disorder characterized by the refusal to maintain a minimally normal body weight, an intense fear of gaining weight, and body image disturbance. Anorexia can be further classified as the **restricting type** (no binge-eating or purging behaviors) or **binge-eating/purging type** (regular binge-eating and purging epidodes; American Psychiatric Association, 2000). Keel, Dorer, Franko, and colleagues (2005) found that eight to nine years after treatment, approximately one-third of women experienced a relapse after being successfully treated for these disorders. Women with higher levels of body image disturbance were more likely to relapse than women with healthier body images.

- bulimia nervosa
- anorexia nervosa
- purging type
- nonpurging type
- restricting type
- binge-eating/purging type

Body image disturbance can also lead to steroid use among men who want to increase their lean muscle mass. A study conducted at the Centers for Disease Control and Prevention in Atlanta, Georgia, reported that, in 1997, 3.7 percent of young men in grades 9 to 12 had used steroids at least once. Although nearly half of these men were using steroids to improve their sports performance, just as many were using steroids to change their physical appearance (Centers for Disease Control and Prevention, 2001).

Smoking. Many smokers (particularly women and adolescents) report that they smoke to maintain or lose weight. Some smokers may even experience an increased urge to smoke when they are exposed to situations that make them feel badly about their bodies (e.g., when looking at photographs of ultra-thin models; Lopez, Drobes, Thompson, & Brandon, 2008). Thus, body image concerns can lead some people to start smoking or to continue smoking (Stice & Shaw, 2003; Wiseman, Turco, Sunday, & Halmi, 1998). However, a longitudinal study of nearly 4,000 men and women between the ages of 18 and 30 found that over a seven-year period, smokers and nonsmokers gained the same amount of weight (Klesges, Ward, Ray, et al., 1998). Apparently, smoking is not as effective a weight management strategy as many people believe.

Health-promoting behaviors

One might expect that body image concerns could prompt people to take better care of their health (Heinberg, Thompson, & Matzon, 2001), perhaps by motivating them to start an exercise program or to eat more healthfully. However, emerging data do not support this hypothesis, at least not among adolescents. A longitudinal study of 2,500 adolescents found that having a poor body image did not motivate adolescents to become more physically active or to eat more fruits and vegetables (Neumark-Sztainer, Paxton, Hannan, et al., 2006). Although study participants with low levels of body satisfaction were more likely to diet to lose weight than participants with higher levels of body satisfaction, they were also more likely to engage in unhealthy weight loss behaviors (e.g., fasting, skipping meals) and to be less physically active. Thus, for adolescents, there appear to be virtually no health advantages associated with being dissatisfied with one's body. Whether a small amount of body dissatisfaction can prompt healthy weight-loss behaviors in adults remains to be seen.

Measurement

Exercise psychologists are interested in understanding the relationship between exercise behavior and body image. In order to study this relationship, however, we need valid and reliable measures of all four dimensions of body image (i.e., perceptual, cognitive, affective, and behavioral). Although many more body image measures exist than can be discussed in this chapter, some of the most common approaches to measuring body image are described next. For an excellent overview of body image measures used by exercise psychologists, see Bane and McAuley (1998).

Perceptual Measures

Perceptual measures of body image assess the level of accuracy of judgments about the size of one's body parts or the body as a whole. Body-part procedures require individuals to indicate the perceived width of a particular body part. One particularly innovative body-part procedure involves using specially designed morphing software to digitally alter a photographic image of a study participant (Stewart, Benson, Michanikou, et al., 2003). Highly sophisticated computer algorithms are applied to distort the arms, legs, and torso so that they appear larger or smaller than the actual size of the participant's body part. Next, the participant is shown the morphed photograph and asked to adjust it to match his or her *perceived* body shape and size (see Exhibit 9.1). A ratio is calculated comparing the actual dimensions of the respondent's body parts (as depicted in the original photograph) with the respondent's perceived dimensions. This ratio indicates the degree to which the person overestimates or underestimates his or her body size and reflects the accuracy of the body image perceptions. Body-part estimation can also be done by simply asking participants to mark their body widths on a sheet of paper attached to a wall. Again, perceived widths are compared with actual body-part widths, and the ratio of over- or underestimation is calculated.

For assessing whole-body perceptions, a commonly used technique requires individuals to view a range of real-life photographic or videotaped images of themselves that have been morphed (modified) to appear larger or smaller than

Examples of an individual's actual body and the corresponding estimated and ideal bodies. exhibit 9.1

ACTUAL	ESTIMATED	IDEAL
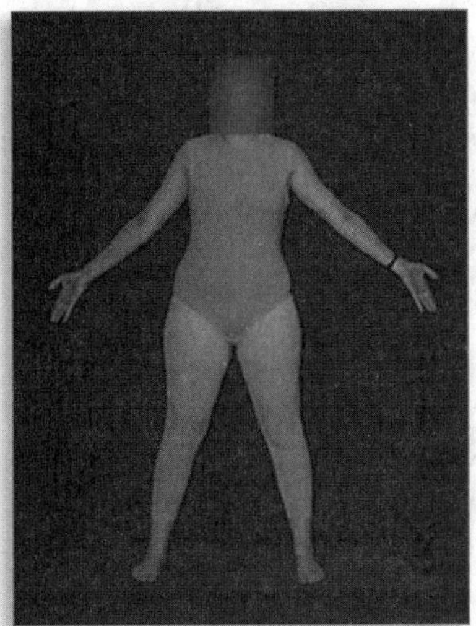	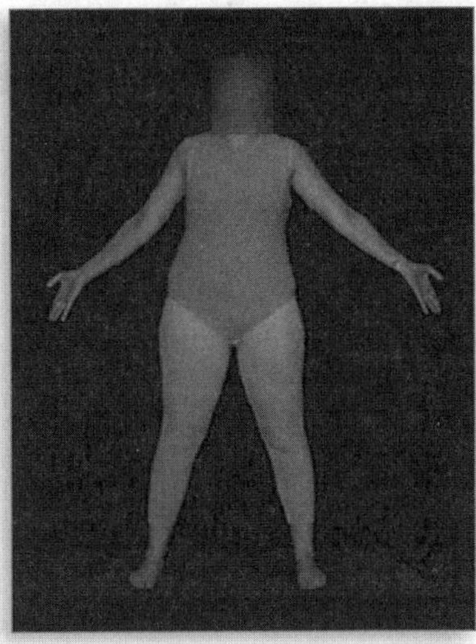	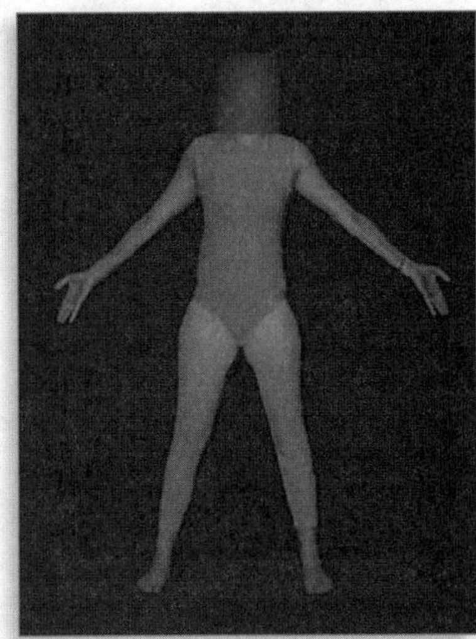

The individual has an actual BMI of 25.3, an estimated BMI of 27.3, and an ideal BMI of 18.3.

Source: Tovée, Benson, Emery, et al. (2003). Used with permission.

actual body size. From the array of images, respondents are asked to choose the one that best represents their actual body size. The difference between what people think they look like and what they actually look like represents the accuracy of their body-size perception. For both the body-part and the whole-body perception tests, when individuals perceive themselves to be different from their actual size, this is evidence of body image disturbance.

Cognitive Measures

Of the four dimensions of body image, there are more measures of the cognitive dimension than any other. Measures of the cognitive dimension typically consist of questionnaires that assess the degree of satisfaction with one's body shape, size, and function, as well as one's attitudes, beliefs, and thoughts about body shape, size, and function.

Degree of satisfaction is usually measured by presenting respondents with a list of various body parts (chest, legs, etc.) or aspects of physical function (energy level, strength, etc.) and asking them to rate their level of satisfaction or dissatisfaction with each item on the list. The Body Esteem Scale (Franzoi & Shields, 1984) is an example of this type of measure.

exhibit 9.2 **Line drawings used as a cognitive measure of body image.**

Respondents are asked to choose the drawing they think best represents their current size and the drawing that best represents their ideal size. The discrepancy between the two chosen figures is taken as an indication of body size dissatisfaction.

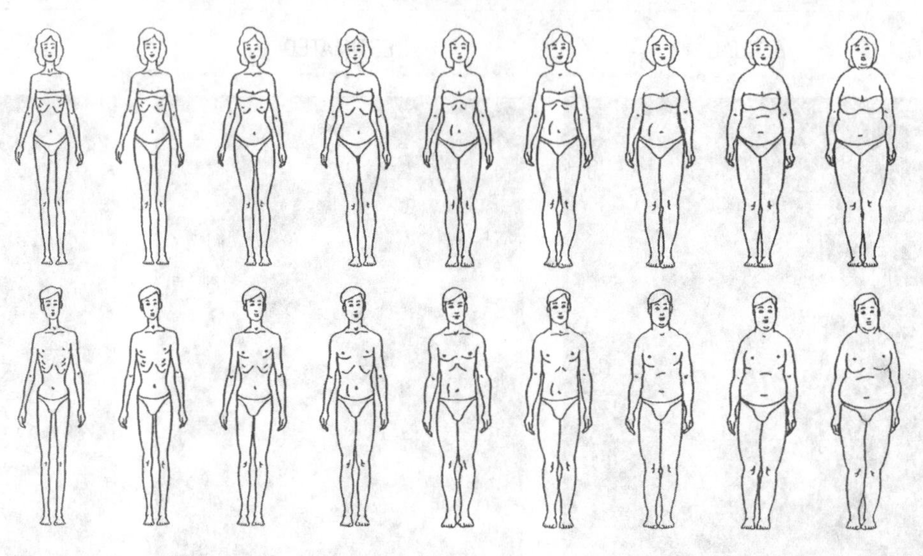

From Thompson, M. A. and Gray, J. J. (1995) Development and validation of a new body assessment scale. *Journal of Personality Assessment, 64*(2), 263. Used by permission of Taylor & Francis Group, www.informaworld.com.

Another way in which satisfaction is measured is by presenting respondents with a series of drawings that represent a range of possible body shapes and sizes, from very thin to very muscled, or from very thin to very overweight, such as the drawings presented in Exhibit 9.2. Respondents are asked to choose the drawing they think best represents their current size and the drawing that best represents their ideal size. The discrepancy between the two chosen figures is taken as an indication of body size dissatisfaction. Likewise, as discussed previously, Stewart and colleagues (2003) have used their body-morphing software to assess body size satisfaction by asking people to create their "ideal" body from a distorted image of their own body (see Exhibit 9.1). The difference in size between the ideal and actual images is also considered an index of body size dissatisfaction.

Attitudes, beliefs, and thoughts about one's body are typically measured using a series of questionnaire items. The Multidimensional Body–Self Relations Questionnaire (MBSRQ; Cash, Winstead, & Janda, 1986) is an example of this type of measure. The most comprehensive cognitive measure of body image, the MBSRQ consists of 10 subscales that assess body image cognitions related to the body's appearance, health, and physical functioning. Two subscales of the MBSRQ are shown in Exhibits 9.3 and 9.4.

Despite being one of the most widely used body image measures, the MBSRQ has been criticized for not adequately assessing men's body image concerns (Cafri & Thompson, 2004). Among men, body image disturbance generally stems from

Appearance evaluation scale from the MBSRQ.* exhibit 9.3

Please indicate the extent to which you agree with each statement.	*Definitely Disagree*	*Mostly Disagree*	*Neither Agree nor Disagree*	*Mostly Agree*	*Definitely Agree*
1. I like my looks just the way they are.	1	2	3	4	5
2. My body is sexually appealing.	1	2	3	4	5
3. Most people would consider me good looking.	1	2	3	4	5
4. I like the way I look without my clothes on.	1	2	3	4	5
5. I like the way my clothes fit me.	1	2	3	4	5
6. I dislike my physique.	1	2	3	4	5
7. I am physically unattractive.	1	2	3	4	5

Note: This scale is scored by reverse-scoring items 6 and 7 and then averaging the scores for all items. Higher scores indicate more positive evaluations of one's appearance.

Source: Cash, Winstead, & Janda (1986).

Body-areas satisfaction scale from the MBSRQ.* exhibit 9.4

Please use this 1 to 5 scale to indicate how satisfied you are with each of the following areas or aspects of your body:	*Very Dissatisfied*	*Mostly Dissatisfied*	*Neither Satisfied nor Dissatisfied*	*Mostly Satisfied*	*Very Satisfied*
1. Face (facial features, complexion)	1	2	3	4	5
2. Hair (color, thickness, texture)	1	2	3	4	5
3. Lower torso (buttocks, hips, thighs, legs)	1	2	3	4	5
4. Mid torso (waist, stomach)	1	2	3	4	5
5. Upper torso (chest or breasts, shoulders, arms)	1	2	3	4	5
6. Muscle tone	1	2	3	4	5
7. Weight	1	2	3	4	5
8. Height	1	2	3	4	5
9. Overall appearance	1	2	3	4	5

Note: This scale is scored by averaging the scores for all items. Higher scores indicate greater body satisfaction.

Source: Cash, Winstead, & Janda (1986).

*The MBSRQ (© Thomas Cash, Ph.D.) is available from its author's website, www.body-images.com. Use of the MBSRQ requires permission of the author.

concerns about not being sufficiently muscular. In contrast, female body image disturbance usually emanates from concerns about not being sufficiently thin. The MBSRQ does an excellent job of measuring concerns about thinness, but it does not adequately measure concerns about muscularity. Recognizing the importance of muscularity to male body image, McCreary and Sasse (2000) developed the Drive for Muscularity Scale, which includes seven items to assess body image cognitions related to the body's muscularity (see Exhibit 9.5).

exhibit 9.5 **Drive for Muscularity Scale.**

Please read each item carefully. Then, for each statement, circle the number that best applies to you.

1	2	3	4	5	6
Always	*Very often*	*Often*	*Sometimes*	*Rarely*	*Never*

I. ITEMS TO ASSESS MUSCULARITY-ORIENTED BODY IMAGE COGNITIONS

I wish that I were more muscular.	1	2	3	4	5	6
I think I would feel more confident if I had more muscle mass.	1	2	3	4	5	6
I think that I would look better if I gained 10 pounds in bulk.	1	2	3	4	5	6
I think that I would feel stronger if I gained a little more muscle mass.	1	2	3	4	5	6
I think that my arms are not muscular enough.	1	2	3	4	5	6
I think that my chest is not muscular enough.	1	2	3	4	5	6
I think that my legs are not muscular enough.	1	2	3	4	5	6

II. ITEMS TO ASSESS MUSCULARITY-ORIENTED BEHAVIORS

I lift weights to build up muscle.	1	2	3	4	5	6
I use protein or energy supplements.	1	2	3	4	5	6
I drink weight-gain or protein shakes.	1	2	3	4	5	6
I try to consume as many calories as I can in a day.	1	2	3	4	5	6
I feel guilty if I miss a weight-training session.	1	2	3	4	5	6
Other people think I work out with weights too often.	1	2	3	4	5	6
I think that my weight-training schedule interferes with other aspects of my life.	1	2	3	4	5	6

Note: This scale is scored by calculating separate sums for the cognition items and the behavior items. Higher scores indicate greater muscularity satisfaction and less use of behaviors to increase muscularity.

From McCreary, D. R., Sasse, D. K., Saucier, D. M., & Dorsch, K. D. (2004). Measuring the drive for masculinity: Factorial validity of the Drive for Muscularity Scale in men and women. *Psychology of Men & Masculinity, 5,* 49–58. Copyright © 2004 by the Educational Publishing Foundation. Adapted with permission.

Affective Measures

In contrast to the multitude of cognitive and perceptual measures of body image that are available, there are relatively few measures of the affective dimension. Affective measures assess feelings such as worry, shame, anxiety, comfort, embarrassment, and pride in relation to the body. Greater negative feelings are associated with greater body image disturbance. An example of an affective measure is the Objectified Body Consciousness Scale (McKinley & Hyde, 1996), which measures people's feelings of shame about their outward appearance and weight. The questionnaire asks respondents to indicate their level of agreement with statements such as "When I can't control my weight, I feel like something must be wrong with me" and "I feel like I must be a bad person when I don't look as good as I could." The Social Physique Anxiety Scale (SPAS; Hart, Leary, & Rejeski, 1989) is another affective measure of body image that has been used extensively in exercise psychology research. **Social physique anxiety** is the anxiety people experience during real or imagined conditions when other people evaluate or "check out" their body. The SPAS assesses the level of that anxiety. The nine-item version of the SPAS is shown in Exhibit 9.6.

■ social physique anxiety

Social Physique Anxiety Scale (nine-item version). **exhibit 9.6**

Read each of the following statements carefully and indicate the degree to which the statement is characteristic or true of you, according to the following scale:

1	2	3	4	5
Not at all characteristic of me	*Slightly characteristic of me*	*Moderately characteristic of me*	*Very characteristic of me*	*Extremely characteristic of me*

1. I wish I wasn't so uptight about my physique/figure.	1	2	3	4	5
2. There are times when I am bothered by thoughts that other people are evaluating my weight or muscular development negatively.	1	2	3	4	5
3. Unattractive features of my physique/figure make me nervous in certain social settings.	1	2	3	4	5
4. In the presence of others, I feel apprehensive about my physique/figure.	1	2	3	4	5
5. I am comfortable with how fit my body appears to others.	1	2	3	4	5
6. It would make me uncomfortable to know others were evaluating my physique/figure.	1	2	3	4	5
7. When it comes to displaying my physique/figure to others, I am a shy person.	1	2	3	4	5
8. I usually feel relaxed when it is obvious that others are looking at my physique/figure.	1	2	3	4	5
9. When in a bathing suit, I often feel nervous about the shape of my body.	1	2	3	4	5

Note: The SPAS is scored by reverse-scoring items 5 and 8 and then summing the scores for all items. Higher scores indicate greater social physique anxiety.

Reprinted, with permission, from E. A. Hart, M. R. Leary, and W. J. Rejeski, 1989. "The measurement of social physique anxiety," *Journal of Sport & Exercise Psychology, 11*(1), 98, table 1.

Another affective aspect of body image—body comfort—can be measured using a body focus procedure (Butters & Cash, 1987). This procedure requires participants to examine their body in a full-length, three-panel mirror for 30 seconds and then to indicate their level of comfort.

Behavioral Measures

Of the four dimensions of body image, the behavioral dimension has the fewest measures. Measures of the behavioral component assess the frequency with which one engages in activities that might be indicative of body image disturbance. These activities fall into three general categories: avoidance behaviors, lifestyle behaviors, and body checking behaviors.

avoidance behaviors ■

Avoidance behaviors are actions performed to divert attention away from the body or to prevent other people from seeing one's body. Examples include wearing baggy clothes, shunning social events, and avoiding physical or sexual intimacy.

lifestyle behaviors ■

Lifestyle behaviors are actions performed with the goal of altering the body or that reflect extensive body image concern. Examples include restrained eating or dieting, excessive exercising, exercising only for the purpose of losing weight (as opposed to improving health), using steroids, weighing oneself repeatedly, and seeking out cosmetic surgery to alter one's appearance.

body checking behaviors ■

Body checking behaviors are actions performed to monitor or assess one's body shape or size. These behaviors are often quite idiosyncratic (i.e., unusual). Examples include pinching parts of the body to measure body fatness, measuring the diameter of one's wrist, and monitoring whether one's thighs rub together while walking.

All three categories of behavior are generally measured using questionnaires that ask participants to self-report the frequency with which they engage in these behaviors. For instance, the Drive for Muscularity Scale shown earlier in Exhibit 9.5 includes seven items that assess behaviors that a man may perform to become bigger and more muscular.

The Body Checking Questionnaire (Reas, Whisenhunt, Netemeyer & Williamson, 2002) consists of three subscales that measure checking behaviors related to general appearance and specific body parts, as well as idiosyncratic (i.e., unusual) checking behaviors. Two of these subscales are shown in Exhibit 9.7. Sometimes, it may also be possible to obtain direct measures (rather than self-report measures) of these activities. For example, it may be possible to observe and record the type of clothing that a person wears to an aerobics class as a direct behavioral index of that person's body image. There has been very little development of valid and reliable direct approaches to measure these behaviors, however.

Research on Body Image and Exercise

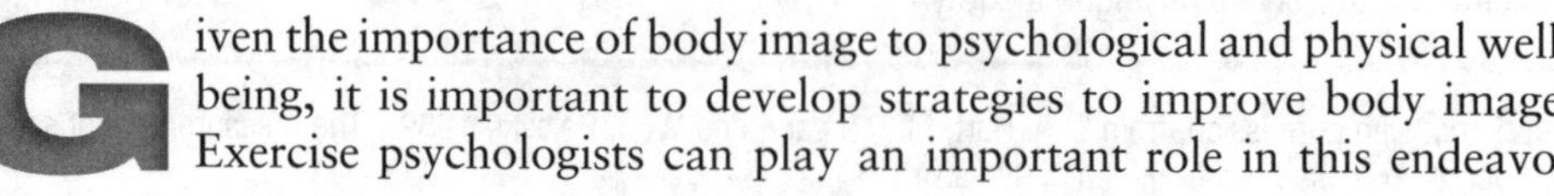

Given the importance of body image to psychological and physical well-being, it is important to develop strategies to improve body image. Exercise psychologists can play an important role in this endeavor

exhibit 9.7 **Two subscales of the Body Checking Questionnaire.**

Circle the number that best describes how often you engage in these behaviors at the present time.

1	2	3	4	5
Never	*Rarely*	*Sometimes*	*Often*	*Very often*

1. I check to see if my thighs spread when I'm sitting down.	1	2	3	4	5
2. I pinch my stomach to measure fatness.	1	2	3	4	5
3. I check the diameter of my wrist to make sure it's the same size as before.	1	2	3	4	5
4. I pinch my upper arms to measure fatness.	1	2	3	4	5
5. I touch underneath my chin to make sure I don't have a "double chin."	1	2	3	4	5
6. I rub (or touch) my thighs while sitting to check for fatness.	1	2	3	4	5
7. I check the diameter of my legs to make sure they're the same size as before.	1	2	3	4	5
8. I check to see if my thighs rub together.	1	2	3	4	5
9. I check to see if my fat jiggles.	1	2	3	4	5
10. I check to make sure my rings fit the same way as before.	1	2	3	4	5
11. I look to see if I have cellulite on my thighs when I am sitting.	1	2	3	4	5
12. I lie down on the floor to see if I can feel my bones touch the floor.	1	2	3	4	5
13. I pinch my cheeks to measure fatness.	1	2	3	4	5

From Reas, D.L., Whisenhunt, B.L., Netemeyer, R., & Williamson, D.A. (2002). Development of the Body Checking Questionnaire: A self-report measure of body checking behaviors. *International Journal of Eating disorders, 31*, 324–333. Reprinted with permission from Elsevier Science.

by studying the effects of exercise on body image and using this information to develop body image–enhancing exercise interventions.

Exercise Can Improve Body Image

Comprehensive narrative and meta-analytic reviews of exercise interventions (Hausenblas & Fallon, 2006; Martin & Lichtenberger, 2002) have led to the conclusion that exercise training can lead to significant improvements in body image among both men and women. The results of Hausenblas and Fallon's meta-analysis indicated that exercise interventions consisting of a *combination* of aerobic training and strength training produced greater improvements in body image than interventions consisting of only aerobic training (e.g., jogging, walking) or only strength training (e.g., lifting weights). Given that the cultural body image ideal for men is lean and muscular, and the female ideal is lean and toned, it makes sense that exercise interventions designed to reduce fat and build muscle would yield the biggest improvements in body image.

When the effects of aerobic- and strength-training interventions were compared in the meta-analysis, there was virtually no difference in the effects of these exercise modalities on body image. However, it is important to note that a meta-analysis compares the average effect observed in one type of study (e.g., studies that employed a strength-training intervention) with the average effect observed in another type of study (e.g., studies that employed an aerobic-training intervention). The studies included in a meta-analysis will vary in their quality, participants involved, measures administered, exercise training protocols, and so on; these factors can influence the outcome of a particular study. Because of differences in the studies used to compare strength and aerobic training, the results of comparisons made in a meta-analysis will not necessarily parallel the results of a single study that *directly* compares the effects of strength training with the effects of aerobic training.

Indeed, in the only published study to have *directly* compared the effects of strength and aerobic training on body image (Tucker & Mortell, 1993), strength training was found to be superior. Tucker and Mortell randomly assigned 30 women to a weight-training program and 30 women to a walking program. Both programs were held three times per week. Body satisfaction was measured at the start of the study and again 12 weeks later. Upon completion of the exercise program, both groups of women showed significant improvements in body image, but those assigned to the weight-training intervention showed greater improvements than did the walkers. However, it should be noted that moderate- and strenuous-intensity exercise have been shown to produce greater improvements in body image than mild intensity exercise (Hausenblas & Fallon, 2006). It is possible that walking was not as effective as weight training because it was performed at a milder intensity. The conflicting findings produced in Hausenblas and Fallon's meta-analysis, compared with Tucker and Mortell's study, suggest that we cannot assume that aerobic exercise is always as effective as strength training for improving body image. Rather, the type and intensity of the activity also need to be considered.

An interesting question is whether exercise is as effective as traditional psychological approaches to improving body image. Unfortunately, this issue has not been well studied. Nonetheless, the results of one experiment (Fisher & Thompson, 1994) have provided encouraging results. You can read about this study in the box on page 245.

Mechanisms of Change

Exhibit 9.8 shows three proposed mechanisms by which exercise might improve body image: improved physical fitness, increased awareness of physical capabilities, and increased self-efficacy.

Improved physical fitness

Fitness reflects one's level of cardiorespiratory endurance (or aerobic fitness), muscular strength and endurance, flexibility, body composition, and ability to perform functional activities such as those associated with daily living.

Exercise versus Psychological Interventions for Improving Body Image

Cognitive behavior therapy (CBT), a type of psychological intervention, has been used successfully to improve body image (Butters & Cash, 1987; Grant & Cash, 1995). In general, CBT consists of strategies such as relaxation training, cognitive restructuring, stress management, and desensitization procedures that individuals are trained to use to improve their thoughts, feelings, perceptions, and behaviors toward their bodies.

One study has shown that exercise can be just as effective as CBT for improving body image. Fifty-four women who scored very low on a measure of body satisfaction were randomly assigned to either a CBT treatment group, an exercise treatment group, or a control group (Fisher & Thompson, 1994). Those assigned to the CBT group participated in six one-hour sessions of therapy over a six-week period. Those assigned to the exercise group participated in a one-hour exercise class each week for six weeks, and were also instructed to exercise on their own at least two additional times per week. Participants in the control group did not receive any intervention. Over the six-week study, the CBT and exercise groups showed significant and similar improvements along the cognitive and affective dimensions of body image. The control group showed no improvement. These findings suggest that exercise is just as good as psychological interventions for improving body image. Of course, unlike psychological interventions, exercise interventions have the added bonus of improving people's health and physical fitness at the same time as they improve body image.

The vast majority of exercise intervention studies have examined body image change in relation to change in just a *single* fitness component—**body composition** (the relative amount of lean body mass vs. fat in the body). Some of these studies have shown no relationship between change in body image and change in body composition (e.g., Lindwall & Lindgren, 2005; McAuley et al., 2002). Some of these studies have shown that changes in body composition are significantly related to the amount of body image change experienced during an exercise intervention, with larger decreases in body fat and body weight leading to greater improvements in body image (e.g., McAuley, Bane, Rudolph, & Lox, 1995; Taylor & Fox, 2005). However, the effects of improved body composition are fairly modest and generally account for less than 10 percent of the total change in body image. Moreover, in some exercise training studies, participants have significantly improved their body image but have shown very little or no significant change in body composition (e.g., Taylor & Fox, 2005). These findings suggest that greater decreases in body weight are not necessarily associated with greater improvements in body image, and that relatively small alterations in body composition can lead to considerably large improvements in body image.

■ body composition

A few studies have examined the relationship between changes in body image and changes in the cardiovascular endurance and muscular strength aspects of physical fitness. Typically, improvements in cardiovascular endurance are not related to improvements in body image (e.g., Lindwall & Lindgren, 2005; Taylor exhibit 9.8 Three proposed mechanisms by which exercise might improve body image.

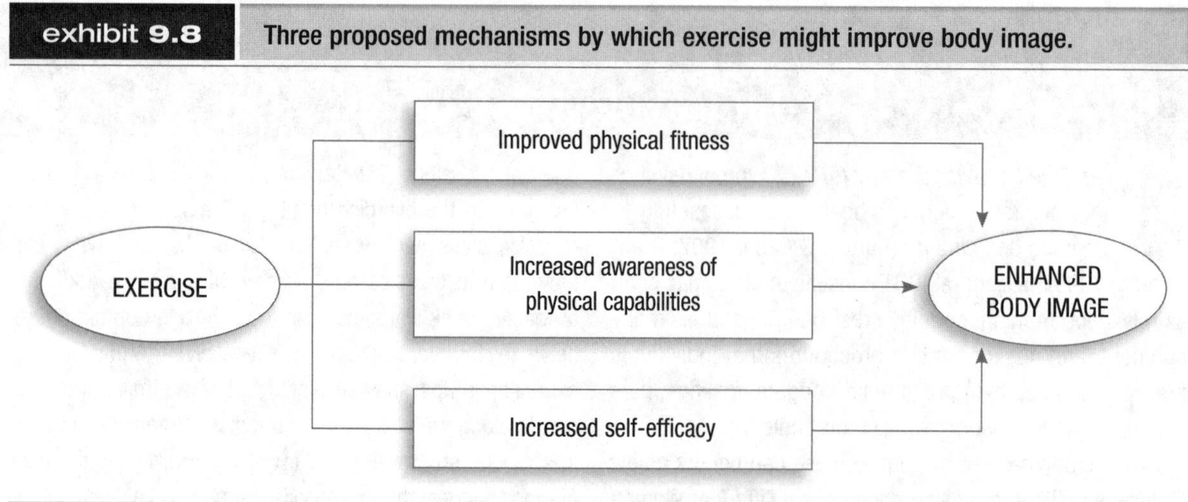

& Fox, 2005), and improvements in strength account for only modest amounts of change in body image. For example, Tucker and Mortell's study (1993) found that changes in strength across a 12-week weight-training program accounted for just 12 percent of the variability in body image change. These results suggest that other variables account for much of the effects of exercise on body image.

Even if changes in muscular strength do account for some of the variability in body image change, it is unknown whether *actual* improvements in strength trigger improvements in body image, or whether the changes in physical appearance that *accompany* increased strength (e.g., improved muscle tone, firmer-looking physique) make people feel better about their bodies. Interestingly, the answer may depend on whether the exerciser is a man or a woman. Preliminary data suggest that following a weight-lifting training program, a combination of improvements in both perceived and actual strength contributed to positive changes in women's body image. In contrast, only perceived improvements in strength seemed to play a role in positively changing men's body image (Martin Ginis, Eng, Arbour, et al., 2005).

Increased awareness of physical capabilities

If changes in body composition do not fully explain the positive effects of exercise on body image, then what does? Perhaps exercise improves body image by making people more aware of their physical capabilities, while reducing the focus on their physical appearance. This shift in awareness might be particularly relevant to women, who, unlike men, tend to place greater value on physical appearance than on physical capabilities or function and, hence, are more inclined to exercise primarily to change their appearance. Because it is virtually impossible for most women to achieve the cultural body ideal through exercise, those who embark on an exercise program with the goal of attaining this ideal are setting themselves up for inevitable failure and continued body dissatisfaction.

It is possible, however, for most women to improve their physical functioning and conditioning through exercise training. When women exercise to improve nonappearance aspects of body image (such as satisfaction with physical function), they are more likely to experience success and satisfaction than when they exercise for appearance-related reasons. This may explain why women who exercise for fitness-related motives express greater body satisfaction than those who exercise for appearance-related motives. Because our culture and the media do not have strictly defined ideals for fitness (i.e., in terms of how fast a woman should be able to run, or how much weight she should be able to lift), women who focus on improving along fitness dimensions are not constantly comparing themselves with an unattainable standard (Martin & Lichtenberger, 2002).

Increased self-efficacy

When exercisers pay attention to their physical capabilities and see themselves improving, it is likely that their physical self-efficacy also improves. Such changes in self-efficacy may lead to changes in body image. This hypothesis is consistent with the exercise and self-esteem model (see Chapter 8), which suggests that exercise-related improvements in physical self-efficacy can lead to more positive feelings about one's body. Indeed, McAuley and his colleagues (2002) found that, over the course of a 12-month study of an exercise intervention for older adults, increases in physical self-efficacy were associated with decreases in social physique anxiety (i.e., the anxiety that people experience in response to others' evaluations of their body). Although self-efficacy was only modestly associated with social physique anxiety, these results do suggest that self-efficacy may account for at least some of the effects of exercise on body image.

Who Benefits Most from Exercise Interventions?

Exercise interventions have the greatest impact on the people who have the poorest body image. In Tucker and Mortell's study (1993), for example, the women who had the poorest body image at the start of the study showed the greatest improvements over the course of the study. It follows, then, that exercise training could be particularly beneficial to people whose body image may be threatened by disease or illness (Martin & Lichtenberger, 2002). Indeed, exercise training has been associated with increased body image satisfaction among women diagnosed with breast cancer (Pinto, Clark, Maruyama, & Feder, 2003), men and women with spinal cord injuries (Hicks, Martin, Latimer, et al., 2003), adolescents with postural deformities (Dekel, Tenenbaum, & Kudar, 1996), and obese women (Foster, Wadden, & Vogt, 1997). These findings speak to the robustness of exercise for improving body image across a variety of special populations.

FOCUS on Breast Cancer, Exercise, and Body Image

Breast cancer is the most frequently diagnosed form of cancer among women, with one in nine developing the disease over the course of her lifetime. Although the incidence of breast cancer has increased over the past 25 years, breast cancer death rates have steadily decreased during this same period. The decline in death rates is largely due to early detection and treatment of breast cancers, before the disease spreads to other parts of the body (Canadian Cancer Society, 2004). Improved survival rates are certainly good news, but it is important to note that breast cancer and its treatments can significantly alter physical appearance. For example, part or all of the breasts might be removed during surgery, chemotherapy might cause hair loss, radiation treatments might alter skin tone and texture, and hormone therapies might result in weight gain. Women often consider these appearance-related changes to be more severe than other treatment side effects such as nausea and fatigue. Thus, it should not be surprising that such changes can have a negative impact on a woman's thoughts, feelings, and beliefs about her body (White, 2002).

Pinto and her colleagues (2003) examined the effects of exercise on the body image of women who had been treated for breast cancer. They recruited 24 sedentary women who had undergone breast cancer surgery, chemotherapy, or radiation treatment. Half of the women participated in a 12-week, supervised exercise program that consisted of 30 minutes of aerobic activity such as treadmill walking, stationary cycling, or rowing, along with some upper body strength-training using hand-held weights. The other half was assigned to a control group and did not exercise over the 12-week study period. At the beginning and end of the study, the women completed questionnaire measures of their feelings about their bodies (i.e., an affective measure of body image). Analyses of the data revealed that body image improved significantly among the women in the exercise group. In contrast, women in the control group reported a decline in body image over the course of the study. Given the small sample size and relatively short duration of the study, these findings cannot be considered conclusive, but the results are encouraging and suggest that women who have had breast cancer may feel better about their bodies by taking up a regular program of physical activity.

ADDITIONAL RESOURCES

Culos-Reed, S.N., Shields, C., & Brawley, L.R. (2005). Breast cancer survivors involved in vigorous team physical activity: Psychosocial correlates of maintenance participation. *Psycho-Oncology, 14,* 594–605.

Jones, L.W., & Courneya, K.S. (2002). Exercise counselling and programming preferences of cancer survivors. *Cancer Practice, 10,* 208–215.

Pinto, B.M., Frierson, G.M., Rabin, C,. Trunzo, J.J., & Marcus, B.H. (2005). Home-based physical activity intervention for breast cancer patients. Journal of Clinical *Oncology, 23,* 3577–3587.

ACTIVITY

Dragon boat racing has become a popular activity among breast cancer survivors.

1. Conduct an Internet search to find answers to the following questions:
   - What is dragon boat racing?
   - Where did it originate?
   - In what countries do cancer survivors participate in dragon boat racing?
   - Is dragon boat racing a competitive sport?
   - What qualities make a successful dragon boat team?
2. Conduct a search of the scientific literature to answer the following questions:
   - What are the physical benefits of dragon boat racing for breast cancer survivors?

- What are the social and psychological benefits of dragon boat racing for breast cancer survivors?
- Are there any risks associated with dragon boat racing for breast cancer survivors?

3. Using the information you have gathered, write a one-page article that would be appropriate for publication in a health magazine. The goal of the article is to educate people about dragon boat racing as a form of exercise for breast cancer survivors.

It is important to note, however, that studies of the effects of exercise on body image have involved mostly adult women. A few studies of exercise training among men have been done, but most of these investigations have involved middle-aged or older individuals. Consequently, little is known about the effects of exercise training on younger men and people drawn from other ethnic groups or socioeconomic strata. Also, little is known about the effects of exercise interventions on children's body image. Yet given that sports participation has been associated with better body image among children (Statistics Canada, 2001), it is suspected that structured exercise interventions could have a similar positive effect. In support of this idea, a case study of six obese children demonstrated that thrice weekly exercise with a personal trainer resulted in improvements in body image (see O'Brien & Martin, 1998). Similarly, in an intervention study involving 30 children who were either overweight or obese, increases in physical activity were strongly correlated with improvements in body image (Goldfield, Mallory, Parker, et al., 2007). This correlation was statistically significant even after changes in body weight were accounted for. In other words, regardless of how much weight a child lost during the study, an increase in physical activity led to more positive feelings about one's body.

Influence of Body Image on Exercise Behavior

Exercise motivation

As discussed earlier in this chapter, it has been presumed that body image concerns can motivate people to exercise. Consistent with this notion, a survey of adult men and women regarding their motivations to participate in exercise programs indicated that the desire to lose weight or increase muscle tone is a primary motive for *starting* an exercise program (Rodgers & Gauvin, 1994). However, the factors that compel a person to *start* exercising—such as body image concerns and the desire to change one's appearance—are not necessarily the same factors that compel a person to *continue* exercising.

Over time, some people who start an exercise program to change their appearance will gradually shift their motives toward exercising for continued physical and psychological well-being (Ingledew, Markland, & Medley, 1998). A shift in motives probably occurs when exercise initiates begin to see and value the fitness and mood-related benefits associated with being active. This is an important psychological step toward becoming a regular exerciser, because long-term maintenance of an exercise program is generally associated with endorsement of physical and psychological motives for exercise rather than with motives related to improving appearance.

For other people, the desire to change their physical appearance will remain their primary motive for exercising. Under such circumstances, long-term exercise adherence is unlikely. Markland and Ingledew (2007) have suggested that having a poor body image leads to less autonomous motivation for exercise (i.e., being motivated to exercise to obtain rewards or avoid punishment; see Chapter 3), perhaps by increasing the perceived pressure to conform to sociocultural body ideals. In turn, low levels of autonomous motivation lead to poorer exercise adherence.

In the short-term, however, body image concerns could influence motivation to participate in certain types of exercise activities. For instance, a cross-sectional study of 571 female fitness-center members found small but statistically significant correlations among body image, appearance-based motives for exercise, and the amount of time spent on aerobic exercise activities and yoga (Prichard & Tiggemann, 2008). Women who scored higher on measures of body dissatisfaction and appearance-based motives for exercise spent more time participating in aerobic exercise activities (e.g., cycling, rowing, running) and less time in yoga classes than women who had less body dissatisfaction and less motivation to exercise for appearance-based reasons. Because aerobic exercise is the type of activity typically recommended for weight loss, it makes sense that body-dissatisfied women would be particularly motivated to engage in this form of activity in order to improve their appearance. Yet paradoxically, when men and women work out primarily for appearance-related motives, exercise may actually exacerbate their body dissatisfaction (Prichard & Tiggemann, 2008; Strelan & Hargreaves, 2005). Exercise is a slow and challenging appearance-improvement tactic, and some people's bodies respond to exercise more than others. For example, there is tremendous variability in the amount of muscle mass that a person can gain from strength training (Hubal, Gordish-Dressman, Thompson, et al., 2005) and the amount of weight that can be lost with diet and exercises (Bouchard, 2008). Exercisers who are motivated primarily by the desire to change their bodies could be setting themselves up for continued disappointment and frustration if they do not see improvements as quickly or profoundly as expected.

Overall, body dissatisfaction seems to be more of a deterrent than an incentive to exercise. As was the case with June—the girl portrayed in the case study at the start of this chapter—body image dissatisfaction can cause some people to avoid exercise completely. Sometimes, people may refuse to exercise because they are worried about looking overweight, uncoordinated, weak, or unfit (Leary, 1992). This phenomenon was demonstrated in a study of Irish adolescents that found that, among teenagers who did not exercise regularly, body image concerns were cited as a major reason for avoiding exercise (Martin, Leary, & O'Brien, 2001).

Likewise, people who are severely overweight or obese frequently indicate that they avoid signing up for exercise programs and joining gyms because they are embarrassed or ashamed of their appearance (Bain, Wilson, & Chaikind, 1989). Unfortunately, even when obese people do take the first step and sign up for exercise programs, concerns about their appearance may prevent them from adhering. For example, in a study of obese women who were part of a walking group, those who had greater anxiety about others' evaluations of their body's appearance (i.e., greater social physique anxiety) had poorer attendance than those who were not as anxious about others' evaluations of their appearance (Treasure, Lox, & Lawton, 1998).

Exercise setting and attire preferences

Exercise setting preferences appear to be influenced by body image concerns. For example, Spink (1992) administered the Social Physique Anxiety Scale (SPAS; discussed earlier in the chapter) to a sample of young women and asked them where they typically exercised. Women who had high scores on the SPAS (that is, women who reported that they experienced very high levels of anxiety when other people evaluated their bodies) were more likely to exercise in private settings (alone at home) than were women who had low scores on the SPAS (women who reported little or no anxiety when other people evaluated their bodies).

In another study, SPAS scores were associated with the spot where women preferred to stand during an aerobics class and the clothes they wore (Brewer, Diehl, Cornelius, et al., 2004). Specifically, women with higher levels of social physique anxiety preferred to stand further away from the instructor during aerobics classes, and they wore less revealing exercise clothing than women with lower levels of social physique anxiety. These findings suggest that standing at the back of an exercise studio and wearing long, baggy exercise attire are strategies that women might use to allay fears that other people will see and evaluate their bodies.

How do women with high social physique anxiety feel when other exercisers in the class wear revealing clothing? Crawford and Eklund (1994) conducted a study that required women to watch a videotaped exercise class in which class members wore conservative aerobics attire (shorts and t-shirts) and a second video in which participants wore revealing aerobics attire (tights and thong leotards). After watching each video, women completed a questionnaire that assessed their feelings toward that particular exercise class. The questionnaire included items such as "I would be comfortable exercising with this class" and "I would feel out of place in this exercise class." Analyses revealed a significant correlation between social physique anxiety and feelings about the exercise classes. Higher levels of social physique anxiety were associated with more negative feelings toward the class that wore the revealing attire and more positive feelings toward the class that wore the conservative attire.

Women with high social physique anxiety also prefer that their exercise leaders wear conservative attire and place more emphasis on health than appearance during exercise classes. In a study of college-aged women with high levels of social physique anxiety, participants were randomly assigned to participate in one of two exercise classes (Raedeke, Focht, & Scales, 2007). In the appearance-oriented class, the exercise instructor wore revealing aerobics attire and made appearance-related comments throughout the exercise session (e.g., "let's get your legs toned so they look good!"). In the health-oriented class, the same instructor wore conservative attire and made health-related (e.g., "work it—let's get fit and healthy!") rather than appearance-related comments. Participants in the health-oriented class enjoyed the class more than those in the appearance-related class. They also reported stronger intentions to join a similar class in the future.

To date, there have been no studies examining the effects of men's body image concerns on their exercise setting and attire preferences. However, it has been shown that men do worry, at least a little, about what other exercisers think of them when they participate in an exercise class for the first time (Martin & Fox, 2001). Also, wearing revealing swimming attire (i.e., a Speedo briefs-style swimsuit) can increase feelings of body shame in some men (Martins, Tiggemann, & Kirkbride, 2007). Thus, it is likely that body image concerns can lead men to have certain preferences for where they exercise and what they wear during exercise.

Practical Recommendations

Given what is known about the effects of body image on exercise participation and the effects of exercise training on body image, several issues should be kept in mind when promoting exercise and developing exercise interventions to improve body image. First, with regard to exercise promotion, it is important that promotional materials show a wide range of body shapes, sizes, and physical abilities. Exercise campaigns that show only ultra-fit models send an inaccurate message that a fit appearance is a prerequisite for joining a gym or starting an exercise program. Consequently, people who are dissatisfied with their bodies may avoid joining a fitness program because they believe that they "don't look good enough" to be seen exercising in public.

Exercise programs should also focus on improving physical function, strength, and endurance rather than on changing physical appearance. Programs that help people to set realistic and attainable goals and that teach people how to monitor progress in terms of functional fitness improvements should have a more positive impact on body image than programs with an emphasis on "building buns of steel" and "fighting flabby abs." In short, to achieve body image change, exercise programs should focus on what people *can* realistically change, rather than draw attention to what they cannot. Granted, many people start exercising to improve their body image, but effort should be directed toward educating or orienting these individuals to the other physical and mental benefits of exercise. Fitness instructors can go one step further in de-emphasizing physical appearance by encouraging participants to wear loose-fitting, comfortable exercise attire, and donning such attire themselves (Raedeke et al., 2007).

Fitness instructors can also play an important role in shaping healthy attitudes toward exercise. People sometimes take an "all or nothing" approach to exercise, believing that if they can't do extreme amounts of strenuous exercise, then there is no point in exercising at all. Of course, any amount of exercise is better than none, and extreme amounts are unhealthy. Fitness instructors can teach people to have a more realistic, healthy approach to physical activity.

With regard to developing interventions to improve body image, the results of a meta-analysis suggest that, in order to see significant gains in body image, exercise intensity should be moderate to high (Hausenblas & Fallon, 2006)—perhaps because this level of exercise is most likely to generate the greatest improvements in physical function, fitness, and self-efficacy. Strength training can be just as effective as aerobic exercise for improving body image.

Some evidence also suggests that people who enjoy their workouts the most show the biggest exercise-related improvements in body image. Tucker and Mortell's (1993) study found that among women assigned to the weight-training group, the better they felt at the conclusion of each training session, the more they tended to gain in body image across the three-month program. It may be that people who enjoy their workouts exercise harder and adhere better than do those who don't enjoy exercising, thus reaping greater improvements in fitness, function, and appearance.

Conclusion

The most recent data suggest that a large proportion of men and women are dissatisfied with their bodies. Overall, body dissatisfaction is a greater deterrent, rather than incentive, to exercise. Exercise psychologists are interested in studying the relationship between body image and exercise-related thoughts, feelings, and behaviors. They are also interested in determining whether exercise can be used to improve body image. Although the research to date has been limited primarily to studies of Caucasian women, the results of these studies suggest that exercise can significantly improve body image. Given the importance of body image to mental and physical well-being, it is encouraging to note that exercise can be a highly effective intervention for alleviating body image disturbance.

what do you know?

1. Identify and describe the four dimensions of body image.
2. Describe two factors that can influence body image formation and disturbance.
3. How does culture shape body image?
4. Why is the assumption that "men have a better body image than women" now being questioned?

5. Give two reasons why body image is important to psychological and physical well-being.
6. Describe one type of measurement strategy for each of the four dimensions of body image.
7. Describe three ways in which exercise may improve body image.
8. How might body image have a demotivating effect on exercise behavior?
9. Why might exercise be particularly useful for improving the body image of people with disease or disability?
10. What type of exercise would you recommend to a woman who wanted to improve her body image? Does the woman's body ideal influence your recommendation?
11. What type of exercise would you recommend to a man who wanted to improve his body image? Does the man's body ideal influence your recommendation?

learning activities

1. Examine how the media portrays exercise and body image for men and women. Choose one popular women's magazine and one popular men's magazine (not fitness magazines). Compare the following across the two magazines:
   a. the number of references to exercise as a way to lose weight and change physical appearance
   b. the number of references to exercise as a way to improve health
   c. the number of advertisements and articles on diets and diet products
   d. the number of models whose bodies could be considered typical or representative of the general population
   e. the number of models whose bodies represent the ultra-trim and ultra-fit cultural ideal
2. Perform the following activities with your classmates:
   a. Ask students to complete the Social Physique Anxiety, Body Areas Satisfaction, Appearance Evaluation, and Drive for Muscularity scales. Have everyone tally their scores for each scale and then submit a brief report listing their scores, their sex, and the number of times per week that they exercise.
   b. Calculate the mean (average) score for each scale for the female students and then for the male students. On what scales did the women score higher than the men? On what scales did the men score higher than the women? Did the men and women have similar scores on any of the scales? Discuss biological, social, and psychological factors that might explain any differences or similarities in scale scores between men and women.

c. Calculate the mean score for each body image scale for women who exercise at least three times per week and then for women who exercise two times or fewer per week. Repeat this procedure for the men. What trends do you notice when you compare female exercisers' and nonexercisers' body image scores? Do similar trends exist for the men? With reference to the mechanisms presented in Exhibit 9.8, explain why differences may exist between exercisers' and nonexercisers' body image scores.

3. The transition from middle school to high school can be challenging for both boys and girls. Many things are changing in their lives, including their bodies. Design an intervention program for young teenagers (ages 13 to 15) with the objective of improving or maintaining a healthy body image.
4. Imagine that you are an instructor at a fitness club and you have been asked to design an exercise program for obese people. Taking into account what you now know about body image and exercise, design a program in which obese people will feel comfortable and that will also lead to changes in their body image.
5. When people exercise in public, they may worry about what other people think of them. For instance, they may worry about looking incompetent or unfit. Ask your classmates to make a list of worries that they have experienced in different public exercise settings (e.g., at a private exercise club, at the campus fitness center, outdoors). How do the worries differ across exercise settings? Do the worries differ for men versus women? How might body image concerns play a role in the different types of worries?
6. A meta-analysis was conducted to examine the relationship between ethnicity and body dissatisfaction among women in the United States (Grabe & Hyde, 2006). Four ethnic groups were examined, representing African American, Asian American, Hispanic, and Caucasian women. Although the differences were not large, African American women were significantly more satisfied with their bodies than Caucasian and Hispanic women. There were no differences between any of the other groups. Discuss the factors that may account for the differences and absence of differences in body dissatisfaction. Should exercise programmers take these factors into consideration when developing exercise plans for women of different ethnicities?

references

American Psychiatric Association (2000). *Diagnostic and statistical manual of mental disorders, fourth edition, text revisions* (DSM-IV-TR). Arlington, VA: American Psychiatric Publishing.

Bain, L.L., Wilson, T., & Chaikind, E. (1989). Participant perceptions of exercise programs for overweight women. *Research Quarterly for Exercise and Sport, 60,* 134–143.

Bane, S., & McAuley, E. (1998). Body image and exercise. In J.L. Duda (Ed.), *Advances in sport and exercise psychology measurement* (pp. 311–324). Morgantown, WV: Fitness Information Technology.

Blouin, A.G., & Goldfield, G.S. (1995). Body image and steroid use in male bodybuilders. *International Journal of Eating Disorders, 18,* 159–165.

Bouchard, C. (2008). Gene-environment interactions in the etiology of obesity: Defining the fundamentals. *Obesity*, 16 (Suppl. 4). 5–10.

Brewer, B.W., Diehl, N.S., Cornelius, A.E., Joshua, M.D., & Van Raalte, J.L. (2004). Exercising caution: Social physique anxiety and protective self-presentational behaviour. *Journal of Science and Medicine in Sport, 7*, 47–55.

Butters, J.W., & Cash, T.F. (1987). Cognitive-behavioral treatment of women's body image satisfaction: A controlled-outcome study. *Journal of Consulting and Clinical Psychology, 55*, 889–897.

Cafri, G., & Thompson, J.K. (2004). Evaluating the convergence of muscle appearance attitude measures. *Assessment, 11*, 224–229.

Canadian Cancer Society. (2004). Cancer information Retrieved from: www.cancer.ca.

Cash, T.F., & Deagle, E.A. (1997). The nature and extent of body-image disturbance in anorexia nervosa and bulimia nervosa: A meta-analysis. *International Journal of Eating Disorders, 22*, 107–125.

Cash, T.F., Morrow, J.A., Hrabosky, J.I., & Perry, A.A. (2004). How has body image changed? A corss-sectional investigation of college women and men from 1983 to 2001. *Journal of Consulting and Clinical Psychology*, 72, 1081–1089.

Cash, T.F., Winstead, B.A., & Janda, L.H. (1986). The great American shape-up. *Psychology Today, 20*(4), 30–37.

Celio, A.A., Zabinski, M.F., & Wilfley, D.E. (2002). African American body images. In T.F. Cash & T. Pruzinsky (Eds.), *Body image: A handbook of theory, research, and clinical practice* (pp. 234–242). New York: Guilford Press.

Centers for Disease Control and Prevention. (2001). *Youth risk behavior survey, 1997* Retrieved from: www.cdc.gov.

Cohen, T., & Esther, M. (1993). Depressed mood and concern with weight and shape in normal young women. *International Journal of Eating Disorders, 14*, 223–227.

Crawford, S., & Eklund, R.C. (1994). Social physique anxiety, reasons for exercise, and attitudes toward exercise settings. *Journal of Sport and Exercise Psychology, 16*, 70–82.

Davison, T.E., & McCabe, M.P. (2005). Relationships between men's ad women's body image and their psychological, social, and sexual functioning. *Sex Roles*, 52, 463–475.

Davison, T.E., & McCabe, M.P. (2006). Adolescent body image and psychosocial functioning. *The Journal of Social Psychology, 146*, 15–30.

Dekel, Y., Tenenbaum, G., & Kudar, K. (1996). An exploratory study on the relationship between postural deformities and body-image and self-esteem in adolescents: The mediating role of physical activity. *International Journal of Sport Psychology, 27*, 183–196.

Eisenberg, M.E., Neumark-Sztainer, D., & Paxton, S.J. (2006). Five-year change in body satisfaction among adolescents. *Journal of Psychosomatic Research, 61*, 521–527.

Feingold, A., & Mazzella, R. (1998). Gender differences in body image are increasing. *Psychological Science, 9*, 190–195.

Fisher, E., & Thompson, J.K. (1994). A comparative evaluation of cognitive behavior therapy (CBT) versus exercise therapy (ET) for the treatment of body image disturbance. *Behavior Modification, 18*, 171–185.

Foster, G.D., Wadden, T.A., & Vogt, R.A. (1997). Body image in obese women before, during, and after weight loss treatment. *Health Psychology, 16*, 226–229.

Franzoi, S.L., & Shields, S.A. (1984). The body esteem scale: Multidimensional structure and sex differences in a college population. *Journal of Personality Assessment, 48*, 173–178.

Furnham, A., Titman, P., & Sleeman, E. (1994). Perception of female body shapes as a function of exercise. *Journal of Social Behavior and Personality, 9*, 335–352.

Goldfield, G.S., Mallory, R., Parker, T., Cunningham, T., Legg, C. Lumb, A., et al. (2007). Effects of modifying physical activity and sedentary behavior on psychosocial adjustment in overweight/obese children. *Journal of Pediatric Psychology, 32*, 783–793.

Grabe, S., & Hyde, J. S. (2006). Ethnicity and body dissatisfaction among women in the United States: A meta-analysis. *Psychological Bulletin, 132*, 622–640.

Grant, J.R., & Cash, T.F. (1995). Cognitive-behavioral body image therapy: Comparative efficacy of group and modest-contact treatments. *Behaviour Therapy, 26*, 69–84.

Hart, E.A., Leary, M.R., & Rejeski, W.J. (1989). The measurement of social physique anxiety. *Journal of Sport and Exercise Psychology, 11*, 94–104.

Hausenblas, H.A., & Fallon, E.A. (2006). Exercise and body image: A meta-analysis. *Psychology & Health, 21* 33–47.

Heinberg, L.J., Thompson, J.K., & Matzon, J.L. (2001). Body image dissatisfaction as a motivator for healthy lifestyle change: Is some distress beneficial? In R.H. Striegel-Moore & L. Smolak (Eds.), *Eating disorders: Innovative directions in research and practice* (pp. 215–232). Washington, DC: American Psychological Association.

Hicks, A.L., Martin, K.A., Latimer, A.E., Ditor, D.S., & McCartney, N. (2003). Long-term exercise training in persons with spinal cord injury: effects on strength, arm ergometry performance and psychological well-being. *Spinal Cord, 41,* 29–33.

Hubal, M.J., Gordish-Dressman, H., Thompson, P.D., Price, T.B., Hoffmann, E.P., Angelopoulos, TJ., et al. (2005). Variability in muscle size and strength gain after unilateral resistance training. *Medicine & Science in Sports & Exercise, 37,* 964–972.

Ingledew, D., Markland, D., & Medley, A.R. (1998). Exercise motives and stages of change. *Journal of Health Psychology, 3,* 477–489.

Keel, P.K., Dorer, D.J., Franko, D.L., Jackson, S.C., & Herzog, D.B. (2005). Postremission predictors of relapse in women with eating disorders. *American Journal of Psychiatry, 162,* 2263–2268.

Kirkcaldy, B.D., Eysenck, M., Furnham, A.F., & Siefen, G. (1998). Gender, anxiety and self-image. *Personality and Individual Differences, 24,* 677–684.

Klesges, R.C., Ward, K.D., Ray, J.W., Cutter, G., Jacobs, D.R., & Wagenknecht, L.E. (1998). The prospective relationships between smoking and weight in a young, biracial cohort: The coronary artery risk development in young adults study. *Journal of Consulting and Clinical Psychology, 66,* 987–993.

Leary, M.R. (1992). Self-presentational processes in exercise and sport. *Journal of Sport and Exercise Psychology, 14,* 339–351.

Lindwall, M., & Lindgren, E.-C. (2005). The effects of a 6-month exercise intervention programme on physical self-perceptions and social physique anxiety in nonphysically active adolescent Swedish girls. *Psychology of Sport and Exercise, 6,* 643–658.

Lopez, E.N., Drobes, D.J., Thompson, J.K., & Brandon, T.H. (2008). Effects of a body image challenge on smoking motivation among college females. *Health Psychology, 27* (suppl.), 243–251.

Markland, D., & Ingledew, D.K. (2007). The relationships between body mass and body image and relative autonomy for exercise among adolescent males and females. *Psychology of Sport ad Exercise, 8,* 836–853.

Martin, K.A., & Fox, L.D. (2001). Group and leadership effects on social anxiety experienced during an exercise class. *Journal of Applied Social Psychology,* 31, 1000–1016.

Martin, K.A., Leary, M.R., & O'Brien, J. (2001). The role of self-presentation in the health practices of a sample of Irish adolescents. *Journal of Adolescent Health, 28,* 259–262.

Martin, K.A., Leary, M.R., & Rejeski, W.J. (2000). Self-presentational concerns in older adults: Implications for health and well-being. *Basic and Applied Social Psychology, 22,* 169–179.

Martin, K.A., & Lichtenberger, C.M. (2002). Fitness enhancement and body image change. In T.F. Cash & T. Pruzinsky (Eds.), *Body images: A handbook of theory, research, and clinical practice* (pp. 414–421). New York: Guilford Press.

Martin Ginis, K.A., Eng, J.J., Arbour, K.P., Hartman, J.W., & Phillips, S.M. (2005). Mind over muscle? Sex differences in the relationship between body image change and subjective and objective physical changes following a 12-week strength-training program. *Body Image, 2,* 363–372.

Martins, Y., Tiggemann, M., & Kirkbride, A. (2007). Those Speedos become them: The role of self-objectification in gay and heterosexual men's body image. *Personality and Social Psychology Bulletin, 33,* 634–647.

McAuley, E., Bane, S.M., Rudolph, D., & Lox, C. (1995). Physique anxiety and exercise in middle-aged adults. *Journal of Gerontology, 50B,* 229–235.

McAuley, E., Marquez, D.X., Jerome, G.J., Blissmer, B., & Katula, J. (2002). Physical activity and physique anxiety in older adults: Fitness and efficacy influences. *Aging & Mental Health, 6,* 222–230.

McCabe, M.P., & Ricciardelli, L.A. (2004). Body image dissatisfaction among males across the lifespan: A review of past literature. *Journal of Psychosomatic Research, 56,* 675–685.

McCreary, D.R., & Sasse, D.K. (2000). Exploring the drive for muscularity in adolescent boys and girls. *Journal of American College Health, 48,* 297–304.

McCreary, D.R., Sasse, D.K., Saucier, D.M., & Dorsch, K.D. (2004). Measuring the drive for muscularity: Factorial validity of the Drive for Muscularity Scale in men and women. *Psychology of Men & Masculinity, 5,* 49–58.

McKinley, N.M., & Hyde, J.S. (1996). The Objectified Body Consciousness Scale. *Psychology of Women Quarterly, 20,* 205–215.

Miller, C.T., & Downey, K.T. (1999). A meta-analysis of heavyweight and self-esteem. *Personality and Social Psychology Review, 31,* 68–84.

Muth, L.L., & Cash, T.F. (1997). Body-image attitudes: What difference does gender make? *Journal of Applied Social Psychology, 21,* 1438–1452.

Neumark-Sztainer, D., Paxton, S.L., Hannan, P.L., Haines, L., & Story M. (2006). Does body dissatisfaction matter? Five-year longitudinal associations between body satisfaction and health behaviors in adolescent females and males. *Journal of Adolescent Health, 39,* 244–251.

O'Brien, J., & Martin, K.A. (1998). Up and running: Interventions in exercise psychology. *Irish Journal of Psychology, 19,* 439–446.

Olivardia, R. (2001). Mirror, mirror on the wall, who's the largest of them all? The features and phenomenology of muscle dysmorphia. *Harvard Review of Psychiatry, 9,* 254–259.

Paxton, S.L., Neumark-Sztainer, D., Hannan, P.L., & Eisenberg, M.E. (2006). Body dissatisfaction prospectively predicts depressive mood and low self-esteem in adolescent girls and boys. *Journal of Clinical Child & Adolescent Pschology, 35,* 339–549.

Phillips, K.A., & Dufresne, R.G., Jr. (2000). Body dysmorphic disorder: A guide for dermatologists and cosmetic surgeons. *American Journal of Clinical Dermatology, 1,* 235–243.

Phillips, K.A., O'Sullivan, R.L., & Pope, H.G. (1997). Muscle dysmorphia. *Journal of Clinical Psychiatry, 58,* 361.

Pickett, T.C., Lewis, R.L., & Cash T.F. (2005). Men, muscles, and body image: Comparisons of competitive bodybuilders, weight trainers, and athletically active controls. *British Journal of Sports Medicine, 39,* 217–222.

Pinto, B.M., Clark, M.M., Maruyama, N.C., & Feder, S.I. (2003). Psychological and fitness changes associated with exercise participation among women with breast cancer. *Psycho-Oncology, 12,* 118–126.

Polivy, J., & Herman, C.P. (2002). Causes of eating disorders. *Annual Review of Psychology, 53,* 187–213.

Prichard, I., & Tiggemann, M. (2008). Relations among exercise type, self objectification, and body image in the fitness centre environment: The role of reasons for exercise. *Psychology of Sport and Exercise, 9,* 855–866.

Raedeke, T.D., Focht, B.C., & Scales, D. (2007). Social environmental factors and psychological responses to acute exercise for socially physique anxious females. *Pschology of Sport and Exercise, 8,* 463–476.

Reas, D.L., Whisenhunt, B.L., Netemeyer, R., & Williamson, D.A. (2002). Development of the Body Checking Questionnaire: A self-report measure of body checking behaviors. *International Journal of Eating disorders, 31,* 324–333.

Ricciardelli, L.A., & McCabe, M.P. (2001). Children's body image concerns and eating disturbance: A review of the literature. *Clinical Psychology Review, 21,* 325–344.

Roberts, A., Cash, T.F., Feingold, A., & Johnson., B.T. (2006). Are Black–White differences in females' body dissatisfaction decreasing? A meta-analytic review. *Journal of Consulting and Clinical Psychology, 74,* 1121–1131.

Rodgers, W.M., & Gauvin, L. (1994). *Contributions and comparisons of personal strivings and outcome expectancies in the understanding of participation motives and exercise adherence* (University of Alberta, Department of Physical Education and Sport Studies Rep. No. 922R010).

Spink, K.S. (1992). Relation of anxiety about social physique to location of participation in physical activity. *Perceptual and Motor Skills, 74,* 1075–1078.

Statistics Canada (2001). *Canadian social trends: Children's participation in sports, 2001.* Retrieved from: www.statcan.ca.

Stewart, A.D., Benson, P.J., Michanikou, E.G., Tsiota, D.G., & Narli, M.K. (2003). Body image perception, satisfaction and somatotype in male and female athletes and non-athletes: Results using a novel morphing technique. *Journal of Sports Sciences, 21,* 815–823.

Stice, E., & Shaw, H. (2003). Prospective relations of body image, eating, and affective disturbances to smoking onset in adolescent girls: How Virginia slims. *Journal of Consulting and Clinical Psychology, 71,* 129–135.

Stice, E., & Whitenton, K. (2002). Risk factors for body image dissatisfaction in adolescent girls: A longitudinal investigation. *Developmental Psychology, 38,* 669–678.

Strelan, P., & Hargreaves, D. (2005). Reasons for exercise and body esteem: Men's responses to self-objectification. *Sex Roles, 53,* 495–503.

Taylor, A.H., & Fox, K.R. (2005). Effectiveness of a primary care exercise referral intervention for changing physical self-perceptions over 9 months. *Health Psychology 24,* 11–21.

Tiggemann, M. (2004). Body image across the adult life span: Stability and change. *Body Image, 1,* 29–41.

Tovée M.J., Benson, P.J., Emery, J.L., Mason, S.M., & Cohen-Tovée, E.M. (2003). Measurement of body size and shape perception in eating-disordered and control observers using body-shape software. *British Journal of Psychology, 94,* 501–516.

Treasure, D.C., Lox, C.L., & Lawton, B.R. (1998). Determinants of physical activity in a sedentary, obese female population. *Journal of Sport and Exercise Psychology, 20,* 218–224.

Tucker, L.A., & Mortell, R. (1993). Comparison of the effects of walking and weight training programs on body image in middle-aged women: An experimental study. *American Journal of Health Promotion, 8,* 34–42.

Veale, D. (2009). Body dysmorphic disorder. In M.M. Antony & M.B Stein (Eds.), *Oxford handbook of anxiety and related disorders* (pp. 541–550). New York: Oxford University Press.

White, C.A. (2002). Body images in oncology. In T.F. Cash & T. Pruzinsky (Eds.), *Body image: A handbook of theory, research, and clinical practice* (pp. 379–386). New York: Guilford Press.

Wiseman, C.V., Turco, R.M., Sunday, S.R., & Halmi, K.A. (1998). Smoking and body image concerns in adolescent girls. *International Journal of Eating Disorders, 24,* 429–433.

10

Stress, Stress Reactivity, and Exercise

KEY TERMS

absolute reactivity
allostasis
allostatic load
cross-stressor adaptation hypothesis
distress
eustress
habituation
homeostasis
primary appraisal
psychophysiology
relative reactivity
secondary appraisal
sensitization
stress
stress response

Jim has recently begun his first semester at the university as a premed student, and every Monday and Wednesday morning he attends a very challenging anatomy and physiology class. From the very first day, Jim has felt that his instructor doesn't like him, which has created a lot of stress for him. He has gotten to the point that he dreads going to lectures, the mere thought of which make his heart race and his blood pressure skyrocket. Jim begins to get physically ill on Monday and Wednesday mornings, and his grades are starting to suffer as a result. He finally seeks help at the student health center and is fortunate enough to get an appointment with a doctor who is an avid exerciser. She suggests that Jim get up an hour earlier on the days of his anatomy and physiology lectures and go for a 20-minute run, preceded and followed up by some stretching. She suggests that he start at an easy pace but recommends that he gradually build up to whatever pace he feels comfortable with. Jim begins the next day and within two weeks is running for 35 minutes every other day. On the days of his anatomy and physiology class, he still feels nervous before class, but he somehow seems more able to handle the stress of the course. He even begins to view it as a challenge rather than an obstacle. The morning run becomes almost ritualistic, and he is certain that it is the most important thing he does to help him "prepare for the challenges of the day."

We live in a world that has become very fast paced. One result from living in such a world is an increasing level of stress. Because of the ever-growing number of stressors in our lives, physical ailments (e.g., cancer, cardiovascular disease, colds) along with depression (Chapter 12) and anxiety and anxiety disorders (Chapter 11) have become increasingly prevalent in our society. It is worth noting that stress can be caused by many different things, such as the following:

- biological sources—substance abuse (alcohol, drugs) and nutritional excess (caffeine, food, sugar)
- psychological sources—perfectionistic attitudes, obsessiveness, compulsiveness, need for control, neuroses (see Chapter 7)
- interpersonal sources—lack of social skills, shyness, insecurity, loneliness, and environmental strain (noise, temperature)

It is also worth noting that many individuals exercise as a way of dealing with or handling stress. This chapter reviews the main concepts of stress and also what is known about the effects that exercise can have on alleviating or ameliorating the stress response.

What Is Stress?

stress ■ **Stress** has been defined as "a state of disharmony, or threatened homeostasis" (Chrousos & Gold, 1992, p. 1245); more simply, stress is what we experience when we face challenges in our lives. These challenges are referred to as *stressors,* and they can be external (e.g., physical threats) or internal (e.g., fear of speaking in public). Although stressors are often
distress ■ thought of as negative (i.e., **distress**—exams, divorces, deadlines), they can also
eustress ■ be positive (i.e., **eustress**—marriage, graduation, job promotion).

In the 1930s Hans Selye borrowed the term *stress* from the field of engineering and used it in conjunction with the results of his initial studies. As noted by Sapolsky (2003), "He attempted to inject his rats daily, but apparently not with a great display of dexterity. Selye would try to inject the rats, miss them, drop them, spend half the morning chasing the rats around the room or vice versa, flailing with a broom to get them out from behind the sink, and so on" (pp. 7–8). Selye found that rats who were exposed to such a variety of unpleasant conditions (stress) developed a variety of physiological changes, including peptic ulcers, enlarged adrenal glands, and atrophied immune tissues. He noted that although the animals were exposed to a variety of stressors, their physiological responses were similar (i.e., the responses were nonspecific); if the animals were exposed to the stressors for an extended period of time, they got sick.

From these initial observations was born the General Adaptation Syndrome (Selye, 1936). When an acute, or short-term, stressor is encountered (e.g., threat of injury, embarrassment, or potential loss), the initial reaction is often referred to as "arousal and alarm." Reflexively, such events set into motion a cascade of immediate physiological adaptations that help to deal with the crisis—that is, the "fight-or-flight" response. The "fight-or-flight" response seems to more accurately reflect the male response; women experiencing stress that is not life-threatening exhibit a behavioral response characterized as the "tend and befriend" response (Taylor, Klein, Lewis, et al., 2000). In fact, these evolutionarily ancient responses are ideal for dealing with such short-term emergencies, eventually returning the body to its more stable resting state. This initial reaction is often followed by feelings of anxiety, irritability, and vulnerability until the stressor is resolved. If the stressor is unresolved and continues, a stage of resistance ensues, characterized by strain, worry, cynicism, and difficulty sleeping. If the stressor becomes prolonged, or chronic, with no resolution, the individual becomes overloaded; this is what Selye referred to as the "stage of exhaustion." The individual experiences sufficient strain to cause fatigue and numerous, insidious stress-related disorders, including anxiety (see Chapter 11) and depression (see Chapter 12).

Physiological and Psychological Responses to Stress

As discussed earlier, although the concept of stress itself is relatively recent, the bodily changes that occur as a result of stressors are evolutionarily ancient (Chrousos & Gold, 1992). The way our body responds to the stress of an exam or an angry roommate is similar to the way the ancient hunter-gatherer's body responded when he encountered a saber-toothed tiger. Over many millennia, the body (including the brain) has evolved ways to deal successfully with the challenges (i.e., stressors) we face. Such successful evolution promotes well-being and, most important, survival. Successful adaptation, however, requires that such challenges occur consistently. When a successful adaptation is developed (success being determined by survival and well-being), such an adaptation is maintained and perhaps then modified over time as changing challenges warrant.

In essence, the **stress response** is initiated when some real or perceived threat (or challenge) is encountered (see Sapolsky, 2003, for a readable discussion). The brain (i.e., the cortex, site of sensory centers, and centers for conscious thought and reasoning) sends a message to the subcortical brain structure called the *amygdala*. The amygdala is thought to be primarily responsible for initiating the stress response. It is also possible that a signal might reach the amygdala without coming from the cortex. The amygdala activates another subcortical brain structure, the hypothalamus, which has separate effects. The lateral hypothalamus activates the sympathetic nervous system (SNS) via the splanchnic nerve, which innervates the adrenal medulla, thus activating the release of the catecholamines epinephrine (E) and norepinephrine (NorE). The paraventricular nucleus of the hypothalamus releases corticotropin releasing hormone (CRH), which has the effect of stimulating the pituitary gland. This causes the release of adrenocorticotropin releasing hormone (ACTH), which acts on the adrenal cortex to stimulate the release of cortisol. Both the catecholamines and cortisol initiate the "fight-or-flight" response, preparing the body for handling the stressor. Ongoing, chronic stress leads to ongoing reactivation of the stress pathways. See Exhibit 10.1, which shows the vicious cycle of stress.

■ stress response

exhibit 10.1 **Vicious cycle of stress.**

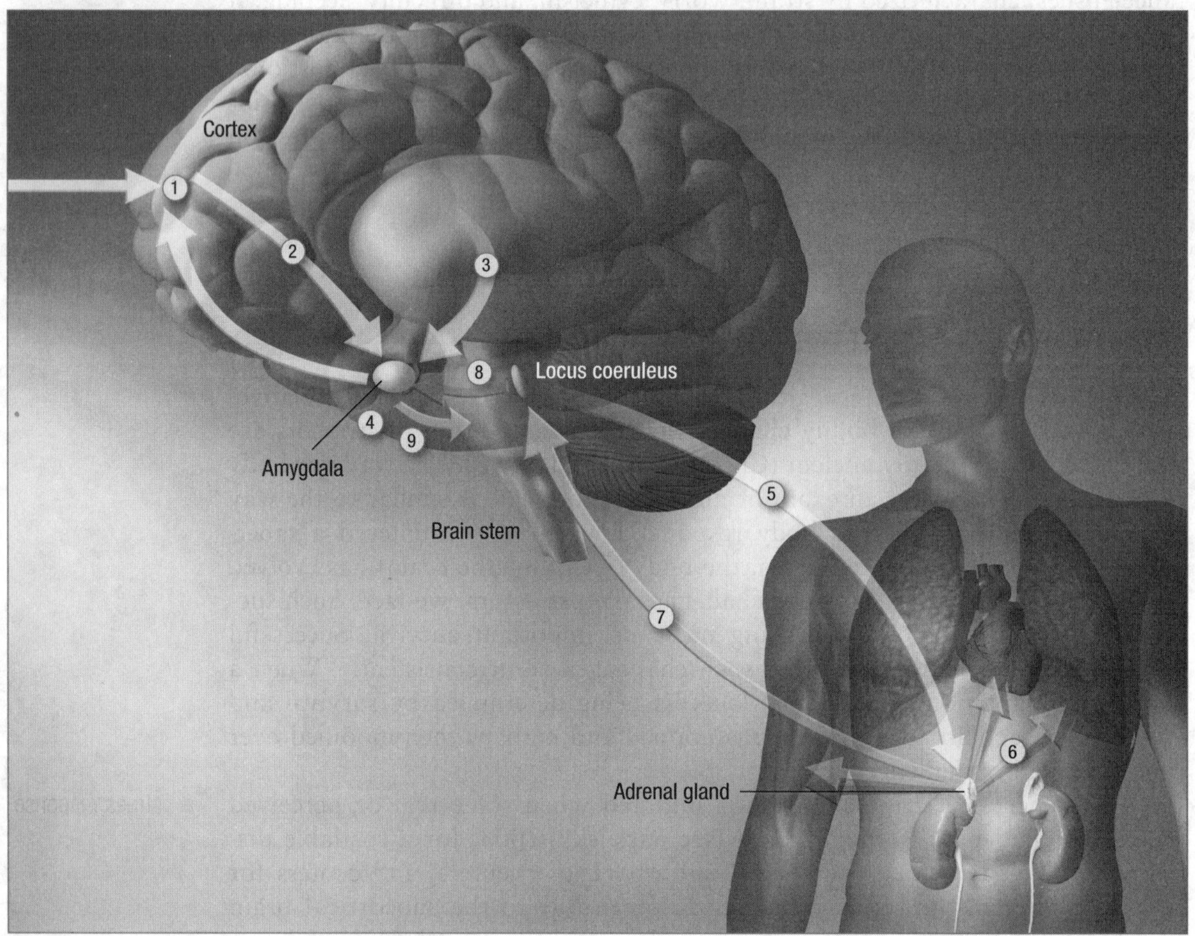

Stress pathways are diverse and involve many regions of the brain in feedback loops that can sometimes greatly amplify a response. The process—simplified somewhat in this diagram—begins when an actual or perceived threat activates the sensory and higher reasoning centers in the cortex (1). The cortex then sends a message to the amygdala, the principal mediator of the stress response (2). Separately, a preconscious signal may precipitate activity in the amygdala (3). The amygdala releases corticotropin-releasing hormone (CRH), which stimulates the brain stem (4) to activate the sympathetic nervous system via the spinal cord (5). In response, the adrenal glands produce the stress hormone epinephrine; a different pathway simultaneously triggers the adrenals to release glucocorticoids. The two types of hormones act on the muscle, heart, and lungs to prepare the body for "fight or flight" (6). If the stress becomes chronic, glucocorticoids induce the locus coeruleus (7) to release norepinephrine, which communicates with the amygdala (8), leading to the production of more CRH (9)—and to ongoing reactivation of stress pathways.

From Sapolsky, R. (September 2003). "Taming stress." *Scientific American, 289,* 87–95. Image by Alfred T. Kamajian. Reprinted with permission of the artist.

One primary aspect of the stress response, as noted above, involves the secretion of two kinds of hormones from the adrenal glands, which are located just above the kidneys:

1. Catecholamines—epinephrine and norepinephrine—are secreted from the adrenal medulla, the inner (middle) area of the adrenal gland.
2. Cortisol is released from the adrenal cortex, the outer layer of the adrenal gland.

Generally, the release of catecholamines is related to activation, effort, or engagement, while the release of cortisol is related more to distress or negative affect. Traditionally, catecholamine release is seen when situations present a challenge to the individual (which are not necessarily threatening), and cortisol release is seen when the individual is faced with a stressor viewed as a threat or an unpleasant challenge. Importantly, the degree of novelty, (lack of) predictability, and (lack of) controllability are influential in modulating the cortisol response.

Researchers have demonstrated that not only physical stressors but also psychological stimuli could elicit the stress response (Lazarus, 1966; Mason, 1975). Lazarus (1968; Folkman & Lazarus, 1985) introduced perceptions of novelty, predictability, and controllability (i.e., appraisals) to highlight the importance of the ongoing interaction between the individual and the environment. A **primary appraisal** (challenge, threat, harm) results from assessing a situation as important yet potentially demanding. A **secondary appraisal** (i.e., assessing one's resources to cope with the situation) can lead to a revision of the initial appraisal. Such a secondary appraisal might involve questioning what options are available and how viable they might be.

■ primary appraisal
■ secondary appraisal

It is also worth noting that perceptions of control can result in different neuroendocrine responses. Frankenhaeuser's work (1991), for example, has shown that a stressor perceived as relatively easy to handle usually invokes more active coping mechanisms (e.g., confronting or dealing with the stress right away) and the release of norepinephrine. As perceptions of control decrease, the levels of anxiety tend to increase, as does the tendency to use more passive coping (e.g., avoidance). This is often accompanied by increases in epinephrine and a decrease in the ratio of norepinephrine to epinephrine. With even greater losses of perceived control, distress levels increase along with greater output of cortisol.

Cognitive models of the stress response (e.g., Lazarus's cognitive-transactional model), particularly as applied to exercise psychology research, have advanced understanding to a large extent. Primarily, they have brought forth the importance of the perception of the stressor to the individual and the impact that perception might have on the stress response. These cognitive models often suffer, however, by failing to incorporate the various interactions with physiological pathways (of both the central and peripheral nervous systems; Dishman & Jackson, 2000) while attempting to explain the stress response.

Combat Stress in Soldiers

A rather unique "real-world" example of the effects of uncontrollable stress on the stress response in humans comes from the work of Charles Morgan and colleagues. Using active-duty soldiers enrolled in U.S. army survival school training, Morgan et al. (2001), using the experiences of American soldiers captured during World War II, the Korean War, and the Vietnam War, documented individual differences in psychobiological responses to intense and uncontrollable stress. This stress involved interrogations following a mock capture, food and sleep deprivation, and problem solving. The entire episode lasted approximately 72 hours. Morgan and colleagues examined both catecholamines and cortisol released during this stressful experience; they found that elevated cortisol was associated with both dissociative thinking (i.e., psychologically disconnecting from the environment) and poorer performance, but catecholamine changes were not. Greater cortisol levels were associated with greater levels of dissociation in individuals who found the stress to be intolerable. Such field experiments allow for much more realistic assessments of the stress response to severe stressors than can typically be achieved in laboratory-based experiments. If possible, it would be interesting to incorporate fitness as a variable in such work to determine the extent to which exercise/fitness might impact the stress response in such situations.

Homeostasis

It should be apparent that a stressor disrupts the relative physiological balance of the body. In 1939, Walter Cannon proposed the term *homeostasis* as a way of describing this balancing of the body's physiological systems, thus furthering the concept of the "milieu interieur" initially developed by French physiologist Claude Bernard in the mid-1800s. Specifically, **homeostasis** is the ability of an organism to change and stabilize its internal environment in spite of constant changes in the external environment. Such internal changes work to return the various bodily systems to equilibrium. The concept of homeostasis has been reconceptualized, to some extent, to refer to a limited number of physiological systems that are essential for survival (e.g., pH, body temperature, glucose levels) and that are kept within a reasonably tight range for optimal function (McEwen & Wingfield, 2003).

homeostasis ■

Allostasis

Whereas homeostasis refers to functioning within a fairly narrow range, **allostasis** is "achieving stability through change" in a wide range of functioning (McEwen & Wingfield, 2003, p. 3). Thus, the concept of allostasis (McEwen, 1998) is a more recent addition to the stress literature. As noted previously, homeostasis relates to the systems needed to maintain life; allostasis reflects the balance these essential coping/adaptation systems (e.g., cardiovascular, immune, metabolic, brain) maintain depending on a variety of factors (e.g., time of day, internal needs, aging, external demands).

allostasis ■

A related concept is **allostatic load,** which is essentially the cost of this coping/adaptation. According to McEwen, this load occurs whenever either the SAM

allostatic load ■

(sympathetic adrenal medullary) or the HPA (hypothalamic-pituitary-adrenocortical) axis becomes overworked (e.g., chronic, unrelenting stress); if neither axis turns off after the stress is removed; or if neither system adequately responds to the stressor itself and causes other systems to become overworked. See Exhibit 10.2 for an illustration of the physical effects of chronic, unrelenting stress.

Importantly, McEwen (1998) noted that individual differences can impact the stress response. The individual's perception or interpretation (appraisal) of the situation can impact this response, as can the physical state of the body itself. The most oft-cited example in this regard is of the physically fit individual who can more easily handle an exercise workload compared to the unfit person. In essence, the SAM and HPA systems are most useful when they respond rapidly

Physical effects of chronic, unrelenting stress. **exhibit 10.2**

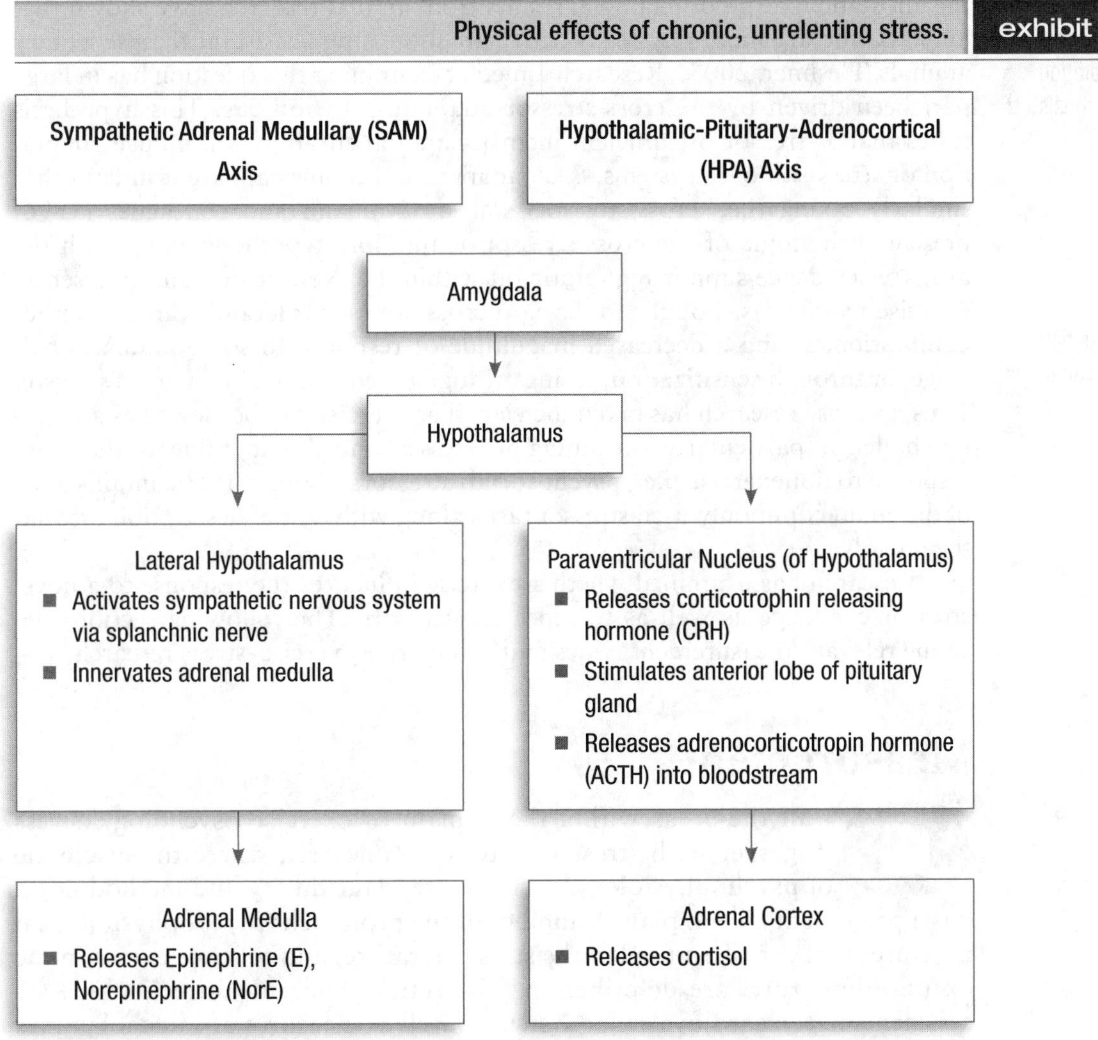

to a stressor and then "turn off" as soon as they are no longer needed. Allostatic load, or the wear and tear on the brain and the body, occurs from ongoing overactivity or inactivity of either system that ultimately results in illness or disease. For example, chronic elevations of heart rate, blood pressure, and metabolism can lead to decreased immune function, memory loss, and increased risk of anxiety and depression. Additionally, a whole host of disorders have been linked to under- and overproduction of cortisol, including depression, panic disorder, anorexia nervosa, chronic fatigue syndrome, and fibromyalgia.

Cross-Stressor Adaptation Hypothesis

Researchers have suspected for some time that regular exercise and/or fitness might beneficially impact the stress response (i.e., exercise/fitness might reduce the allostatic load). For example, results from animal research have shown that animals who are more physically active are more stress-resistant than sedentary animals (Fleshner, 2005). Research aimed at examining this question has in large part been driven by the **cross-stressor adaptation hypothesis.** This hypothesis states that a stressor of sufficient intensity and/or duration will induce adaptation of stress response systems. Such adaptation becomes apparent under other similarly taxing (i.e., cross-stressor) states. Sothmann and colleagues (1996) presented the logic of the cross-stressor adaptation hypothesis along with the available evidence supporting/refuting it within the exercise domain. In essence, exercise training is thought to develop cross-stressor tolerance through either **habituation,** seeing a decreased magnitude of response to some familiar challenge, or through **sensitization,** seeing an augmented response to a novel stressor. Thus, exercise research has taken the view that exercise can be viewed as a familiar challenge (particularly as training progresses) and should influence the stress response to nonexercise (i.e., psychosocial) stressors. Exhibit 10.3 contains a list of different, commonly used stressor tasks along with a brief description of what they involve.

cross-stressor adaptation hypothesis ■

habituation ■

sensitization ■

Research has examined whether exercise influences the response to a novel stressor challenge as well as to repeated stressors. The following sections describe relevant measurement issues and summarize exercise–stress research.

Measurement

Of all the areas within the domain of exercise psychology, stress (together with stress reactivity) is one area where the discipline of **psychophysiology,** with its attendant theory and methodology, has a prominent role to play. A number of the prominent psychophysiological measures that are often used in the stress literature, and to some extent in the exercise literature, are described in this section. Such measures include assessments of the cardiovascular system as well as measures of catecholamines and cortisol.

psychophysiology ■

Common stressor tasks/situations. exhibit 10.3

ACTIVE STRESSORS—tasks/situations in which the individual's response leads to a particular outcome; the response is under the individual's control

Laboratory Stressors

- Stroop Color and Word Test: Color words (e.g., red, blue, yellow) are presented with a conflict—the words appear in a different color than the word itself (e.g., the word "blue" appears in the color green). The individual is supposed to ignore the word and state the color of the letters of the word (the correct answer in this case would be green).
- Mental Arithmetic: Individual is asked to perform mathematical operations (e.g., division, multiplication) for some length of time, usually with time and performance pressure.
- Reaction Time (RT) tasks: Individual is supposed to respond as rapidly as possible to some presented stimulus. Could be *Performance RT* task, requiring rapid response to receive reward/reinforcement (e.g., stickers, points, money), or *Avoidance RT* task, requiring rapid response to avoid punishment or unpleasant event (e.g., electric shock, noxious noise).
- Others (includes cognitive tasks involving memory or quizzes)

Real-Life Stressors

- Public speech
- Defense of doctoral dissertation
- Combat stress in soldiers (see the box earlier in the chapter)
- Parachuting, driving race car, flying airplane

PASSIVE STRESSORS—tasks/situations in which the individual's response has no bearing on the outcome; he or she has no control over the situation; it often involves pain or noise that is unavoidable

Laboratory Stressors

- Films that elicit (usually negative) emotional reactions (e.g., of victims of car accidents, combat)
- Exposure to unpleasant/aversive sounds (e.g., loud burst of white noise) or other stimuli (e.g., cold pressor test) with no ability to change or control them

Real-Life Stressors

- Dental procedures (e.g., filling a cavity, root canal)
- In-flight emergencies

Self-Report Measurement

The exercise–stress response literature has incorporated a variety of measures of the stress response. The easiest measure to obtain is self-reported stress, whether this is in terms of perceived stress magnitude or frequency. One of the most widely used self-report measures is the Perceived Stress Scale (PSS; Cohen, Kamarck, & Mermelstein, 1983), which measures the degree to which situations in one's life are viewed as stressful. See Exhibit 10.4 for the items in this scale.

exhibit 10.4 Perceived Stress Scale.

The questions in this scale ask you about your feelings and thoughts **during the last month**. In each case, you will be asked to indicate by circling *how often* you felt or thought a certain way.

0	*1*	*2*	*3*	*4*
Never	*Rarely*	*Sometimes*	*Often*	*Very often*

1. In the last month, how often have you been upset because of something that happened unexpectedly?	0	1	2	3	4
2. In the last month, how often have you felt that you were unable to control the important things in your life?	0	1	2	3	4
3. In the last month, how often have you felt nervous and "stressed"?	0	1	2	3	4
4. In the last month, how often have you felt confident about your ability to handle your personal problems?	0	1	2	3	4
5. In the last month, how often have you felt that things were going your way?	0	1	2	3	4
6. In the last month, how often have you found that you could not cope with all the things that you had to do?	0	1	2	3	4
7. In the last month, how often have you been able to control irritations in your life?	0	1	2	3	4
8. In the last month, how often have you felt that you were on top of things?	0	1	2	3	4
9. In the last month, how often have you been angered because of things that were outside of your control?	0	1	2	3	4
10. In the last month, how often have you felt difficulties were piling up so high that you could not overcome them?	0	1	2	3	4

Scoring: PSS scores are obtained by reversing responses (e.g., 0 = 4, 1 = 3, 2 = 2, 3 = 1, & 4 = 0) to the four positively stated items (items 4, 5, 7, & 8) and then summing across all scale items. A short 4 item scale can be made from questions 2, 4, 5, and 10 of the PSS 10 item scale.

Respondents rate these items using a response format ranging from "never" to "very often." Such instruments can be useful in assessing stress levels in large groups and for gaining insight into the level of stress an individual perceives he or she is experiencing. Unfortunately, exclusive reliance on self-report does not help much in uncovering the physiological mechanisms underlying the stress response and determining whether exercise training aids in alleviating the allostatic load.

Psychophysiology

Psychophysiology is a scientific discipline that examines cognitive, emotional, and behavioral events through their manifestation as physiological processes and events. In essence, psychophysiology attempts to infer the psychological significance of cognitive, emotional, and/or behavioral events from the concomitant physiological events. It assumes that the various aspects of the psychological "domain" are embodied phenomena, that is, they can be revealed through bodily responses. This is not to say that one can simply measure heart rate to gauge the amount of anxiety a person might be experiencing. Instead, such psychophysiological relationships tend to be complex, often linked through patterns of responses and further revealed by how these patterns unfold over time (see Cacioppo, Tassinary, & Berntson, 2000). The discipline itself has a rich measurement history, having developed relatively noninvasive measures of most (if not all) bodily systems. This includes measurement of electrical activity in muscle, brain, and the cardiovascular system; endocrine function; and immune function. Importantly, a great deal of research and theory has been developed to better understand physiological function and how it might relate to and explain psychological phenomena. In particular, many of these measurement technologies have been instrumental in our current understanding of the stress response.

Cardiovascular Measurement

Clearly, the most frequently used physiological measures in this literature involve the cardiovascular system. Of the available cardiovascular measures, heart rate (HR) and blood pressure (BP) responses have been examined most often. For example, in a review of 34 studies by Crews and Landers (1987), 30 (88 percent) of the studies used measures of HR and BP (for the BP measures, however, 13 reported systolic BP and 17 reported diastolic BP). Absolute levels of these measures have been examined, as have changes in these measures from a baseline value. Unfortunately, using fairly gross measures of cardiovascular function like HR and BP does not give much insight into why or how any resultant changes occurred. Heart rate increases might occur because of combinations of activity in both the sympathetic and parasympathetic branches of the autonomic system (increases [or decreases] in both, or a change in one and no change in the other). For example, as van Doornen, de Geus, and Orlebeke (1988) point out, a HR increase during exercise is due largely to a withdrawal of vagal influence (i.e., parasympathetic dominance decreases); during the stress response to a psychosocial stressor, the HR increase is due largely to increased sympathetic activity. As they note, using a beta-blocker (a pharmacological agent that influences sympathetic activity but not parasympathetic activity) eliminates the increase seen during stress but not during exercise.

Beyond overall measures of HR, more specific aspects of the HR response can be informative. For example, HR variability, or the pattern of HR change over time, can provide insight regarding the stress response, particularly the extent to which heart rate is being modulated by parasympathetic influence. Larger amounts of variability indicate strong parasympathetic influence on the heart, which is useful in controlling the stress response.

Van Doornen and colleagues (1988) also stress the importance of including measures beyond systolic BP and diastolic BP to understand the vascular nature of the stress response. Noninvasive measures of both cardiac output (amount of blood ejected by the heart in one minute into the circulation) and total peripheral resistance (resistance to blood flow by the body's blood vessels, excluding those in the lungs) are useful in this regard. Impedance cardiography is a technique that provides measures of blood flow changes, from which can be derived measures of stroke volume (SV; the amount of blood ejected by a single beat of the heart). When combined with HR (HR × SV), estimates of cardiac output can be obtained (Stern, Ray, & Quigley, 2001).

Another useful measure for assessing sympathetic influences on the heart is the pre-ejection period (the period of time immediately before blood is pumped from the heart into the circulation), which is thought to reflect the force of contraction or contractility of the heart (Stern et al., 2001).

Hormonal Measurement

In addition to cardiovascular measures, assessments of catecholamines and cortisol are important for understanding the stress response. Indices of such variables can be obtained directly in animal studies (Dishman & Jackson, 2000); in human studies they are often derived from plasma, urine, or salivary samples. It is important to realize that such measures often have a diurnal variation (i.e., daily peaks and valleys). For example, cortisol is known to peak before waking in the morning, with additional peaks occurring around midday and again during early evening (Lovallo & Thomas, 2000). Such conditions are important for research design.

Human Exercise–Stress Research

Although a great deal has been, and continues to be, learned from animal studies (see Dishman & Jackson, 2000), only exercise research involving humans will be discussed here. Numerous studies have examined self-reports of stress or perceived stress and whether exercise influences these perceptions. In general, people report feeling less stress following acute exercise bouts and feeling less stressed in general when they are physically active as opposed to being sedentary. Reliance on self-report can be problematic, however. Because of widespread media reports of the exercise–stress reduction link, individuals might report feeling less stress following exercise because they think that is what is supposed to happen (i.e., a placebo effect). This may be independent of whether they actually feel less stress. As stated previously, self-reports of stress also fail to provide information about any physiological and/or behavioral changes that may occur following either acute exercise or exercise training. What follows next is a presentation of research examining the influence of exercise on the stress response in a number of domains.

Cardiovascular Fitness

In 1987, Crews and Landers published their findings of a review of 34 studies examining the effects of aerobic fitness on the response to psychosocial stressors (again, refer to Exhibit 10.3 for examples). The studies included in the review had used a variety of measures of the stress response, including heart rate, systolic blood pressure, diastolic blood pressure, self-report, and catecholamines (NorE, E). The basic question was quite simple: Do individuals possessing greater levels of aerobic fitness have a reduced stress response compared to less fit individuals? This would provide some evidence either supporting or refuting the viability of the cross-stressor adaptation hypothesis. Based on the results of their review, Crews and Landers concluded that, regardless of how the stress response was measured, more fit individuals had a sizably smaller stress response than unfit individuals.

Although the work by Crews and Landers has been widely cited as evidence for positive fitness effects on stress, at least in terms of cardiovascular reactivity, two more recent reviews of the fitness-stress reactivity literature paint a less optimistic picture. For example, Forcier, Stroud, Papandonatos, and colleagues (2006) conducted a meta-analysis examining the effects of physical fitness on cardiovascular reactivity (HR, SBP, DBP) and recovery from psychosocial stressors. While their results favored a fitness effect, it was much less marked than that reported by Crews and Landers. Forcier and colleagues analysis essentially showed that physically fit individuals have a smaller HR and SBP reactivity response to such stressors and also have a faster HR recovery when such stressors are over. They estimated that fit individuals have about a 15 to 25 percent reduction in reactivity relative to unfit individuals, which could have important clinical implications. In contrast to both the Crews and Landers review and the Forcier et al. review, Jackson and Dishman (2006) concluded that the evidence does *not* support the hypothesis of reduced reactivity to stressors in more fit individuals. They did find evidence for a slightly faster recovery following stressor offset in more fit individuals, but noted that such an effect was rather small.

Given Crews and Landers' conclusion (1987), it would seem reasonable to assume that exercise training would have stress-buffering effects; as noted above, however, not all scientists are in agreement with that assessment. For example, in a review of exercise-training studies and the effects that training had on the stress response, Peronnet and Szabo (1993) stated, "Examination of these longitudinal studies suggests that there are no clearly identifiable changes in sympathetic response to psychosocial stress after physical exercise training as revealed by direct sympathetic indices, such as circulating catecholamines" (p. 206). Clearly, this is in marked contrast to the Crews and Landers conclusion. Consistent with Peronnet and Szabo, Buckworth and Dishman (2002) noted

FOCUS on Spinal Cord Injury

A spinal cord injury (SCI) causes structural damage to the spinal cord, resulting in the impairment or loss of motor and sensory function. *Tetraplegia* (also known as quadriplegia) is the condition associated with an injury at the cervical level of the spinal cord. *Paraplegia* reflects an injury at the thoracic, lumbar, or sacral level. Prior to World War II, most people lived for only a few days after a SCI. With medical advances, however, people with SCI can now expect to live almost as long as those without. In fact, in North America alone, approximately half a million people are living with such an injury (Spinal Cord Injury Information Network, 2009).

Given the catastrophic and life-altering nature of a spinal cord injury, it is not surprising that people with such an injury report high levels of stress. Their stress is partly a reflection of the day-to-day struggles associated with living with a SCI; it is also a consequence of the severe and chronic pain that plagues most people who have a SCI.

Researchers at McMaster University examined whether a nine-month exercise-training program could reduce stress in this population (Latimer, Martin Ginis, Hicks, & McCartney, 2004). Participants were 34 men and women with a SCI, randomly assigned to an exercise condition or a waiting list (control) condition. Twice a week, participants in the exercise condition engaged in supervised aerobic and resistance-training activities. The resistance exercises worked upper-body muscle groups, such as the shoulders, that are prone to overuse injuries and pain in people with SCI. Participants in the control group were instructed to continue with their normal activities and were invited to participate in the exercise program at the end of the nine-month study. Questionnaire measures of stress and pain were administered every three months to all participants throughout the study.

At the end of the study, the experimental group reported significantly less stress and pain than the control group. Furthermore, statistical analyses indicated that a decrease in pain during the first six months of the study led to a decrease in stress at the end of the study. The study authors suggested that training injury-prone muscle groups prevented the exacerbation of pain symptoms, which, in turn, reduced a major source of stress. The results of this study highlight the importance of designing exercise interventions for people with SCI that will reduce their pain. When the pain dissipates, so does the stress.

ADDITIONAL RESOURCES

Arbour-Nicitopoulos, K.P., Ginis, K.A., & Latimer, A.E. (2009). Planning, leisure-time physical activity, and coping self-efficacy in persons with spinal cord injury: A randomized controlled trial. *Archives of Physical Medicine & Rehabilitation, 90,* 2003–2011.

Latimer, A.E., & Martin Ginis, K.A. (2005). The theory of planned behavior in prediction of leisure time physical activity among individuals with spinal cord injury. *Rehabilitation Psychology, 50,* 389–396.

Scelza, W.M., Kalpakjian, C.Z., Zemper, E.D., & Tate, D.G. (2005). Perceived barriers to exercise in people with spinal cord injury. *American Journal of Physical Medicine and Rehabilitation, 84,* 576–583.

SCI Action Canada, www.sciactioncanada.ca

ACTIVITY

The study by Latimer et al. (2004) examined stress and pain in spinal cord–injured individuals before and after a nine-month exercise intervention. They reported using questionnaire measures of stress every three months during the study. Use the information in the chapter to complete the following:

1. What other avenues besides self-report could be used to gauge the stress response, and what measures of stress could be used to assess changes in

the stress response over time? Create a table such as the one below, and complete the cells with these alternate measures and what changes you would expect to see from the beginning to the end of the nine-month exercise intervention.

2. Would you expect similar or different responses if you were to use a different sample of participants? For example, would "normal," otherwise healthy college students be expected to have similar or different responses? Why or why not?

SYSTEM	MEASURE	EXPECTED CHANGE FROM EXERCISE INTERVENTION
Self-report	Questionnaire	Reduction in self-reported stress

that studies done so far do not support the notion that exercise training and/or high levels of cardiovascular fitness translate into a reduced response to psychosocial stressors, a position supported by the Jackson and Dishman (2006) meta-analysis. The Buckworth and Dishman viewpoint is based on the lack of evidence showing that training results in a reduced sympathetic response (i.e., plasma levels of NorE and E; sympathetic nerve activity) to psychosocial stress. They note that training does not usually change indices of sympathetic activity (e.g., levels of NorE, sympathetic nerve activity) at rest. It has been demonstrated that the sympathetic response is reduced after exercise training, but only at absolute intensities (i.e., all participants train at the same workload regardless of fitness level); when similar relative intensities are examined (i.e., exercise workload is adjusted based on fitness, age, gender, etc.) the sympathetic response is similar. In other words, "exercise training seems to increase the capacity of the sympathetic nerves to respond to maximal exercise, but does not change their responses to exercise of the same relative strain as before training" (Buckworth & Dishman, 2002, p. 83).

After examining longitudinal exercise-training studies, Perronet and Szabo (1993) concluded that the mechanisms responsible for the sympathetic aspect of the psychosocial stress response and the response to exercise stress are different. While this may ultimately be true, research suggests that aerobic fitness might confer stress-buffering effects to psychosocial stressors. For example, Boutcher has conducted a number of studies, both cross-sectional and longitudinal, providing evidence that cardiovascular fitness may indeed protect against the potentially damaging stress response and allostatic load. In one cross-sectional comparison, Boutcher, Nugent, McLaren, and Weltman (1998) found a low-

absolute reactivity ■ relative reactivity ■

er absolute HR response to mental arithmetic and Stroop tasks in aerobically trained individuals. They distinguished between **absolute reactivity,** the absolute value of HR during stress in this case, and **relative reactivity,** a change in HR during stress from a baseline value. As Boutcher and colleagues note, the lower absolute HR of aerobically trained individuals during stress could be due, at least in part, to a lower resting HR. It has been argued that this lower resting HR is why such individuals appear to have a smaller reaction to stress (Buckworth & Dishman, 2002), but in reality their reaction is similar in magnitude to the less fit person. Boutcher (2004) argues instead that the lower resting HR and absolute HR during stress could actually be a cardio-protective effect brought about by the exercise training. More specifically, he suggests that the lower heart rate effectively results in the individual spending more total time in a more "stable" state during the blood pressure cycle (i.e., during diastole, that portion of the cycle when there is less change in the rate of blood flow and when blood flow itself is primarily unidirectional).

Boutcher (2004) also discusses the possibility that a reduced absolute HR response is due to greater dominance of the parasympathetic system at rest coupled with a smaller sympathetic response while encountering a stressor. By measuring heart rate variability, which provides an indirect assessment of the level of parasympathetic influence on the heart, it has been shown that the HR response to a stressor is more a function of parasympathetic withdrawal and less a function of increased sympathetic activity in trained individuals (Boutcher et al., 1998; Franks & Boutcher, 2003). The parasympathetic withdrawal effect is potentially important from the standpoint of catecholamine sparing. In other words, if the elevated HR response is due to more of a withdrawal of parasympathetic influence than to an increase in sympathetic activity, fewer catecholamines will be released in response to the stressor (see Exhibit 10.1), which can theoretically lead to a reduced allostatic load and, ultimately, reduced likelihood of disease and disability.

In another example, a study by Spalding, Lyon, Steel, and Hatfield (2004) examined the cardiovascular responses to psychosocial stressors that occurred before and after six weeks of either aerobic training (30–45 minutes per session [which included a 10 minute warm-up and a 5 minute cool-down], three to five times per week), weight training (40–45 minutes per session [including a 10–15 minute warm-up], three to five sessions per week), and a no-training control treatment (no regular or new exercise participation, maintenance of customary level of activity). The male and female participants were assessed for baseline values, randomly assigned to one of the three treatment groups for six weeks, and then assessed again. Heart rate, systolic BP, and diastolic BP (along with the resultant rate pressure product [RPP; HR × systolic BP], an indirect measure of workload placed on the heart and of myocardial oxygen consumption) were measured before, during, and following the stressor. The psychosocial stress protocol involved a six-minute mental arithmetic task with progressively greater levels of auditory distraction. Results revealed a reduction in cardiovascular activity in response to aerobic training during stress, as well as at rest and during recovery from stress. In particular, the RPP was markedly lower during stress and recovery from stress in the group trained aerobically, especially compared to the no-treatment control group. HR and systolic BP were also lowered significantly in the aerobically trained group compared to the weight-trained and no-treatment groups. Thus, Spalding and colleagues (2004) concluded that the aerobic training employed in their study, which did yield a significant improvement in aerobic fitness, also conferred a stress-buffering effect during stress exposure and during recovery from stress.

A final example highlights the more real-world nature of the fitness–stress relationship. A study conducted by King, Baumann, O'Sullivan, and colleagues (2002) examined the effect of a year-long exercise intervention (compared to a year-long nutrition education program) on cardiovascular stress reactivity in initially sedentary women who were caring for a relative with dementia. Participants' heart rate and blood pressure reactivity were assessed at the beginning and end of the intervention in response to a 6-minute period during which participants were asked to discuss those "aspects of her caregiving experience that she found to be most frustrating or disturbing" (p. M29). Results showed that the participants in the exercise intervention had significantly smaller blood pressure reactivity, both systolic and diastolic (4–9 mmHg smaller, about twice that reported in the Forcier et al. [2006] meta-analysis), following the intervention than did their nutrition education counterparts; this reflected an improvement in the relationship between chronic stress and cardiovascular pathology. As noted above, this study is a very practical application of the exercise–stress paradigm in a real-world setting.

HPA Axis Response

While most exercise–stress research has tended to focus on cardiovascular and catecholamine reactivity, some research has examined the hypothalamic-pituitary-adrenal cortical (HPA) axis response to psychosocial stressors. Traustadottir, Bosch, and Matt (2005) examined whether adaptations known to occur within the HPA axis in response to physical stress (e.g., blunted cortisol response to exercise performed at the same absolute intensity, greater maximal capacity of the adrenal glands) also occur in response to psychosocial stress (i.e., cross-stressor adaptation). They were also interested in whether aerobic fitness influenced that response. To examine these questions, Traustadottir and colleagues had 10 young (19–36 years old) and 26 older (59–81 years old) women perform a battery of psychosocial stressors. All of the younger women were classified as unfit; roughly half of the older women were also classified as unfit, while the other half were classified as fit. The battery of tests, referred to as the Matt Stress Reactivity Protocol (MSRP), consisted of the Stroop Color and Word Test, mental arithmetic, an anagram task (a series of letters needing to be unscrambled to form words; time urgency usually stressed), a cold pressor task (subjects placed their hands in buckets of ice water for as long as they could, up to three minutes), and an interpersonal interview, in that order. The entire MSRP lasted approximately 30 minutes. Heart rate, blood pressure, and plasma cortisol were assessed 45 minutes prior to beginning the protocol, at the conclusion of each of the tasks, and during recovery from the protocol.

Whereas the MSRP resulted in significant elevations in cardiovascular and endocrine responses, the endocrine responses, specifically the cortisol response, were modified by fitness. The older fit women had significantly lower cortisol responses to the stressors than their older unfit counterparts. This difference in response to stress occurred in spite of there being no significant differences at baseline between the groups. It is worth noting that even during the recovery time period, cortisol responses were still elevated above baseline values for the older unfit group. Although the cortisol effects were pronounced, no differences existed for adrenocorticotropin releasing hormone response, nor for any of the cardiovascular measures, between the fit and unfit. Thus, aerobic fitness did blunt the stress response in these older women. Traustadottir and colleagues (2005) interpreted this as evidence that aerobic fitness can influence sensitivity to stress, ultimately affecting the HPA axis in the direction of a reduced cortisol response to psychosocial stress.

The conclusion reached by Traustadottir and colleagues has been confirmed in at least two studies since then. An initial study by Rimmele, Zellweger, Marti, and colleagues (2007) compared responses of highly trained (i.e., elite sportsmen) to those of otherwise healthy but sedentary men in a 10-minute psychosocial stressor challenge. The Trier Social Stress Test (TSST) consists of a five-minute public speaking task (in this case, participants had to engage in a mock job interview), followed by a five-minute mental arithmetic task involving serial subtraction. Oral responses are given during the serial subtraction task, and both tasks are performed in front of two evaluators (unfamiliar to the participants). Previous research had shown the TSST to alter both HPA axis and cardiovascular responses significantly. Rimmele et al. (2007) found the elite sportsmen had significantly smaller reactivity (i.e., smaller increase) in both HR and salivary cortisol compared to their sedentary counterparts. It could be argued that one reason for the different response is simply due to the fact that elite sportsmen are exposed to socially threatening situations more often through competition and thus have different responses because of this.

A follow-up study (Rimmele, Seiler, Marti, et al., 2009) replicated and extended the findings from the earlier study. Similar groups were tested (elite sportsmen vs. sedentary men), but a third, intermediate group consisting of amateur sportsmen was added. Thus, these participants would likely have the same exposure to the socially threatening situations, but they do not train at the same level as the elite sportsmen. The participants were again subjected to the TSST, and the results were similar for the elite sportsmen compared to the sedentary group—that is, reduced HR and cortisol reactivity during the stressor task. The amateur sportsmen had a cortisol response that was similar to the sedentary group, but they had a HR response that was similar to the elite group. Thus, the overall findings from both studies were consistent with the Traustadottir et al. work (2005), namely that physical activity seems to have a blunting effect on the HPA axis. Furthermore, it appears that physical activity has faster effects on the sympathetic nervous system as both groups of sportsmen showed a smaller increase in HR response to the stressor.

Immunity

The stress response can also have a potent impact on immune function. As Fleshner pointed out (2005), exposure to a stressor is immunomodulatory; it has the ability to change one or more of the immune functions. The immune system can be negatively impacted (i.e., immunosuppressive) or positively impacted (i.e., immunopotentiated). In groundbreaking work, LaPerriere and colleagues (1990) examined the impact of exercise training as a way of buffering stressors. In a group of asymptomatic men at risk for AIDS, LaPerriere and coworkers showed that those who exercised for five weeks prior to receiving notification of their HIV-1 status had little change in psychological and immunological measures when they were notified of testing positive for HIV-1. A control group of men who did not exercise showed significant immunologic changes indicative of reduced immunocompetence (i.e., decreased natural killer cell activity) along with significant increases in anxiety and depression following positive HIV-1 notification. Thus, the exercise training was, at least in part, instrumental in attenuating the stressful influence of a real-life stressor—discovering that one has the virus that causes AIDS—both psychologically as well as immunologically.

Reactivity versus Recovery

A key issue, which historically has been overlooked in the exercise research but is now recognized as important (Forcier et al., 2006; Jackson & Dishman, 2006), is the examination of reactivity to a stressor as opposed to the recovery from the stressor once it is over. For example, in an interesting review, Gal and Lazarus (1975) noted that emotional arousal in response to a stressful event might be reflected not in the *magnitude* of the hormonal response but rather in the *duration* of that response. Citing data from a study of combat soldiers, they noted that, while an "attacking" company had a more marked rise in corticosteroids (i.e., cortisol) in response to combat than a "defending" company, the defending company took twice as long to recover as the attacking company from the combat (13 days versus 6 days). This finding fits nicely with their thesis that participating in physical/motor activity of some sort, as opposed to being passive, helps to cope with a stressor. It is also worth noting that recovery from a stressor might be as important as the actual reactivity to it.

Sinyor, Schwartz, Peronnet, and colleagues (1983) performed one of the earliest controlled laboratory studies to examine the effects of exercise training on the stress response during reactivity to the stressor as well as during recovery from the stressor. They examined reactivity in 15 trained and 15 untrained men, using cardiovascular (HR), biochemical (E, NorE, cortisol), and subjective (arousal, anxiety) indices of the stress response to a 17-minute stressor (mental arithmetic with white noise as a distracter, a 23-item quiz, and the Stroop Color and Word Test). They found that the trained individuals had a significantly lower HR response immediately following the stressor and for the first 10 minutes into recovery, along with lower self-reported stress, compared to the untrained group. They also showed that the trained group had a more rapid peak in the NorE response during the stressor, followed by a decline to baseline values. Sinyor et al. concluded that the trained individuals had a faster recovery from the stressor, in essence dealing with it and then getting over it.

Recall the findings from two of the studies already mentioned. Spalding and colleagues (2004) showed lower HR and RPP levels during recovery from a psychosocial stressor in a group of aerobically trained individuals compared to weight-trained or non-trained individuals. Likewise, Traustadottir and colleagues (2005) found elevated cortisol levels in older unfit women during recovery from a stress battery compared to a group of older fit women. Thus, while the evidence for a stress-buffering effect of exercise may not be particularly compelling at present, evidence suggests that fitness or exercise training may provide a more rapid recovery from the stressor once it is no longer present. This shorter duration stress response could have the effect of reducing the allostatic load and overall wear and tear on the body. This is clearly an area that requires more research attention.

Mechanism to Explain Exercise Effect: Physiological Toughness Model

Clearly, exercise–stress research has much to uncover regarding how exercise might help to ameliorate the stress response, reducing the allostatic load and, ultimately, disease risk. A potentially useful model for explaining not only the reaction to stressors but also the recovery from stressors has been available for some time. Even though it has not received the kind of attention it perhaps deserves, it is worth describing the model because it perhaps clearly fits within the stress paradigm and, more important, because of the role it suggests for exercise in dealing with stress.

The "physiological toughness" model (Dienstbier, 1989, 1991) offers a psychophysiological framework for explaining how exercise not only reduces the immediate effects of stress but also enhances the recovery from stressors. In essence, the model postulates that intermittent yet regular exposure to stressors can lead, through specific patterns of neuroendocrine change, to psychological coping and emotional stability (e.g., reduced stress and anxiety). The basic premise is that regular (though not constant) experiences with stressors (e.g., regular exercise) results in a variety of physiological changes, including the following:

- increased catecholamine capacity in the central nervous system
- reduced levels of resting catecholamines in the periphery
- greater catecholamine capacity and responsiveness along with fairly rapid dissipation of these catecholamines after cessation of a stressor
- delayed or reduced basal HPA axis response (i.e., less cortisol)

Dienstbier (1989, 1991) further proposed that these physiological changes lead to adaptive performance in challenge/threat situations, emotional stability, enhancement of immune system function, and greater stress tolerance. When confronted with a challenge or a threat, the sympathetic nervous system response, in conjunction with the adrenal medulla, is fast and strong. For example, the release of E or NorE in response to a challenge would be rapid, with a large outpouring of these catecholamines (along with cortisol suppression) occurring fairly quickly after the onset of the stressor (refer back to Exhibit 10.1). Importantly, this arousal response quickly returns to baseline when the stressor is removed. Catecholamines dissipate fairly quickly from the system once they are released. An HPA-axis arousal response, with its concomitant adrenal cortical outpouring of cortisol (Exhibit 10.1), is considered a less adaptive response in Dienstbier's model. This response is much more indicative of the "untough" individual. Whereas catecholamines act quickly, cortisol takes much longer to reach its peak and stays in the system much longer. In other words, the untough response is similar to continuing to react to the stressor even after the stressor itself has stopped. Recall that Jackson and Dishman (2006) found a slightly faster recovery for more fit (i.e., tough) individuals, a finding that would support the physiological toughness model.

The compelling feature of Dienstbier's model is the psychophysiological nature of it. The model has specific predictions for the interaction of appraisals and the physiological responses that ensue. The model predicts that if an individual appraises a stressor as a *challenge,* this would lead to a more pronounced catecholamine response (rather than a cortisol response) and corresponding feelings of energy. Such appraisals would be derived from a sense of control and expected success. Appraising a stressor as a *threat,* on the other hand, would lead to a more pronounced cortisol response and its concomitant feelings of tension.

As Dienstbier (1989, 1991) notes, however, this interaction goes both ways. The perception of the arousal experienced in response to a stressor impacts on the appraisal process. The two different responses thus become self-sustaining. That is, when the "physiologically tough" individual has a more adaptive (i.e., catecholamine) response to stress, he or she has a more positive perception (i.e., more energy, confidence), which increases the likelihood of positive appraisals of similar stressors in the future. The opposite is also true: the "untough" individual has a less adaptive (i.e., cortisol) response to a stressor with a concomitant negative perception (i.e., tension, anxiety), which increases the likelihood of negative appraisals of similar stressors in the future. This model, while certainly attractive, has not received the kind of attention it probably deserves as a way of better understanding the stress response in the exercise paradigm.

Practical Recommendations

For those who use exercise as a way of dealing with the daily stressors of life, it is probably a good idea to arrange to exercise when it will be most helpful. Thus, a morning workout might help some people to get ready to take on the day's challenges, a noontime workout might provide a much needed break in the day to recharge the batteries, or some might find a workout later in the day a useful method for "purging" the tensions and worries of the day. This is obviously something that will need to be determined by each person on an individual basis.

Conclusion

Given the current level of understanding, it seems likely that exercise can be useful in reducing the stress response. Whether this is in terms of reduced reactivity to the stressor itself or in terms of faster recovery from the stressor remains unclear. A great deal of careful work is necessary to elucidate both aspects of the stress response and the potential buffering effects that exercise might have. Regardless of what is eventually found, it is clear that exercise can be beneficial, leading to a reduced allostatic load and, ultimately, to reduced risk of disease and disability.

what do you know?

1. Define stress.
2. What is the difference between eustress and distress?
3. How is homeostasis distinguished from allostasis?
4. What role do appraisals play in the stress response?
5. How is the concept of allostatic load important in the context of stress? What implications does allostatic load have for health?
6. What is the main prediction of the cross-stressor adaptation hypothesis?
7. How is absolute reactivity different from relative reactivity when examining the stress response?

8. What is the difference between an active stressor and a passive stressor?
9. Can exercise training provide any useful benefits in the recovery from stressors? If so, in what ways?
10. What is the expected pattern of the stress response in someone who is considered "physiologically tough"? Describe this pattern in terms of both the appraisal and neuroendocrine aspects.

learning activity

Over the course of a month, track how much exercise or physical activity you engage in (frequency, intensity, duration, mode). Also track the kinds of stressors you encounter, in terms of how much stress they cause for you, whether you can do anything about the stressor, and how long the stressor lasts. Finally, assess how much stress you perceive for yourself. This can be done on a daily basis or at the end of the month-long observation period. Is there any relationship between your level of activity and your perceived stress?

references

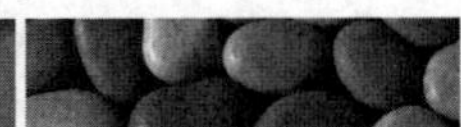

Boutcher, S.H. (2004). The psychophysiology of sport and physical activity. In T. Morris & G. Summers (Eds.), *Sport psychology: Theories, applications, & issues* (pp. 513–525). Brisbane, Australia: John Wiley.

Boutcher, S.H., Nugent, F.W., McLaren, P.F., & Weltman, A.L. (1998). Heart period variability of trained and untrained men at rest and during mental challenge. *Psychophysiology, 35,* 16–22.

Buckworth, J., & Dishman, R.K. (2002). Stress. In J. Buckworth & R.K. Dishman, *Exercise psychology* (pp. 75–89). Champaign, IL: Human Kinetics.

Cacioppo, J.T., Tassinary, L.G., & Berntson, G.G. (2000). Psychophysiological science. In J.T. Cacioppo, L.G. Tassinary, & G.G. Berntson (Eds.), *Handbook of psychophysiology,* 2nd ed. (pp. 3–23). New York: Cambridge University Press.

Cannon, W. (1939). *The wisdom of the body* (Rev. ed.). New York: Norton.

Chrousos, G.P., & Gold, P.W. (1992). The concepts of stress and stress system disorders: Overview of physical and behavioral homeostasis. *Journal of the American Medical Association, 267*(9), 1244–1252.

Cohen, S., Kamarck, T., & Mermelstein, R. (1983). A global measure of perceived stress. *Journal of Health and Social Behavior, 24,* 385–396.

Crews, D.J., & Landers, D.M. (1987). A meta-analytic review of aerobic fitness and reactivity to psychosocial stressors. *Medicine & Science in Sports and Exercise, 19,* 114–120.

Dienstbier, R.A. (1989). Arousal and physiological toughness: Implications for mental and physical health. *Psychological Bulletin, 96,* 84–100.

Dienstbier, R.A. (1991). Behavioral correlates of sympathoadrenal reactivity: The toughness model. *Medicine & Science in Sports & Exercise, 23,* 846–852.

Dishman, R.K., & Jackson, E.M. (2000). Exercise, fitness, and stress. *International Journal of Sport Psychology, 31,* 175–203.

Fleshner, M. (2005). Physical activity and stress resistance: Sympathetic nervous system adaptations prevent stress-induced immunosuppression. *Exercise & Sport Sciences Reviews, 33,* 120–126.

Folkman, S., & Lazarus, R.S. (1985). If it changes it must be a process: Study of emotion and coping during three stages of a college examination. *Journal of Personality & Social Psychology, 48,* 150–170.

Forcier, K., Stroud, L.R., Papandonatos, G.D., Hitsman, B., Reiches, M., Krishnamoorthy, J., & Niaura, R. (2006). Links between physical fitness and cardiovascular reactivity and recovery to psychological stressors: A meta-analysis. *Health Psychology, 25(6)*, 723–739.

Frankenhaeuser, M. (1991). The psychophysiology of workload, stress, and health: Comparison between the sexes. *Annals of Behavioral Medicine, 13*, 197–204.

Franks, P.W., & Boutcher, S.H. (2003). Cardiovascular response of trained preadolescent boys to mental challenge. *Medicine & Science in Sports & Exercise, 35*, 1429–1435.

Gal, R., & Lazarus, R.S. (1975). The role of activity in anticipating and confronting stressful situations. *Journal of Human Stress, 1*, 4–20.

Jackson, E.M., & Dishman, R.K. (2006). Cardiorespiratory fitness and laboratory stress: A meta-regression analysis. *Psychophysiology, 43*, 57–72.

King, A.C., Baumann, K., O'Sullivan, P., Wilcox, S., & Castro, C. (2002). Effects of moderate-intensity exercise on physiological, behavioral, and emotional responses to family caregiving: A randomized controlled trial. *Journals of Gerontology A: Biological Sciences & Medical Sciences, 57*, M26–M36.

LaPerriere, A.R., Antoni, M.H., Schneiderman, N., Ironson, G., Klimas, N., Caralis, P., & Fletcher, M.A. (1990). Exercise intervention attenuates emotional distress and natural killer cell decrements following notification of positive serologic status for HIV-1. *Biofeedback & Self-Regulation, 15*, 229–242.

Latimer, A.E., Martin Ginis, K.A., Hicks, A.L., & McCartney, N. (2004). An examination of the mechanisms of exercise-induced change in psychological well-being among people with spinal cord injury. *Journal of Rehabilitation Research & Development, 41*, 643–652.

Lazarus, R.S. (1966). *Psychological stress and coping.* New York: McGraw-Hill.

Lazarus, R.S. (1968). Emotions and adaptation: Conceptual and empirical relations. In W.J. Arnold (Ed.), *Nebraska symposium on motivation* (Vol. 16, pp. 175–266). Lincoln: University of Nebraska Press.

Lovallo, W.R., & Thomas, T.L. (2000). Stress hormones in psychophysiological research: Emotional, behavioral, and cognitive implications. In J.T. Cacioppo, L.G. Tassinary, & G.G. Berntson (Eds.), *Handbook of psychophysiology*, 2nd ed. (pp. 342–367). New York: Cambridge University Press.

Mason, J.W. (1975). Emotion as reflected in patterns of endocrine integration. In L. Levi (Ed.), *Emotions: Their parameters and measurement* (pp. 143–181). New York: Raven Press.

McEwen, B.S. (1998). Stress, adaptation, and disease: Allostasis and allostatic load. *Annals of the New York Academy of Sciences, 840*, 33–44.

McEwen, B.S., & Wingfield, J.C. (2003). The concept of allostasis in biology and biomedicine. *Hormones & Behavior, 43*, 2–15.

Morgan, C.A., Wang, S., Rasmusson, A., Hazlett, G., Anderson, G., & Charney, D.S. (2001). Relationship among plasma cortisol, catecholamines, neuropeptide Y, and human performance during exposure to uncontrollable stress. *Psychosomatic Medicine, 63*, 412–422.

Peronnet, F., & Szabo, A. (1993). Sympathetic response to acute psychosocial stressors in humans: Linkage to physical exercise and training. In P. Seraganian (Ed.), *Exercise psychology: The influence of physical exercise on psychological processes* (pp. 172–217). New York: Wiley.

Rimmele, U., Seiler, R., Marti, B., Wirtz, P.H., Ehlert, U., & Heinrichs, M. (2009). The level of physical activity affects adrenal and cardiovascular reactivity to psychosocial stress. *Psychoneuroendocrinology, 34*, 190–198.

Rimmele, U., Zellweger, B.C., Marti, B., Seiler, R., Mohiyeddini, C., Ehlert, U., & Heinrichs, M. (2007). Trained men show lower cortisol, heart rate and psychological responses to psychosocial stress compared with untrained men. *Psychoneuroendocrinology, 32*, 627–635.

Sapolsky, R. (2003). Taming stress. *Scientific American, 289*(3), 88–95.

Selye, H. (1936). A syndrome produced by diverse noxious agents. *Nature, 138*, 32.

Sinyor, D., Schwartz, S.G., Peronnet, F., Brisson, G., & Seraganian, P. (1983). Aerobic fitness level and reactivity to psychosocial stress: Physiological, biochemical, and subjective measures. *Psychosomatic Medicine, 45*, 205–217.

Sothmann, M.S., Buckworth, J., Claytor, R.P., Cox, R.H., White-Welkley, J.E., & Dishman, R.K. (1996). Exercise training and the cross-stressor adaptation hypothesis. *Exercise & Sport Sciences Reviews, 24*, 267–287.

Spalding, T.W., Lyon, L.A., Steel, D.H., & Hatfield, B.D. (2004). Aerobic exercise training and cardiovascular reactivity to psychological stress in sedentary young normotensive men and women. *Psychophysiology, 41*, 552–562.

Spinal Cord Injury Information Network. (2009). Facts and Figures at a Glance, 2009. Accessed March 25, 2010, www.nscisc.uab.edu/public_content/facts_figures_2009.aspx.

Stern, R.M., Ray, W.J., & Quigley, K.S. (2001). *Psychophysiological recording, 2nd ed.* New York: Oxford University Press.

Taylor, S.E., Klein, L.C., Lewis, B.P., Gruenewald, T.L., Gurung, R.A., & Updegraff, J.A. (2000). Biobehavioral responses to stress in females: Tend-and-befriend, not fight-or-flight. *Psychological Review, 107(3),* 411–429.

Traustadottir, T., Bosch, P.R., & Matt, K.S. (2005). The HPA axis response to stress in women: Effects of aging and fitness. *Psychoneuroendocrinology, 30,* 392–402.

van Doornen, L.J.P., de Geus, E.J.C., & Orlebeke, J.F. (1988). Aerobic fitness and the physiological stress response: A critical evaluation. *Social Science & Medicine, 3,* 303–307.

11

Anxiety and Exercise

KEY TERMS

anxiety disorders
anxiety sensitivity
anxiolytic
clinical anxiety
distraction/time-out hypothesis
double blind
exercise sensitivity
generalized anxiety disorder
mental disorders
mental health
mental health problems
mental illness
obsessive–compulsive disorder
panic disorder
phobias
post-traumatic stress disorder
state anxiety
thermogenic hypothesis
trait anxiety

Amanda is in the middle of her second semester of her freshman year at college. Unlike Jim, a fellow student in her anatomy and physiology class who is experiencing stress as a result of the challenging lectures, Amanda is having significantly greater problems. She has begun experiencing a variety of symptoms including difficulty sleeping, persistent feelings of tension, difficulty concentrating, and occasional but increasing feelings of panic in ordinary situations. Being in a university setting, she visits the student health center and sees a physician who collaborates with an exercise psychology professor in various research projects. Because of this connection, rather than immediately prescribing a tranquilizer type of medication, her physician has Amanda undergo some different tests, including measuring her resting muscle activity, and asking her to complete a questionnaire that assesses her general feelings of anxiety and nervousness. The results of these tests reveal that Amanda has unusually high levels of muscle tension and anxiety. As a result, her physician prescribes an exercise program for her. This includes brisk walking between classes as well as using the university's fitness center. At the fitness center she is to engage in aerobic exercise, choosing an activity that she thinks she would enjoy. Amanda finds that walking on a treadmill at the same brisk pace she uses while walking on campus seems to work best for her. She follows this routine for 30 minutes every other day for the next six weeks. Upon her return visit to her physician, the same tests (muscle tension, anxiety) reveal that her resting level of muscle activity as well as her feelings of nervousness and anxiety have been reduced significantly. Her sleeping problems have abated, as have her panic episodes. Amanda also finds she is able to concentrate much better during her classes and while studying.

Exercise has the effect of defusing anger and rage, fear and anxiety. Like music, it soothes the savage in us that lies so close to the surface. It is the ultimate tranquilizer.

—GEORGE SHEEHAN, *HOW TO FEEL GREAT 24 HOURS A DAY*

Mental Health Versus Mental Illness

mental health ■ mental illness ■ mental disorders ■

Mental health is defined in the Surgeon General's Report on Mental Health as "a state of successful performance of mental function, resulting in productive activities, fulfilling relationships with other people, and the ability to adapt to change and to cope with adversity" (USDHHS, 1999, p. 4). **Mental illness,** on the other hand, is the term used to refer collectively to all diagnosable mental disorders (p. 5). **Mental disorders** "are health conditions that are characterized by alterations in thinking, mood, or behavior (or some combination thereof) associated with distress and/or impaired functioning" (USDHHS, 1999, p. 4).

mental health problems ■

Mental illnesses are distinguished from "mental health problems" based on the criterion that **mental health problems** refer to signs and symptoms of insufficient intensity or duration to meet the criteria for any mental disorders, but are sufficient to warrant active efforts in health promotion, prevention, and treatment. In other words, a person with mental health problems may display some signs or symptoms of a mental illness, for example, anxiety or depression, but would not be considered sufficiently ill to receive a diagnosis of a particular mental disorder. Perhaps it would be helpful to conceptualize the relationship as a continuum, with mental health at one end and mental illness on the other (see Exhibit 11.1). In such a conceptualization, mental health problems would occur somewhere between the two endpoints, but nearer the mental illness pole (Leith, 1994).

exhibit 11.1 **Continuum showing relationship of mental health problems to a mental illness–mental health continuum.**

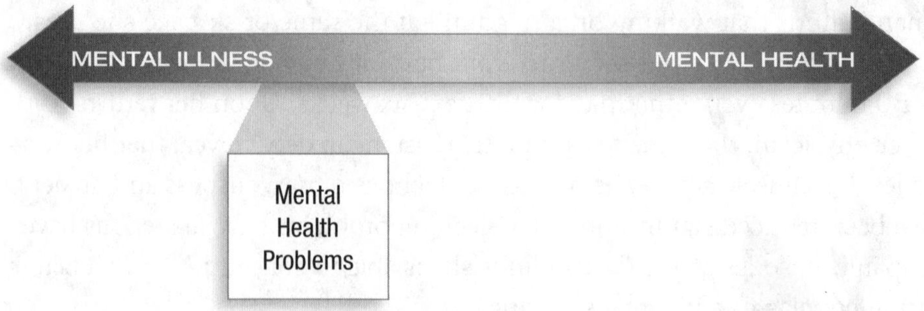

MENTAL ILLNESS ⟷ MENTAL HEALTH

Mental Health Problems

Defining Anxiety

As noted in Chapter 10, stress can lead to mental health problems, including anxiety. Chronic stress can come from many things, including lack of sleep, juggling busy schedules, poor dietary habits, deadlines, work pressures, and dealing with rush hour traffic, to name but a few. The individual who, because of such chronic stress, begins to feel that he or she must always be "on guard" is experiencing anxiety. This is a feeling that goes beyond normal feelings of fear. In fact, the Surgeon General's Report on Mental Health refers to anxiety as the "pathological counterpart of normal fear, manifest by disturbances of mood, as well as of thinking, behavior, and physiological activity" (USDHHS, 1999, p. 233). The anxiety becomes **clinical anxiety** when it results in behavioral and cognitive changes, when it occurs even without some eliciting event, and when the response is disproportionate and unmanageable (American Psychiatric Association, 2000, p. 299A–C). Because of ever-increasing stressors in our lives, anxiety and anxiety disorders (along with mood disorders; see Chapter 12) have become increasingly prevalent problems in our society. The traditional view has held that a stimulus perceived as a threat results in an acute stress response. As discussed in Chapter 10, this response is often characterized by increased arousal (through a complex set of interactions between the brain and the sympathetic nervous system, along with the secretion of hormones from the adrenal glands, namely epinephrine and cortisol), but this is not exactly the same as anxiety. In several ways, even though stress and anxiety are often viewed as synonymous, anxiety is more than increased arousal in that:

■ clinical anxiety

1. the perception and concern over the threat are disproportionate to the actual threat,
2. cognitive and behavioral actions are undertaken to avoid the symptoms of an anxiety attack,
3. the anxiety is usually experienced far longer than the arousal lasts,
4. the anxiety can occur in the absence of an actual threat; that is, even a perceived threat can result in anxiety (USDHHS, 1999).

Thus, Amanda, who experiences panic attacks in ordinary situations, is experiencing *anxiety;* Jim, whose response to his anatomy and physiology class is less severe, is experiencing *stress.*

As noted in the Surgeon General's Report, the anxiety disorders (i.e., clinical anxiety) are the most prevalent of the mental disorders (Regier, Farmer, Rae, et al., 1990). **Anxiety disorders** include **panic disorder, phobias** (social phobia, agoraphobia), **generalized anxiety disorder, obsessive–compulsive disorder,** and **post-traumatic stress disorder.** They, like depression, contribute significantly to the disease and disability burden of the nation. Indeed, anxiety disorders can often lead to or become depression if not treated successfully, and the two often co-occur (i.e., comorbidity can be as much as 40 percent). See Exhibit 11.2 for a description of some of these disorders.

■ anxiety disorders
■ panic disorder
■ phobias
■ generalized anxiety disorder
■ obsessive–compulsive disorder
■ post-traumatic stress disorder

exhibit 11.2 Characteristics of main anxiety disorders (clinical anxiety).

PANIC DISORDER

- Intense fear and discomfort associated with physical and mental symptoms, including:
  - Sweating, trembling, shortness of breath, chest pain, nausea
  - Fear of dying or loss of control of emotions
- Induces urge to escape or run away, and often results in seeking emergency help (e.g., hospital)
- Frequently accompanied by major depressive disorder
- Twice as common in women as in men

AGORAPHOBIA

- Severe, pervasive anxiety when in situations perceived to be difficult to escape from, or complete avoidance of certain situations (e.g., crowded areas, alone outside of home, travel in bus or plane)
- Often seen after onset of panic disorder
- Twice as common in women as in men

SOCIAL PHOBIA (SOCIAL ANXIETY DISORDER)

- Marked, persistent anxiety in social situations (e.g., public speaking)
  - Possibility of embarrassment or ridicule is crucial factor
  - Individual is preoccupied with concern that others will notice the anxiety symptoms (e.g., trembling, sweating, halting/rapid speech)
- Accompanied by anticipatory anxiety days or weeks prior to feared event
- More common in women than in men

OBSESSIVE–COMPULSIVE DISORDER

- Obsessions, such as recurrent thoughts or images that are perceived as inappropriate or forbidden, elicit anxiety
- Individual perceives loss of control, thus acts on impulses or thoughts
- Compulsions, including behaviors or thoughts, reduce anxiety associated with obsessions
  - Include overt behavior (e.g., hand washing) and mental acts (e.g., counting, praying)
  - Take long periods of time to complete
- Disorder has fluctuating course, including periods of increased symptoms, usually linked with life stressors
- Equally common in women and men

GENERALIZED ANXIETY DISORDER

- Defined by worry lasting more than six months, along with multiple symptoms (e.g., muscle tension, poor concentration, insomnia, irritability)

Characteristics of main anxiety disorders (clinical anxiety), continued. **exhibit 11.2**

- Anxiety and worry not attributable to other conditions (e.g., panic disorder, phobias)
- Disorder has fluctuating course, including periods of increased symptoms, usually linked with life stressors
- Twice as common in women as in men

POST-TRAUMATIC STRESS DISORDER

- Anxiety and behavioral disturbances following exposure to extreme trauma (e.g., combat, physical assault), which persist for more than one month
- Dissociation—symptom involving perceived detachment from emotional state or body—is critical feature
- Symptoms also include generalized anxiety, hyperarousal, avoidance of situations that trigger memories of trauma, recurrent thoughts
- Occurs in about 9 percent of those exposed to extreme trauma

Source: American Psychiatric Association (2000); USDHHS (1999), pp. 234–237.

Prevalence

Two nationwide probability surveys highlight the prevalence of such disabling mental conditions. In 1994, the National Comorbidity Survey's 23.4 percent one-year prevalence rate for any mental disorder (Kessler, McGonagle, Zhao, et al., 1994) included an 18.7 percent one-year prevalence rate for any anxiety disorder, which means that within a given year, 18.7 percent of the U.S. adult population will have a diagnosable anxiety disorder. The more recent National Comorbidity Survey Replication study indicated an 18.1 percent one-year prevalence rate for any anxiety disorder (Kessler, Chiu, Demler, & Walters, 2005). Of those individuals diagnosed with an anxiety disorder, roughly 22.8 percent were categorized as serious (in terms of severity), 33.7 percent were moderate, and 43.5 percent were classified as mild. Another survey, the Epidemiological Catchment Area Study (Regier, Narrow, Rae, et al., 1993) estimated a 19.5 percent one-year prevalence rate for any mental disorder, including 13.1 percent for any anxiety disorder. From these studies, best estimates of the one-year prevalence rates have been calculated to be 16.4 percent for any anxiety disorder (USDHHS, 1999). Although Kessler et al. (2005) caution against making interpretations regarding trends over time, anxiety disorders continue to be the most prevalent of the mental disorders.

As is the case for depression (see Chapter 12), the prevalence of these disabling mental conditions creates an economic burden both in terms of treatment and in lost productivity. Beyond the immeasurable human suffering, it has been estimated that annual costs associated with anxiety disorders are likely

FOCUS on Chronic Obstructive Pulmonary Disease

Chronic obstructive pulmonary disease (COPD) is the fourth-leading cause of death among adults in the United States. The term COPD refers to a number of lung conditions characterized by airflow limitation and shortness of breath (or "dyspnea"). In people aged 65 years or older, approximately 34 out of every 1,000 have the disease (National Center for Health Statistics, 1982–1995).

Rates of anxiety disorders, particularly generalized anxiety disorder (GAD) and panic disorder, are much higher in patients with COPD than in the general population. Compared to the general population, the prevalence of GAD is at least three times greater among patients with COPD. Likewise, the prevalence rates for panic disorder are more than five times greater in these patients than in the general population. As high anxiety can have a negative impact on the physical and psychological well-being of people with COPD, interventions to reduce anxiety in this population need to be developed (Brenes, 2003).

Exercise appears to be a promising intervention strategy. Emery (1994) conducted a 30-day rehabilitation program for 64 people with COPD. The program included aerobic exercise, strength training, education about the disease, psychosocial counseling, and stress management. Sessions were held five days a week for four hours each. At the end of the study, patients reported significant reductions in the severity of their anxiety symptoms. Of course, given the use of multiple intervention components—not just exercise—and the lack of a control group, Emery could not conclude that exercise caused the observed changes in anxiety. Consequently, he conducted a second study of 79 people with COPD.

This second study used a randomized, controlled design (Emery, Schein, Hauck, & MacIntyre, 1998). Patients were randomly assigned to one of three conditions: (1) COPD education and stress-management counseling, (2) COPD education and stress-management counseling *plus* exercise, or (3) a waiting list (control condition). The exercise component of the intervention consisted of 37 sessions of aerobic and strength training over the course of the 10-week study. At the end of the study, it was found that patients who received the education and stress management *plus* exercise intervention experienced a statistically significant reduction in anxiety that was not demonstrated in the other two conditions. This finding indicates that in people with COPD, exercise has an effect on anxiety above and beyond the effects of education and stress management alone.

ADDITIONAL RESOURCES

Coventry, P.A., & Hind, D. (2007). Comprehensive pulmonary rehabilitation for anxiety and depression in adults with chronic obstructive pulmonary disease: Systematic review and meta-analysis. *Journal of Psychosomatic Research, 63,* 551–565.

De Godoy, D.V., & de Godoy, R.F. (2003). A randomized controlled trial of the effect of psychotherapy on anxiety and depression in chronic obstructive pulmonary disease. *Archives of Physical Medicine and Rehabilitation, 84,* 1154–1157.

Trappenburg, J.C., Troosters, T., Spruit, M.A., Vandebrouck, N., Decramer, M., & Gosselink, R. (2005). Psychosocial conditions do not affect short-term outcome of multidisciplinary rehabilitation in chronic obstructive pulmonary disease. *Archives of Physical Medicine and Rehabilitation, 86,* 1788–1792.

ACTIVITY

Do some research to determine other conditions or diseases that, like COPD, have higher rates of anxiety than are found in the general population. Once you have identified these conditions/diseases, determine whether exercise might help reduce anxiety in individuals with that condition/disease. If exercise can be useful, outline an exercise program that could be prescribed. Be sure to support your prescription with a defensible rationale for the exercise you have chosen. *Hint:* examine the exercise interventions in other studies to get ideas.

more than twice the approximately $42 billion estimated in the United States in 1990 (PAGAC, 2008). Greenberg et al. (1999) estimated a cost of $1,542 per year for each person afflicted with an anxiety disorder. A more recent analysis by Marciniak, Lage, Dunayevich, et al. (2005) estimated the medical cost for a patient with any anxiety disorder at approximately $6,500. Costs then increased depending on the specific type of anxiety disorder (e.g., generalized anxiety disorder was associated with an additional cost of about $2,100). Of the costs associated with the anxiety disorders, it is estimated that about 31 percent is spent for psychiatric treatment (e.g., counseling, hospitalization), 54 percent is spent in nonpsychiatric medical treatment (e.g., emergency room treatment), 10 percent in indirect workplace costs (e.g., reduced productivity, absence due to sickness, early retirement), and approximately 5 percent on prescription costs and mortality (i.e., anxiety-induced suicide). It is worth noting that the vast majority (88 percent) of the costs to the workplace are derived from lost productivity rather than absenteeism itself. Anxiety is also a predisposing factor in drug and substance abuse, which further adds to the cost of the disorder.

Symptomatology

Anxiety can be manifested both psychologically and physiologically, and is characterized by one or more of the following:

1. unpleasant feelings (e.g., uncertainty over what to do, feeling overwhelmed)
2. bodily symptoms resulting from activation of the autonomic nervous system (e.g., muscle tension, autonomic hyperactivity)
3. changes in cognitions (e.g., recurrent obsessions or compulsions; irrational fear of objects, activities, or situations)
4. changes in behavior (e.g., avoidance of situations)
5. vigilance (e.g., being on the lookout for danger or a problem)

Patients with clinical anxiety are often distinguished from those with "normal" anxiety on the basis of the number and intensity of symptoms, degree of suffering, and degree of dysfunction. Thus, using established criteria like those found in the *Diagnostic and Statistical Manual of Mental Disorders*, 4th ed. (DSM–IV) or DSM–IV-TR (text revision), clinical anxiety is diagnosed when anxiety responses occur in the absence of an eliciting event, are disproportionate, and are unmanageable (American Psychiatric Association, 2000).

Anxiety need not manifest itself to the extent that it becomes clinical, however. Often, when we perceive that a situation exceeds our capabilities for effectively coping with it or feel uncertain of our control over the situation, we experience stress. When our appraisal becomes negative, anxiety is often the result. This is a state characterized by worry, self-doubt, nervousness, and tension, but it is also a state that disrupts thought processes and behavior and alters physiological functioning. When anxiety affects these processes to such an extent that normal behavior is disrupted, it becomes clinical.

Treatment

Traditional treatment protocols for anxiety (e.g., medication, psychotherapy), while readily available and generally effective, are often expensive and time consuming (as is the case with depression; see Chapter 12). Medications, such as tranquilizers and antidepressants, are often used. Benzodiazepines—drugs that inhibit neurotransmitter systems (e.g., diazepam)—have sedative effects. Antidepressants (e.g., clomipramine, a tricyclic antidepressant, or specific serotonin reuptake inhibitors such as sertraline and fluoxetine) are also used to treat anxiety because of their anti-anxiety properties. Both classes of medication often require that they be taken for extended periods of time, often up to four to six months. Furthermore, pharmacological treatments often cause numerous side effects (e.g., withdrawal symptoms when medication is stopped). Psychotherapy, while certainly helpful, can also be problematic, primarily in terms of the length of the treatment (which also means greater financial cost). Cognitive-behavioral therapies help to (1) determine the cause-and-effect relationships among the person's thoughts, feelings, and behaviors and (2) develop strategies for attenuating symptoms and reducing avoidant behaviors (USDHHS, 1999). Time-limited therapies (i.e., therapy conducted within a finite time frame, for example, 12 weeks) are often used to assist the individual in directly coping with the anxiety and its symptoms.

For quite some time, the use of physical activity (i.e., exercise) has been examined as a potential tool in both the prevention and the treatment of anxiety. Indeed, the National Institute of Mental Health identified examination of the **anxiolytic** (i.e., anxiety-reducing) effects of exercise as an important topic (Morgan & Goldston, 1987). Some of the anxiety disorders (e.g., phobias) are thought to be unaffected by exercise because they are linked to specific situations or objects (Dunn, Trivedi, & O'Neal, 2001). This view, however, is not uniformly accepted (Johnsgard, 1989, 2004). A fairly extensive body of literature examining the relationship between exercise and anxiety has developed over the past 40 years. The remainder of this chapter presents the major findings of this work, both for normal anxiety and for anxiety sufficient to be considered clinical. Before examining the research on exercise and anxiety, however, we first examine the ways in which anxiety is assessed and measured.

anxiolytic ■

Measurement

An understanding of the difference between state and trait forms of anxiety is necessary as background to the ways in which anxiety is measured. **State anxiety** is a noticeable but *transient* emotional state characterized by feelings of apprehension and heightened autonomic nervous

state anxiety ■

system activity, such as increased heart rate, sweaty palms, increased breathing rate, and increased muscle tension. Thus, state anxiety is assessed by asking individuals to respond based on how they feel "right now, at this moment." For example, respondents are asked to indicate the extent to which they "feel calm," "feel relaxed," or "are presently worrying over possible misfortunes."

Conversely, **trait anxiety** reflects a more general predisposition to respond with apprehension, worry, and nervousness across many situations. For example, individuals with high trait anxiety would respond with increased restlessness, lack of confidence, difficulty in making decisions, and a feeling of inadequacy in most of the situations in which they find themselves. Thus, trait anxiety is assessed by asking subjects to respond based on how they "generally feel." So, for example, they are asked the extent to which they "generally feel this way, that is, how they feel on average" to items like "I feel satisfied with myself," "I feel like a failure," "I wish I could be as happy as others seem to be," and "I take disappointments so keenly that I can't put them out of my mind." Finally, because measures of trait anxiety are conceptually analogous to the personality construct of neuroticism (see Chapter 7), some studies have used measures that assess this construct (see examples from Chapter 7). Because trait anxiety is a general feeling of anxiety, it makes sense to assess trait anxiety before and after *chronic* exercise programs rather than before and after *single* bouts of exercise. Anxiety in pre–post studies of single bouts of exercise is primarily assessed by using state anxiety measures because the goal is to assess the currently experienced level of anxiety.

■ trait anxiety

Psychological Measures

As stated earlier, anxiety can be manifested both psychologically and physiologically, and therefore it can be assessed in a variety of ways. The most common method for the psychological assessment of anxiety in exercise studies is through the use of self-report inventories. Easily the most popular inventory has been the 40-item Spielberger State–Trait Anxiety Inventory (STAI; Spielberger, 1979, 1983; see Exhibit 11.3), followed by the Tension subscale of the Profile of Mood States (McNair, Droppleman, & Lorr, 1981), and the anxiety subscale of the Multiple Affect Adjective Check List (MAACL; Zuckerman & Lubin, 1965).

Physiological Measures

In addition to psychological measures for assessing anxiety, numerous measures of physiological activation or arousal (e.g., increased heart rate, muscle tension, feelings of being jittery or shaky) have been used. Because anxiety often occurs with increased activity in skeletal muscles, measures of muscle tension, via electromyography (EMG), have been used to index anxiety. Notable in this regard is the work of Herbert deVries (e.g., deVries & Adams, 1972; see an example of this research later in this chapter in the section on "Exercise Versus Other Treatments").

exhibit 11.3 Sample items from The State–Trait Anxiety Inventory.

The State-Trait Anxiety Inventory consists of 20 State items (identified as Scale Y1) and 20 Trait items (identified as Scale Y2).

This scale is used to respond to items:

1	2	3	4
Not At All	*Somewhat*	*Moderately So*	*Very Much So*

The following is a sample of five items from the complete 40-item scale.

"State" means "How I feel at this moment"

Examples from the State scale:

I feel calm.	1	2	3	4
I feel at ease.	1	2	3	4
I feel frightened.	1	2	3	4

"Trait" means "How I usually am"

Examples from the Trait scale:

I am a steady person.	1	2	3	4
I lack self-confidence.	1	2	3	4

Because higher scores are indicative of greater levels of anxiety, in the scoring of the scales, some items are reverse scored (e.g., a response of 1 to "I feel calm" would be scored as a 4 since not feeling very calm would be indicative of greater levels of anxiety) in order to arrive at a total for State and a total for Trait. Respondents' scores are typically compared with a normative group (e.g., college-aged students) to understand relative anxiety.

Anxiety can also be reflected in the cardiovascular system through measures of blood pressure and heart rate, through the electrodermal system (skin responses—galvanic skin response, palmar sweating, skin temperature), and through the central nervous system (e.g., electroencephalography or EEG—measure of electrical activity in the brain). Although anxiety responses are likely to have neurochemical components (e.g., increases in catecholamines and cortisol), measures of these components have not been used much in the human exercise–anxiety literature. This is largely because of the expense involved in collecting and analyzing data reflecting these kinds of variables. It is worth pointing out, however, that a fairly sizable amount of research using both human and animal models has made considerable progress into the neurochemistry of anxiety and how such pathways may be influenced by exercise (e.g., Dishman, 1997; O'Connor, Raglin, & Martinsen, 2000).

Research on Exercise and Anxiety

In the exercise–anxiety literature, exercise can be classified as either *acute* or *chronic* in nature. As defined in Chapter 1, acute exercise involves single bouts of exercise at some level of intensity or duration. Chronic exercise, on the other hand, typically involves a regular program lasting for weeks or months and is usually designed to improve aerobic capacity, although increases in strength can be seen from chronic resistance programs. Well over 100 studies have been documented in this literature (including both the acute and chronic exercise studies). Physical activity/exercise is believed to be a useful tool in alleviating anxiety and anxiety disorders. Physicians, at least to some extent, prescribe exercise to their patients. A survey in *Physician and Sportsmedicine* indicated that 60 percent of the 1,750 physicians surveyed prescribed exercise for those suffering from anxiety (Ryan, 1983). We turn now to a summary of the evidence accumulated on the anxiety–exercise relationship to date.

Evidence for Preventive Effects

Various studies have indicated that exercise can play a role in preventing anxiety symptoms and disorders. A cross-sectional, epidemiological study by Stephens (1988), examining four separate large adult samples (ranging in size from 3,025 to 23,791), found greater self-reported physical activity to be associated with better mental health, including fewer symptoms of anxiety (and fewer symptoms of depression). Another large-scale, population-based study conducted in the Netherlands with more than 19,000 adolescent and adult twins and their families showed that exercisers had lower trait (i.e., more general) anxiety scores than those individuals who didn't exercise (deMoor, Beem, Stubbe, et al., 2006). A third study, by Goodwin (2003), used data from the National Comorbidity Survey to examine the relationship between regular physical activity ("how often do you get physical exercise—either on your job or in a recreational activity?") and mental disorders, including a variety of anxiety disorders (e.g., generalized anxiety disorder, panic attack, agoraphobia). From a sample of 5,877 adults between 15 and 54 years of age, 63 percent (3,707) responded that they regularly exercised, with the remainder (2,170) reporting that they exercised occasionally, rarely, or never. The analyses showed that regular physical activity was associated with reduced chances of having generalized anxiety disorder, agoraphobia, panic attack, specific phobias, and social phobia. These relationships remained even after controlling for a variety of demographic and self-reported illness variables. It is also interesting to note that a dose-response effect was evident in these data, namely, the frequency of reported anxiety disorders increased as the level of physical activity decreased. For example, panic attacks occurred in 3.32 percent of those reporting regular exercise, 4.85 percent reporting occasional exercise, 7.33 percent who exercised rarely, and 8.52 percent who never exercised. Generalized anxiety disorder showed a similar dose effect, occurring in 2.26 percent of those who exercised regularly, 2.97 percent of occasional exercisers, 5.93 percent of those who rarely exercised, and 6.49 percent of those who never exercised. Goodwin (2003) concluded that these results provide evidence of the potential link between regular exercise and a reduced likelihood of a variety of anxiety disorders.

This link is not always the case, however. Taylor and colleagues (2004) used another large database (i.e., 2001 Behavioral Risk Factor Surveillance System) of almost 42,000 U.S. adults to examine the potential links between physical activity and mental health. Using the Healthy People 2010 guidelines for physical activity, they found that those who were completely inactive were at significantly greater risk of having anxiety symptoms on at least 14 of the previous 30 days. Somewhat surprisingly, adults who were physically active, but not at a level that satisfied the Healthy People 2010 recommendation, were actually at less risk of experiencing anxiety symptoms than those who were active at a level that met or exceeded the recommendation (Taylor et al., 2004). It is worth noting that this relationship persisted only in those over the age of 40. Taylor and coworkers concluded that some physical activity was better than none when it came to protecting against anxiety symptoms, but more physical activity was not necessarily better. Clearly this relationship needs further examination.

In addition, studies have consistently shown that individuals who are physically fit have less anxiety than do their unfit counterparts. A review by Landers and Petruzzello (1994) concluded that physically fit individuals have less anxiety than those who are unfit. This could be the result of fitter individuals leading healthier lifestyles (e.g., more activity, better nutrition). For example, when they reviewed studies examining the effects of exercise training programs (which often lead to increased fitness), Landers and Petruzzello concluded that, in addition to an increase in fitness, trait levels of anxiety decrease following such activity protocols. In studies that have examined levels of neuroticism, this has been seen to decline over the length of a training program. This effect seems to be more pronounced as the length of the training program is increased (Petruzzello, Landers, Hatfield, Kubitz, & Salazar, 1991). There could, of course, be other explanations for this relationship independent of fitness. Overall, the evidence supports the idea that involvement in physical activity on a consistent basis serves to provide a buffer against anxiety symptoms and anxiety disorders (Physical Activity Guidelines Advisory Committee, 2008).

Evidence for Use as Treatment

The preventive effects of exercise are clearly important, but it is also important to determine the extent to which exercise can be useful as a treatment for anxiety problems once they have manifested themselves. Although the literature focused exclusively on clinical samples is relatively scant, some evidence does suggest that exercise can be useful in the treatment of mental disorders, and several calls have been made for using exercise as a treatment for such problems (Callahan, 2004; Chung & Baird, 1999). As discussed in Chapter 12, Johnsgard (1989) presents numerous case study examples in *The Exercise Prescription for Depression and Anxiety* of how exercise has been useful in the treatment of both anxiety and mood disorders in his patients. For example, he presents the case of a woman suffering from agoraphobia (fear of public places) wherein he was able to help treat her phobia with brief but ever-increasing durations of exercise. Other, more carefully controlled studies conducted with clinically anxious samples highlight the utility of such an "exercise prescription." Some of these studies are presented below.

Whereas a fair amount of research has examined the utility of exercise for those with clinical depression, fewer research studies have examined the efficacy of exercise in treating the anxiety disorders. Some studies have suggested that initially low-fit and highly anxious individuals have the most to gain from exercise training from a psychological perspective. Martinsen, Hoffart, and Solberg (1989) demonstrated that both aerobic (walk/jog) and nonaerobic (muscular strength, flexibility) exercise resulted in significant psychological improvements in 79 in-patients with anxiety disorders. The treatment protocol involved 60 minutes of exercise three times per week over the course of eight weeks.

Sexton, Maere, and Dahl (1989) examined the effects of an eight-week exercise program (walking, jogging) in 52 symptomatic neurotics with a follow-up six months post-program. Participants were patients with a nonpsychotic diagnosis using the DSM–III (the precursor to the currently used DSM–IV and DSM–IV-TR). Both walking and jogging significantly reduced anxiety and depression, with these changes being maintained at follow-up. In fact, at follow-up a significant relationship was noted between aerobic capacity and anxiety levels, with greater fitness levels related to lower anxiety. This finding provides evidence that an increase in fitness, and not just in physical activity level, is associated with anxiety reduction. Sexton and colleagues noted the importance of the finding that vigorous exercise was not necessary for improvements in the psychological variables, with walking and running yielding equivalent effects. The study further reinforces the point made earlier that moderate-intensity exercise is sufficient to decrease anxiety even in clinical populations. These researchers also noted that the patients rated exercise as more important than medication and psychotherapy in their improvement.

Meyer et al. (1998) examined the influence of 45 to 60 minutes of running three times per week over the course of 10 weeks in patients with DSM–III-Revised diagnosed panic disorder with or without agoraphobia compared to pharmacotherapy (clomipramine) or control. After the 10 weeks of treatment, the exercise group showed significant clinical improvement in their anxiety relative to the control condition and similar levels of improvement to the clomipramine group.

Broocks et al. (1998), in a randomized, placebo-controlled clinical trial, assigned 46 outpatients diagnosed with moderate to severe panic disorder to either a

10-week exercise treatment (running three times per week; $n = 16$), pharmacotherapy (112.5 mg/d of clomipramine; $n = 15$), or placebo treatment ($n = 15$). Results revealed that, for the Hamilton Rating Scale measure of anxiety, exercise was as effective as the drug treatment in reducing self-reported anxiety, with both being superior to the placebo. The drug treatment resulted in an earlier improvement in anxiety symptoms (after four weeks), but was equivalent to the exercise treatment at the end of the 10-week trial (see Exhibit 11.4). The drug treatment did improve both patient- and observer-rated panic and agoraphobia intensity and frequency of attacks to a greater extent than did exercise, but, again, exercise was superior to placebo in reducing the frequency and intensity of these conditions. This is particularly salient given the call by Salmon (2001) for more studies examining the utility of exercise in dealing with panic disorder. Some researchers have proposed that exercise might actually induce panic attacks in panic-prone individuals, but this is based more on flawed logic than on experimental evidence. O'Connor, Smith, and Morgan (2000) point out that exercise, both acute and chronic, is safe for panic disorder patients and that, generally, panic patients show anxiety reductions following exercise similar to those seen in nonanxious individuals.

In addition to their work examining exercise and panic disorder, O'Connor et al. (2000) have noted that more work is needed to examine the effect of exercise on another anxiety disorder, namely generalized anxiety disorder. As Goodwin (2003) demonstrated, exercise should be helpful in this regard. Merom and colleagues (2008) conducted a recent study through an outpatient clinic that provided group cognitive behavioral therapy (GCBT) to individuals with diagnosed panic disorder, social phobia, or generalized anxiety disorder. In this work, a home-based walking program or educational sessions were added to the GCBT, and self-reported anxiety, stress, and depression were assessed before and after the 8 to 10-week

exhibit 11.4 **The effect of exercise, drug treatment, and placebo on anxiety symptoms.**

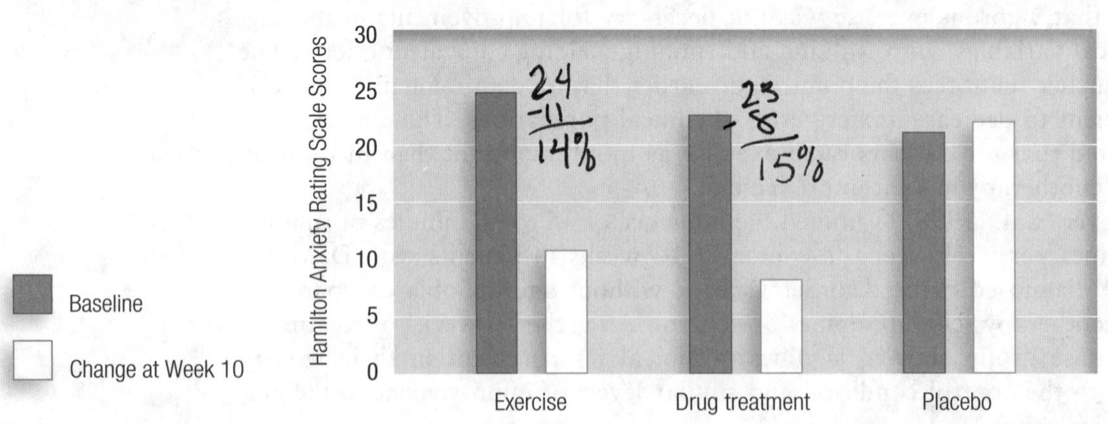

Source: Adapted from Broocks, Bandelow, Pekrun, et al. (1998).

intervention. The exercise intervention consisted of gradually increasing the number of 30-minute moderate-intensity exercise sessions (e.g., brisk walking), with an ultimate goal of 150 minutes of accumulated exercise per week. For those who completed the intervention, after controlling for several potential confounding factors, the GCBT-plus-exercise group showed a sizable reduction in anxiety, stress, and depression scores. The researchers noted that the exercise intervention effect may have been larger had the program lasted more than 8 to 10 weeks.

Noting that many cognitive behavioral therapy protocols involve exposure to anxiety-related arousal symptoms, Broman-Fulks and Storey (2008) conducted a follow-up to an earlier study by Broman-Fulks, Berman, Rabian, and Webster (2004) to examine whether acute exercise sessions could reduce **anxiety sensitivity,** that is, fear of anxiety and anxiety-related sensations. They noted that anxiety sensitivity is crucial in the etiology of panic disorder and other anxiety disorders. The earlier (2004) study showed that six 20-minute bouts of both low- and high-intensity exercise over a two-week period were effective at reducing anxiety sensitivity. The follow-up work (Broman-Fulks & Storey, 2008) randomly assigned 24 individuals with high scores on an anxiety sensitivity index to either an exercise group or a no-exercise control group. The exercise group again completed six 20-minute bouts of aerobic exercise over a two-week period. Results showed a significant reduction in anxiety sensitivity, but only for the exercise group. As a result, Broman-Fulks and Storey suggested that exercise may be an effective intervention for individuals with high levels of anxiety sensitivity, especially if they need a quick reduction in that sensitivity.

■ anxiety sensitivity

The Relationship Between Exercise and Anxiety

In a comprehensive review of the exercise–anxiety literature, Petruzzello and colleagues (1991) conducted a meta-analysis of more than 100 studies that had examined the exercise–anxiety relationship. This review actually included three meta-analyses: one each for acute exercise–state anxiety research, for chronic exercise–trait anxiety research, and for studies using psychophysiological concomitants of anxiety (e.g., EMG, cardiovascular measures). A number of other meta-analyses have appeared since 1991 (Long & van Stavel, 1995; McDonald & Hodgdon, 1991; PAGAC, 2008; Schlicht, 1994; Wipfli, Rethorst, & Landers, 2008), but none has been as comprehensive or shown any striking differences from the earlier review.

Aerobic exercise and anxiety

Easily the most noteworthy finding from the 1991 meta-analysis by Petruzzello and colleagues was that anxiety is reduced following exercise, but only exercise of an aerobic nature. Importantly, no consistent differences have been found among the various modes of aerobic exercise (e.g., walking, jogging, running, swimming, cycling, aerobics). These reductions occur for *state* anxiety following *acute* exercise and for *trait* anxiety following *chronic* exercise. Anxiety reductions occur regardless of how the anxiety is operationalized:

1. Reductions are seen in self-report measures (questionnaires).
2. Reductions are seen in measures of muscular tension (EMG).
3. Reductions are seen in cardiovascular measures (heart rate, blood pressure).
4. Alterations consistent with reduced anxiety are seen in central nervous system measures (e.g., EEG alpha activity).

Anaerobic exercise and anxiety

In contrast to the findings regarding aerobic exercise and anxiety, Petruzzello et al. (1991) found that anaerobic or resistance exercise seems to result in slight *increases* in anxiety. These findings contrast with the effects of this form of exercise on depression (see Chapter 12). A number of studies that have appeared since 1991 support the conclusion that resistance training slightly increases anxiety. A review of these later studies involving resistance exercise (Raglin, 1997) indicates that the picture has not really changed—reductions in state anxiety are not consistently seen following resistance exercise. Speculation for the lack of change in anxiety, and even increased anxiety in some cases, revolves around issues related to subject (in)experience with the activity and exercise intensity. At least some support has been shown for the intensity explanation. Raglin, Turner, and Eksten (1993) found that after 30 minutes of resistance exercise at 70–80 percent of the individual's 1-repetition maximum (1-RM), anxiety actually increased briefly but returned to baseline levels within 20 minutes. Bartholomew and Linder (1998) showed reductions in state anxiety following 20 minutes of self-rated "light" intensity weight training (in men but not women); however, state anxiety was increased following self-rated moderate and "high" intensity activity. These elevated anxiety levels were short lived, dissipating within 5–15 minutes following completion of the exercise. In a second study using intensity based on estimated 1-RMs, Bartholomew and Linder (1998) showed that low-intensity (40–50 percent 1-RM) resistance exercise resulted in decreased anxiety 15 and 30 minutes post-exercise, but anxiety was significantly increased up to 15 minutes following high-intensity (75–85 percent 1-RM) exercise. The Physical Activity Guidelines Advisory Committee (2008) concluded, based on six randomized controlled trials published since 1995, that the magnitude of anxiety reduction does not differ depending on exercise mode, with resistance exercise resulting in similar reductions in anxiety compared to aerobic exercise. Like the studies cited above, it appears that light- to moderate-intensity resistance exercise may result in reduced anxiety. More vigorous intensities still seem to either increase anxiety or result in no change (e.g., Cassilhas, Viana, Grassmann, et al., 2007).

It is also possible that the unchanged/increased anxiety may result from measurement problems. As articulated by Ekkekakis, Hall, and Petruzzello (1999; and initially by Rejeski, Hardy, & Shaw, 1991), studies using the State–Trait Anxiety Inventory (STAI) to measure anxiety (which includes the vast majority of all exercise studies) may be erroneously reflecting increased "anxiety" that is little more than increased activation or arousal (e.g., increased heart rate). The STAI includes numerous items that were designed to reflect perceived activation based on the notion that changes in such perceptions of activation would be related to changes in anxiety (e.g., jitteriness). With exercise, however, such changed perceptions may be more reflective of actual changes in autonomic activity consistent with the demands of the exercise. Thus, an individual might respond that he or she is more "jittery" or less calm *immediately* following exercise, particularly resistance exercise, which is a normal outcome of the exertion of the activity, but the STAI reflects this as increased anxiety.

Acute exercise and anxiety

In the acute exercise studies, the anxiolytic effect seen following exercise is transient. Studies examining the anxiety responses for an extended period suggest that the effect seems to last for about two to four hours following acute exercise. In other words, anxiety reduction does not last indefinitely, but anxiety instead returns to pre-exercise levels after some period of time (Petruzzello et al., 1991). Interestingly, this psychological change parallels some physiological changes that occur following exercise (e.g., post-exercise hypotension or reduced blood pressure). Many studies have shown reductions in blood pressure following exercise, and numerous studies have also shown reductions in anxiety, leading to speculation that the two might be linked. Given that participants in chronic exercise programs also show reduced trait anxiety, it is possible that, over time, pre-exercise levels become reduced, that is, a new baseline is achieved. Anxiety reduction, however, does take place following a single bout of aerobic activity. For example, a baseline level of anxiety prior to an acute exercise session might be a score of 35 (possible scores ranging from 20 to 80). Following the exercise bout, this anxiety level might drop to 28. The next day, prior to an exercise session, the anxiety level might again be 35. Over a period of 12 to 16 weeks of consistent exercise, the baseline level of anxiety might drop to 30. With this reduction in baseline anxiety, anxiety following a single exercise bout might fall to 25 but return to the pre-exercise level of 30 before the next exercise session.

Exercise versus other treatments

An important question that has been asked in the exercise–anxiety literature is: To what extent does exercise reduce anxiety as well as, or better than, other common treatments for anxiety (e.g., meditation, relaxation, or quiet rest—or not doing anything)? Exercise has been shown to be better at reducing anxiety than not doing anything and has also been shown to be as effective as other known anxiety-reducing treatments. A study conducted by Bahrke and Morgan (1978) shows this quite nicely. In this work, 75 men were randomly assigned to 20 minutes of exercising on a treadmill, meditating, or sitting quietly in a sound-dampened chamber reading a *Reader's Digest* magazine (which has come to be known as the "quiet rest" condition). Comparisons were made of anxiety levels pre-treatment, post-treatment, and then 10 minutes post-treatment. State anxiety was reduced across all three conditions, and there were no differences among the three (see Exhibit 11.5). The pessimist might view this as evidence that exercise

exhibit 11.5 The effect of exercise on anxiety compared to meditation and no treatment.

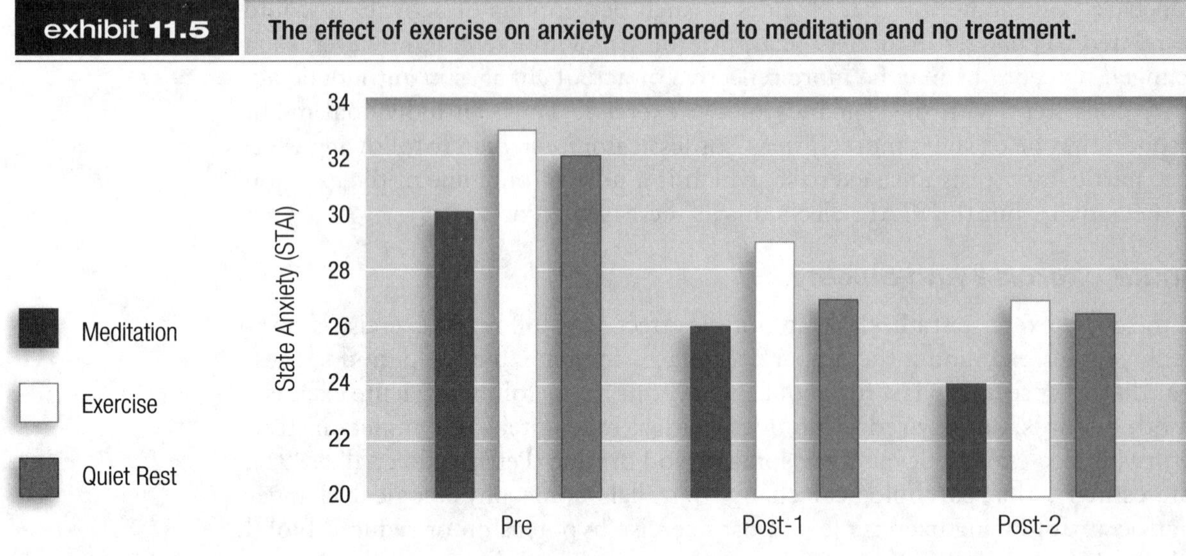

Source: Adapted from Bahrke & Morgan (1978).

is not necessary for anxiety reduction. The optimist, however, would suggest that while exercise is perhaps no better than other anxiety-reducing treatments, it is just as good. Furthermore, numerous physiological benefits accrue from physical activity that would not be achieved from other treatments. Another beneficial aspect of exercise over other treatments is that the anxiety-reducing effects seem to last longer following exercise. For example, Raglin and Morgan (1987) showed that anxiety was still reduced below pre-treatment levels three hours following exercise but not quiet rest.

Another common treatment for anxiety is pharmacotherapy (i.e., medication). Limited evidence shows that exercise may be more effective than anti-anxiety drugs (e.g., diazepam). In a classic study, deVries and Adams (1972) recruited 10 older adults (52 to 70 years old) with anxiety/tension problems (e.g., difficulty concentrating, excessive muscle tension, nervousness). Each of these individuals underwent five different treatment conditions three separate times:

1. 400 mg capsule containing meprobamate, a commonly used anti-anxiety drug at the time
2. 400 mg placebo capsule containing lactose (a sugar pill)
3. 15 minutes of walking at an intensity to elicit a heart rate (HR) of 100 bpm (about 67 percent of the individual's maximal heart rate)
4. 15 minutes of walking at an intensity to elicit a HR of 120 bpm (about 80 percent of the individual's maximal heart rate)
5. a control condition (sat quietly and read)

As is often done in drug studies, conditions (1) and (2) were done in **double blind** fashion (i.e., neither the subjects nor the experimenters interacting with the subjects knew whether the subjects were receiving the drug or the placebo) to reduce expectancy effects. DeVries and Adams assessed anxiety through EMG measures taken before and after each treatment condition. Of the five conditions, only the exercise at the lower intensity (i.e., 100 bpm) elicited a significant reduction in muscle tension (although it is worth noting that the higher-intensity exercise condition nearly achieved significance as well). The control, drug, and placebo conditions were essentially the same and did not reduce muscle tension. Clearly more work is needed in this area, but these results suggest that exercise may be more effective than anti-anxiety drugs. Indeed, deVries consistently referred to the "tranquilizer effect of exercise" (1981). One of the only other studies examining the effectiveness of exercise relative to anxiety medication was done by Broocks and colleagues (1998) and was discussed earlier in the chapter. Given the widespread use of anti-anxiety (i.e., tranquilizer) medications, more research in this area is needed (see Martinsen & Stanghelle, 1997).

■ double blind

Before turning to a discussion about what we don't know about exercise and anxiety, we provide a summary of what we do know in Exhibit 11.6.

What we don't know

Although we have learned a great deal regarding exercise and anxiety reduction, much, unfortunately, remains unknown. This is particularly true with respect to dose–response issues (i.e., intensity, duration).

It has been suggested that thresholds exist for the achievement of anxiety reduction. For example, Dishman (1986) proposed that exercise of at least 70 percent of aerobic capacity sustained for at least 20 minutes would yield anxiety reduction. Raglin and Morgan (1987) suggested that a more moderate intensity (greater than 60 percent of maximum) was sufficient. The minimum intensity needed for anxiety reduction, however, has been poorly investigated. Ekkekakis and Petruzzello (1999), summarizing studies that specifically examined dose–response issues, concluded that evidence shows state anxiety and tension (measured via the Profile of Mood States [POMS], which is discussed in Chapter 13) are sensitive to exercise intensity effects. They found that higher intensities led to increases in anxiety/tension and lower intensities resulted in no change or decreases

Consensus statements regarding exercise and anxiety. **exhibit 11.6**

1. Exercise can be associated with reduced state anxiety.
2. Long-term exercise is usually associated with reductions in neuroticism and trait anxiety.
3. Exercise can result in the reduction of various stress indices.
4. Exercise can have beneficial emotional effects across all ages and both genders.

Source: Adapted from Morgan & Goldston (1987).

(but remember the caveat raised earlier regarding the potential problems with measuring anxiety in the exercise context). Clearly more work is needed before any firm conclusions can be made and certainly before any recommendations about minimal exercise intensity levels can be made.

As for the issue of minimum duration of exercise needed to achieve anxiety-reducing effects, the meta-analysis by Petruzzello and colleagues (1991) noted that exercise durations of fewer than 20 minutes were as effective as durations of greater than 20 minutes for reducing anxiety. Thus, research at this point shows that the anxiety-reducing effect that is achieved by exercise is present regardless of the duration of that exercise. Recommendations like those made by Dishman for a minimum duration of 20 minutes are thus sufficient but not necessarily accurate. The PAGAC report (2008) essentially concluded the same thing—minimal and/or optimal durations or intensities are still unknown regarding anxiety reduction. Clearly, more research is needed for a definitive answer, but reductions in anxiety can apparently be realized simply by exercising aerobically.

Another problematic issue for the field is the extent to which anxiety reduction occurs for individuals suffering from clinical levels of anxiety. The vast majority of the research in this area has examined the reduction of anxiety symptoms (usually via self-report) in people who are not clinically anxious. The PAGAC report (2008) does detail that approximately 60 percent of the randomized controlled trials conducted since 1995 have used individuals, usually patients with some medical condition (e.g., cancer, cardiovascular disease), but not necessarily suffering from clinical anxiety. In fact, one rather curious conclusion of the meta-analysis by Wipfli and colleagues (2008) was that future research be conducted with clinical samples, as only 3 of the 49 studies they reviewed used such clinical samples. This was echoed in the Ekkekakis editorial (2008), which noted that the authors acknowledged that "in nearly all (46 of 49) of the studies reviewed, the participants were not clinically anxious" (p. 48). Clearly, this is work that needs to be done before clear recommendations can be made regarding exercise as a treatment for clinically anxious individuals.

Mechanisms of Change

We do not yet have a definitive picture of the mechanisms responsible for the anxiety-reducing effect of exercise. Many of the mechanisms that have been proposed to explain the anxiolytic effect are the same as those proposed to explain depression reduction. Thus, the interested reader can turn to Chapter 12 for a discussion of the mastery, endorphin, monoamine, and social interaction hypotheses. Two additional mechanisms, the thermogenic and the distraction/time-out hypotheses, have also been proposed as explanations for anxiety reduction with exercise.

Thermogenic hypothesis

Derived from research showing that treatments that elevate body temperature (e.g., sauna bathing, warm showers) produce therapeutic benefits (e.g., reduced muscle tension), the **thermogenic hypothesis** states that the elevated body temperature resulting from exercise may also lead to observed psychological changes, such as reduced anxiety. In essence, exercise is thought to result in elevated body temperature. This temperature increase is sensed by the brain, a muscular relaxation response is triggered, and this relaxation is fed back to the brain and interpreted as relaxation or reduced anxiety. This is probably the most systematically studied of the proposed mechanisms. At present, research seems to indicate that the elevated body temperature is probably not directly responsible for the psychological changes (Koltyn, Shake, & Morgan, 1993; Petruzzello, Landers, & Salazar, 1993; Youngstedt, Dishman, Cureton, & Peacock, 1993). The thermogenic hypothesis remains tenable, however, in part because it could very well be that brain temperature and not body temperature is what drives the affective response and decrease in anxiety. Some evidence shows that the temperature of the brain is regulated independently from the body, although this independence is not completely accepted, and researchers have not yet been able to directly measure exercise-related increases in brain temperature in humans. Thus more work is needed to determine the effects of exercise on brain temperature before the thermogenic hypothesis can be accepted or ruled out.

■ thermogenic hypothesis

Distraction/time-out hypothesis

The **distraction/time-out hypothesis** grew out of the findings from the Bahrke and Morgan (1978) study described earlier, wherein 20 minutes of treadmill exercise, noncultic meditation, or sitting quietly in a sound-dampened chamber reading a *Reader's Digest* magazine were compared from pre-treatment to post-treatment and 10 minutes post-treatment. Essentially no differences existed across the three conditions. This particular hypothesis, stated simply, says that the anxiety-reducing effects seen with exercise are due to the distraction it provides from the normal routine. It allows the stressed, anxious, depressed person to "leave behind" or take a time-out from his or her cares and worries. Other distraction "therapies" have also been shown to reduce anxiety and depression (e.g., meditation, relaxation, quiet rest). As noted earlier, however, the effect of exercise may be qualitatively different from other cognitively based therapies because the exercise effect lasts longer. The distraction hypothesis remains a possible explanation for anxiety and depression reduction; however, it appears that the exercise-related anxiety and depression reduction is the consequence of more than simply taking time away from one's daily routine, given the available evidence.

■ distraction/time-out hypothesis

Practical Recommendations

As is the case with depression, the "minimal" level of exercise activity is currently unknown, but it seems clear that exercise or physical activity done on a regular basis can be useful in alleviating anxiety as well as in protecting against the anxiety that we might ordinarily succumb to as a result of our busy, stressful lives if we remained sedentary. As Amanda discovered in the chapter-opening scenario, an exercise regime can reduce anxiety and anxiety-related symptoms. The type of exercise *does* seem to matter, as only aerobic forms of exercise seem to be effective in reducing anxiety. This conclusion may change as more studies examine anaerobic/resistance types of exercise. Those suffering from more severe forms of anxiety may also find relief in exercise therapies, but these individuals should certainly consult with a mental health–care provider before beginning an exercise program.

Conclusion

As with exercise and depression, it seems reasonable to propose that exercise can be helpful in reducing anxiety in the short term and in reducing general tension, nervousness, and worry, thus increasing emotional stability over the longer term. Exercise can also be successful in treating clinical manifestations of anxiety, such as panic disorder, phobias, and generalized anxiety disorder, although more research with clinically anxious populations is needed. The current state of research is summarized in Exhibit 11.6. Much remains to be done, however, not the least of which is determining what causes this reduced level of anxiety and determining what "doses" of exercise reliably yield such effects.

what do you know?

1. What is the difference between mental health and mental illness?
2. What percentage of adults in the United States suffer from some type of mental health problem in a given year?
3. What percentage of adults in the United States suffer from some type of anxiety disorder in a given year?
4. What are some of the symptoms associated with panic disorder?
5. What is known from cross-sectional and prospective studies regarding the association between (lack of) activity and anxiety?
6. To reduce anxiety, how long must exercise programs be?
7. What is the optimal "dosage" in terms of type, frequency, intensity, and duration needed for anxiety reduction?
8. What kind of exercise is best for anxiety reduction?
9. Can exercise be useful in the treatment of clinical manifestations of anxiety? What evidence exists to support this answer?
10. Which hypothesis for explaining the exercise-anxiety relationship relies on changes in temperature?

learning activities

1. Imagine two groups of individuals. Group 1 scores relatively high on trait anxiety and Group 2 scores relatively low on trait anxiety. Based on what you know from the chapter, describe these different groups in terms of the levels of physical activity you suspect they have.
2. Choose a day when your perceived stress level is fairly high. Go for a brisk 15-minute walk. Before you go, using the scale below, mark a "B" for "before" on the line to indicate how you feel at that time relative to being either very tense/anxious or very calm/relaxed. When you return from your walk, mark an "A" for "after" to indicate how you feel. After you've rated how you feel, answer the following questions:
   a. Is there any change in the location of your A vs. your B?
   b. Based on the results, how would you rate the walk in terms of its ability to influence your anxiety level? Why do you think the score changed (or didn't change)?

Tense or anxious — Calm or relaxed

references

American Psychiatric Association (2000). *Diagnostic and statistical manual of mental disorders* (4th ed., text rev.). Arlington, VA: Author.

Bahrke, M.S., & Morgan, W.P. (1978). Anxiety reduction following exercise and meditation. *Cognitive Therapy and Research, 4,* 323–333.

Bartholomew, J.B., & Linder, D.E. (1998). State anxiety following resistance exercise: The role of gender and exercise intensity. *Journal of Behavioral Medicine, 21,* 205–219.

Brenes, G.A. (2003). Anxiety and chronic obstructive pulmonary disease: Prevalence, impact, and treatment. *Psychosomatic Medicine, 65,* 963–970.

Broman-Fulks, J.J., Berman, M.E., Rabian, B.A., & Webster, M.J. (2004). Effects of aerobic exercise on anxiety sensitivity. *Behaviour Research & Therapy, 42,* 125–136.

Broman-Fulks, J.J., & Storey, K.M. (2008). Evaluation of a brief aerobic intervention for high anxiety sensitivity. *Anxiety, Stress & Coping, 21,* 117–128.

Broocks, A., Bandelow, B., Pekrun, G., George, A., Meyer, T., Bartmann, U., Hillmer-Vogel, U., & Ruther, E. (1998). Comparison of aerobic exercise, chloripramine, and placebo in the treatment of panic disorder. *American Journal of Psychiatry, 155,* 603–609.

Callahan, P. (2004). Exercise: A neglected intervention in mental health care? *Journal of Psychiatric & Mental Health Nursing, 11,* 476–483.

Cassilhas, R.C., Viana, V.A.R., Grassmann, V., Santos, R.T., Santos, R.F., Tufik, S., & Mello, M.T. (2007). The impact of resistance exercise on the cognitive function of the elderly. *Medicine & Science in Sports & Exercise, 39,* 1401–1407.

Chung, Y.B., & Baird, M.K. (1999). Physical exercise as a counseling intervention. *Journal of Mental Health Counseling, 21,* 124–135.

deMoor, M.H.M., Beem, A.L., Stubbe, J.H., Boomsma, D.I., & deGeus, E.J.C. (2006). Regular exercise, anxiety, depression and personality: A population-based study. *Preventive Medicine, 42,* 273–279.

DeVries, H.A. (1981). Tranquilizer effect of exercise: A critical review. *Physician and Sportsmedicine, 9*(11), 47–54.

DeVries, H.A., & Adams, G.M. (1972). Electromyographic comparison of single doses of exercise and meprobamate as to effects on muscular relaxation. *American Journal of Physical Medicine, 51,* 130–141.

Dishman, R.K. (1986). Mental health. In V. Seefeldt (Ed.), *Physical activity and well-being* (pp. 303–341). Reston, VA: American Association for Health, Physical Education, Recreation and Dance.

Dishman, R.K. (1997). The norepinephrine hypothesis. In W.P. Morgan (Ed.), *Physical activity & mental health* (pp. 199–212). Washington, DC: Taylor & Francis.

Dunn, A.L., Trivedi, M.H., & O'Neal, H.A. (2001). Physical activity dose–response effects on outcomes of depression and anxiety. *Medicine and Science in Sports and Exercise, 33* (Supplement), S587–S597.

DuPont, R.L., Rice, D.P., Miller, L.S., Shiraki, S.S., Rowland, C.R., & Harwood, H.J. (1996). Economic cost of anxiety disorders. *Anxiety, 2,* 167–172.

Ekkekakis, P. (2008). The genetic tidal wave finally reached our shores: Will it be a catalyst for a critical overhaul of the way we think and do science? *Mental Health & Physical Activity, 1,* 47–52.

Ekkekakis, P., Hall, E.E., & Petruzzello, S.J. (1999). Measuring state anxiety in the context of acute exercise using the State Anxiety Inventory: An attempt to resolve the brouhaha. *Journal of Sport and Exercise Psychology, 21,* 205–229.

Ekkekakis, P., & Petruzzello, S.J. (1999). Acute aerobic exercise and affect: Current status, problems and prospects regarding dose–response. *Sports Medicine, 28,* 337–374.

Emery, C.F. (1994). Effects of age on physiological and psychological functioning among COPD patients in an exercise program. *Journal of Aging and Health, 6,* 3–16.

Emery, C.F., Schein, R.L., Hauck, E.R., & MacIntyre, N.R. (1998). Psychological and cognitive outcomes of a randomized trial of exercise among patients with chronic obstructive pulmonary disease. *Health Psychology, 17,* 232–240.

Goodwin, R.D. (2003). Association between physical activity and mental disorders among adults in the United States. *Preventive Medicine, 36,* 698–703.

Greenberg, P.E., Sisitsky, T., Kessler, R.C., Finkelstein, S.N., Berndt, E.R., Davidson, J.R., Ballenger, J.C., & Fyer, A.J. (1999). The economic burden of anxiety disorders in the 1990s. *Journal of Clinical Psychiatry, 60,* 427–435.

Johnsgard, K.W. (1989). *The exercise prescription for depression and anxiety.* New York: Plenum.

Johnsgard, K. (2004). *Conquering depression and anxiety through exercise.* Amherst, NY: Prometheus Books.

Kessler, R.C., Chiu, W.T., Demler, O., & Walters, E.E. (2005). Prevalence, severity, and comorbidity of 12-month DSM-IV disorders in the National Comorbidity Survey Replication. *Archives of General Psychiatry, 62,* 617–627.

Kessler, R.C., McGonagle, K.A., Zhao, S., Nelson, C.B., Hughes, M., Eshleman, S., Wittchen, H.U., & Kendler, K.S. (1994). Lifetime and 12-month prevalence of DSM-III-R psychiatric disorders in the United States: Results from the National Comorbidity Survey. *Archives of General Psychiatry, 51,* 8–18.

Koltyn, K.F., Shake, C.L., & Morgan, W.P. (1993). Interaction of exercise, water temperature and protective apparel on body awareness and anxiety. *International Journal of Sport Psychology, 24,* 297–305.

Landers, D.M., & Petruzzello, S.J. (1994). Physical activity, fitness, and anxiety. In C. Bouchard, R.J. Shephard, & T. Stephens (Eds.), *Physical activity, fitness, and health: International proceedings and consensus statement* (pp. 868–882). Champaign, IL: Human Kinetics.

Leith, L.M. (1994). *Foundations of exercise and mental health.* Morgantown, WV: Fitness Information Technology.

Long, B.C., & van Stavel, R. (1995). Effects of exercise training on anxiety: A meta-analysis. *Journal of Applied Sport Psychology, 7,* 167–189.

Marciniak, M.D., Lage, M.J., Dunayevich, E., Russell, J.M., Bowman, L., Landbloom, R.P., & Levine, L.R. (2005). The cost of treating anxiety: The medical and demographic correlates that impact total medical costs. *Depression & Anxiety, 21,* 178–184.

Martinsen, E.W., Hoffart, A., & Solberg, O.Y. (1989). Aerobic and non-aerobic forms of exercise in the treatment of anxiety disorders. *Stress Medicine, 5,* 115–120.

Martinsen, E.W., Sandvik, L., & Kolbjornsrud, O.B. (1989). Aerobic exercise in the treatment of nonpsychotic mental disorders: An exploratory study. *Nordic Journal of Psychiatry, 43,* 521–529.

Martinsen, E.W., & Stanghelle, J.K. (1997). Drug therapy and physical activity. In W.P. Morgan (Ed.), *Physical activity and mental health* (pp. 81–90). Washington, DC: Taylor & Francis.

McDonald, D.G., & Hodgdon, J.A. (1991). *Psychological effects of aerobic fitness training: Research and theory.* New York: Springer-Verlag.

McNair, D.M., Droppleman, L.F., & Lorr, M. (1981). *Manual for the Profile of Mood States.* San Diego, CA: Educational and Industrial Testing Service.

Merom, D., Phongsavan, P., Wagner, R., Chey, T., Marnane, C., Steel, Z., Silove, D., & Bauman, A. (2008). Promoting walking as an adjunct intervention to group cognitive behavioral therapy for anxiety disorders: A pilot group randomized trial. *Journal of Anxiety Disorders, 22,* 959–968.

Meyer, T., Broocks, A., Bandelow, B., Hillmer-Vogel, U., & Ruther, E. (1998). Endurance training in panic patients: Spiroergometric and clinical effects. *International Journal of Sports Medicine, 19,* 496–502.

Morgan, W.P., & Goldston, S.E. (Eds.). (1987). *Exercise and mental health.* Washington, DC: Hemisphere.

National Center for Health Statistics (1982–1995). National Health Interview Survey. Hyattsville, MD: U.S. Department of Health and Human Services.

O'Connor, P.J., Raglin, J.S., & Martinsen, E.W. (2000). Physical activity, anxiety and anxiety disorders. *International Journal of Sport Psychology, 31*(2), 136–155.

O'Connor, P.J., Smith, J.C., & Morgan, W.P. (2000). Physical activity does not provoke panic attacks in patients with panic disorder: A review of the evidence. *Anxiety, Stress and Coping, 13,* 333–353.

Petruzzello, S.J., Landers, D.M., Hatfield, B.D., Kubitz, K.A., & Salazar, W. (1991). A meta-analysis on the anxiety-reducing effects of acute and chronic exercise: Outcomes and mechanisms. *Sports Medicine, 11,* 143–182.

Petruzzello, S.J., Landers, D.M., & Salazar, W. (1993). Exercise and anxiety reduction: Examination of temperature as an explanation for affective change. *Journal of Sport and Exercise Psychology, 15,* 63–76.

Physical Activity Guidelines Advisory Committee (PAGAC) (2008). *Physical Activity Guidelines Advisory Committee Report, 2008.* Washington, DC: U.S. Department of Health and Human Services.

Raglin, J.S. (1997). Anxiolytic effects of physical activity. In W.P. Morgan (Ed.), *Physical activity and mental health* (pp. 107–126). Washington, DC: Taylor & Francis.

Raglin, J.S., & Morgan, W.P. (1987). Influence of exercise and quiet rest on state anxiety and blood pressure. *Medicine and Science in Sports and Exercise, 19,* 456–463.

Raglin, J.S., Turner, P.E., & Eksten, F. (1993). State anxiety and blood pressure following 30 min of leg ergometry or weight training. *Medicine & Science in Sports & Exercise, 25,* 1044–1048.

Regier, D.A., Farmer, M.E., Rae, D.S., Locke, B.Z., Keith, S.J., Judd, L.L., & Goodwin, F.K. (1990). Comorbidity of mental disorders with alcohol and other drug abuse: Results from the Epidemiologic Catchment Area (ECA) Study. *Journal of the American Medical Association, 264,* 2511–2518.

Regier, D.A., Narrow, W.E., Rae, D.S., Manderscheid, R.W., Locke, B.Z., & Goodwin, F.K. (1993). The de facto U.S. mental and addictive disorders service system: Epidemiologic Catchment Area prospective 1-year prevalence rates of disorders and services. *Archives of General Psychiatry, 50,* 85–94.

Rejeski, W.J., Hardy, C.J., & Shaw, J. (1991). Psychometric confounds of assessing state anxiety in conjunction with acute bouts of vigorous exercise. *Journal of Sport and Exercise Psychology, 13,* 65–74.

Ryan, A.J. (1983). Exercise is medicine. *Physician and Sportsmedicine, 11,* 10.

Salmon, P. (2001). Effects of physical exercise on anxiety, depression, and sensitivity to stress: A unifying theory. *Clinical Psychology Review, 21*(1), 33–61.

Schlicht, W. (1994). Does physical exercise reduce anxious emotions? A meta-analysis. *Anxiety, Stress and Coping, 6,* 275–288.

Sexton, H., Maere, A., & Dahl, N.H. (1989). Exercise intensity and reduction in neurotic symptoms. *Acta Psychiatrica Scandinavica, 80,* 231–235.

Spielberger, C.D. (1979). Preliminary manual for the State–Trait Personality Inventory (STPI). Unpublished manuscript.

Spielberger, C.D. (1983). *Manual for the State–Trait Anxiety Inventory (Form Y).* Palo Alto, CA: Consulting Psychologists Press.

Stephens, T. (1988). Physical activity and mental health in the United States and Canada: Evidence from four population surveys. *Preventive Medicine, 17,* 35–47.

Taylor, M.K., Pietrobon, R., Pan, D., Huff, M., & Higgins, L.D. (2004). Healthy People 2010 physical activity guidelines and psychological symptoms: Evidence from a large nationwide database. *Journal of Physical Activity & Health, 1,* 114–130.

U.S. Department of Health and Human Services. (1999). *Mental health: A report of the Surgeon General.* Rockville, MD: U.S. Department of Health and Human Services, Substance Abuse and Mental Health Services Administration, Center for Mental Health Services, National Institutes of Health, National Institute of Mental Health.

Wipfli, B.M., Rethorst, C.D., & Landers, D.M. (2008). The anxiolytic effects of exercise: A meta-analysis of randomized trials and dose-response analysis. *Journal of Sport & Exercise Psychology, 30,* 392–410.

Youngstedt, S.D., Dishman, R.K., Cureton, K.J., & Peacock, L.J. (1993). Does body temperature mediate anxiolytic effect of acute exercise? *Journal of Applied Physiology, 74,* 825–831.

Zuckerman, M., & Lubin, B. (1965). *Manual for the Multiple Affect Adjective Checklist.* San Diego, CA: Educational and Industrial Testing Service.

12

Depression and Exercise

KEY TERMS

anthropological hypothesis
bipolar disorder
cyclothymia
depressive disorder
disability adjusted life years (DALYs)
dysthymia
effect size
endorphin hypothesis
mastery hypothesis
moderating factors
monoamine hypothesis
neurogenesis
social interaction hypothesis

John retired from his job as a professor at the university in May. By the end of August, he is rather despondent. His wife, Mary, doesn't know what to do anymore. He frequently rises at 2:00 or 3:00 in the morning and then often sleeps two or three hours during the day. John has loads of free time to putter in his workshop, something he had always wanted to do but didn't have the time, but even this doesn't bring him any happiness. Finally, in a last effort to help, Mary makes an appointment for John to see a clinical psychologist. Susan, the psychologist is a firm believer in the value of exercise for helping those with depression, and she sees John as a perfect candidate. He hasn't been involved in any regular physical activity since his days as a college athlete. Susan suggests that John begin walking with Mary every night after dinner. She suggests this for two reasons: one, John will get started on an exercise program; two, he will be able to spend some time with Mary, who Susan senses is a supportive spouse who could be helpful in John's transition period. John is initially skeptical, but he takes the daily walk more to satisfy Mary than anything else. After the first few nights, however, John initiates the walk. Their walks become longer and then more vigorous, and within a few weeks John and Mary are walking for an hour at a time. Both start losing weight, and John's despondency noticeably improves. They become a regular fixture around the neighborhood during the late afternoons and early evenings.

> In all of my years on the trails and roadways, I have never seen depressed walkers.
>
> —KEITH W. JOHNSGARD (1989, p. 166)

I would like to suggest that running should be viewed as a wonder drug, analogous to penicillin, morphine, and the tricyclics. It has a profound potential in preventing mental and physical disease and in rehabilitation after various diseases have occurred.

—WILLIAM P. MORGAN (CITED IN JOHNSGARD, 1989, p. 119)

There are many ways to distract or self-medicate ourselves. Some eventually add to our misery, some are dangerous, and others are lethal. None can match the beneficence of physical activity.

—KEITH W. JOHNSGARD (2004, p. 273)

Defining Depression

According to the *Diagnostic and Statistical Manual of Mental Disorders,* 4th edition, Text Revision (DSM–IV-TR), depression falls under a category of mental disorders that the DSM classifies as "mood disturbances" and includes disorders that influence mood regulation *beyond the usual variations between sadness and happiness/excitement* (American Psychiatric Association, 1994, 2000). As such, depression is a mental disorder characterized primarily by altered mood. Four major mood disorders were covered in the first Surgeon General's Report on Mental Health, released at the end of the twentieth century (USDHHS, 1999). The four major disorders are **depressive disorder** (unipolar major depression), **bipolar disorder, dysthymia,** and **cyclothymia** (see Exhibit 12.1).

depressive disorder ■
bipolar disorder ■
dysthymia ■
cyclothymia ■

Definitions of depression can vary widely, "from episodes of unhappiness that affect most people from time to time, to persistent low mood and inability to find enjoyment" (Biddle & Mutrie, 2001, p. 207). Depression is often characterized by the presence of one or more of the following (see also Exhibit 12.2):

- sustained feelings of sadness or elation
- feelings of guilt or worthlessness
- disturbances in appetite
- disturbances in sleep patterns
- lack of energy (anergia)
- difficulty concentrating
- loss of interest in all or most activities
- problems with memory
- thoughts of suicide
- hallucinations

A student might be depressed upon receiving the results of an exam on which he did very poorly, but this usually subsides and motivates the student to

Characteristics of major depressive disorders. **exhibit 12.1**

MAJOR DEPRESSIVE DISORDER

- Depressed mood, loss of interest or pleasure are primary symptoms
  - Not driven by physiological causes (e.g., drugs) or medical condition (e.g., hypothyroidism)
- Other symptoms can vary widely
- Episodes last approximately nine months if untreated
  - 80 to 90 percent remit within two years of first episode
  - 50 percent will recur
- Symptoms cause significant impairment in social, work, or other important areas

BIPOLAR DISORDER

- One or more episodes of mania or mixed episodes of mania and depression
  - Mania can range from pure euphoria/elation to irritability
  - Thoughts are grandiose or delusional
  - Decreased need for sleep
  - Easily distracted, with racing thoughts
  - Excessive involvement in pleasurable activities that are likely to have painful consequences (e.g., unrestrained shopping spree, sexual indiscretions)
- Higher familial prevalence (i.e., stronger genetic component)

DYSTHYMIA

- Chronic form of depression
- Fewer than five persistent symptoms
- Duration of approximately two years for adults, approximately one year for children
- Increased susceptibility to major depression
- Seldom remits spontaneously
- Women twice as likely to be diagnosed as men

CYCLOTHYMIA

- Marked by manic and depressive states, but of insufficient intensity/duration to diagnose as bipolar or major depressive
- Increased risk of developing bipolar disorder

Source: USDHHS (1999, p. 247).

exhibit 12.2 DSM–IV criteria for major depressive disorders.

1. Depressed mood most of the day, nearly every day, as indexed by self-report or observations made by others
2. Diminished interest/pleasure in all or most activities, as indexed by self-report or observations of others
3. Significant weight loss when not dieting or weight gain (change of greater than 5 percent body weight in a month), decreased or increased appetite nearly every day
4. Insomnia or hypersomnia
5. Psychomotor agitation or retardation, observable by others
6. Fatigue or loss of energy when no physical work has been performed
7. Feelings of worthlessness or excessive/inappropriate guilt
8. Inability to think or concentrate
9. Recurrent thoughts of death or suicide

Note: Major depression may be diagnosed when five or more of the symptoms have been present during the same two-week period and represent a change from previous functioning. At least one of the symptoms is either depressed mood or loss of interest or pleasure.

Source: USDHHS (1999, p. 247).

study harder, take better notes, or be better prepared for the next exam. More severe depression might take the form of an unexplainably depressed mood. A student might be unable to concentrate sufficiently to work on an assignment, lack the motivation to begin or continue, and experience feelings of worthlessness because of this. Or, as in the case of John in the chapter-opening scenario, a person might lack interest in previously pleasurable activities.

Prevalence of Depression

The Surgeon General's Report on Mental Health (USDHHS, 1999) noted that mental illness is relatively prevalent in the United States. The disease burden that such disorders create has been seriously underestimated. **Disability adjusted life years (DALYs)** provide a measure of the disease burden (Murray & Lopez, 1996). DALYs estimate the years of healthy life lost due to premature death and years lived with a disability of specified severity and duration. Using DALYs, mental illnesses rank second only to cardiovascular problems in disease burden within industrialized nations. As noted in the Surgeon General's report, a number of mental illnesses (e.g., bipolar disorder, panic disorder, post-traumatic stress disorder, schizophrenia, obsessive–compulsive disorder) contribute significantly to the disease and disability burden attributed to these kinds of illnesses. Of the mental illnesses, major depression, when compared with different disease conditions,

disability adjusted life years (DALYs)

was second only to ischemic heart disease and ranked ahead of cardiovascular disease, alcohol use, and traffic accidents in disease and disability burden.

It has been repeatedly estimated that, every year, approximately 20 to 25 percent of adults in the United States suffer from some diagnosable form of mental health problem, including severe and disabling mental disorders (Centers for Disease Control and Prevention, 1998; Kessler, Chiu, Demler, et al., 2005). In adults, mood disorders (e.g., major depression, bipolar disorder) rank within the top 10 causes of disability worldwide (Murray & Lopez, 1996).

Two large, nationwide probability surveys published in the mid-1990s, and a third published in 2005 (Kessler et al., 2005), highlight the prevalence of such disabling mental conditions. The Epidemiological Catchment Area Study (Regier, Narrow, Rae, et al., 1993) estimated a 19.5 percent one-year prevalence rate for any mental disorder, including a 7.1 percent one-year prevalence rate for any mood disorder. The National Comorbidity Survey (Kessler, McGonagle, Zhao, et al., 1994) estimated a 23.4 percent one-year prevalence rate for any mental disorder, which means that within a given year, 23.4 percent of the U.S. adult population will have a diagnosable mental disorder. This translates to approximately 44 million people. This included an 11.1 percent one-year prevalence rate for any of the mood disorders. Findings from the National Comorbidity Survey Replication (Kessler et al., 2005) essentially mirrored the results of the original National Comorbidity Survey, with one-year prevalence estimates for any mental disorder rising somewhat to 26.2 percent. From these studies, best estimates of the one-year prevalence rates have been calculated to be 7.1 percent for any mood disorder (i.e., depressive disorders) and 21.0 percent for any mental disorder (USDHHS, 1999). It is worth pointing out that similar estimates obtained in the mid-1980s (Robins, Helzer, Weissman, et al., 1984) were notably lower (approximately 4 percent one-year prevalence), which prompted Thayer (2001) to speculate that an even greater increase might have occurred for mild to moderate depression. This seems to be supported by recent data (Kessler et al., 2005).

The prevalence of mood disorders creates an economic burden in terms of both mortality (i.e., depression-related suicides) and morbidity (i.e., direct medical costs, workplace costs). Estimates of this economic burden for depression went from approximately $44 billion in 1990 (Greenberg, Stiglin, Finkelstein, & Berndt, 1993) to more than $83 billion in 2000 (Greenberg, Kessler, Birnbaum, et al., 2003). In 1990, costs associated with depression broke down to about 28 percent spent for direct treatment and rehabilitation, 17 percent for mortality, and another 55 percent for both excessive absenteeism and reduced work productivity (Greenberg et al., 1993). In 2000, these costs changed somewhat, with about 31 percent spent for direct treatment and rehabilitation, 7 percent for mortality, and 62 percent for absenteeism and reduced work productivity (Greenberg et al., 2003). A study completed by Wang, Beck, Berglund, and colleagues (2004) specifically examined the effect of depression (and other chronic conditions such as allergies, asthma, back pain, and headaches) on work productivity. Of the conditions studied, depression was the only one associated with reduced productivity and task focus. Wang et al. (2004) estimated that this was equivalent to 2.3 days of absences from work each month. In addition, because depression significantly increases the risk of other potentially chronic diseases (e.g., cancer, cardiovascular disease), its costs go beyond the disease itself. As staggering as these figures are, they say nothing about the burdens created on the individuals and their families in terms of decreased quality of life.

Symptomatology

As indicated earlier, depression can be either a mental problem or a mental illness, and nonclinical or clinical depending on the severity and duration of symptoms. Clearly, not all forms of depression reach clinical levels. It is quite normal to experience sadness, distress, or grief in times of stress and during tragedy (e.g., death of a loved one, severe illness, job loss). Such instances of dysphoria (negative or aversive mood) are usually not as pervasive or as long lasting as when such symptoms reach clinical levels. As with clinical manifestations, symptoms of mild to moderate depression can include difficulty concentrating, disturbed sleep, changes in appetite, and fatigue or loss of energy (see Exhibit 12.2).

Causes

The causes of depression are not well understood. Both physiological and psychosocial factors interact, often in response to some stressful event in the person's life (e.g., death of a loved one, divorce, or retirement as in John's case in the chapter-opening scenario). As noted in the Surgeon General's report, there is tremendous individual variation in such responses. Factors such as heredity, coping skills, and social support influence the degree to which depression is manifested, or if it is manifested at all (USDHHS, 1999).

monoamine hypothesis

Investigations of the causes of depression have focused on biological factors like neurotransmitter deficiencies. For example, the **monoamine hypothesis** proposes that the cause for depression is depleted levels of the monoamines (the main neurotransmitters): serotonin, dopamine, norepinephrine, and epinephrine. The functions of neurotransmitters result in brain states like the level of arousal, attention, and coloring of information with emotion (USDHHS, 1999). Ultimately, the monoamine hypothesis has been found to be an insufficient explanation for depression because a complicated mental disorder like depression is a result of interactions among neurotransmitter levels, genetics, information from the environment, experience, gender, and social support. Certainly, understanding the causes of depression will be important in developing and refining the most appropriate and effective treatments, but there appears to be a long way to go before such discoveries are made.

Treatment

Although depression has been linked with mortality and morbidity worldwide (ESEMeD/MHEDEA 2000 Investigators, 2004; Lawlor & Hopker, 2001), it often goes untreated. When depressed individuals do seek help from a physician, it is often not for their depression. This reluctance to seek treatment is partly due to the stigma that is still associated with mental illness (USDHHS, 1999). When the depression is treated, it is often done through pharmacological means (e.g., antidepressant drugs like sertraline, imipramine). Often there is a lack of compliance when such drug treatments are prescribed (see Lawlor & Hopker). In addition, traditional treatment protocols (e.g., medication, psychotherapy) are often expensive; the costs include both the expense of the direct treatment and indirect costs such as lost productivity and reduced quality of life. For example, medications can often have unwanted side effects (e.g., drowsiness, weight gain, sexual side-effects), which can result in difficulty concentrating at work and an inability to perform normal functions effectively. Clearly, if other treatments can be shown to have utility in the management of mental disorders, at the very least these would provide additional options in the treatment toolbox for the therapist.

It has been suspected for quite some time, at least within the exercise science community, that physical activity might be a useful tool in both the prevention and treatment of depression. Much of the impetus for the work that has been done over the past 40 years could be traced back to the pioneering efforts of William P. Morgan. His early work noting the lower fitness levels in depressed patients compared with nonhospitalized controls (Morgan, 1968, 1969, 1970) is probably the earliest work in the modern era to demonstrate the potential utility of exercise in dealing with mental health problems. Before examining further the research that has used exercise in both the prevention and treatment of mental health problems, it would be instructive to discuss their assessment.

Measurement of Depression

In exercise depression research, depression is measured in two ways: (1) using standard classification criteria and determining if the individual satisfies these criteria through a clinician-administered interview and (2) using self-report measures.

Standard Classification Criteria

Easily the major tool in the diagnosis of mental disorders is the *Diagnostic and Statistical Manual of Mental Disorders,* 4th edition (DSM–IV, which has undergone a text revision; American Psychological Association, 1994, 2000). The DSM–IV-TR provides extensive guidelines for psychologists and psychiatrists to use in diagnosing and classifying nearly 400 mental disorders. The current diagnostic system allows for a detailed assessment, incorporating different aspects (mental, emotional, physical) of an individual's life, to provide the most complete context possible for making a proper diagnosis. The Research Diagnostic Criteria (RDC; Spitzer, Endicott, & Robins, 1978) and the International Classification of Diseases (ICD-10; World Health Organization, 1993) provide other standard classification criteria.

Self-Report Measures

Studies of clinical and mild to moderate depression employ a number of standardized self-report measures (i.e., questionnaires). Perhaps the two most common and well validated are the Beck Depression Inventory (BDI and the more recent BDI-II; Beck, Steer, & Brown, 1996) and the Zung Self-Rating Depression Scale. Other commonly used instruments include the Hamilton Depression Rating Scale (Hamilton, 1960), the Patient Health Questionnaire-9 (Kroenke, Spitzer, & Williams, 2001), the Symptom Rating Test (Kellner & Sheffield, 1973), the Depression subscale of the Profile of Mood States (POMS), the Geriatric Depression Scale, and the Center of Epidemiologic Studies–Depression (CES-D) scale.

The CES-D scale (see Exhibit 12.3) asks the individual to indicate how frequently he or she has experienced certain events over the past seven days, using a rating from 0 (rarely or none of the time, less than one day) to 3 (most or all of the time, five to seven days). All of these measures essentially derive a "level" of depression, with higher scores indicating greater levels of depression. For example, on the CES-D, scores could range from 0 to 60. A score of 16 or more indicates that the individual experienced some level of depression over the past week. It is important to note that a qualified mental health professional should be consulted to make a reliable clinical diagnosis of depression.

In many exercise studies, the depression score obtained on the questionnaire of choice is usually examined before and after a single bout of exercise or, more commonly, before and after some type of exercise training program lasting several weeks or months.

Research on Exercise and Depression

Since the late 1960s, systematic research has been conducted to examine the relationship between exercise and mental health. This section presents evidence for the beneficial effects of exercise on depression, from mild to moderate levels of depression to clinical manifestations of the disorder.

Physical activity/exercise has been shown to be a useful tool in the treatment of such mental disorders/disabilities, whether mild/moderate or severe, and it might be a useful treatment strategy when the goal is to return those who suffer from such debilitating mental problems to a more productive, independent lifestyle (PAGAC, 2008; this is not a universally accepted view, however. See deGeus & deMoor, 2008; Lawlor & Hopker, 2001; Salmon, 2001). There is even some evidence that physicians use exercise as at least part of the treatment for depressive disorders. A survey published in *The Physician and Sportsmedicine* (albeit a survey of physicians who read this particular publication, which may introduce at least some bias) revealed that of the 1,750 physicians who participated in the survey, 85 percent prescribed exercise for patients suffering from depression (Ryan, 1983). Perhaps more important, evidence from numerous epidemiological surveys indicates that a lifestyle of regular physical activity may be

Center for Epidemiologic Studies–Depression (CES-D) scale. **exhibit 12.3**

Below is a list of the ways you might have felt or behaved. Please tell me how often you have felt this way during the past week.

	DURING THE PAST WEEK			
	Rarely or none of the time (less than 1 day)	*Some or a little of the time (1–2 days)*	*Occasionally or a moderate amount of time (3–4 days)*	*Most or all of the time (5–7 days)*
1. I was bothered by things that usually don't bother me.	☐	☐	☐	☐
2. I did not feel like eating; my appetite was poor.	☐	☐	☐	☐
3. I felt that I could not shake off the blues even with help from my family or friends.	☐	☐	☐	☐
4. I felt that I was just as good as other people.	☐	☐	☐	☐
5. I had trouble keeping my mind on what I was doing.	☐	☐	☐	☐
6. I felt depressed.	☐	☐	☐	☐
7. I felt that everything I did was an effort.	☐	☐	☐	☐
8. I felt hopeful about the future.	☐	☐	☐	☐
9. I thought my life had been a failure.	☐	☐	☐	☐
10. I felt fearful.	☐	☐	☐	☐
11. My sleep was restless.	☐	☐	☐	☐
12. I was happy.	☐	☐	☐	☐
13. I talked less than usual.	☐	☐	☐	☐
14. I felt lonely.	☐	☐	☐	☐
15. People were unfriendly.	☐	☐	☐	☐
16. I enjoyed life.	☐	☐	☐	☐
17. I had crying spells.	☐	☐	☐	☐
18. I felt sad.	☐	☐	☐	☐
19. I felt that people disliked me.	☐	☐	☐	☐
20. I could not get "going."	☐	☐	☐	☐

SCORING: Zero for answers in the first column, 1 for answers in the second column, 2 for answers in the third column, 3 for answers in the fourth column. The scoring of positive items is reversed. Possible range of scores is zero to 60, with the higher scores indicating the presence of more symptomatology.

Source: National Institute of Mental Health (NIMH).

exhibit 12.4

Prevalence of major depressive disorder in adults based on frequency of self-reported physical activity.

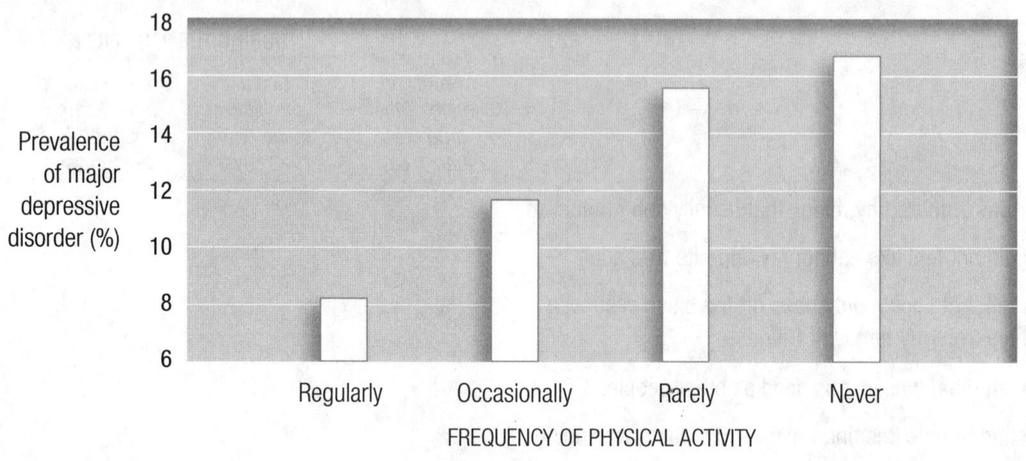

Source: Adapted from Goodwin (2003).

influential in preventing such debilitating mental disorders from developing or at least reducing the risk of such disorders. This has particular importance, because as Morgan (1994) pointed out, the widespread nature of depression makes both pharmacological and psychotherapeutic treatments less desirable owing to the time, money, and potential side effects involved.

Evidence for Preventive Effects

Numerous cross-sectional epidemiological studies have examined the role of exercise in promoting and maintaining mental health (preventing mental illness). Stephens (1988), in four separate samples of U.S. and Canadian adults (sample size ranging from 3,025 to 23,791), found self-reported physical activity to be associated with better mental health, which included fewer symptoms of anxiety and depression. In another sample, Hassmen, Koivula, and Uutela (2000) noted that Finnish adults who exercised less frequently (fewer than 2–3 times per week) had greater reporting of depressive symptoms on the Beck Depression Inventory discussed earlier, a commonly used tool for assessing such symptoms.

Goodwin's (2003) analysis of the National Comorbidity Survey data from almost 6,000 adults ages 15 to 54 years old (57 percent female), showed a dose–response relationship with major depression, dysthymia, and bipolar disorder. In each case, the likelihood of experiencing the mental disorder increased as frequency of self-reported physical activity decreased—from regularly, to occasionally, to rarely, to never (see Exhibit 12.4). In a similarly large sample (approximately 6,700; 19 percent female), Galper, Trivedi, Barlow, and colleagues (2006) examined relationships between cardiorespiratory fitness and habitual physical activity with depressive symptoms as assessed via the CES-D (data taken from the Aerobics Center Longitudinal Study). Again, a dose–response relationship emerged for the fitness–depressive symptoms relationship (in both men and women) such that high cardiorespiratory fitness was associated with the lowest depressive symptomatology, low fitness was associated with the highest symptomatology, and moderate fitness was in between. Habitual physical activity showed a similar graded relationship with depressive symptoms. As level of activity went from "inactive" (defined as less than one mile per week of walking, jogging or running), to "insufficiently active" (1 to 10 miles per week), to either "sufficiently active" or "highly active" (more than 10 miles per week), depressive symptoms decreased significantly, with little difference between sufficiently active and highly active.

A number of prospective studies have provided further evidence for a link between physical activity and depression prevention. Prospective studies are able to examine how the risk of developing depression plays out over a period of time. Farmer and colleagues (1988) found that women who were sedentary or engaged in little activity were twice as likely to develop depression (measured using the CES-D) over an eight-year follow-up period as those who were at least moderately active. Furthermore, inactivity at baseline was a strong predictor of continued depression at follow-up. In the Alameda County Study, Camacho, Roberts, Lazarus, and colleagues (1991) found an association between inactivity and incidence of depression from 1965 to 1983. The relative risk of developing depression was significantly greater for men and women at both follow-up periods (1974, 1983) if they had been inactive in 1965. Those who were inactive at baseline but who had become active (at either moderate or high levels) by one of the follow-up periods were at no greater risk than were those who were active at baseline, highlighting the potential importance of physical activity in warding off depression. Similarly, Paffenbarger, Lee, and Leung (1994), in a sample of more than 21,000 college alumni, found that physical activity at baseline was negatively associated with depression 25 years later (i.e., more activity predicted lower depression). Mobily, Rubenstein, Lemke, O'Hara, and Wallace (1996), in a sample of 2,084 older men and women, found that, of individuals who reported (using the CES-D) greater numbers of depressive symptoms at baseline, those who subsequently became daily walkers had a greater likelihood of reduced depressive symptoms at the three-year follow-up. Finally, Lampinen, Heikkinen, and Ruoppila (2000) examined physical activity and depressive symptoms in 663 Finnish adults from 1988 to 1996. Their findings revealed that those individuals who reduced the intensity of their exercise over the eight-year span of the study had greater symptoms of depression (measured with a modified version of the Beck Depression Inventory). In contrast, those participants who either increased the level of their activity or at least maintained the same level showed reduced depressive symptoms.

A study by Motl, Birnbaum, Kubik, and Dishman (2004) examined the relationships between physical activity and depression (as measured by the CES-D scale; Exhibit 12.3) in a sample of 4,594 adolescents over a two-year period. They found that both initial levels of physical activity and changes in level of physical activity were associated with levels of depression. Specifically, those adolescents who were more physically active initially had lower levels of depression. Also, those who became less active over time had increased levels of depression, whereas those who became more active over time had decreased levels of depression.

All together, these cross-sectional and prospective studies show an association between (lack of) activity and depression across the age spectrum. Specifically, people who are less active or sedentary are at greater risk for depression than are people who are more active. Said another way, physical activity seems to offer a defense against depressive symptoms (PAGAC, 2008). Perhaps not surprisingly, the connection between the growing lack of physical activity and increasing incidence and prevalence of mental health problems in industrialized nations has led numerous investigators to suggest that the decline of physical activity is largely responsible for the rise of mental health problems (Johnsgard, 1989, 2004; Martinsen, 2002; Thayer, 2001). The consistent finding has been that the least active individuals have the greatest incidence of mental health problems. Thus, regular physical activity can potentially be useful in preventing mental disorders or in reducing their risk of occurrence.

Evidence for Use of Exercise as Treatment

Although the evidence for preventive effects of exercise on depression is noteworthy, whether exercise can be a useful treatment once mental disorders, and in particular severely disabling forms of such disorders, have manifested themselves is a question that is still being addressed in ongoing research. Research examining the utility of exercise in treating samples with clinical manifestations of depression has not been extensive, especially compared to research examining the effects of exercise on reducing depressive symptoms in nonclinical samples. However, there has been a more concerted effort of late to examine the efficacy of exercise as another therapeutic option for treating clinical depression. The exercise–depression literature includes studies examining exercise effects on those with mild to moderate levels of depression and on clinical samples. Clearly, some evidence suggests that exercise can be useful in the treatment of clinical as well as nonclinical depression. In his book *The Exercise Prescription for Depression and Anxiety,* clinical psychologist Keith Johnsgard (1989) cites numerous case study examples of how exercise has been useful in the treatment of both anxiety and mood disorders in his patients. The box on page 325 presents a synopsis of one of the cases.

Other, more carefully controlled studies have highlighted the utility of such an "exercise prescription." Research summaries of the exercise–depression literature have taken the form of both the more traditional "narrative" reviews and the more recently used "quantitative" reviews, commonly referred to as *meta-analyses* (see box in Chapter 5). In the following sections, we examine the evidence found in some of these studies for the effectiveness of exercise in reducing symptoms of depression.

Sample Case Study Synopsis

One of Johnsgard's cases involved a man who had lost his wife to suicide and who was struggling with a great deal of depression and guilt. Johnsgard prescribed a two-pronged approach to treatment: symptom prescription and exercise therapy. The symptom prescription involved requiring the patient to ruminate for an hour each day on nothing but his guilt feelings. The exercise therapy involved walking/jogging for the same hour each day. Johnsgard is convinced that the two treatments had a substantive interaction effect. The patient "recovered" fairly quickly, with Johnsgard noting that the patient came to realize that he had control over his guilt ruminations. The exercise had an effect of its own as well. Johnsgard speculated that the exercise might have resulted in greater activation of the antidepressant neurotransmitters in the patient's brain, that the tranquilizing effect of the exercise allowed the individual to sleep better, and that the patient had more energy.

Source: Johnsgard (1989).

Depression reduction

This section reviews what is currently known regarding the effects of exercise on depressive symptoms. The first quantitative review of this literature appeared in 1990 in a meta-analysis by North, McCullagh, and Tran, but several substantive meta-analytic reviews have appeared since. Although the North review was important as the first quantitative review of the exercise–depression literature, it was limited in that it mixed subject samples who were not diagnosed or classified with clinical depression (i.e., at least mild to moderate depression) with those who were. For example, 22 studies used subjects classified as either depressed or "feeling down," 39 studies used "apparently healthy" or athlete samples, and 11 studies used patient samples (i.e., undergoing hemodialysis, post myocardial infarction, schizophrenic). This limitation notwithstanding, based on the effect sizes, the primary findings reported by North and colleagues were:

1. Exercise resulted in decreased depression.
2. Certain factors moderated exercise treatment effects while others did not.
3. Exercise was as effective as, and sometimes more effective than, traditional therapies (e.g., medication, psychotherapy).

Subsequent meta-analyses, which have included only studies examining participants diagnosed as having depression, have essentially confirmed these findings (e.g., Craft & Landers, 1998; Lawlor & Hopker, 2001; PAGAC, 2008).

Decreased depression. Perhaps the most important finding from these reviews is that exercise results in decreased depression, yielding a fairly substantial effect. This is interpreted to mean that depression is reduced fairly sizably as a result of exercise of some sort.

Exercise and Participant Variables

FROM THE META-ANALYSES STUDYING THE EFFECTS OF EXERCISE ON DEPRESSION

EXERCISE VARIABLES

■ *Mode of exercise.* One important factor was whether the kind of exercise matters. North and colleagues (1990) found no differences among various modes of exercise, although only two studies (out of 66) examined nonaerobic types of exercise. Subsequent reviews have confirmed this finding (Craft & Landers, 1998, Lawlor & Hopker, 2001; PAGAC, 2008; Rethorst, Wipfli, & Landers, 2009). Thus, whether people engage in weight training, walking, jogging, or various other aerobic activities, the reduction of depression appears to be similar. Although requiring further examination, it is potentially interesting that the PAGAC (2008) review noted a larger reduction in depression occurring for continuous exercise activities as opposed to intermittent activity.

■ *Length of exercise program.* In studies examining exercise training, the length of the exercise program was apparently not as important as "just doing it." On examining programs ranging in length from fewer than four weeks to more than 24 weeks, no one particular program length resulted in greater reductions in depression than any other. It is interesting to note, from the effect sizes presented in North et al. (1990), Craft and Landers (1998), and Rethorst et al. (2009), that it appears that as the length of the program increases, particularly with clinically depressed samples, the degree of depression reduction also increases. Because so few studies have examined longer exercise programs, however, the apparently greater reduction in depression seen in longer exercise programs warrants further investigation. Of note, the Lawlor and Hopker (2001) review found no difference across interventions ranging from fewer than eight weeks to more than eight weeks, although their analysis indicated the depression-reducing effect actually weakened as the intervention length increased.

■ *Exercise intensity.* Findings for other important exercise variables have not been as consistent as the findings for mode and length of the exercise program. Exercise intensity, a factor important to developing the most effective exercise prescription, has not been examined consistently enough (or, more likely, not reported consistently enough) for any comparisons to be made. However, a recent study by Chu, Buckworth, Kirby, and Emery (2009) did explicitly examine different levels of exercise intensity in women with mild to moderate depressive symptoms. Participants were randomly assigned to one

Moderating factors. As stated in Chapter 5, *moderating factors* are variables that could influence or "moderate" the treatment effects. In these quantitative reviews, the moderating factors considered were (1) exercise variables and (2) participant variables (see the above box).

Effectiveness of exercise versus traditional treatments. Reviews have also examined the effectiveness of exercise compared to other typical treatments for depression. It has been noted that exercise reduced depression better than did no treatment, a waiting list control treatment (designed to control for expectancy effects; see the box on page 328), and other enjoyable activities (i.e., nonexercise activities of choice). Exercise has been shown to be as effective as more tradition-of three 10-week treatment groups: a stretching control group, a low-intensity aerobic exercise group (40–55 percent $\dot{V}O_2$reserve), or a high-intensity aerobic exercise group (65–75 percent $\dot{V}O_2$reserve). Groups met once each week for a supervised session (30–40 minutes of treadmill exercise for the exercise groups, 30 minutes of stretching and flexibility for the control group) and then were to complete three to four unsupervised sessions on their own. Results showed a significant reduction in depressive symptoms for all three groups; additional analyses revealed significantly fewer symptoms in the high-intensity exercise group at both 5 and 10 weeks of training compared to the low-intensity and control groups, which were not significantly different from one another. Although the higher-intensity exercise training resulted in a greater reduction of depressive symptoms, this change was unrelated to changes in fitness. Coupled with the conclusion from the Physical Activity Guidelines Advisory Committee Report (PAGAC, 2008), more systematic work is needed to delineate the optimal intensity needed for depression reduction.

■ *Duration or frequency.* As for duration or frequency of exercise bouts, neither had any systematic influence on degree of depression reduction. Clearly, much work remains to be done to uncover any systematic influences of the exercise "dose."

■ *Acute versus chronic.* Another factor of interest in the meta-analysis was whether the exercise was acute or chronic. The depression reduction occurred for both acute and chronic exercise; in other words, depression was reduced following single bouts of exercise and following longer-term programs of physical activity.

PARTICIPANT VARIABLES

In addition to studying exercise variables, quantitative reviews have been able to examine a variety of participant variables that might serve as moderating factors, including age, gender, and race/ethnicity.

■ *Age.* It apparently doesn't matter whether participants are young (less than 18 years old), college-aged (18 to 24 years old), or middle-aged (25 to 64 years of age): exercise appears to result in decreased depression for all ages.

■ *Gender.* The anti-depressant effect was similar for both men and women.

■ *Race/ethnicity.* A final participant variable of interest is whether depression reduction differs based on race or ethnicity. The PAGAC review (2008) concluded that, because of poor reporting of the racial and/or ethnic makeup of participant samples, it is difficult to make any conclusions to date regarding any moderation of exercise effects based on race or ethnicity.

al therapies such as relaxation, psychotherapy, and in some instances medication (see below for more extended discussion of this issue). Pinquart, Duberstein, and Lyness (2007) presented a less positive review, however. Their quantitative review of interventions used in clinically depressed older adults noted that physical exercise had a medium effect size and concluded that "the available data suggest that cognitive and/or behavioral treatments are more effective than physical exercise" (p. 652) at reducing depression.

Finally, exercise in conjunction with psychotherapy yielded the best depression-reducing effects. Perhaps the strongest conclusion to be taken from the meta-analysis by North et al. (1990) is that exercise can apparently be a cost-effective treatment for depression. Exercise also has the added benefit of improved

Waiting List Control

In a waiting list control, individuals are recruited to a study with the understanding that there is currently no room for them in the treatment protocol, but that as soon as there is room they will be included. Thus, the individual has an expectancy of being a participant in the study protocol and should respond in ways that the actual participants would, with the exception of any actual treatment effects. Ethically, at the conclusion of the experimental protocol, these waiting list control subjects should be offered the opportunity to receive the actual treatment protocol.

physical health, which can of course help in the prevention of an ever-expanding list of physical maladies. Although reviews are no substitute for original research, they do provide answers to questions and highlight deficiencies in the literature (see also Biddle & Mutrie, 2001).

Clinical depression

As pointed out in the meta-analytic review of exercise effects on clinical depression by Craft and Landers (1998), changes in the health-care climate with respect to limits on treatment therapies (in terms of both time and money) highlight the need for examination of other, less costly treatment options. As with nonclinical levels of depression, exercise has been used, and is being examined more frequently, as a viable option for the treatment of clinical levels of depression (Berk, 2007; Brosse, Sheets, Lett, & Blumenthal, 2002; Dunn, Trivedi, & O'Neal, 2001; O'Neal, Dunn, & Martinsen, 2000). With the aggregate findings presented above as a background, we now examine the effects of exercise on clinical depression in several select studies.

In perhaps the classic exercise–depression study, Greist and colleagues (1979) compared the effects of running to time-limited and time-unlimited psychotherapy in patients with minor clinical depression as defined by research diagnostic criteria (RDC). Time-limited psychotherapy involves receiving therapy for a specific amount of time (e.g., 16 weeks), whereas time-unlimited psychotherapy does not put time constraints on the therapy. The running treatment (three times per week for 12 weeks) was shown to be as effective as both forms of psychotherapy, with continued improvement at a three-week follow-up.

Martinsen and colleagues have also contributed greatly to our knowledge regarding exercise effects in patients suffering from anxiety and depressive disorders. Martinsen, Medhus, and Sandvik (1985) studied the effects of aerobic exercise in 43 hospitalized psychiatric patients diagnosed with major depression (classified according to DSM–III criteria). Individuals were randomly assigned to either exercise or occupational therapy (control) groups in addition to standard psychotherapy and pharmacotherapy for nine weeks. The exercise group patients had significant reductions in depressive symptoms relative to the control group. Interestingly, patients rated exercise as the most important component of the comprehensive treatment they received. More than 90 percent of the subjects continued to exercise regularly on their own, with 65 percent exercising aerobically for two or more hours per week one to two years later.

Martinsen, Hoffart, and Solberg (1989) demonstrated that both aerobic and nonaerobic (muscular strength, flexibility) exercise resulted in significant psychological improvements in 99 clinically depressed in-patients who met DSM–III-R criteria for major depression, dysthymic disorder, or nonspecified depressive disorders. Singh, Clements, and Fiatarone (1997) conducted a randomized, controlled trial with 32 individuals (who averaged 71.3 years of age) diagnosed with major or minor depression or dysthymia (DSM–IV criteria). A randomized controlled trial is the best experimental design, because individuals are selected to represent accurately the population from which they are drawn, and then these individuals are randomly assigned to either the treatment or a control condition. In this study, the exercise involved a 10-week program of supervised progressive resistance training (three times per week). An attention-control group, designed to prevent expectancy effects, met twice a week and received lectures and videos on health education. Exercise patients had significant reductions in depression, as measured by the BDI and Hamilton Depression Rating Scale, compared with controls after the 10-week intervention. A significant increase in strength was seen in the exercise group, with intensity of training serving as a significant predictor of depression reduction. In other words, people who trained harder had greater reductions in depression, a finding that may have dose-response implications.

Singh, Clements, and Fiatarone Singh (2001) reported in a follow-up study that the 10 weeks of supervised weight lifting was followed by 10 weeks of unsupervised exercise. Exercise patients had significant reductions in BDI depression compared with controls at both 20 weeks and 26 months of follow-up. Nearly 75 percent of the exercise patients were no longer classified as depressed based on BDI scores, compared to 36 percent of control patients. See Exhibit 12.5.

Results of the Singh, Clements and Fiatarone Singh (2001) study. **exhibit 12.5**

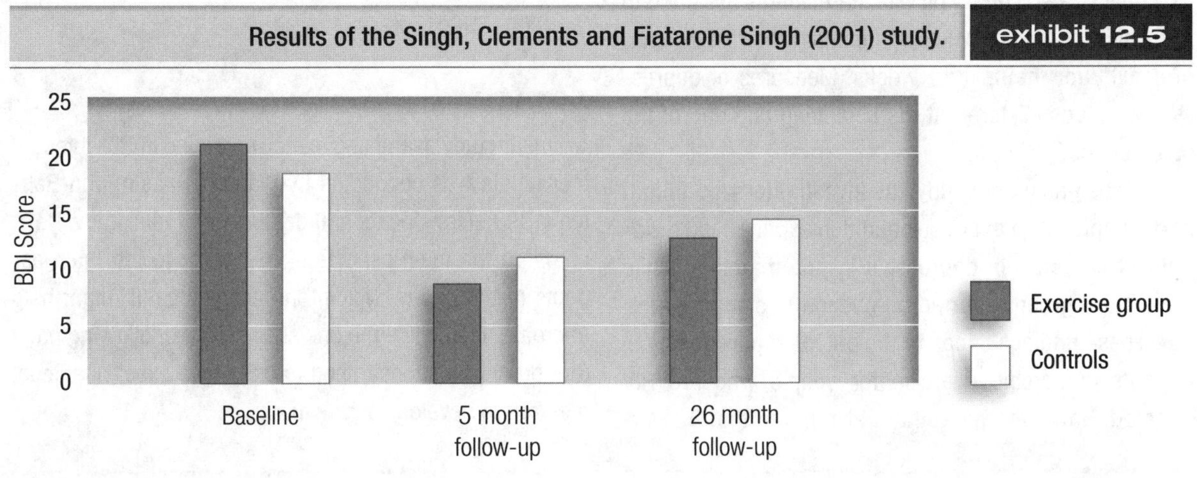

FOCUS on Human Immunodeficiency Virus (HIV)

Among people living with HIV—the virus that causes acquired immunodeficiency syndrome (AIDS)—depression is the most common reason for psychiatric evaluation and treatment. Depression is reported among HIV-infected persons at nearly twice the rate reported by the general population (Kessler, et al., 1994). Indeed, in a nationally representative study of adults receiving care for HIV infection in the United States, more than one third experienced clinical depression during the previous 12 months (Bing, Burnam, Longshore, et al., 2001). This is cause for concern given that depressive symptoms might be associated with more rapid immune decline, accelerated mortality, and drug nonadherence in HIV patients. Thus, it is important to find strategies to manage and alleviate depressive symptomatology in this population.

Neidig and her colleagues examined whether aerobic exercise could reduce depressive symptomatology in adults infected with HIV (Neidig, Smith, & Brashers, 2003). Sixty patients were randomly assigned to a 12-week aerobic exercise–training program or to a waiting list (control condition). Those in the exercise condition attended three supervised one-hour training sessions per week that involved aerobic activity performed on a treadmill or a stationary bicycle. Participants assigned to the waiting list were asked to maintain their usual level of activity for the next 12 weeks. Measures of depression were administered at the beginning and end of the study period.

At the end of the study, the investigators found that participants in the exercise condition experienced a significant decrease in depressive symptomatology while the control group reported no change in symptomatology. These findings speak to the potential psychological benefits of aerobic exercise for people who are HIV infected. However, the authors also noted that 40 percent of people assigned to the exercise condition were unable to complete the study. Those who dropped out were often among the working poor and reported abrupt changes in employment, unreliable transportation, and increased family responsibilities as reasons for study withdrawal. Therefore, although exercise training does seem to be effective for reducing depression in people who are HIV-positive, transportation, child care, and other services may need to be provided to help less economically advantaged individuals reap the benefit of exercise.

ADDITIONAL RESOURCES

Ciccolo, J.T., Jowers, E.M., & Bartholomew, J.B. (2004). The benefits of exercise training for quality of life in HIV/AIDS in the post-HAART era. *Sports Medicine, 34,* 487–499.

Lox, C.L., McAuley, E., & Tucker, R.S. (1995). Exercise as an intervention for enhancing subjective well-being in an HIV-1 population. *Journal of Sport and Exercise Psychology, 17,* 345–362.

Nixon, S., O'Brien, K., Glazier, R.H., & Tynan, A.M. (2005). Aerobic exercise interventions for adults living with HIV/AIDS. *Cochrane Database of Systematic Reviews, 18*(2), CD001796.

ACTIVITY

A similar study examining exercise training in HIV-infected individuals was conducted by Wagner, Rabkin, and Rabkin (1998). First, locate and get a copy of this study. Next, compare the main aspects of this study to the main aspects of the one by Neidig and colleagues. It might help to create a table like the one shown on the following page (but do not feel constrained to use these exact headings; feel free to develop your own).

Study	Participant sample (describe in terms of age, gender, etc.)	Exercise (length, intensity, duration, etc.)	Depression measure(s)	Main results
Neidig et al.				
Wagner et al.				

Using the information in the table, compare and contrast the two studies. From this analysis, what conclusions might you draw regarding the effects of exercise on depression in individuals with HIV?

In another study designed to examine the utility of exercise as a potential treatment for mild to moderate major depressive disorder, Dunn and colleagues (2005) randomly assigned 80 adults (20–45 years of age) to one of four different exercise treatments or to an exercise placebo control (stretching and flexibility) condition. The exercise treatments varied by their total energy expenditure (low dose: 7 kcal/kg/week; "public health dose": 17.5 kcal/kg/week) and frequency (three or five days per week). The "public health dose" (PHD) was designed to be consistent with public health recommendations for physical activity. Thus, the four exercise conditions were low dose (LD) for either three (LD/3) or five (LD/5) days per week, or PHD for either three (PHD/3) or five (PHD/5) days per week. This allowed an assessment of whether a dose-response relationship existed between exercise and depression reduction. Using the Hamilton Depression Rating Scale as the primary outcome measure of depression, Dunn and colleagues showed a 47 percent reduction in depression for the PHD condition following 12 weeks of treatment, a reduction significantly greater than that seen in the other treatment conditions; there was no effect of frequency (i.e., PHD/3 and PHD/5 were not different). Furthermore, 42 percent of the PHD participants had remission of depressive symptoms. Both the LD and the placebo conditions showed reductions in depression, although the reductions were not significantly different from one another (30 percent and 29 percent respectively).

Blumenthal, Babyak, Moore, and colleagues (1999), in their Standardized Medical Intervention and Long-term Exercise (SMILE) study, randomly placed 156 patients with major depressive disorder in one of three 16-week treatments:

1. exercise training (three times per week at 70 to 85 percent of maximum heart rate)

2. pharmacotherapy (sertraline, an antidepressant medication)
3. combined exercise and pharmacotherapy

At the conclusion of the 16-week treatment period, Blumenthal et al. noted that there were significant reductions in depressive symptoms for all three treatment groups. More specifically, 60 percent of the participants in the exercise training group, 66 percent in the combined exercise and therapy group, and 69 percent in the pharmacotherapy group were classified as no longer being clinically depressed as rated by a clinician who didn't know which group the participants were in. The clinician's rating was made based on DSM-IV criteria for major depression disorder. When the clinician's rating was combined with a Hamilton Depression score of 6 or more, the percentage in each group deemed no longer clinically depressed dropped somewhat (47 percent in the exercise and combined treatment groups, 56 percent in the pharmacotherapy group), but there were still no significant differences among the treatment groups.

Blumenthal et al. did note that there were differences in response to the various treatments over time. Specifically, the medication treatment group showed the fastest decrease in symptoms, with the greatest difference occurring by week 4. However, by the end of the treatment protocol, all three treatments had reduced depressive symptoms to an equivalent level. They also noted that those who were less severely depressed at treatment onset showed a more rapid reduction in depressive symptoms, but again all three treatments resulted in similar depressive symptom reduction by the end of the 16-week treatment intervention. The bottom line from this particular study is that exercise, as a treatment for clinical levels of depression, was as effective as both the drug and the combined drug and exercise treatments at the end of the 4-month treatment intervention.

In a follow-up with 133 of the original 156 participants six months after completion of the formal treatment phase, Babyak, Blumenthal, Herman, et al. (2000) found that the exercise-group participants had lower rates of depression (30 percent) than either those in the medication (52 percent) or combination (55 percent) groups when the presence of major depressive disorder was defined by either an interviewer diagnosis (DSM–IV criteria) or a Hamilton Depression Rating Scale score of greater than 7. Perhaps even more revealing is what happened to the 83 patients who were assessed as being in remission at the end of the formal treatment phase (at four months). To be classified as being in remission meant that the individual no longer met DSM–IV criteria for major depressive disorder and had a Hamilton Depression Rating Scale score of less than 8 after the treatment. At the six-month post-treatment follow-up, those in the exercise group were significantly more likely to be either fully or partially recovered, with only 8 percent experiencing a relapse (i.e., recurrence of depression). By contrast, 38 percent of those in the medication group and 31 percent in the combination exercise–medication group had relapsed six months after the end of formal treatment (see Exhibit 12.7). Babyak and colleagues noted that continuing to exercise on one's own was related to a reduced likelihood of being diagnosed as depressed even after formal treatment had stopped.

In spite of the positive effects of exercise in the Blumenthal et al. (1999) and Babyak et al. (2000) studies, not having a control group meant the researchers were not able to rule out alternative explanations for the outcomes (e.g., research staff attention and support, statistical regression toward the mean). In an effort to ascribe depression reduction more definitively to the treatment itself, Blumenthal, Babyak, Doraiswamy, and colleagues (2007) conducted a prospective, randomized controlled trial with 202 adults (153 females) diagnosed with major depressive disorder. These individuals were randomly assigned to one of four possible treatment conditions: supervised group exercise (45 minutes of walking/jogging on a treadmill at 70–85 percent heart rate reserve [included a 10-minute warm-up and 5-minute cool-down], three times per week for 16 weeks); home-based exercise (same exercise as the supervised group, but done at home with little contact from research staff); anti-depressant medication (daily

Status of patients diagnosed as remitted following four months of either exercise, medication, or an exercise-and-medication combined treatment when reassessed six months following the end of treatment. exhibit 12.7

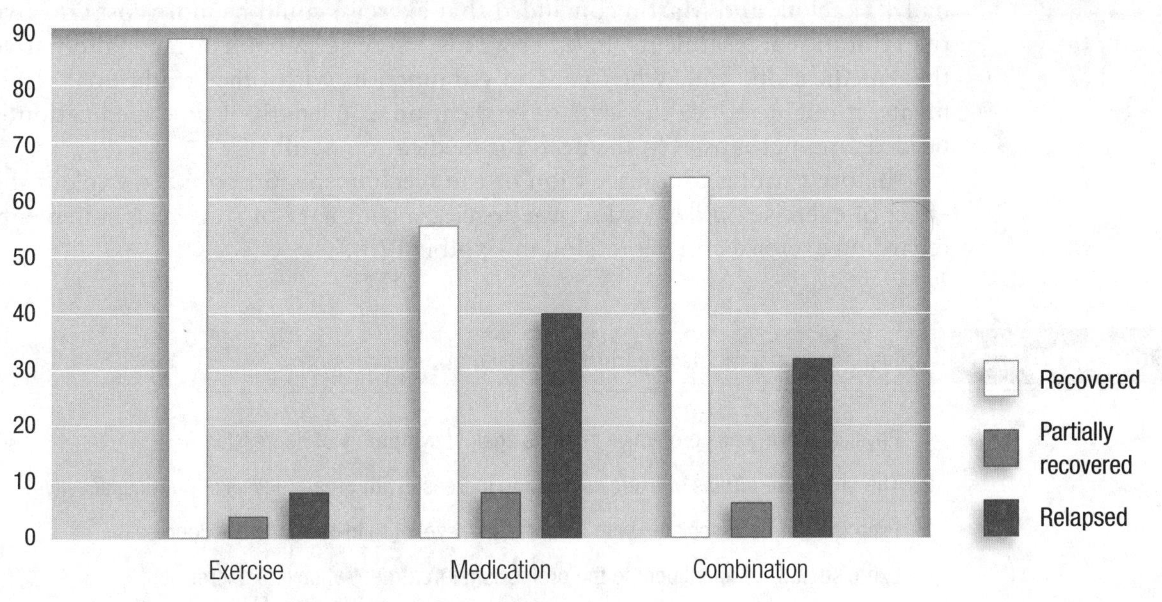

From Babyak et al. (2000). Exercise treatment for major depression: Maintenance of therapeutic benefit at 10 months. *Psychosomatic Medicine, 62*(5), 633–638. Reprinted with permission of the author.

dosage dependent on response; initial dose of 50 mg with additional dosages up to 200 mg); and placebo group (identical pill as the anti-depressant condition without active medication). Both "drug" conditions were administered in double-blind fashion. Results indicated that the exercise treatments were similar to the anti-depressant medication, with all three resulting in greater depression reduction compared to the placebo group (40 to 47 percent vs. 31 percent). Blumenthal et al. (2007) noted, however, that depression reduction was reasonably high in the placebo group, leading to the conclusion that at least a portion of the "therapeutic response" could have been caused by expectations on the part of the individual, attention from research staff, and monitoring of symptoms throughout the study.

In light of the generally positive findings, Tkachuk and Martin (1999) noted in their review of the literature that significant improvements could be obtained in those who are clinically depressed. Such improvements were seen with exercise training of:

1. at least five weeks duration
2. three times per week of supervised aerobic or nonaerobic activity
3. low to moderate intensity (50 percent maximum heart rate)
4. durations of 20 to 60 minutes

Follow-up assessments have shown maintenance of improvements up to one year post-treatment, particularly when some level of activity is continued. Finally, Tkachuk and Martin concluded that exercise could be more cost effective than traditional treatments. In other words, exercise can be a cheaper alternative than medication, and, when used in conjunction with other traditional treatments, it might reduce the level of medication, the length of time medication is needed, and perhaps even the need for medication at all.

Before turning to a discussion of the mechanisms proposed to explain the effect of exercise on depression, we provide a summary of consensus statements regarding exercise and depression in Exhibit 12.8.

exhibit 12.8 **Consensus statements regarding exercise and depression.**

1. Physical activity has protective benefits against symptoms of depression.
2. The protective effects of exercise seem to increase with greater levels of physical activity.
3. Exercise can be associated with a decreased level of mild-to-moderate depression.
4. Exercise may be an adjunct to the professional treatment of severe depression.
5. Optimal types and/or amounts of physical activity are not known.

Source: Adapted from Morgan & Goldston (1987) and PAGAC (2008).

Mechanisms of Change

As the research discussed in the preceding section shows, a primary objective of the work examining the effects of exercise on depression is "simply" to demonstrate that there is an effect. Equally important is the interest in understanding why such changes occur. Pursuing this understanding often involves the search for the mechanisms underlying such effects. In the domain of exercise and depression reduction, a number of plausible mechanisms have been discussed, and research is beginning to examine such possibilities systematically. Among these mechanisms are those that are primarily physiological in nature on the one hand, and those that are primarily psychological on the other. The ultimate explanation will likely not be one or the other, but rather a combination of biopsychosocial explanations. (Many of these same explanations are also posited to explain the reductions in anxiety associated with exercise; see Chapter 11.)

Anthropological hypothesis

■ anthropological hypothesis

Labeled the **anthropological hypothesis** (Martinsen, 2002), one potential explanation for the link between physical activity and depression reflects an evolutionary perspective. As Martinsen has pointed out, humans have spent the vast majority of their existence in lifestyles that emphasize physical activity. Whether as hunter–gatherers or even as recently as in the early twentieth century, when manual labor still predominated, our lifestyles typically required large amounts of physical activity on a daily basis. Only within the last 50–75 years or so has technology progressed to the point that such vigorous forms of activity are no longer necessary for our survival. Interestingly, it is also within the past 50–75 years or so that incidences of depression have increased dramatically. It seems highly unlikely that this has been coincidental. Given the epidemiological evidence linking physical activity with decreased depression, it may very well be that we are "violating our genetic warranty" (Johnsgard, 1989, 2004) by not engaging in more regular physical activity. In other words, the anthropological hypothesis suggests that human beings are genetically designed to be physically active. If we violate this genetic predisposition by being sedentary, then perhaps it is not surprising that we subsequently face a host of health problems, including depression.

Endorphin hypothesis

■ endorphin hypothesis

The explanation for the depression-reducing effects of exercise that clearly has been the most popular with the media is the **endorphin hypothesis** (see Hoffmann, 1997). This hypothesis has been discussed as a possible explanation in nearly every exercise–depression literature review. The essence of the hypothesis is that during stress (e.g., exercise) the body produces endorphins. Endorphins, or endogenous opioids, are neuropeptides—"informational substances" (Pert, 1997) that make communication between neurons possible—and are thought to be analogous to the drug morphine. The name *endorphin* is derived from the combination of the terms "endogenous" (naturally occurring) and "morphine." Simply, endorphins are the body's own natural painkillers. Thus, if endorphins are released during exercise and exercise makes us feel better (e.g., less depressed), then the increased endorphins could be the reason why.

A recent study using positron emission tomography (PET), an imaging technique that highlights metabolically active brain areas, drew a lot of attention to the endorphin–exercise relationship. Boecker, Sprenger, Spilker, and colleagues (2008) reported strong negative relationships between self-reported euphoria and endorphin receptor availability following two hours of running; that is, greater euphoria was associated with reduced receptor availability. Reduced receptor availability suggests that endorphins are occupying the receptor sites and theoretically exerting their effect. This study provided the first evidence that exercise can influence endorphin activity in the human brain, but much remains to be done before any conclusive statements can be made (Dishman & O'Connor, 2009). At this point, however, it appears that for every solid study that supports the endorphin hypothesis, there is an equally solid study that refutes it. Clearly, more work is needed before any firm conclusions can be reached.

Monoamine hypothesis

The monoamine hypothesis has been proposed as another mechanism to explain the depression-reducing effects of exercise. This hypothesis has been divided into more specific hypotheses in recent years, evolving into the serotonin hypothesis (Chaouloff, 1997) and the norepinephrine hypothesis (Dishman, 1997). In essence, these hypotheses attempt to explain the effects of exercise on depression through the alteration of brain neurotransmitters like serotonin, norepinephrine, and dopamine. All of these neurotransmitters have been implicated in the regulation of emotion, variously enhancing or inhibiting emotion, and are also altered through exercise (e.g., increased release, increased uptake, etc.). In other words, exercise can increase the rate at which neurotransmitters are produced, released into the spaces between neurons (allowing communication between neurons), or taken up by neurons (again resulting in either a facilitation or inhibition of the neuronal action).

neurogenesis ■

Another recent addition to the list of explanations is the theory that exercise might help to alleviate depression because it causes **neurogenesis**—the synthesis of new neurons in the brain, particularly in brain areas shown to be affected by depression (Ernst, Olson, Pinel, et al., 2006). This has been referred to as the adult-neurogenesis hypothesis of major depressive disorder (Ernst et al., 2006). One way in which neurogenesis is thought to occur is through exercise, which leads to increased levels of brain-derived neurotrophic factor (BDNF), a growth factor that is critical in the promotion of neuronal survival and regeneration. Mounting evidence points to exercise as an important component of the expression of BDNF in the central nervous system. As with most explanations, the answer awaits the outcome of future research.

Much of the evidence for these hypotheses is based on animal research, largely because it is rather difficult to assess levels of these neurotransmitters in intact humans. It remains to be seen to what extent these hypotheses will ultimately help explain the effects of exercise on depression; undoubtedly they will.

Mastery hypothesis

A psychological explanation for the depression-reducing effects of exercise is the **mastery hypothesis** (see Biddle & Mutrie, 2001). This hypothesis posits that the psychological effects of exercise are derived from the sense of accomplishment or mastery that is felt on completing a task. This is thought to give individuals a sense of greater self-worth or personal control over their environment and can help them in coping with their problems. (See Chapter 8 for more information.) This explanation has been examined in several recent studies. Craft (2005) sought to determine whether an exercise intervention (nine weeks, three sessions per week, at 50–75 percent $HR_{reserve}$) would alleviate depression in clinically depressed women and to what extent mastery might be an explanation for any depression reduction seen. A significant reduction in depression was seen, with some of the women in the exercise group showing notable changes by the third week of the intervention; these women also had significantly increased levels of coping self-efficacy. In essence, those women who reported less depression following the exercise intervention also felt they had greater capability to deal with potential obstacles that might have otherwise prevented them from continuing with such a program. Chu and colleagues (2009) showed that self-efficacy and coping self-efficacy were increased over a 10-week intervention, but no specific effects were seen relative to the exercise intervention. That is, the sense of mastery that occurred was not exclusive to the exercise intervention. Thus, while it remains a possible explanation for the effects of exercise on reducing depression, the mastery hypothesis awaits further work.

■ mastery hypothesis

Using a research design that would allow the determination of "temporal precedence"—that is, determining which variable might precede another and thus being able to ascribe a degree of causality to it—White, Kendrick, and Yardley (2009) sought to determine whether changes in self-efficacy, self-esteem, or mood as a result of exercise led to subsequent reductions in depression in a sample of 39 adults aged 18 to 45 and described as at least mildly depressed (32 women, 7 men). Although the outcome did not allow the researchers to determine whether any of the potential mechanisms caused the reductions in depression, White and colleagues asserted that, because of the magnitude of change and the temporal sequence of change, self-efficacy and mood were stronger candidate mechanisms than self-esteem. Of particular interest, they noted that changes in positive affect were particularly large relative to either negative affect or self-efficacy. Based on this outcome, they suggested that "physical activity may particularly tackle the loss of pleasurable engagement, that is, the low PA [positive affect] element of depression" (White et al., p. 50). This presents an interesting possibility for future research to examine.

Social interaction hypothesis

social interaction hypothesis

The **social interaction hypothesis,** quite simply, proposes that the reason exercise reduces depression is that it provides an opportunity for the individual to interact with others. Certainly, some (perhaps many) people enjoy exercising in a social setting (e.g., aerobics class, running with a partner). It is quite clear, however, that while this explanation may account, in part, for the depression reduction following exercise, it cannot be the sole explanation. The social interaction idea completely fails when data from laboratory studies and more ecologically valid settings show that exercising alone also results in reduced levels of depression. The study with adult depressives by Blumenthal and colleagues (1999) showed significant reductions in depression following 16 weeks of aerobic exercise, effects that are not accounted for by any social interaction influences.

As noted earlier, any of these proposed mechanisms may be operating to drive the changes in depression typically seen with exercise. It remains to be determined to what extent these (or others) might actually explain the effects.

Practical Recommendations

As noted by Johnsgard (1989), research consistently "shows that 30 minutes of aerobic exercise three times a week will significantly reduce depression" (p. 280). The "minimal" level of exercise activity (i.e., frequency, duration, intensity) is currently unknown, but it seems clear that exercise done on a regular basis can be useful in the treatment of depression as well as in protecting against depression that we might ordinarily succumb to if we remained sedentary. The type of exercise does not seem to matter, as both aerobic and nonaerobic (e.g., weight training) forms of exercise seem to be effective in reducing depression.

Those suffering from more severe forms of depression can also find relief in exercise therapies. As demonstrated by Susan, the psychologist in the chapter-opening scenario, mental health professionals clearly need to be educated as to the value of exercise as another tool at their disposal in helping patients suffering from subclinical and clinical levels of depression. Obviously, medical clearance from a physician should be obtained before any exercise program is prescribed (Tkachuk & Martin, 1999). Three classes of risk factors and the attendant cautions associated with exercise for each are presented in Exhibit 12.9. Tkachuk and Martin also provide guidelines for the use of exercise therapy that should prove useful. Included among their recommendations are the following:

1. Obtain information about the individual's past experiences with exercise to determine enjoyable/disliked activities as a way of enhancing adherence to the exercise program.
2. Exercise with the individual for support and to provide a model of correct behavior.

Risk categories for medical exams before beginning an aerobic training program. exhibit 12.9

LEVEL OF RISK	POPULATION		RISK FACTORS	TYPE OF PROGRAM	PRIOR PHYSICAL EXAM
Low	men < 45 yrs. women < 55 yrs.	No more than one:	Family history of coronary artery disease, cigarette smoking, hypertension	Moderate Vigorous	No No
Moderate	men ≥ 45 yrs. women ≥ 55 yrs.	Two or more:	Hypercholesterolemia, impaired fasting glucose, obesity, sedentary lifestyle	Moderate Vigorous	No Yes
High	All	One or more:	Known cardiovascular, pulmonary, or metabolic disease, ischemia, dizziness/ syncope, orthopnea/ paroxysmal nocturnal dyspnea, ankle edema, palpitations/ tachycardia, intermittent claudication, known heart murmur, unusual fatigue	All	Yes

Source: Housh, Housh, & deVries (2011), *Applied Exercise and Sport Physiology,* 3rd ed. (Scottsdale, AZ: Holcomb Hathaway).

3. Help to make the exercise adaptable to the individual's lifestyle (e.g., walking to work, including household activities).
4. Use the individual's environment to foster activity (e.g., parks, home equipment).
5. Monitor exercise dosage (i.e., frequency, intensity, duration), modifying as the individual's level of fitness changes.
6. Help the individual to understand that setbacks may occur and to devise strategies for dealing with them (discussed in Chapter 4).

Conclusion

Given the information presented herein, it would seem reasonable to promote the value of regular physical activity. The evidence from epidemiological/prospective studies fairly clearly links lack of physical activity with increased risk for and prevalence of mental disorders. While not a universally agreed upon position (see Salmon, 2001, for example), it also seems reasonable to propose that physical activity be carefully considered as an important part of any treatment regimen for depression. We may certainly make the case that exercise can indeed be a valuable tool in the treatment "toolbox" for those suffering from mental disorders and disabilities. At the very least, the consensus statements regarding exercise and depression that appear in Exhibit 12.8 seem to be warranted. Beyond the positive mental health effects, physical activity concomitantly leads to the improvement of physical health as well, further reducing the risks of debilitating chronic disease conditions.

what do you know?

1. What are some of the symptoms associated with mild to moderate depression?
2. What is the major tool used in the diagnosis of mental disorders?
3. What is known from the cross-sectional and prospective studies regarding the association between (lack of) activity and depression?
4. How long do exercise programs need to be to result in reductions in depression?
5. What is the optimal "dosage" in terms of type, frequency, intensity, and duration needed for depression reduction?
6. Can exercise be useful in the treatment of clinical levels of depression? What evidence is there to support this answer?
7. What is the basis for the anthropological hypothesis as a mechanism to explain the exercise–depression relationship?
8. Which hypothesis for explaining the exercise–depression relationship relies on changes in neuropeptides?

learning activities

1. Imagine that your help as an expert in exercise psychology has been solicited by a clinical psychologist who is designing an exercise program as part of the treatment plan for a patient suffering from depression. Using the guidelines outlined by Tkachuk and Martin (1999), describe the exercise therapy that you would recommend.
2. Develop an argument that you would use in trying to convince an individual suffering from mild to moderate depression that he should consider beginning an exercise program as a way of dealing with the depression. You will need to be as convincing as you can, so you should incorporate reasons for exercising from many different approaches (e.g., both physical and psychological).

references

American Psychiatric Association. (1994). *Diagnostic and statistical manual of mental disorders* (4th ed.). Arlington, VA: Author.

American Psychiatric Association. (2000). *Diagnostic and statistical manual of mental disorders* (4th ed., text revision). Arlington, VA: Author.

Babyak, M.A., Blumenthal, J.A., Herman, S., Khatri, P., Doraiswamy, P.M., Moore, K.A., Craighead, W.E., Baldewicz, T.T., & Krishnan, K.R. (2000). Exercise treatment for major depression: Maintenance of therapeutic benefit at 10 months. *Psychosomatic Medicine, 62*(5), 633–638.

Bahrke, M.S., & Morgan, W.P. (1978). Anxiety reduction following exercise and meditation. *Cognitive Therapy and Research, 2,* 323–333.

Beck, A.T., Steer, R.A., & Brown, G.K. (1996). Manual for the Beck Depression Inventory-II. San Antonio, TX: Psychological Corporation.

Berk, M.,(2007). Should we be targeting exercise as a routine mental health intervention? *Acta Neuropsychiatrica, 19,* 217–218.

Biddle, S.J.H., & Mutrie, N. (2001). Depression and other mental illnesses. In S.J.H. Biddle & N. Mutrie, Eds., *Psychology of physical activity: Determinants, well-being and interventions* (pp. 202–235). London: Routledge.

Bing, E.G., Burnam, A., Longshore, D., Fleishman, J.A., Sherbourne, C.D., London, A.S., et al. (2001). Psychiatric disorders and drug use among human immunodeficiency virus–infected adults in the United States. *Archives of General Psychiatry, 58,* 721–728.

Blumenthal, J.A., Babyak, M.A., Doraiswamy, P.M., Watkins, L., Hoffman, B.M., Barbour, K.A., Herman, S., Craighead, W.E., Brosse, A.L., Waugh, R., Hinderliter, A., & Sherwood, A. (2007). Exercise and pharmacotherapy in the treatment of major depressive disorder. *Psychosomatic Medicine, 69,* 587–596.

Blumenthal, J.A., Babyak, M.A., Moore, K.A., Craighead, W.E., Herman, S., Khatri, P., Waugh, R., Napolitano, M.A., Forman, L.M., Appelbaum, M., Doraiswamy, P.M., & Krishnan, K.R. (1999). Effects of exercise training on older patients with major depression. *Archives of Internal Medicine, 159,* 2349–2356.

Boecker, H., Sprenger, T., Spilker, M.E., Henriksen, G., Koppenhoefer, M., Wagner, K.J., Valet, M., Berthele, A., & Tolle, T.R. (2008). The runner's high: Opioidergic mechanisms in the human brain. *Cerebral Cortex, 18*(11), 2523–2531.

Brosse, A.L., Sheets, E.S., Lett, H.S., & Blumenthal, J.A. (2002). Exercise and the treatment of clinical depression in adults: Recent findings and future directions. *Sports Medicine, 32,* 741–760.

Camacho, T.C., Roberts, R.E., Lazarus, N.B., Kaplan, G.A., & Cohen, R.D. (1991). Physical activity and depression: Evidence from the Alameda County Study. *American Journal of Epidemiology, 134,* 220–231.

Centers for Disease Control and Prevention. (1998). Self-reported frequent mental distress among adults: United States, 1993–1996. *Morbidity and Mortality Weekly Report, 47*(16), 325–331.

Chaouloff, F. (1997). The serotonin hypothesis. In W.P. Morgan (Ed.), *Physical activity and mental health* (pp. 179–198). Washington, DC: Taylor & Francis.

Chu, I.H., Buckworth, J., Kirby, T.E., & Emery, C.F. (2009). Effect of exercise intensity on depressive symptoms in women. *Mental Health & Physical Activity, 2,* 37–43.

Craft, L.L. (2005). Exercise and clinical depression: Examining two psychological mechanisms. *Psychology of Sport & Exercise, 6,* 151–171.

Craft, L.L., & Landers, D.M. (1998). The effect of exercise on clinical depression and depression resulting from mental illness: A meta-analysis. *Journal of Sport and Exercise Psychology, 20,* 339–357.

deGeus, E.J.C., & deMoor, M.H.M. (2008). A genetic perspective on the association between exercise and mental health. *Mental Health & Physical Activity, 1,* 53–61.

Dishman, R.K. (1997). The norepinephrine hypothesis. In W.P. Morgan (Ed.), *Physical activity and mental health* (pp. 199–212). Washington, DC: Taylor & Francis.

Dishman, R.K., & O'Connor, P.J. (2009). Lessons in exercise neurobiology: The case of endorphins. *Mental Health & Physical Activity, 2,* 4–9.

Dunn, A.L., Trivedi, M.H., & O'Neal, H.A. (2001). Physical activity dose-response effects on outcomes of depression and anxiety. *Medicine and Science in Sports and Exercise, 33* (Supplement), S587–S597.

Dunn, A.L., Trivedi, M.H., Kampert, J.B., Clark, C.G., & Chambliss, H.O. (2005). Exercise treatment for depression: Efficacy and dose response. *American Journal of Preventive Medicine, 28,* 1–8.

Ernst, C., Olson, A.K., Pinel, J.P.J., Lam, R.W., & Christie, B.R. (2006). Antidepressant effects of exercise: Evidence for an adult-neurogenesis hypothesis? *Journal of Psychiatry & Neuroscience, 31,* 84–92.

ESEMeD/MHEDEA 2000 Investigators. (2004). 12-month comorbidity patterns and associated factors in Europe: Results from the European Study of Epidemiology of Mental Disorders (ESEMeD) project. *Acta Psychiatrica Scandinavica, Supplement 420,* 28–37.

Farmer, M.E., Locke, B.Z., Moscicki, E.K., Dannenberg, A.L., Larson, D.B., & Radloff, L.S. (1988). Physical activity and depressive symptoms: The NHANES I epidemiological follow-up study. *American Journal of Epidemiology, 128,* 1340–1351.

Goodwin, R. D. (2003). Association between physical activity and mental disorders among adults in the United States. *Preventive Medicine, 36,* 698–703.

Galper, D.I., Trivedi, M.H., Barlow, C.E., Dunn, A.L., & Kampert, J.B. (2006). Inverse association between physical inactivity and mental health in men and women. *Medicine & Science in Sports & Exercise, 38,* 173–178.

Greenberg, P.E., Kessler, R.C., Birnbaum, H.G., Leong, S.A., Lowe, S.W., Berglund, P.A., & Corey-Lisle, P.K. (2003). The economic burden of depression in the United States: How did it change between 1990 and 2000? *Journal of Clinical Psychiatry, 64,* 1465–1475.

Greenberg, P.E., Stiglin, L.E., Finkelstein, S.N., & Berndt, E.R. (1993). The economic burden of depression in 1990. *Journal of Clinical Psychiatry, 54*(11), 405–418.

Greist, J.H., Klein, M.H., Eischens, R.R., Faris, J.W., Gurman, A.S., & Morgan, W.P. (1979). Running as a treatment for depression. *Comprehensive Psychiatry, 20,* 41–54.

Hamilton, M. (1960). A rating scale for depression. *Journal of Neurology, Neurosurgery and Psychiatry, 23,* 56–62.

Hassmen, P., Koivula, N., & Uutela, A. (2000). Physical exercise and psychological well-being: A population study in Finland. *Preventive Medicine, 30,* 17–25.

Hoffmann, P. (1997). The endorphin hypothesis. In W.P. Morgan (Ed.), *Physical activity and mental health* (pp. 163–177). Washington, DC: Taylor & Francis.

Housh, T.J., Housh, D.J., & deVries, H.A. (2006). *Applied exercise and sport physiology* (2nd ed.). Scottsdale, AZ: Holcomb Hathaway.

Johnsgard, K. (2004). *Conquering depression and anxiety through exercise.* Amherst, NY: Prometheus Books.

Johnsgard, K.W. (1989). *The exercise prescription for depression and anxiety.* New York: Plenum.

Kellner, R., & Sheffield, B.F. (1973). A self-rating scale of distress. *Psychological Medicine, 3,* 88–100.

Kessler, R.C., Chiu, W.T., Demler, O., Merikangas, K.R., & Walters, E.E. (2005). Prevalence, severity, and comorbidity of 12-month DSM–IV disorders in the National Comorbidity Survey Replication. *Archives of General Psychiatry, 62,* 590–592.

Kessler, R.C., McGonagle, K.A., Zhao, S., Nelson, C.B., Hughes, M., Eshleman, S., Wittchen, H.U., & Kendler, K.S. (1994). Lifetime and 12-month prevalence of DSM–III-R psychiatric disorders in the United States: Results from the National Comorbidity Survey. *Archives of General Psychiatry, 51,* 8–18.

Kroenke, K., Spitzer, R.L., & Williams, J.B. (2001). The PHQ-9: Validity of a brief depression severity measure. *Journal of General Internal Medicine, 16,* 606–613.

Lampinen, P., Heikkinen, R.-L., & Ruoppila, I. (2000). Changes in intensity of physical exercise as predictors of depressive symptoms among older adults: An eight-year follow-up. *Preventive Medicine, 30,* 371–380.

Lawlor, D.A., & Hopker, S.W. (2001). The effectiveness of exercise as an intervention in the management of depression: Systematic review and meta-regression analysis of randomized controlled trials. *British Medical Journal, 322,* 1–8.

Martinsen, E.W. (2002). The role of exercise in the management of depression. In D.L. Mostofsky & L.D. Zaichowsky (Eds.), *Medical and psychological aspects of sport and exercise* (pp. 205–214). Morgantown, WV: Fitness Information Technology.

Martinsen, E.W., Hoffart, A., & Solberg, O. (1989). Comparing aerobic with nonaerobic forms of exercise in the treatment of clinical depression: A randomized trial. *Comprehensive Psychiatry, 30*(4), 324–331.

Martinsen, E.W., Medhus, A., & Sandvik, L. (1985). Effects of aerobic exercise on depression: A controlled study. *British Medical Journal, 291,* 109.

Mobily, K.E., Rubenstein, L.M., Lemke, J.H., O'Hara, M.W., & Wallace, R.B. (1996). Walking and depression in a cohort of older adults: The Iowa 65+ Rural Health Study. *Journal of Aging and Physical Activity, 4,* 119–135.

Morgan, W.P. (1968). Selected physiological and psychomotor correlates of depression in psychiatric patients. *Research Quarterly, 39,* 1037–1043.

Morgan, W.P. (1969). A pilot investigation of physical working capacity in depressed and non-depressed psychiatric males. *Research Quarterly, 40,* 859–861.

Morgan, W.P. (1970). Physical working capacity in depressed and non-depressed psychiatric females: A preliminary study. *American Corrective Therapy Journal, 24,* 14–16.

Morgan, W.P. (1994). Physical activity, fitness, and depression. In C. Bouchard, R.J. Shephard, & T. Stephens (Eds.), *Physical activity, fitness, and health: International proceedings and consensus statement* (pp. 851–867). Champaign, IL: Human Kinetics.

Morgan, W.P., & Goldston, S.E. (Eds.). (1987). *Exercise and mental health.* Washington, DC: Hemisphere.

Motl, R.W., Birnbaum, A.S., Kubik, M.Y., & Dishman, R.K. (2004). Naturally occurring changes in physical activity are inversely related to depressive symptoms during early adolescence. *Psychosomatic Medicine, 66,* 336–342.

Murray, C.J.L., & Lopez, A.D. (1996). *The global burden of disease: A comprehensive assessment of mortality and disability from diseases, injuries, and risk factors in 1990 and projected to 2020.* Cambridge, MA: Harvard School of Public Health.

Neidig, J.L., Smith, B.A., & Brashers, D.E. (2003). Aerobic exercise training for depressive symptom management in adults living with HIV infection. *Journal of the Association of Nurses in AIDS Care, 14,* 30–40.

North, T.C., McCullagh, P., & Tran, Z.V. (1990). Effect of exercise on depression. *Exercise & Sport Sciences Reviews, 18,* 379–415.

O'Neal, H.A., Dunn, A.L., & Martinsen, E.W. (2000). Depression and exercise. *International Journal of Sport Psychology, 31*(2), 110–135.

Paffenbarger, R.S., Lee, I.M., & Leung, R. (1994). Physical activity and personal characteristics associated with depression and suicide in American college men. *Acta Psychiatrica Scandinavica, Suppl. 377,* 16–22.

Pert, C.B. (1997). *Molecules of emotion.* New York: Scribner.

Physical Activity Guidelines Advisory Committee (PAGAC) (2008). *Physical Activity Guidelines Advisory Committee Report, 2008.* Washington, DC: U.S. Department of Health and Human Services.

Pinquart, M., Duberstein, P.R., & Lyness, J.M. (2007). Effects of psychotherapy and other behavioral interventions on clinically depressed older adults: A meta-analysis. *Aging & Mental Health, 11,* 645–657.

Regier, D.A., Narrow, W.E., Rae, D.S., Manderscheid, R.W., Locke, B.Z., & Goodwin, F.K. (1993). The de facto U.S. mental and addictive disorders service system: Epidemiologic Catchment Area prospective 1-year prevalence rates of disorders and services. *Archives of General Psychiatry, 50,* 85–94.

Rethorst, C.D., Wipfli, B.M., & Landers, D.M. (2009). The antidepressive effects of exercise: A meta-analysis of randomized trials. *Sports Medicine, 39,* 491–511.

Robins, L.N., Helzer, J.E., Weissman, M.M., Orvaschel, H., Gruenberg, E., Burke, J.D., Jr., & Regier, D.A. (1984). Lifetime prevalence of specific psychiatric disorders in three sites. *Archives of General Psychiatry, 41*(10), 949–958.

Ryan, A.J. (1983). Exercise is medicine. *Physician & Sportsmedicine, 11,* 10.

Salmon, P. (2001). Effects of physical exercise on anxiety, depression, and sensitivity to stress: A unifying theory. *Clinical Psychology Review, 21,* 33–61.

Singh, N.A., Clements, K.M., & Fiatarone, M.A. (1997). A randomized controlled trial of progressive resistance training in depressed elders. *Journal of Gerontology, 52A*(1), M27–M35.

Singh, N.A., Clements, K.M., & Fiatarone Singh, M.A. (2001). The efficacy of exercise as a long-term antidepressant in elderly subjects: A randomized, controlled trial. *Journal of Gerontology: Medical Sciences, 56A*(1), M497–M504.

Spitzer, R.L., Endicott, J., & Robins, E. (1978). Research diagnostic criteria: Rationale and reliability. *Archives of General Psychiatry, 35,* 773–782.

Stephens, T. (1988). Physical activity and mental health in the United States and Canada: Evidence from four population surveys. *Preventive Medicine, 17,* 35–47.

Thayer, R.E. (2001). *Calm energy: How people regulate mood with food and exercise.* New York: Oxford.

Tkachuk, G.A., & Martin, G.L. (1999). Exercise therapy for patients with psychiatric disorders: Research and clinical implications. *Professional Psychology: Research and Practice, 30*(3), 275–282.

U.S. Department of Health and Human Services. (1999). *Mental health: A report of the Surgeon General.* Rockville, MD: U.S. Department of Health and Human Services, Substance Abuse and Mental Health Services Administration, Center for Mental Health Services, National Institutes of Health, National Institute of Mental Health.

Wagner, G., Rabkin, J., & Rabkin, R. (1998). Exercise as a mediator of psychological and nutritional effects of testosterone therapy in HIV+ men. *Medicine & Science in Sports & Exercise, 30*(6), 811–817.

Wang, P.S., Beck, A.L., Berglund, P., McKenas, D.K., Pronk, N.P., Simon, G.E., & Kessler, R.C. (2004). Effects of major depression on moment-in-time work performance. *American Journal of Psychiatry, 161,* 1885–1891.

White, K., Kendrick, T., & Yardley, L. (2009). Change in self-esteem, self-efficacy and the mood dimensions of depression as potential mediators of the physical activity and depression relationship: Exploring the temporal relation of change. *Mental Health & Physical Activity, 2,* 44–52.

World Health Organization (1993). *The ICD-10 classification of mental and behavioral disorders: Diagnostic criteria for research.* Geneva: World Health Organization.

13

Emotional Well-Being and Exercise

KEY TERMS

affect
categorical approach
circumplex model
dimensional approach
emotional well-being
emotions
energetic arousal
exercise dependence syndrome
iceberg profile
lactate threshold
moods
overtraining
primary exercise dependence
secondary exercise dependence
staleness syndrome
tense arousal
ventilatory threshold

Nick and Stephanie both turned 40 in the past year. They have two kids, ages 11 and 13, who are both very involved in school and sports activities. Nick and Steph find themselves so busy with going to work; carpooling kids to practices, games, and social functions; and doing their household chores that they have no time for themselves. At the end of the day, they both collapse onto the couch, usually with a glass of wine or beer, and vegetate in front of the television until it is time for bed (if they don't fall asleep on the couch first!). They usually sleep later than they had planned, yet wake up tired and immediately stressed out at the prospect of yet another crazy day.

This kind of schedule goes on for quite a while until Steph runs across a book at the local bookstore that catches her attention. Written by Robert Thayer, a psychologist from the California State University at Long Beach, it is titled *Calm Energy: How People Regulate Mood with Food and Exercise.* It sounds interesting, so Steph buys it and begins reading it at her first opportunity. To her surprise, she has a hard time putting it down, largely because so much of what she reads strikes a chord. She is particularly taken by the sections of the book dealing with the energizing effects of exercise and its mood-improving capabilities.

Steph formulates a plan: She and Nick will get up 45 minutes earlier than usual and take their golden retriever for a 30-minute walk around the neighborhood. This will accomplish two major goals—she and Nick can spend some time together at the beginning of the day to discuss the day's activities and to just talk to each other without being interrupted by phone calls and kids. It will also get them some much-needed exercise. It takes some getting used to the earlier wake-up time, but before too long Nick and Steph find themselves looking forward to their early morning walks. They feel like they have much more energy during the day and much less tension, both of which make their daily activities much easier. Within two months, Nick and Steph have begun incorporating some running into their exercise routines. It seems like the more exercise they incorporate, the better they feel. They sleep better, handle stress much better, and are generally just a lot more pleasant to be around. They marvel at how something like exercise can actually leave them feeling energized.

> Everyone knows the effect of physical exercise on the mood: how much more cheerful and courageous one feels when the body has been toned up, than when it is "run down." ...Our moods are determined by the feelings which come up from our body. Those feelings are sometimes of worry, breathlessness, anxiety; sometimes of peace and repose. It is certain that physical exercise will tend to train the body toward the latter feelings. The latter feelings are certainly an essential ingredient in all perfect human character.
>
> —**WILLIAM JAMES (1899, pp. 220–221)**

The vast majority of research examining psychological changes associated with exercise and physical activity has traditionally focused on reductions in negative emotions like anxiety and depression (see Chapters 11 and 12). Given the prevalence of such mental-health problems, this is certainly an important endeavor. Yet, when it comes to recommending exercise and physical activity, the focus tends to be on making the activity more enjoyable or more tolerable rather than on the mental-health benefits. For example, the National Institutes of Health Consensus Development Panel on Physical Activity and Cardiovascular Health (1996), and more recently the American College of Sports Medicine (2006), suggest that activities such as walking and other moderate-intensity activities will likely improve adherence rates over more strenuous activities. The assumption of recommending moderate-intensity exercise seems to be that if the activity is more enjoyable or less aversive, then rates of exercise adherence might improve and the benefits of physical activity can be more readily experienced. This is likely true; however, an approach that focuses on benefits may be effective as well. Consider that one of the most consistently reported effects from exercise of even mild intensities is an increase in feelings of energy, such as experienced by Nick and Stephanie in the chapter-opening scenario. For example, O'Connor and Puetz (2005), in a review of physical activity and feelings of energy and fatigue, noted that such feelings have a strong link with health and quality of life. They further point out that all of the epidemiological evidence they reviewed showed a positive relationship between regular physical activity and energy. Such an effect might be particularly salient for those suffering from physical and mental conditions characterized, in part, by feelings of low energy and fatigue (e.g., heart disease, cancer, HIV, depression). Importantly, physical activity can have similar energy-enhancing/fatigue-reducing effects in otherwise mentally and physically healthy individuals as well. Additionally, Thayer (1987) has consistently shown that a 10-minute walk is more effective, not only at increasing energy but also at reducing tension, than eating a candy bar or smoking cigarettes. It has also been shown that people tend to do what makes them feel good (Emmons & Diener, 1986). Thus, if exercise can be shown to have the ability to improve psychological states, exercise programs might be developed to capitalize on such effects so that people not only begin exercise programs but stick with them.

Defining Emotional Well-Being

The concept of emotional well-being is an aspect of mental health—related to anxiety and depression yet also distinct from them—that has recently gained more research attention in the exercise domain. Simply put, **emotional well-being** is a greater amount of positive affect than negative affect, along with favorable thoughts such as satisfaction with life. It should be easy to see that if exercise reduces negative emotions like stress, anxiety, and depression, and increases positive emotions like energy and vigor, then it should also result in better emotional well-being. Exercise and physical activity have also been shown to result in greater self-confidence and self-esteem and improved cognitive function (see Chapter 8; see also McAuley & Rudolph, 1995), which serve to bolster well-being.

■ emotional well-being

Unfortunately, a number of issues involved in the examination of such psychological states in the exercise literature continue to be problematic. These issues include how such states are conceptualized, how and when they are measured, and issues related to what is often called the "dose–response" relationship.

Conceptualization Issues: Affect, Emotions, or Moods?

It has been noted that an unfortunate tendency in the exercise psychology literature has been to equate the terms *affect, emotion,* and *mood* as if they all refer to the same thing (see Ekkekakis & Petruzzello, 2000). This has led to a great deal of confusion and messiness in the literature. It is a reasonable and defensible position to claim that these terms represent distinct constructs and should thus not be used as synonyms. Affect, emotion, and mood can be viewed as related to one another, yet each has important differences from the others.

Emotions (e.g., fear, guilt, pride) are states elicited following an appraisal wherein an object, person, or event is determined to impact or have the potential to impact the goals or the well-being of the individual. An emotion is an immediate response to a specific stimulus (e.g., an impending speech elicits anxiety, winning a race elicits joy) that requires some level of cognitive input. Perhaps more simply, emotions occur following mental processing that attaches some meaning to an event.

■ emotions

Like emotions, **moods** (e.g., irritation, cheerfulness) are subjective states, have a cognitive basis, and can enhance or interfere with purposive behavior. Moods can be distinguished from emotions in at least three important ways:

■ moods

FOCUS on Overweight, Sedentary Adults

Anyone paying attention to the news is aware that the adult population of the United States is becoming increasingly overweight (67%; National Center for Health Statistics, 2007). This has clear implications for adult health and well-being. It has been reported that, even though physical activity is important in weight-loss programs, adherence to physical activity programs decreases with increasing levels of body weight, body fat, and body mass index (BMI). When physical activity is used by overweight adults as a weight-management strategy, roughly 20 percent report exercising at the minimum recommended levels (Centers for Disease Control and Prevention, 2000). This becomes even more problematic because, for weight loss to be successful, energy expenditure needs to be significantly sustained. As reported by Ekkekakis and Lind (2006), frustration with weight-loss progress is a major reason for lack of adherence to exercise programs, yet weight loss becomes difficult at such minimal exercise levels.

Ekkekakis and Lind (2006) also note that individuals who are overweight tend to have reduced tolerance to higher intensity exercise, perceive the activity as requiring more effort, and prefer self-chosen over imposed physical activity. It is important to examine the relationship between exercise intensity and affective and exertional responses to that activity to more fully understand adherence in overweight and obese individuals. In an effort to do just that, Ekkekakis and Lind examined affective and exertional responses to imposed versus self-selected exercise intensities in a group of overweight, sedentary women.

A group of sedentary (inactive for at least the previous 12 months), middle-aged (approximately 43 years old) women were recruited for the study. Whereas nine of the women were of normal weight (BMI < 25 kg/m^2), 16 were considered overweight, having an average BMI of 31.1 kg/m^2. On the first day, all of the participants completed a graded exercise test to determine their peak aerobic capacity. On a separate day, they completed a 20-minute session of treadmill exercise at a speed of their own choosing. Finally, on a third day, the participants exercised again for 20 minutes, except during this session the speed was set at a level 10 percent faster than the self-selected speed from the second exercise session. In addition to measuring heart rate during each exercise session, perceived exertion (via the rating of perceived exertion [RPE] scale) and affect (using the Feeling Scale [FS]) were assessed every five minutes during the exercise (with affect also being assessed at the start). It was found that the overweight individuals had higher perceptions of exertion regardless of the exercise intensity (self-selected vs. imposed), but affective responses were differentially influenced by exercise intensity. For the overweight individuals, the imposed intensity resulted in a steady decline in affect (i.e., they felt worse as the session went along); affect remained stable during the self-selected condition.

Ekkekakis and Lind speculated that lower adherence to exercise programs in overweight individuals might be due to less pleasurable experiences during exercise, particularly since such exercise is often prescribed/imposed by an exercise leader/personal trainer. Whether this reduced pleasure/increased displeasure is due to negative appraisals of exercise, some physiological differences (e.g., impaired thermoregulation), or an increase in negative symptoms (e.g., muscle aches) remains to be determined. It seems reasonable at this point not only to incorporate physiological parameters (e.g., heart rate, percentage of aerobic capacity) into the design of exercise programs for overweight individuals, but also to pay greater attention to how the individual feels during such activities. As noted, people will tend to do what feels good (Emmons & Diener, 1986), so it makes sense to examine affective responses more carefully to better understand adherence issues.

ADDITIONAL RESOURCES

Ekkekakis, P., Lind, E., & Vazou, S. (2010). Affective responses to increasing levels of exercise intensity in normal-weight, overweight, and obese middle-aged women. *Obesity, 18*(1), 79–85.

Stewart, K.J., Turner, K.L., Bacher, A.C., DeRegis, J.R., Sung, J., Tayback, M., & Ouyang, P. (2003). Are fitness, activity, and fatness associated with health-related quality of life and mood in older persons? *Journal of Cardiopulmonary Rehabilitation, 23,* 115–121.

Treasure, D.C., Lox, C.L., & Lawton, B. (1998). Determinants of physical activity in a sedentary, obese female population. *Journal of Sport and Exercise Psychology, 20,* 218–224.

ACTIVITY

In a manner similar to the Ekkekakis and Lind study, do a self-study (or use a roommate or friend). Using the Self-Assessment Inventory (the AD ACL) included later in the chapter (see Exhibit 13.3), complete the inventory before and within five minutes after completing a session of your (or your roommate's/friend's) preferred or favorite exercise. Complete the inventory again in the same fashion before and following a similar duration bout of some other form of aerobic exercise (i.e., not your favorite). How do the results compare to those from Ekkekakis and Lind? What is similar and what is different between the two studies? Make a list of these differences and speculate as to why these differences might have something to do with any differences you noted between the two exercise bouts.

1. Moods usually imply a longer course of time, whereas emotions are rather short-lived.
2. Antecedents or causes of emotions can usually be identified, whereas moods come and go with sometimes unidentifiable causes.
3. Emotions are usually more intense and variable than moods.

■ affect

Unlike emotions and moods, **affect** (e.g., tension, calmness) is a more general "valenced" response, that is, a good–bad/pleasure–displeasure feeling. Thus, all emotions and moods are subsumed under affect. Affect is thought to be more basic than emotion for at least two reasons: Affect is evolutionarily more primitive, and affect does not require thought processes to precede it. Understanding the more primitive nature of affect is valuable because basic affective responses can be elicited through "hard-wired" mechanisms, very similar to eliciting a reflexive response. For example, consider the feeling of unpleasantness in response to pain. The immediate response to pain does not require a detailed cognitive analysis before the feeling can be labeled as pain and, indeed, such "cognitive elaboration" could be dangerous to the individual. Any valenced response is an affect but not necessarily an emotion, because, as stated previously, cognitive elaboration is not needed for affect. For example, affect is present when an infant cries because she feels distress, but the infant cannot feel sadness because she has not yet developed the cognitive appraisal capacity necessary to determine sadness (Ekkekakis & Petruzzello, 2000).

Measurement

In this section, we discuss various measures used to assess affective states, including generalized and exercise-specific measures.

Generalized Measures

Generalized measures are measures of mood or affect that are not specific to any context. They include the Profile of Mood States (POMS), the Positive and Negative Affect Schedule (PANAS), and the Activation-Deactivation Adjective Check List (AD ACL).

Profile of Mood States. The POMS (McNair, Lorr, & Droppleman, 1971/1981) has been one of the most popular self-report instruments used in the exercise (and sport) psychology literature. Originally developed for use in psychiatric populations, the POMS has been employed to examine mood changes occurring in response to various exercise manipulations for nearly 40 years. The POMS is a 65-item adjective rating scale that yields scores on six different mood subscales:

- tension–anxiety
- depression–dejection
- anger–hostility
- vigor–activity
- fatigue–inertia
- confusion–bewilderment

Respondents rate each of the 65 adjectives (e.g., exhausted, alert, terrified, ready to go, miserable, tense, confused, uneasy, fatigued) along a 5-point scale ranging from 0 (not at all) to 4 (extremely) according to how they feel. The response set, which is essentially the instructions given to respondents for making their assessments, can be varied to reflect how the individual feels "right now," "today," "over the past week," "over the past month," "over the past year," or "over a lifetime." The problem with using an instrument like the POMS is that it assesses only six distinct mood states. These six states may not be the only mood states in the entire domain of mood. Use of the POMS in an exercise study implicitly assumes that only the six moods that it measures are affected by an exercise manipulation when other moods could also be affected, such as excitement or boredom. It is also worth noting that because of its length, the POMS poses problems when a researcher wants to measure mood multiple times in a single exercise session. Because of concerns about its length, the original 65-item measure has been modified, and shorter versions and alternative versions are now available. In spite of their brevity, however, these shorter versions still suffer from the assumptions made about which moods they assess.

Positive and Negative Affect Schedule. The PANAS (Watson, Clark, & Tellegen, 1988), another relatively popular measure in the exercise domain, is a 20-item self-report instrument based on the two-dimensional (positive affect, negative affect) model proposed by Watson and Tellegen (1985). As such, it provides measures of the two orthogonal (i.e., conceptually independent) dimensions of positive affect (PA) and negative affect (NA). See Exhibit 13.1. As with the POMS, respondents rate each of the 20 adjectives (e.g., interested, distressed,

The dimensions of positive affect and negative affect as assessed by the PANAS. **exhibit 13.1**

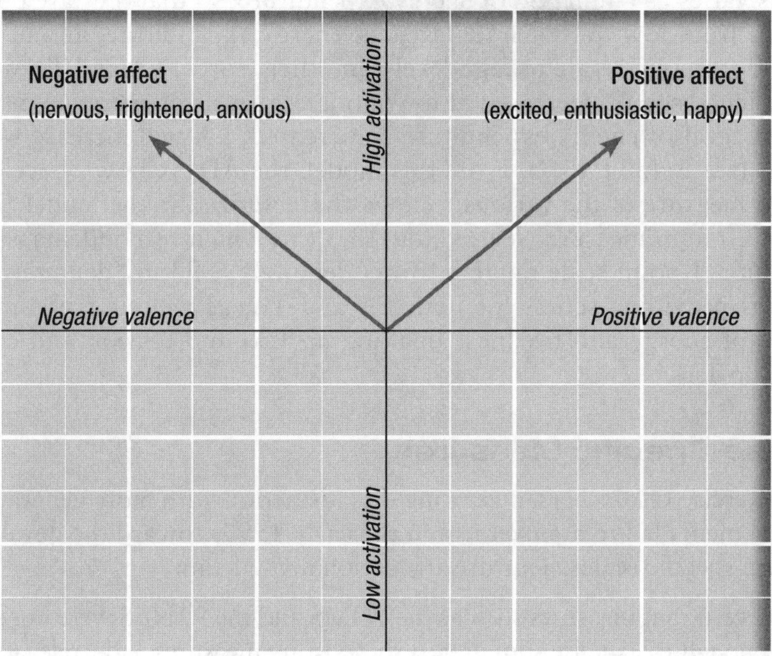

excited, jittery, ashamed) along a 5-point scale ranging from 1 (very slightly or not at all) to 5 (extremely) according to how they feel. Possible time frames for these assessments range from "you feel this way right now, that is, at the present moment" to "you generally feel this way, that is, how you feel on average." One of the problems with the PANAS is that it measures only the high-activation ends of PA and NA and not the low-activation ends (see Exhibit 13.1). Thus, it is useful for measuring high-activation states like excitement or enthusiasm (PA) and nervousness or fright (NA), but not low-activation states like relaxation or calmness (PA) and sadness or tiredness (NA). Such shortcomings have been rectified in a later version of the PANAS, the PANAS-X (Watson & Clark, 1994), but this revised measure has not yet been used in the exercise literature.

Activation-Deactivation Adjective Check List (AD ACL). The AD ACL (Thayer, 1986, 1989) was developed based on a theoretical framework incorporating two bipolar dimensions of activation and arousal. The first dimension, termed **energetic arousal** (EA), is characterized by energy–sleep and refers to feelings ranging from energy, vigor, and liveliness to feelings of fatigue and tiredness. EA is proposed to follow a circadian rhythm and, importantly for the exercise domain, to reflect changes in gross physical activity. The second dimension, termed **tense arousal** (TA), is characterized by tension–placidity

■ energetic arousal

■ tense arousal

and refers to feelings ranging from subjective tension to placidity, quietness, and stillness. Thayer (1989) proposed that the relationship between the two dimensions varies as a function of energy expenditure, so that they are positively correlated from low to moderate levels of energy expenditure, and negatively correlated from moderate to high levels. In other words, EA and TA will both be either increased or decreased at low/moderate levels of energy expenditure, but as the level of energy expenditure is increased, EA will increase while TA decreases (see Exhibit 13.2). From this model, the AD ACL was developed to provide a measure of the various feelings characterized in the model. The AD ACL is a 20-item measure (see Exhibit 13.3), in which respondents rate their feelings on a 4-point scale ranging from "definitely feel" to "definitely do not feel," thus providing scores for both EA and TA, as well as the component subscales of energy and tiredness (making up EA) and tension and calmness (making up TA).

Exercise-Specific Measures

Among exercise researchers, a growing dissatisfaction with more general self-report instruments led to a movement in the early 1990s toward the development of exercise-specific scales. This dissatisfaction arose from:

1. A concern that measures such as the POMS and the PANAS were not sensitive enough to exercise stimuli (i.e., the existing measures had irrelevant items or items that didn't seem to change in response to exercise manipulations).

exhibit 13.2 A diagram of the relationships between energetic arousal (EA) and tense arousal (TA).

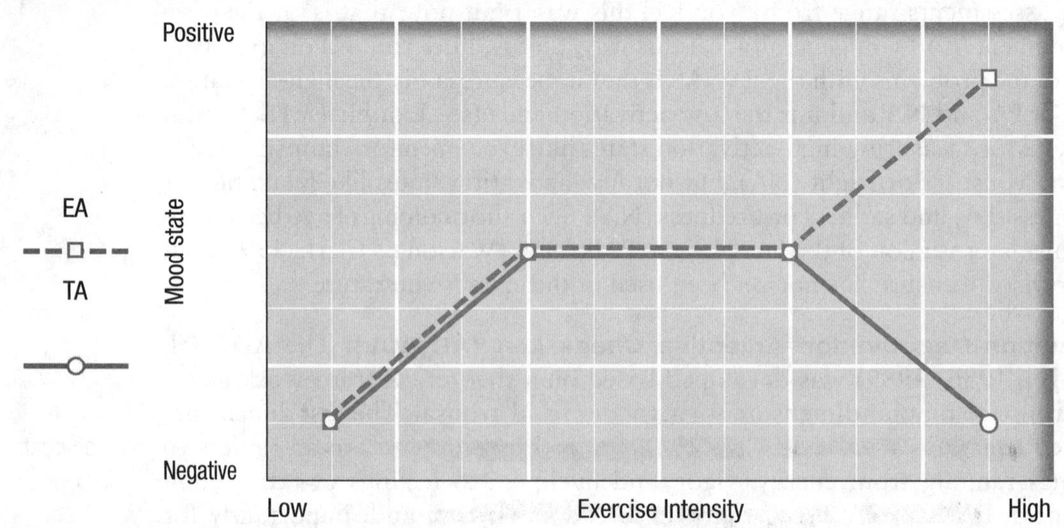

Source: Thayer (2001).

Self-Assessment Inventory: Thayer's Activation-Deactivation Adjective Check List (AD ACL). **exhibit 13.3**

INSTRUCTIONS: Following are some adjectives that describe people's feelings. Please read each of the adjectives and then indicate how you are feeling *at this particular moment,* by circling the appropriate response. There are no right or wrong answers, so do not spend too much time on any one item. Check to make sure you have responded to all the items.

	Definitely feel	*Feel slightly*	*Cannot decide*	*Definitely do not feel*
1. Active	✓✓	✓	?	no
2. Placid	✓✓	✓	?	no
3. Sleepy	✓✓	✓	?	no
4. Jittery	✓✓	✓	?	no
5. Energetic	✓✓	✓	?	no
6. Intense	✓✓	✓	?	no
7. Calm	✓✓	✓	?	no
8. Tired	✓✓	✓	?	no
9. Vigorous	✓✓	✓	?	no
10. At rest	✓✓	✓	?	no
11. Drowsy	✓✓	✓	?	no
12. Fearful	✓✓	✓	?	no
13. Lively	✓✓	✓	?	no
14. Still	✓✓	✓	?	no
15. Wide-awake	✓✓	✓	?	no
16. Clutched-up	✓✓	✓	?	no
17. Quiet	✓✓	✓	?	no
18. Full-of-pep	✓✓	✓	?	no
19. Tense	✓✓	✓	?	no
20. Wakeful	✓✓	✓	?	no

Note: The AD ACL is scored by assigning the following scores: ✓✓ = 4, ✓ = 3, ? = 2, and no = 1. The scores for each subscale are then summed, with subscale adjectives as follows: Energy (active, energetic, vigorous, lively, full-of-pep); Tired (sleepy, tired, drowsy, wide-awake, wakeful); Tension (jittery, intense, fearful, clutched-up, tense); Calmness (placid, calm, at-rest, still, quiet). Scoring for "wakeful" and "wide-awake" must be reversed for the Tiredness subscale. To derive the Energetic Arousal (EA) and Tense Arousal (TA) dimensions, see Thayer (1989, Appendix I) or www.csulb.edu/~thayer/thayer/adacl.htm for additional instructions.

2. A concern that exercise has unique and distinct properties (i.e., affect is somehow changed in the exercise context in ways that are not seen in other contexts) that existing measures failed to detect. It is worth noting that, to date, no evidence has shown that exercise has such distinct, unique properties. Thus, existing affect measures *should* work just fine in assessing any effective changes occurring as a result of exercise.

Out of this dissatisfaction, three multi-item scales—Exercise-induced Feeling Inventory (EFI), Subjective Exercise Experiences Scale (SEES), and Physical Activity Affect Scale (PAAS)—and one single-item scale—Feeling Scale (FS)—were developed.

Exercise-induced Feeling Inventory (EFI). The EFI (Gauvin & Rejeski, 1993) is a 12-item measure of exercise-induced feeling states. It is composed of four subscales (positive engagement, revitalization, physical exhaustion, and tranquility) thought to reflect aspects of the affective experience associated with exercise that were not available with other instruments. These subscales are supposedly analogous to enthusiasm, energy, fatigue, and calmness (Gauvin & Spence, 1998). Responses are made on a 5-point scale ranging from 0 (do not feel) to 4 (feel very strongly).

Subjective Exercise Experiences Scale (SEES). The SEES (McAuley & Courneya, 1994) is also a 12-item scale designed to measure the subjective experiences unique to exercise, with specific attention to the positive dimensions of affect in response to exercise. The SEES is composed of three subscales, namely positive well-being, psychological distress, and fatigue. Psychological well-being is analogous to positive affect, whereas psychological distress is analogous to negative affect. Ratings are made along a 7-point scale ranging from 1 (not at all) to 7 (very much so). Among other things (see the extensive discussion of the EFI by Ekkekakis & Petruzzello, 2001a, and the SEES by Ekkekakis & Petruzzello, 2001b), it has been noted that some potential redundancy exists within and between the EFI and SEES (Lox, Jackson, Tuholski, et al., 2000).

Physical Activity Affect Scale (PAAS). In an effort to capitalize on the unique aspects of both the EFI and the SEES while at the same time reducing the overlap between them, Lox and colleagues (2000) developed the PAAS, an instrument consisting of the Psychological Distress subscale of the SEES and the subscales of the EFI. This resulted in another 12-item exercise-specific measure using the same response format as the EFI (a 5-point scale of 0 to 4 ranging from "do not feel" to "feel very strongly"). This comparatively new instrument has not been used very extensively in the literature to this point.

Feeling Scale (FS). Finally, the FS (Hardy & Rejeski, 1989) is a single-item measure of valence or hedonic tone (good–bad/pleasant–unpleasant), with responses made along an 11-point continuum ranging from –5 (very bad) to +5 (very good) with 0 as a neutral midpoint. It was designed for use as an in-task (i.e., during exercise) measure of affect and has been used in numerous studies to measure affect during acute exercise bouts.

Perhaps the biggest drawback of all four of the exercise-specific scales is the fact that each was developed in the absence of a guiding theoretical framework (see Ekkekakis & Petruzzello, 2000, 2001a, 2001b for extensive critiques). It is also worth noting that among the EFI, SEES, and PAAS, none has been shown to satisfactorily address the two concerns (see above) that led to their development. For these types of reasons, scientists need to exert great care when deciding on the most appropriate affect measure to use in their research.

Research Issues

Before examining the research, we first look at the following important issues related to the study of exercise-related affect: categorical versus dimensional approaches, temporal dynamics of affective response, and dose–response issues.

Categorical Versus Dimensional Approaches

One of the underlying assumptions of the vast majority of research examining the affective/emotional/mood responses to exercise is that exercise influences certain affect/emotions/moods. Thus, the field is rife with studies examining anxiety and depression responses to exercise and with studies all using the same measure (e.g., POMS). This tendency seems to reflect a **categorical approach,** an approach that assumes that affective states (be they emotions, moods, or affect) are distinct and have unique properties and antecedents. Thus, the implicit assumption is that exercise can reduce anxiety or depression but does not have any other influence on affective states. For example, this approach implicitly assumes that exercise cannot improve energy or increase relaxation or minimize fatigue. In contrast is the less-often used **dimensional approach,** which assumes that affective states are interrelated and can be accurately captured by a small number of dimensions (as few as two). For example, using the dimensions of activation and valence, a much more informative picture of the affective dynamics accompanying a bout of exercise might emerge. Each approach has its advantages and disadvantages. The main advantages attributed to dimensional models are their broader, more encompassing scope and their parsimony. Thus, with as little as two dimensions, exercise might be shown to result in increased energy during and immediately following activity and increased relaxation during the recovery from activity.

■ categorical approach

■ dimensional approach

Little is actually known about the nature of the affective changes that occur in response to bouts of exercise (e.g., how affect might change over time, the kind of affect actually being experienced). Given the limited knowledge, dimensional models provide a desirable approach to studying such affective phenomena (see Biddle & Mutrie, 2001; Ekkekakis & Petruzzello, 2002).

Consider the following, which indicates the utility in using a dimensional approach to study affect in the exercise domain:

> [The dimensional] approach seems better suited to the understanding of exercise and affect because the models stemming from it are intended to be broad, encompassing conceptualizations of affective experience. Because the affective experience that accompanies exercise has not been thoroughly described, a model of affect that has a wider breadth is more likely to capture the essence of exercise-induced affect than a model that, at the outset, limits the focus of investigation to specific emotions. (Gauvin & Brawley, 1993, p. 152)

circumplex model

A potentially useful dimensional model is the two-dimensional circumplex model of affect, which has been described extensively by Russell (1980, 1997) and Ekkekakis and Petruzzello (1999, 2002). The **circumplex model** describes affective states along the perimeter of a circle defined by the dimensions of affective valence (pleasure–displeasure) and activation. These two dimensions form four quadrants (see Exhibit 13.4) that can be characterized by the various combinations of valence and activation:

1. pleasant–activated, reflecting excitement, enthusiasm, energy
2. pleasant–unactivated, reflecting relaxation and calmness
3. unpleasant–unactivated, reflecting boredom, fatigue, depression
4. unpleasant–activated, reflecting anxiety, tension, distress

Researchers have only recently begun to examine affective responses to exercise from this framework (see the following section), but it has the potential to handle the problematic issues in the area. It provides a more general representation of affect, allows for both positive and negative affective states, and is a more parsimonious approach to studying affect in the exercise domain. The AD ACL provides measures of affect that can be used within such a dimensional framework (see Exhibit 13.4).

Temporal Dynamics of Affective Responses

Another extremely important issue in the study of exercise-related affect is the timing of the measurement of affective responses. The vast majority of the literature before 1998 had been content to study responses before and after an acute bout of exercise. Only recently has there been any systematic investigation into the responses *during* a bout of exercise. This distinction is potentially very important for understanding the temporal dynamics associated with affective responses to exercise. It is possible that affect experienced during an exercise bout can be quite distinct from the affective change reported from before to after exercise. For example, whereas exercise done at more moderate intensities might result in the same post-exercise affective states as more vigorous intensities, the responses during the exercise at different intensities might be very divergent. This would obviously have important implications in exercise prescription. If a person does not feel well during an exercise bout, even if he feels better afterward, he might be less inclined to continue the activity. The post-exercise positive feelings might not be sufficient to "override" the negative feelings during exercise. Important theoretical implications might arise from attempts to elucidate the mechanisms underlying such affective responses. If

The circumplex model of affect. **exhibit 13.4**

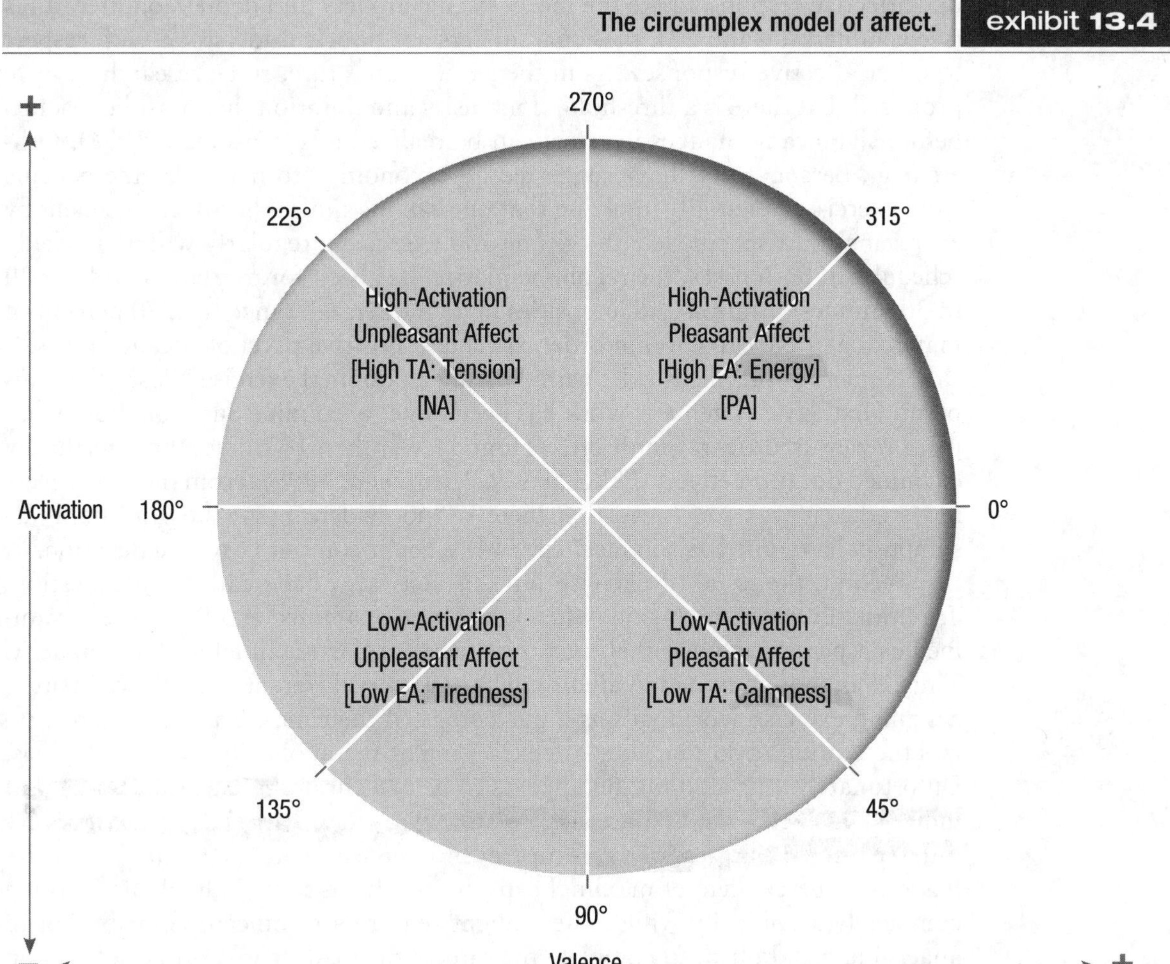

Reprinted from *Psychology of Sport and Exercise,* Vol. 3, Ekkekakis, P. and Petruzzello, S. J., Analysis of the affect measurement conundrum in exercise psychology, IV. A conceptual case for the affect circumplex, p. 39. Copyright 2002, with permission from Elsevier Science.

affective responses during exercise are different from those seen following exercise, explanations for these changes need to be incorporated into theoretical models. Without such incorporation, the models are grossly incomplete and can never adequately explain the affective responses to exercise stimuli.

Dose–Response Issues

The final methodological issue to be addressed before a synopsis of the literature concerns the dose–response effect. Specifically, it is currently very popular to speculate as to the intensity and duration of exercise that yields the most optimal affective response. Like the more specific anxiety and depression literatures (see Chapters 11 and 12), these parameters are poorly understood with respect to other affective responses. As in the anxiety literature, some researchers have proposed that there is a threshold of intensity and duration that must be reached before significant changes in affect can be realized (e.g., Dishman, 1986). Others (e.g., Berger, 1994) have suggested a "taxonomy" to maximize the benefits from exercise, essentially implying that one can maximize the affective benefit by exercising for a specific length of time and exercising regularly within a weekly schedule. In both cases, the recommendation has been for exercise of at least 20 to 30 minutes duration and intensities in a "moderate" range (i.e., 70 percent of maximal aerobic capacity) in order to achieve positive psychological changes.

Numerous problems exist with deriving an optimal exercise "dosage" at this point. First, little systematic work has been done to examine duration. For example, a review of dose–response effects found fewer than 10 studies that specifically examined duration effects (Ekkekakis & Petruzzello, 1999). From these relatively few studies it was concluded that there is "no evidence that the 'threshold' assumption has some basis in fact" (p. 354) when it comes to exercise duration.

Second, the issue of exercise intensity has also been called into question. Traditionally, intensity (again, when it has been examined at all) has been examined as a percentage of either maximal heart rate or maximal aerobic capacity. Thus, even though two individuals might have very different maximal capacities, assigning exercise workloads as a percentage of their maximal capacity relativizes the workload so that they are exercising at metabolically equivalent levels. Unfortunately, this assumption appears to be inaccurate. It has been shown that individuals exercising at the same relative workload can end up having very different metabolic responses. Thus, even exercise at a "moderate" intensity based on a percentage of maximal capacity results in some individuals working completely aerobically while others might require a significant contribution of anaerobic metabolism to complete the same workload. It was proposed that an approach that accounts for individually determined metabolic landmarks might be more useful in the study of exercise intensity effects (Ekkekakis & Petruzzello, 1999). In particular, the **lactate threshold** has been suggested as one such landmark (Ekkekakis, 2003). This is the point at which lactate concentrations in the blood exceed the rate at which lactate is removed from the blood, resulting in excess lactate and a shift toward increasing supplementation by anaerobic energy systems during exercise. The ventilatory threshold, another threshold that has been shown to be reasonably closely correlated with the lactate threshold, is thought to reflect the same basic shift toward increasing anaerobic energy system supplementation during more and more intense exercise. It is also a noninvasive way of estimating such changes in energy metabolism. A growing number of studies are using the lactate or ventilatory threshold as a basis for prescribing exercise intensity, and such research is showing promising results (see Ekkekakis, Parfitt, & Petruzzello, in press; see also the discussion of Bixby, Spalding, & Hatfield, 2001, and Ekkekakis, Hall, & Petruzzello, 2008, later in this chapter).

lactate threshold ■

Research on Affective Response to Exercise

This section summarizes research examining the affective responses to exercise, beyond that examining anxiety or depression responses. We emphasize studies that relate to the dose–response effect, that is, those studies that have examined varying levels of intensity, duration, or their combination. This selective review also focuses on research that has examined before- and after-exercise responses (easily a larger body of research) and research that has examined in-task exercise responses. To date, little systematic work has been done to examine affective responses to resistance exercise (see Arent, Landers, Matt, & Etnier, 2005, and Bartholomew, Moore, Todd, et al., 2001, for exceptions). Because so little evidence is currently available, the research reviewed in the next section focuses on affective responses to aerobic exercise. Clearly, examination of affective responses to resistance forms of exercise is important and needs more research attention.

Before- and After-Exercise Responses

Much of the early research examining the psychological responses to exercise was conducted using either the POMS or the State–Trait Anxiety Inventory (STAI; see Chapter 11). As noted by Biddle and Mutrie (2001), the relationship between exercise and mood (using the POMS) suggests a positive association between exercise and vigor and a negative association between exercise and moods like tension, anger, confusion, and fatigue. This is similar to the pattern referred to as the "iceberg profile" by Morgan (1984; see discussion later in this chapter and Exhibit 13.6). In general, research has shown that exercise seems to increase positive mood states (see Reed & Buck, 2009; Reed & Ones, 2006) and to reduce negative mood states.

An interesting paradoxical effect of exercise on affect or mood is the energizing effect that is so often reported. As noted by Thayer (2001), moderate amounts of exercise usually energize the exerciser. Thayer discusses how exercise can be used to boost energy levels when one is tired or energy levels are low. He discusses the following practical self-experiment: he suggests conducting a self-rating of energy at night while lounging around watching television (he suggests a scale from 1 to 7, with 1 being the least energy an individual usually feels and 7 being the most). He then suggests getting up and going for a 10-minute brisk walk, followed by another self-rating of energy. More often than not, feelings of energy increase. Such a practical self-regulatory technique is the result of numerous research studies where this effect has been shown. For example, in one of the first studies to document this effect, Thayer (1987) showed that 10 minutes of brisk walking significantly elevated feelings of energy for up to 120 minutes following the walk. Similar research by Saklofske, Blomme, and Kelly (1992) showed increased energy and decreased tension following walks of 4 and 10 minutes in duration. In a series of studies using both naturalistic and more controlled laboratory settings, Ekkekakis, Hall, Van Landuyt, and Petruzzello

(2000) showed that 10 to 15 minutes of walking was consistently associated with increased activation and more positive affective valence, in essence reflecting increased energy and decreased tension.

Although systematic examinations of exercise intensity beyond brisk walking have been relatively infrequent, their typical finding is that positive affect tends to increase from pre- to post-exercise following exercise intensities that are not exhaustive (Reed & Ones, 2006). Two studies are representative of these effects. First, Steptoe, Kearsley, and Walters (1993) showed, using the tension–anxiety, vigor, and depression–dejection subscales of the POMS, that vigor increased from pre- to post-exercise following cycling at both 50 percent and 70 percent of aerobic capacity; tension was decreased below pre-exercise levels by 30 minutes of recovery. In addition to these POMS subscales, Steptoe and colleagues used items reflective of exhilaration. Again, similar to the vigor effects, exhilaration was increased following exercise and stayed elevated during recovery. In a second study, Tate and Petruzzello (1995) examined affective responses to 30 minutes of cycling at 55 percent and 70 percent of maximal aerobic capacity. Affect was assessed using the AD ACL before, during, and following the exercise bouts. In this study, no affective changes were seen in the 55 percent intensity condition. Cycling at 70 percent resulted in significant increases in energetic arousal during and following exercise.

In general, it appears that positively valenced affective states (e.g., energy, vigor, exhilaration) are increased following moderate-intensity exercise (see also Reed & Ones, 2006), and negatively valenced affective states (e.g., fatigue, tension) are either unchanged or reduced following moderate exercise. Following high-intensity exercise, negative affective states may be increased and positive affective states decreased, particularly in less fit individuals. In more fit individuals, however, even high-intensity exercise may result in improved positive affect after the exercise (see Ekkekakis & Petruzzello, 1999).

In-Task Exercise Responses

If exercise can make people feel better, because of either increased energy or decreased tension and fatigue, why don't more people exercise? (See, for example, Backhouse, Ekkekakis, Biddle, et al., 2007.) As Thayer noted, "The extensive evidence about the value of exercise should have the gyms packed, the running tracks crowded, and the sidewalks filled with throngs of people walking. But they aren't" (2001, p. 32). It may very well be that even though people feel better *after* exercise, how they feel *during* exercise may be part of the problem. The work of Emmons and Diener (1986) nicely pointed out that the affect experienced during an activity is a good predictor of future engagement in that activity. As postulated by hedonic theory (Ekkekakis, 2009; Kahneman, 1999; Williams, 2008), a person is not likely to continue an activity that does not bring enjoyment or is not fun to do. In spite of the abundance of research examining pre- to post-exercise changes in affect, studies examining "in-task" affective responses have been rare, although there has been a move to change that shortcoming (see Ekkekakis et al., in press).

With the advent of single-item and relatively brief multi-item self-report scales for measuring affect, assessing affect during exercise has become more viable. As noted earlier, one scale, the Feeling Scale (FS), has begun to get much more use in this regard. For example, Hardy and Rejeski (1989) showed that across four-minute exercise bouts of increasing intensity (30 percent, 60 percent, and 90 percent of maximal aerobic capacity), affect, as measured by the FS, became progressively more negative. Parfitt and colleagues (Parfitt & Eston, 1995; Parfitt, Eston, & Connolly, 1996; Parfitt, Markland, & Holmes, 1994) showed similar findings. Parfitt and Eston showed that FS ratings were generally lower in a condition involving cycling at 90 percent of maximal aerobic capacity compared to 60 percent, with some additional differences occurring between active compared to inactive participants. Parfitt et al. (1994) also showed lower FS ratings in a 90 percent intensity exercise condition relative to exercise at 60 percent. In a study comparing low- and high-active women, Parfitt et al. (1996) showed that low-active women felt less positive at a higher level of perceived exertion (RPE = 17) than at a lower level (RPE = 9), along with being less positive than high-active women at all levels of exertion.

Another interesting aspect of some of the research examining in-task affective responses has been the relationship of these responses to ongoing physiological changes. In the work of Hardy and Rejeski (1989), relationships between FS and ratings of perceived exertion became progressively more negative as intensity increased from 30 percent to 90 percent of maximal aerobic capacity. In other words, as the intensity increased, perceptions of exertion increased while FS ratings decreased, indicating more displeasure at greater exercise intensity. Feeling Scale ratings were also negatively correlated with various physiological measures like ventilation, heart rate, respiratory rate, and oxygen consumption, reflecting decreased pleasure or increased displeasure with increasing physiological activation.

Acevedo, Rinehardt, and Kraemer (1994) found that as exercise intensity (in this case, running speed) increased, perceived exertion showed a corresponding increase, along with heart rate and blood lactate, but FS ratings became progressively less positive. Feeling Scale ratings were negatively related to the physiological variables of HR and lactate across all of the workloads. When examining the comparison of FS and perceived exertion, Acevedo and colleagues found moderate to strong negative relationships at the lower and highest intensities, but very small correlations at more moderate intensities. Finally, at the highest intensities, the variability in the FS ratings increased relative to the lower and moderate intensities, a finding that led the researchers to suggest the importance of examining individual difference factors that might influence such affective responses. Ekkekakis, Kavouras, Casa, et al. (1997) showed similar effects in a study using cycling exercise in the heat and under conditions of dehydration. They showed a progressive decline in affective valence (i.e., an increase in displeasure) from the beginning to the end of the exercise bout.

ventilatory threshold ■

In another study, Bixby and colleagues (2001) compared cycle ergometer exercise at two different intensities, one that corresponded to the **ventilatory threshold** (VT) and another that was significantly below the ventilatory threshold. Conceptually analogous to lactate threshold, ventilatory threshold is the point at which the ventilatory equivalent for oxygen continues to increase without a concomitant increase in the ventilatory equivalent for carbon dioxide. Bixby and colleagues used a visual analogue mood scale, a simple rating scale in which an individual indicates his or her current mood state by placing a mark along a horizontal line anchored with the words "worst mood" on one end and "best mood" at the other. With this instrument, Bixby et al. showed that during exercise below the VT, mood improved at 20 minutes into the exercise bout and then remained elevated for the remainder of the exercise and for a period of time during recovery. In contrast, exercise performed at the VT resulted in a worsening of mood at 10 minutes into the exercise bout, which remained that way until the recovery period.

Two additional studies are worthy of mention here. Acevedo, Kraemer, Haltom, and Tryniecki (2003) examined changes in perceived exertion and affective responses to exercise below, at, and above the lactate threshold. Consistent with Bixby et al., this latter group found that as exercise intensity increased, affect became increasingly less positive and more negative. These findings led them to propose that affect experienced during exercise could be important for enhancing adherence to exercise programs. Similarly, Parfitt, Rose, and Burgess (2006) showed that 20 minutes of exercise at an intensity exceeding the lactate threshold resulted in substantially more negative affective responses than exercise below the lactate threshold or at a self-selected intensity. Interestingly, the self-selected intensity ended up being not significantly different from the lactate threshold.

Finally, work reported by Van Landuyt, Ekkekakis, Hall, and Petruzzello (2000) highlighted the importance of in-task measures of affect in understanding how individuals might get from their pre-exercise affective state to the post-exercise affective state. In a moderate-intensity (60 percent of predicted maximal aerobic capacity) bout of cycling, there was essentially no change in FS ratings over the course of the 30-minute bout. This lack of change was masked, however, by the fact that about half of the participants (48 percent) reported an improvement in affective valence (reflected by increased FS scores), 35 percent reported a decline in affect (decreased FS scores), and about 17 percent reported no change. In other words, the lack of change at the group level concealed the fact that some individuals actually felt better during exercise while others felt worse. This work is useful in illustrating that even moderate-intensity bouts of exercise do not necessarily result in positive affective changes *during* the activity, even though pre- to post-exercise changes with such moderate-intensity activity are generally positive.

To summarize, the general conclusion that can be derived from the available research is that affect gets progressively more negative as exercise intensity increases. Moderate-intensity exercise generally results in more positive affective changes, but this is not a universal phenomenon and individual difference factors need to be carefully examined in this regard (Ekkekakis et al., in press).

Research Exemplar

As an example of how the problems described earlier can be addressed, consider the work of Hall, Ekkekakis, and Petruzzello (2002). Affective responses to three distinct levels of exercise intensity were examined before and after as well as during a graded treadmill protocol to the point at which the person could no longer continue. Affect was assessed using the dimensions of valence and activation contained in the circumplex model, and exercise intensity was standardized across individuals. Affect was measured using both multi-item and single-item instruments. The Feeling Scale (FS) was used as a measure of affective valence, and the Felt Arousal Scale (FAS) of the Telic State Measure (Svebak & Murgatroyd, 1985) was used as a single-item measure of perceived activation. Both the FS and FAS were used to assess affect during exercise and were obtained every minute of the exercise protocol. The Activation-Deactivation Adjective Check List (AD ACL) was used to provide a measure of the four quadrants of circumplex affective space discussed earlier (refer back to Exhibit 13.4) and was completed before and at the end of the exercise as well as 10 and 20 minutes following the exercise bout. Exercise intensity was standardized by using the ventilatory threshold (VT). Once the time point at which the VT occurred was determined, the following were selected for analysis: the FS and FAS ratings made at the first two minutes, the minute of the VT, two minutes following the VT, the last two minutes of the bout, and during the two minutes immediately following completion of the exercise bout.

The results of the study showed the following: Pre- to post-exercise responses on the AD ACL revealed beneficial affective responses, indexed by increased energetic arousal (EA) along with decreased tense arousal (TA, refer back to Exhibit 13.5). During exercise, however, affective valence became increasingly negative after the ventilatory threshold was reached and continued to be negative until volitional exhaustion was reached. Interestingly, this affective negativity rebounded completely when the exercise was stopped (Exhibit 13.5). These findings were interpreted as indicating that exercise at intensities requiring increasingly greater levels of anaerobic metabolism can have a substantial negative affective impact, albeit a relatively temporary one. Essentially the same pattern of findings has been seen in several recent investigations with a variety of different kinds of participants: young healthy adults (Ekkekakis et al., 2008); healthy college men and women (Kilpatrick, Kraemer, Bartholomew, et al., 2007); sedentary middle-aged women (Lind, Joens-Matre, & Ekkekakis, 2005); sedentary men and women (Parfitt et al., 2006); sedentary women (Rose & Parfitt, 2007); and sedentary young women (Welch, Hulley, Ferguson, & Beauchamp, 2007). Importantly, findings such as these could have implications for the design and implementation of exercise programs. To the extent that exercise programs can be individualized so that the exerciser does not experience negative affect during the activity, individuals might be better able to stick with their exercise regimens (Ekkekakis, 2009).

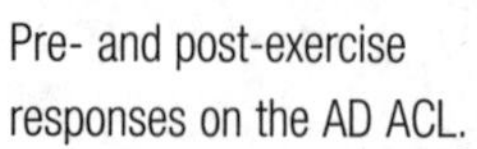

exhibit 13.5 Affective responses to a graded exercise protocol.

Pre- and post-exercise responses on the AD ACL.

EA = Energetic arousal
TA = Tense arousal

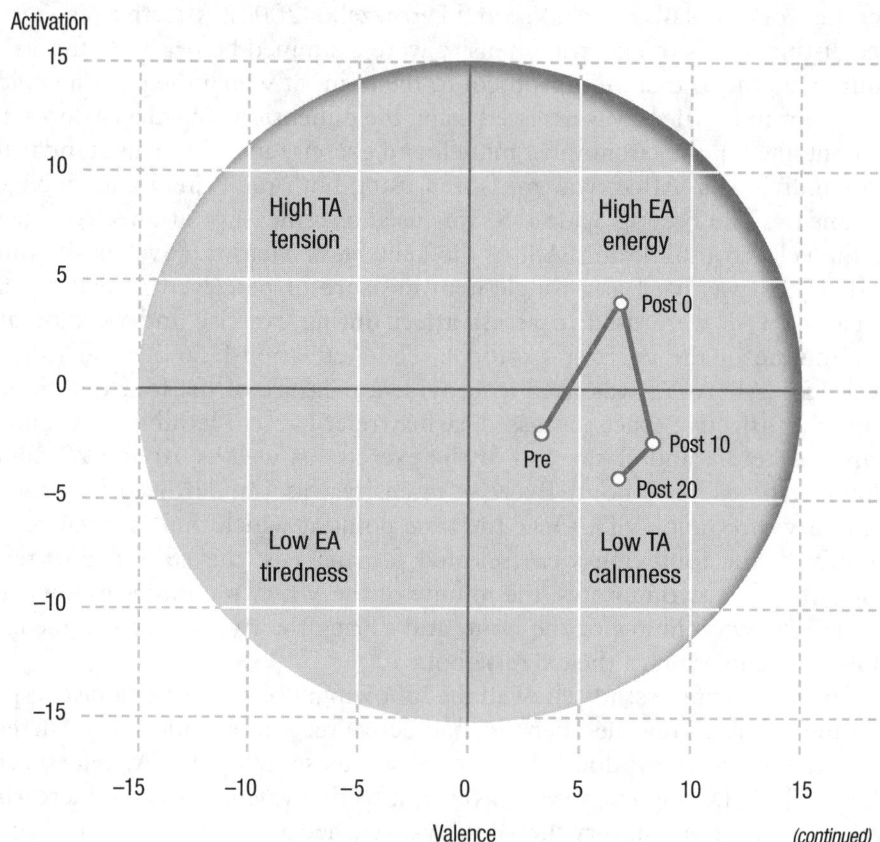

(continued)

Negative Psychological Effects of Exercise on Emotional Well-Being

Although the psychological effects associated with exercise are generally regarded as positive, this is not always the case. A number of negative psychological effects can take place with more extreme levels of exercise.

Overtraining, the Staleness Syndrome, and Depression

overtraining ■ It has been well documented that with overtraining in endurance athletes, the staleness syndrome often results. **Overtraining** occurs when the individual trains at a greater level than he or she might be accustomed to in terms of frequency, intensity, and duration. Such a pattern of training is used to help athletes adapt to greater levels of training

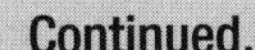

Continued. exhibit 13.5

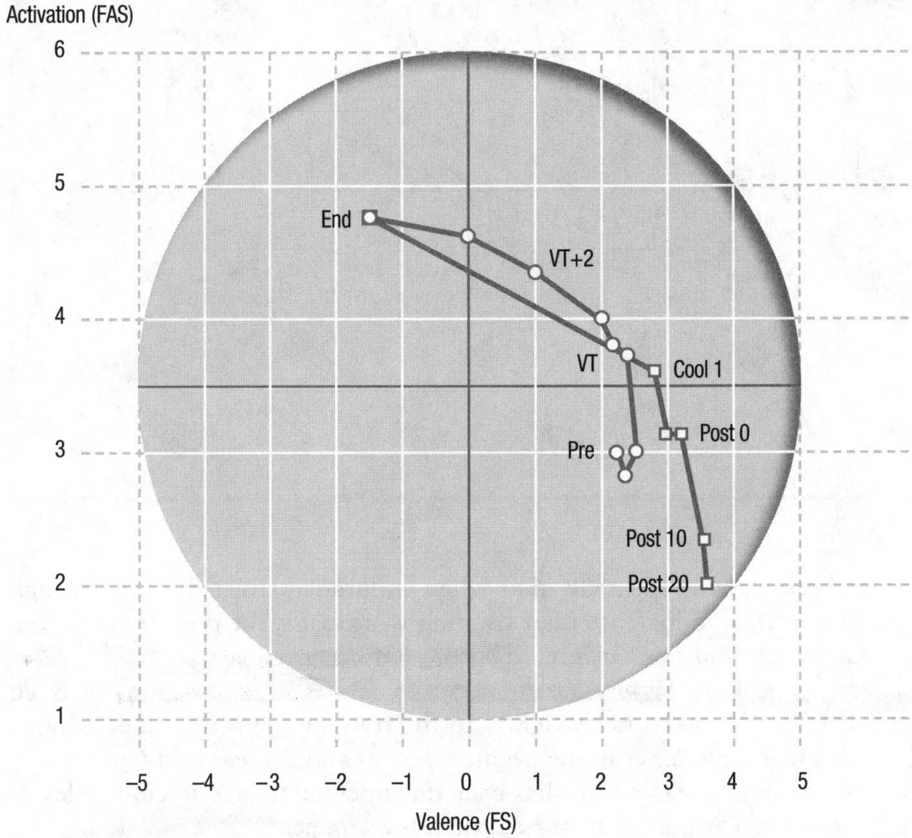

Responses across the stages of exercise, cool-down, and recovery on the FS and FAS.

VT = Ventilatory threshold

From Hall, Ekkekakis, & Petruzzello (2002, pp. 56, 59). Reproduced with permission from *The British Journal of Health Psychology.* © The British Psychological Society.

stress so that when they reduce the amount of training in preparation for important competitions (e.g., the Olympics) their bodies respond with better performances than were achievable prior to the overtraining. One negative aspect of such overtraining is that some individuals develop the **staleness syndrome,** characterized by increased negative mental health (depression, anxiety, fatigue, reduced energy) and poorer performance. Overtraining can also lead to clinical depression in elite athletes.

■ staleness syndrome

Morgan's Mental Health Model (1984) describes the psychological profile of the elite athlete, relative to the population average, as being above average on positive factors and below average on negative factors. This has been popularly referred to as the **"iceberg profile"** because, when scores from the POMS subscales are plotted on the POMS profile sheet, athletes typically have scores on the vigor subscale that fall above the 50th percentile and scores on the tension, confusion, anger, fatigue, and depression subscales that fall below the 50th percentile. Connecting the points on the profile sheet results in what looks like an iceberg (see Exhibit 13.6).

■ iceberg profile

exhibit 13.6 **The "iceberg profile."**

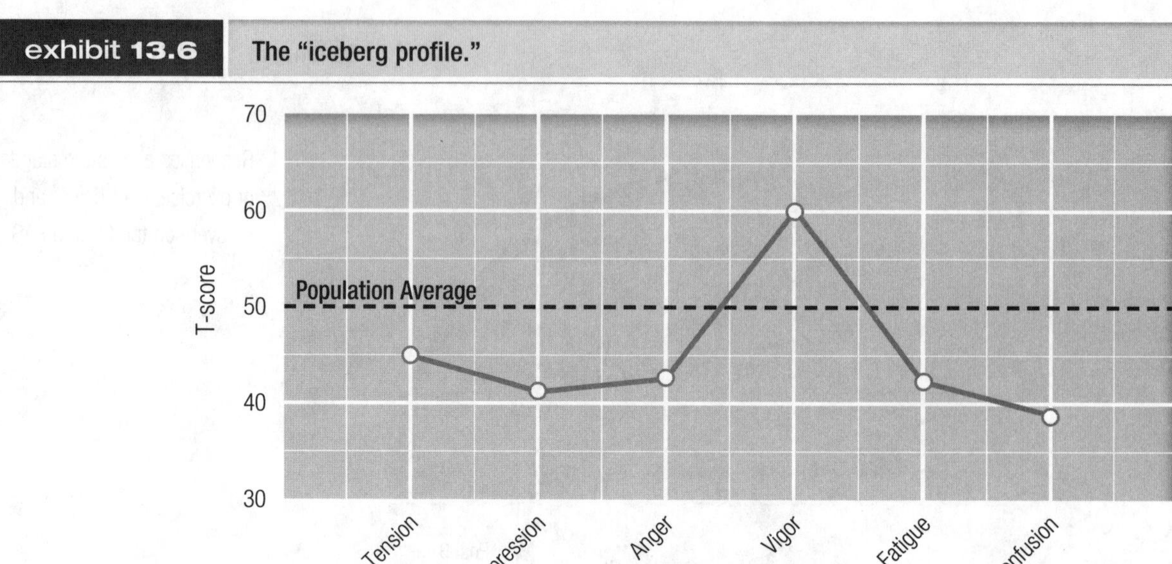

Source: Morgan (1984).

It has been shown repeatedly that when endurance athletes move through their training cycle and increase their training workloads, the typical profile begins to flatten out and even inverts. That is, with increasing workloads, vigor scores decrease and scores on the five "negative" mood subscales increase. Such an effect is typically linked fairly tightly to the training load (Raglin & Moger, 1999), with greater increases in the negative scores and decreases in vigor as the amount of training increases. This has been documented to lead to clinical levels of depression, and the only known treatment is to reduce the training load.

exhibit 13.7 **Terminology used in the study of exercise dependence.**

Exercise dependence, *also* running dependence
Addiction, *also* running addiction, exercise addiction, negative addiction
Obligatory exercise
Exercise commitment
Excessive exercise
Commitment to physical activity, *also* excessive commitment to running
Attitudinal commitment
Compulsive runner
High-intensity running
Habitual running

Source: Hausenblas & Symons Downs (2002).

Exercise Dependence Syndrome

Another phenomenon that has received much more attention in the literature is what is referred to as the **exercise dependence syndrome.** Unfortunately, this phenomenon has been referred to by various labels (see Exhibit 13.7), and numerous measures have been used to document its existence, all of which have led to a great deal of confusion. As defined by Hausenblas and Symons Downs (2002), exercise dependence is "a craving for leisure-time physical activity, resulting in uncontrollable excessive exercise behavior, that manifests in physiological (e.g., tolerance/withdrawal) and/or psychological (e.g., anxiety, depression) symptoms" (p. 90). One of the points raised by Symons Downs, Hausenblas, and Nigg (2004) in their review of the exercise dependence literature is the need for better operational definitions of exercise dependence. To that end, their suggested criteria are listed in Exhibit 13.8.

■ exercise dependence syndrome

exhibit 13.8

Operational definitions of the multidimensional nature of exercise dependence with sample items from the Exercise Dependence Scale.

1. Tolerance
   - Need for increased amount of exercise to achieve desired effect
     "I continually increase my exercise intensity to achieve the desired effects/benefits."
   - Diminished effect with continuation of same amount of exercise
     "I feel less of an effect/benefit with my current exercise."
2. Withdrawal
   - Withdrawal symptoms (e.g., anxiety, fatigue, disturbed sleep) when exercise is missed
     "I feel tense if I cannot exercise."
   - Exercise relieves or helps avoid withdrawal symptoms
     "I exercise to avoid feeling irritable."
3. Intention effects: Exercise often lasts longer than was originally intended
   "I often exercise longer than I intend."
4. Loss of control: Persistent desire and/or unsuccessful effort to control exercise (e.g., cut back)
   "I am unable to reduce how long I exercise."
5. Time: Lots of time spent in activities needed to obtain exercise
   "I organize my life around my exercise."
6. Conflict: Giving up of important social, occupational, and relationship activities because of exercise
   "I decline social invitations because they interfere with my exercise."
7. Continuance: Exercise is maintained in spite of knowledge that it is problematic from either physical (e.g., injury) or psychological perspectives
   "I exercise despite persistent physical problems."

Source: Symons Downs, Hausenblas, & Nigg (2004).

It is worth noting that exercise dependence is often a part of an eating disorder. Pierce (1994) discusses the distinction between primary and secondary exercise dependence, noting that the main distinction is derived from the individual's objective for exercising. In **primary exercise dependence**, the exercise is an end in itself. Any alterations of body composition or diet are done to enhance exercise performance. Other features associated with primary exercise dependence include the following: exercise tolerance, manifested as a progressively increasing volume of exercise (e.g., increasing levels of intensity and/or duration, or increased frequency of exercise) or a regular (e.g., daily) stereotyped activity that may or may not be at a high volume; exercising alone; or lying about exercise (e.g., telling a spouse that one is going shopping and then working out instead). In **secondary exercise dependence**, exercise is used exclusively to control body composition. This is seen quite often in individuals with eating disorders (e.g., anorexia nervosa). Pierce also discusses a number of factors associated with exercise dependence, including psychological, behavioral, and physiological. Pierce notes that there is a positive relationship between exercise dependence and anxiety, compulsiveness, and rigidity, along with a negative association with self-esteem. Perhaps obviously, in terms of behavior, a positive association exists between exercise dependence and exercise volume (e.g., frequency, duration).

primary exercise dependence ■

secondary exercise dependence ■

Several psychobiological mechanisms have been proposed as explanations for exercise dependence (Hamer & Karageorghis, 2007). The *affect regulation hypothesis* postulates that exercise acts to enhance positive affect and reduce negative affect. Originally proposed by Tomkins (as cited in Hamer & Karageorghis) as an explanation of smoking behavior, Hamer and Karageorghis discuss the "negative exerciser" as a person who exercises to reduce stress and other negative feelings (e.g., depression, anxiety) in contrast to the "positive exerciser," the person who exercises to increase positive feelings (e.g., energy, vigor). Either of these types of exercisers could be exercise dependent. With respect to exercise dependence, the habitual exerciser experiences mood disturbances upon withdrawal from exercise (i.e., when he or she is unable to engage in a planned routine). Thus, the person who runs to feel good ends up experiencing more negative feelings when she is unable to run.

One problem with the studies relates to the issue of why the habitual exerciser stopped exercising. For example, if the exercise cessation was caused by injury, it is difficult to tease out which part of the mood disturbance is due to the injury and which might be due to the inability to exercise. Another problem in these studies is when affect is measured. For example, a study by Mondin, Morgan, Piering, and colleagues (1996) had regular exercisers (who may or may not have been exercise dependent) perform an acute bout of exercise on the first day of the study, after which they completed a measure of their mood state. Over the next three days, participants completed mood measures at the same time each day but abstained from their regular exercise routine. Mondin et al. reported that mood became progressively more negative over the days with no exercise. However, the researchers compared the mood measures on the days with no exercise to the mood state reported *following* an acute bout of exercise, which is known to result in reductions in negative and/or increases in positive mood. Was the increasing negative mood on non-exercise days due to the lack of exercise, or was it just the normal mood response that appeared to be more negative because it was being compared to a day with exercise?

A recent investigation by Niven, Rendell, and Chisholm (2008) essentially replicated the work by Mondin et al., but they did not assess initial affect following an acute exercise bout. Niven and colleagues had 58 healthy women who exercised regularly (i.e., at least four days per week) complete measures of affect and body image, and then they randomly asked half of the women to abstain from exercising for a 72-hour period. Like Mondin et al., Niven and colleagues found that "hedonic tone" (i.e., pleasure–displeasure) became less pleasurable, a measure of positive affect became less positive, and measures of negative affect and body image became more negative during the abstinence period. It is worth pointing out that Niven et al. were very careful to describe the stoppage of exercise as abstinence rather than as exercise deprivation or withdrawal. As alluded to earlier, in studies like these it is unethical to impose cessation of exercise on an individual. Indeed, it could be argued that a truly "dependent" exerciser would likely not stop their exercise regimen for anything. In many, if not all, of the exercise dependence research done with humans, the participants willingly refrain from exercising, which is an important distinction in this research.

Another psychobiological explanation is the *anorexia analogue hypothesis*. Originally proposed by Yates, Leehey, and Shisslak (1983), the idea is that compulsive exercise serves as a male counterpart of the eating disorder anorexia nervosa (which is a predominantly female disorder, with women comprising 95 percent of individuals diagnosed as having anorexia nervosa). Yates and colleagues proposed the hypothesis on the basis of similarities in personality profiles (inhibition of anger, unreasonably high expectations for themselves, ability to tolerate physical discomfort, denial of incapacity, tendency toward depression) between obligatory male runners and patients suffering from anorexia nervosa. Thus, the idea is that whereas women with this particular personality profile are more likely to be anorexic, men with a similar profile are more likely to exhibit exercise dependence. This hypothesis has received only limited support in the literature.

In the *endorphin hypothesis,* the individual is thought to exercise to excess because of an actual physical dependence on the chemical released during exercise, a dependence sometimes referred to as "addiction." Whether exercise dependence is an addiction is a debatable issue. Experts have not yet agreed that such addictions can actually occur with exercise, or the extent to which such dependence might occur. Endorphins are known to be released in response to stress, and exercise is certainly a form of stress (see Chapter 10). The endorphin hypothesis suggests that it is the release of those endorphins that the individual's body craves, leading to more exercise to result in more endorphin release, and the cycle repeats itself. Animal research gives some limited support to this hypothesis, whereby chronic exercise may lead to tolerance of endorphins. This tolerance results in greater doses of exercise (i.e., increased intensity, longer duration, greater frequency) to yield the same psychological effect.

The psychophysiological hypothesis (also referred to as the *energy conservation–sympathetic arousal hypothesis;* see Thompson & Blanton, 1987) posits that because the effect of training is a decrease in sympathetic nervous system output (e.g., catecholamines—epinephrine and norepinephrine), an increase in fitness can potentially result in a state of lethargy, fatigue, and decreased arousal. This state motivates the individual to increase the training dose, thereby increasing catecholamine output and satisfying the physiological "need." This creates a vicious cycle, however, because eventually the individual adapts to the increased training load, decreasing catecholamines and increasing the negative feelings. To date, this particular hypothesis has not been specifically tested within an exercise dependence paradigm.

Although some individuals clearly exercise excessively, caution is certainly warranted at this stage of knowledge development when drawing conclusions about exercise dependence. For one thing, it is very difficult to study truly exercise-dependent individuals, if for no other reason than they are unwilling (or unable) to stop exercising and will not do so voluntarily. Thus, it is impossible to determine how their physical and psychological states vary as a function of their exercise levels and exercise withdrawal. By definition, an individual could not be dependent on exercise if there were no withdrawal symptoms upon cessation of exercise. In fact, Baekeland (1970), in his initial study attempting to examine the effects of exercise deprivation on sleep, was unable to recruit any individual who ran more than five or six days per week! In many cases it is possible to study truly dependent exercisers only when they become injured, but in those cases it is difficult to discern whether the affective responses are due to the deprivation or to the injury. Finally, because of the definitional and measurement problems that have plagued this area of research to this point, it is difficult to measure how serious a problem exercise dependence is in terms of its prevalence within the population.

Practical Recommendations

It would appear that one of the most reasonable things individuals can do regarding exercise and their emotional well-being is simply to become more aware of how they feel when they do or do not exercise. As Thayer (2001) outlines in his book, one way to do this is through self-study. This is a fairly simple activity, but one that could pay great dividends. As Thayer shows, self-study involves thinking about how energetic or tense you feel at different times of the day. It is also important to note how you feel before and after any exercise that you might do on a given day. You might find it advantageous to try to schedule exercise time during periods of the day when you usually experience low energy, as it has been fairly clearly shown that one of the best benefits of exercise is increased energy and decreased tension—as Nick and Stephanie discovered in the chapter-opening scenario.

As with other aspects of mental health, the amount of exercise required to achieve increased positive or decreased negative feelings is currently not known. It does seem apparent that exercise that is not excessive ("excessive" could be defined simply as activity being done every day for more than one hour at a time, particularly when it is not part of some sort of athletic training regimen) results in more positive affective responses, particularly if done below the ventilatory threshold. Perhaps the simplest rule of thumb to follow is that if you can carry on a conversation while exercising, the intensity is not too high. Such types of exercise will likely result in positive (or at least not negative) experiences during and following the exercise, thus increasing the likelihood that the exercise will be performed again (and again and again).

It is important to point out that this is a rapidly changing area of study. Much remains to be learned about dose–response effects, and new research is being reported every week that is helping to detail these kinds of effects. It does seem clear that, in addition to the reduction in depression and anxiety, exercise has much to offer, and better understanding these benefits will be useful in designing exercise programs that people not only engage in but also enjoy.

Conclusion

The study of the psychological outcomes of exercise is becoming increasingly recognized as an important endeavor. In spite of the relatively long history of research examining such outcomes, however, we continue to have a fairly limited knowledge of what effects exercise has and how these effects might influence exercise behavior, whether that be adherence to a regular program of activity or dropping out from such programs. Given the health benefits that accrue from exercise, a better understanding of the psychological outcomes could have a very worthwhile influence on behavior.

what do you know?

1. What is the definition of emotional well-being?
2. Distinguish among emotions, moods, and affect.
3. What two things led to the dissatisfaction with existing affective measures and the development of exercise-specific measures?
4. What are the two major advantages attributed to using a dimensional approach to study affect?
5. What general conclusions can be drawn regarding the before-to-after affective responses to exercise?
6. What is the metabolic landmark that seems to provide a fairly reliable indication of when, *during* exercise, affect shifts from good to bad or positive to negative?
7. Distinguish between primary and secondary exercise dependence.
8. What is the basis for the energy conservation–sympathetic arousal hypothesis?
9. Based on what is currently known, is exercise dependence a widespread problem?

learning activities

1. To gain a better understanding of the relationship between exercise and affect, conduct a self-experiment. Over the course of two weeks, do a simple rating of energy and tension before and after a scheduled exercise session. Use a rating from 1 to 7 for each, with 1 being none or very little and 7 being a great deal or very much. On non-exercise days, rate yourself using the same scale at approximately the same times of the day that you would exercise. After the two-week period, compare the ratings from before and after the exercise session. What differences are apparent? What happens when you compare the affect on exercise days with the affect experienced on non-exercise days?
2. Use the circumplex approach to examining affective responses. Using the circumplex diagram below, in which the dimensions of activation and valence are represented, try the following exercises. Incorporate the following time points as appropriate:

- Moderate Exercise
  - Pre-exercise
  - 5 minutes
  - 15 minutes
  - Immediately post-exercise
  - 20 minutes post-exercise
- Intense Exercise
  - Pre-exercise
  - 5 minutes
  - 15 minutes
  - Immediately post-exercise
  - 20 minutes post-exercise

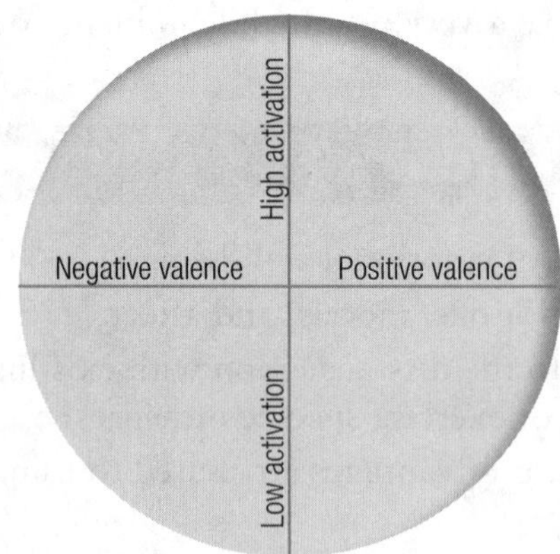

a. Describe two different intensities of exercise, noting how they differ in terms of intensity. Label one type as "moderate" and the other as "intense."
b. Draw the expected response to a 20-minute bout of the "moderate" exercise.
c. Draw the expected response to a 20-minute bout of the "intense" exercise, incorporating the same time points.
d. What are the major differences in the two drawings? Why do these differences occur?

references

Acevedo, E.O., Kraemer, R.R., Haltom, R.W., & Tryniecki, J.L. (2003). Perceptual responses proximal to the onset of blood lactate accumulation. *Journal of Sports Medicine & Physical Fitness, 43,* 267–273.

Acevedo, E.O., Rinehart, K.F., & Kraemer, R.R. (1994). Perceived exertion and affect at varying intensities of running. *Research Quarterly for Exercise & Sport, 65,* 372–376.

American College of Sports Medicine (2006). *ACSM's guidelines for exercise testing and prescription* (7th ed.). Philadelphia, PA: Lippincott Williams & Wilkins.

Arent, S.M., Landers, D.M., Matt, K.S., & Etnier, J.L. (2005). Dose-response and mechanistic issues in the resistance training and affect relationship. *Journal of Sport & Exercise Psychology, 27,* 92–110.

Backhouse, S.H., Ekkekakis, P., Biddle, S.J.H., Foskett, A., & Williams, C. (2007). Exercise makes people feel better but people are inactive: Paradox or artifact? *Journal of Sport & Exercise Psychology, 29,* 498–517.

Baekeland, F. (1970). Exercise deprivation: Sleep and psychological reactions. *Archives of General Psychiatry, 22,* 365–369.

Bartholomew, J.B., Moore, J., Todd, J., Todd, T., & Elrod, C.C. (2001). Psychological states following resistant exercise of different workloads. *Journal of Applied Sport Psychology, 13,* 399–410.

Berger, B.G. (1994). Coping with stress: The effectiveness of exercise and other techniques. *Quest, 46,* 100–119.

Biddle, S.J.H., & Mutrie, N. (2001). *Psychology of physical activity: Determinants, well-being and interventions.* New York: Routledge.

Bixby, W.R., Spalding, T.W., & Hatfield, B.D. (2001). Temporal dynamics and dimensional specificity of the affective response to exercise of varying intensity: Differing pathways to a common outcome. *Journal of Sport and Exercise Psychology, 23,* 171–190.

Centers for Disease Control and Prevention. (2000). Prevalence of leisure-time physical activity among overweight adults: United States, 1998. *Morbidity & Mortality Weekly Reports, 49,* 326–330.

Dishman, R.K. (1986). Mental health. In V. Seefeldt (Ed.), *Physical activity and well-being* (pp. 303–341). Reston, VA: AAHPERD.

Ekkekakis, P. (2003). Pleasure and displeasure from the body; Perspectives from exercise. *Cognition & Emotion, 17,* 213–239.

Ekkekakis, P. (2009). Let them roam free? Physiological and psychological evidence for the potential of self-selected exercise intensity in public health. *Sports Medicine, 39,* 857–888.

Ekkekakis, P., Hall, E.E., & Petruzzello, S.J. (2008). The relationship between exercise intensity and affective responses demystified: To crack the 40-year-old nut, replace the 40-year-old nutcracker! *Annals of Behavioral Medicine, 35,* 136–149.

Ekkekakis, P., Hall, E.E., Van Landuyt, L.M., & Petruzzello, S.J. (2000). Walking in (affective) circles: Can short walks enhance affect? *Journal of Behavioral Medicine, 23,* 245–275.

Ekkekakis, P., Kavouras, S.A., Casa, D.J., Herrera, J.A., Armstrong, L.E., Maresh, C.M., & Petruzzello, S.J. (1997). Affective responses to a bout of exhaustive exercise in the heat in dehydrated and rehydrated states: In search of physiological correlates. In R. Lidor & M. Bar-Eli (Eds.), *Innovations in sport psychology: Linking theory and practice* (pp. 253–254). Proceedings of the IX World Congress of Sport Psychology.

Ekkekakis, P., & Lind, E. (2006). Exercise does not feel the same when you are overweight: The impact of self-selected and imposed intensity on affect and exertion. *International Journal of Obesity, 30*(4), 652–660.

Ekkekakis, P., Parfitt, G., & Petruzzello, S.J. (in press). The effect of intensity on the pleasure or displeasure people feel when they exercise: Decennial update and progress towards a tripartite rationale for exercise intensity prescription.

Ekkekakis, P., & Petruzzello, S.J. (1999). Acute aerobic exercise and affect: Current status, problems and prospects regarding dose–response. *Sports Medicine, 28,* 337–374.

Ekkekakis, P., & Petruzzello, S.J. (2000). Analysis of the affect measurement conundrum in exercise psychology. I. Fundamental issues. *Psychology of Sport and Exercise, 1,* 71–88.

Ekkekakis, P., & Petruzzello, S.J. (2001a). Analysis of the affect measurement conundrum in exercise psychology. II. A conceptual and methodological critique of the Exercise-Induced Feeling Inventory. *Psychology of Sport and Exercise, 2,* 1–26.

Ekkekakis, P., & Petruzzello, S.J. (2001b). Analysis of the affect measurement conundrum in exercise psychology. III. A conceptual and methodological critique of the Subjective Exercise Experiences Scale. *Psychology of Sport and Exercise, 2,* 205–232.

Ekkekakis, P., & Petruzzello, S.J. (2002). Analysis of the affect measurement conundrum in exercise psychology. IV. A conceptual case for the affect circumplex. *Psychology of Sport and Exercise, 3,* 35–63.

Emmons, R.A., & Diener, E. (1986). A goal-affect analysis of everyday situational choices. *Journal of Research in Personality, 20,* 309–326.

Felson, D.T., Lawrence, R.C., Dieppe, P.A., Hirsch, R., Helmick, C.G., Jordan, J.M., et al. (2000). Osteoarthritis: New insights, part I: The disease and its risk factors. *Annals of Internal Medicine, 133,* 635–646.

Focht, B.C., Gauvin, L., & Rejeski, W.J. (2004). The contribution of daily experiences and acute exercise to fluctuations in daily feeling states among older, obese adults with knee osteoarthritis. *Journal of Behavioral Medicine, 27,* 101–121.

Gauvin, L., & Brawley, L.R. (1993). Alternative psychological models and methodologies for the study of exercise and effect. In P. Seraganian (Ed.), *Exercise psychology: The influence of physical exercise on psychological processes* (pp. 146–171). New York: John Wiley.

Gauvin L., & Rejeski, W.J. (1993). The Exercise-Induced Feeling Inventory: Development and initial validation. *Journal of Sport and Exercise Psychology, 15,* 403–423.

Gauvin, L., & Spence, J.C. (1998). Measurement of exercise-induced changes in feeling states, affect, mood, and emotions. In J.L. Duda (Ed.), *Advances in sport and exercise psychology measurement* (pp. 325–336). Morgantown, WV: Fitness Information Technology.

Hall, E.E., Ekkekakis, P., & Petruzzello, S.J. (2002). The affective beneficence of vigorous exercise revisited. *British Journal of Health Psychology, 7,* 47–66.

Hamer, M., & Karageorghis, C.I. (2007). Psychobiological mechanisms of exercise dependence. *Sports Medicine, 37,* 477–484.

Hardy, C.J., & Rejeski, W.J. (1989). Not what, but how one feels: The measurement of affect during exercise. *Journal of Sport and Exercise Psychology, 11,* 304–317.

Hausenblas, H.A., & Symons Downs, D. (2002). Exercise dependence: A systematic review. *Psychology of Sport and Exercise, 3,* 89–123.

James, W. (1899). Untitled. *American Physical Education Review, 4,* 220–221.

Kahneman, D. (1999). Objective happiness. In D. Kahneman, E. Diener, & N. Schwarz (Eds.), *Well-being: Foundations of hedonic psychology* (pp. 3–25). New York: Russell Sage Foundation.

Kilpatrick, M., Kraemer, R., Bartholomew, J., Acevedo, E., & Jarreau, D. (2007). Affective responses to exercise are dependent on intensity rather than total work. *Medicine & Science in Sports & Exercise, 39,* 1417–1422.

Lind, E., Joens-Matre, R.R., & Ekkekakis, P. (2005). What intensity of physical activity do previously sedentary middle-aged women select? Evidence of a coherent pattern from physiological, perceptual, and affective markers. *Preventive Medicine, 40,* 407–419.

Lox, C.L., Jackson, S., Tuholski, S.W., Wasley, D., & Treasure, D.C. (2000). Revisiting the measurement of exercise-induced feeling states: The Physical Activity Affect Scale (PAAS). *Measurement in Physical Education and Exercise Science, 4,* 79–95.

McAuley, E. (1994). Physical activity and psychosocial outcomes. In C. Bouchard, R.J. Shephard, & T. Stephens (Eds.), *Physical activity, fitness, and health: International proceedings and consensus statement* (pp. 551–568). Champaign, IL: Human Kinetics.

McAuley, E., & Courneya, K.S. (1994). The Subjective Exercise Experiences Scale (SEES): Development and preliminary validation. *Journal of Sport and Exercise Psychology, 16,* 163–177.

McAuley, E., & Rudolph, D. (1995). Physical activity, aging, and psychological well-being. *Journal of Aging and Physical Activity, 3,* 67–96.

McNair, D.M., Lorr, M., & Droppleman, L.F. (1971). *Manual for the profile of mood states.* San Diego, CA: Educational and Industrial Testing Service.

Mondin, G.W., Morgan, W.P., Piering, P.N., Stegner, A.J., Stotesbury, C.L., Trine, M.R., & Wu, M. (1996). Psychological consequences of exercise deprivation in habitual exercisers. *Medicine and Science in Sports and Exercise, 28,* 1199–1203.

Morgan, W.P. (1984). Selected psychological factors limiting performance: A mental health model. *American Academy of Physical Education Papers, 18,* 70–80.

National Center for Health Statistics. (2007). *Selected health conditions and risk factors, United States, 2005–2006.* Hyattsville, MD: Author.

National Institutes of Health Consensus Development Panel on Physical Activity and Cardiovascular Health. (1996). Physical activity and cardiovascular health. *Journal of the American Medical Association, 276,* 241–246.

Niven, A., Rendell, E., & Chisholm, L. (2008). Effects of 72-h of exercise abstinence on affect and body dissatisfaction in healthy female regular exercisers. *Journal of Sports Sciences, 26,* 1235–1242.

O'Connor, P.J., & Puetz, T.W. (2005). Chronic physical activity and feelings of energy and fatigue. *Medicine & Science in Sports & Exercise, 37,* 299–305.

Parfitt, G., & Eston, R. (1995). Changes in ratings of perceived exertion and psychological affect in the early stages of exercise. *Perceptual and Motor Skills, 80,* 259–266.

Parfitt, G., Eston, R., & Connolly, D. (1996). Psychological affect at different ratings of perceived exertion in high- and low-active women: A study using a production protocol. *Perceptual & Motor Skills, 83,* 1035–1042.

Parfitt, G., Markland, D., & Holmes, C. (1994). Responses to physical exertion in active and inactive males and females. *Journal of Sport and Exercise Psychology, 16,* 178–186.

Parfitt, G., Rose, E.A., & Burgess, W.M. (2006). The psychological and physiological responses of sedentary individuals to prescribed and preferred intensity exercise. *British Journal of Health Psychology, 11,* 39–53.

Pierce, E.F. (1994). Exercise dependence syndrome in runners. *Sports Medicine, 18,* 149–155.

Raglin, J.S., & Moger, L. (1999). Adverse consequences of physical activity: When more is too much. In J.M. Rippe (Ed.), *Lifestyle medicine* (pp. 998–1004). Malden, MA: Blackwell Science.

Reed, J., & Buck, S. (2009). The effect of regular aerobic exercise on positive-activated affect: A meta-analysis. *Psychology of Sport & Exercise, 10,* 581–594.

Reed, J., & Ones, D.S. (2006). The effect of acute aerobic exercise on positive activated affect: A meta-analysis. *Psychology of Sport & Exercise, 7,* 477–514.

Rose, E.A., & Parfitt, G. (2007). A quantitative analysis and qualitative explanation of the individual differences in affective responses to prescribed and self-selected exercise intensities. *Journal of Sport & Exercise Psychology* , *29,* 281–309.

Russell, J.A. (1980). A circumplex model of affect. *Journal of Personality and Social Psychology, 39,* 1161–1178.

Russell, J.A. (1997). How shall an emotion be called? In R. Plutchik & H.R. Conte (Eds.), *Circumplex models of personality and emotions* (pp. 205–222). Washington, DC: American Psychological Association.

Saklofske, D.H., Blomme, G.C., & Kelly, I.W. (1992). The effect of exercise and relaxation on energetic and tense arousal. *Personality and Individual Differences, 13,* 623–625.

Steptoe, A., Kearsley, N., & Walters, N. (1993). Acute mood responses to maximal and submaximal exercise in active and inactive men. *Psychology and Health, 8,* 89–99.

Svebak, S., & Murgatroyd, S. (1985). Metamotivational dominance: A multimethod validation of reversal theory constructs. *Journal of Personality and Social Psychology, 48,* 107–116.

Symons Downs, D., Hausenblas, H.A., & Nigg, C.A. (2004). Factorial validity and psychometric examination of the Exercise Dependence Scale–Revised. *Measurement in Physical Education and Exercise Science, 8,* 183–201.

Tate, A.K., & Petruzzello, S.J. (1995). Varying the intensity of acute exercise: Implications for changes in affect. *Journal of Sports Medicine and Physical Fitness, 35,* 295–302.

Thayer, R.E. (1986). Activation–deactivation adjective check list: Current overview and structural analysis. *Psychological Reports, 58,* 607–614.

Thayer, R.E. (1987). Energy, tiredness, and tension effects of a sugar snack versus moderate exercise. *Journal of Personality and Social Psychology, 52,* 119–125.

Thayer, R.E. (1989). *The biopsychology of mood and arousal.* New York: Oxford University Press.

Thayer, R.E. (2001). *Calm energy: How people regulate mood with food and exercise.* New York: Oxford University Press.

Thompson, J.K., & Blanton, P. (1987). Energy conservation and exercise dependence: A sympathetic arousal hypothesis. *Medicine and Science in Sports and Exercise, 19,* 91–99.

Van Landuyt, L.M., Ekkekakis, P., Hall, E.E., & Petruzzello, S.J. (2000). Throwing the mountains into the lakes: On the perils of nomothetic conceptions of the exercise–affect relationship. *Journal of Sport and Exercise Psychology, 22,* 208–234.

Watson, D., & Clark, L.A. (1994). *The PANAS-X: Manual for the positive and negative affect schedule–Expanded form.* Unpublished manuscript, University of Iowa, Iowa City.

Watson, D., Clark, L.A., & Tellegen, A. (1988). Development and validation of brief measures of positive and negative affect: The PANAS scales. *Journal of Personality and Social Psychology, 54,* 1063–1070.

Watson, D., & Tellegen, A. (1985). Toward a consensual structure of mood. *Psychological Bulletin, 98,* 219–235.

Welch, A.S., Hulley, A., Ferguson, C., & Beauchamp, M.R. (2007). Affective responses of inactive women to a maximal incremental exercise test: A test of the dual-mode model. *Psychology of Sport & Exercise, 8,* 401–423.

Williams, D.M. (2008). Exercise, affect, and adherence: An integrated model and a case for self-paced exercise. *Journal of Sport & Exercise Psychology, 30,* 471–496.

Yates, A., Leehey, K., & Shisslak, C.M. (1983). Running—an analogue of anorexia? *New England Journal of Medicine, 308*(5), 251–255.

14

Cognitive Function and Exercise

KEY TERMS

amplitude
angiogenesis
attentional network
attentional resources
brain-derived neurotrophic factor (BDNF)
cardiovascular fitness hypothesis
cognitive function
error-related negativity (ERN)
event-related potential (ERP)
executive control
functional magnetic resonance imaging (fMRI)
interference control
latency
neurogenesis
neuroimaging
P300 (P3)
response inhibition
selective improvement hypothesis
stopping
stopping task
synaptic plasticity
task switching
working memory

Nola is a kinesiology major at a large research university. Students in her program are encouraged to get involved in faculty members' research projects. After looking over her options, Nola decides to work in the laboratory of a professor who is studying the effects of exercise on cognitive processing. As a result of her experience, Nola strongly encourages her grandparents, George and Phyllis, to become more physically active. Using what she has learned from working in the lab, Nola recommends that her grandparents begin walking together each evening after dinner. When the weather gets colder, George and Phyllis join a group of older adults who walk inside the local mall every morning before it opens for business. When she sees her grandparents over the holidays, Nola is amazed by how much more alert and "with it" they seem. George and Phyllis have even lost a little bit of weight, and they comment to Nola that they feel so much better and are no longer having as much trouble remembering where they put things. As she listens to them, Nola realizes that she is seeing living proof of the research she has been assisting with—older adults really can improve their cognitive functioning by exercising.

The connection between exercise and the brain's ability to process information is one of many examples of the connection between mind and body. Researchers have been examining the relationship between exercise and cognitive functioning for at least the past 50 years. However, it has really only been since the turn of the 21st century that a combination of several elements—solid research design, sophisticated new imaging technology, and complementary research using animal models—has provided new and more definitive insights into the effect that exercise can have on cognitive function, as well as brain structure and function.

Numerous anecdotal reports suggest that exercise facilitates cognitive processing, but other reports seem to indicate debilitating effects of exercise on cognitive function. Many reviews of the exercise–cognitive function literature have concluded that the evidence is mixed, leaning definitively neither one way nor the other. This confusion has resulted partly from:

- comparing acute and chronic exercise studies,
- the variety of measures of cognitive functioning that have been used, and
- variations in when cognitive processing was assessed relative to the exercise itself (i.e., before, during, or after).

One major review using meta-analytic techniques (see Chapter 5 for definition/description of meta-analysis) concluded that acute and chronic exercise result in better cognitive functioning, with the overall effect for chronic exercise programs being approximately twice that for acute exercise (Etnier et al., 1997). The overall effect was rather modest, and the authors noted that many of the studies conducted to that point had serious methodological and design issues that prevented unambiguous conclusions.

This chapter presents the current thinking regarding the effects of exercise on cognitive processing, taking a lifespan perspective. That is, evidence from research examining the effects of exercise on cognitive processing in older and younger individuals will be presented, as youth and old age are the parts of the developmental continuum when cognitive processing is either in development or in decline, respectively, and thus time frames when exercise, if it influences cognitive processing at all, would have its largest effects. This chapter also examines the effects of both acute and chronic exercise on cognitive functioning.

One of the most significant systematic investigations into the relationship between physical activity/fitness and cognitive function, if not the first, was conducted by Waneen Spirduso. In her seminal 1975 work, she examined simple and choice reaction times (RTs) in four groups of "sportsmen": an older, active (OA) group (average age 57.2 yrs); an older, nonactive (ONA) group (56.3 yrs); a young, active (YA) group (23.6 yrs); and a young, nonactive (YNA) group (25.4 yrs). The results were striking: the older racquet sportsmen were significantly faster on both simple and choice RTs and movement times than non-exercisers of the same age. Because the differences could have been due to the emphasis on hand-eye coordination in racquet sports, Spirduso and Clifford (1978) conducted a follow-up study, adding a group of old and young runners to the study design. This allowed Spirduso to address whether it was physical activity itself or a specific *kind* of physical activity that resulted in better cognitive performance. Spirduso and Clifford essentially replicated the initial study, finding that the older runners and racquet sportsmen had simple and choice RTs that were similar to the young exercisers (i.e., young exercisers were fastest, older non-exercisers slowest). Baylor and Spirduso (1988) replicated the same effect in females. While these were certainly not the first studies to examine these relationships, Spirduso's pioneering work ignited research in the area. This interest is generated partly by the desire to determine whether regular physical activity can prevent the decline in cognitive function so typically seen with advancing age, and perhaps even offer protection against some of the most ravaging diseases, like Alzheimer's disease. Indeed, some researchers are asking whether physical activity might reverse cognitive decline that has already occurred. In addition to examining the effects of physical activity at the latter end of the lifespan, a growing number of researchers are examining the same effects at the other end of the lifespan, namely in children and adolescents.

Defining Cognitive Function

■ cognitive function

Cognitive function can be defined as the process whereby an individual is able to perceive, recognize, or understand thoughts and ideas. Cognitive functioning involves the abilities to concentrate or divide one's attention among several things, to learn and remember, to make a plan of action and effectively execute that plan, to self-regulate activities, to recognize objects or things, to evaluate, to construct in one's mind, to think logically, and to solve problems. It also encompasses a variety of mental tasks, including tests of perception (e.g., critical flicker fusion, which identifies the point where a flickering visual stimulus appears as a continuous stimulus); verbal tests; academic achievement tests; tests of short-term (i.e., working) and long-term memory, reaction time, and reasoning abilities; and intelligence testing. This is certainly not an exhaustive list, but it gives a sense of the breadth of the processes made possible by cognitive function.

Studies of Older Adults

It is fairly well established that, with advancing age, the brain changes in both its structure and its function. For example, gray and white matter within the brain decrease, while at the same time the brain's ventricles increase in size. Such atrophy has been associated with decreased cognitive function, indicated by decreased performance on numerous neuropsychological tests (namely, compromised function on tests of memory, attention, and decision making). Because this atrophy is seen so readily in older adults, it is logical to assume that if exercise has any beneficial effects on cognitive function, these effects should be observable in this population.

Chronic Exercise

The effects of regular or chronic exercise on cognitive function can be examined in at least two different ways. First, *cross-sectional studies* compare the performance of long-term exercisers to that of sedentary individuals, to determine whether fitness across the lifespan can preserve cognitive function. This type of approach answers questions such as: Is the loss of brain structure and function inevitable, or can physical activity reduce these losses? Can fitness help a person maintain brain function? Unfortunately, the difficulty of teasing apart differences

FOCUS on Alzheimer's Disease

Aging is often associated with declines of function in a variety of ways, both physical and mental. One of the more pernicious cognitive insults is the onset of Alzheimer's disease (AD). It has been estimated that 26.6 million individuals suffered from AD in 2006, with this number expected to reach more than 100 million adults worldwide by 2050 (Brookmeyer, Johnson, Ziegler-Graham, & Arrighi, 2007). In the United States, 4.5 million adults suffer from AD, and it is estimated that up to 14 million will be diagnosed by 2030 (Yu & Kolanowski, 2009). Alzheimer's disease is a disease of progressive cognitive decline, often accompanied by disrupted function and neuropsychiatric symptoms, frequently evolving into dementia. Obviously, determining whether regular physical activity can prevent or reduce the risk of developing AD is an important research endeavor.

As the prospective studies have shown, involvement in regular physical activity is associated with a reduction in the risk for developing AD or dementia (Etgen et al., 2010; Larson et al., 2006). What about those who already suffer with AD? Does exercise offer any relief of symptoms or perhaps even reverse the cognitive decline? This is a fairly new area of research within the exercise domain, but some studies do appear to offer some promise. First, a meta-analysis of 30 randomized trials conducted between 1970 and 2003 revealed that exercise could be a useful treatment for older adults suffering from cognitive impairment (Heyn, Abreu, & Ottenbacher, 2004). This analysis included studies that randomized participants to either an exercise intervention or a control group. Participants were 65 years old, or older, with clinically diagnosed cognitive impairment or dementia. Heyn and colleagues (2004) showed that exercise training not only resulted in improved physical function (e.g., strength, fitness, functional performance), but also resulted in an improvement in cognitive function of more than half a standard deviation—a sizable effect.

A more recent randomized clinical trial conducted by Lautenschlager, Cox, Flicker, and colleagues (2008) demonstrated that exercise in individuals who were at risk for AD could result in some improvement in cognitive function. More specifically, after fairly stringent screening for severe cognitive impairment and clinical depressive symptoms, participants with mild cognitive impairment were randomly assigned to either a "usual care" control group or an exercise intervention group. Control group participants received educational materials regarding memory loss and other health-related information, whereas the exercise group participants engaged in at least 150 minutes of physical activity per week. This was accomplished primarily by having the participants exercise in three sessions per week of 50 minutes per session. At the end of the 24-week intervention, the participants in the exercise group showed a modest improvement in cognitive function compared to the usual care group. Furthermore, the exercise group participants continued to show better cognitive function 18 months after the conclusion of the intervention.

Although the results of such exercise research appear promising, working with such a population can present unique challenges. For example, as noted by Heyn et al. (2004), it can be difficult to motivate individuals suffering from AD to exercise. There is also a need to individualize exercise programs for such individuals. Indeed, one of the points raised by Lautenschlager and colleagues (2008) was the utility of an intervention that was individualized and provided feedback to participants regarding their progress. Much remains to be done, but it is possible that someday a diagnosis of AD or perhaps even dementia may not be as ominous as it currently is.

ADDITIONAL RESOURCES

Galik, E.M., Resnick, B., & Pretzer-Aboff, I. (2009). "Knowing what makes them tick": Motivating cognitively impaired older adults to participate in restorative care. *International Journal of Nursing Practice, 15,* 48–55.

Honea, R.A., Thomas, G.P., Harsha, A., Anderson, H.S., Donnelly, J.E., Brooks, W.M., & Burns, J.M. (2009). Cardiorespiratory fitness and preserved medial temporal lobe volume in Alzheimer disease. *Alzheimer Disease & Associated Disorders, 23,* 188–197.

Yu, F., Kolanowski, A.M., Strumpf, N.E. & Eslinger, P.J. (2006). Improving cognition and function through exercise intervention in Alzheimer's disease. *Journal of Nursing Scholarship, 38,* 358–365.

ACTIVITY

You have been assigned to present an activity program to a residential care facility that specializes in caring for older adults with Alzheimer's disease and/or dementia. Your task is to develop an exercise program that can be used in the facility to assist the staff with helping the residents to begin and, you hope, stay with an exercise program. To do this successfully—that is, to convince the administration of the facility to begin the exercise program—do the following:

1. Search the research literature and find the best available information regarding the kind of exercise to use. This should include the typical information: type, frequency, intensity, and duration.
2. Search the literature to determine the most effective strategies that can be used with this population to help motivate them to engage in the exercise program and, more perhaps important, to adhere to the program. After all, the benefits they may obtain from the exercise program will be apparent only if they stick with it.
3. Put your information together into a presentation that you can deliver to the care facility's administration.

in nutrition, medical care, education, and other factors that may differ between regular exercisers and sedentary individuals hinders cross-sectional comparisons. By contrast, *longitudinal studies* treat exercise as an intervention, often asking sedentary individuals to engage in a program of regular exercise over a period of weeks or months. The longitudinal approach circumvents self-selection issues (e.g., individuals with intact cognitive functioning abilities also engage in exercise, but exercise may or may not influence their cognitive function). This approach can also answer questions about whether declines in cognitive function can be reversed. In the following sections, we will discuss studies of both types that have examined the effects of chronic exercise on cognitive function.

Observational studies

One way to get a sense of the impact that physical activity may have on cognitive functioning is to examine the results from large-scale epidemiological or observational studies. Several of these studies were prospective in nature—that is, individuals were examined at one point in time and then re-examined at some later time to determine the extent to which characteristics that were present at the initial assessment predicted outcomes at the later assessment. For example, Larson and colleagues (2006) studied nearly 1,750 adults over the age of 65 who had no cognitive impairment. The researchers obtained baseline measurements of cognitive and physical function, along with the subjects' frequency of various exercise activities. Participants were contacted again approximately six years later. Individuals who reported engaging in exercise activities at least three times per week at baseline were 34 percent less likely to develop dementia or Alzheimer's disease later in life. Similar results were shown in a community-based study in Germany (Etgen et al., 2010).

Measures of Executive Control

Physical activity and exercise seem to exert their greatest influence on the aspects of cognitive function referred to as *executive control,* and researchers have devised several methods to measure executive control. Researchers often use the Eriksen flanker task (Eriksen & Eriksen, 1974) to examine how well a person is able to process relevant information and/or ignore or discriminate relevant from irrelevant information. The basic task involves presenting an array of symbols or letters (e.g., >>>>>, >><>> or HHHHH, HHSHH) to the individual, who attempts to respond based on the symbol or letter in the middle, which is flanked by either compatible or incompatible symbols or letters. Compatible stimuli (e.g., SSSSS) result in faster and more accurate responses than incompatible stimuli (e.g., SSHSS).

Task switching, another useful test of executive control processes, measures "cost" of switching between two different tasks. Researchers measure the reaction time for trials in which the subject switches between tasks and the time for trials in which the subject continues performing the same task. The difference in reaction time gives an index of this cost. See Exhibit 14.1, which shows the effect of a walking program on task switching from the Kramer et al. (1999) exercise intervention study (see the description of this study in the "Intervention Studies" section later in this chapter).

Another task commonly used for assessing executive control processes is the Stroop Color and Word Test. In this task, the participant is asked to identify the color of the ink that a word is printed in, while ignoring the word itself. When the word itself is the name of a color, the word interferes with the cognitive process of naming the ink color. Different ink colors (e.g., red, blue, yellow, green) and different categories of words are used, providing three different types of stimuli: (1) incongruent, where the word is the name of a color that is different from the ink color in which it is printed (e.g., the word "BLUE" printed in red ink); (2) congruent, where the word is the name of the ink color in which it is printed (e.g., the word "BLUE" printed in blue ink); and (3) neutral, where the word is unrelated to the ink color (e.g., the word "RUN" printed in green ink). Studies using this task often show a large decrease in both speed and accuracy for incongruent versus congru-

Effect of a walking program on task switching.

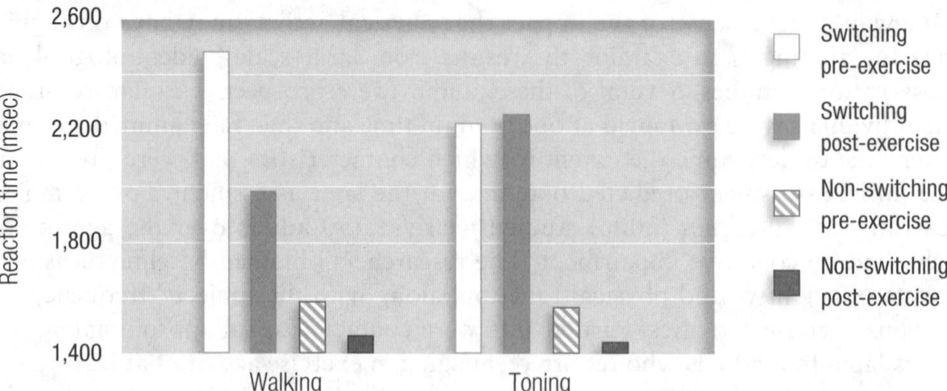

The walking group is able to switch tasks faster than the toning group; hence, the walking group's cost of switching is lower.

From Kramer, A.F., Hahn, S., Cohen, N.J., Banich, M.T., McAuley, E., Harrison, C.R., Chason, J., Vakil, E., Bardell, L., Boileau, R.A., Colcombe, A. Aging, fitness, and neurocognitive function. *Nature, 400(29),* 418–419.

ent trials. For example, a recent study conducted by Smiley-Oyen, Lowry, Francois, et al. (2008) showed significantly slower response times when participants went from congruent trials (e.g., mean RT = 846 msec) to incongruent trials (e.g., mean RT = 1315 msec).

Although all of the executive control tasks described here may be used as behavioral tasks—that is, we can examine reaction times and response accuracy (e.g., % correct, # of errors) for any executive control task—these tasks are often combined with electrophysiological (e.g., event-related potentials) or **neuroimaging** (e.g., functional magnetic resonance imaging) techniques to obtain another level of information regarding the cognitive processing of information within the central nervous system. **Functional magnetic resonance imaging** (fMRI) is a special type of MRI that provides a very specific and detailed picture of brain activity, based on neuronal activity and the subsequent metabolism and blood flow changes in brain tissue, in almost real time. See Exhibit 14.2 for an example.

Example of fMRI data. **exhibit 14.2**

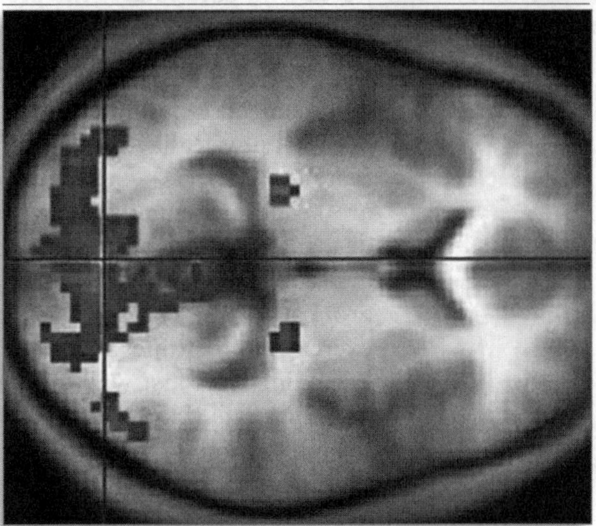

The image shows the regions of activation in a comparison between a task involving a complex moving visual stimulus and a rest condition (viewing a black screen). The activations are shown (as is typical) against a background based on the average structural images from the subjects in the experiment.

Source: http://en.wikipedia.org/wiki/Image:FMRI.jpg.

Another prospective study examined whether aerobic fitness was related to cognitive function measured six years later. Nearly 350 community-dwelling adults aged 55 and older performed a graded treadmill test to assess their aerobic capacity. Six years later, they underwent an extensive cognitive test battery (Barnes, Yaffe, Satariano, & Tager, 2003). Aerobic fitness was positively associated with later cognitive function, suggesting that aerobic fitness may buffer against the development of cognitive impairment so often seen in advancing age. Overall, the findings from studies like these indicate that even modest levels of physical activity and/or fitness seem to have a positive influence on cognitive functioning. This effect seems to be particularly significant for cognitive tasks involving executive control and attention in middle-aged and older adults.

Executive control processes (Hillman, Erikson & Kramer, 2008) are those that control cognitive functions oriented toward goal-directed behavior (Etnier & Chang, 2009). Such processes include scheduling, planning, **working memory** (the ability to hold relevant information in one's mind for relatively short periods of time), **interference control** (the ability to deal with distraction), task coordination, and multi-tasking. Such tasks do not become automatic over time

- executive control
- working memory
- interference control

or with practice (Colcombe & Kramer, 2003). They have been shown to decline substantially with advancing age, as do the brain regions that are known to support them, particularly the prefrontal cortex.

Intervention studies: Effects on cognitive function

Although observational studies can certainly offer insight into the relationship between physical activity and cognitive functioning, they cannot directly manipulate the subjects' exercise or physical activity. Experiments and interventions are needed to elucidate the nature of the relationship and to explore the underlying mechanisms. In one of the first exercise intervention studies, Dustman and colleagues (1984) randomly assigned middle-aged and older men to three groups: (1) an aerobic exercise group (n = 13, average age 60.6 yrs), which exercised three times per week for 60 minutes in each session for four months, beginning with fast walking/slow jogging and with a goal of increasing exercising heart rate (HR) to 70–80% of their $HR_{reserve}$ and maintaining that intensity for longer times as fitness improved; (2) an exercise control group (n = 15, 62.3 yrs), which performed strength and flexibility exercises but was encouraged to keep exercise HR below a level that would yield any aerobic benefit; and (3) a non-exercise control group (n = 15, 57.4 yrs), which performed no exercise at all. All participants underwent a battery of tests of cognitive function (e.g., RT, Stroop) before and after the completion of the four-month intervention.

The researchers found that the aerobic exercise group had an increase in their aerobic capacity (i.e., $\dot{V}O_2max$) of 27 percent; the exercise control group, although it did not engage in any aerobic activity, still had a 9 percent increase in their aerobic capacity. The aerobic exercise group showed the largest improvement on the battery of neuropsychological tests. Although the exercise control group also showed an overall significant improvement, the aerobic exercise group improved in cognitive performance to a significantly greater degree than the exercise controls and the non-exercise controls. The aerobic exercise group showed significant improvement on nearly every task (seven of eight), the exercise controls improved on two of the tasks, and the non-exercise controls improved on only one task. Interestingly, the aerobic exercise group was the only group to show any improvement on the lone executive control task—the Stroop. Dustman and colleagues (1984) concluded that physically unfit older adults who participate in programs of regular exercise can improve their fitness and, importantly, their cognitive function.

Several interventions followed from Dustman's seminal work, but numerous methodological and design issues prevented the drawing of any clear conclusions from these studies regarding the effectiveness of exercise as an intervention. As highlighted by Kramer and Erickson (2007a), these problems involved:

1. the methods by which cardiovascular fitness was assessed,
2. aspects of the training programs (e.g., length, intensity, duration),
3. the choice of cognitive processes assessed, and
4. subject characteristics, particularly age.

In an effort to discern some consistencies, Colcombe and Kramer (2003) conducted a meta-analytic review of exercise training studies. They examined the results of studies conducted between 1966 and 2001 to address the question of whether fitness has an effect on cognitive function and whether this effect is moderated by any other factors (e.g., age, length of training, exercise intensity, nature of cognitive tasks). The overall results suggested a clear, significant influence of aerobic fitness training on cognitive function, although it had selective effects. Exercisers had significantly greater improvements on controlled tasks (those tasks requiring some level of cognitive control); for example:

- a choice reaction time task (pressing one key when presented with a certain stimulus and a different key when a different stimulus is presented),
- spatial tasks, that is, transferring and then remembering information presented visually and spatially (e.g., viewing a line drawing and then replicating it from memory), and
- speed tasks, that is, tasks that assess the speed with which an individual can respond to a stimulus (e.g., simple reaction time task).

The strongest, most robust effects were seen for cognitive tasks involving executive control processes; for these, exercise had a nearly 30 percent greater effect than a control comparison (see Exhibit 14.3).

Training programs that included aerobic training along with strength and flexibility training were superior to programs of aerobic exercise only. The effects also seemed to be greatest when exercise session length exceeded 30 minutes (Colcombe & Kramer, 2003).

Effects of aerobic fitness training on executive control processes. **exhibit 14.3**

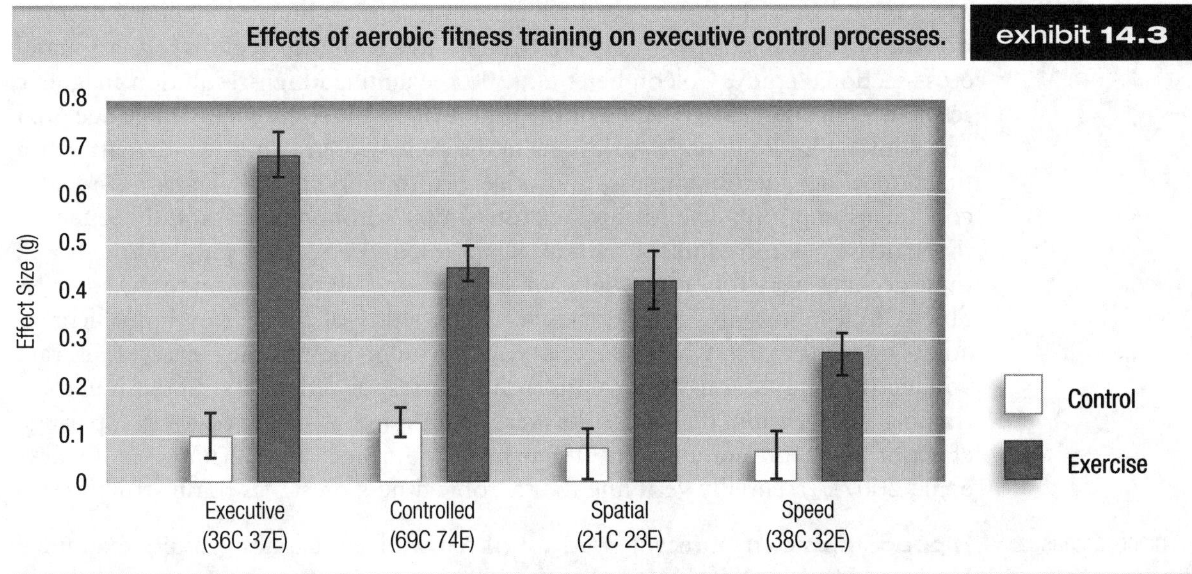

From Colcombe, S. & Kramer, A.F., Fitness effects on the cognitive function of older adults: a meta-analytic study. *Psychological Science (14),* 125–130.

In perhaps the best exercise intervention to follow after Dustman's work, Kramer and colleagues (1999) examined the effects of exercise on cognitive tasks that required executive control and were mediated by the frontal regions of the brain: (1) task-switching, (2) a response compatibility test, which measures the ability to ignore task-irrelevant stimuli, and (3) **stopping,** or aborting a preprogrammed action. The researchers randomly assigned 124 healthy but sedentary adults between the ages of 60 and 75 to a 6-month intervention consisting of either walking (three times per week, increasing to 40 minutes per session at an intensity of 60–65% $\dot{V}O_2max$, with an emphasis on increasing aerobic capacity) or stretching/toning (three times per week, 40 min/session, with an emphasis on increasing flexibility but not aerobic capacity). The exercise intervention resulted in a significant improvement in aerobic capacity (5.1% increase in $\dot{V}O_2max$) for the walking group but not for the stretching/toning group (2.8% decrease in $\dot{V}O_2max$). Although response times were similar between the groups on the less complex cognitive tasks, for tasks that depended on executive control processes, cognitive performance improved significantly in the aerobically trained participants. For example, the walkers became significantly faster at switching between tasks, relative to the stretching and toning group (refer back to Exhibit 14.1).

stopping ■

Intervention studies: Effects on the structure and operation of the brain

Relatively few studies have examined the effects of physical activity interventions on the brain itself, more specifically on the structure of the brain (see Exhibit 14.4) and its operation (Kramer & Eriksen, 2007b). One of the reasons speculated for the decline in cognitive function typically seen with advancing age is the age-related loss of both gray and white matter in the brain, particularly in anterior brain regions (e.g., frontal, pre-frontal, and temporal regions). In an initial cross-sectional study, Colcombe et al. (2003) examined high-resolution magnetic resonance imaging (MRI) scans of the brains of 55 older adults (average age 66.5 yrs), looking for systematic variations in the density of gray and white matter as a function of age, aerobic fitness, and other health markers (e.g., hypertension, alcohol consumption). The researchers found that, although substantial declines in tissue density occurred in the frontal, temporal, and parietal regions of the brain, these declines were offset (i.e., substantially reduced) in proportion to the subject's fitness. In a follow-up six-month intervention study of 59 healthy but sedentary adults aged 60 to 79, Colcombe et al. (2006) found significant increases in brain volume (both gray and white matter) that corresponded to a six-month aerobic training intervention. These results were interpreted as evidence for a "sparing" effect of fitness on brain tissue. Others have confirmed this sparing effect (Marks et al., 2007), essentially verifying that aerobic fitness preserves brain structure.

hippocampus ■

Hippocampus. In a recent study, Eriksen and colleagues (2009) examined brain structure, specifically in the hippocampus, a subcortical area of the brain known to influence spatial memory. Memory is another aspect of executive control that often weakens with aging. The researchers assessed aerobic fitness in

The structure of the brain. **exhibit 14.4**

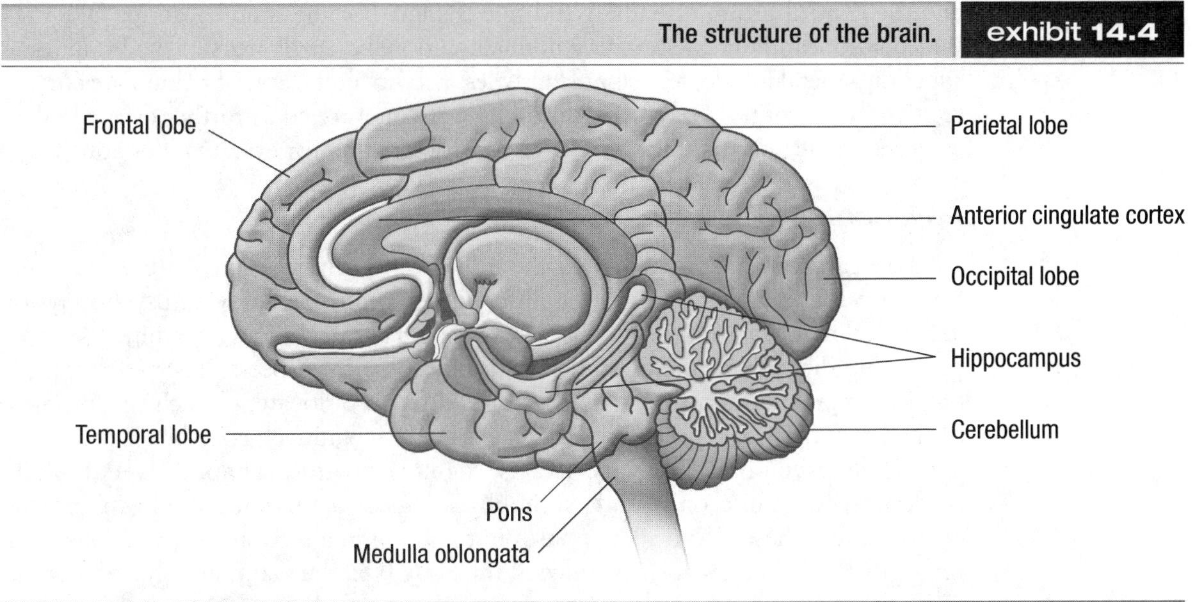

165 older adults (average age 66.6 yrs; 109 females), along with performance on a spatial memory task and MRI scans of the left and right hippocampi. Confirming previous studies, they found that levels of aerobic fitness were associated with hippocampal volume. Furthermore, greater fitness and hippocampal volume were associated with better spatial memory performance. Work in animals had previously shown clear and profound effects of exercise on the hippocampus (see, for example, Cotman, Berchtold & Christie, 2007), but this was the first demonstration of the relationship in humans.

■ attentional network

Attentional network. The **attentional network** is neural circuitry involved in various aspects of executive control processes. Colcombe et al. (2004) conducted two separate studies of the attentional network. The first, a cross-sectional study of 41 older adults (average age ~67 yrs) found that high-fit individuals were able to deal with conflicting visual cues, as assessed via the flanker task, more effectively than lower-fit individuals. Furthermore, fMRI scans showed that the high-fit individuals had greater activation of the attentional network than did the low-fit individuals. In other words, those brain regions thought to be crucial to attentional processes were more active in the high-fit group while they performed the attentional task.

In the second study, a six-month randomized control trial, the researchers compared the effects of cardiovascular training (resulting in a 10 percent increase in aerobic capacity) to a non-training control group (stretching and toning; 3% increase). They also examined brain areas implicated in different aspects of executive control and the attentional network, namely, the superior parietal lobule, which is involved in attentional selection and the resolution of response conflict, and the anterior cingulate cortex, which is sensitive to response conflict. Consistent with previous research, the aerobic group had a significant reduction in their conflict time (11%), and the control group essentially did not change. For the training goup, fMRI revealed significantly greater activity in the attentional control areas of the brain (e.g., superior parietal lobule) and significantly less activity in the anterior cingulate cortex, relative to the control group. These results were interpreted as further evidence that exercise training can enhance executive control functioning, even in older adults.

Psychophysiological studies

Some researchers have investigated the influence of physical activity, exercise, and fitness on cognitive function from a different perspective, employing psychophysiological techniques to examine such relationships. These techniques examine cognitive processing through its manifestation as a physiological process. The psychophysiological approach sacrifices some precision in terms of locating which specific area of the brain may be most active during particular cognitive tasks, but it offers the advantage of temporal specificity. That is, cognitive processing happens very rapidly, on the order of milliseconds, and psychophysiological methodologies allow researchers to capture these electrical responses in the brain in almost real time. Measuring these electrical changes at the surface of the body (i.e., the scalp) greatly reduces the technological burden and the expense of conducting such investigations.

event-related potential ■

Studies using a psychophysiological approach focus on a methodology that uses the **event-related potential (ERP)**—a measured brain response evoked from some type of stimulus (e.g., visual, auditory). The brain potential is time-locked to the stimulus; thus, knowing when a stimulus is presented allows us to examine the subsequent brain potentials (responses). The brain potential (response) is detected at the surface of the scalp by sensors placed over particular brain regions, and these sensors are connected to a recording device. The brain potential is part of the ongoing brain activity, but when several of these measured responses are averaged together they become distinct from the ongoing brain activity, and the resultant waveform reflects the processing of information invoked by the stimulus. Two key features of ERP are its **latency,** (the time when the potential occurs relative to the presentation of the stimulus), and its **amplitude,** whether the potential deflects up or down.

latency ■

amplitude ■

P300 (P3) ■

attentional resources ■

One of the most commonly studied components of an ERP is a positive-going waveform referred to as the **P300** or the **P3,** so labeled because it occurs approximately 300 milliseconds after the stimulus is presented (see Exhibit 14.5) (although it can occur anywhere from 300 to 800 milliseconds after the stimulus). It is believed to reflect the allocation of **attentional resources** (which can be thought of as the amount of brain activity needed to attend to the task) and the updating of memory. Thus, the amplitude of the P300—the magnitude of the deflection in a positive direction—reflects the proportion of attentional resources the brain needs to engage in the task. A larger amplitude means the allocation of more attentional resources. On the other hand, the latency of the P300 is a measure of the speed with which a stimulus is classified; that is, a longer latency means the central nervous system requires a longer time to process the stimulus.

We can invoke the P300 (and various other ERPs), by using the measures of cognitive function described earlier. For example, researchers often use the flanker task

A representation of commonly studied ERPs. **exhibit 14.5**

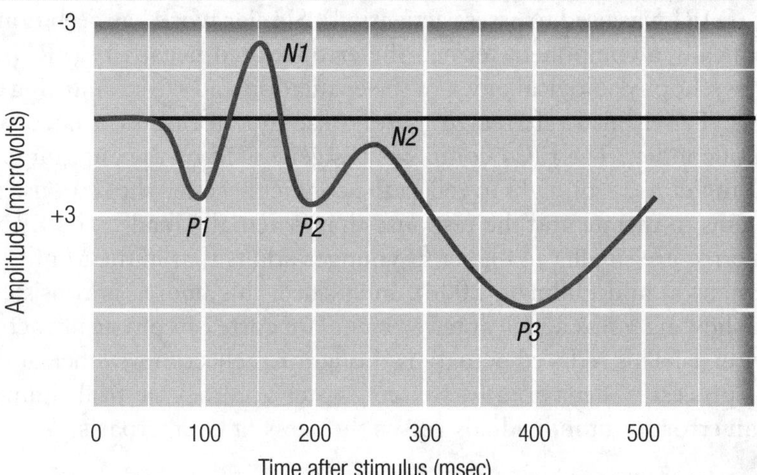

In ERP nomenclature, positive components go *down,* and they are referenced according to when they occur relative to the stimulus being presented. For example, the time point labeled "0" would correspond to stimulus presentation. The point labeled "P3" is the P300, meaning it is a positive-going deflection occurring approximately 300 milliseconds (reflecting latency) after the stimulus presentation.

paradigm in conjunction with the P300. In this case, the P300 is examined by presenting a subject with a group of symbols and asking about the compatibility of the middle symbol with the flanking symbols. Longer latencies are considered to indicate longer times to process the stimulus while greater amplitude is thought to reflect the allocation of more resources to process the information contained in the stimulus.

Numerous studies have examined the effects of fitness on cognitive functioning, as reflected in the P300, in older adults. Older adults typically show increased P300 latencies and smaller amplitudes, and researchers have sought to determine whether fitness and/or regular exercise ameliorates these declines. As Hillman et al. (2008) have noted, the results of such work reveal quite clearly that individuals with higher levels of aerobic fitness have larger P300 amplitudes and faster latencies, compared to less fit individuals. Like the MRI and fMRI studies, these studies showed that physical activity is beneficial for cognitive tasks, particularly those requiring greater levels of executive control.

For example, in a study by Hillman, Kramer, Belopolsky, and Smith (2006), 32 older and 34 younger active and sedentary participants engaged in a task-switching paradigm. Response speed (i.e., RT), response accuracy, and P300s (both amplitude and latency) were recorded. In the active participants, P300 amplitudes were greater and RTs tended to be faster, relative to the sedentary participants. This finding suggests that fitness enhances both processing of stimuli and responding to stimuli.

Researchers have also studied the effects of fitness on the functioning of the anterior cingulate cortex, a part of the brain sensitive to response conflict. Recall the work of Colcombe and colleagues (2004), described earlier, demonstrating that an aerobically trained group of older adults showed less activity in the anterior cingulate cortex (fMRI was used to assess activation). Similar work has been done using ERPs, specifically a component termed the **error-related negativity (ERN)**, which provides a psychophysiological index of the evaluation and self-monitoring of one's own actions. This is also referred to as response-monitoring associated with the evaluation of conflict. The ERN component is generated by the anterior cingulate cortex and, therefore, is thought to reflect the conflict between the response that the stimulus seems to dictate and the response that is actually made. The ERNs after making an error are smaller in higher fit younger adults that in their unfit counterparts (Themanson and Hillman, 2006). In essence, this finding is consistent with fMRI data showing a less active anterior cingulate cortex in physically active and/or fit individuals. This reduced activity is thought to reflect more efficient conflict-monitoring processes. Behaviorally, we see greater accuracy on trials immediately following an error for fit individuals versus their less fit counterparts.

error-related negativity ■

Acute Exercise Studies

We can expect a program of regular exercise to result in improvements in cognitive function and even reverse the loss of function seen with aging. It is reasonable to ask whether a single bout of exercise has any facilitating or debilitating effects on cognitive function.

Acute exercise has positive, albeit small, effects on cognitive function (Etnier et al., 1997). Recently, researchers have examined these effects, including a relationship between accumulated blood lactate resulting from high-intensity exercise (see Chapter 13) and an effect on RT and divided attention (Coco et al., 2009). Essentially, as lactate levels increased with increasing exercise intensity, RT slowed, execution time on the divided attention task slowed, and the subjects made more errors and omissions. These results appear to reflect a debilitating effect of increasing exercise intensity on cognitive processing.

Davranche and McMorris (2009) examined the effect of a vigorous bout of acute exercise (20 min of cycling at the ventilatory threshold, VT) on cognitive processing during the exercise. Subjects completed 5 blocks of 64 trials each of a cognitive task referred to as the *Simon task,* which requires a quick button press according to the color of a stimulus presented to the left or right of a fixation point. In compatible trials, stimuli appear in a specific location on a computer screen that corresponds to where the response is to be made, in incompatible trials, the stimuli appear in some other location. In this study, the color of the stimulus required either a right (green stimulus) or left (red stimulus) button press response, regardless of whether the stimulus appeared to the left or right on the computer screen. RT was faster during exercise but **response inhibition** (withholding a response rather than making one) appeared to be worse during exercise.

response inhibition ■

Using a more moderate-intensity exercise stimulus, Davranche, Hall, and McMorris (2009) also examined the effect of acute cycling exercise (50% maximal aerobic power) on executive function, using the Eriksen flanker task. Results showed that cognitive processing was facilitated during exercise, with RTs significantly faster in the exercise condition than a non-exercise control. One study found no influence of acute treadmill exercise (30 min at 83% HR_{max}) on measures of action monitoring (e.g., ERNs) in either higher or lower fit adults (Themanson & Hillman, 2006).

As with chronic exercise research, clearly much remains to be learned regarding the effects of acute exercise on cognitive processing. Much more systematic investigation of dose-response (i.e., intensity, duration) effects is necessary, as well as assessment of the duration of any effects on cognitive processing. In one study, subjects performed a **stopping task** (a task requiring the suppression of a response after a specific stimulus) during and following 30 minutes of cycling exercise (performed at 40% maximal aerobic power). They demonstrated a beneficial effect (i.e., faster RT) during and for up to 52 minutes following the exercise (Joyce, Graydon, McMorris, and Davranche, 2009). Finally, research is necessary to examine different modes of activity.

■ stopping task

The little work to date that has examined the effects of resistance exercise seems to indicate that this form of exercise may have beneficial effects (Chang & Etnier, 2009a, 2009b). Obviously, a single bout of exercise may not in and of itself produce health and fitness outcomes, but it appears that single bouts of activity may have utility in the short term, in terms of enhancing the processing of information. The intervention studies already presented suggest that single bouts of activity, when accumulated over weeks and months, can have profound positive effects on cognitive processing.

Childhood and Adolescence: The Other End of the Lifespan Spectrum

Clearly, research on older adults is important for the health, well-being, and quality of life of the older segment of the population. With the increasing levels of inactivity in children, it is important that the link between activity and cognitive functioning be examined in younger populations, as well. There is increasing evidence that physical activity and exercise can have a significant impact on the cognitive functioning of children and adolescents.

Physical Fitness

Recently, researchers have been more systematically examining the influence of exercise on cognitive processing in preadolescents. Several initial studies have shown promising relationships between physical fitness and academic achievement. For example, the California Department of Education studied nearly 10,000 students in the 5th, 7th, and 9th grades to examine the relationship between physical fitness and academic achievement (2001). The researchers used a standardized achievement test and the Fitnessgram fitness test and found a small but positive relationship between fitness and academic performance in each of the three grade levels. In a similar study of 3rd and 5th grade students, Castelli, Hillman, Buck, and Erwin (2007) sought to determine which component of fitness (aerobic capacity, muscular fitness, or body composition) influenced academic achievement, which was decomposed into reading and mathematics. The researchers showed that, after controlling for age, sex, and poverty index, aerobic capacity predicted performance on both mathematics and reading achievement tests (i.e., higher fitness predicted better performance), and body composition predicted performance negatively (i.e., greater body fat predicted worse performance). In another study, sedentary children were assigned to a no-exercise control condition or to either 20 or 40 minutes of daily after-school physical activity for 15 weeks. The children who had 40 minutes of daily activity performed best on the cognitive assessment that was used (Davis et al., 2007). Such findings further support conclusions from other studies (e.g., Coe et al., 2006; Sallis et al., 1999) and several authors (e.g., Trudeau & Shephard, 2008), as well as the results of a meta-analysis of cognitive function and physical activity in children (Sibley & Etnier, 2003).

A cross-sectional study using more specific measures of cognitive functioning as opposed to measures of academic achievement, showed that high-fit children (average age 9.6 yrs) responded significantly faster and more accurately than low-fit children to a rarely occurring target stimulus. High-fit children had larger P300 amplitudes in response to the rarely occurring target stimulus. This is thought to reflect greater allocation of attentional resources and a reduction of conflict during response selection—that is, better cognitive function (Hillman, Castelli, & Buck, 2005). A separate study of a sample of 7 to 12 year olds performing the Stroop task revealed the same effect: aerobic fitness predicted performance on the Stroop task, independent of age, body composition, and intelligence (Buck, Hillman, & Castelli, 2008). Hillman and colleagues (2009) showed similar neuroelectric effects in higher and lower fit children (average age 9.4 yrs) performing a flanker task. Again, higher fit children were more accurate in responding and had larger P300 amplitudes, indicating greater allocation of attentional resources.

A study of 35 higher and lower fit adolescents showed that fitness was associated with better cognitive task preparation and more efficient executive control processes. However, neither fitness nor an acute bout of moderate exercise (20 min at 60% HR_{max}) had any effect on allocation of attentional resources or memory control, as indexed by the P300 (Stroth et al., 2009).

Acute Exercise

Hillman and colleagues (2009) have also examined the effects of acute exercise on cognitive function in children. In this study, preadolescent children walked on a treadmill for 20 minutes at a moderate intensity. Before and after the exercise, the children performed several cognitive tasks, including the flanker task. Results showed better accuracy of responding following exercise, along with larger P300 amplitudes and better performance on a test of academic achievement. As the researchers noted, although some studies have shown no improvement in cognitive function following exercise, the fact that no published reports have shown a detrimental effect of physical activity suggests that physical activity does not "hinder academic performance and may lead to improved physical and mental health" (p. 1044).

Clearly this work is in its early stages, but given the potential importance of physical activity not only for children's physical health but also for their cognitive health, this area should become the subject of systematic research. If subsequent research can substantiate and extend the current knowledge base, physical activity programs for children—including more physical activity–oriented physical education—can be developed to start them on a healthful path early and to help them avoid the losses that accrue with age.

Mechanisms and Hypotheses

Several explanations have been put forward in an attempt to explain how exercise might influence cognitive functioning. The **selective improvement hypothesis** proposes that exercise that results in improved cardiorespiratory fitness fosters selective as opposed to generalized improvements. More specifically, frontal lobe mediated executive control tasks, which suffer the largest decrements with age, should show the greatest improvements with exercise training (Kramer et al., 1999). Several studies have supported this hypothesis (e.g., Kramer et al., 1999; Smiley-Oyen et al., 2008). Somewhat similar to the selective improvement hypothesis, the **cardiovascular fitness hypothesis** asserts that some measure of cardiovascular fitness improvement is needed for improvements in cognitive function to take place. Evidence in support of this hypothesis is mixed; several studies show improved cardiovascular fitness in association with improved cognitive function, and several show improvement in cognitive function unrelated to changes in cardiovascular fitness.

- selective improvement hypothesis
- cardiovascular fitness hypothesis

Why does exercise seem to bring about improved cognitive functioning? In addition to the above hypotheses, researchers have suggested several mechanisms to explain exercise effects. For one, exercise may induce increases in several kinds of growth factors important for neuronal and brain health. These growth factors provide signals for **synaptic plasticity** (the ability of connections between neurons to change in strength), cell proliferation and differentiation (together referred to as **neurogenesis**), and learning. Among these nerve growth factors, **brain-derived neurotrophic factor (BDNF)** has been studied most frequently; it is essential for hippocampal function, synaptic plasticity and adaptability, and learning. In animal studies, exercise increases BDNF in several brain regions, with the most robust and enduring response occurring in the hippocampus, a key brain structure for learning and memory (Cotman, Berchtold & Christie, 2007). Another growth factor, termed *insulin-like growth factor (IGF-1),* has been shown to regulate exercise-dependent stimulation of new capillary growth (i.e., **angiogenesis**) along with neurogenesis in the hippocampus (Cotman et al., 2007). Angiogenesis is important for supplying the oxygen and nutrients to the nerves. It has also been speculated that exercise can increase the number of synapses in frontal and parietal gray matter, which would obviously be important given the frontal-lobe connection with executive function. Finally, exercise may cause increased blood supply to brain regions supporting executive control functions. All of these changes (i.e., neurogenesis, angiogenesis,

- synaptic pasticity
- neurogenesis
- brain-derived neurotrophic factor (BDNF)
- angiogenesis

increased blood supply) provide the structural and metabolic resources necessary for successful cognitive functioning (Dustman et al., 1984).

Practical Recommendations

A growing body of evidence seems to show that moderate exercise can be a useful tool to protect against and perhaps even prevent the decline in cognitive function and brain deterioration that so often accompanies advancing age. Some evidence concludes that greater amounts of physical activity seem to further reduce the likelihood of cognitive decline; in addition, some evidence suggests that such moderate activity may even be able to reverse already-existing decrements in cognitive functioning. As Erickson and Kramer (2009) stated, "we can safely argue that an active lifestyle with moderate amounts of aerobic activity will likely improve cognitive and brain function and reverse the neural decay frequently observed in older adults" (p. 24).

Practically speaking, at present little more can be definitely said other than "just do it." A combination of aerobic and nonaerobic exercise activities (e.g., walking/jogging plus weight training) may provide more beneficial effects than either aerobic or nonaerobic activities alone, but more work is needed to make this definitive. As discussed in Chapter 2, most major organizations (e.g., Centers for Disease Control & Prevention, National Institute on Aging, American College of Sports Medicine) recommend at least 150 minutes of moderate-intensity activity (roughly 30 minutes per day), or 75 minutes of vigorous-intensity activity, per week, including both aerobic and muscle-strengthening exercises. In addition, exercises to increase/maintain balance and flexibility are often recommended. Again, much remains to be done before a definitive "prescription" can be made regarding the optimal "dose" of exercise for optimal cognitive effects.

In addition to any cognitive benefits that may come from being physically active, the exercising individual also accumulates many physical benefits. These benefits, in combination, become even more important as we age.

Conclusion

Clearly, much work remains to be done as we come to understand the effects of exercise on cognitive functioning. As Hillman, Erickson, and Kramer (2008) observe,

> Future research might be able to answer questions such as: when is it best to begin? What are the best varieties, intensities, frequencies and durations of exercise? Is it ever too late to start an exercise programme? Can exercise be used to reduce the deleterious effects of neurodegenerative diseases? (p. 63)

Answers to these questions, and others not yet asked, will be crucial in helping us take full advantage of the benefits that exercise has to offer to improve cognitive health.

what do you know?

1. What is cognitive function, and what are some of the ways it is measured?
2. What happens to the human brain, in terms of brain structure, as it ages?
3. What kind of cognitive processes seem to improve to the greatest extent as a result of chronic exercise interventions?
4. Why is the hippocampus an important brain structure in terms of cognitive function?
5. What kinds of imaging techniques have been used to determine the brain areas that are most active during the performance of various cognitive processing tasks?
6. What are the two key aspects of the event-related potential, in terms of what they reveal about cognitive functioning?
7. When researchers examine cognitive functioning, what is perhaps the most commonly studied component of the event-related potential? Why is it important to study?
8. What seems to be the relationship between cognitive processing and physical fitness in children?
9. What is the main argument of the selective improvement hypothesis?
10. What is BDNF?

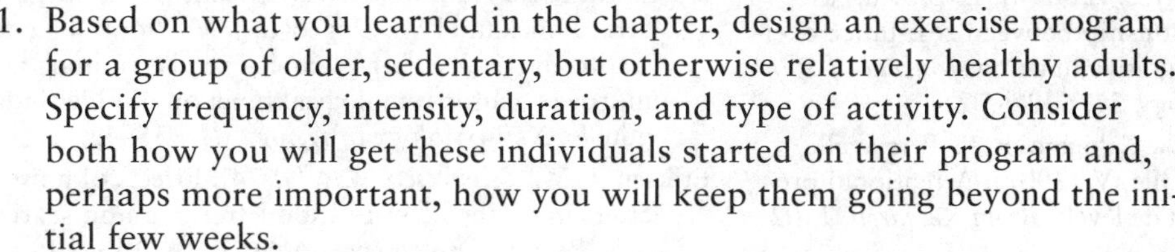

learning activities

1. Based on what you learned in the chapter, design an exercise program for a group of older, sedentary, but otherwise relatively healthy adults. Specify frequency, intensity, duration, and type of activity. Consider both how you will get these individuals started on their program and, perhaps more important, how you will keep them going beyond the initial few weeks.
2. If you wished to assess changes in cognitive functioning in this group, what aspects of cognitive functioning would you measure and why?
3. You are part of a team charged with developing a convincing argument for why all grade schools in the country should include daily physical education in the curriculum. Your role is to make the case for this daily requirement on cognitive grounds. That is, your task is to put together as strong an argument as you can that daily physical education will help the children in their academic performance, understanding that others will argue that taking time away from academic classes will hurt the students' academic performance. Present as convincing a case as you can, using the available evidence to support your arguments.

references

Barnes, D.E., Yaffe, K., Satariano, W.A., & Tager, I.B. (2003). A longitudinal study of cardiorespiratory fitness and cognitive function in healthy older adults. *Journal of the American Geriatrics Society, 51(4),* 459–465.

Baylor, A.M., & Spirduso, W.W. (1988). Systematic aerobic exercise and components of reaction time in older women. *Journal of Gerontology, 43,* 121–126.

Buck, S.M., Hillman, C.H., & Castelli, D.M. (2008). The relation of aerobic fitness to stroop task performance in preadolescent children. *Medicine & Science in Sports & Exercise, 40(1),* 166–172.

Brookmeyer, R., Johnson, E., Ziegler-Graham, K., & Arrighi, H.M. (2007). Forecasting the global burden of Alzheimer's disease. *Alzheimers & Dementia, 3,* 186–191.

California Department of Education (CDE) (2001). California physical fitness test: Report to the governor and legislature. Sacramento, CA: California Department of Education Standards and Assessment Division.

Castelli, D.M., Hillman, C.H., Buck, S.M., & Erwin, H.E. (2007). Physical fitness and academic achievement in third- and fifth-grade students. *Journal of Sport & Exercise Psychology, 29,* 239–252.

Chang, Y.K., & Etnier, J.L. (2009a). Effects of an acute bout of localized resistance exercise on cognitive performance in middle-aged adults: A randomized controlled trial study. *Psychology of Sport & Exercise, 10,* 19–24.

Chang, Y.K., & Etnier, J.L. (2009b). Exploring the dose-response relationship between resistance exercise intensity and cognitive function. *Journal of Sport & Exercise Psychology, 31,* 640–656.

Coco, M., Di Corrado, D., Calogero, R.A., Perciavalle, V., Maci, T., Perciavalle, V. (2009). Attentional processes and blood lactate levels. *Brain Research, 1302,* 205–211.

Coe, D.P., Pivarnik, J.M., Womack, C.J., Reeves, M.J., & Malina, R.M. (2006). Effect of physical education and activity levels on academic achievement in children. *Medicine & Science in Sports & Exercise, 38(8),* 1515–1519.

Colcombe, S., & Kramer, A.F. (2003). Fitness effects on the cognitive function of older adults: a meta-analytic study. *Psychological Science, 14,* 125–130.

Colcombe, S.J., Erickson, K.I., Raz, N., Webb, A.G., Cohen, N.J., McAuley, E., & Kramer, A.F. (2003). Aerobic fitness reduces brain tissue loss in aging humans. *Journal of Gerontology: Biological Science & Medical Science, 58A(2),* 176–180.

Colcombe, S.J., Erickson, K.I., Scalf, P.E., Kim, J.S., Prakash, R., McAuley, E., Elavsky, S., Marquez, D.X., Hu, L., & Kramer, A.F. (2006). Aerobic exercise training increases brain volume in aging humans. *Journal of Gerontology: Biological Science & Medical Science, 61A(11),* 1166–1170.

Colcombe, S.J., Kramer, A.F., Erickson, K.I., Scalf, P., McAuley, E., Cohen, N.J., Webb, A., Jerome, G.J., Marquez, D.X., & Elavsky, S. (2004). Cardiovascular fitness, cortical plasticity, and aging. *Proceedings of the National Academy of Sciences, 101(9),* 3316–3321.

Cotman, C.W., Berchtold, N.C., & Christie, L.A. (2007). Exercise builds brain health: Key roles of growth factor cascades and inflammation. *Trends in Neuroscience, 30(9),* 464–472.

Davis, C.L., Tomporowski, P.D., Boyle, C.A., Waller, J.L., Miller, P.H., Naglieri, J.A., Gregoski, M. (2007). Effects of aerobic exercise on overweight children's cognitive functioning: a randomized controlled trial. *Research Quarterly for Exercise & Sport, 78(5),* 510–519.

Davranche, K., Hall, B., & McMorris, T. (2009). Effects of acute exercise on cognitive control during an Eriksen flanker task. *Journal of Sport & Exercise Psychology, 31,* 628–639.

Davranche, K., McMorris, T. (2009). Specific effects of acute moderate exercise on cognitive control. *Brain & Cognition, 69,* 565–570.

Dustman, R.E., Ruhling, R.O., Russell, E.M., Shearer, D.E., Bonekat, H.W., Shigeoka, J.W., Wood, J.S., & Bradford, D.C. (1984). Aerobic exercise training and improved neuropsychological function of older individuals. *Neurobiology of Aging, 5(1),* 35–42.

Eriksen, C.W., & Eriksen, B.A. (1974). Effects of noise letters upon the identification letter in a non-search task. *Perception & Psychophysics, 16,* 143–149.

Erickson, K.I., & Kramer, A.F. (2009). Aerobic exercise effects on cognitive and neural plasticity in older adults. *British Journal of Sports Medicine, 43,* 22–24.

Erickson, K.I., Prakash, R.S., Voss, M.W., Chaddock, L., Hu, L., Morris, K.S., White, S.M., Wójcicki, T.R., McAuley, E., & Kramer, A.F. (2009). Aerobic fitness is associated with hippocampal volume in elderly humans. *Hippocampus, 19(10),* 1030–1039.

Etgen, T., Sander, D., Huntgeburth, U., Poppert, H., Forstl, H., & Bickel, H. (2010). Physical activity and incident cognitive impairment in elderly persons: The INVADE Study. *Archives of Internal Medicine, 170(2),* 186–193.

Etnier, J.L., & Chang, Y. (2009). The effect of physical activity on executive function: A brief commentary on definitions, measurement issues, and the current state of the literature. *Journal of Sport & Exercise Psychology, 31*, 469–483.

Etnier, J.L., Salazar, W., Landers, D.M., Petruzzello, S.J., Han, M., & Nowell, P. (1997). The influence of physical fitness and exercise upon cognitive functioning: A meta-analysis. *Journal of Sport & Exercise Psychology, 19*, 249–277.

Heyn, P., Abreu, B.C., & Ottenbacher, K.J. (2004). The effects of exercise training on elderly persons with cognitive impairment and dementia: A meta-analysis. *Archives of Physical Medicine & Rehabilitation, 84*, 1694–1704.

Hillman, C.H., Buck, S.M., Themanson, J.B., Pontifex, M.B., & Castelli, D.M. (2009). Aerobic fitness and cognitive development: Event-related brain potential and task performance indices of executive control in preadolescent children. *Developmental Psychology, 45(1)*, 114–129.

Hillman, C.H., Castelli, D.M., & Buck, S.M. (2005). Aerobic fitness and neurocognitive function in healthy preadolescent children. *Medicine & Science in Sports & Exercise, 37*, 1967–1974.

Hillman, C.H., Erickson, K.I., & Kramer, A.F. (2008). Be smart, exercise your heart: exercise effects on brain and cognition. *Nature Reviews: Neuroscience, 9(1)*, 58–65.

Hillman, C.H., Kramer, A.F., Belopolsky, A.V., Smith, D.P. (2006). A cross-sectional examination of age and physical activity on performance and event-related brain potentials in a task switching paradigm. *International Journal of Psychophysiology, 59(1)*, 30–39.

Hillman, C.H., Pontifex, M.B., Raine, L.B., Castelli, D.M., Hall, E.E., & Kramer, A.F. (2009). The effect of acute treadmill walking on cognitive control and academic achievement in preadolescent children. *Neuroscience, 159(3)*, 1044–1054.

Joyce, J., Graydon, J., McMorris, T., & Davranche, K. (2009). The time course effect of moderate intensity exercise on response execution and response inhibition. *Brain & Cognition, 71*, 14–19.

Kramer, A.F., & Erikson, K.I. (2007a). Capitalizing on cortical plasticity: Influence of physical activity on cognition and brain function. *Trends in Cognitive Sciences, 11(8)*, 342–348.

Kramer, A.F., & Erikson, K.I. (2007b). Effects of physical activity on cognition, well-being, and brain: Human interventions. *Alzheimer's & Dementia, 3*,S45–S51.

Kramer, A.F., Hahn, S., Cohen, N.J., Banich, M.T., McAuley, E., Harrison, C.R., Chason, J., Vakil, E., Bardell, L., Boileau, R.A., & Colcombe, A. (1999). Aging, fitness, and neurocognitive function. *Nature, 400(29)*, 418–419.

Larson, E.B., Wang, L., Bowen, J.D., McCormick, W.C., Teri, L., Crane, P., & Kukull, W. (2006). Exercise is associated with reduced risk for incident dementia among persons 65 years of age and older. *Annals of Internal Medicine, 144(2)*, 73–81.

Lautenschlager, N.T., Cox, K.L., Flicker, L., Foster, J.K., van Bockxmeer, F.M., Xiao, J., Greenop, K.R., & Almeida, O.P. (2008). Effect of physical activity on cognitive function in older adults at risk for Alzheimer disease: A randomized trial. *Journal of the American Medical Association, 300(9)*, 1027–37.

Marks, B.L., Madden, D.J., Bucur, B., Provenzale, J.M., White, L.E., Cabeza, R., & Huettel, S.A. (2007). Role of aerobic fitness and aging on cerebral white matter integrity. *Annals of the New York Academy of Sciences, 1097*, 171–174.

Sallis, J.F., McKenzie, T.L., Kolody, B., Lewis, M., Marshall, S., & Rosengard, P. (1999). Effects of health-related physical education on academic achievement: project SPARK. *Research Quarterly for Exercise & Sport, 70(2)*, 127–134.

Sibley, B.A., & Etnier, J.L. (2003). The relationship between physical activity and cognition in children: A meta-analysis. *Pediatric Exercise Science,15*, 243–256.

Smiley-Oyen, A.L., Lowry, K.A., Francois, S.J., Kohut, M.L., & Ekkekakis, P. (2008). Exercise, fitness, and neurocognitive function in older adults: the "selective improvement" and "cardiovascular fitness" hypotheses. *Annals of Behavioral Medicine, 36(3)*, 280–291.

Spirduso, W.W. (1975). Reaction and movement time as a function of age and physical activity level. *Journal of Gerontology, 30*, 435–440.

Spirduso, W.W., & Clifford, P. (1978). Replication of age and physical activity effects on reaction and movement times. *Journal of Gerontology, 33*, 26–30.

Stroth, S., Kubesch, S., Dieterle, K., Ruchsow, M., Heim, R., & Kiefer, M. (2009). Physical fitness, but not acute exercise modulates event-related potential indices for executive control in healthy adolescents. *Brain Research, 1269*, 114–124.

Themanson, J.R., & Hillman, C.H. (2006). Cardiorespiratory fitness and acute aerobic exercise effects on neuroelectric and behavioral measures of action monitoring. *Neuroscience, 141(2)*, 757–767.

Trudeau, F., & Shephard, R.J. (2008). Physical education, school physical activity, school sports and academic performance. *International Journal of Behavioral Nutrition & Physical Activity, 5*, 10.

Yu, F., & Kolanowski, A. (2009). Facilitating aerobic exercise training in older adults with Alzheimer's disease. *Geriatric Nursing, 30*, 250–259.

15

Health-Related Quality of Life and Exercise

KEY TERMS

activities of daily living (ADL)
control beliefs
disease-specific measures
generic measures
health-related quality of life (HRQoL)
individual difference factors
objective measures
optimism
pessimism
proxy measures
quality-adjusted life years (QALY)
quality of life (QoL)
subjective measures

Harry is 92 years old and lives by himself in a small house in the city. He cooks and cleans for himself and walks to the corner stores a couple of times each week to buy groceries and to take care of other errands. He meets friends at a community center every Tuesday and Thursday to play cards and to participate in an exercise class for seniors. Although Harry is fairly active in his daily life, health problems prevent him from walking long distances and performing strenuous activities. He has chronic obstructive pulmonary disease (COPD), which leaves him breathless after walking more than a block. Arthritis in his hips and shoulders makes it painful for him to do heavy lifting and bending. Fortunately, a neighbor helps out by mowing Harry's lawn in the summers and shoveling snow from his sidewalk in the winters.

Family members have offered to move Harry to a retirement facility where staff would take care of all his chores—shopping, cleaning, cooking, and so on. Harry insists, however, that despite his aches and pains, he actually feels healthiest and happiest when he is moving around the community and taking care of himself. He fears that if he no longer *had* to be physically active in his daily life, his physical functioning might decline with lack of use and he would no longer be able to stay independent and do the things that he enjoys. Harry realizes that being physically active in his daily life—even at a relatively low level—helps preserve his level of physical function, his independence, and his ability to participate in community life, and it contributes to his overall health and happiness. In other words, physical activity contributes to his overall quality of life and more specifically to his health-related quality of life.

Quality of Life

quality of life (QoL) ■

Quality of life (QoL) is used to describe both subjective and objective evaluations of the "goodness" of one's life overall, and the goodness of all of the various domains that make up one's life. In general, subjective evaluations reflect people's own perceptions of the "goodness" or quality of their lives. Objective evaluations are typically measures of various aspects of one's life that can be made by someone other than the individual, such as a health-care worker or researcher.

Exhibit 15.1 presents the various dimensions that the World Health Organization (1993) has identified and defined as components of quality of life, along with the factors that comprise each of those dimensions.

exhibit 15.1 The World Health Organization's dimensions of quality of life.

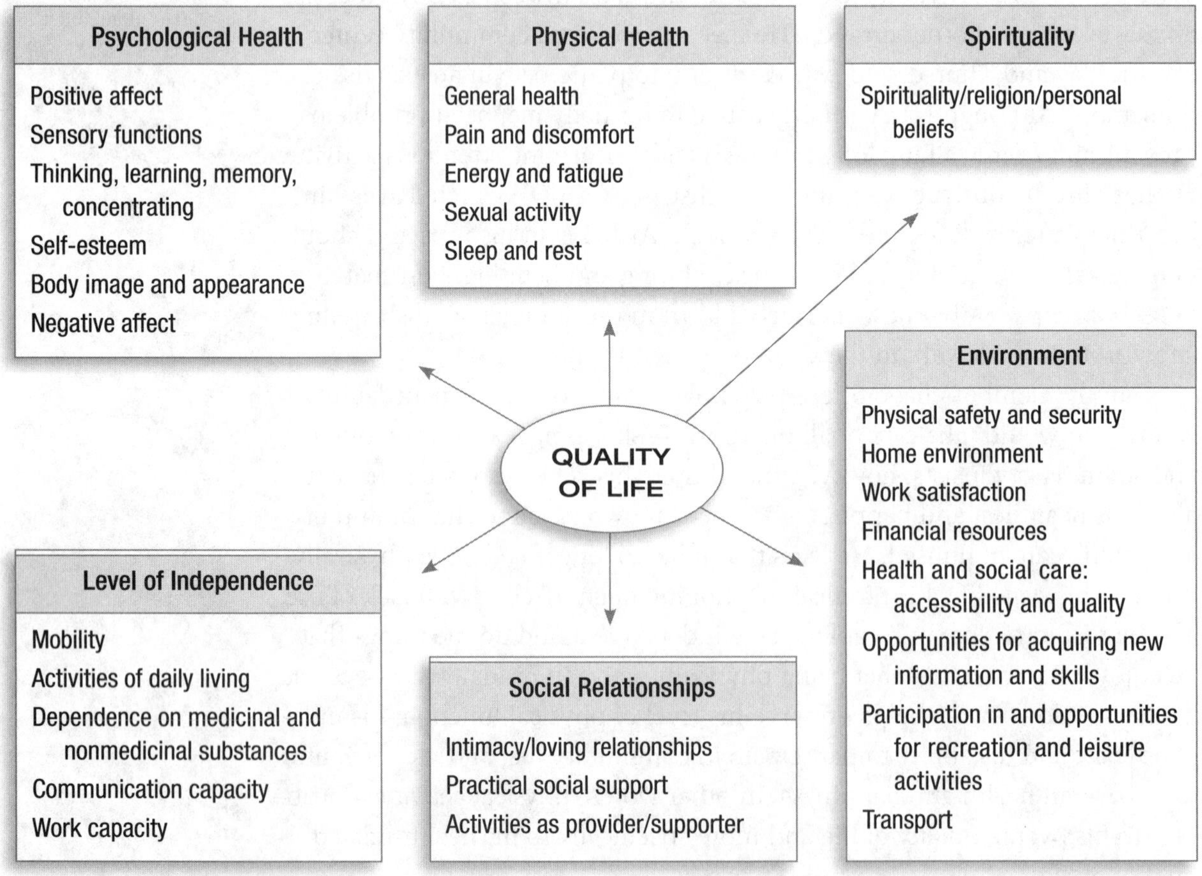

QUALITY OF LIFE

Psychological Health
- Positive affect
- Sensory functions
- Thinking, learning, memory, concentrating
- Self-esteem
- Body image and appearance
- Negative affect

Physical Health
- General health
- Pain and discomfort
- Energy and fatigue
- Sexual activity
- Sleep and rest

Spirituality
- Spirituality/religion/personal beliefs

Environment
- Physical safety and security
- Home environment
- Work satisfaction
- Financial resources
- Health and social care: accessibility and quality
- Opportunities for acquiring new information and skills
- Participation in and opportunities for recreation and leisure activities
- Transport

Level of Independence
- Mobility
- Activities of daily living
- Dependence on medicinal and nonmedicinal substances
- Communication capacity
- Work capacity

Social Relationships
- Intimacy/loving relationships
- Practical social support
- Activities as provider/supporter

Source: Adapted from World Health Organization (1993).

Defining Health-Related Quality of Life

Health-related quality of life (HRQoL) is a subcomponent of QoL that reflects the "goodness" of those dimensions of life that can be affected by health and by health interventions, such as one's physical function, emotional well-being, and ability to fulfill family and other social roles.

■ health-related quality of life (HRQoL)

Researchers and clinicians often disagree on the specific dimensions that are part of HRQoL, but there is a general consensus regarding the broad core dimensions that should be considered when measuring HRQoL in most populations. These dimensions include the following:

- Physical functioning, including aerobic fitness, strength, endurance, balance, flexibility, and the ability to perform activities of daily living (ADL) such as walking, climbing stairs, carrying heavy objects, and dressing and bathing oneself. This dimension also includes physical self-concept.
- Emotional functioning and well-being, including depression, anxiety, anger/hostility, and feelings of happiness, hope, and tranquility.
- Social functioning and ability to fulfill social roles, including involvement with community and social groups and the ability to fulfill the role of spouse, parent, employee, caregiver, and so forth.
- Cognitive functioning, including memory, attention, concentration, comprehension, problem solving, and decision making.
- Health status, including physical health, symptoms, and states (e.g., energy, fatigue, pain, sleep).

Some researchers include other core dimensions in their definitions of HRQoL, such as sexual functioning and intimacy, and work productivity. Yet unlike the dimensions listed previously, these additional dimensions might not be relevant to many populations, so we have not included them in our list of broad core dimensions. For instance, sexual functioning and intimacy would not be a relevant construct when assessing the HRQoL of children. Similarly, work productivity would not be relevant to the HRQoL of children, retired people, or individuals whose health status prevents them from working.

Why Is HRQoL Important to Exercise Psychologists?

The past several decades have seen an increased recognition that health should not be defined simply as the absence of disability and disease (i.e., the biomedical definition of health). Rather, consistent with a biopsychosocial definition, health is now conceptualized as a positive state of physical, mental, and social well-being (World Health Organization, 1947). Previously, most interests were focused on developing interventions to improve physical health only. With acceptance of the biopsychosocial definition has come greater interest among researchers (including exercise psychologists and other exercise scientists), clinicians (physicians, physiotherapists), and patients in identifying therapeutic techniques that will enhance *all three* components of health. As a result of this shift in focus, exercise psychologists are interested in HRQoL for at least three reasons:

1. HRQoL is an important index of treatment effectiveness

Because HRQoL reflects patients' satisfaction with all three health components—physical, mental, and social—it has become an important benchmark for determining the effectiveness of exercise interventions as well as virtually every other type of clinical intervention (e.g., pharmacological, surgical). Traditionally, clinical researchers (researchers who study the effects of clinical interventions) tended to be interested only in the effects of treatment on objective medical outcomes associated with morbidity (i.e., illness, injury) and mortality (i.e., death). Yet it is now apparent that in order to get a complete understanding of the broad range of psychological and social effects of exercise and other treatments on patients, researchers need to augment traditional medical outcome measures with measures of HRQoL. Thus, most exercise intervention studies now include measures of HRQoL as well as traditional measures of disability and disease. In fact, the U.S. National Institutes of Health (NIH) now mandate the inclusion of measures of HRQoL in most clinical studies of therapeutic interventions. It is no longer sufficient to demonstrate that an intervention has positive physical benefits for a patient. Researchers must also demonstrate that the intervention does not have a negative effect on quality of life, as the side effects of some treatments might be worse than the symptoms of the disease being treated.

2. Improvements in HRQoL are recognized as an important benefit of exercise

In recent years, there has been a dramatic increase in the number of studies examining exercise for the treatment of diseases such as osteoarthritis, cancer, diabetes, and heart disease, and for the prevention of physical and cognitive declines associated with aging. These studies have generated considerable knowledge regarding the therapeutic benefits of exercise. Consequently, physical activity is being used increasingly by clinicians and health promoters as a therapeutic modality for treating chronic disease and disability and for preventing age-related declines. (See Exhibit 15.2.)

For example, the Canadian Heart and Stroke Foundation recognizes exercise as an essential component of cardiac rehabilitation programs for individuals who have experienced an infarction or other cardiac event. The American Arthritis Foundation recommends exercise as a strategy for managing arthritis symptoms (e.g., pain and stiffness) and preventing further joint damage (Arthritis Foundation, 2009). The American College of Sports Medicine (2009)

Seniors, exercise, and quality of life. **exhibit 15.2**

Exercise is being used increasingly as a therapeutic modality to help older adults maintain their quality of life. Consequently, more and more exercise programs are being developed for seniors. The man and the woman shown here belong to an exercise facility known as "The Club," which is housed in the Shalom Village long-term care facility for older adults in Ontario, Canada. The Club features group exercise classes as well as specialized weight-training equipment for older adults (e.g., weight machines that can be adjusted in one-pound increments). Anybody can join The Club. The only restriction is that you must be at least 75 years old.

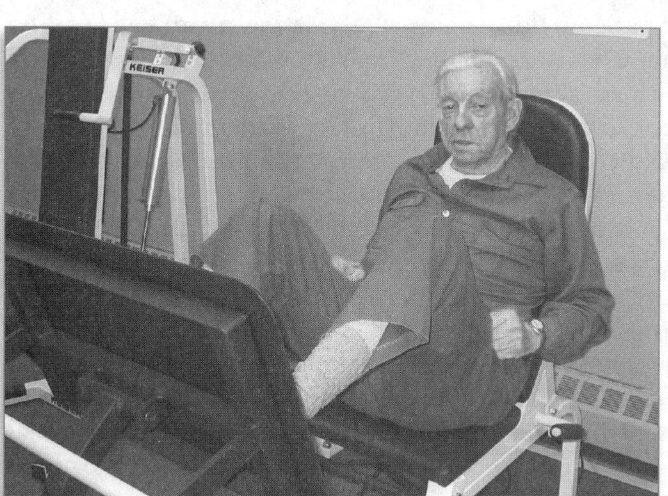

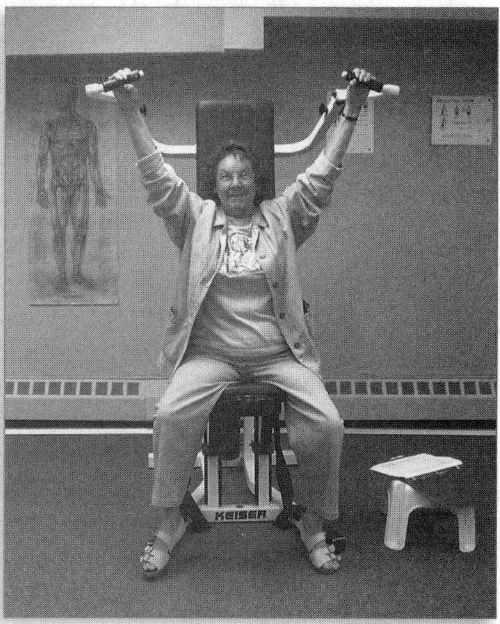

advocates exercise participation among older adults (including the frail elderly) and provides guidelines for prescribing exercise to this population.

Interestingly, clinicians and health promoters are not recommending exercise solely for its physical benefits; they are also endorsing the use of exercise to enhance HRQoL. For example, in addition to highlighting the physical benefits of exercise to people who have had a stroke or heart attack, the Heart and Stroke Foundation also recommends exercise as a means to help these patients feel better about themselves, their physical abilities, and their lives. Specifically, the Heart and Stroke Foundation of Canada (2009) states:

> Physical activity can be a lifesaver—literally. When you're active 30 to 60 minutes a day, most days of the week, you can dramatically lower your risk of heart disease and stroke. . . . Adding more activity to your daily life may also reduce stress levels, increase energy and improve sleep and digestion. Because physical activity makes you feel better about yourself, you're more likely to make healthy lifestyle choices and to avoid bad ones such as smoking, overeating or drinking too much alcohol.

This recommendation reflects an increasing trend toward the use of physical activity by health practitioners and promoters to improve HRQoL among people with disease and disability—populations that tend to report poorer HRQoL than people who are healthy (Ware, Kosinski, Bayliss, et al., 1995; Yost, Haan, Levine, & Gold, 2005).

3. Knowledge of a patient's HRQoL is useful for prescribing exercise

An increased interest in HRQoL among researchers and clinicians reflects a growing appreciation of the patient's thoughts and feelings with regard to prescribed treatments. How patients think and feel about the treatment (e.g., do they enjoy exercising? After exercising, do they feel better or are they completely fatigued and unable to perform activities of daily living?) is just as important as the medical outcomes derived from treatment. In fact, patients often consider the psychological and social consequences of a treatment to be *more* important than the medical consequences. By asking patients about the effects of exercise on their HRQoL, we can gain an understanding of the effects of the intervention on the whole person. Such a holistic understanding allows us to make better decisions about exercise prescription. For instance, if patients do not report any improvements in their HRQoL, then this may indicate that they do not perceive any meaningful benefits from exercise (Gillison, Skevington, Sato, et al., 2009). The exercise prescription could then be adjusted so patients do improve in ways that are considered personally meaningful. Patients could also receive additional counseling or information to help them become more aware of what they have gained from exercise.

Measurement

As mentioned earlier, exercise psychologists use HRQoL to assess the effectiveness of exercise interventions. But in order to use HRQoL for these purposes, we must be able to measure it. Two general approaches exist for measuring HRQoL—the objective approach and the subjective approach.

Objective Approaches to Measuring HRQoL

objective measures ■ In general, **objective measures** of HRQoL are measures that (1) can be made by someone other than the patient, and (2) are quantitative (i.e., numeric) in nature. Objective measures can be used to assess individual HRQoL components or overall HRQoL. Examples of objective measures of the physical function component are the number of pounds a person can bench press and the distance he can walk in six minutes. Examples of objective measures of the health status component are the number of days a patient was confined to a hospital bed over the past month and the number of pain relief capsules she took over the course of a week.

In addition to objective measures of individual HRQoL components, there are also objective measures of overall HRQoL. An example of an objective measure of one's overall HRQoL is to estimate a person's life expectancy in **quality-adjusted life years** (QALY; Kaplan & Bush, 1982). This approach involves calculating a numeric value that indicates the quality of one's remaining years of life. The logic behind this approach is that people with poorer health might have the same life *expectancy* as healthier individuals, but the *quality* of their remaining years might not be as good as that of a healthier person. QALY are calculated by multiplying life expectancy by the value assigned to that person's level of health (see the following box). QALY values can then be used to compare the HRQoL of healthy people with that of individuals who have a particular disease or disability, or to compare the HRQoL between groups of people with different types of disease or disability. The QALY approach can also be used to measure the effectiveness of health interventions such as exercise. For instance, among people who have incurred a spinal cord injury and who have paraplegia or quadriplegia, it has been estimated that an exercise training program could increase their QALY by 10 percent (Noreau & Shephard, 1995). Likewise, it has been demonstrated that men who exercise consistently from the age of 35 to 65 will live more QALY over that 30-year period than will men who are sedentary during that same time frame (Hatziandreu, Koplan, Weinstein, et al., 1988).

■ quality-adjusted life years

QALY are not typically used by clinicians or exercise scientists, but they are a commonly used index within the field of health economics. In order to determine whether a particular intervention is cost effective, health economists can estimate how much a particular intervention costs for each additional QALY that is gained. For instance, a Dutch study examined the cost-effectiveness of providing three weeks of intensive exercise therapy to arthritic patients who had recently been admitted to the hospital (Bulthuis, Mohammad, Braakman-Jansen, et al., 2008). Changes in their QALY were examined over a one-year period and compared with changes in QALY among control patients who did not receive exercise therapy. At the end of the study, patients who received exercise therapy had a greater increase in QALY than control patients. Every one-year increase in QALY was associated with a decrease of 718 euros in health-care costs (about $1,000 U.S.), reflecting the tendency for people in the exercise condition to spend fewer days in a hospital than those in the control condition. Based on these results, the authors concluded that exercise is a cost-effective intervention for people with arthritis because it improves their quality of life while decreasing the medical costs associated with their treatment. Bulthuis and colleagues recommended that intensive exercise therapy become standard for arthritic patients upon discharge from hospital.

Although exercise was deemed to be cost effective in the Dutch study, other studies could find that a particular exercise intervention is too expensive relative to its effects on quality of life. Under these circumstances, although it is beneficial, the intervention may not be recommended because it is not cost effective. As

The QALY Approach

DESCRIPTION OF HEALTH STATE	VALUATION
No problems	1.000
No problems walking about; no problems with self-care; some problems with performing usual activities; some pain or discomfort; not anxious or depressed	0.760
Some problems walking about; some problems washing or dressing self; some problems with performing usual activities; moderate pain or discomfort; moderately anxious or depressed	0.516
No problems walking about; some problems washing or dressing self; unable to perform usual activities; some pain or discomfort; not anxious or depressed	0.329
Some problems walking about; no problems with self-care; no problems with performing usual activities; moderate pain or discomfort; extremely anxious or depressed	0.222
Some problems walking about; unable to wash or dress self; unable to perform usual activities; moderate pain or discomfort; moderately anxious or depressed	0.079
Confined to bed; unable to wash or dress self; unable to perform usual activities; extreme pain or discomfort; moderately anxious or depressed	–0.429

Phillips C. *What is a QALY?,* 2nd ed. London: Hayward Medical Communications, 2009. Kindly reproduced by permission of Hayward Medical Communications,

To illustrate the concept of QALY, consider the following example. The average life expectancy for the American population is 77.7 years (USDHHS, 2009). Consider two 50-year-old men living in the United States, Raj and Luis. Raj is in perfect health, but Luis has health problems that have left him with mild physical disability, some chronic pain, and feelings of depression and anxiety. Although both men have the same life expectancy—they are both expected to live nearly 28 more years—the QALY approach suggests that given differences in their health status, the *quality* of their remaining years will be very different. Specifically, using the valuations in the table above, Raj can expect to live 28 quality-adjusted life years (28 expected years multiplied by the life quality value of 1.0). In contrast, after adjusting for the quality of his life, Luis has only 14.45 QALY (28 expected years multiplied by the life quality value of 0.516).

such, the use of QALY can be controversial—some exercise treatments may not be implemented if it is calculated that the benefits to patients are outweighed by the financial costs of providing the treatment.

The QALY approach is considered objective because it assumes all people who have similar health problems have the same "goodness" of life, regardless of how these people *feel* about their health and the impact of their health on their lives. For example, the QALY approach would consider all people who have the same symptoms as Harry (in the scenario at the beginning of this chapter) to have the same health-related quality of life. It also assumes that better health and reduced symptomatology will automatically lead to better quality of life. This assumption is common to all objective measures of HRQoL—they are based on the assumption that the better the characteristics of a particular HRQoL domain (e.g., the more weight a person can lift, the less pain a person experiences, the better a person's cholesterol levels), the better one's HRQoL. But does reducing the amount of cholesterol in one's blood, for example, necessarily mean that a person's goodness of life will improve? Of course not. And do all people with arthritis and lung disease experience the same goodness of life as Harry, who has these same conditions? Again, the answer is no. As these questions illustrate, HRQoL is not simply a reflection of the actual or objective characteristics of a person's health. Rather, HRQoL reflects how people think and feel about their health and the impact of their health on their lives. In other words, an individual's *subjective* perceptions of health also influence one's HRQoL. A subjective approach to measuring HRQoL takes these perceptions into account.

Subjective Approaches to Measuring HRQoL

■ subjective measures

Subjective measures of HRQoL focus on assessing the individual's *perceptions* of the quality or goodness of the various domains that constitute HRQoL. This is usually done through the administration of a questionnaire that asks patients to rate either their *level* of functioning in one or more HRQoL domains or their *satisfaction* with their functioning in one or more HRQoL domains. An example of a question that could be used to assess level of emotional functioning, for instance, is, "Over the past week, how happy have you felt?" An example of a question that could be used to assess satisfaction with emotional functioning is, "Over the past week, how satisfied have you been with the amount of happiness you have felt?"

Given that researchers cannot agree on how to define HRQoL, you probably will not be surprised to learn that researchers also cannot agree on the best subjective measure of HRQoL. Indeed, one research report noted that more than 150 different questionnaires had been used to measure HRQoL in just 75 different medical studies (Gill & Feinstein, 1994). Some of these questionnaires are designed to measure perceptions of *individual* HRQoL domains, and some are designed to measure perceptions of one's *overall* HRQoL. Although it is beyond the scope of this chapter to discuss these measures in depth, in the following paragraphs we provide some information on two frequently used HRQoL questionnaires. The first, the SF-36, is an example of a questionnaire used to assess perceived *level* of functioning across various individual HRQoL domains. The second questionnaire, the PQOL, is an example of a questionnaire used to assess *satisfaction* with functioning and is a measure of one's overall HRQoL.

Measuring perceived level of functioning

In studies of exercise as well as virtually every other type of health intervention, the most widely used measure of HRQoL is the 36-item Short-Form Health Survey (Ware & Sherbourne, 1992). This questionnaire—also known as the "SF-36"—assesses patients' perceptions of their level of functioning with regard to the following dimensions of HRQoL: general health, physical functioning, social functioning, mental health, bodily pain, and vitality. The SF-36 questions assess patients' perceptions of their symptoms and the extent to which symptoms impact on their daily functioning. For example, the SF-36 pain subscale asks respondents to rate how much pain they have experienced in the past four weeks and how much pain has interfered with their normal daily activities over the past four weeks. The SF-36 is considered a **generic measure** of HRQoL because it was not designed for any particular patient population. Rather, it is considered an appropriate measure of HRQoL for people with virtually any type of disease or disability. In contrast, some subjective measures of HRQoL are considered **disease-specific,** because they were designed to measure HRQoL only among people with a specific disease or disabling condition, such as arthritis or asthma.

generic measures ■

disease-specific measures ■

The SF-36 has been used to demonstrate the positive effects of exercise interventions on HRQoL across a wide range of clinical populations, such as the frail elderly (Schectman & Ory, 2001), cardiac rehabilitation patients (Arthur, Gunn, Thorpe, et al., 2007), women with breast cancer (Segal, Evans, Johnson, et al., 2001), and people with Type 2 diabetes (Kirk, Higgins, Hughes, et al., 2001). In general, these studies have shown that exercise can improve scores on the SF-36. However, the effects of exercise on the various dimensions measured by the SF-36 tend to vary across populations. For example, when the survey was used in a study of patients participating in a home-based cardiac rehabilitation program, the researchers found that, after three months of exercise, participants significantly improved on *all* HRQoL dimensions (Salvetti, Filho, Serrantes, & de Paolo, 2008). In contrast, a study of women with breast cancer found that physical functioning was the only HRQoL dimension that improved after 26 weeks of training (Segal et al., 2001). Taken together, these results suggest that exercise can improve various dimensions of HRQoL, as measured by the SF-36. However, researchers and clinicians should not expect to see exercise-induced improvements on all of the dimensions in all patient populations.

Measuring satisfaction with functioning

Whereas HRQoL measures of perceived *level* of functioning assess *how much* patients have been impacted by symptoms and interventions, measures of *satisfaction* with functioning assess how patients *feel* about the impact of symptoms and interventions. An example of a questionnaire that assesses *satisfaction with functioning* is the Perceived Quality of Life Scale (PQOL; Patrick, Danis, Southerland, & Hong, 1988). This 19-item scale measures satisfaction with physical, social, and cognitive functioning. These aspects of functioning are considered important to people with disease or disability and can be affected by disease and treatment. Exhibit 15.3 shows some of the items that are included in the PQOL.

Using the PQOL, exercise has been shown to be an effective intervention for improving HRQoL. For example, after 20 weeks of training, patients with osteoarthritis who were randomly assigned to an aquatic exercise class had higher PQOL scores than nonexercising patients in a control condition (Patrick, Ramsey, Spencer, et al., 2001). Similarly, in a trial of men and women with a spinal

Sample items from the Perceived Quality of Life Scale. **exhibit 15.3**

1. How dissatisfied or satisfied are you with your physical health? (P)
2. How dissatisfied or satisfied are you with how well you care for yourself, for example, preparing meals, bathing, or shopping? (P)
3. How dissatisfied or satisfied are you with how well you think and remember? (C)
4. How dissatisfied or satisfied are you with how well you carry on a conversation, for example, speaking clearly, hearing others, or being understood? (C)
5. How dissatisfied or satisfied are you with how often you see or talk to your family and friends? (S)
6. How dissatisfied or satisfied are you with your contribution to your community, for example, a neighborhood, religious, political, or other group? (S)

The PQOL scale measures satisfaction with physical (P), cognitive (C), and social (S) functioning. All items are rated on a scale ranging from 0 (extremely dissatisfied) to 10 (extremely satisfied).

Source: Patrick, Danis, Southerland, & Hong (1988).

cord injury, those assigned to an exercise training group demonstrated greater improvements on the PQOL after nine months of exercise training than those assigned to a control group. In fact, after nine months, the control group experienced a decrement in their PQOL scores (Hicks, Martin, Latimer, et al., 2003).

Proxy versus patient measures of HRQoL

As previously mentioned, subjective measures of HRQoL reflect the patient's perceptions of his or her health. When people rate their own HRQoL, this is referred to as a *patient measure* of HRQoL. Sometimes it is difficult or impossible for people to rate their own HRQoL, however, because they have physical or cognitive limitations that prevent them from completing HRQoL questionnaires. In these circumstances, other people (e.g., health-care providers, family members) may be asked to complete the HRQoL measure on the patient's behalf. When other people are asked to rate a patient's HRQoL, this is referred to as a **proxy measure** of HRQoL.

■ proxy measure

Although proxy measures of HRQoL can provide important information about the patient's quality of life, proxy and patient measures cannot be considered equal. In general, significant others and health-care providers tend to underestimate patients' self-reported HRQoL (Pickard & Knight, 2005). In other words, patients tend to have more positive perceptions of their own HRQoL than do people who provide proxy measures of HRQoL. Furthermore, it may be very difficult for a proxy to rate certain dimensions of a patient's HRQoL. For instance, studies have shown that parents tend to be quite good at estimating aspects of their child's HRQoL that can be easily observed, such as the child's physical functioning and health status. Conversely, parent and child ratings of HRQoL dimensions that are more difficult to observe, such as emotional well-being and social functioning, tend to match up less frequently (Eiser & Morse, 2001). If a proxy cannot observe and assess the patient's functioning in a particular HRQoL dimension, then it is difficult, if not impossible, for the proxy to provide an accurate assessment of the patient's HRQoL. Exhibit 15.4 provides an example of standardized questionnaires that are used to measure a child's HRQoL from both the parent's perspective (i.e., proxy measure of HRQoL) and the child's perspective (i.e., patient measure of HRQoL). These measures could be administered to the parent and child by a researcher or clinician.

Objective Versus Subjective Measures—Which Are Best?

When treating patients with exercise, we need to ask ourselves what is more important—how *we* as researchers and health-care professionals rate their HRQoL (objective approach), or how *they* (or their proxies) perceive their HRQoL (subjective approach). When compared to objective measures of HRQoL, patients' subjective perceptions of their HRQoL are usually more closely associated with important health-related outcomes such as their physical and psychological functioning, their adherence to treatment, and their ability to cope successfully with illness (Neill, Branch, De Jong, et al., 1985). Given that subjective measures are a better and more meaningful predictor of important health-related outcomes, the vast majority of studies that have examined the effects of exercise on HRQoL have used a subjective approach to HRQoL measurement. Before beginning a discussion of HRQoL and exercise, we first present some individual characteristics that can affect subjective perceptions of HRQoL.

exhibit 15.4 **Sample items from standardized questionnaires used to measure a child's HRQoL from both the parent's and child's perspectives.**

CHILD'S PERSPECTIVE

In the past ONE month, how much of a problem has this been for you . . .

About My Health and Activities (problems with . . .)	*Never*	*Almost Never*	*Sometimes*	*Often*	*Almost Always*
1. It is hard for me to walk more than one block	0	1	2	3	4
2. It is hard for me to run	0	1	2	3	4
3. It is hard for me to do sports activity or exercise	0	1	2	3	4
4. It is hard for me to lift something heavy	0	1	2	3	4
5. It is hard for me to take a bath or shower by myself	0	1	2	3	4
6. It is hard for me to do chores around the house	0	1	2	3	4
7. I hurt or ache	0	1	2	3	4
8. I have low energy	0	1	2	3	4

(continued)

Sample items from standardized questionnaires used to measure a child's HRQoL from both the parent's and child's perspectives, continued. exhibit 15.4

How I Get Along with Others (problems with . . .)	*Never*	*Almost Never*	*Sometimes*	*Often*	*Almost Always*
1. I have trouble getting along with other kids	0	1	2	3	4
2. Other kids do not want to be my friend	0	1	2	3	4
3. Other kids tease me	0	1	2	3	4
4. I cannot do things that other kids my age can do	0	1	2	3	4
5. It is hard to keep up when I play with other kids	0	1	2	3	4

PARENT'S PERSPECTIVE

In the past ONE month, how much of a problem has your child had with . . .

Physical Functioning (problems with . . .)	*Never*	*Almost Never*	*Sometimes*	*Often*	*Almost Always*
1. Walking more than one block	0	1	2	3	4
2. Running	0	1	2	3	4
3. Participating in sports activity or exercise	0	1	2	3	4
4. Lifting something heavy	0	1	2	3	4
5. Taking a bath or shower by him- or herself	0	1	2	3	4
6. Doing chores around the house	0	1	2	3	4
7. Having hurts or aches	0	1	2	3	4
8. Low energy level	0	1	2	3	4

Social Functioning (problems with . . .)	*Never*	*Almost Never*	*Sometimes*	*Often*	*Almost Always*
1. Getting along with other children	0	1	2	3	4
2. Other kids not wanting to be his or her friend	0	1	2	3	4
3. Getting teased by other children	0	1	2	3	4
4. Not able to do things that other children his or her age can do	0	1	2	3	4
5. Keeping up when playing with other children	0	1	2	3	4

Effect of Individual Difference Factors on Perceptions of HRQoL

Individual differences can affect people's perceptions of their HRQoL. For example, two people with the exact same scores on objective measures of HRQoL (e.g., the same symptoms, the same number of QALYs) can have very different scores on subjective measures. The disparity between subjective and objective measures of HRQoL reflects differences in how people think and feel about their lives. Three **individual difference factors** that can affect HRQoL perceptions are personality characteristics, personal beliefs, and personal values.

individual difference factors ■

Personality Characteristics

One personality characteristic that can affect HRQoL perceptions is optimism. **Optimism** is a dispositional tendency to expect that good things will be plentiful in the future and that bad things will be scarce. Optimistic people have a positive orientation toward life, whereas **pessimism** refers to people who have a negative life orientation (Scheier & Carver, 1985). To use an old adage, optimists are people who believe that the glass is "half full," whereas pessimists see the same glass as "half empty." Individuals with an optimistic personality tend to report better HRQoL than those with a pessimistic personality. For example, in a study of women diagnosed with breast cancer, patients with high scores on a measure of optimism reported better HRQoL one year after surgery than patients who were more pessimistic (Schou, Ekeberg, Sandvik, et al., 2005). Another study compared women who had been identified as pessimistic versus optimistic before receiving a diagnosis of breast cancer. Nearly 10 years after their diagnosis, the optimistic women reported better HRQoL than the pessimistic women (Petersen, Clark, Novotny, et al., 2008). Optimists may report a better HRQoL than pessimists because they are more likely to take control of their health by pursuing HRQoL-enriching activities such as exercise. In contrast, pessimists tend to be more passive and may be less likely to actively make changes to improve their HRQoL.

optimism ■

pessimism ■

The personality traits of extraversion and neuroticism may also be related to HRQoL. People who score high on measures of extraversion tend to be warm, socially outgoing individuals who enjoy the company of others. People who score high on the trait of neuroticism tend to be anxious individuals who worry a lot and are prone to feelings of guilt (Eysenck & Eysenck, 1969). In their study of more than 800 adults, a group of Japanese researchers found that higher levels of neuroticism were associated with poorer HRQoL, while higher levels of extraversion were associated with better HRQoL (Yamaoka, Shigehisa, Ogoshi, et al., 1998). In children, also, neuroticism has been found to be an important predictor of HRQoL. In a study of children who had been hospitalized for treatment of motor vehicle and other accidental injuries, higher levels of neuroticism were associated with poorer HRQoL one month after the injury. One year after injury, children with higher levels of neuroticism had smaller increases in

HRQoL than children who were low in neuroticism (Vollrath & Landolt, 2005). One possible explanation for these findings is that highly neurotic individuals experience considerable negative affect in their daily lives (after all, these are people who are worried and anxious much of the time), and their persistent negativity taints their perception of their HRQoL. Conversely, extraverts experience considerable positive affect in their daily lives, and these feelings are reflected in more positive perceptions and evaluations of their HRQoL.

Personal Beliefs

Among people with disease or disability, a better HRQoL is associated with a stronger belief about one's level of control over aspects of the illness (e.g., beliefs about one's ability to control pain and other symptoms), its treatment (e.g., beliefs about one's ability to accept or decline a particular treatment), and the ability to care for oneself and perform activities of daily living (e.g., beliefs about one's ability to get dressed, eat, and move about without assistance). In contrast, poorer HRQoL is typically reported among people who believe that they have little control over their illness and their lives, and who lack the ability to perform daily tasks (Kempen, Jelicic, & Ormel, 1997). Exercise may help to improve these **control beliefs.** For example, in a study of older adults, exercise was shown to enhance patients' beliefs in their ability to perform a variety of activities of daily living (Martin Ginis, Latimer, Brawley, et al., 2006). Likewise, exercise has been shown to increase COPD patients' perceptions of their ability to control their breathing-related symptoms (Lacasse, Wong, Guyatt, et al., 1996). Thus, exercise might help to improve HRQoL by enhancing people's beliefs about their ability to control aspects of their lives that may be hampered by disease or illness and about their ability to control symptoms of the illness.

■ control beliefs

Religious and spiritual beliefs are another type of belief that is related to HRQoL. A review of the scientific research on health, religion, and spirituality by Larson, Sawyers, and McCullough (1997) concluded that greater religious participation is associated with more positive perceptions along the HRQoL dimensions of physical, social, and psychological well-being, and with more positive perceptions of one's quality of life overall. Interestingly, it seems that regardless of how religious beliefs are expressed—as church attendance and membership, praying, reading religious books, or watching religious television programs—simply having these beliefs is associated with more positive HRQoL perceptions (Levin & Taylor, 1998).

Preliminary research suggests that HRQoL is also associated with the *strength* of one's spiritual beliefs. The term "spirituality" refers to a belief system that focuses on self-transcendence, self-actualization, and finding integrity and meaning in one's life. People can have a sense of spirituality without ascribing to an organized religion. Although researchers are only just beginning to explore the relationship between spirituality and HRQoL, the existing data indicate a positive relationship between these constructs. For instance, in a study of men with prostate cancer, those who scored higher on a measure of spirituality reported better HRQoL than those who had lower scores (Zavala, Maliski, Kwan, et al., 2009).

Personal Values

A central determinant of HRQoL perceptions is the value that one places on a particular life domain. For example, among people with similar objective levels of physical functioning, the importance that a person places on physical functioning will influence whether that person is satisfied or dissatisfied with physical functioning. For instance, in a study of older adults with knee osteoarthritis (Rejeski, Martin, Miller, et al., 1998), researchers identified patients who reported significant functional impairment. They then measured the value that these impaired patients placed on the HRQoL domain of physical function, and their level of satisfaction with their physical function. Interestingly, impaired patients who placed high value on function reported significantly less satisfaction with their physical function than did impaired patients who placed low value on function. As this study demonstrates, when people believe that their lives lack something that they consider personally valuable (e.g., the ability to be physically active, personal relationships, a fulfilling career), this has a greater negative impact on their HRQoL than when their lives lack something that they don't consider valuable.

Research on HRQoL and Exercise

ur discussion of the research on health-related quality of life focuses on two broad areas: the effects of exercise on perceptions of HRQoL, and who benefits from exercise interventions.

The Effects of Exercise on Perceptions of HRQoL

So far in this book, we have studied exercise psychology concepts primarily within the context of understanding physical activity that is performed to improve some aspect(s) of physical fitness (i.e., what we defined in Chapter 2 as "exercise") among people who are already in relatively good general health. Yet for many people with chronic disease and disability, such as Harry, the goal of an exercise intervention is not so much to increase their physical fitness but simply to help them regain or maintain the functional capacity (i.e., strength, endurance) to perform the activities they want or need to do in their daily lives. These activities are commonly referred to as **activities of daily living (ADL)**. Therefore, when studying the effects of exercise training on HRQoL, exercise psychologists conceptualize exercise training programs in very broad terms. These programs might include activity performed at a sufficient intensity to increase physical fitness (e.g., aerobic and strength-training programs) as well as moderate- and low-intensity activity (e.g., Tai Chi and some walking programs) that is not nec-

activities of daily living (ADL) ■

essarily intense enough to increase fitness but can help a person maintain or attain the ability to perform activities of daily living such as shopping, climbing stairs, or doing laundry.

As mentioned in the earlier section describing the SF-36 measure of HRQoL, not all dimensions of HRQoL are likely to be affected by exercise. For example, sensory function—seeing, speaking, hearing—is sometimes considered an HRQoL dimension (for instance, in studies of patients being treated for head and neck cancers), but it is unlikely to be improved through an exercise intervention. The following five dimensions of HRQoL, however, have been identified as those most likely to be affected by exercise training programs (Rejeski, Brawley, & Shumaker, 1996):

1. Perceptions of physical functioning

A meta-analysis of 56 exercise intervention studies concluded that exercise results in significant improvements in perceptions of physical functioning (Gillison et al., 2009). These effects were demonstrated in healthy adult populations and across a wide range of patient populations such as the frail elderly and people with arthritis, kidney disease, spinal cord injury, and heart disease, to name just a few. For example, in a six-month study of older adults (with mean age of 73 years), those who had been randomly assigned to a twice weekly Tai Chi exercise program reported higher levels of physical functioning than those who were assigned to a control condition (Li, Harmer, McAuley, et al., 2001). Specifically, when compared with the control group, people in the Tai Chi condition reported better performance of vigorous and moderate physical activities as well as activities of daily living. Another study examined perceived level of physical functioning among a group of adults with COPD (Nakamura, Tanaka, Shigematsu, et al., 2008). Patients were randomly assigned to a walking-plus-strength-training condition, a walking-plus-recreational-activities condition (e.g., games to improve balance, agility, and coordination), or a control condition that did not exercise. After 12 weeks, the walking-plus-strength-training condition saw a large improvement in perceptions of physical functioning, while the walking-plus-recreation condition saw a smaller improvement. Perceptions of physical functioning decreased in the control group.

Physical self-concept, which reflects how an individual feels about one's physical self in general (see Chapter 8), is also included under the HRQoL domain of physical function. Although HRQoL researchers have not studied physical self-concept as thoroughly as perceived level and satisfaction with physical functioning, people with chronic disease or disability can improve their self-concept through exercise. For instance, in a study of adolescents who had been diagnosed with cancer (Keats, Courneya, Danielsen, & Whitsett, 1999), patients who maintained an active lifestyle throughout the cancer experience (i.e., pre-diagnosis, during cancer treatment, and after cancer treatment) had a better physical self-concept than those who were inactive throughout the entire cancer experience or those who became inactive after diagnosis.

2. Perceptions of health status

Exercise training has been shown to improve perceptions of physical health and symptom severity across a wide range of populations. For example, exercise training programs have been shown to improve the perceived "goodness" of health among older adults (Wallace, Buchner, Grothaus, et al., 1998), patients with heart disease (e.g., Denollet & Brutsaert, 1995), and individuals with knee osteoarthritis (Rejeski, Ettinger, Martin, & Morgan, 1998). Symptom severity has also been shown to improve following exercise training. For instance, in a review of studies examining the effects of exercise training on people with fibromyalgia—a chronic condition characterized by the symptoms of widespread joint and muscle pain, and exceptional sensitivity at specific pressure points on the body (e.g., at the second rib, at the mid-point of the trapezius muscle)—the authors concluded that aerobic exercise may be effective for reducing pain and pressure point discomfort (Busch, Barber, Overend, et al., 2007). Thus, it seems that exercise can help to alleviate some disease-related symptoms and might provide patients with a strategy for managing or controlling these symptoms.

Evidence suggests that exercise can help to alleviate the uncomfortable side effects of certain disease treatments. For example, chemotherapy has severe side effects including nausea and fatigue. In a study of women undergoing chemotherapy treatment for breast cancer, Winningham and MacVicar (1988) examined the effects of exercise on nausea. Those women who were assigned to a thrice-weekly program of exercise on a cycle ergometer had larger decreases in nausea than women assigned to a placebo or a control condition. Similarly, Mock and colleagues (2001) found, in a sample of women undergoing chemotherapy or radiation treatment for breast cancer, that those who were assigned to a thrice-weekly walking program reported significantly less fatigue than women in a control condition.

3. Perceptions of emotional well-being

As described in Chapters 10, 11, 12, and 13, exercise is associated with improvements in numerous aspects of emotional well-being among the general population, such as decreased depression and anxiety, and increased positive affect. The effects of exercise on emotional well-being have also been demonstrated in the elderly as well as various patient populations. For instance, exercise training has been shown to decrease feelings of depression and anxiety among the elderly (Wallace et al., 1998), patients with COPD (Emery, Schein, Hauck, & MacIntyre, 1998), breast cancer survivors (Segar, Katch, Roth, et al., 1998), and people with spinal cord injury (Martin Ginis, Latimer, McKechnie, et al., 2003).

Although the majority of exercise and HRQoL studies have focused on changes in negative affect, such as anxiety and depression, some studies have shown that exercise can also increase feelings of positive affect. For example, a study of older adults showed that, over a five-year period, increases in physical activity had a significant effect on happiness (Elavsky, McAuley, Motl, et al., 2005). That is, people who reported the greatest increases in physical activity experienced the greatest improvements in their level of happiness.

exhibit 15.5

Exercise training has been shown to significantly improve health-related quality of life among people with various types of diseases and disability.

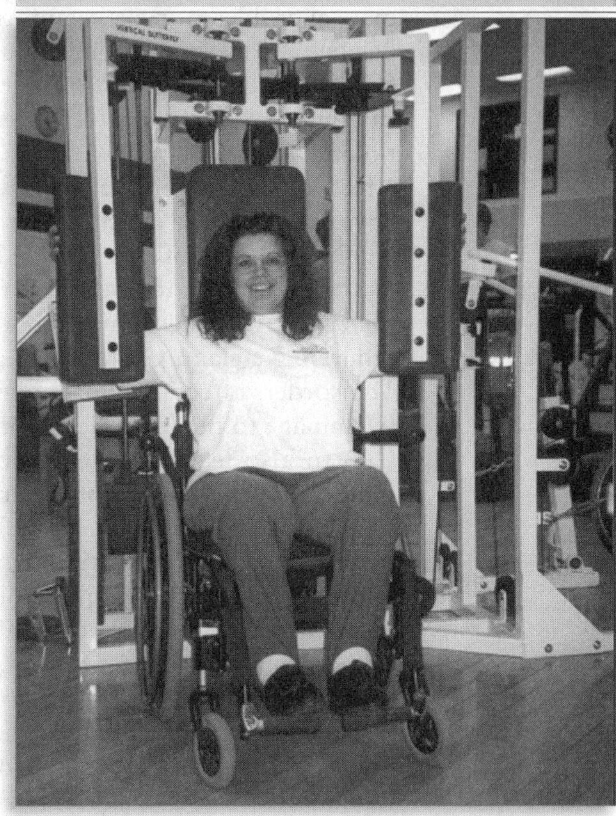

4. Perceptions of social functioning

The relationship between exercise and the social functioning dimension of HRQoL has not yet been well studied. Nevertheless, some evidence suggests that exercise can positively affect patient perceptions of aspects of their social lives. For instance, a review of studies of frail elderly men and women indicated that a regular exercise program can have positive effects on their perceptions of social functioning (Schechtman & Ory, 2001). Specifically, elderly individuals who were randomly assigned to an exercise program reported that their health interfered with their social activities less often than did individuals assigned to a control condition. Similar positive results have been found in studies of other clinical populations, such as individuals with diabetes (Wiesinger, Pleiner, Quittan, et al., 2001), fibromyalgia (Mannerkorpi, Nyberg, Ahlmen, & Ekdahl, 2000), and clinical depression (Singh, Clements, & Fiatarone, 1997).

It is important to note that people with chronic disease and disability do not need to exercise in social settings (e.g., in group exercise classes or at a gym) in order to improve their social functioning. Patients who exercise alone experience improvements in social functioning that are just as large as the improvements experienced by patients who exercise in group settings (Gillison et al., 2009). Although this finding may seem counterintuitive, the social contacts established in an exercise class probably don't have a meaningful impact on a patient's broader social life. Rather, the effects of exercise on social functioning are most likely transmitted through improvements in physical functioning, which enable exercisers to move about their communities and interact with friends and family more easily and more frequently.

In addition, exercise may enhance the social confidence of people with disease and disability by reducing concerns about being perceived by others as "disabled" or "frail" (Taub, Blinde, & Greer, 1999). People with physical disabilities have reported that the physical gains made during exercise give them more confidence in social situations (Martin, Latimer, Francoeur, et al., 2002; Taub et al., 1999).

5. Perceptions of cognitive functioning

As discussed in Chapter 14, a relatively large body of literature exists on the topic of physical activity's effects on objective measures of cognition. In these studies, exercise has been shown to improve objective indices of cognitive performance on tasks related to processing and sorting information (e.g., performing mathematical problems or sorting information into groups) and planning and initiating behaviors (e.g., performing a reaction time test). Yet, despite the *objective* benefits of exercise on cognition, very little research has examined whether exercise can improve people's perceptions of, and satisfaction with, their cognitive functioning. A demonstration of these *subjective* benefits is critical to determining the effects of exercise on the cognitive dimension of HRQoL. Although few studies have examined the effects of exercise on this dimension of HRQoL, the existing studies suggest that exercise can be beneficial to both children and adults.

For instance, in one study, researchers examined the effects of exercise on the cognitive dimension of HRQoL among children with cerebral palsy (Verschuren, Ketelaar, Gorter, et al., 2007). Cerebral palsy (CP) refers to a group of disorders affecting body movement and muscle coordination that are caused by damage to the brain during its development. The brain damage that caused CP can also lead to other problems that affect perception, cognition, communication, and behavior. Over the course of an eight-month study, children who participated in a twice-weekly exercise class had greater improvements in perceived cognitive functioning than children assigned to a control condition. Specifically, parents of children in the exercise condition (the parents had provided proxy measures of HRQoL) reported significantly greater improvements in their children's concentration, reading, learning, and verbal expression than did parents of children in the control condition.

Another study examined the effects of a twice-weekly, aerobic- and resistance-training exercise program on HRQoL among men infected with the human immunodeficiency virus (HIV; Fillipas, Oldmeadow, Bailey, & Cherry, 2006). Cognitive impairment is a frequent complication of HIV infection, so it is important to measure changes in the cognitive dimension of HRQoL when studying interventions designed to improve HRQoL in this population. Examples of items used to measure perceptions of cognitive functioning in people with HIV are: "How much of the time, during the past month, did you have difficulty reasoning and solving problems, for example, making plans, making decisions, learning new things?" and "How much of the time, during the past month, did you have trouble keeping your attention on any activity for long?" (Wu, Rubin, Mathews, et al., 1991). At the end of their six-month study, Fillipas and colleagues found that men in the exercise condition had significantly larger improvements in perceived cognitive functioning than men in the control condition.

Taken together, these studies indicate that exercise can improve *perceptions* of cognitive functioning among children and adults who may have cognitive impairments as the result of injury or disease. Much remains to be learned, however, about the role of exercise in improving people's *satisfaction* with their cognitive functioning and the effects of exercise on cognitive HRQoL among a wider range of populations.

Who Benefits from Exercise Interventions?

Both narrative reviews and meta-analyses have documented the positive effects of exercise on HRQoL across a wide range of populations. For instance, Rejeski and his colleagues (1996) conducted a narrative review of studies examining the effects of exercise on HRQoL among three patient populations: people with cardiovascular disease, pulmonary disease, or arthritis. The authors concluded that exercise is associated with improvements in all five dimensions of HRQoL reviewed previously in this chapter. Similarly, meta-analyses have shown that exercise training is associated with significant improvements in various dimensions of HRQoL in both healthy individuals (Gillison et al., 2009) and among people with chronic health conditions such as multiple sclerosis (Motl & Gosney, 2008) and heart failure (van Tol, Huijsmans, Kroon, et al., 2006). Taken together, these extensive reviews have provided compelling evidence that exercise can lead to significant improvements in the HRQoL of healthy people as well as individuals with a wide range of physical disabilities and diseases. (For a discussion of HRQoL and exercise in people with intellectual disabilities, see the following box.)

Interestingly, reasons for exercising can influence the effects of an exercise intervention on HRQoL. Gillison and colleagues examined the effects of exercise on HRQoL across three groups: (1) people who participated in an exercise program in order to improve their health or prevent disease (e.g., people who had risk factors for, but who had not yet developed, heart disease), (2) people who exercised as part of their rehabilitation following a health threat but who were expected to make a full recovery (e.g., people who had received treatment for cancer), and (3) people who exercised to manage a disease that could not be cured (e.g., people who exercised as a strategy to manage symptoms of fibromyalgia). The authors reported the effects of exercise on two HRQoL dimensions that they labeled "physical health" and "psychological health" (refer back to Exhibit 15.1 for examples of these dimensions as defined by the World Health Organization). People who exercised for health promotion or disease prevention, as opposed to rehabilitation or disease management purposes, showed the largest gains in both the physical and psychological health dimensions.

It is not yet clear why the purpose of the exercise program influences the effects of exercise interventions. Perhaps people in health promotion/disease prevention programs are generally healthier and thus are able to adhere better and exercise harder than people in rehabilitation and disease management programs. With greater exercise, participants may derive greater improvements in HRQoL. Another possibility is that people with certain health conditions may not perceive any benefit of exercise on the symptoms or complications that they consider most problematic. For instance, a woman who exercises to manage the symptoms of fibromyalgia may find that although exercise alleviates her pain, it

FOCUS on Intellectual Disabilities

Most of the studies highlighted in this chapter have focused on people with physical disabilities. Very little research has examined whether exercise can enhance the health-related quality of life of people with other types of disabilities such as intellectual or developmental disabilities. In one of the few studies to examine exercise and HRQoL among people with intellectual disabilities, researchers from the University of Illinois tested the effects of a fitness and health education program among 53 adults with Down syndrome (Heller, Hsieh, & Rimmer, 2004). Down syndrome, which occurs in approximately 1 in every 800 live births, is a genetic condition that causes delays in intellectual and physical development (National Association for Down Syndrome, www.nads.org, 2010). Adults with Down syndrome have low fitness levels and tend to lead sedentary lives—characteristics that place them at an elevated risk for various health problems including obesity. They are also predisposed to a variety of secondary health conditions, and their health declines at an earlier age than in the general population (Heller et al., 2004). Not surprisingly, these myriad health issues can compromise HRQoL. Physical activity has been identified as a potential strategy for improving the health status (USDHHS, 2002) and HRQoL of people with Down syndrome.

Participants in the study conducted by Heller and colleagues (2004) were randomly assigned to a treatment or control group. The treatment group participated in a 12-week, three-day-per-week exercise and health education program. The exercise program consisted of 30–35 minutes of aerobic exercise and 15 minutes of muscular strength and endurance exercises. Over the course of the study, the treatment group experienced a significant increase in overall life satisfaction and a small decrease in depression. The control group did not show any change in life satisfaction or depression. These findings indicate the potential benefits of exercise interventions for enhancing HRQoL among people with intellectual disabilities and highlight the importance of making fitness programs available to this population.

ADDITIONAL RESOURCES

Dodd, K.J., & Shields, N.A. (2005). Systematic review of the outcomes of cardiovascular exercise programs for people with Down syndrome. *Archives of Physical Medicine and Rehabilitation, 86,* 2051–2058.

Horvat, M., & Franklin, C. (2001). The effects of the environment on physical activity patterns of children with mental retardation. *Research Quarterly for Exercise and Sport, 72,* 189–195.

Whitt-Glover, M.C., O'Neill, K.L., & Stettler, N. (2006). Physical activity patterns in children with and without Down syndrome. *Pediatric Rehabilitation, 9,* 158–164.

ACTIVITY

People with Down syndrome and other types of intellectual and developmental disabilities face a wide range of barriers to physical activity participation. After reading the studies listed above, complete the following:

1. Make a list of specific physical activity barriers that confront people with intellectual and developmental disabilities.
2. Develop a list of strategies to overcome each barrier.
3. Consider the feasibility of implementing these strategies in your community. For example, consider what resources would be required and what individuals or agencies would be responsible for implementing each strategy.
4. Summarize your points in a position paper outlining why it is important for people with intellectual and developmental disabilities to become more physically active and how your community can help.

does not improve the feelings of chronic fatigue that interfere with her daily life. As such, she may not report any improvements in her perceptions of, or satisfaction with, her physical and psychological health.

Although exercise is associated with improvements in all five domains, some HRQoL domains may show greater improvements following an exercise intervention than others. For example, in a series of studies examining the effects of exercise on the HRQoL of community-dwelling older adults, an exercise intervention was shown to have a small but significant effect on emotional functioning, an even smaller (and nonsignificant) effect on social functioning, and no effect whatsoever on health perceptions (Schectman & Ory, 2001). One reason for the differential effects of exercise on HRQoL domains could be that people typically start out lower on some domains than others, so they have more room for improvement on certain domains. Another possibility is that exercise simply has greater effects on some domains than on others.

Some evidence also suggests that exercise can further enhance HRQoL among people who are already receiving some other type of HRQoL intervention. For example, one experiment examined the effects of exercise on the HRQoL of heart failure patients who were already receiving the maximum recommended drug therapy (Pozehl, Duncan, Krueger, & VerMass, 2003). Drug therapy has been shown to reduce the key symptoms of dyspnea and fatigue in people with heart failure and to improve their overall quality of life. At the end of a 12-week study, patients who had received drug therapy *plus* an exercise intervention scored higher on the SF-36 than patients who had received only drug therapy. Similarly, Courneya and colleagues (Courneya, Friedenreich, Sela, et al., 2003) examined the effects of exercise on cancer survivors over and above the effects of group psychotherapy—an intervention that has been shown to improve quality of life in this population (Blake-Mortimer, Gore-Felton, Kimerling, et al., 1999). Over the course of a 10-week study, people randomly assigned to receive psychotherapy plus an exercise intervention showed greater improvements in HRQoL than people who received psychotherapy alone. Taken together, the results of these two studies speak to the potency of exercise as an HRQoL-enhancing intervention: It can have positive benefits beyond those achievable by other standard forms of treatment.

The relationship between changes in HRQoL and objective changes in disease status and physical fitness

The positive effects of exercise on HRQoL are generally unrelated to exercise-related improvements in objective indices of disease status or physical fitness. For example, in a study of men who were HIV positive, a 12-week exercise intervention was shown to significantly improve perceptions of their emotional and physical functioning, despite no change in an objective index of disease status—the number of CD4 cells present (Lox, McAuley, & Tucker, 1995). Similarly, a study of exercise among adults with COPD showed that improvements in objective measures of physical fitness were unrelated to improvements in perceived health status and emotional well-being (Wijkstra, Van Altena, Kraan, et al., 1994). Thus, a person does not need to experience objective improvements in physical fitness in order to derive the HRQoL-enhancing benefits of exercise.

The lack of an association between improvements in HRQoL and improvements in objective indices of disease status and fitness may seem counterintuitive. As emphasized throughout this chapter, however, HRQoL is not simply a reflection of one's objective health status and level of functioning. Rather, HRQoL reflects *perceptions of, and thoughts and feelings about* one's health status and functioning. Thus, in order for exercise to have an effect on HRQoL, people must be able to perceive improvements in their own health and function.

The relationship between changes in HRQoL and perceived changes in important aspects of one's life

How meaningful are changes in "maximal workload" or "maximal oxygen consumption" to the average older adult with COPD? Not very; most people have no idea how to interpret the results of these objective measures of physical fitness. Likewise, are changes in CD4 cell counts the only aspect of health that a person with HIV cares about? Probably not. Instead, for many people with disease and disability, the changes in their ability to perform tasks that are important in their daily lives—such as climbing stairs, dealing with their emotions, and participating in family and community life (e.g., Sutherland, Lockwood, & Boyd, 1990)—are often what is important. When exercise leads to perceived improvements in the ability to perform these important tasks, such improvements are usually more meaningful to people than are changes in objective measures of fitness or disease. As a result, when considering the impact of exercise on their HRQoL, people tend to focus on whether exercise has had an impact on valued aspects of their lives.

Practical Recommendations

Based on the information provided in this chapter, we can offer several practical recommendations for designing exercise interventions to enhance HRQoL. First, in order for exercise to enhance HRQoL, people must be able to *perceive* improvements in their level of functioning. Interventionists can help make people more aware of their functional gains by regularly asking them about their level of functioning in their daily lives (e.g., how many stairs can they climb, how much help do they need to get dressed or bathe, how many days were they confined to bed in the past week), or periodically testing participants' ability to perform activities of daily living (e.g., opening heavy doors, getting in and out of a car). Changes in the perceived difficulty with which these tasks are performed or the amount of help that the person needs to do these tasks can be recorded over the course of an exercise intervention and brought to the participant's attention. Often, people don't realize that they have made progress unless they are given the opportunity to see how far they have come.

Second, people must realize the *value* of exercise to their HRQoL. In many cases, people may not understand how certain exercises can be of benefit to them. For example, older people may wonder why a fitness leader is asking them to perform exercises to strengthen their biceps and triceps. The exercise leader could explain how each of these exercises relates to the performance of activities of daily living such as carrying a laundry basket or pushing oneself out of a bathtub. When people realize that exercise-induced strength gains result in meaningful changes to their daily functioning, exercise is more likely to have a positive effect on HRQoL.

Third, people should be encouraged to engage in various different types of physical activity, as some types of activity may affect certain components of HRQoL more than others. For example, participation in an exercise class that focuses on strength training would likely provide a greater sense of improved physical functioning than participation in an exercise class that focuses on stretching and flexibility. Similarly, although *structured* exercise has been shown to enhance perceptions of physical functioning, individuals should also be encouraged to engage in short bouts of *unstructured* activity throughout the day (e.g., walking to a friend's house, gardening, grocery shopping, taking a pet for a walk). Performing these activities can increase beliefs about the level of control a person has over his or her life. Because improved control beliefs might lead to increased perceptions of HRQoL, it is important to encourage people to perform activities that will give them a greater sense of power over their lives. An exercise programmer might further increase control beliefs by reminding participants that, by exercising, they are taking charge of an aspect of their well-being.

Conclusion

Health-related quality of life reflects the perceived goodness of the various aspects of one's life that can be affected by health and health interventions. It is a subcomponent of the broader concept of "quality of life," which reflects objective and subjective evaluations of the *overall* goodness of one's life. HRQoL is also considered an important benchmark for determining the effectiveness of health treatments and for making treatment decisions. As exercise is being used increasingly as a treatment for people with disease and disability, exercise psychologists are interested in determining the effects of exercise interventions on HRQoL. Although researchers often disagree on how best to define and measure HRQoL, evidence shows that exercise can play a role in improving at least five different dimensions of HRQoL: physical function, health status, emotional well-being, social function, and cognitive function. People exercising for health promotion and disease prevention tend to experience greater improvements in HRQoL than people exercising for rehabilitation or disease management purposes. Interestingly, exercise interventions do not need to cause objective improvements along dimensions such as disease status or physical fitness in order for improvements in HRQoL to occur. Rather, improvements in HRQoL seem to be related to perceived improvements in the ability to perform daily activities that the individual considers important or meaningful.

what do you know?

1. What is the difference between quality of life (QoL) and health-related quality of life (HRQoL)?
2. Identify and briefly describe the five core dimensions of HRQoL that are generally agreed on by researchers and clinicians.
3. What is the main difference between subjective and objective measures of HRQoL?
4. Give two examples of objective measures of HRQoL.
5. What is meant by "quality-adjusted life years"?
6. Describe the subjective approach to measuring HRQoL.
7. What is meant by the "proxy approach" to measuring HRQoL?
8. In studies of exercise interventions, why is the subjective approach generally considered better than the objective approach?
9. Which dimensions of HRQoL are most likely to be affected by exercise training?
10. To what extent do changes in disease status and physical fitness affect HRQoL?
11. Give examples of populations that have shown exercise-related improvements in HRQoL. Who is most likely to improve, and why?
12. Identify and describe three individual difference variables that can affect perceptions of HRQoL.

learning activities

1. Use your knowledge of HRQoL to make decisions about exercise prescription for the following two cases:

   Case 1. You are studying the effects of aerobic exercise on the progression of a newly identified disease. Although blood samples reveal that exercise is curbing disease progress, patients are so fatigued after working out and experience such a large increase in pain due to exercise that they are unable to perform activities of daily living or to socialize with their families and friends. Thus, despite medical improvements, patients have significant decrements in their HRQoL. Should you recommend exercise as a treatment for this disease? Defend your position.

Case 2. You have been asked to implement an exercise training program at a local nursing home where the caregivers are hoping to decrease the risk of heart disease among residents. After six months of light chair exercises (exercises performed while seated), no improvement is seen in participants' risk for heart disease. However, participants note that since starting the exercise program, they have felt happier with their ability to walk short distances and their level of energy for participating in social activities. When their families visit, family members remark that the patients seem more positive. Do you continue the exercise program even though it is not producing any change in risk for heart disease? Construct an argument defending your position to present to the director of the home.

2. Conduct a literature search to find exercise intervention studies that have used the SF-36 scale to measure changes in HRQoL. Choose two studies that involved two different populations (e.g., arthritis patients and the elderly). Compare and contrast the effects of exercise on SF-36 scores for these two different groups of people.
3. Develop an exercise training program for the frail elderly that has the specific goal of improving their HRQoL. Pay careful attention to:
   a. the types of exercises and activities that you prescribe
   b. the instructions and information that you give participants about the relationship between exercise and HRQoL
   c. strategies to enhance perceptions of improvement and control.
4. Choose a particular disease or disability (e.g., heart disease, hearing loss) and conduct an Internet search to find a questionnaire measuring HRQoL designed specifically for people who have this condition. If you were to administer this measure to patients at the start of an exercise program and then three months into the exercise program, how do you think their responses to the questionnaire would change?
5. People with chronic disease and disability cannot derive exercise-related improvements in HRQoL unless, of course, they are able to exercise. Environmental barriers are a primary deterrent to exercise among people with chronic disease and disability, particularly among those with a mobility impairment (i.e., people who use a wheelchair, cane, or other mobility aid to move about their communities). For these individuals, it is often difficult or even impossible to use public exercise facilities.
   a. Choose a particular population with a mobility impairment (e.g., people with arthritis, spinal cord injury, multiple sclerosis) and generate a list of physical activity barriers that this population would face.
   b. Conduct an audit or survey of a local fitness facility to determine whether the facility would be accessible to your population of choice. Your audit could include an evaluation of features such as the availability and proximity of wheelchair-accessible parking, ramps and elevators, the spacing in and around exercise equipment (i.e., is there enough space for

a wheelchair to move about?), the height of drinking fountains and service desks, and the availability of staff to help these exercisers.

c. Write a report that summarizes the accessible and inaccessible elements of the facility and makes recommendations to improve accessibility.

references

American College of Sports Medicine (2009). Position stand: Exercise and physical activity for older adults. *Medicine and Science in Sports and Exercise, 41,* 1510–1530.

Arthritis Foundation (2009). *Exercise and arthritis.* Retrieved May 25, 2009, from www.arthritis.org/exercise-intro.php.

Arthur, H.M., Gunn, E., Thorpe, K.E., Martin Ginis, K.A., Mataseje, L., McCartney, N., & McKelvie, R.S. (2007). Effect of aerobic vs. combined aerobic-strength training on 1-year, post-cardiac rehabilitation outcomes in women after a cardiac event. *Journal of Rehabilitation Medicine, 39,* 730–735.

Blake-Mortimer, C., Gore-Felton, R., Kimerling, J.M., Turner-Cobb, K., & Spiegel, D. (1999). Improving the quality and quantity of life among patients with cancer: A review of the effectiveness of group psychotherapy. *European Journal of Cancer, 35,* 1581–1586.

Bulthuis, Y., Mohammad, S., Braakman-Jansen, L.M., Drossaers-Bakker, K.W., & van de Laar, M.A. (2008). Cost-effectiveness of intensive exercise therapy directly following hospital discharge in patients with arthritis: Results of a randomized controlled clinical trial. *Arthritis & Rheumatism, 59,* 247–254.

Busch, A.J., Barber, K.A., Overend, T.J., Peloso, P.M., & Schachter, C.L. (2007).Exercise for treating fibromyalgia syndrome. *Cochrane Database of Systematic Reviews, 4:* CD003786.

Courneya, K.S., Friedenreich, C.M., Sela, R.A., Quinney, A., Rhodes, R.E., & Handman, M. (2003). The group psychotherapy and home-based physical exercise (GROUP-HOPE) trial in cancer survivors: Physical fitness and quality of life outcomes. *Psycho-Oncology, 12,* 357–374.

Denollet, J., & Brutsaert, D.L. (1995). Enhancing emotional well-being by comprehensive rehabilitation in patients with coronary heart disease. *European Heart Journal, 16,* 1070–1078.

Eiser, C., & Morse, R. (2001). Can parents rate their child's health-related quality of life? Results of a systematic review. *Quality of Life Research, 10,* 347–357.

Elavsky, S., McAuley, E., Motl, R.W., Konopack, J.F., Marquez, D.X., Hu, L., Jerome, G.J., & Diener, E. (2005). Physical activity enhances long-term quality of life in older adults: Efficacy, esteem, and affective influences. *Annals of Behavioral Medicine, 30,* 138–145.

Emery, C.F., Schein, R.L., Hauck, E.R., & MacIntyre, N.R. (1998). Psychological and cognitive outcomes of a randomized trial of exercise among patients with chronic obstructive pulmonary disease. *Health Psychology, 17,* 232–240.

Eysenck, S.B., & Eysenck, H.J. (1969). Scores of three personality variables as a function of age, sex, and social class. *British Journal of Social and Clinical Psychology, 8,* 69–76.

Fillipas, S., Oldmeadow, L.B., Bailey, M.J., & Cherry, C.L. (2006). A six-month, supervised, aerobic and resistance exercise program improves self-efficacy in people with human immunodeficiency virus: A randomised controlled trial. *Australian Journal of Physiotherapy, 52,* 185–190.

Gill, T.M., & Feinstein, A.R. (1994). A critical appraisal of the quality of quality-of-life measurements. *Journal of the American Medical Association, 272,* 619–631.

Gillison, F.B., Skevington, S.M., Sato, A., Standage, M., & Evangelidou, S. (2009). The effects of exercise interventions on quality of life in clinical and healthy populations; A meta-analysis. *Social Science & Medicine, 68,* 1700–1710.

Hatziandreu, E.I., Koplan, J.P., Weinstein, M.C., Caspersen, C.J., & Warner, K.E. (1988). A cost-effectiveness analysis of exercise as a health promotion activity. *American Journal of Public Health, 78,* 1417–1421.

Heart and Stroke Foundation of Canada (2009). *Basic principles of physical activity.* Retrieved July 1, 2009, from www.heartandstroke.on.ca.

Heller, T., Hsieh, K., & Rimmer, J.H. (2004). Attitudinal and psychosocial outcomes of a fitness and health education program on adults with Down syndrome. *American Journal of Mental Retardation, 109,* 175–185.

Hicks, A.L., Martin, K.A., Latimer, A.E., Ditor, D.S., & McCartney, N. (2003). Long-term exercise training in persons with spinal cord injury: Effects on strength, arm ergometry performance and psychological well-being. *Spinal Cord, 41,* 29–33.

Kaplan, R.M., & Bush, J.W. (1982). Health-related quality of life measurement for evaluation research analysis. *Health Psychology, 1,* 61–80.

Keats, M.R., Courneya, K.S., Danielsen, S., & Whitsett, S.F. (1999). Leisure-time physical activity and psychosocial well-being in adolescents after cancer diagnosis. *Journal of Pediatric Oncology Nursing, 16,* 180–188.

Kempen, G.I., Jelicic, M., & Ormel, J. (1997). Personality, chronic medical morbidity, and health-related quality of life among older persons. *Health Psychology, 16,* 539–546.

Kirk, A.F., Higgins, L.A., Hughes, A.R., Fisher, B.M., Mutrie, N., Hillis, S., & MacIntyre, P.D. (2001). A randomized, controlled trial to study the effects of exercise consultation on the promotion of physical activity in people with type 2 diabetes: Pilot study. *Diabetic Medicine, 11,* 877–882.

Lacasse, Y., Wong, E., Guyatt, G.H., King, D., Cook, D.J., & Goldstein, R.S. (1996). Meta-analysis of respiratory rehabilitation in chronic obstructive pulmonary disease. *The Lancet, 348,* 1115–1119.

Larson, D.B., Sawyers, J.P., & McCullough, M.E. (1997). *Scientific research on spirituality and health: A consensus report.* Rockville, MD: National Institute for Healthcare Research.

Levin, J.S., & Taylor, R.J. (1998). Panel analyses of religious involvement and well-being in African Americans: Contemporaneous vs. longitudinal effects. *Journal of the Scientific Study of Religion, 37,* 695–709.

Li, F., Harmer, P., McAuley, E., Duncan, T.E., Duncan, S.C., Chaumeton, N., & Fisher, K.J. (2001). An evaluation of the effects of tai chi exercise on physical function among older persons: A randomized controlled trial. *Annals of Behavioral Medicine, 23,* 139–146.

Lox, C.L, McAuley, E., & Tucker, R.S. (1995). Exercise as an intervention for enhancing subjective well-being in an HIV-1 population. *Journal of Sport and Exercise Psychology, 17,* 345–362.

Mannerkorpi, K., Nyberg, B., Ahlmen, M., & Ekdahl, C. (2000). Pool exercise combined with an education program for patients with fibromyalgia syndrome: A prospective, randomized study. *Journal of Rheumatology, 10,* 2473–2481.

Martin, K.A., Latimer, A.E., Francoeur, C., Hanley, H., & Watson, K. (2002). Sustaining exercise motivation and participation among people with spinal cord injury: Lessons learned from a 9-month intervention. *Palaestra, 18,* 38–40.

Martin Ginis, K.A., Latimer, A.E., Brawley, L.R., Jung, M.E., & Hicks, A. (2006). Weight training to activities of daily living: Helping older adults make a connection. *Medicine and Science in Sports and Exercise, 38,* 116–121.

Martin Ginis, K.A., Latimer, A.E., McKechnie, K., Ditor, D.S., McCartney, N., Hicks, A.L., Bugaresti, J., & Craven, C. (2003). Using physical activity to enhance subjective well-being among people with spinal cord injury: The mediating influence of stress and pain. *Rehabilitation Psychology, 48,* 157–164.

Mock V., Pickett, M., Ropka, M.E., Muscari, E., Stewart, K.J., Rhodes, V.A., McDaniel, R., Grimm, P.M., Krumm, S., & McCorkle, R. (2001). Fatigue and quality of life outcomes of exercise during cancer treatment. *Cancer Practice, 9,* 119–127.

Motl, R.W., & Gosney, J.L. (2008). Effect of exercise training on quality of life in multiple sclerosis: A meta-analysis. *Multiple Sclerosis, 14,* 129–135.

Nakamura, Y., Tanaka, K., Shigematsu, R., Nakagaichi, M., Inoue, M., & Homma, T. (2008). Effects of aerobic training and recreational activities in patients with chronic obstructive pulmonary disease. *International Journal of Rehabilitation Research, 31,* 275–283.

National Association for Down Syndrome. (2010). Down syndrome facts. www.nads.org/pages_new/facts.htm.

Neill, W.A., Branch, L.G., De Jong, G., Smith, N.E., Hogan, C.A., Corcoran, P.J., Jette, A.M., Balasco, E.M., & Osberg, S. (1985). Cardiac disability: The impact of coronary heart disease on patients' daily activities. *Archives of Internal Medicine, 145,* 1642–1647.

Noreau, L., & Shephard, R.J. (1995). Spinal cord injury, exercise and quality of life. *Sports Medicine, 20,* 226–250.

Patrick, D.L., Danis, M., Southerland, L.I., & Hong, G. (1988). Quality of life following intensive care. *Journal of General Internal Medicine, 3,* 218–223.

Patrick, D.L., Ramsey, S.D., Spencer, A.C., Kinne, S., Belza, B., & Topolski, T.D. (2001). Economic evaluation of aquatic exercise for persons with osteoarthritis. *Medical Care, 39,* 413–424.

Petersen, L.R., Clark, M.M., Novotny, P., Kung, S., Sloan, J.A., Patten, C.A., Vickers, K.S., Rummens, T.A., Frost, M.H., & Culligan, R.C. (2008). Relationship of optimism-pessimism and health-related quality of life in breast cancer survivors. *Journal of Psychosocial Oncology, 26,* 15–32.

Philips, C., & Thompson, G. (2001). *What Is a QALY?* Kent, UK: Hayward Medical Communications.

Pickard, A.S., & Knight, S.J. (2005). Proxy evaluation of health-related quality of life: A conceptual framework for understanding multiple proxy perspectives. *Medical Care, 43,* 493–499.

Pozehl, B., Duncan, K., Krueger, S., & VerMass, P. (2003). Adjunctive effects of exercise training in heart failure patients receiving maximum pharmacologic therapy. *Progress in Cardiovascular Nursing, 18,* 177–183.

Rejeski, W.J., Brawley, L.R., & Shumaker, S.A. (1996). Physical activity and health-related quality of life. *Exercise and Sport Science Reviews, 24,* 71–108.

Rejeski, W.J., Ettinger, W.H., Martin, K.A., & Morgan, T. (1998). Treating disability in knee osteoarthritis with exercise therapy: A central role for self-efficacy and pain. *Arthritis Care Research, 11,* 94–101.

Rejeski, W.J., Martin, K.A., Miller, M.E., Ettinger, W.H., & Rapp, S. (1998). Perceived importance and satisfaction with physical function in patients with knee osteoarthritis. *Annals of Behavioral Medicine, 20,* 141–148.

Salvetti, M.X., Filho, J.A.O., Serrantes, D.M., & de Paolo, A.A.V. (2008). How much do the benefits cost? Effects of a home-based training programme on cardiovascular fitness, quality of life, programme cost and adherence for patients with coronary disease. *Clinical Rehabilitation, 22,* 987–996.

Schectman, K.B., & Ory, M.G. (2001). The effects of exercise on the quality of life of frail older adults: A preplanned meta-analysis of the FICSIT trials. *Annals of Behavioral Medicine, 23,* 186–197.

Scheier, M.F., & Carver, C.S. (1985). Optimism, coping, and health: Assessment and implications of generalized outcome expectancies. *Health Psychology, 4,* 219–247.

Schou, I., Ekeberg, O., Sandvik, L., Hjermstad, M.J., & Ruland, C.M. (2005). Multiple predictors of health-related quality of life in early stage breast cancer: Data from a year follow-up study compared with the general population. *Quality of Life Research, 14,* 1813–1823.

Segal, R., Evans, W., Johnson, D., Smith, J., Colletta, S., Gayton, J., Woodard, S., Wells, G., & Reid, R. (2001). Structured exercise improves physical functioning in women with stages I and II breast cancer: Results of a randomized controlled trial. *Journal of Clinical Oncology, 19,* 657–665.

Segar, M.L., Katch, V.L., Roth, R.S., Weinstein Garcia, A., Portner, T.I., Glickman, S.G., Haslanger, S., & Wilkins, E.G. (1998). The effect of aerobic exercise on self-esteem and depressive and anxiety symptoms among breast cancer survivors. *Oncology Nursing Forum, 25,* 107–113.

Singh, N.A., Clements, K.M., & Fiatarone, M.A. (1997). A randomized controlled trial of progressive resistance training in depressed elders. *Journals of Gerontology: Series-A: Biological Sciences and Medical Sciences, 52A,* M27–M35.

Sutherland, H.J., Lockwood, G.A., & Boyd, N.F. (1990). Ratings of the importance of quality of life variables: Therapeutic implications for patients with metastatic breast cancer. *Journal of Clinical Epidemiology, 43,* 661–666.

Taub, D.E., Blinde, E.M., & Greer, K.R. (1999). Stigma management through participation in sport and physical activity: Experiences of male college students with physical disabilities. *Human Relations, 52,* 1469–1484.

Tsevat, J., Sherman, S.N., McElwee, J.A., Mandell, K.L., Simbarti, L.A., Sonnenberg, F.A., & Fowler, F.J. (1999). The will to live among HIV-infected patients. *Annals of Internal Medicine, 131,* 194–198.

U. S. Department of Health and Human Services. (2002). Closing the gap: A national blueprint for improving the health of individuals with mental retardation. Report of the Surgeon General's Conference on Health Disparities and Mental Retardation. Rockville, MD: Office of the Surgeon General.

U. S. Department of Health and Human Services (2009). Deaths: Final data for 2006. *National Vital Statistics Reports, 57*(14).

van Tol, B.A., Huijsmans, R.J., Kroon, D.W., Schothorst, M., & Kwakkel, G. (2006). Effects of exercise training on cardiac performance, exercise capacity and quality of life in patients with heart failure: A meta-analysis. *European Journal of Heart Failure, 8,* 841–850.

Verschuren, O., Ketelaar, M., Gorter, J.W., Helders, P.J., Uiterwaal, C.S., & Takken, T. (2007). Exercise training program in children and adolescents with cerebral palsy: A randomized controlled trial. *Archives of Pediatrics & Adolescent Medicine, 161,* 1075–1081.

Vollrath, M., & Landolt, M.A. (2005). Personality predicts quality of life in pediatric patients with unintentional injuries: A 1-year follow-up study. *Journal of Pediatric Psychology, 30,* 481–431.

Wallace, J.I., Buchner, D.M., Grothaus, L., Leveille, S., Tyll, L., LaCroix, A.Z., & Wagner, E.H. (1998). Implementation and effectiveness of a community-based health promotion program for older adults. *Journal of Gerontology, 53A,* 301–306.

Ware, J.E., Kosinski, M., Bayliss, M.S., McHorney, C.A., et al. (1995). Comparison of methods for the scoring and statistical analysis of SF-36 health profile and summary measures: Summary of results from the medical outcomes study. *Medical Care, 33* (Supplement), 264–279.

Ware, J.E., & Sherbourne, C.D. (1992). The MOS 36-item short-form health survey (SF-36): I. Conceptual framework and item selection. *Medical Care, 30,* 473–483.

Whitt-Glover, M.C., O'Neill, K.L., & Stettler, N. (2006). Physical activity patterns in children with and without Down syndrome. *Pediatric Rehabilitation, 9,* 158–164.

Wiesinger, G.F., Pleiner, J., Quittan, M., Fuchsjager-Mayrl, G., Crevanna, R., Nuhr, M.J., Francesconi, C., Seit, H.P., Francesconi, M., Fialka-Moser, V., & Wolzt, M. (2001). Health related quality of life in patients with long-standing insulin dependent (type 1) diabetes mellitus: Benefits of regular exercise training. *Wiener Klinische Wochenschrift, 113,* 670–675.

Wijkstra, P.J., Van Altena, R., Kraan, J., Otten, V., Postma, D.S., & Koeter, G.H. (1994). Quality of life in patients with chronic pulmonary obstructive disease improves after rehabilitation at home. *The European Respiratory Journal, 7,* 269–273.

Winningham, M.L., & MacVicar, M.G. (1988). The effect of aerobic exercise on patient reports of nausea. *Oncology Nursing Forum, 15,* 447–450.

World Health Organization. (1947). *Definition of health* [On-line]. Available: www.who.int/aboutwho/en/definition.html.

World Health Organization. (1993). WHOQOL Study Protocol. WHO (MNH/PSF/93.9).

Wu, A.W., Rubin, H.R., Mathews, W.C., Ware, J.E., Brysk, L.T., Hardy, W.D., Bozzette, S.A., Spector, S.A., & Richman, D.D. (1991). A health status questionnaire using 30 items from the Medical Outcomes Study. *Medical Care, 29,* 786–798.

Yamaoka, K., Shigehisa, T., Ogoshi, K., Haruyama, K., Watanabe, M., Hayashi, F., & Hayashi, C. (1998). Health-related quality of life varies with personality types: A comparison among cancer patients, non-cancer patients and healthy individuals in a Japanese population. *Quality of Life Research, 6,* 535–544.

Yost, K.J., Haan, M.N., Levine, R.A., & Gold, E.B. (2005). Comparing SF-36 scores across three groups of women with different health profiles. *Quality of Life Research, 14,* 1251–1261.

Zavala, M.W., Maliski, S.L., Kwan, L., Fink, A., & Litwin, M.S. (2009). Spirituality and quality of life in low-income men with metastatic prostate cancer. *Psycho-Oncology, 18,* 753–761.

Glossary

absolute reactivity The absolute value of heart rate during stress.

abstinence violation effect In behavior change, when a single lapse in behavior causes an individual to give up trying to change a behavior, resulting in a full relapse.

academic self-concept A subdomain of general self-concept, encompassing the primary learning domains of English, math, history, and science.

accelerometer A small device worn at the waist that detects acceleration of a limb (e.g., leg) to provide data related to the amount of activity performed over time.

acquired immune deficiency syndrome (AIDS) An infectious disease caused by the HIV virus (human immunodeficiency virus), which damages the body's immune system, leaving the person vulnerable to a large number of illnesses.

action planning Forming concrete plans that specify when, where, and how a person will translate his or her behavioral (e.g., exercise) intentions into action.

action stage Transtheoretical model stage at which a person is exercising at recommended levels for health and fitness.

activities of daily living (ADL) Actions completed during the normal course of the day such as going up and down stairs, carrying groceries, and walking.

activity log A self-report measure in which activities are written in notebooks or recorded in a variety of electronic mediums.

activity trait A subtrait of extraversion that reflects a tendency to be busy and energetic and with a preference for fast-paced living.

acute Short-term, temporary.

adherence Maintaining an exercise regimen for a prolonged period of time.

adoption The beginning stage of an exercise regimen.

affect A general, valenced response to a stimulus that does not require thought processes to precede it.

affective dimension of body image Feelings experienced in relation to the body's appearance and function.

affective state Temporary positive or negative feelings that influence, and are influenced by, exercise behavior.

agoraphobia An anxiety disorder characterized by severe, pervasive anxiety when in situations perceived to be difficult to escape (e.g., fear of being in crowds), or complete avoidance of certain situations.

agreeableness In the Five Factor Model, compatibility with others.

all-cause mortality rates Death by any cause.

allostasis The process of an organism's adaptation to a stressor promoted by the autonomic nervous systems and the hypothalamic-pituitary-adrenal cortical (HPA) axis.

allostatic load The cost of an organism's coping/adaptation to a stressor promoted by the autonomic nervous systems and the hypothalamic-pituitary-adrenal cortical (HPA) axis.

amotivation The absence of motivation and/or lack of intention to engage in a behavior.

amplitude A key feature of event-related potential that measures whether the potential deflects up or down.

androgynous A term that refers to an individual who scores high on both the expressive and instrumental personality dimensions.

angiogenesis The formation of new capillaries, the stimulation of which is exercise-dependent.

anorexia nervosa An eating disorder characterized by the refusal to maintain a minimally healthy weight, an intense fear of gaining weight, body image disturbance, and, in women, absence of at least three consecutive menstrual cycles.

antecedent cue A cue that precedes a behavior in classical conditioning.

anthropological hypothesis An explanation for the link between physical activity and depression based on evolutionary theory.

anxiety disorders A category of mental health disorders characterized by excessive or inappropriate expression of anxiety.

anxiety sensitivity Fear of anxiety and anxiety-related sensations.

anxiolytic Anxiety reducing.

arthritis A category of more than 100 conditions that involve inflammation of the joints, pain, stiffness, and occasionally swelling.

attentional network The neural circuitry involved in various aspects of executive control processes.

attentional resources The amount of brain activity needed to attend to a task and to update memory.

attitude An individual's positive or negative evaluations of a something (e.g., physical activity).

autonomic nervous system A branch of the nervous system that controls physiological functioning relatively automatically (e.g., heart rate, blood pressure, respiration).

avoidance behaviors With regard to body image, actions performed to divert attention away from the body or to prevent other people from seeing one's body.

behavioral approaches An approach to physical activity interventions in which one teaches the behavioral management skills necessary for both successful adoption and maintenance of behavior changes.

behavioral coping strategies Strategies that involve the development and implementation of overt plans to manage high-risk situations.

behavioral dimension With regard to body image, things we do that reflect our positive or negative perceptions, thoughts, and feelings about our bodies.

behavioral economics A model of behavior that integrates stimulus-response theory with research on cognitive psychology and decision making in order to understand how people allocate time and effort to various behavioral options.

behavioral medicine A field of medicine that focuses on the interrelationships of behavioral, physical, and psychosocial factors in the understanding of healthful living and the treatment of illness, disease, and disability.

behavioral processes In the transtheoretical model, behaviors that a person undertakes in order to change aspects of the environment that can affect exercise participation.

behavioral reactance The phenomenon whereby people respond in a direction opposite to the direction being advocated.

binge eating/purging type A type of anorexia involving regular binge-eating and purging episodes.

biopsychosocial approach The belief that the body, mind, and social environment influence one another and, ultimately, behavior.

bipolar disorder A mood disorder characterized by one or more episodes of mania or mixed episodes of mania and depression.

body checking behaviors Actions, usually idiosyncratic performed to monitor or assess one's body shape or size.

body composition The relative amount of lean body mass versus fat in the body.

body dysmorphic disorder A serious psychiatric condition characterized by excessive preoccupation with some aspect of physical appearance (e.g., breast size, body weight, or facial features).

body ideal An individual's perception of how his or her body should look and function.

body image A multidimensional construct that reflects how one sees, thinks, feels, and behaves toward one's own body; includes perceptual, cognitive, affective, and behavioral dimensions.

body image disturbance Negative self-evaluations along any or all of the body image dimensions.

body-part procedures A perceptual measurement of body image based on the perceived width of a particular body part.

body reality An individual's *actual* physical characteristics, such as height, weight, strength, and disease. When body reality is the same as or similar to body ideal, this is usually indicative of a healthy body image. When body reality is dissimilar to body ideal, there may be body image disturbance.

brain derived neurotrophic factor (BDNF) A protein that is essential for hippocampal function, synaptic plasticity and adaptability, and learning

bulimia nervosa An eating disorder characterized by binge eating and dramatic behaviors to compensate for overeating (e.g., self-induced vomiting, strenuous exercise, inappropriate use of diuretics and/or laxatives).

cancer A disease of the cells characterized by unrestricted cell growth that usually results in the formation of a tumor. Cancer is the second most frequent cause of death in North America.

cardiovascular fitness hypothesis The idea that some measure of cardiovascular fitness improvement is needed for improvements in cognitive function to take place.

categorical approach An approach that assumes that affective states are distinct and have unique properties and antecedents.

cerebrotonia Sheldon's term for the tense, introverted, socially restrained, and inhibited personality associated with the ectomorph somatotype.

change talk Statements regarding one's desires, abilities, and reasons for change.

chronic Long-term, relatively permanent.

chronic obstructive pulmonary disease (COPD) Respiratory disease characterized by permanently reduced airflow; includes both emphysema and chronic bronchitis. One of the five leading causes of death in North America; 80 percent of cases in the United States are related to smoking.

circumplex model A model that describes affective states along the perimeter of a circle defined by the dimensions of affective valence and activation.

classical conditioning A theory that a reflexive behavior can be elicited through repeated pairings of the behavior with an antecedent cue.

clinical anxiety Having enough anxiety symptoms at a sufficient intensity to meet criteria for a clinical disorder requiring some form of therapeutic intervention (e.g., psychotherapy, medication).

cognitive behavior therapy (CBT) A form of psychotherapy in which individuals are trained to use strategies (such as relaxation training and stress management) to replace negative thought patterns with thoughts that will lead to positive feelings and behaviors.

cognitive coping strategies The use of nonobservable thought processes—such as self-talk and visualization—to overcome disruptive thoughts and feelings.

cognitive dimension of body image How we think about or evaluate our body in terms of both its appearance and function.

cognitive functioning The ability to concentrate or divide one's attention among several things, to learn and remember, to make a plan of action and effectively execute that plan, to self-regulate activities, to recognize objects or things, to evaluate, to construct in one's mind, and to think logically and solve problems.

cognitive restructuring The process of changing how one thinks about a situation or event.

community-wide campaigns Physical activity interventions that engage different community members and organizations in the development and delivery of information aimed at increasing physical activity.

companionship support A reflection of the availability of people with whom one can exercise, such as a friend, family member, or group.

conscientiousness In the Five Factor Model, the number of goals an individual is focused on and the level of self-discipline used to accomplish those goals.

consciousness raising Increasing one's awareness and memory of the benefits of physical activity.

consequent reinforcement A reward that follows a behavior.

constitutional theory A theory that individuals possess certain body types (somatypes) that determine personality.

contemplation stage The stage in which a person intends to start exercising within the next six months.

contextual motivation A relatively stable pattern of motivation experienced in a particular context.

control beliefs A person's perception of how much power they have over their bodies, an illness, and their lives.

coping efficacy Self-efficacy for overcoming barriers or challenges to exercise.

core The portion of personality that includes our perceptions of the external world and our self, and our basic attitudes, values, interests, and motives.

cross-stressor adaptation hypothesis The hypothesis that states that a stressor of sufficient intensity and/or duration will induce adaptation of the stress response systems.

cues-to-action Stimuli in the environment or within the person that prompt a particular behavior.

cues-to-decision Stimuli that initiate a process of deciding whether or not to perform a behavior.

cultural body ideal In Western society, the rigidly defined ideal body weight/type glamorized by the media (also called *media ideal*).

cultural tailoring Adapting or targeting informational interventions to specific cultural groups.

cyclothymia A mood disorder characterized by manic and depressive states, but of insufficient intensity/duration to diagnose as bipolar or major depressive disorder.

decisional balance A model that reflects how people perceive the pros and cons of changing their behavior.

depressive disorder A mental illness characterized by one or more of the following: sustained feelings of sadness, feelings of guilt or worthlessness, disturbances in appetite, disturbances in sleep patterns, lack of energy, difficulty concentrating, loss of interest in all or most activities, problems with memory, thoughts of suicide, hallucinations.

descriptive studies Studies that simply describe characteristics of a sample, or between variables within a sample.

diabetes A disease in which the body is unable properly to use and store glucose, leading to a buildup of glucose in the bloodstream, or hyperglycemia.

dimensional approach An approach that assumes that affective states are interrelated and can be accurately captured by a small number of dimensions.

disability-adjusted life years (DALYs) A measure of a person's disease burden that estimates the years of healthy life lost due to premature death and years lived with a disability of specified severity and duration.

disease-specific measures An assessment of people with a specific disease or disabling condition.

dispositional approach A perspective on personality that emphasizes the person; examples include biological theories and trait theories.

distraction/time-out hypothesis A hypothesis that suggests that the anxiety- and depression-reducing effects of exercise are due to the distraction it provides from the normal routine.

distress Stressors that are negative.

double-blind experiments Experiments in which neither the subjects nor the experimenters know which subjects are receiving a drug or a placebo.

Down syndrome A genetic condition that causes delays in intellectual and physical development.

dysthymia Chronic form of depression.

ecosystem System formed by the interaction of a community of living things with one another and with their physical environment.

ectomorph A body type characterized by linearity, tallness, and leanness; in constitutional theory, individuals with this body type are characterized as tense, introverted, socially restrained, and inhibited.

effect size Estimates of the magnitude of an effect.

emotional dimension of body image *See affective dimension of body image.*

emotional support The expression of encouragement, caring, empathy, and concern toward a person.

emotional well-being A greater amount of positive affect than negative affect along with favorable thoughts such as satisfaction with life.

emotions States of feeling elicited following an appraisal in which an object (a person or event) is determined to impact on the well-being of the individual.

empathy The ability to identify with another person and understand his or her feelings.

endomorph A body type characterized by plumpness, fatness, and roundedness; in constitutional theory, this body type is linked with affection, sociability, relaxation, and joviality.

endorphin hypothesis An explanation for anxiety- and depression-reducing effects of exercise based on the body's production of endorphins during exercise.

energetic arousal (EA) A dimension of the AD ACL characterized by feelings ranging from energy, vigor, and liveliness to feelings of fatigue and tiredness.

environmental and policy approaches Approaches to physical activity interventions in which one changes the structure of physical and organizational environments to provide safe, attractive, and convenient places for physical activity.

epidemic Anything that affects a large number of people; the study of patterns of disease, injury, and disability, and their risk factors and causes.

epidemiology The study of epidemics, dealing with the incidence, distribution, and control of disease in a population.

error-related negativity (ERN) A psychophysiological index of the evaluation and self-monitoring of one's own actions.

eustress Stressors that are positive.

event-related potential (ERP) A brain response evoked from some type of stimulus.

executive control Processes that control cognitive functions oriented toward goal-directed behavior.

exercise A form of leisure physical activity (as opposed to occupational or household physical activity) that is undertaken in order to achieve a particular objective (e.g., improved appearance, improved cardiorespiratory fitness, reduced stress).

exercise buddies Individuals who provide one another with different types of social support—not just during workouts, when they can motivate and distract one another, but also in-between workouts when exercisers might need help overcoming slips in motivation or self-confidence.

exercise contract A contract that specifically describes the amount of exercise to which a person will commit and that might also include the promise of a positive enforcer for fulfilling the contract.

exercise dependence syndrome A craving for leisure-time physical activity, resulting in uncontrollable excessive exercise behavior that manifests in physiological and/or psychological symptoms.

exercise psychology A field of study concerned with the application of psychological principles to the promotion and maintenance of leisure physical activity (exercise), and the psychological and emotional consequences of leisure physical activity.

exercise science A field devoted to the study of all aspects of sport, recreation, exercise/fitness, and rehabilitative behavior.

exosystem All of the external systems that influence the microsystems.

expectancy value approach A theory that motivation is predicated on the individual's expected behavioral outcome and the value placed on the predicted outcome.

experiential processes Techniques for increasing a person's awareness of, and changing their thoughts and feelings about, themselves and their exercise behavior.

expressive personality A personality characterized by such traits as understanding, sympathy, affection, and compassion.

external regulation The process of engaging in a behavior for the purpose of obtaining an external reward or avoiding an externally applied punishment.

extinction Withholding a positive stimulus after a behavior in order to decrease the likelihood of that behavior happening in the future.

extraversion-introversion dimension In Eysenck's personality theory, the dimension of the personality driven by the level of arousal in the cortex of the brain.

extraverts In Eysenck's personality theory, individuals with low base levels of cortical arousal who seek opportunities for additional stimulation.

extrinsic motivation Motivation that is induced by a force outside the individual.

extrinsic reinforcers Motivation driven by a force outside the individual.

fibromyalgia A chronic condition characterized primarily by widespread pain throughout the body and uncontrollable fatigue.

fitness appraisal A physical activity intervention designed to provide people with personalized information about their level of fitness.

functional capacity An individual's physical ability to perform the daily activities that she or he wants or needs to do.

functional magnetic resonance imaging (fMRI) A special type of MRI that provides a specific and detailed picture of brain activity, based on neuronal activity and the subsequent metabolism and blood flow changes in brain tissue, in almost real time.

generalized anxiety disorder An anxiety disorder characterized by worry lasting more than six months, along with multiple symptoms (e.g., muscle tension, poor concentration, insomnia, irritability).

generic measures of HRQoL Measures designed to assess multiple aspects of HRQoL across a wide range of patient populations (e.g., the SF-36).

global motivation The degree of motivation normally experienced by an individual across most behavioral domains.

global self-esteem An individual's overall self-esteem based on his or her self-esteem in the various domains of life.

goal-setting Behavioral process whereby specific strategies are developed that enhance motivation to achieve an objective.

goal-setting worksheet A place for exercisers to make a detailed plan for achieving success and to record daily progress notes.

group cohesion The tendency of a group to stick together and remain united in pursuit of its objectives.

habituation The decreased magnitude of response to some familiar challenge.

hardiness A personality construct defined as a sense of control over events; commitment, dedication, or involvement in everyday life; and a tendency to perceive life events as challenges and opportunities rather than as stressors.

health-damaging behaviors Behaviors that could lead to a state of illness or injury, such as steroid use, smoking, or using illicit drugs.

health-promoting behaviors Behaviors that could lead to improvements in health or that help to maintain an existing state of good health, such as exercising regularly, eating a well-balanced diet, and getting sufficient sleep.

health psychology A field of psychology that is concerned with psychological processes related to health and health care and is therefore not limited to the health behavior of exercise.

health-related quality of life (HRQoL) Subjective perceptions of the "goodness" of those aspects of life that can be affected by health and health interventions.

health risk appraisals Opportunities provided within the community for people to be screened, without cost, for diseases such as diabetes or cardiovascular disease.

healthy body ideal A realistic goal for health and fitness for one's unique and personal body shape.

healthy body image Positive self-evaluations in the perceptual, cognitive, affective, and behavioral dimensions of body image.

heart disease (also coronary heart disease) Illnesses that result from the narrowing and blocking of the coronary arteries that enmesh the heart and supply it with oxygen-rich blood; the leading cause of death in North America.

heart rate monitor An instrument that uses a transmitter attached to a chest band residing over the heart to emit a signal that is displayed on a special wristwatch.

hippocampus A part of the limbic system that is a key brain structure for learning and memory.

homeostasis The ability of an organism to change and stabilize its internal environment in spite of constant changes in the external environment.

human immunodeficiency virus (HIV) The virus that causes acquired immunodeficiency syndrome (AIDS).

iceberg profile Psychological profile of elite athletes based on various mood states.

identified regulation The process of engaging in behavior motivated by personal goals.

imagery Picturing an object or behavior in the mind using some or all of the body's senses (sight, sound, touch, taste, smell).

implementation intentions Developing a strong mental association between a situational cue and a specific behavior.

individual difference factors Personal factors about a person that may influence the consequences of participation in physical activity

information approach An approach to physical activity interventions in which one tries to change knowledge and attitudes about the benefits of and opportunities for physical activity.

informational support Giving directions, advice, or suggestions about how to exercise and providing feedback regarding the exerciser's progress.

instrumental conditioning A principle that states that a new behavior can be learned, or an existing behavior can be changed, by pairing that behavior with a consequence. A positive consequence will increase the likelihood of the behavior occurring again in the future. A negative consequence will decrease its probability of occurring in the future.

instrumental personality A personality characterized by traits such as risk taking, independence, aggression, and competitiveness.

instrumental support Providing tangible, practical assistance that will help a person achieve exercise goals.

integrated regulation The process of engaging in a behavior in order to confirm one's sense of self.

intensity preference A predisposition to select a particular level of physical effort when given the opportunity to choose the level.

intensity tolerance A trait that influences one's ability to continue exercising at an imposed level of physical effort even when the activity becomes uncomfortable or unpleasant.

interactionist perspective A behavioral model that views both the individual and the situation in which the individual is involved as important in determining behavior.

interference control How one deals with distractions.

intervention studies In exercise psychology, research that examines the effectiveness of some type of intervention strategy to change people's thoughts, feelings, or behaviors regarding physical activity.

intrinsic motivation Motivation that emanates from within a person.

intrinsic reinforcers Rewards that come from within the self, such as feeling good about one's body, feeling a sense of accomplishment at the end of a workout, or simply experiencing the physical and emotional sense of well-being that accompanies exercise.

introjected regulation The process of engaging in a behavior in response to a self-imposed source of pressure.

introverts In Eysenck's personality theory, individuals with higher base levels of cortical activation, who tend to augment incoming stimulation to avoid further arousal.

knee osteoarthritis A form of arthritis characterized by the degeneration of the cartilage in the knee joint, resulting in painful areas of the joint where bone rubs against bone.

lactate threshold The point at which lactate concentrations in the blood exceed the rate at which lactate is removed from the blood, resulting in excess lactate and a shift toward anaerobic metabolism.

lapse A brief period of inactivity (session, week) that precedes resumption of the regular exercise regimen.

latency A measure of the speed with which a stimulus is classified.

learning approaches Theories about personality that focus on the environment; includes conditioning or behaviorist theories and social learning theories.

learning theory A theory that explains how people learn new behaviors.

learning/situational An approach to studying personality that emphasizes how the environment influences a person's behavior.

leisure Time spent outside of work or household activities.

lifestyle behaviors In regard to body image, actions performed with the goal of altering the body or that reflect extensive body image concern.

limbic system The collection of brain structures responsible for emotional responding.

longitudinal studies Study design that allows researchers to monitor changes in behavior across a relatively long period of time (i.e., years) in the same group of people.

macrosystem Encompasses all other systems; it is the larger sociocultural context in which a person resides and includes cultural values, political philosophies, economic patterns, and social conditions.

maintenance stage The stage at which a person has been exercising at recommended levels for a prescribed period of time (e.g., six months).

major depressive disorder A mood disorder characterized by depressed mood most of the day nearly every day and loss of interest or pleasure in all or most activities.

mass media campaign Physical activity interventions that reach people using some medium other than personal contact with a health professional or provider; a means for reaching large numbers of people that is less expensive than face-to-face services.

mastery The process of accomplishing or completing a goal; the thorough learning and performance of a skill, technique, or behavior.

mastery hypothesis A hypothesis that explains the effect of exercise on depression and anxiety by positing that these effects are derived from the sense of accomplishment or mastery felt upon completion of a task.

medical body ideal The body weight at which mortality rates are lowest for a person of a given height.

medical model The use of traditional forms of medicine (e.g., pharmacology) for improving physical and/or mental health.

mental disorders Health conditions characterized by alterations in thinking, mood, or behavior associated with distress and/or impaired functioning.

mental health According to the U.S. surgeon general, a state of successful performance of mental function, resulting in productive activities, fulfilling relationships with other people, and the ability to adapt to change and to cope with adversity.

mental health problems Signs and symptoms of insufficient intensity or duration to meet the criteria for mental disorders, but sufficient to potentially warrant active efforts in health promotion, prevention, and treatment.

mental illness The term used to refer to all diagnosable mental disorders.

mesomorph A body type characterized by wide muscular shoulders and narrow hips-the classic athletic body type; in constitutional theory, individuals with this body type are thought to be adventurous, risk-taking, dominant, aggressive, and leaders.

mesosystem Location where interactions between the microsystems take place.

meta-analyses Quantitative reviews and syntheses of research studies.

microsystem The immediate systems in which people interact; in a physical activity context, they are environments where people might be physically active or where they might receive support for being physically active.

model A visual representation of a phenomenon or behavior.

moderating factors Variables that could influence the strength of an intervention or the relationship between two variables.

monamine hypothesis An explanation for the effect of exercise on depression based on the alteration of brain neurotransmitters such as serotonin, norepinephrine, and dopamine.

moods Subjective states of feeling that have a cognitive basis and that can enhance or interfere with purposive behavior.

morbidity Disease.

motivation The degree of determination, drive, or desire with which an individual approaches or avoids a behavior.

motivational interviewing A counseling technique that provides people with the opportunity to talk about and resolve their mixed feelings so that they can move forward with change.

muscle dysmorphia A special type of body dysmorphic disorder (BDD) characterized by a preoccupation with muscularity.

negative reinforcers Unpleasant or aversive stimuli that, when withdrawn after a behavior, will increase the frequency of that behavior in the future.

neurogenesis Cell proliferation and differentiation.

neuroimaging Image techniques to get another level of information regarding how the cognitive processing of information is handled within the central nervous system.

neuroticism A personality trait associated with activity of the limbic system and the autonomic nervous system and characterized by more labile and longer-lasting autonomic reactions.

neuroticism-stability dimension In Eysenck's personality theory, the dimension associated with limbic system activity and the autonomic nervous system.

non-academic self-concept A subdomain of general self-concept, comprising social, emotional, and physical self-concept.

noncompliance Failure to maintain an exercise regimen prescribed by a health-care professional.

nonpurging type A type of bulimia involveing regular use of compensatory behaviors such as fasting or excessive exercising, but no purging episodes.

norm A pattern of behaviors or beliefs common to members of a particular group or society.

objective measures Measures that can be made by someone other than the patient; usually quantitative in nature.

obsessive-compulsive disorder An anxiety disorder characterized by obsessions, such as recurrent thoughts or images perceived as inappropriate or forbidden, that elicit anxiety and compulsions, including behaviors or thoughts, that reduce the anxiety associated with obsessions.

optimism A general personal tendency to expect more good experiences than bad experiences in one's own life.

osteoporosis A disease characterized by low bone mass and deterioration of bone tissue.

overprotectiveness The quality of going to extremes in trying to protect another person from harm.

overtraining Training at a level greater than an individual is accustomed to in terms of frequency, intensity, and duration.

P300 (P3) A component of event-related potential that is a positive-going waveform that occurs approximately 300 milliseconds after stimulus is presented. It is thought to reflect the allocation of attentional resources.

panic disorder An anxiety disorder characterized by intense fear and discomfort associated with physical and mental symptoms, including sweating, trembling, shortness of breath, chest pain, nausea, fear of dying, or loss of control of emotions.

past performance accomplishments The degree of success perceived by an individual who has previously engaged in activities similar to, or the same as, the current behavior.

pedometer A small device typically attached to either the waistband or shoe to provide data such as the number of steps taken and distance covered over a period of time.

perceived behavioral control (PBC) The degree of personal control an individual perceives he or she has over a behavior.

perceived competence An individual's judgment of his or her abilities and potential success in specific situations, activities, skills, or domains.

perceptual dimension of body image The picture of our own body that we form in our mind.

personality The underlying, relatively stable, psychological structures and processes that organize human experience and shape a person's actions and reactions to the environment.

personality core A reflection of who we are developed from early environmental interactions; it includes such things as our perceptions of the external world, perceptions of self, basic attitudes, values, interests, motives, and our self-concept.

pessimism A general personal tendency to expect more bad than good experiences in one's own life.

phobia An anxiety disorder characterized by an exaggerated, irrational fear of an object or class of objects.

physical activity Any bodily movement produced by skeletal muscles that results in energy expenditure.

physical activity epidemiology The study of the "epidemic" of physical inactivity concerned with the five "W's" of exercise (who exercises; where, when, and why they do so; and what they do).

physical activity recall A self-report measure that asks the respondent to recall the mode, frequency, intensity, and duration of the activity performed for a specific period of time in the past.

physical self-concept An individual's judgment of his or her general physical abilities.

physiological state Temporary physical condition of the body (e.g., feelings of pain and fatigue or rapid heart rate).

physiological toughness model A psychophysiological model that postulates that exposure to stressors can lead to psychological coping and emotional stability.

point-of-decision prompt A physical activity intervention that involves placing a sign at points where people must choose between two activities, e. g., taking the elevator versus walking up the stairs; such messages are effective because they remind people that they are about to have an opportunity to engage in some physical activity.

positive reinforcer Any intrinsic or extrinsic reward that increases the likelihood of a person repeating a behavior.

post-traumatic stress disorder An anxiety disorder characterized by anxiety and behavioral disturbances following exposure to extreme trauma (e.g., combat, physical assault) that persist for more than one month.

precontemplation stage A stage in which a person has no intention to start exercising in the foreseeable future.

predictive studies Exercise research that has attempted to predict future exercise behavior.

preparation stage The stage at which a person performs tasks (such as getting medical clearance or buying exercise equipment) that will prepare him or her for starting an exercise program.

primary appraisal An initial assessment of a situation's importance and its potential challenges, threats, and possibilities of harm.

primary exercise dependence A psychological condition in which exercise is an end in itself.

proxy measures Measures completed by other people when asked to rate a patient's HRQoL because the patient has some physical or cognitive limitation that prevents him or her from completing the questionnaire.

psychobiological model A model of behavior that advocates considering both biological and psychological factors.

psychology A field of study concerned with the various mental processes people experience and use in all aspects of their lives.

psychophysiology A scientific discipline that examines cognitive, emotional, and behavioral events through their manifestation as physiological processes and events.

psychoticism-superego dimension In Eysenck's personality theory, the dimension of personality that is driven by hormonal function.

public policy Government statements or rules that are meant to influence people's behavior.

punishment An unpleasant or uncomfortable stimulus after a behavior that serves to decrease the probability of that behavior happening in the future.

purging type A type of bulimia that involves regular episodes of self-induced vomiting or the misuse of laxatives or diuretics.

quality-adjusted life years (QALY) An objective, numerical measure of QL that represents the number of years a person is expected to live, adjusted for (or taking into account) health problems that may affect the quality of those remaining years.

quality of life (QoL) The overall "goodness" of a person's life; includes both subjective and objective evaluations of all the factors that contribute to one's life.

Rating of Perceived Exertion Scale (RPE) A scale used by an individual to rate the intensity of the physical activity in which he or she is engaging.

RE-AIM A framework (Reach, Efficacy, Adoption, Implementation, Maintenance) to guide the evaluation of physical activity and other health interventions in the real world.

rehabilitation psychology An area of psychology that deals with the relationship between psychological factors and the physical rehabilitation process.

reinforcement management The process of developing strategies for rewarding or reinforcing oneself when exercise goals are met.

relapse Failure to resume regular exercise following a lapse in activity.

relative reactivity The relative value of heart rate during stress from a baseline value.

response inhibition Withholding a response rather than making one.

restricting type A type of anorexia that involves no binge-eating or purging behaviors but rather limiting eating to the point of not maintaining a minimally normal body weight.

role-related behaviors Variable, daily behaviors influenced by the particular context in which we find ourselves.

scheduling efficacy Confidence in one's abilities to schedule and manage exercise behavior.

secondary appraisal A follow-up assessment of a situation's importance and its potential; the assessment can possibly modify a primary appraisal and may include considering what options are available and how viable they might be.

secondary exercise dependence A psychological condition in which exercise is used exclusively to control body composition.

sedentary Chronic (long-term) pattern of inactivity.

selective improvement hypothesis The idea that exercise results in improved cardiorespiratory fitness but that it results in selective as opposed to generalized improvements.

self-concept The way in which we see or define ourselves.

self-confidence Confidence in one's self and in one's powers and abilities. In the physical activity setting, an individual's perception of his or her ability to perform certain physical activities.

self-determination Autonomous, self-dependent behavior.

self-efficacy The extent to which individuals believe they will be successful in performing the desired behavior given the abilities they possess and the situation in which they find themselves.

self-esteem The evaluative or affective consequence of one's self-concept.

self-liberation Activities that strengthen one's commitment to change and the belief that one can change.

self-monitoring Paying attention to one's own thoughts, feelings, and behaviors and gauging them against a standard.

self reevaluation The process by which individuals consider how they feel about their exercise behavior.

self-schemata An individual's domain-specific identities, e.g., exercise identity.

self-talk The statements we make to ourselves, which can be used to increase confidence, regulate arousal, and focus effort in order to overcome high-risk situations.

sensitization The augmented response to a novel stressor.

situational motivation Motivation experienced in a particular activity at a specific point in time.

social anxiety disorder *See social phobia.*

social approaches An approach to physical activity interventions in which one creates social environments that facilitate and enhance behavior change.

social cognitive approach A psychological approach that views exercise behavior as being influenced by human cognition and external stimuli.

social control Measures and actions taken by a group to force compliance with traditions, perceptions, or rules.

social ecological models A model that takes the approach that individual-level factors are only one of multiple levels of influence on behavior.

social facilitation The phenomenon by which people increase their effort and performance when others are watching them.

social influence Real or imagined pressure to change one's behavior, attitudes, or beliefs.

social interaction hypothesis A hypothesis that proposes that the reason exercise reduces depression is that it provides an opportunity for the individual to interact with others.

social persuasion Verbal and nonverbal tactics used by others in an attempt to increase a person's self-efficacy.

social phobia A marked, persistent anxiety in social situations.

social physique anxiety The anxiety people experience during real or imagined conditions when their bodies are evaluated by others.

social self-concept An individual's judgment of his or her general ability to interact positively with others.

social support The degree of perceived comfort, caring, assistance, and information that a person receives from others.

somatotonia Sheldon's term for the adventurous, risk-taking, dominant, and aggressive personality he associated with the mesomorph somatotype.

Specific Measures of HRQoL Measures designed to measure the most valued domains of HRQoL among people with a particular disease or disability.

spinal cord injury (SCI) Neurological damage in the spine that results in the loss of motor control, sensation, and reflexes. The damage may be caused by disease or an injury.

staleness syndrome An aspect of overtraining characterized by increased negative mental health.

state anxiety A noticeable but transient emotional state characterized by feelings of apprehension and heightened autonomic nervous system activity.

stereotypes A set of beliefs—true or false—about the characteristics of people who belong to a particular group.

stimulus control The process of placing cues in the environment that will remind people to be more physically active.

stopping A measure of the ability to stop or abort a preprogrammed action.

stopping task A task that requires the suppression of a response given a specific stimulus.

stress The physical and emotional tension we feel when we face challenges in our lives.

stress response The body's immediate physiological adaptations to an encounter with an acute stressor (i.e., "fight-or-flight" response).

subjective measures Measures of a patient's perceptions of the quality or goodness of various domains; usually qualitative in nature.

subjective norm A construct that focuses on the degree to which the individual feels social pressure to perform a behavior.

subsequent reinforcement A reward that follows a behavior.

synaptic plasticity The ability of the connections between neurons to change in strength.

Tai Chi A Chinese martial art characterized by soft, slow, flowing movements that emphasize force rather than strength.

task switching A behavioral measure of the cost of switching between two different tasks.

tense arousal (TA) A dimension of the AD ACL characterized by feelings ranging from subjective tension to placidity, quietness, and stillness.

theory An explanation about why a behavior or phenomenon occurs.

thermogenic hypothesis A hypothesis that states that elevated body temperature resulting from exercise can also lead to psychological changes such as reduced anxiety.

trait anxiety A general predisposition to respond across many situations with apprehension, worry, and nervousness.

traits Relatively enduring, highly consistent internal attributes.

transtheoretical model (TTM) A behavioral model that integrates elements from across a variety of theories and models of behavior.

Type A behavior pattern (TABP) A personality type marked by anger, hostility, and sense of urgency that has been implicated in cardiovascular disease; sometimes called coronary-prone personality.

typical responses Our fairly predictable behaviors and ways of reacting to our environment.

validation Comparing oneself with others in order to gauge progress and to confirm that one's thoughts, feelings, problems, and experiences are "normal."

ventilatory threshold (VT) The point at which the ventilatory equivalent for oxygen continues to increase without a concomitant increase in the ventilatory equivalent for carbon dioxide.

vicarious experiences The process of experiencing a sensation, situation, or behavior via imagined participation in another individual's encounter; a source of self-efficacy.

visceratonia Sheldon's term for the affectionate, sociable, relaxed, and jovial personality he associated with the endomorph somatotype.

visualization (or mental imagery) Seeing and feeling an experience in one's mind.

working memory Being able to hold relevant information in one's mind for relatively short periods of time.

Author Index

Subject Index